Participate

in a transformative

moment in history!

When students undertake a

Critical Mission,

they learn to read and analyze

sources, interpret maps and

timelines, and think like a

historian.

>> In this Critical Mission, students play a role in the impeachment of Andrew Johnson. They need to advise Edmund G. Ross, who represents the crucial swing vote in Congress, on how to vote.

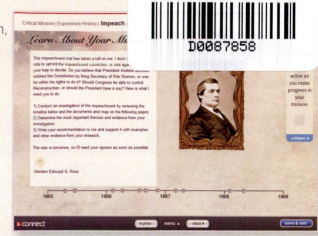

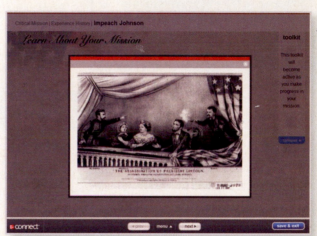

<< A brief video provides students with context by reviewing the historical events leading up to the impeachment.

<< Students then read documents and examine maps to gather evidence and choose themes before writing their opinion for or against conviction.

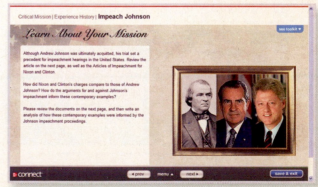

⌃ Part 2 of the mission brings students to modern times by asking them to consider how Johnson's impeachment impacted more recent impeachment controversies.

Connect *to success in history*

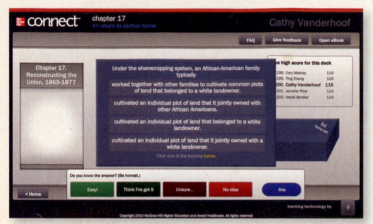

<< Connect's **LearnSmart**, an adaptive learning system, provides students with remediation based not just on right or wrong answers, but also the confidence they feel in answering the question.

>> All Connect activities are linked to learning objectives, such as helping students understand the **geographical context** for historical events.

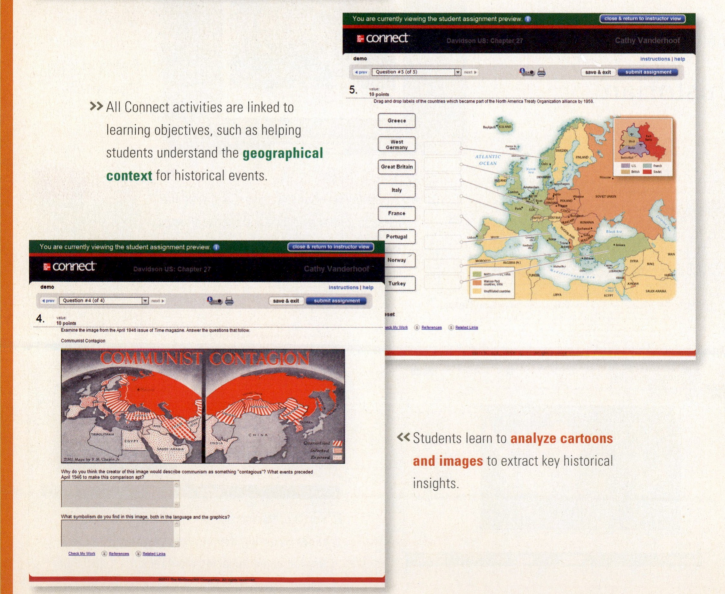

<< Students learn to **analyze cartoons and images** to extract key historical insights.

Independent research shows that students' grades improve with **Connect**, a learning platform that shows them what they know and what they still need to learn.

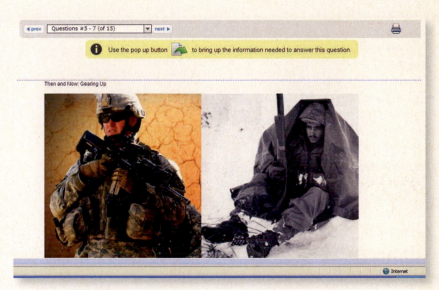

⌃ Linked to the "Then and Now" feature in the text, these comparisons help students make the **connection between past and current events.**

⌃ **Dueling Documents** provide practice in analyzing and comparing primary source accounts of the same historical event.

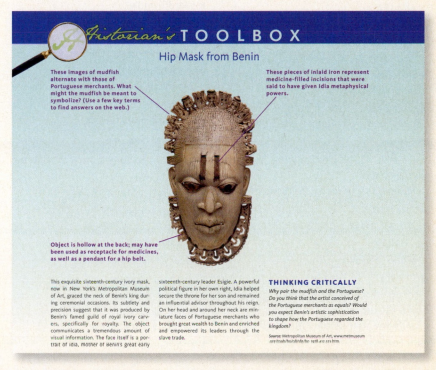

⌃ **Historian's Toolbox** helps students learn how to examine an artifact or image from the past in the way a historian would.

We would like to express our deep appreciation to the following individuals who contributed to the development of this program:

Reviewers of U★S: A Narrative History

Mary Adams,
City College of San Francisco

Chris Bell,
Edmonds Community College

Roger Bowerman,
Glendale Community College

Jeffrey Brown,
New Mexico State University

Ann Chirhart,
Indiana State University

Patty Colman,
Moorpark College

Clarissa Confer,
California University of Pennsylvania

Cara Converse,
Moorpark College

Aaron Cowen,
Slippery Rock University

David Dalton,
College of the Ozarks

Brandon Franke,
Blinn College

Christos Frentzos,
Austin Peay State University

George Gastil,
Grossmont College

Frank Gilbert,
Southeastern Oklahoma State University

Jim Good,
Lone Star College, North Harris

Patricia Gower,
University of the Incarnate Word

Debbie Hargis,
Odessa College

Tom Heiting,
Odessa College

Carol Keller,
San Antonio College

Dennis Kortheuer,
California State University, Long Beach

Mary Lewis,
Jacksonville College

Tammi Littrel,
Chadron State College

Bob McConaughy,
Austin Community College

Russell Mitchell,
Tarrant County College, Southeast

Michael Namorato,
University of Mississippi

Bret Nelson,
San Jacinto College, North

Alison Ollinger-Riefstahl,
Mercyhurst Northeast College

Edward Richey,
University of North Texas

Joaquin Riveya-Martinez,
Texas State University, San Marcos

Stephen Rockenbach,
Virginia State University

Michele Rotunda,
Rutgers University, Newark

Steven Short,
Collin College

Maureen Melvin Sowa,
Bristol Community College

Rita Thomas,
Northern Kentucky University

Richard Trimble,
Ocean County College

Salli Vargis,
Georgia Perimeter College

William Wantland,
Mount Vernon Nazarene University

Chad Wooley,
Tarrant County College

Connect History Board of Advisors

Charles Ambler,
University of Texas, El Paso

Tramaine Anderson,
Tarrant County College

Mario Bennekin,
Georgia Perimeter College

Cassandra Cookson,
Lee College

Nancy Duke,
Daytona State College

Wendy Gunderson,
Collin County Community College

Aimee Harris,
El Paso Community College

Stephen Lopez,
San Jacinto College

Jan McCauley,
Tyler Junior College

Mark Newell,
Ramapo College of New Jersey

Jessica Patton,
Tarrant County College

Penne Restad,
University of Texas, Austin

Manfred Silva,
El Paso Community College, Northwest

Richard Straw,
Radford University

David Stricklin,
Dallas Baptist University

Paddy Swiney,
Tulsa Community College, Southeast

Teresa Thomas,
Austin Community College

Armando Villarreal,
Tarrant County College

Roger Ward,
Collin County Community College

Connect History and LearnSmart Subject Matter Experts

Jeff Bowersox, Chris Brooks,
Rachel Burstein, Beatrice Burton,
Rebecca Cerling, Javier Collazo,
Maura Cunningham, Zachary Doleshal,
Nancy Duke, Shennette Garrett-Scott,
Patricia Goldsworthy, Drew Gonrowski,
Amanda Guidotti, Lawrence Gutman,
Aimee Harris, Giovanni Hortua,
Jonathan Hunt, Michael Johnson,
Sara Kimble, Aki Maehara,
Suzanne McFadden, Brian McNeil,
Aragorn Storm Miller, Rebecca Nykwest,
Emily Pace, Marc Palen, Andrew Peterson,
Michelle Reeves, Linda Scherr,
Kimberly Shepard, Xia Shi, Richard Straw,
David Villarreal, Ingrid Wilkerson,
Scott Williams, Chad Wooley, David Yeatts

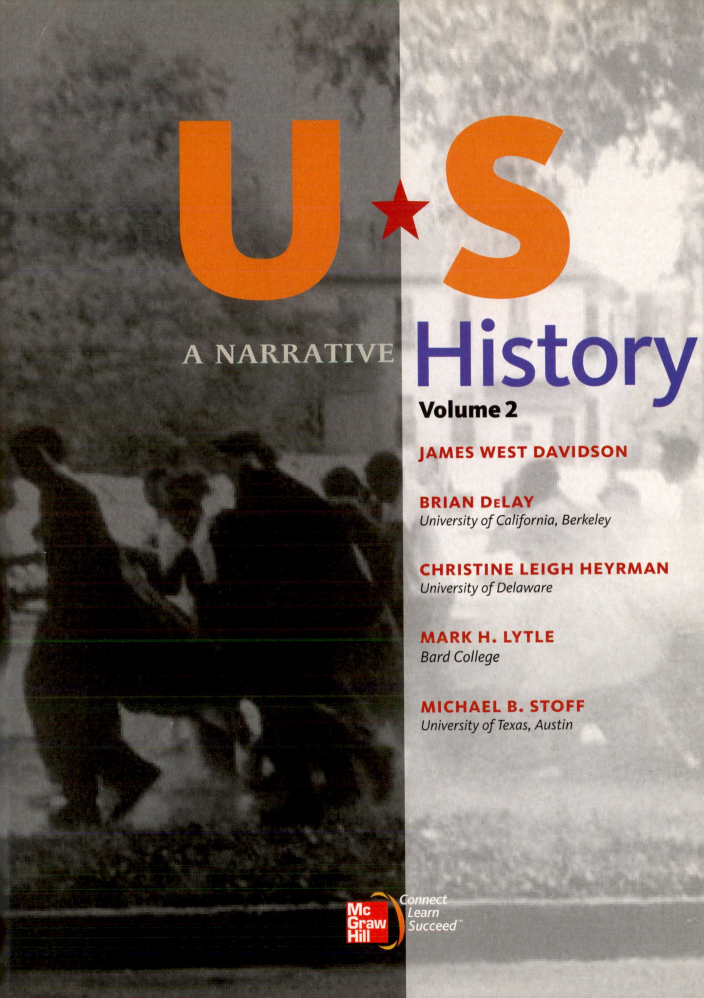

U★S History

A NARRATIVE

Volume 2

JAMES WEST DAVIDSON

BRIAN DeLAY
University of California, Berkeley

CHRISTINE LEIGH HEYRMAN
University of Delaware

MARK H. LYTLE
Bard College

MICHAEL B. STOFF
University of Texas, Austin

McGraw Hill

Connect
Learn
Succeed™

U.S.: A Narrative History

AUTHORS

James West Davidson   Brian DeLay

Christine Leigh Heyrman   Mark H. Lytle   Michael B. Stoff

VICE PRESIDENT AND EDITOR IN CHIEF **Michael J. Ryan**

PUBLISHER **Christopher Freitag**

SPONSORING EDITOR **Matthew Busbridge**

DIRECTOR OF DEVELOPMENT **Nancy Crochiere**

DEVELOPMENT EDITOR **Cynthia Ward**

CONNECT DEVELOPMENT EDITOR **Laura Wilk**

EDITORIAL COORDINATOR **Jaclyn Mautone**

EDITORIAL INTERN **Megan Ruggiero**

MARKETING MANAGER **Stacy Ruel**

MARKETING SPECIALIST **Jen Nelson**

PRODUCTION EDITOR **Mel Valentin**

MANUSCRIPT EDITOR **Stacey Sawyer**

ART MANAGER **Robin Mouat**

COVER DESIGNER **Cassandra Chu**

INTERIOR DESIGNER **Maureen McCutcheon**

PHOTO RESEARCH COORDINATOR **Nora Agbayani**

PHOTO RESEARCHERS **Deborah Bull, NY; Jullie Chung**

MEDIA PROJECT MANAGER **Sarah B. Hill**

BUYER **Laura Fuller**

The McGraw·Hill Companies

Mc Graw Hill
Connect
Learn
Succeed™

US/A Narrative History, Volume 2

Published by MCGraw-Hill, and imprint of The McGraw-Hill Companies, Inc. 1221 Avenue of the American, New York, NY, 10020. Copyright © 2012 by The McGraw-Hill Companies, Inc. All rights reserved. No part of this publication may be reproduced or distributed in any form or by any means or stored in a database or retrieval system, without the prior written consent of The McGraw-Hill Companies, Inc., including, but not limited to, in any network or other electronic storage or transmission, or broadcast for distance learning.

Some ancillaries including electronic and print components may not be available to customer outside the United States. PRINTED IN THE UNITED STATES OF AMERICA.

3 4 5 6 7 8 9 0 QVS/QVS 9 8 7 6 5 4 3

ISBN: 978-0-07-742077-2

MHID: 0-07-742077-2

This text was set in 10/12 Celeste Book by Laserwords Private Limited, and printed on acid-free 45# Orion Gloss by Quad/Graphics.

Cover image credits (clockwise): Hulton Archive/Getty Images; Rubberball/Getty Images; Corbis; Daniel Arsenault/Getty Images; (back cover): Purestock/Getty Images.

Because this page cannot legibly accommodate all acknowledgment for copyrighted material, credits appear at the end of the book, and constitute an extension of this copyright page.

Library of Congress Cataloging in Publication Data

Davidson, James West.
  US : a narrative history / James West Davidson, Brian DeLay, Christine Leigh Heyrman.—6th ed.
    p. cm.
  Includes bibliographical references and index.
  ISBN-13: 978-0-07-742076-5 (alk. paper)
  ISBN-10: 0-07-742076-4 (alk. paper)
  ISBN-13: 978-0-07-338566-2 (v. 1)
  ISBN-10: 0-07-338566-2 (v. 1)
  [etc.]
1. United States—History. I. DeLay, Brian, 1971– II. Heyrman, Christine Leigh. III. Title.
  E178.1.D23 2011
  973—dc22
                                                        2011016596

www.mhhe.com

WHAT'S NEW IN U*S

HIGHLIGHTS IN VOL. 2:

>> **HISTORIAN'S TOOLBOX** is a new feature box appearing in many chapters. Historical images and artifacts—including sheet music, a voting machine, cereal box ring, a home appliance advertisement, a farmworker's altar and a lynching post-card, among others—show how historians analyze visual clues and material culture.

>> **REVIEW QUESTIONS** immediately following each section within the chapter help students retain information by asking them to reconstruct what they've read.

>> **EXPANDED COVERAGE OF ENVIRONMENTAL HISTORY** in most chapters shows both how the environment has shaped American history—from flu pandemics to the Galveston flood and Hurricane Katrina—and how Americans have shaped the environment—from the effects of suburban development to the damage of Agent Orange and the Gulf oil spill of 2010. Chapter 23, "The Future of Energy," discusses the fateful decision to power automobiles using leaded gasoline rather than ethyl alcohol.

>> **COVERAGE OF THE HISTORY OF GLOBAL WARMING:** Chapter 19 (The New Industrial Order) notes early research and speculation into the topic; Chapter 31 adds coverage of a clash over the causes of global warming; and Chapter 32 ends with a new section, "Short, Medium, Long" describing current environmental challenges, including proposals to address global warming, the BP oil spill and the Gulf's hypoxic zone (with a new map).

>> **GLOBAL HISTORY COVERAGE DEEPENED:** In Chapter 25, "The Golden Age of Radio and Film" adds coverage of how Hitler used film as propaganda. In Chapter 32, the introduction to "The New Migration" is updated with current statistics; "The Internet Revolution" has been updated to include more on social networking sites, virtual communities, and a Historian's Toolbox analyzing worldwide web traffic.

U*S
BRIEF CONTENTS

Contents

20 THE RISE OF AN URBAN ORDER 1870–1900

21 THE POLITICAL SYSTEM UNDER STRAIN AT HOME AND ABROAD
1877–1900

22 THE PROGRESSIVE ERA
1890–1920

Whatever the weather
We only reach welfare
together

32 THE UNITED STATES IN A GLOBAL COMMUNITY
1989–PRESENT

Features

About the Authors

James West Davidson

Received his Ph.D. from Yale University. A historian who has pursued a full-time writing career, he is the author of numerous books, among them *After the Fact: The Art of Historical Detection* (with Mark H. Lytle), *The Logic of Millennial Thought: Eighteenth-Century New England,* and *Great Heart: The History of a Labrador Adventure* (with John Rugge). He is co-editor with Michael Stoff of the *Oxford New Narratives in American History,* in which his own most recent book appears: *'They Say': Ida B. Wells and the Reconstruction of Race.*

Brian DeLay

Received his Ph.D. from Harvard and is an Associate Professor of History at the University of California, Berkeley. He is a frequent guest speaker at teacher workshops across the country and has won several prizes for his book *War of a Thousand Deserts: Indian Raids and the U.S.-Mexican War.*

Christine Leigh Heyrman

Is the Robert W. and Shirley P. Grimble Professor of American History at the University of Delaware. She received a Ph.D. in American Studies from Yale University and is the author of *Commerce and Culture: The Maritime Communities of Colonial Massachusetts, 1690–1750.* Her book *Southern Cross: The Beginnings of the Bible Belt* was awarded the Bancroft Prize. She is currently writing a book about evangelical views of Islam in the early nineteenth century.

Mark H. Lytle

A Ph.D. from Yale University, is Professor of History and Chair of the Environmental Studies Program at Bard College. He has served two years as Mary Ball Washington Professor of American History at University College, Dublin, in Ireland. His publications include *The Origins of the Iranian-American Alliance, 1941–1953, After the Fact: The Art of Historical Detection* (with James West Davidson), *America's Uncivil Wars: The Sixties Era from Elvis to the Fall of Richard Nixon,* and most recently, *The Gentle Subversive: Rachel Carson, Silent Spring, and the Rise of the Environmental Movement.* He is also co-editor of a joint issue of the journals *Diplomatic History* and *Environmental History* dedicated to the field of environmental diplomacy.

Michael B. Stoff

Is Associate Professor of History and Director of the Plan II Honors Program at the University of Texas at Austin. The recipient of a Ph.D. from Yale University, he has been honored many times for his teaching, most recently with election to the Academy of Distinguished Teachers. He is the author of *Oil, War, and American Security: The Search for a National Policy on Foreign Oil, 1941–1947,* co-editor (with Jonathan Fanton and R. Hall Williams) of *The Manhattan Project: A Documentary Introduction to the Atomic Age,* and series co-editor (with James West Davidson) of the *Oxford New Narratives in American History.* He is currently working on a narrative of the bombing of Nagasaki.

There were swaying chimneys, tottering walls, streets impassable from piles of brick, stones, and rubbish," reported one journalist in Richmond at war's end. "Men stood speechless, haggard . . . gazing at the desolation." In this photograph, the need for a time exposure made residents walking the streets look like ghosts. Many must have felt that way in defeat, though newly freed African Americans were exultant.

RECONSTRUCTING
the Union

17

>> **AN AMERICAN STORY**

A SECRET SALE AT DAVIS BEND

Joseph Davis had had enough. Well on in years and financially ruined by the war, he decided to sell his Mississippi plantations Hurricane and Brierfield to Benjamin Montgomery and his sons in November 1866. Such a sale was common enough after the war, but this transaction was bound to attract attention, since Joseph Davis was the elder brother of Jefferson Davis. Indeed, before the war the ex-Confederate president had operated Brierfield as his own plantation, even though his brother retained legal title to it. But the sale was unusual for another reason—so unusual that the parties involved agreed to keep it secret. The plantation's new owners were black, and Mississippi law prohibited African Americans from owning land. >>

1865–1877

Though a slave, Benjamin Montgomery had been the business manager of the two Davis plantations before the war. He had also operated a store on Hurricane Plantation with his own line of credit in New Orleans. In 1863 Montgomery fled to the North, but when the war was over, he returned to Davis Bend, where the federal government had confiscated the Davis plantations and was leasing plots of the land to black farmers. Montgomery quickly emerged as the leader of the African American community at the Bend.

Then, in 1866, President Andrew Johnson pardoned Joseph Davis and restored his lands. Davis was now over 80 years old and lacked the will and stamina to rebuild, yet unlike many ex-slaveholders, he felt bound by obligations to his former slaves. Convinced that with encouragement African Americans could succeed in freedom, he sold his land secretly to Benjamin Montgomery. Only when the law prohibiting African Americans from owning land was overturned in 1867 did Davis publicly confirm the sale to his former slave.

For his part, Montgomery undertook to create a model society at Davis Bend based on mutual cooperation. He rented land to black farmers, hired others to work his own fields, sold supplies on credit, and ginned and marketed the crops. The work was hard indeed: Davis Bend's farmers faced the destruction caused by the war, several disastrous floods, insects, droughts, and declining

↑ *A Visit from the Old Mistress,* by Winslow Homer, captures the conflicting, often awkward emotions felt by both races after the war.

cotton prices. Yet before long, cotton production exceeded that of the prewar years. The Montgomerys eventually acquired 5,500 acres, which made them reputedly the third largest planters in the state, and they won national and international awards for the quality of their cotton. Their success demonstrated what African Americans, given a fair chance, might accomplish.

The experiences of Benjamin Montgomery were not those of most black southerners, who did not own land or have a powerful white benefactor. Yet all African Americans shared Montgomery's dream of economic independence. As one black veteran noted: "Every colored man will be a slave, and feel himself a slave until he can raise him own bale of cotton and put him own mark upon

it and say this is mine!" Blacks could not gain effective freedom simply through a proclamation of emancipation. They needed economic power, including their own land that no one could unfairly take away. And political power too, if the legacy of slavery was to be overturned.

How would the Republic be reunited, now that slavery had been abolished? War, in its blunt way, had roughed out the contours of a solution, but only in broad terms. The North, with its industrial might, would be the driving force in the nation's economy and retain the dominant political voice. But would African Americans receive effective power? How would North and South readjust their economic and political relations? These questions lay at the heart of the problem of Reconstruction. «

PRESIDENTIAL RECONSTRUCTION

Throughout the war Abraham Lincoln had considered Reconstruction his responsibility. Elected with less than 40 percent of the popular vote in 1860, he was acutely aware that once the states of the Confederacy were restored to the Union, the Republicans would be weakened unless they ceased to be a sectional party. By a generous peace, Lincoln hoped to attract former Whigs in the South, who supported many of the Republicans' economic policies, and build up a southern wing of the party.

Lincoln's 10 Percent Plan >>
Lincoln outlined his program in a Proclamation of **Amnesty** and Reconstruction, issued in December 1863. When a minimum of 10 percent of the qualified voters from 1860 took a **loyalty oath** to the Union, they could organize a state government. The new state constitution had to abolish slavery and provide for black education, but Lincoln did not insist that high-ranking Confederate leaders be barred from public life.

> **amnesty** general pardon granted by a government, usually for political crimes.
>
> **loyalty oath** oath of fidelity to the state or to an organization.

Lincoln indicated that he would be generous in granting pardons to Confederate leaders and did not rule out compensation for slave property. Moreover, while he privately advocated limited black suffrage in the disloyal southern states, he did not demand social or political equality for black Americans. In Louisiana, Arkansas, and Tennessee he recognized pro-Union governments that allowed only white men to vote.

The Radical Republicans found Lincoln's approach much too lenient. Strongly antislavery, Radical members of Congress had led the struggle to make emancipation a war aim. Now they led the fight to guarantee the rights of former slaves, or freedpeople. The Radicals believed that it was the duty of Congress, not the president, to set the terms under which states would regain their rights in the Union. Though the Radicals often disagreed on other matters, they were united in a determination to readmit southern states only after slavery had been ended, black rights protected, and the power of the planter class destroyed.

Under the direction of Senator Benjamin Wade of Ohio and Representative Henry Winter Davis of Maryland, Congress formulated a much stricter plan of Reconstruction. The Wade-Davis bill required half the white adult males to take an oath of allegiance before drafting a new state constitution, and it restricted political power to the hard-core Unionists. Lincoln vetoed this

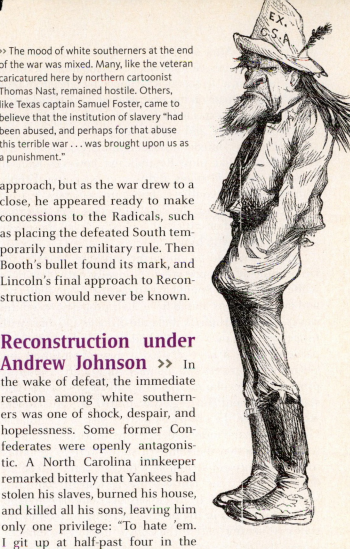

>> The mood of white southerners at the end of the war was mixed. Many, like the veteran caricatured here by northern cartoonist Thomas Nast, remained hostile. Others, like Texas captain Samuel Foster, came to believe that the institution of slavery "had been abused, and perhaps for that abuse this terrible war . . . was brought upon us as a punishment."

approach, but as the war drew to a close, he appeared ready to make concessions to the Radicals, such as placing the defeated South temporarily under military rule. Then Booth's bullet found its mark, and Lincoln's final approach to Reconstruction would never be known.

Reconstruction under Andrew Johnson >>
In the wake of defeat, the immediate reaction among white southerners was one of shock, despair, and hopelessness. Some former Confederates were openly antagonistic. A North Carolina innkeeper remarked bitterly that Yankees had stolen his slaves, burned his house, and killed all his sons, leaving him only one privilege: "To hate 'em. I git up at half-past four in the morning, and sit up till twelve at night, to hate 'em." Most Confederate soldiers were less defiant, having had their fill of war. Even among hostile civilians the feeling was widespread that the South must accept northern terms. A South Carolina paper admitted that "the conqueror has the right to make the terms, and we must submit."

This psychological moment was critical. To prevent a resurgence of resistance, the president needed to lay out in unmistakable terms what white southerners had to do to regain their old status in the Union. Perhaps even a clear and firm policy would not have been enough. But with Lincoln's death, the executive power came to rest in far less capable hands.

Andrew Johnson, the new president, had been born in North Carolina and eventually moved to Tennessee, where he worked as a tailor. Barely able to read and write when he married, he rose to political power by portraying himself as the champion of the people against the wealthy planter class. "Some day I will show the stuck-up aristocrats who is running the country," he vowed as he began his political career. Although he accepted emancipation as one consequence of the war, Johnson lacked any concern for the welfare of African Americans. "Damn the negroes," he said during the war, "I am fighting these traitorous aristocrats, their masters." After serving in Congress and as military governor of Tennessee following its occupation by Union forces, Johnson, a Democrat, was tapped by Lincoln in 1864 as his running mate on the rechristened "Union" ticket.

The Radicals expected Johnson to uphold their views on Reconstruction, and on assuming the presidency he spoke of trying Confederate leaders and breaking up planters' estates. Unlike most Republicans, however, Johnson strongly supported states' rights, and his political shortcomings sparked conflicts almost immediately. Scarred by his humble origins, he became tactless and inflexible when challenged or criticized, alienating even those who sought to work with him.

Johnson moved to return the southern states to the Union quickly. He prescribed a loyalty oath that most white southerners would have to take to regain their civil and political rights and to have their property, except for slaves, restored. High Confederate officials and those with property worth over $20,000 had to apply for individual pardons. Once a state drafted a new constitution and elected state officers and members of Congress, Johnson promised to revoke martial law and recognize the new state government. Suffrage was limited to white citizens who had taken the loyalty oath. This plan was similar to Lincoln's, though more lenient. Only informally did Johnson stipulate that the southern states were to renounce their ordinances of secession, repudiate the Confederate debt, and ratify the Thirteenth Amendment abolishing slavery, which had been passed by Congress in January 1865 and was in the process of being ratified by the states. (It became part of the Constitution in December.)

The Failure of Johnson's Program ≫

The southern delegates who met to construct new governments were in no mood to follow Johnson's recommendations. Several states merely repealed instead of repudiating their ordinances of secession, rejected the Thirteenth Amendment, or refused to repudiate the Confederate debt.

Nor did the new governments allow African Americans any political rights or provide in any effective way for black education. In addition, each state passed a series of laws, often modeled on its old slave code, that applied only to African Americans.

black codes laws passed by southern states in 1865 and 1866, modeled on the slave codes in effect before the Civil War. The codes did grant African Americans some rights not enjoyed by slaves, but their primary purpose was to keep African Americans as propertyless agricultural laborers.

These "**black codes**" did give African Americans some rights that had not been granted to slaves. They legalized marriages from slavery and allowed black southerners to hold and sell property and to sue and be sued in state courts. Yet their primary intent was to keep African Americans as propertyless agricultural laborers with inferior legal rights. The new freedpeople could not serve on juries, testify against whites, or work as they pleased. Mississippi prohibited them from buying or renting farmland, and most states ominously provided that black people who were vagrants could be arrested and hired out to landowners. Many northerners were incensed by the restrictive black codes, which violated their conception of freedom.

Southern voters under Johnson's plan also defiantly elected prominent Confederate military and political leaders to office. At this point, Johnson could have called for new elections or admitted that a different program of Reconstruction was needed. Instead he caved in. For all his harsh rhetoric, he shrank from the prospect of social upheaval, and as the lines of ex-Confederates waiting to see him lengthened, he began issuing special pardons almost as fast as they could be printed. Publicly Johnson put on a bold face, announcing that Reconstruction had been successfully completed. But many members of Congress were deeply alarmed, and the stage was set for a serious confrontation.

⌃ Andrew Johnson was a staunch Unionist, but his contentious personality and inflexibility masked a deep-seated insecurity, which was rooted in his humble background. As a young man, he worked and lived in this rude tailor shop in Greeneville, Tennessee.

Johnson's Break with Congress >> The
new Congress was by no means of one mind. A small
number of Democrats and a few conservative Republicans
backed the president's program of immediate and uncondi-
tional restoration. At the other end of the spectrum, a larger
group of Radical Republicans, led by Thaddeus Stevens,
Charles Sumner, Benjamin Wade, and others, was bent on
remaking southern society in the image of the North. Reconstruction must "revolutionize Southern institutions, habits,
and manners," insisted Representative Stevens, ". . . or all our
blood and treasure have been spent in vain."

As a minority the Radicals needed the aid of the moderate Republicans, the largest bloc in Congress. Led by William Pitt Fessenden and Lyman Trumbull, the moderates
had no desire to foster social revolution or promote racial
equality in the South. But they wanted to keep Confederate leaders from reassuming power, and they were convinced that the former slaves needed federal protection.
Otherwise, Trumbull declared, the freedpeople would "be
tyrannized over, abused, and virtually reenslaved."

The central issue dividing Johnson and the Radicals
was the place of African Americans in American society.
Johnson accused his opponents of seeking "to Africanize
the southern half of our country," while the Radicals championed civil and political rights for African Americans.
The only way to maintain loyal governments and develop
a Republican party in the South, Radicals argued, was to
give black men the ballot. Moderates agreed that the new
southern governments were too harsh toward African
Americans, but they feared that too great an emphasis on
black civil rights would alienate northern voters.

In December 1865, when southern representatives to
Congress appeared in Washington, a majority in Congress
voted to exclude them. Congress also appointed a joint
committee, chaired by Senator Fessenden, to look
into Reconstruction.

The growing split with the president
became clearer when Congress passed a
bill extending the life of the Freedmen's
Bureau. Created in March 1865, the bureau
provided emergency food, clothing, and
medical care to war refugees (including white southerners) and took charge
of settling freedpeople on abandoned
lands. The new bill gave the bureau the
added responsibilities of supervising
special courts to resolve disputes involving freedpeople and establishing schools
for black southerners. Although this bill
passed with virtually unanimous Republican support, Johnson vetoed it.

Johnson also vetoed a civil rights bill
designed to overturn the more flagrant provisions of the black codes. The law made

African Americans citizens of the United States and
granted them the right to own property, make contracts,
and have access to courts as parties and witnesses. For
most Republicans Johnson's action was the last straw,
and in April 1866 Congress overrode his veto. Congress
then approved a slightly revised Freedmen's Bureau bill
in July and promptly overrode the president's veto. Johnson's refusal to compromise drove the moderates into
the arms of the Radicals.

The Fourteenth Amendment >> To pre-
vent unrepentant Confederates from taking over the reconstructed state governments and denying African Americans
basic freedoms, the Joint Committee on Reconstruction
proposed an amendment to the Constitution, which passed
both houses of Congress with the necessary two-thirds vote
in June 1866.

The amendment guaranteed repayment of the national
war debt and prohibited repayment of the Confederate
debt. To counteract the president's wholesale pardons, it
disqualified prominent Confederates from holding office.
Because moderates balked at giving the vote to African
Americans, the amendment merely gave Congress the
right to reduce the representation of any state that did
not have impartial male suffrage. The practical effect of
this provision, which Radicals labeled a "swindle," was to
allow northern states to retain white suffrage, since unlike
southern states they had few African Americans in their
populations and thus would not be penalized.

The amendment's most important provision, Section
1, defined an American citizen as anyone born in the
United States or naturalized, thereby automatically making African Americans citizens. Section 1 also prohibited
states from abridging "the privileges or immunities" of
citizens, depriving "any person of life, liberty, or
property, without due process of law," or denying "any person . . . equal protection of the
laws." The framers of the amendment probably intended to prohibit laws that applied
to one race only, such as the black codes,
or that made certain acts felonies when
committed by black but not white people,
or that decreed different penalties for the
same crime when committed by white
and black lawbreakers. The framers probably did not intend to prevent segregation (the legal separation of the races) in
schools and public places.

Johnson denounced the amendment and
urged southern states not to ratify it. Ironically, of the seceded states only the president's
own state ratified the amendment, and Congress readmitted Tennessee with no further
restrictions. The telegram sent to Congress by

⚡ Thaddeus Stevens, Radical
leader in the House.

Voters soundly repudiated Johnson, as the Republicans won more than a two-thirds majority in both houses of Congress. The Radicals had reached the height of their power, propelled by genuine alarm among northerners that Johnson's policies would lose the fruits of the Union's victory. Johnson was a president virtually without a party.

 REVIEW

What were Lincoln's and Andrew Johnson's approaches to Reconstruction, and why did Congress reject Johnson's approach?

a longtime foe of Johnson officially announcing Tennessee's approval ended: "Give my respects to the dead dog in the White House."

The Election of 1866 >> When Congress blocked his policies Johnson undertook a speaking tour of the East and Midwest in the fall of 1866 to drum up popular support. But the president found it difficult to convince northern audiences that white southerners were fully repentant. Only months earlier white mobs in Memphis and New Orleans had attacked black residents and killed nearly 100 in two major race riots. "The negroes now know, to their sorrow, that it is best not to arouse the fury of the white man," boasted one Memphis newspaper. When the president encountered hostile audiences during his northern campaign, he made matters only worse by trading insults and proclaiming that the Radicals were traitors.

Not to be outdone, the Radicals vilified Johnson as a traitor aiming to turn the country over to former rebels. Resorting to the tactic of "waving the **bloody shirt**," they appealed to voters by reviving bitter memories of the war. In a classic example of such rhetoric, Governor Oliver Morton of Indiana proclaimed that "every bounty jumper, every deserter, every sneak who ran away from the draft" was a Democrat; every "New York rioter in 1863 who burned up little children in colored asylums called himself a Democrat. In short, the Democratic party may be described as a common sewer."

bloody shirt political campaign tactic of "waving the bloody shirt," used by Republicans against Democrats; it invoked the deaths and casualties from the Civil War as a reason to vote for Republicans as the party of the Union, rather than the Democrats, who had often opposed the war.

CONGRESSIONAL RECONSTRUCTION

With a clear mandate in hand congressional Republicans passed their own program of Reconstruction, beginning with the first Reconstruction Act in March 1867. Like all later pieces of Reconstruction legislation, it was repassed over Johnson's veto.

Placing the 10 unreconstructed states under military commanders, the act provided that in enrolling voters, officials were to include black adult males but not former Confederates, who were barred from holding office under the Fourteenth Amendment. Delegates to the state conventions were to frame constitutions that provided for black suffrage and disqualified prominent ex-Confederates from office. The first state legislatures to meet under the new constitution were required to ratify the Fourteenth Amendment. Once these steps were completed and Congress approved the new state constitution, a state could send representatives to Congress.

White southerners found these requirements so obnoxious that officials took no steps to register voters. Congress then enacted a second Reconstruction Act, also in March, ordering the local military commanders to put the machinery of Reconstruction into motion. Johnson's efforts to limit the power of military commanders produced a third act, passed in July, that upheld their

Opinion

If the North won the war, how well did it win the peace?

superiority in all matters. When the first election was held in Alabama to ratify the new state constitution, whites boycotted it in sufficient numbers to prevent a majority of voters from participating. Undaunted, Congress passed the fourth Reconstruction Act (March 1868), which required ratification of the constitution by only a majority of those voting rather than those who were registered.

By June 1868 Congress had readmitted the representatives of seven states. Texas, Virginia, and Mississippi did not complete the process until 1869. Georgia finally followed in 1870.

THE SOUTHERN STATES DURING RECONSTRUCTION

Post-Emancipation Societies in the Americas >>
With the exception of Haiti's revolution (1791–1804), the United States was the only society in the Americas in which the destruction of slavery was accomplished by violence. But the United States, uniquely among these societies, enfranchised former slaves almost immediately after the emancipation. Thus in the United States former masters and slaves battled for control of the state in ways that did not occur in other post-emancipation societies. In most of the Caribbean, property requirements for voting left the planters in political control. Jamaica, for example, with a population of 500,000 in the 1860s, had only 3,000 voters.

Moreover, in reaction to political efforts to mobilize disfranchised black peasants, Jamaican planters dissolved the assembly and reverted to being a Crown colony governed from London. Of the sugar islands, all but Barbados adopted the same policy, thereby blocking the potential for any future black peasant democracy. Nor did any of these societies have the counterparts of the Radical Republicans, a group of outsiders with political power that promoted the fundamental transformation of the post-emancipation South. These comparisons highlight the radicalism of Reconstruction in the United States, which alone saw an effort to forge an interracial democracy.

The Land Issue >>
While the political process of Reconstruction proceeded, Congress debated whether land should be given to former slaves to foster economic independence. At a meeting with Secretary of War Edwin Stanton near the end of the war, African American leaders declared: "The way we can best take care of ourselves is to have land, and till it by our own labor." The Second Confiscation Act of 1862 had authorized the government to seize and sell the property of supporters of the rebellion. In June 1866, however, President Johnson ruled that confiscation laws applied only to wartime.

After more than a year of debate Congress rejected all proposals to give land to former slaves. Given Americans' strong belief in self-reliance, little sympathy existed for the idea that government should support any group. In addition, land redistribution represented an attack on property rights, another cherished American value. "A division of rich men's lands amongst the landless," argued the *Nation,* a Radical journal, "would give a shock to our whole social and political system from which it would hardly recover without the loss of liberty." By 1867 land reform was dead.

> **After more than a year of debate, Congress rejected all proposals to give land to former slaves.**

Impeachment >>
Throughout 1867 Congress routinely overrode Johnson's vetoes, but the president undercut congressional Reconstruction in other ways. He interpreted the new laws narrowly and removed military commanders who vigorously enforced them. Congress responded by restricting his power to issue orders to military commanders in the South. It also passed the Tenure of Office Act, which forbade Johnson to remove any member of the cabinet without the Senate's consent. The intention of this law was to

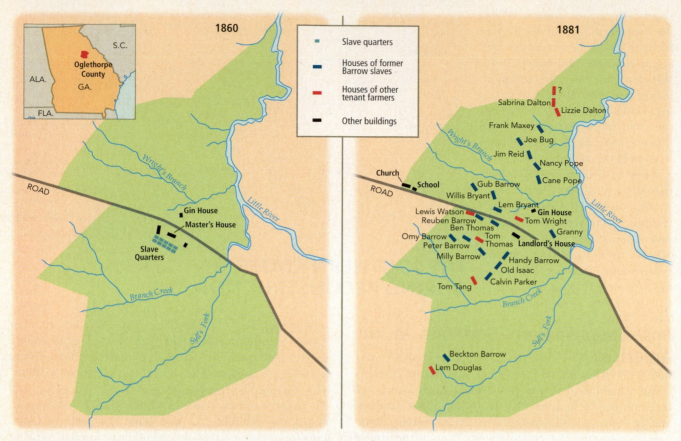

GEORGIA PLANTATION AFTER THE WAR

After emancipation, sharecropping became the dominant form of agricultural labor in the South. Black families no longer lived in the old slave quarters but dispersed to separate plots of land that they farmed themselves. At the end of the year each sharecropper turned over part of the crop to the white landowner.

prevent him from firing Secretary of War Edwin Stanton, the only remaining Radical in the cabinet.

When Johnson tried to dismiss Stanton in February 1868, the House of Representatives angrily approved articles of impeachment. The articles focused on the violation of the Tenure of Office Act, but the charge with the most substance was that Johnson had acted to systematically obstruct Reconstruction legislation. In the trial before the Senate, his lawyers argued that a president could be impeached only for an indictable crime, which Johnson clearly had not committed. The Radicals countered that impeachment applied to political offenses and not merely criminal acts. In May 1868 the Senate voted 35 to 19 to convict, one vote short of the two-thirds majority needed. The seven Republicans who joined the Democrats in voting for acquittal were uneasy about using impeachment as a political weapon.

 **REVIEW**

What was Congress's approach to Reconstruction, and why did it not include a provision for giving land to former slaves?

RECONSTRUCTION IN THE SOUTH

As the power of the Radicals in Congress waned, the fate of Reconstruction increasingly hinged on developments in the southern states themselves. Power in these states rested with the new Republican parties, representing a coalition of black and white southerners and transplanted northerners.

Black and White Republicans >> Once African Americans received the right to vote, black men constituted as much as 80 percent of the Republican voters in the South. They steadfastly opposed the Democratic party with its appeal to white supremacy. But during Reconstruction African Americans never held office in proportion to their voting strength. No African American was ever elected governor. And only in South Carolina, where more than 60 percent of the population was black, did they control even one house of the legislature. Between 15 and 20 percent of the state officers and 6 percent of members of Congress (2 senators and 15 representatives) were black. Only in South Carolina did black officeholders approach their proportion of the population.

Those who held office came from the top levels of African American society. Among state and federal officeholders, perhaps 80 percent were literate, and over a quarter had been free before the war, both marks of distinction in the black community. Their occupations also set them apart: many were professionals (mostly clergy), and of the third who were farmers, nearly all owned land. In their political and social values, African American leaders were more conservative than the rural black population, and they showed little interest in land reform.

Black citizens were a majority of the voters only in South Carolina, Mississippi, and Louisiana. Thus in most of the South the Republican party had to secure white votes to stay in power. Opponents scornfully labeled white southerners who allied with the Republican party **scalawags**, yet an estimated quarter of white southerners at one time voted Republican. They were primarily Unionists from the upland counties and hill areas and largely yeoman farmers. Such voters were attracted by Republican promises to rebuild the South, restore prosperity, create public schools, and open isolated areas to the market with railroads.

> **scalawags** white southerners who supported the Republican party.

The other group of white Republicans in the South were known as **carpetbaggers.** Originally from the North, they allegedly had arrived with all their worldly possessions stuffed in a carpetbag, ready to loot and plunder the defeated South. Some did, certainly, but northerners moved south for a variety of reasons. Though carpetbaggers made up only a small percentage of Republican voters, they controlled almost a third of the offices. More than half of all southern Republican governors and nearly half of Republican members of Congress were originally northerners.

> **carpetbaggers** northern white Republicans who came to live in the South after the Civil War. Most were veterans of the Union army; many were teachers, Freedman's Bureau agents or investors in cotton plantations.

The Republican party in the South had difficulty maintaining unity. Scalawags were especially susceptible to the race issue and social pressure. "Even my own kinspeople have turned the cold shoulder to me because I hold office under a Republican administration," testified a Mississippi white Republican. As black southerners pressed for greater recognition, white southerners increasingly defected to the Democrats. Carpetbaggers, in contrast, were less sensitive to race, although most felt that their black allies should be content with minor offices. The animosity between scalawags and carpetbaggers, which grew out of their rivalry for party honors, was particularly intense.

Reforms under the New State Governments >>

The new southern state constitutions enacted several significant reforms. They devised fairer systems of legislative representation and made many previously appointive offices elective. The Radical state governments also assumed some responsibility for social welfare and established the first statewide systems of public schools in the South.

All the new constitutions proclaimed the principle of equality and granted black adult males the right to vote. On social relations they were much more cautious. No state outlawed segregation, and South Carolina and Louisiana were the only ones that required integration in public schools (a mandate that was almost universally ignored). Sensitive to status, mulattoes pushed for prohibition of social discrimination, but white Republicans refused to adopt such a radical policy.

Economic Issues and Corruption >>

With the southern economy in ruins at the end of the war, problems of economic reconstruction were severe. The new Republican governments encouraged industrial development by providing subsidies, loans, and even temporary exemptions from taxes. These governments also largely rebuilt the southern railroad system, offering lavish aid to railroad corporations. In the two decades after 1860, the region doubled its manufacturing establishments, yet the South steadily slipped further behind the booming industrial economy of the North.

The expansion of government services offered temptations for corruption. Southern officials regularly received bribes and kickbacks for awarding railroad charters, franchises, and other contracts. The railroad grants and new social services such as schools also left state governments in debt, even though taxes rose in the 1870s to four times the rate in 1860.

Corruption, however, was not only a southern problem but a national one. During these years, the Democratic Tweed Ring in New York City alone stole more money than all the southern Radical governments combined. Moreover, corruption was hardly limited to southern Republicans: many Democrats and white business leaders participated. Louisiana governor Henry Warmoth, a carpetbagger, told a congressional committee: "Everybody is demoralizing down here. Corruption is the fashion."

Corruption in Radical governments existed, but southern Democrats exaggerated its extent for partisan purposes. They opposed honest Radical regimes just as bitterly as notoriously corrupt ones. In the eyes of most white southerners, the real crime of the Radical governments was that they allowed black citizens to hold some offices and tried to protect the civil rights of black Americans. Race was white conservatives' greatest weapon. And it would prove the most effective means to undermine Republican power in the South.

✔ REVIEW

What roles did African Americans, southern whites, and northern whites play in the Reconstruction governments of the South?

BLACK ASPIRATIONS

Emancipation came to slaves in different ways and at different times. Betty Jones's grandmother was told about the Emancipation Proclamation by another slave while they were hoeing corn. Mary Anderson received the news from her master near the end of the war when Sherman's army invaded North Carolina. Whatever the timing, freedom meant a host of precious blessings to people who had been in bondage all their lives.

Experiencing Freedom ≫

The first impulse was to think of freedom as a contrast to slavery. Emancipation immediately released slaves from the most oppressive aspects of bondage—the whippings, the breakup of families, the sexual exploitation. Freedom also meant movement, the right to travel without a pass or white permission. Above all, freedom meant that African Americans' labor would be for their own benefit. One Arkansas freedman, who earned his first dollar working on a railroad, recalled that when he was paid, "I felt like the richest man in the world."

Freedom included finding a new place to work. Changing jobs was one concrete way to break the psychological ties of slavery. Even planters with reputations for kindness sometimes saw most of their former hands depart. The cook who left a South Carolina family, despite the offer of higher wages than her new job's, explained: "I must go. If I stays here I'll never know I'm free."

Symbolically, freedom meant having a full name. African Americans now adopted last names, most commonly the name of the first master in the family's oral history as far back as it could be recalled. Most, however, retained their first name, especially if the name had

been given to them by their parents (as most often had been the case). Whatever the name, black Americans insisted on making the decision themselves.

The Black Family ≫

African Americans also sought to strengthen the family in freedom. Since slave marriages had not been recognized as legal, thousands of former slaves insisted on being married again by proper authorities, even though this was not required by law. Those who had been forcibly separated in slavery and later remarried confronted the dilemma of which spouse to take. Laura Spicer, whose husband had been sold away in slavery, wrote him after the war seeking to resume their marriage. In a series of wrenching letters, he explained that he had thought her dead, had remarried, and had a new family. "You know it never was our wishes to be separated from each other, and it never was our fault. I had rather anything to had happened to me most than ever have been parted from you and the children," he wrote. "As I am, I do not know which I love best, you or Anna." Declining to return, he closed, "Laura, truly, I have got another wife, and I am very sorry."

As in white families, black husbands deemed themselves the head of the family and acted legally for their wives. They often insisted that their wives would not work in the fields as they had in slavery. "The [black] women say they never mean to do any more outdoor work," one planter reported, "that white men support their wives and they mean that their husbands shall support them." In negotiating contracts, a father also demanded the right to control his children and their labor. All these changes were designed to insulate the black family from white control.

The Schoolhouse and the Church ≫

In freedom, the schoolhouse and the black church became essential institutions in the black community. "My Lord, Ma'am, what a great thing learning is!" a South Carolina freedman told a northern teacher. "White folks can do what they likes, for they know so much more than we." At first, northern churches and missionaries, working with the Freedmen's Bureau, set up black schools in the South. Tuition at these schools represented 10 percent or more of a laborer's monthly wages, yet these schools were full. Eventually, states established public school systems, which by 1867 enrolled 40 percent of African American children.

Black adults, who often attended night classes, had good reasons for seeking literacy. They wanted to be able to read the Bible, to defend their newly gained civil and political rights, and to protect themselves

SAML. DOVE wishes to know of the whereabouts of his mother, Areno, his sisters Maria, Neziah, and Peggy, and his brother Edmond, who were owned by Geo. Dove, of Rockingham county, Shenandoah Valley, Va. Sold in Richmond, after which Saml. and Edmond were taken to Nashville, Tenn., by Joe Mick; Areno was left at the Eagle Tavern, Richmond

Respectfully yours,
SAML. DOVE.
Utica, New York, Aug. 5, 1865–3m

⌃ During the decades before the Civil War many slave families were split when individual slaves were sold to new masters. This Tennessee newspaper advertisement shows one way that freed people sought to deal with the consequences.

from being cheated. Both races saw that education would undermine the servility that slavery had fostered.

The teachers in the Freedmen's Bureau schools were primarily northern middle-class white women sent south by northern missionary societies. "I feel that it is a precious privilege," Esther Douglass wrote, "to be allowed to do something for these poor people." Many saw themselves as peacetime soldiers, struggling to make emancipation a reality. Indeed, hostile white southerners sometimes destroyed black schools and threatened and even murdered white teachers. Then there were the everyday challenges: low pay, run-down buildings, few books, classes of 100 or more children. By 1869 most teachers in these Freedmen's Bureau schools were black, trained by the bureau.

Most slaves had attended white churches or services supervised by whites. Once free, African Americans quickly established their own congregations led by black preachers. Mostly Methodist and Baptist, black churches were the only major organizations in the African American community controlled by blacks themselves. A white missionary reported that "the Ebony preacher who promises perfect independence from White control and direction carried the colored heart at once." Just as in slavery, religion offered African Americans a place of refuge in a hostile white world and provided them with hope, comfort, and a means of self-identification.

New Working Conditions >>
As a largely propertyless class, blacks in the postwar South had no choice but to work for white landowners. Except for paying wages, whites wanted to retain the old system of labor, including close supervision, gang labor, and physical punishment. Determined to remove all emblems of servitude, African Americans refused to work under these conditions, and they demanded time off to devote to their own interests. Because of shorter hours and the withdrawal of children and women from the fields, blacks' output declined by an estimated 35 percent in freedom. They also refused to live in the old slave quarters located near the master's house and instead erected cabins on distant parts of the plantation. Wages initially were $5 or $6 a month plus provisions and a cabin; by 1867, they had risen to an average of $10 a month.

These changes eventually led to the rise of sharecropping. Under this arrangement African American families farmed separate plots of land and then at the end of the year divided the crop, normally on an equal basis, with

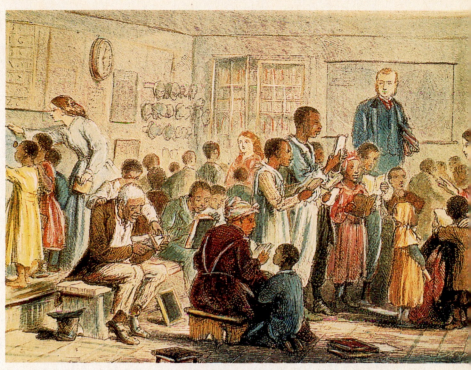

After living for years in a society in which teaching slaves to read and write was usually illegal, freedpeople viewed literacy as a key to securing their newfound freedom. Blacks were not merely "anxious to learn," a school official in Virginia reported, they were "crazy to learn."

the white landowner. Sharecropping had higher status and offered greater personal freedom than being a wage laborer. "I am not working for wages," one black farmer declared in defending his right to leave the plantation at will, "but am part owner of the crop and as [such,] I have all the rights that you or any other man has." Although black per capita agricultural income increased 40 percent in freedom, sharecropping was a harshly exploitative system in which black families often sank into perpetual debt.

The task of supervising the transition from slavery to freedom on southern plantations fell to the Freedmen's Bureau, a unique experiment in social policy supported by the federal government. Assigned the task of protecting freedpeople's economic rights, approximately 550 local agents regulated working conditions in southern agriculture after the war. The racial attitudes of Bureau agents varied widely, as did their commitment and competence.

Most agents required written contracts between white planters and black laborers, specifying wages and the conditions of employment. Although agents sometimes intervened to protect freedpeople from unfair treatment, they also provided important help to planters. They insisted that black laborers not leave at harvesttime, they arrested those who violated their contracts or refused to sign new ones at the beginning of the year, and they preached the need to be orderly and respectful.

Because of such attitudes, freedpeople increasingly complained that Bureau agents were mere tools of the planter class. One observer reported: "Doing justice seems to mean seeing that the blacks don't break contracts and compelling them to submit cheerfully."

The primary means of enforcing working conditions were the Freedmen's Courts, which Congress created in 1866 in order to avoid the discrimination African Americans received in state courts. These new courts functioned as military tribunals, and often the agent was the entire court. The sympathy black laborers received varied from state to state. But since Congress was opposed to creating any permanent welfare agency, it shut down the Bureau, and by 1872 it had gone out of business. Despite its mixed record, it was the most effective agency in protecting blacks' civil and political rights. Its disbanding signaled the beginning of the northern retreat from Reconstruction.

Planters and a New Way of Life >>
Planters and other white southerners faced emancipation with dread. "All the traditions and habits of both races had been suddenly overthrown," a Tennessee planter recalled, "and neither knew just what to do, or how to accommodate themselves to the new situation." Slavery had been a complex institution that welded black and white southerners together in intimate relationships. The old ideal of a paternalistic planter, which required blacks to act subservient and grateful, gave way to an emphasis on strictly economic relationships. Only with time did planters develop new norms to judge black behavior.

After the war, however, planters increasingly embraced the ideology of segregation. Since emancipation significantly reduced the social distance between the races, white southerners sought psychological separation and kept dealings with African Americans to a minimum. By the time Reconstruction ended, white planters had developed a new way of life based on the institutions of sharecropping and segregation, and undergirded by a militant white supremacy.

While most planters kept their land, they did not regain the economic prosperity of the prewar years. Cotton prices began a long decline, and southern per capita income suffered as a result. By 1880 the value of southern farms had slid 33 percent below the level of 1860.

> "All the traditions and habits of both races had been suddenly overthrown," a Tennessee planter recalled, "and neither knew just what to do, or how to accommodate themselves to the new situation."

 **REVIEW**

In what ways were the church and the school central to African American hopes after the Civil War?

THE ABANDONMENT OF RECONSTRUCTION

On Christmas Day 1875 a white acquaintance approached Charles Caldwell in Clinton, Mississippi, and invited him to have a drink. A former slave, Caldwell was a state senator and the leader of the Republican party in Hinds County. But the black leader's fearlessness made him a marked man. Only two months earlier, Caldwell had fled the county to escape an armed white mob. Despite threats against him, he had returned home to vote in the November state election. Now, as Caldwell and his "friend" raised their glasses in a holiday toast, a gunshot exploded through the window and Caldwell collapsed, mortally wounded. He was taken outside, where his assassins riddled his body with bullets. He died alone in the street.

Charles Caldwell shared the fate of a number of black Republican leaders in the South during Reconstruction. Resorting to violence and terror, southern whites challenged the commitment of the federal government to sustaining Reconstruction. After Andrew Johnson was acquitted in May 1868 at his impeachment trial, the crusading idealism of the Republican party began to wane. Ulysses S. Grant was hardly the cause of this change, but he certainly came to symbolize it.

The Grant Administration >>
In 1868 Grant was elected president—and Republicans were shocked. Their candidate, a great war hero, had won by a margin of only 300,000 votes. Furthermore, with an estimated 450,000 black Republican votes cast in the South, a majority of whites had voted Democratic. The election helped convince Republican leaders that an amendment securing black suffrage throughout the nation was necessary.

THE FIFTEENTH AMENDMENT.

CELEBRATED MAY 19? 1870.

⌃ The Fifteenth Amendment, ratified in 1870, secured the right of African American males to vote as free citizens. In New York, black citizens paraded in support of Ulysses S. Grant for president (*center*). But citizenship was only one component of what African Americans insisted were central aspects of their freedom. What other features of a free life does the poster champion?

In February 1869 Congress sent the Fifteenth Amendment to the states for ratification. It forbade any state to deny the right to vote on grounds of race, color, or previous condition of servitude. It did not forbid literacy and property requirements, as some Radicals wanted, because the moderates feared that only a conservative version of the amendment could be ratified. As a result, when the amendment was ratified in March 1870, loopholes remained that eventually allowed southern states to **disfranchise** African Americans.

> **disfranchisement** denial of a citizen's right to vote.

Advocates of women's suffrage were bitterly disappointed when Congress refused to outlaw voting discrimination on the basis of sex as well as race. The Women's Loyal League, led by Elizabeth Cady Stanton and Susan B. Anthony, had pressed for first the Fourteenth and then the Fifteenth Amendment to recognize that women had a civic right to vote. But even most Radicals were unwilling to back women's suffrage, contending that black rights had to be ensured first. As a result, the Fifteenth Amendment divided the feminist movement. Although disappointed that women were not included in its provisions, Lucy Stone and the American Woman Suffrage Association urged ratification. Stanton and Anthony, however, denounced the amendment and organized the National Woman Suffrage Association to work for passage of a new amendment giving women the ballot. The division hampered the women's rights movement for decades to come.

When Ulysses S. Grant was a general his quiet manner and well known resolution served him well. As president he proved much less certain of his goals and therefore less effective at corralling politicians than at maneuvering troops.

>> Grant swings from a trapeze while supporting a number of associates accused of corruption. Among those holding on are Secretary of the Navy George M. Robeson (*top center*), who was accused of accepting bribes for awarding Navy contracts; Secretary of War William W. Belknap (*top right*), who was forced to resign for selling Indian post traderships; and the president's private secretary, Orville Babcock (*bottom right*), who was implicated in the Whiskey Ring scandal. Although not personally involved in the scandals during his administration, Grant was reluctant to dismiss from office supporters accused of wrongdoing.

A series of scandals wracked his administration, so much so that "Grantism" soon became a code word in American politics for corruption, cronyism, and venality. Although Grant did not profit personally, he remained loyal to his friends and displayed little zeal to root out wrongdoing. Nor was Congress immune from the lowered tone of public life. In such a climate ruthless state machines, led by men who favored the status quo, came to dominate the party.

As corruption in both the North and the South worsened, reformers became more interested in cleaning up government than in protecting black rights. Congress in 1872 passed an amnesty act, allowing many more ex-Confederates to serve in southern governments. That same year liberal Republicans broke with the Republican party and nominated for president Horace Greeley, the editor of the New York *Tribune*. A one-time Radical, Greeley had become disillusioned with Reconstruction and urged a restoration of home rule in the South as well as adoption of civil service reform. Democrats decided to back the Liberal Republican ticket. The Republicans renominated Grant, who, despite the defection of a number of prominent Radicals, won an easy victory.

Growing Northern Disillusionment >>

During Grant's second term Congress passed the Civil Rights Act of 1875, the last major piece of Reconstruction legislation. This law prohibited racial discrimination in public accommodations, transportation, places of amusement, and juries. At the same time Congress rejected a ban on segregation in public schools, which was almost universally practiced in the North as well as the South. The federal government made little attempt to enforce the law, however, and in 1883 the Supreme Court struck down its provisions, except the one relating to juries.

Despite passage of the Civil Rights Act many northerners were growing disillusioned with Reconstruction. They were repelled by the corruption of the southern governments, they were tired of the violence and disorder that accompanied elections in the South, and they had little faith in black Americans. William Dodge, a wealthy New York capitalist and an influential Republican, wrote in 1875 that the South could never develop its resources "till confidence in her state governments can be restored, and this will never be done by federal bayonets." It had been a mistake, he went on, to make black southerners feel "that the United States government was their special friend, rather than those . . . among whom they must live and for whom they must work. We have tried this long enough," he concluded. "Now let the South alone."

As the agony of the war became more distant, the Panic of 1873, which precipitated a severe four-year depression, diverted public attention to economic issues. Battered by the panic and the corruption issue, the Republicans lost a shocking 77 seats in Congress in the 1874 elections, and along with them control of the House of Representatives for the first time since 1861.

"The truth is our people are tired out with the worn out cry of 'Southern outrages'!!" one Republican concluded. "Hard times and heavy taxes make them wish the 'ever lasting nigger' were in hell or Africa." More and more, Republicans spoke about cutting loose the unpopular southern governments.

The Triumph of White Supremacy ≫

Meanwhile, southern Democrats set out to overthrow the remaining Radical governments. Already white Republicans in the South felt heavy pressure to desert their party. To poor white southerners who lacked social standing, the Democratic appeal to racial solidarity offered special comfort. The large landowners and other wealthy groups that led southern Democrats objected less to black southerners voting, since they were confident that if outside influences were removed, they could control the black vote.

Democrats also resorted to economic pressure to undermine Republican power. In heavily black counties, newspapers published the names of black residents who cast Republican ballots and urged planters to discharge

≪ "Brute Might Makes Right. Shoot Suffrage to Death," reads the sign above the figure. By the time this cartoon appeared in 1879, terror tactics had "redeemed" the South for white Democrats.

them. But terror and violence provided the most effective means to overthrow the radical regimes. A number of paramilitary organizations broke up Republican meetings, terrorized white and black Republicans, assassinated Republican leaders, and prevented black citizens from voting. The most notorious of these organizations was the Ku Klux Klan, which along with similar groups functioned as an unofficial arm of the Democratic party.

In the war for supremacy, contesting control of the night was paramount to both southern whites and blacks. Before emancipation masters regulated the nighttime hours, with a system of passes and patrols that chased slaves who went hunting or tried to sneak a visit to a family member at a neighboring plantation. For slaves the night provided precious free time: to read, to meet for worship, school or dancing. During Reconstruction African Americans actively took back the night for a host of activities, including torchlight political parades and meetings of such organizations as the Union League. Part of the Klan's mission was to recoup this contested ground and to limit the ability of African Americans to use the night as they pleased. When indirect threats of violence were not enough (galloping through black neighborhoods rattling fences with lances), beatings and executions were undertaken—again, facilitated by the dark of night.

What became known as the Mississippi Plan was inaugurated in 1875, when Democrats decided to use as much violence as necessary to carry the state election. Local papers trumpeted, "Carry the election peaceably if we can, forcibly if we must." Recognizing that

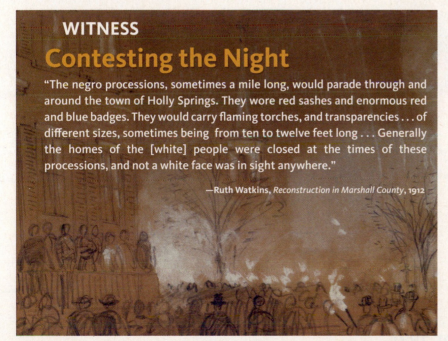

WITNESS

Contesting the Night

"The negro processions, sometimes a mile long, would parade through and around the town of Holly Springs. They wore red sashes and enormous red and blue badges. They would carry flaming torches, and transparencies . . . of different sizes, sometimes being from ten to twelve feet long . . . Generally the homes of the [white] people were closed at the times of these processions, and not a white face was in sight anywhere."

—Ruth Watkins, *Reconstruction in Marshall County*, 1912

northern public opinion had grown sick of repeated federal intervention in southern elections, the Grant administration rejected the request of Republican governor Adelbert Ames for troops to stop the violence. Bolstered by terrorism, the Democrats swept the election in Mississippi. Violence and intimidation prevented as many as 60,000 black and white Republicans from voting, converting the normal Republican majority into a Democratic majority of 30,000. Mississippi had been "redeemed."

> **Even under redeemer governments, African Americans did not return to the social position they had occupied before the war.**

The Disputed Election of 1876 >>

The 1876 presidential election was crucial to the final overthrow of Reconstruction. The Republicans nominated Ohio governor Rutherford B. Hayes to oppose Samuel Tilden of New York. Once again violence prevented an estimated quarter of a million Republican votes from being cast in the South. Tilden had a clear majority of 250,000 in the popular vote, but the outcome in the Electoral College was in doubt

Redeemers southerners who came to power in southern state governments from 1875 to 1877, claiming to have "redeemed" the South from Reconstruction. The Redeemers looked to undo many of the changes wrought by the Civil War.

because both parties claimed South Carolina, Florida, and Louisiana, the only reconstructed states still in Republican hands.

To arbitrate the disputed returns Congress established a 15-member electoral commission. By a straight party vote of 8 to 7, the commission awarded the disputed electoral votes—and the presidency—to Hayes.

When angry Democrats threatened a filibuster to prevent the electoral votes from being counted, key Republicans met with southern Democrats and reached an informal understanding, later known as the Compromise of 1877. Hayes's supporters agreed to withdraw federal troops from the South and not oppose the new Democratic state governments. For their part, southern Democrats dropped their opposition to Hayes's election and pledged to respect African Americans' rights.

Without federal support, the last Republican southern governments collapsed, and Democrats took control of the remaining states of the Confederacy. By 1877, the entire South was in the hands of the **Redeemers**, as they called themselves. Reconstruction and Republican rule had come to an end.

Racism and the Failure of Reconstruction >>

Reconstruction failed for a multitude of reasons. The reforming impulse behind the Republican party of the 1850s had been battered and worn down by the war. The new materialism of industrial America inspired a jaded cynicism in many Americans. In the South, African American voters and leaders inevitably lacked a certain amount of education and experience; elsewhere, Republicans were divided over policies and options.

Yet beyond these obstacles, the sad fact remains that the ideals of Reconstruction were most clearly defeated by a deep-seated racism that permeated American life. Racism stimulated white southern resistance, undercut northern support for black rights, and eventually made northerners willing to write off Reconstruction, and with it the welfare of African Americans. Although Congress could pass a constitutional amendment abolishing slavery, it could not overturn at a stroke the social habits of two centuries.

Candidate (Party)	Electoral Vote (%)	Popular Vote (%)
Rutherford B. Hayes (Republican)	185 (50)	4,034,311 (48)
Samuel J. Tilden (Democrat)	184 (50)	4,288,546 (51)
Minor parties	–	93,895 (1)
Nonvoting territories		

ELECTION OF 1876

What factors in the North and the South led the federal government to abandon Reconstruction in the South?

With the overthrow of Reconstruction, the white South had won back some of the power it had lost in 1865—but not all. In the longer term, the political equations of power had been changed. Even under redeemer governments, African Americans did not return to the social position they had occupied before the war. They were no longer slaves, and black southerners who walked dusty roads in search of family members, sent their children to school, or worshiped in their own black churches knew what a momentous change this was. Even under the exploitative sharecropping system, black income rose significantly in freedom. Then, too, the guarantees of "equal protection" and "due process of law" had been written into the Constitution and would be available for later generations to use in championing once again the Radicals' goal of racial equality.

But this was a struggle left to future reformers. For the time being, the clear trend was away from change or hope—especially for former slaves like Benjamin Montgomery and his sons, the owners of the old Davis plantations in Mississippi. In the 1870s bad crops, lower cotton prices, and falling land values undermined the Montgomerys' financial position, and in 1875 Jefferson Davis sued to have the sale of Brierfield invalidated. Following the overthrow of Mississippi's Radical government, a white conservative majority of the court awarded Brierfield to Davis in 1878. The Montgomerys lost Hurricane as well.

The waning days of Reconstruction were times filled with such ironies: of governments "redeemed" by violence, of Fourteenth Amendment rights being used by conservative courts to protect not black people but giant corporations, of reformers taking up other causes. Increasingly, the industrial North focused on an economic task: integrating both the South and the West into the Union. In the case of both regions, northern factories sought to use southern and western raw materials to produce goods and to find national markets for those products. Indeed, during the coming decades European nations also scrambled to acquire natural resources and markets. In the onrushing age of imperialism, Western nations would seek to dominate newly acquired colonies in Africa and Asia, with the same disregard for their "subject peoples" that was seen with African Americans, Latinos, and Indians in the United States.

Disowned by its northern supporters and unmourned by public opinion, Reconstruction was over.

CHAPTER SUMMARY

Presidents Abraham Lincoln and Andrew Johnson and the Republican-dominated Congress each developed a program of Reconstruction to quickly restore the Confederate states to the Union.

- Lincoln's 10 percent plan required that 10 percent of qualified voters from 1860 swear an oath of loyalty to begin organizing a state government.
- Following Lincoln's assassination, Andrew Johnson changed Lincoln's terms and lessened Reconstruction's requirements.
- The more radical Congress repudiated Johnson's state governments and eventually enacted its own program of Reconstruction, which included the principle of black suffrage.
  - Congress passed the Fourteenth and Fifteenth Amendments and also extended the life of the Freedmen's Bureau, a unique experiment in social welfare.
  - Congress rejected land reform, however, which would have provided the freedpeople with a greater economic stake.
  - The effort to remove Johnson from office through impeachment failed.
- The Radical governments in the South, led by black and white southerners and transplanted northerners, compiled a mixed record on matters such as racial equality, education, economic issues, and corruption.
- Reconstruction was a time of both joy and frustration for former slaves.
  - Former slaves took steps to reunite their families and establish black-controlled churches.
  - They evidenced a widespread desire for land and education.
  - Black resistance to the old system of labor led to the adoption of sharecropping.
  - The Freedmen's Bureau fostered these new working arrangements and also the beginnings of black education in the South.
- Northern public opinion became disillusioned with Reconstruction during the presidency of Ulysses S. Grant.
- Southern whites used violence, economic coercion, and racism to overthrow the Republican state governments.
- In 1877 Republican leaders agreed to end Reconstruction in exchange for Rutherford B. Hayes's election as president.
- Racism played a key role in the eventual failure of Reconstruction.

Additional Reading

Historians' views of Reconstruction have dramatically changed over the past half century. Modern studies offer a more sympathetic assessment of Reconstruction and the experience of African Americans. Indicative of this trend is Eric Foner, *Reconstruction* (1988), and his briefer treatment (with photographic essays by Joshua Brown) *Forever Free: the Story of Emancipation and Reconstruction* (2005). Michael Les Benedict treats the clash between Andrew Johnson and Congress in *The Impeachment and Trial of Andrew Johnson* (1973). Political affairs in the South during Reconstruction are examined in Dan T. Carter, *When the War Was Over* (1985), and Thomas Holt, *Black over White* (1977), an imaginative study of black political leadership in South Carolina. Hans Trefousse, *Thaddeus Stevens: Nineteenth-Century Egalitarian* (1997), provides a sympathetic reassessment of the influential Radical Republican.

Leon Litwack, *Been in the Storm So Long* (1979), sensitively analyzes the transition of enslaved African Americans to freedom. Heather Andrea Williams, *Self-Taught: African American Education in Slavery and Freedom* (2005), illustrates the black drive for literacy and education. James L. Roark, *Masters without Slaves* (1977), discusses former slaveholders' adjustment to the end of slavery. The dialectic of black-white relations is charted from the antebellum years through Reconstruction and beyond in Steven Hahn, *A Nation under Our Feet: Black*

Significant Events

Louisiana, Arkansas, and Tennessee establish governments under Lincoln's Reconstruction Plan

Freedmen's Bureau established; Johnson becomes president; presidential Reconstruction completed; Thirteenth Amendment ratified

1864   **1865–1866**   **1865**   **1866**   **1867–1868**

Black codes enacted

Civil rights bill passed over Johnson's veto; Memphis and New Orleans riots; Ku Klux Klan organized

Constitutional conventions in the South; Blacks vote in southern elections

Political Struggles in the Rural South from Slavery to the Great Migration (2003). Two excellent studies of changing labor relations in southern agriculture are Julie Saville, *The Work of Reconstruction* (1995), and John C. Rodrigue, *Reconstruction in the Cane Fields* (2001). For contrasting views of the Freedman's Bureau see George R. Bentley, *A History of the Freedman's Bureau* (1955)—favorable—and Donald Nieman, *To Set the Law in Motion* (1979)—more critical. William Gillette, *Retreat from Reconstruction, 1869–1879* (1980), focuses on national politics and the end of Reconstruction, while Michael Perman, *The Road to Redemption* (1984), looks at developments in the South.

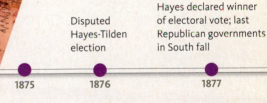

Johnson impeached
but acquitted;
Fourteenth
Amendment ratified;
Grant elected
president

Disputed
Hayes-Tilden
election

Compromise of 1877;
Hayes declared winner
of electoral vote; last
Republican governments
in South fall

1867 1868 1870 1875 1876 1877

Congressional
Reconstruction
enacted; Tenure
of Office Act
passed

Fifteenth
Amendment
ratified

Civil Rights Act;
Mississippi Plan

African Americans wait on a levee, as many Exodusters did in moving to Kansas in 1879 and 1880. Often traveling with few resources, they found the journey uncertain. In the foreground a young child sleeps on the only bedding available.

The New South and the

18

›› AN AMERICAN STORY

"COME WEST"

The news spread across the South during the late 1870s. Perhaps a man came around with a handbill, telling of cheap land; or a letter might arrive from friends or relatives and be read aloud at church. The news spread in different ways, but in the end, the talk always spelled KANSAS.

Few black farmers had been to Kansas themselves. More than a few knew that the abolitionist John Brown had made his home there before coming east to raid Harpers Ferry. Black folks, it seemed, might be able to live more freely in Kansas: "They do not kill Negroes here for voting," wrote one black settler to a friend. **››**

1870–1890

Trans-Mississippi West

St. Louis learned of these rumblings in the first raw days of March 1879, as steamers from downriver began unloading freedpeople in large numbers. By the end of 1879 crowds overwhelmed the wharves and temporary shelters. The city's black churches banded together to house the "refugees," feed them, and help them continue toward Kansas. The "Exodusters," as they became known, pressed westward, many of the black emigrants settling in growing towns such as Topeka and Kansas City

The thousands of Exodusters who poured into Kansas were part of a human flood westward. It had many sources: played-out farms of New England and the South, crowded cities, much of Europe. Special trains brought the settlers to the plains, all eager to start anew. But the optimism of boomers black and white could not mask the serious strains in the rapidly expanding nation, especially in the South and the lands west of the Mississippi—the trans-Mississippi West. As largely agricultural regions, they struggled to find their place in the new age of industry emerging from Reconstruction.

In the South, despite a strong push to industrialize, white supremacy undercut economic growth. Sharecropping and farm tenancy mushroomed, and a system of racial violence and caste replaced slavery. For its part, the booming West began to realize some of the dreams of democratic antebellum reformers: for free land, for a transcontinental railroad, for colleges to educate its people. Yet the West, too, built a society based on racial violence and hierarchy that challenged hopes for a more democratic future.

By the end of the nineteenth century both the South and the West had assumed their place as suppliers of raw materials, providers of foodstuffs, and consumers of finished goods. A nation of "regional nations" hardly equal in stature was thus drawn together in the last third of the nineteenth century, despite the growing frustrations of inhabitants old and new. ‹‹

THE SOUTHERN BURDEN

It was just such regional inequities that infuriated Henry Grady, the editor of the *Atlanta Constitution.* He liked to tell the story of the poor cotton farmer buried in a pine coffin in the pine woods of Georgia. Only the coffin had been made not in Georgia but in Cincinnati. Despite its own rich resources, Grady fumed, the "South didn't furnish a thing on earth for that funeral but the corpse and the hole in the ground!" The irony of the story was the tragedy of the South. The region had human and natural resources aplenty but, alas, few factories to manufacture the goods it needed.

In the 1880s Grady campaigned to bring about a "New South" based on bustling industry, cities, and commerce. The business class and its values would displace the old planter class as southerners raced "to out-Yankee the Yankee." Like modern alchemists they would transform resources into riches. The region encompassed a third of the nation's farmlands, vast tracts of lumber, and rich deposits of coal, iron, oil, and fertilizers. To overcome the destruction of the Civil War and the loss of slaveholding wealth, apostles of the New South campaigned to catch up with the industrial North.

For all the hopeful talk of industry, the economy of the postwar South remained agricultural, tied to crops such as tobacco, rice, sugar, and especially cotton. By using fertilizers, planters were able to introduce cotton into areas once considered marginal.

Yet from 1880 to 1900 world demand for cotton grew slowly, and prices fell. As farms in other parts of the country became larger, more efficient, and tended by fewer workers per acre, southern farms shrank. This reflected the breakup of large plantations, but it also resulted from a high birthrate. Across the country, the number of children born per mother was dropping, but in the South, large families remained common. More children meant more farmhands. Thus each year, fewer acres of land were available for each person to cultivate.

Tenancy and Sharecropping ›› To freedpeople across the South, the end of slavery brought hopes of economic independence. After the war a hopeful John Solomon Lewis rented land to grow cotton in Tensas Parish, Louisiana. A depression in the 1870s dashed his dreams. "I was in debt," Lewis explained, "and the man I rented land from said every year I must rent again to pay the other year, and so I rents and rents and each year I gets deeper and deeper in debt."

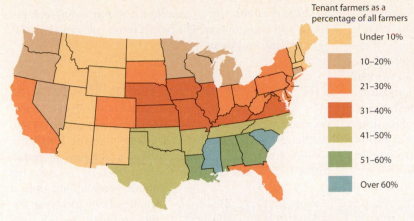

Tenant farmers as a
percentage of all farmers

Under 10%

10–20%

21–30%

31–40%

41–50%

51–60%

Over 60%

⌃ TENANT FARMERS, 1900 Tenant farming dominated southern agriculture after the Civil War. But note that by 1900 it also accounted for much of the farm labor in the trans-Mississippi West, where low crop prices, high costs, and severe environmental conditions forced independent farmers into tenancy.

Lewis was impoverished like most small farmers in the cotton South. Despite the breakup of some plantations, the South's best lands remained in the hands of the largest plantation owners. Few freed-people or poor white southerners had money to acquire property. Like Lewis, most rented land—perhaps a plot of 15 to 20 acres—as tenants in hopes of buying someday. Since cotton was king and money scarce, rents were generally set in pounds of cotton rather than dollars. Usually the amount added up to between one-quarter and one-half the value of the crop.

Among the most common and exploitative forms of farm tenancy was sharecropping. Unlike renters, who leased land and controlled what they raised, sharecroppers simply worked a parcel of land in exchange for a share of the crop, usually a third after debt was deducted. It was rarely enough to make ends meet. Like other forms of tenancy, sharecropping left farmers in perpetual debt.

This system might not have proved so ruinous if the South had possessed a fairer system of credit. Before selling crops in the fall, farmers without cash had to borrow money in the spring to buy seeds, tools, and other necessities. Most often the only source of supplies was the local store, where prices for goods bought on credit could be as much as 60 percent higher. As security for the merchant's credit, the only asset most renters and sharecroppers could offer was a mortgage, or "lien," on their crops. The lien gave the shopkeeper first claim on the crop until the debt was paid off.

lien legal claim against property used to obtain a loan, which must be paid when the property is sold.

Year after year tenants and croppers borrowed against their harvests to use the land they farmed. Most landlords insisted that sharecroppers grow profitable crops such as cotton rather than things they could eat. They also required that raw cotton be ginned, baled, and marketed through their mills—at a rate they controlled. Sharecropping, crop liens, and monopolies on ginning and marketing added up to

inequality, crushing poverty, and **debt peonage** for the South's small farmers.

debt peonage paying off a debt through labor when the debtor lacks sufficient cash or other assets.

The slide of sharecroppers and tenants into debt peonage occurred elsewhere in the cotton-growing world. In India, Egypt, and Brazil agricultural laborers gave up **subsistence farming** to raise cotton as a cash crop during the American Civil War, when the North prevented southern cotton

subsistence farming farming in which individuals and families produce most of what they need to live on.

from being exported to textile manufacturers in Europe. But when prices fell as American cotton farming revived after the war, growers borrowed to make ends meet, as in the U.S. South. In Egypt interest rates soared sometimes to 60 percent. The pressures on cotton growers led them to revolt in the mid-1870s. In India growers attacked prominent moneylenders. In Brazil protesters destroyed land records and refused to pay taxes.

Southern Industry >>

The crusade for a New South did bring change. From 1869 to 1909 industrial production grew faster in the South than it did nationally. A boom in railroad building after 1879 furnished the region with good transportation. In two areas, cotton textiles and tobacco, southern advances were striking. With cotton fiber

⌃ This girl had been working in a cotton mill in Whitnel, North Carolina, for about a year, sometimes on the night shift. She made 48 cents a day. When asked how old she was, she hesitated, then said, "I don't remember." But she added, confidentially, "I'm not old enough to work, but do just the same."

and cheap labor close at hand, 400 cotton mills were humming by 1900, when they employed almost 100,000 workers.

Most new textile workers were white southerners escaping competition from black farm laborers or fleeing the hardscrabble life of the mountains. Entire families worked in the mills. Older men had the most trouble adjusting. They lacked the experience, temperament, and dexterity to tend spindles and looms in cramped mills. Only over time, as farm folk adapted to the tedious rhythm of factories, did southerners become competitive with workers from other regions of the United States and western Europe.

The tobacco industry also thrived in the New South. Before the Civil War, American tastes had run to cigars, snuff, and chewing tobacco. In 1876, James Bonsack invented a machine to roll cigarettes. That was just the device Washington Duke and his son James needed to boost the fortunes of their growing tobacco business. Cigarettes suited the new urban market in the North. Unlike chewing tobacco and snuff, they were, in the words of one observer, "clean, quick, and potent." Between 1860 and 1900, Americans spent more money on tobacco than on clothes or shoes.

Gentlemens' Delight

Manufactured by B.H. WATSON, Lynchburg, Va.

 Tobacco and sex became entwined in the nineteenth century, as this label for B. H. Watson's "Gentlemen's Delight" tobacco reveals. A bare-shouldered woman, her dark hair tumbling behind her, beckons buyers to purchase the product that promises nothing but the delight on the label's title.

In the postwar era the South possessed over 60 percent of the nation's timber resources. With soaring demand from towns and cities, lumber and turpentine became the South's chief industries and employers. The environmental costs were high. In the South as elsewhere, over-cutting and other logging practices stripped hillsides bare. As spring rains eroded soil and unleashed floods, forests lost their capacity for self-renewal. With them went the golden eagles, peregrine falcons, and other native species.

The iron and steel industry most disappointed promoters of the New South. The availability of coke as a fuel made Chattanooga, Tennessee, and Birmingham, Alabama, major centers for foundries. By the 1890s the Tennessee Coal, Iron, and Railway Company (TCI) of Birmingham was turning out iron pipe for gas, water, and sewer lines vital to cities. Unfortunately, Birmingham's iron deposits were ill suited to produce the kinds of steel in demand. In 1907 TCI was sold to the giant U.S. Steel Corporation, controlled by northern interests.

The pattern of lost opportunity was repeated in other southern industries. Under the campaign for a New South, all grew dramatically in employment and value, but not enough to end poverty. The South remained largely rural, agricultural, and poor.

The Sources of Southern Poverty »

Why did poverty persist in the New South? Three factors peculiar to the South best explain the region's poverty. First, the South began to industrialize later than the Northeast, so northerners had a head start on learning new manufacturing techniques. It was difficult to catch up, because the South commanded only a small technological community to guide its industrial development. Northern engineers and mechanics seldom followed northern capital into the region. Few experts were available to adapt modern technology to southern conditions or to teach southerners how to do it themselves.

Education might have overcome the problem by upgrading the region's workforce were it not for a second factor: school budgets. No region spent less on schooling than the South. Southern leaders, drawn from the ranks of the upper class, cared little about educating poor whites and openly resisted educating black southerners. Education, they contended, "spoiled" otherwise contented workers by leading them to demand higher wages and better conditions.

Lack of education aggravated the third and central source of southern poverty: the isolation of its labor force. In 1900 agriculture still dominated the southern economy. It required unskilled, low-paid sharecroppers and wage laborers. Southerners feared outsiders, whether capitalists, industrialists, or experts in technology, who might spread discontent among workers. So southern states discouraged social services and opportunities that might have attracted human and financial resources, keeping their workforce secluded and uneducated. Despite what some southerners believed, the South remained poor because it received too little, not too much, outside investment.

✔ REVIEW

What factors explain the failure of the campaign for a "New South"?

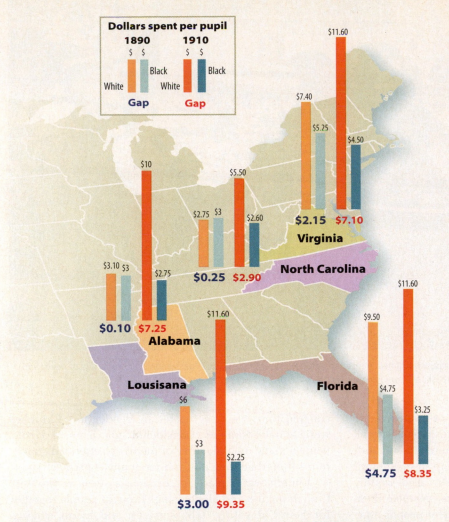

Dollars spent per pupil

1890	1910
White / Black	White / Black
Gap	**Gap**

Virginia
$11.60
$7.40
$5.25
$4.50
$2.15 **$7.10**

North Carolina
$2.75 $3
$5.50
$2.60
$0.25 **$2.90**

$10

$3.10 $3
$2.75
Alabama
$0.10 **$7.25**

Florida
$11.60
$9.50
$4.75
$3.25
$4.75 **$8.35**

Lousisana
$11.60
$6
$3
$2.25
$3.00 **$9.35**

SPENDING ON EDUCATION IN THE SOUTH BEFORE AND AFTER DISFRANCHISEMENT

With disfranchisement and segregation, education was separate, but hardly equal, for blacks and whites. In these states, after blacks were disfranchised, spending on white students rose while spending on black students decreased. [*Source:* Data from Robert A. Margo, *Disfranchisement, School Finance, and the Economics of Segregated Schools in the U.S. South, 1890-1910* (New York: Garland Press, 1985), table I-1.]

LIFE IN THE NEW SOUTH

Many a southern man, noted a son of the region, loved "to toss down a pint of raw whiskey in a gulp, to fiddle and dance all night, to bite off the nose or gouge out the eye of a favorite enemy, to fight harder and love harder than the next man, to be known far and wide as a hell of a fellow." Life in the New South was a constant struggle to balance this masculinized love of sport and leisure with the pull of a more feminized Christian piety.

Divided in its soul the South was also divided by race. After the Civil War some 90 percent of African Americans continued to live in the rural South. Without slavery, however, white southerners lost the system of social control that had defined race relations. Over time they substituted a new system of racial separation that eased but never eliminated white fear of black Americans.

Rural Life >> Pleasure, piety, race, and gender—all divided southern life in town and country alike. Southern males loved hunting. For rural people a successful hunt could add meat and fish to a scanty diet. Hunting also offered welcome relief from heavy farmwork, and for many boys a path to manhood. Seeing his father and brothers return with wild turkeys, young Edward McIlhenny longed "for the time when I would be old enough to hunt this bird."

The thrill of illicit pleasure drew many southern men to events of violence and chance, including cockfighting. Gambling between bird owners and among spectators only heightened the thrills. Such sport and the harddrinking, sometimes brutal culture that accompanied it offended churchgoing southerners. They condemned as sinful "the beer garden, the baseball, the low theater, the dog fight and cock fight and the ring for the pugilist and brute."

Many southern customs involved no such disorderly behavior. Worksharing festivals such as house raisings, log rollings, and quiltings gave isolated farm folk the chance to break their daily routine, to socialize, and to work for a common good. These events, too, were generally segregated along gender lines. Men did the heavy chores and competed in contests of physical prowess. Women shared more domestic tasks such as quilting. These community gatherings also offered young southerners an opportunity for courtship. In one courting game, the young man who found a rare red ear of corn "could kiss the lady of his choice"—although in the school, church, or home under adult supervision, such behavior was discouraged.

For rural folk a trip to town brought special excitement and a bit of danger. Saturdays, court days, and holidays provided an occasion to mingle. For men the saloon, the blacksmith shop, or the storefront was a place to do business and to let off steam. Few men went to town without participating in social drinking. When they turned to roam the streets, the threat of brawling and violence drove most women away.

⚞ For Baptists in the South, the ceremony of adult baptism included immersion, often in a nearby river. The ritual symbolized the waters of newfound faith washing away sins. Here, a black congregation looks on, some holding umbrellas to protect against the sun.

The Church >>

At the center of southern life stood the church as a great stabilizer and custodian of social order. "When one joined the Methodist church," a southern woman recalled, "he was expected to give up all such things as cards, dancing, theatres, in fact all so called worldly amusements." Many devout southerners pursued these ideals, although such restraint asked more of people, especially men, than most were willing to show except perhaps on Sunday.

By 1870 southern churches were segregated by race. Indeed, the black church was the only institution controlled by African Americans after slavery and thus a principal source of leadership and identity in addition to comfort. Within churches both black and white, congregations were segregated by gender, too. Churches were female domains. Considered guardians of virtue, women made up a majority of members, attended church more often than men did, and ran many church activities.

Church was a place to socialize as well as worship. Church picnics and all day sings brought people together for hours of eating, talk, services, and hymn singing. Weekly rituals could not match the fervor of a weeklong camp meeting. In the late summer or early fall, town and countryside alike emptied as folks set up tents in shady groves and listened to two or three ministers preach day and night, in the largest event of the year. The camp meeting refired evangelical faith while celebrating traditional values of home and family.

⚟ A long line of African American voters waits to cast ballots in Caddo Parish, Louisiana, 1897. Clearly, interest in voting remained high among black citizens. Two years later Louisiana followed the lead of other Southern states in disfranchising most of its black voters (as well as many poor whites).

Segregation >> After Reconstruction white northerners and southerners achieved sectional harmony by sacrificing the rights of black citizens. During the 1880s "Redeemer" governments (pages 350–351) moved to formalize a new system of **segregation,** or racial separation. Redeemers were white Democrats who came to power in southern states vowing to end the Republican rule that had been established during Reconstruction.

> **segregation** system, imposed through law and custom, of separating people by race.

The pressure to reach a new racial accommodation in the South increased as more African Americans moved into southern towns and cities, competing for jobs with poor whites. One way to preserve the social and economic superiority of white southerners, poor as well as rich, was to separate blacks as an inferior caste. Within 20 years every southern state had enacted segregation as law. The earliest laws legalized segregation in trains and other public conveyances. Soon a web of "Jim Crow" statutes separated the races in almost all public places except streets and stores. (The term "Jim Crow," to denote a policy of segregation, originated in a song of the same name sung in minstrel shows of the day.) In 1896 the Supreme Court again upheld the policy of segregation. *Plessy v. Ferguson* upheld a Louisiana law requiring segregated railroad facilities. Racial separation did not constitute discrimination, the Court argued, so long as accommodations for both races were equal. In reality, of course, such separate facilities were seldom equal and always stigmatized African Americans.

By the turn of the century segregation was firmly in place, stifling economic competition between the races and reducing African Americans to second-class citizenship. Many kinds of employment, such as work in the textile mills, went largely to whites. Skilled and professional black workers generally served black clients only. Blacks could enter some white residences only as servants and hired help, and then only by the back door. They were barred from juries and usually received far stiffer penalties than whites for the same crimes. Any African American who crossed the color line risked violence. Some were tarred and feathered, others whipped and beaten, and many lynched. Of the 187 lynchings averaged each year of the 1890s, some 80 percent occurred in the South, where the victims were usually black.

 **REVIEW**

How did segregation work as an instrument of social control?

WESTERN FRONTIERS

The black Exodusters flooding into the treeless plains of Kansas in the 1870s and 1880s were only part of the vast migration west. Looking beyond the Mississippi

in the 1840s and 1850s, "overlanders" moved over land (as opposed to sailing around the southern tip of South America), setting their sights on California and Oregon in search of opportunity and "free" land.

Those without money or power found opportunity elusive. They also found Indians and "Hispanos" (settlers of Spanish descent), who hardly considered the land free for use by Anglos. And they discovered the West was not one frontier but many, all moving in different directions. Before the Civil War the frontier for easterners had moved westward beyond the Mississippi to the timberlands of Missouri, but skipped over the Great Plains, as the overlanders settled in California and Oregon. A mining frontier pushed east from the Pacific coast, following diggers into the Sierra Nevada. For Texans the frontier moved from south to north as cattle ranchers sought new grazing land, as had the ancestors of the Hispanic rancheros

⩔ Luring settlers west became big business for railroad companies in the late nineteenth century. They stood to profit three times over: from the sale of lands they owned; from the passenger traffic generated by settlement; and from the goods and commodities shipped to and from settlers. The Burlington and Missouri River Railroad distributed this circular, which promised cheap land in Iowa and Nebraska with loans at low interest rates. What other inducements did the company offer to coax buyers to come west and purchase land?

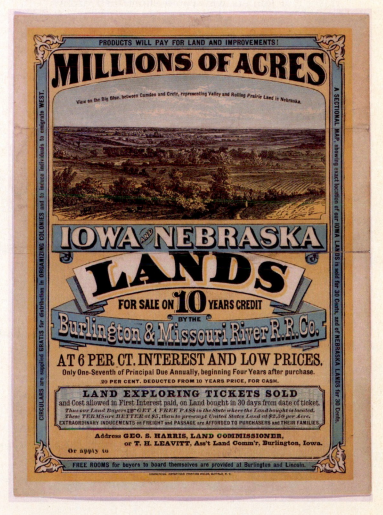

of the Southwest. For American Indians the frontier was constantly shifting and disrupting their ways of life.

Western Landscapes >>

The varied landscapes of the West begin with the region between the 98th meridian and the West Coast—the Great Plains. It receives less than 20 inches of rain a year, making it a treeless expanse of prairie grass and dunes that the first Anglo settlers called "the Great American Desert."

The Great Plains are only part of the trans-Mississippi West. Beyond the plains the jagged peaks of the Rocky Mountains stretch from Alaska to New Mexico. Beyond the mountains lies the Great Basin of Utah, Nevada, and eastern California, where temperatures climb above 100 degrees. Near the coast the towering Sierra Nevada and the Cascades rise, rich in minerals and lumber, and then slope into the temperate shores of the Pacific.

Already in the 1840s, the Great Plains and mountain frontier comprised a complex web of cultures and environments. The horse, for example, had been introduced into North America by Spanish colonizers. By the eighteenth century horses were grazing on prairie grass across the Great Plains. By the nineteenth century the Comanche, Cheyenne, Apache, and other tribes had become master riders and hunters who could shoot their arrows with deadly accuracy at a full gallop. The new mobility of the Plains Indians far extended the area in which they could hunt buffalo. Their lives shifted from settled, village-centered agriculture to a more nomadic existence.

Indian Peoples and the Western Environment >>

Some whites embraced the myth of the Indian as "noble savage" who lived in perfect harmony with the natural world. To be sure, Plains Indians were inventive in using scarce resources. Cottonwood bark fed horses in winter, while the buffalo supplied not only meat but also bones for tools, fat for cosmetics, and sinews for thread. Yet Indians could not help but alter the world around them, not always for the better. Plains Indians hunted buffalo by stampeding herds over cliffs, which often led to waste. They irrigated crops and set fires to improve vegetation. By the mid-nineteenth century some tribes had become so enmeshed in the white fur trade that they over-trapped their own hunting grounds.

Ecological diversity produced a stunning variety of tribes and Indian peoples who nonetheless shared experiences and values. Most tribes were small kinship groups of 300 to 500 people in which the well-being of all outweighed the needs of each member. Although some tribes were materially better off than others, the gap between rich and poor within tribes was seldom large. Such small material differences often promoted communal decision making. The Cheyenne, for example, employed a council of 44 to advise the chief.

The cultures of western Indians were remarkably varied, ranging from the nomadic Plains tribes to the more settled peoples of the northwest coast who lived off the sea. This Sioux woman gathers firewood; the photograph was taken by Edward Curtis, who spent many years recording the faces and lives of the native peoples of the West.

Indians also shared a reverence for nature, whatever their actual impact on the natural world. They believed human beings were part of an interconnected world of animals, plants, and other natural elements. All had souls of their own but were bound together, as if by contract, to live in balance through the ceremonial life of the tribe and the customs related to specific plants and animals. The Taos of New Mexico believed that each spring the pregnant earth issued new life. To avoid disturbing "mother" earth, they walked in bare feet or soft moccasins and removed the hard shoes from their horses.

Whites and the Western Environment: Competing Visions >>

As discoveries of gold and silver lured white settlers into Indian territory, many adopted the decidedly un-Indian outlook of Missouri politician William Gilpin. Only a lack of vision prevented the opening of the West for exploitation, Gilpin told an Independence, Missouri, audience in 1849. What was most needed: cheap lands for farms and a railroad linking the two coasts "like ears on a human head." In his expansive view, land was nothing sacred, only property to be employed. Indians were merely obstacles.

By 1868 a generous Congress had granted western settlers their two greatest wishes: free land under the Homestead Act of 1862, and a transcontinental railroad. As the new governor of Colorado, Gilpin crowed about the West's near limitless possibilities for growth. Scarce water and

NATURAL ENVIRONMENT OF THE WEST

With the exception of the Pacific Northwest few areas west of the 20-inch rainfall line receive enough annual precipitation to support agriculture without irrigation. Consequently, water has been the key to development west of the 98th meridian, an area that encompasses more than half the country.

rainfall did not daunt him for he believed in the widely accepted theory that "rain follows the plow." Early climatologist Cyrus Thomas and amateur scientist Charles Dana Wilbur popularized the notion that plowing dry land released moisture into the air, thereby increasing cloud cover and rainfall. Settlers and speculators in the United States justified their actions as transforming "desert into a farm or garden," as did wheat growers cultivating marginal land in southern Australia. An unusually wet cycle from 1878 to 1886 helped to sustain the myth in the states. The fact that such human activity actually did increase precipitation locally (by robbing rain from nearby areas) undermined skeptics who rightly argued that plowing produced no change in climate over large regions.

Unlike the visionary Gilpin, John Wesley Powell knew something about water and farming. In 1869 and 1871 Powell had led scientific expeditions down the Green and Colorado rivers through the Grand Canyon. Navigating the swirling rapids that blocked his way, he returned to warn Congress that developing the West required more scientific planning. Much of the region had not yet been mapped nor its resources identified.

In 1880 Powell became director of the recently formed U.S. Geological Survey. He, too, had a vision of the West, but one based on the limits of its environment. The key was water, not land. Unlike the water-drenched East, water in the parched West should be treated as community rather than private property. The practice would benefit many rather than a privileged few owners at the headwaters. Powell suggested that the federal government establish political boundaries defined by large watersheds and regulate the distribution of the scarce resource. But his scientific realism could not overcome the popular vision of the West as the American Eden. Powerful interests ensured that development occurred with the same laissez-faire credo that ruled the East.

 **REVIEW**

How did Indian conceptions of the environment compare and contrast with white conceptions?

THE WAR FOR THE WEST

Beginning in 1848 a series of gold and silver discoveries signaled the first serious interest by white settlers in the arid and semiarid lands beyond the Mississippi, where many Indian nations had been forced to migrate. To open more land, federal officials introduced in 1851 a policy of "concentration." Tribes were pressured into signing treaties limiting the boundaries of their hunting grounds to "reservations"—the Sioux to the Dakotas, the Crow to Montana, the Cheyenne to the foothills of Colorado— where they would be taught to farm.

Such treaties often claimed that their provisions would last "as long as waters run," but time after time land-hungry pioneers broke the promises of their government by squatting on Indian lands and demanding federal protection. The government, in turn, forced more restrictive agreements on the western tribes. This cycle of agreements made and broken was repeated, until a full-scale war for the West raged between whites and Indians.

Contact and Conflict >> The policy of concentration began in the Pacific Northwest and produced some of the earliest clashes between whites and Indians. In an oft-repeated pattern, white encroachment led to Indian resistance and war and war to Indian defeat.

By 1862 the lands of the Santee Sioux had been whittled down to a strip 10 miles wide and 150 miles long along the Minnesota River in present-day South Dakota. Lashing out in frustration, the tribe attacked several undefended white settlements along the Minnesota frontier. In response, General John Pope arrived in St. Paul declaring his intention to wipe out the Sioux. When Pope's forces captured 1,800 Sioux, white Minnesotans were outraged that President Lincoln ordered only 38 hanged.

The campaign under General Pope was the opening of a guerrilla war that continued off and on for some 30 years. The conflict gained momentum in November 1864 when a force of Colorado volunteers under Colonel John Chivington fell upon a band of friendly Cheyenne gathered at Sand Creek under army protection. Chief Black Kettle raised an American flag to signal friendship, but Chivington would have none of it. "Kill and scalp all, big and little," he told his men. The troops massacred well over 100, including children holding white flags of truce and mothers with babies in their arms. In 1865 virtually all Plains Indians joined in the First Sioux War to drive whites from their lands.

War was only one way in which contact with whites undermined tribal cultures. Liquor and disease killed more Indians than combat. On the Great Plains the railroad disrupted the migratory patterns of the buffalo and thus the patterns of the hunt. Tourist parties came west to bag the buffalo from railside. As hides became popular back east, commercial companies hired hunters who could kill more than 100 bison an hour. Military commanders promoted the butchery as a way of weakening Indian resistance. In three short years, from 1872 to 1874, approximately nine million members of the herd were slaughtered. Reduced rainfall, competitive domesticated animals, and new diseases, aided by Indian hunters themselves nearly wiped the plains clean of bison by 1883. In other areas mines, crops, grazing herds, and fences disturbed traditional hunting and farming lands of many tribes.

Custer's Last Stand—and the Indians' >>
The Sioux War ended in 1868 with the signing of the Treaty of Fort Laramie. It established two large Indian reservations, one in Oklahoma and the other in the Dakota Badlands. Only six years later, however, Colonel George Armstrong Custer led an expedition into Paha Sapa, the sacred Black

Opinion
Could whites and Indians have lived together peaceably in the trans-Mississippi American West?

Hills of the Sioux. He marched in search of the Sioux and in violation of the treaty of 1868. Custer, a Civil War veteran, already had a reputation as a "squaw killer" for his cruel warfare against Indians in western Kansas. To open the Black Hills to whites, his expedition spread rumors of gold "from the grass roots down." Prospectors poured into Indian country. Federal authorities tried to force yet another treaty to gain control of the Black Hills. When negotiations failed, President Grant ordered all "hostiles" in the area driven onto the reservations.

In the summer of 1876 several army columns, including Custer's Seventh Cavalry of about 600 troops, marched into Indian country. Custer, eager for glory, arrived at the Little Big Horn River a day earlier than the other columns.

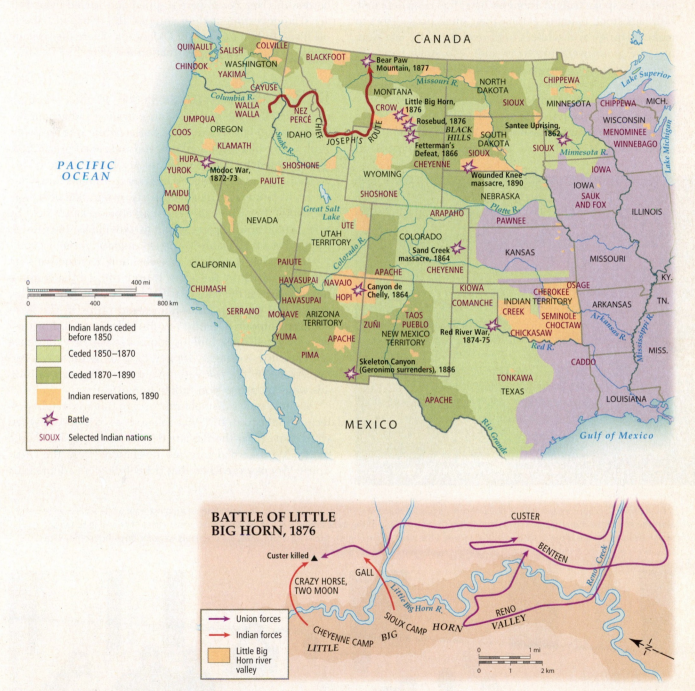

THE INDIAN FRONTIER

As conflict erupted between Indian and white cultures in the West, the government sought increasingly to concentrate tribes on reservations. Resistance to the reservation concept helped unite the Sioux and the Cheyenne, traditionally enemies, in the Dakotas during the 1870s. Along the Little Big Horn River the impetuous Custer underestimated the strength of his Indian opponents and attacked before the supporting troops of Reno and Benteen were in a position to aid him.

- Hispanos were increasingly subjected to similar exploitation but resisted and adapted more effectively to the intrusions of white culture and market economy.
- In a pattern that became typical for western mining, ranching, and agriculture, small operators first grabbed quick profits and then were followed by large corporations that increased both the scale and the wealth of these industries.

Additional Reading

The themes of change and continuity have characterized interpretations of southern history after Reconstruction. For years C. Vann Woodward's classic *The Origins of the New South* (1951) dominated thinking about the region with its powerful argument for a changing South. Edward Ayers, *The Promise of the New South* (1992), offers a fresh, comprehensive synthesis that sees both change and continuity. Gavin Wright, *Old South, New South* (1986), destroys the myth of the southern colonial economy. Ted Ownby, *Subduing Satan* (1990), provides a valuable discussion of southern social life, especially the role of religion. On the issue of race relations see Steven Hahn, *Under Our Feet: Black Political Struggles in the Rural South from Slavery to the Great Migration* (2003).

The contours of western history were first mapped by Fredrick Jackson Turner in his famous address "The Significance of the Frontier in American History" (1893) but have been substantially reshaped by Richard White, *"It's Your Own Misfortune and None of My Own": A New History of the American West* (1992); Patricia Limerick, *A Legacy of Conquest: The Unbroken Past of the American West* (1987); and Donald Worster, *Rivers of Empire* (1985). Each describes the history of the West less as a traditional saga of frontier triumphs than as an analysis of how the region and its resources have been exploited by various peoples and cultures. Heather Cox Richardson's *West From Appomattox: The Reconstruction of America After the Civil War* (2007) ties the North, South, and West together in this sweeping history of the aftermath of the Civil War. She uses the cowboy as a central image of disenchantment with Radical Republican rule and intrusive government. For a beautifully written and superbly researched study of the Great Plains as a contested zone among environment, animals, and people, see Elliott West's *The Contested Plains: Indians, Goldseekers, and the Rush to Colorado* (1998). On John Wesley Powell and his seminal role in the West, see Donald Worster, *A River Running West: The Life of John Wesley Powell* (2001). Sarah Deutsch, *No Separate Refuge: Culture, Class, and Gender on an Anglo-Hispanic Frontier in the American Southwest, 1880–1940* (1987), develops the concept of regional community in New Mexico and Colorado, and Robert M. Utley offers an excellent survey of American Indians in *The Indian Frontier of the American West 1846–1890* (1984). On the growing literature of ethno-racial identity in the West, see Neil Foley, *White Scourge: Mexicans, Blacks, and Poor Whites in Texas Cotton Culture* (1997), and David Gutiérrez, *Walls and Mirrors: Mexican Americans, Mexican Immigrants, and the Politics of Ethnicity* (1995). For an excellent account of the African American experience in shaping the West, see Quintard Taylor, *In Search of the Racial Frontier: African Americans in the American West, 1528–1990* (1998).

1883	1887	1889	1890	1892	1896

Dawes Severalty Act

Union violence at Coeur d'Alene, Idaho; Wyoming range wars

Plessy v. Ferguson upholds separate but equal doctrine

Civil Rights Cases

Oklahoma opened to settlement

Ghost Dance Indian religious revival; Wounded Knee

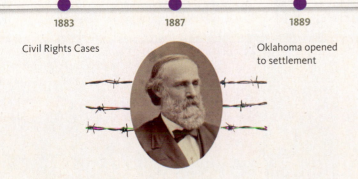

19 The New

>> AN AMERICAN STORY

SCAMPERING THROUGH AMERICA

It was so dark that Robert Ferguson could not see his own feet. Inching along the railroad tracks, he suddenly pitched forward as the ground vanished beneath him and found himself wedged between two railroad ties, his legs dangling in the air. Ferguson, a Scot visiting America in 1866, had been in Memphis only two days earlier, ready to take the "Great Southern Mail Route" east some 850 miles to Washington. >>

Industrial Order

1870–1900

Things had gone badly from the start. A broken river bridge not 50 miles outside of Memphis had forced him to take a ferry across the river and then a bumpy 10-mile ride on a mule-drawn truck to where the track was supposed resume—and didn't. Disheartened, he and his fellow travelers returned to Memphis abroad a train, only to have it derail just outside the city.

When a few passengers decided to hike the remaining distance, Ferguson tagged along. It was then that he fell between the tracks. At dawn he discovered to his horror that the tracks led onto a flimsy, high river bridge. Ferguson had trouble managing the trestle even in daylight.

Less than 20 years later rail passengers traveled in relative luxury. T. S. Hudson, another British tourist, launched a self-proclaimed "Scamper Through America" in 1882. It took him just 60 days to travel from England to San Francisco and back. He crossed the continental United States on a ticket booked by a single agent in Boston. Such speed and centralization would have been unthinkable in 1866, when, in any case, the transcontinental railroad was still three years from completion.

Hudson's trains had Pullman Palace cars with posh sleeping quarters, full meals, and air brakes that smoothed stops. Bridges appeared where none had been before, including a "magnificent" steel-and-stone span held up by three giant arches across the Mississippi at St. Louis. Hudson also found himself in the midst of a communications revolution. Traveling across the plains, he was struck by the number of telephone poles along the route.

What made America in the 1880s so different from the 1860s was a new industrial order. The process of industrialization had begun at least three decades before the Civil War when small factories produced light consumer goods such as clothing, shoes, and furniture. Manufacturers catered to local markets made up mostly of farmers and merchants. After the 1850s the industrial economy matured, with larger factories, more machines, greater efficiency, and national markets.

The transformation, remarkable as it was, brought pain along with the progress. Virgin forests vanished from the Pacific Northwest, the hillsides of Pennsylvania and West Virginia were pockmarked with open-pit mines, and the rivers of the Northeast grew toxic with industrial wastes. In 1882, the year Hudson scampered by rail across America, an average of 675 people were killed on the job every week. Like most Americans, workers scrambled—sometimes literally—to adjust. Change came nonetheless. Industrialization swept from Great Britain to the European continent to America. Almost overnight, the republic of merchants and small farmers turned into an industrial powerhouse. «

THE DEVELOPMENT OF INDUSTRIAL SYSTEMS

The new industrial order can best be understood as a web of complex industrial systems. Look, for example, at the bridge across the Mississippi that Hudson so admired. When James B. Eads constructed its soaring arches in 1874, he needed steel, most likely made from iron ore mined in northern Michigan. Giant steam shovels scooped up the ore and loaded whole freight cars in a few strokes.

A transportation system—railroads, boats, and other carriers—moved the ore to Pittsburgh, where giant mills furnished the labor and machinery to finish the steel. The capital to create such factories came itself from a system of finance, linking investment banks and stock markets to entrepreneurs in need of money. Only with a national network of industrial systems could the Eads bridge be built and a new age of industry arise.

Natural Resources and Industrial Technology »

The earliest European settlers had marveled at the "merchantable commodities" of America, from the glittering silver mines of the Spanish empire to the continent's hardwood forests. What set the new industrial economy apart from that older America was the scale and efficiency of using resources. New technologies made it possible to employ natural riches in ways undreamed of only decades earlier.

Iron, for example, had been forged into steel swords as far back as the Middle Ages. In the 1850s inventors in England and America discovered a cheaper way—called the Bessemer process—to convert large quantities of iron into steel. Steel was lighter than iron, could support 20 times as much weight, and lasted 20 years instead of 3. Steel tracks soon carried most rail traffic; steel girders replaced the old cast iron frames in buildings; steel cables supported new suspension bridges.

Industrial technology made some natural resources more valuable. New distilling methods transformed a thick, smelly liquid called *petroleum* into kerosene for lighting lamps, oil for lubricating machinery, and paraffin for making candles. Beginning in 1859, new drilling techniques began to tap vast pools of petroleum below the surface. About the same time, Frenchman Etienne Lenoir constructed the first practical internal combustion engine. After 1900 new vehicles such as gasoline-powered carriages turned the oil business into a major industry.

The environmental price of industrial technology soon became evident. Coal mining, logging, and the industrial wastes of factories were only the most obvious sources of environmental degradation. When engineers tried to cleanse the polluted Chicago River by reversing its flow, they succeeded only in shifting pollution to rivers downstate.

Systematic Invention >> Industrial technology rested on invention. For sheer inventiveness, the 40 years following the Civil War have rarely been matched in American history. Between 1790 and 1860, 36,000 **patents** were registered with the government. Over the next three decades the U.S. Patent Office granted more than half a million.

> **patent** legal document issued by the government giving the holder exclusive rights to use, make, and sell a process, product, or device for a specified period of time.

One fact helps to account for the growth. The process of invention became systematized. Small-scale inventors were replaced by orderly "invention factories"—forerunners of expensive research labs. No one did more to bring system, order, and profitability to invention than Thomas Alva Edison. After developing a more efficient stock ticker, he set himself up as an independent inventor. For the next five years, Edison patented a new invention almost every five months.

Edison was determined to bring system and order to the process of invention. Only then could breakthroughs come in a steady and profitable stream. He moved 15 of his workers to Menlo Park, New Jersey, where in 1876 he created an "invention factory." Like a manufacturer, Edison subdivided the work among gifted inventors, engineers, toolmakers, and others. This orderly bureaucracy soon evolved into the Edison Electric Light Company. It was soon delivering not only light bulbs but a unified

WITNESS
An Englishman Visits Pittsburgh in 1898

"I spent the day seeing the [steel] works where the Bessemer rails are turned out. . . . All nations are jumbled up here, the poor living in tenement dens or wooden shanties thrown up or dumped down (better expression) with very little reference to roads or situation. . . . It is a most chaotic city, and as yet there is no public spirit or public consciousness to make the conditions healthy. . . . It is industrial greatness with all the worst industrial abuses on the grandest scale."

—Charles Philips Trevelyan, April 15, 1898,
Letters from North America and the Pacific

Production (millions of tons)

1914

31

14

5.5

4

3.5

1880   2.0   .75   2.0   .40   .50

United States   Germany   Great Britain   Russia   France

STEEL PRODUCTION, 1880 AND 1914

While steel production jumped in western industrial nations from 1880 to 1914, it skyrocketed in the United States because of rich resources, cheap labor, and aggressive management.

<< In 1901 Spindletop Hill, just south of Beaumont, Texas, yielded a gusher that began the modern oil industry. Known as "black gold," oil became one of the most profitable businesses in the world, but drilling for it was dangerous, especially for workers at the well-head. Wells could ignite, producing a deadly blast and then a fire that might last for days, as the photo shows.

pushing barges down rivers and carrying passengers and freight across the oceans. Between 1870 and 1900 the value of American exports tripled. Eventually the rail and water transportation systems fused. By 1900 railroad companies owned nearly all of the country's domestic steamship lines.

electrical power system—central stations to generate electric current, wired to users, all powering millions of small bulbs in homes and businesses—to its customers.

George Eastman revolutionized photography by making the consumer a part of his inventive system. In 1888 Eastman marketed the "Kodak" camera at the affordable price of $25. The small black box weighed two pounds and contained a strip of celluloid film that replaced hundreds of pounds of photography equipment. After 100 snaps of the shutter, the owner simply sent the camera back to the factory and waited for the developed photos, along with a reloaded camera, to return by mail, all for $10.

What united these innovations was the notion of rationalizing inventions—of making a systematic business out of them. By 1913 Westinghouse Electric, General Electric, U.S. Rubber Company, and other firms had set up research laboratories. And by the middle of the century research labs had spread beyond business to the federal government, universities, trade associations, and labor unions.

Transportation and Communication >>

Abundant resources and new inventions remained worthless to industry until they could be moved to processing plants, factories, and offices. With more than 3.5 million square miles of land in the United States, distance alone was daunting. Where 100 miles of railroad track would do for shipping goods in Germany and England, 1,000 miles was necessary in America.

An efficient internal transportation network tied the country into an emerging international system. By the 1870s railroads crisscrossed the country, and steam-powered ships (introduced before the Civil War) were

A thriving industrial nation also required effective communication. Information was a precious commodity, as essential as resources or technology to industry. In 1844 Samuel Morse succeeded in tapping out the first message over an electrical wire between cities. Communication using Morse's code of dots and dashes became virtually instantaneous. So useful to railroads was the telegraph that they allowed poles and wires to be set along their rights-of-way in exchange for free telegraphic service. By the turn of the century a million miles of telegraph wire handled some 63 million messages a year, not to mention those flashing across underwater cables to China, Japan, Africa, and South America.

A second innovation in communication, the telephone, vastly improved on the telegraph. Alexander Graham Bell, a Scottish immigrant, was teaching the deaf when he began experimenting with ways to transmit speech electrically. In 1876 he transmitted his famous first words to his young assistant: "Mr. Watson, come here! I want you." No longer did messages require a telegraph office, unwieldy dots and dashes, and couriers to deliver the translated messages. Communication could be instantaneous *and* direct. Before the turn of the century the Bell-organized American Telephone and Telegraph Company combined more than 100 local companies to furnish business and government with long-distance service. The telephone patent proved to be the most valuable ever granted.

Finance Capital >> As industry grew, so did the demand for investment capital—the money spent on land, buildings, and machinery. The need for capital was great especially because so many new industrial systems

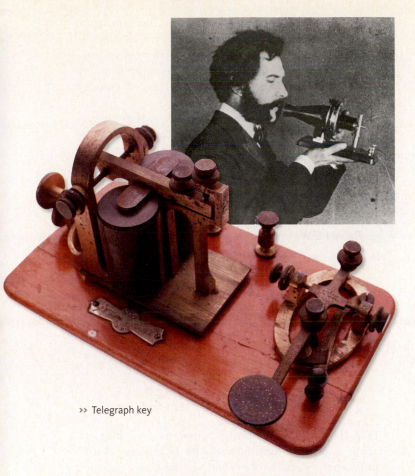

>> Telegraph key

railroad magnate Cornelius Vanderbilt once boasted. "Hain't I got the power?"

To survive over the long term, business leaders could not depend on ruthlessness alone. They needed ingenuity, an eye for detail, and the gift of foresight. The growing scale of enterprise and need for capital, for example, led them to adapt an old device, the corporation, to new needs.

The corporation had several advantages over more traditional forms of ownership, the single owner and the partnership. A corporation could raise large sums quickly by selling "stock certificates," or shares in its business. It could also outlive its owners (or stockholders), because it required no legal reorganization if one died. It limited liability, since owners were no longer personally responsible for corporate debts. And it separated owners from day-to-day management of the company. Professional managers could now operate complex businesses. So clear were these advantages that before the turn of the century, corporations were making two-thirds of all manufactured products in the United States.

An International Pool of Labor >> No

new industrial order could have been created without an abundant pool of labor. In 1860 it took about 4.3 million workers to run all the factories, mills, and shops in the United States. By 1900 there were approximately 20 million industrial workers in America.

In part, the United States relied on a vast global network to fill its need for workers. In Europe as well as Latin America, Asia, Africa, and the Middle East, seasonal migrations provided a rich source of workers for many nations, including the United States. Mechanization, poverty, oppression, and ambition pushed many of these rural laborers from farms into industrial cities and to other continents once steamships made transoceanic travel easier.

Between 1870 and 1890 more than 8 million immigrants arrived in the United States, another 14 million by 1914. Some came from Asia and Latin America, but most came from Europe and settled in industrial cities. Like migratory laborers elsewhere, they hoped to find work, fatten their purses, and go home. According to one estimate, between 25 and 60 percent of all immigrants returned to their homelands from the United States during these years.

Immigrants relied on well-defined migration chains of friends and family. A brother might find work with other Slavs in the mines of Pennsylvania; or the daughter of Greek parents, in a New England textile mill filled with relatives. Labor contractors also served as a funnel to industry. Tough and savvy immigrants themselves, they met newcomers at the docks and train stations with contracts. Among Italians they were known as *padrones;*

were being put into place at once. Each often required enormous start-up costs. Industrial processes involving so many expensive systems could not take shape until someone raised the money to finance them.

For the first three-quarters of the nineteenth century investment capital had come mostly from the savings of firms. In the last half of the century "capital deepening"— a process essential for industrialization—took place. Simply put, as national wealth increased, people began to save and invest more of their money. This meant that more funds could be lent to companies seeking to start up or expand.

Savings and investment grew more attractive with the development of a complex network of financial institutions. Commercial and savings banks, investment houses, and insurance companies gave savers new opportunities to channel money to industry. The New York **Stock Exchange,** in existence since 1792, linked eager investors with money-hungry firms.

stock exchange market at which shares of ownership in corporations are bought and sold.

The Corporation >> For those business leaders

with the skill to knit the industrial pieces together, large profits awaited. This was the era of the notorious "robber baron." And to be sure, sheer ruthlessness went a long way in the fortune-building game. "Law? Who cares about law!"

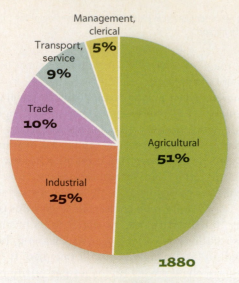

1880

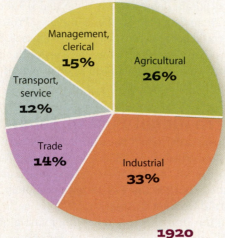

1920

OCCUPATIONAL DISTRIBUTION, 1880 AND 1920

Between 1880 and 1920, management and industrial work—employing white- and blue-collar workers—grew at the expense of farm work.

among Mexicans, as *enganchistas*. By 1900 they controlled two-thirds of the labor in New York.

A massive migration of rural Americans—some 11 million between 1865 and 1920—provided a home-grown source of labor. Driven from the farm by machines or bad times or just following dreams of a new life, they moved first to small, then to larger cities. Most lacked the skills for high-paying work. But they spoke English, and many could read and write. In iron and steel cities as well as in coal-mining towns, the better industrial jobs and supervisory positions went to them. Others found work in retail stores or offices and slowly entered the new urban middle class of white-collar workers.

Most African Americans continued to work the fields of the South. About 300,000 moved to northern cities between 1870 and 1910. Like the new immigrants they were trying to escape discrimination and follow opportunity.

One by one they brought their families. Discrimination still dogged them, but they found employment. Usually they worked in low-paying jobs as day laborers or laundresses and domestic servants. Black entrepreneurship also thrived as black-owned businesses served growing black communities.

Mexicans, too, came in search of jobs, mainly in agriculture but also in industry. They helped to build the transcontinental railroad. After the turn of the century, a small number turned farther north for jobs in the tanneries, meat-packing plants, foundries, and rail yards of Chicago and other midwestern industrial cities.

 REVIEW

What factors led to the development of industrial systems?

RAILROADS: AMERICA'S FIRST BIG BUSINESS

In 1882, the year T. S. Hudson scampered across America, clocks in New York and Boston were 11 minutes and 45 seconds apart. Stations often had several clocks showing the time on different rail lines, along with one displaying "local mean time." In 1883, without consulting anyone, the railroad companies divided the country into four time zones an hour apart to clean up this inefficient mess. Congress did not get around to making the division official until 1916.

At the center of the new industrial systems lay the railroads, moving people and freight, spreading communications, reinventing time, tying the nation together. Railroads also stimulated economic growth, simply because they required so many resources to build—coal, wood, glass, rubber, brass, and, by the 1880s, 75 percent of all U.S. steel. By lowering transportation costs railroads allowed manufacturers to reduce prices, attract more buyers, and increase business. Perhaps most important, as America's first big business they devised new techniques of management, soon adopted by other companies.

A Managerial Revolution >> To the men who ran them, railroads provided a challenge in organization and finance. In the 1850s one of the largest industrial enterprises in America, the Pepperell textile mills of Maine, employed about 800 workers. By the early 1880s the Pennsylvania Railroad had nearly 50,000 people on its payroll. From paying workers to setting schedules and rates to determining costs and profits, everything required a level of coordination unknown in earlier businesses.

The so-called trunk lines devised new systems of management. Scores of early companies had serviced local networks of cities and communities, often with fewer than 50 miles of track. During the 1850s longer trunk lines emerged east of the Mississippi to connect the shorter branches, or "feeder" lines. By the outbreak of the Civil War, with four great trunk lines under a single management, railroads linked the eastern seaboard with the Great Lakes and western rivers.

The operations of large lines spawned a new managerial elite, beneath owners but with wide authority over operations. Daniel McCallum, superintendent of the New York and Erie in the 1850s, laid the foundation for this system by drawing up the first table of organization for an American company. A tree trunk with roots represented the president and board of directors; five branches constituted the main operating divisions; leaves stood for the local agents, train crews, and others. Information moved up and down the trunk so that managers could get reports to and from the separate parts.

These managerial techniques soon spread to other industries. Local superintendents were responsible for daily activities. Central offices served as corporate nerve centers, housing divisions for purchases, production, transportation, sales, and accounting. A new class of middle managers ran them and imposed new order on business operations. Executives, managers, and workers were being taught to operate in increasingly precise and coordinated ways.

Competition and Consolidation >> While managers made operations more systematic, the fierce struggle among railroad companies to dominate the industry was anything but precise and rational. In the 1870s and 1880s the pain of railroad competition began to tell.

The most savage and costly competition came over the prices charged for shipping goods. Managers lowered prices, or "rates," for freight that was shipped in bulk, on long hauls, or on return routes, since the cars were empty any way. They used "rebates"—secret discounts to preferred customers—to drop prices below the posted rates of competitors and then recouped the losses by overcharging small shippers like farmers. When the economy

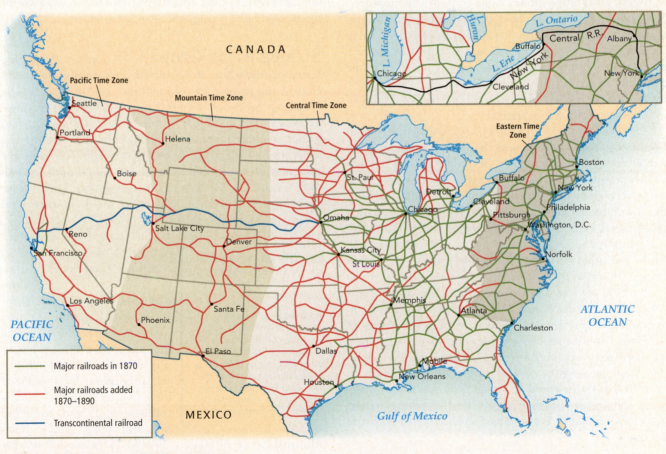

RAILROADS, 1870–1890

By 1890 the railroad network stretched from one end of the country to the other, with more miles of track than in all of Europe combined. New York and Chicago, linked by the New York Central trunk line, became the new commercial axis.

plunged or a weak line sought to improve its position, rate or price wars broke out. By 1880, 65 lines had declared bankruptcy.

Consolidation worked better than competition. During the 1870s railroads created regional federations to pool traffic, set prices, and divide profits among members. Without the force of law, however, these regional federations failed. Members broke ranks by cutting prices in hopes of quick gain. In the end, rate wars died down only when weaker lines failed or stronger ones bought up competitors.

The Challenge of Finance >> Earlier in the nineteenth century many railroads relied on state governments for financial help. Backers also looked to counties, cities, and towns for bonds and other forms of aid. People took stock in exchange for land or labor, particularly those living near the ends of rail lines who stood to gain most from construction. In the 1850s and 1860s western promoters went to Washington for federal assistance. Congress loaned $65 million to six western railroads and granted some 131 million acres of land.

Federal aid helped to build only part of the nation's railroads. Most of the money came from private investors. The New York Stock Exchange expanded rapidly as railroad corporations began to trade their stocks there. Large investment banks developed financial networks to track down money at home and abroad. By 1898 a third of the assets of American life insurance companies had gone into railroads, while Europeans owned nearly a third of all American railroad securities.

Because investment bankers played such large roles in funding railroads, they found themselves advising companies about their business affairs. If a company fell into bankruptcy, bankers sometimes served as the "receivers" who oversaw the property until financial health returned. By absorbing smaller lines into larger ones, eliminating rebates, and stabilizing rates, the bankers helped to reduce competition and impose order and centralization on railroads and other corporations. In the process, they often gained control of the companies they advised.

By 1900 the new industrial systems had transformed American railroads. Some 200,000 miles of track were in operation, 80 percent of it owned by only six groups of railroads. Time zones allowed for coordinated schedules; standardized track permitted easy cross-country freighting. Soon passengers were traveling 16 billion miles a year. To that traffic could be added farm goods, raw materials, and factory-finished products. Everything moved with new regularity that allowed businesses to plan and prosper.

 **REVIEW**

How did the railroads contribute to the rise of big business?

THE GROWTH OF BIG BUSINESS

In 1865, near the end of the Civil War, 26-year-old John D. Rockefeller sat blank-faced in the office of his Cleveland oil refinery, about to conclude the biggest deal of his life. Rockefeller's business was thriving, but he had fallen out with his partner over how quickly to expand. Rockefeller was eager to grow fast; his partner was not. They dissolved their partnership and agreed to bid for the company. Bidding opened at $500, rocketed to $72,500, and abruptly stopped. "The business is yours," said the partner. The men shook hands, and a thin smile crept across Rockefeller's angular face.

Twenty years later, Rockefeller's Standard Oil Company controlled 90 percent of the nation's refining capacity and an empire that stretched well beyond Cleveland. Trains swept Standard executives to New York, Philadelphia, and other eastern cities. It was a fitting form of transportation for Rockefeller's company, because railroads were the key to his oil empire. They pioneered the big business systems on which he was building. And they carried his oil products for discounted rates, giving him the edge to squeeze out rivals.

Strategies of Growth >> First a bedeviling business riddle had to be solved: how to grow and still control the ravages of competition? In Michigan in the 1860s salt producers found themselves fighting for their existence. The presence of too many salt makers had begun an endless round of price-cutting that was driving everyone out of business. Seeing salvation in combination, they drew together in the nation's first pool. In 1869 they formed the Michigan Salt Association. They voluntarily agreed to allocate production, divide markets, and set prices—at double the previous rate.

consumer goods products such as food and clothing that fill the needs and wants of individuals.

horizontal combination strategy of business growth (sometimes referred to as "horizontal integration") that attempts to stifle competition by combining more than one firm involved in the same level of production, transportation, or distribution into a single firm.

Salt processing and other industries that specialized in **consumer goods** had low start-up costs, so they were often plagued by competition. **Horizontal combination**—joining together loosely with rivals that offered the same goods or services—had saved Michigan salt producers. By the 1880s there was a whiskey pool, a cordage pool, and countless rail and other pools. Such informal pools ultimately proved to be unenforceable and therefore unsatisfactory. (After 1890 they were also considered illegal restraints on trade.) But other forms of horizontal growth, such as formal mergers, spread in the wake of an economic panic in the 1890s.

Some makers of consumer products worried less about direct competition and concentrated on boosting efficiency and sales. They adopted a vertical-growth strategy in which one company gained control of two or more stages of a business. Take Gustavus Swift, a New England butcher, for example. Swift moved to Chicago in the mid-1870s, aware of the demand for fresh beef in the East. He acquired new refrigerated railcars to ship meat from western slaughterhouses and a network of ice-cooled warehouses in eastern cities to store it. By 1885 he had created the first national meatpacking enterprise, Swift and Company.

Swift moved upward, closer to consumers, by putting together a fleet of wagons to distribute his beef to retailers. He moved down toward raw materials, extending and coordinating the purchase of cattle at the Chicago stockyards. By the 1890s Swift and Company was a fully integrated, vertically organized corporation operating on a nationwide scale.

Vertical growth generally moved producers of consumer goods closer to the marketplace in search of high-volume sales. The Singer Sewing Machine Company and the McCormick Harvesting Machine Company created their own retail sales arms. Manufacturers began furnishing ordinary consumers with technical information, credit, and repair services. Advertising expenditures grew, to some $90 million by 1900, in an effort to identify markets, shape buying habits, and increase sales.

Carnegie Integrates Steel >> Industrialization encouraged vertical integration in heavy industry but more often in the opposite direction, toward reliable sources of raw materials. These firms made products for big users such as railroads and factory builders. Their markets were easily identified and changed little. For them, success lay in securing limited raw materials and in holding down costs.

Andrew Carnegie led the way in steel. A Scottish immigrant, he worked his way up from bobbin boy to expert telegrapher to superintendent of the Pennsylvania Railroad's western division at the age of 24. A string of wise investments paid off handsomely. Among other things, he owned a locomotive factory and an iron factory that became the nucleus of his steel empire.

In 1872, on a trip to England, Carnegie chanced to see the Bessemer process in action. Awestruck and dreaming of the profits to be made from cheap steel, he rushed home to build the biggest steel mill in the world. It opened in 1875, in the midst of a severe depression. Over the next 25 years, Carnegie added mills at Homestead and elsewhere in Pennsylvania and moved from railroad-building to city-building.

Carnegie succeeded, in part, by taking advantage of the boom-and-bust business cycle. He jumped in during hard times, building and buying when equipment and businesses were cheap. But he also found skilled managers who employed the administrative techniques of the railroads. And Carnegie knew how to compete. He scrapped machinery, workers, even a new mill to keep costs down and undersell competitors. The final key to Carnegie's success was expansion. His empire spread horizontally by purchasing rival steel mills and constructing new ones. It spread vertically, buying up sources of supply, transportation, and eventually sales. Controlling such an integrated system, Carnegie could ensure a steady flow of materials from mine to mill and market, as well as profits at every stage. In 1900 his company turned out more steel than Great Britain and netted $40 million.

> ## Carnegie jumped in during hard times, building and buying when equipment and businesses were cheap. But he also found skilled managers.

Rockefeller and the Great Standard Oil Trust >> John D. Rockefeller accomplished in oil what Carnegie achieved in steel. And he went further, developing an innovative business structure—the trust—that promised greater control than even Carnegie's integrated system. At first Rockefeller grew horizontally by buying out or joining other refiners. To cut costs he also expanded vertically, with oil pipelines, warehouses, and barrel factories. By 1870, when he and five partners formed the Standard Oil Company of Ohio, his high-quality, low-cost products set a competitive standard.

Because the oil refining business was a jungle of competitive firms, Rockefeller proceeded to twist arms. He bribed rivals, spied on them, created phony companies, and slashed prices. His decisive edge came from the railroads. Desperate for business, they granted Standard Oil not only rebates on shipping rates but also "drawbacks," a fee from the railroad for any product shipped by a rival oil company. Within a decade Standard dominated American refining with a vertically integrated empire that stretched from drilling to selling.

Throughout the 1870s Rockefeller kept his empire stitched together through informal pools and other business combinations. But they were weak and afforded him too little control. He could try to expand further, except that corporations were restricted by state law. In Rockefeller's home state of Ohio, for example, corporations could not own plants in other states or own stock in out-of-state companies.

⌃ Carnegie steel furnaces, Braddock, Pennsylvania, on the banks of the Monongahela River were opened in 1875 as part of the J. Edgar Thomson Steel Works. Named for the president of the Pennslyvania Railroad, the mill was capable of producing as much as 255 tons of steel rails a day, many of which went into the construction of the Pennsylvania Railroad line.

In 1879 Samuel C. T. Dodd, chief counsel of Standard Oil, came up with a new device, the "trust." The stockholders of a corporation surrendered their shares "in trust" to a central board of directors with the power to control all property. In exchange, stockholders received certificates of trust that paid hefty dividends. Since it did not literally own other companies, the trust violated no state law, many of which sought to limit the power of big businesses by preventing one corporation from owning stock in another.

trust business arrangement in which owners of shares in a business turn over their shares "in trust" to a board with power to control those businesses for the benefit of the trust.

In 1882 the Standard Oil Company of Ohio formed the country's first great **trust.** It brought Rockefeller what he sought so fiercely: centralized management of the oil industry. Other businesses soon created trusts of their own—in meat-packing, wire-making, and farm machinery, for example. Just as quickly, trusts became notorious for crushing rivals and controlling prices.

The Mergers of J. Pierpont Morgan »

The trust was only a stepping-stone to an even more effective means of avoiding competition, managing people, and controlling business: the corporate merger. The merging of two corporations—one buying out another—remained impossible until 1889, when New Jersey began to permit corporations to own other companies through what became known as the "holding company" (a company that held stock in other companies). Many industries converted their trusts into holding companies, including Standard Oil, which moved to New Jersey in 1899.

Two years later came the biggest corporate merger of the era. It was the creation of a financial wizard named J. Pierpont Morgan. His orderly mind detested the chaotic competition that threatened his profits. "I like a little competition," Morgan used to say, "but I like combination more." After the Civil War he had taken over his father's powerful investment bank. For the next 50 years the House of Morgan played a part in consolidating almost every major industry in the country.

Morgan's greatest triumph came in steel. In 1901 a colossal steel war loomed between Andrew Carnegie and other steelmakers. Morgan convinced Carnegie to put a price tag on his company. When a messenger brought the scrawled reply back—over $400 million—Morgan merely nodded and said, "I accept this price." He then bought Carnegie's eight largest competitors and announced the formation of the United States Steel Corporation. The mammoth holding company produced nearly two-thirds of all American steel. Its value of $1.4 billion exceeded the national debt and made it the country's first billion-dollar corporation.

What Morgan helped to create in steel was rapidly coming to pass in other industries. A wave of mergers swept through American business after the depression of 1893. As the economy plunged, cutthroat competition bled businesses until they were eager to sell out. Giants sprouted almost overnight. By 1904 in each of 50 industries one firm came to account for 60 percent or more of the total output.

Corporate Defenders >>
As Andrew Carnegie's empire grew, so did his social conscience. Preaching a "gospel of wealth," he urged the rich to act as agents for the poor, "doing for them better than they would or could do for themselves." "The man who dies rich . . . dies disgraced," he warned. He devoted more and more of his time to philanthropy by creating foundations and endowing libraries and universities with some $350 million in contributions.

Defenders of the new corporate order were less troubled than Carnegie about the rough-and-tumble world of big business. They justified the system by stressing the opportunity created for individuals by economic growth. Through frugality, acquisitiveness, and discipline—the sources of cherished American individualism—they believed anyone could rise like Andrew Carnegie.

When most ordinary workers failed to follow in Carnegie's footsteps, defenders blamed the individual. Failures were lazy, ignorant, or morally depraved, they said. British philosopher Herbert Spencer added the weight of science by applying Charles Darwin's theories of evolution to society. He maintained that in society, as in biology, only the "fittest" survived. The competitive social jungle doomed the unfit to poverty and rewarded the fit with property and privilege.

Spencer's American apostle, William Graham Sumner, argued that competition was natural and had to proceed without any interference, including government regulation. Millionaires were simply the "product of natural selection." Such "social Darwinism" found strong support among turn-of-the-century business leaders. The philosophy certified their success even as they worked to destroy the very competitiveness it celebrated.

Corporate Critics >>
Meanwhile, a group of radical critics mounted a powerful attack on corporate capitalism. Henry George, a journalist and self-taught economist, proposed a way to redistribute wealth in *Progress and Poverty* (1879). George attacked larger landowners as the source of inequality. They bought property while it was cheap and then held it until the forces of society—labor, technology, and speculation on nearby sites—had increased its value. George proposed to do away with all taxes except a single tax on these "unearned" profits to end monopoly landholding. "Single-tax" clubs sprang up throughout the country, and George nearly won the race for mayor of New York in 1886.

The journalist Edward Bellamy tapped the same popular resentment against the inequalities of corporate capitalism. In his utopian novel, *Looking Backward* (1888), a fictional Bostonian falls asleep in 1887 and awakens Rip Van Winkle–like in the year 2000. The competitive, caste-ridden society of the nineteenth century is gone. In its place is an orderly utopia, managed by a benevolent government trust. "Fraternal cooperation" and shared abundance reign. Like George's ideas, Bellamy's philosophy inspired a host of clubs around the nation. His followers demanded redistribution of wealth, civil service reform, and nationalization of railroads and utilities.

Less popular but equally hostile to capitalism was the

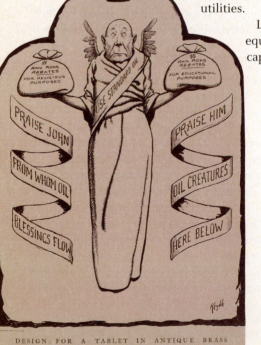

DESIGN FOR A TABLET IN ANTIQUE BRASS
TO BE PLACED IN THE CHICAGO UNIVERSITY

<< This drawing is from a 1905 edition of Collier's magazine, famous for exposing corporate abuses. Here it mocks John D. Rockefeller, head of the Standard Oil Company, as the new God of the industrial age by parodying the Protestant doxology of thanks: "Praise God from whom all blessings flow, Praise him all creatures here below!"

Socialist Labor party, formed in 1877. Under Daniel De Leon, a West Indian immigrant, it stressed class conflict and called for a revolution to give workers control over production. De Leon refused to compromise his radical beliefs, and the **socialists** ended up attracting more intellectuals than workers. Some immigrants found its class consciousness appealing, but most rejected its radicalism and rigidity. A few party members bent on gaining greater support revolted and in 1901 founded the more successful Socialist Party of America. Workers were beginning to organize their own responses to industrialism.

socialism philosophy of social and economic organization in which the means of producing and distributing goods are owned collectively or by government.

By the mid-1880s, in response to the growing criticism of big business, several states in the South and West had enacted laws limiting the size of corporations. But state laws proved all too easy to evade when New Jersey and Delaware eased their rules to cover the whole nation.

In 1890 the public clamor against trusts finally forced Congress to act. The Sherman Antitrust Act relied on the only constitutional authority Congress had over business: its right to regulate interstate commerce. The act outlawed "every contract, combination in the form of trust or otherwise, or conspiracy, in restraint of trade or commerce." The United States stood practically alone among industrialized nations in regulating the size of business combinations.

Its language was purposefully vague, but the Sherman Antitrust Act did give the government the power to break up trusts and other big businesses. So high was the regard for the rights of private property, however, that few in Congress expected the government to exercise that power or the courts to uphold it. They were right. In 1895 the Supreme Court dealt the law a major blow by severely limiting its scope. *United States v. E. C. Knight Co.* held that businesses involved in manufacturing (as opposed to "trade or commerce") lay outside the authority of the Sherman Act. Not until after the turn of the century would the law be used to bust a trust.

The Costs of Doing Business >>
The heated debates between the critics and the defenders of industrial capitalism made clear that the changes in American society were two-edged. Big businesses helped to rationalize the economy, to increase national wealth, and to tie the country together. Yet they also concentrated power, corrupted politics, and made the gap between rich and poor more apparent than ever.

More to the point, the practices of big business subjected the economy to enormous disruptions. The banking system could not always keep pace with the demand for capital, and businesses failed to distribute enough of their profits to sustain the purchasing power of workers. The supply of goods periodically outstripped demand,

BOOM AND BUST BUSINESS CYCLE, 1865–1900

Between 1865 and 1900, industrialization produced great economic growth but also wild swings of prosperity and depression. During booms, productivity soared and near-full employment existed. But the rising number of industrial workers meant high unemployment during deep busts.

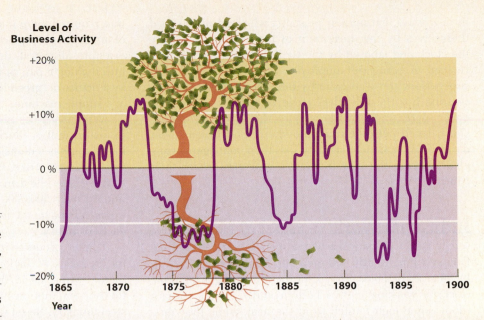

Level of Business Activity

+20%

+10%

0 %

−10%

−20%

1865   1870   1875   1880   1885   1890   1895   1900

Year

and then the wrenching cycle of boom and bust set in. Three severe depressions—1873–1879, 1882–1885, and 1893–1897—rocked the economy in the last third of the nineteenth century. With hard times came fierce competition and ruthless cost cutting.

Some of the costs were unclear at the time. Although anyone could see the environmental impact of industrialization, the long-term effects were less apparent. In the nineteenth century most people, scientists included, assumed that nature would maintain its own balance, largely unaffected by human action. And for the handful of observers interested in climate change only the most basic calculations were possible.

It took a Brit and a Swede consumed with discovering the cause of the prehistoric Ice Age to work out the climatic ramifications of new smokestack industries. In 1859 British scientist John Tyndall took up the question of precisely what in the atmosphere *prevented* the Earth from freezing. By testing the "coal gas" (gas emitted by burning coal) from a jet in his laboratory, he found that methane and carbon dioxide captured heat. Historically such gases had come from volcanic eruptions and other natural occurrences, but growing amounts were now being thrown aloft by industry.

In Sweden Svante Arrhenius carried the idea a step further in 1896. If heat-trapping gases raised global temperatures even slightly, warmer air would absorb more of the most potent heat trapper of all—water vapor—raising temperatures still higher. A new and dramatic cycle of climate change might spread across the planet. With the age of industry in its infancy, few paid attention to the implications for what would later be called "global warming."

 REVIEW

What strategies and structures did businesses use to grow and at what costs?

Opinion

Who deserves more credit for making the United States an industrial powerhouse, industrialists or workers?

THE WORKERS' WORLD

At seven in the morning Sadie Frowne sat at her sewing machine in a Brooklyn garment factory. Her boss, a man she barely knew, dropped a pile of unfinished skirts next to her. She pushed one under her needle and began to rock her foot on the pedal that powered her machine. Sometimes Sadie pushed the skirts too quickly, and the needle pierced her finger. "The machines go like mad all day because the faster you work the more money you get," she explained of the world of industrial work in 1902.

The cramped sweatshops, the vast steel mills, the dank tunnels of the coal fields—all demanded workers and required them to work in new ways. Farmers or peasants who had once timed themselves by the movement of the sun now lived by the clock and labored by the twilight of gaslit factories. Instead of being self-employed, they had to deal with supervisors and were paid by the piece or hour. Not the seasons but the relentless cycle of machines set their pace. Increasingly, workers bore the brunt of depressions, faced periodic unemployment, and toiled under dangerous conditions as they like their managers struggled to bring the new industrial processes under their control.

Industrial Work >>

In 1881 the Pittsburgh Bessemer Steel Company opened its new mill in Homestead, Pennsylvania. Nearly 400 men and boys went to work in its 60 acres of sheds. They kept the mill going around the clock by working in two 12-hour shifts. In the furnace room, some men fainted from the heat, while the vibration and screeching of machinery deafened others. There were no breaks, even for lunch.

Few industrial laborers worked under such conditions, but the Homestead mill reflected common characteristics of industrial work: the use of machines for mass production; the division of labor into intricately organized, often repetitive tasks; and the dictatorship of the clock. At the turn of the century, two-thirds of all industrial work came from large-scale mills.

Under such conditions labor paid dearly for industrial progress. By 1900 most of those earning wages in industry worked six days a week, 10 hours a day. They held jobs that required more machines and fewer skills. Repetition of small chores replaced fine craftwork. In the 1880s, for example, almost all the 40 different steps that had gone into making a pair of shoes by hand could be performed by a novice or "green hand" with a few days of instruction at a simple machine.

With machines also came danger. Tending furnaces in a steel mill or plucking tobacco from cigarette-rolling machines was tedious. If a worker became bored or tired, disaster could strike. Each year from 1880 to 1900 industrial mishaps killed an average of 35,000 wage earners and injured over 500,000. Workers and their families could expect no payment from employers or government for death or injury.

Higher productivity and profits were the aims, and for Frederick W. Taylor, efficiency was the way to achieve them. During the 1870s and 1880s Taylor undertook careful time-and-motion studies of workers' movements in the steel industry. He set up standard procedures and offered pay incentives for beating his production quotas. On one occasion he designed 15 ore shovels, each for a separate task. One hundred forty men were soon doing the work of 600. By the early twentieth century "Taylorism" was a full-blown philosophy, complete with its own professional society. "Management engineers" prescribed routines from which workers could not vary.

For all the high ideals of Taylorism, ordinary laborers refused to perform as cogs in a vast industrial machine. In a variety of ways they worked to maintain control. Many European immigrants continued to observe the numerous Saint's days and other religious holidays of their homelands, regardless of factory rules. When the pressure of six-day weeks became too stifling, workers took an unauthorized "blue Monday" off. Or they slowed down to reduce the grueling pace. Or they simply walked off the job. Come spring and warm weather, factories reported turnover rates of 100 percent or more.

For some, seizing control of work was more than a matter of survival or self-respect. Many workers regarded themselves as citizens of a democratic republic. They expected to earn a "competence"— enough money to support and educate their families and enough time to stay abreast of current affairs. Few but highly

<< This machine tool shop in West Lynn, Massachusetts, photographed in the mid-1890s, suggests something of the growing scale of factory enterprise in the late nineteenth century—and also of the extraordinary dangers that workers in these early manufacturing shops faced.

skilled workers could realize such democratic dreams. More and more, labor was being managed as another part of an integrated system of industry.

Children, Women, and African Americans >>

In the mines of Pennsylvania nimble-fingered eight-year-olds snatched bits of slate from amid the chunks of coal. In Illinois glass factories "dog boys" dashed with trays of red-hot bottles to the cooling ovens. By 1900 the industrial labor force included some 1.7 million children, more than double the number 30 years earlier. Parents often had no choice. As one union leader observed, "Absolute necessity compels the father . . . to take the child into the mine to assist him in winning bread for the family." On average, children worked 60 hours a week and carried home paychecks a third the size of those of adult males.

> **On average, children worked 60 hours a week and carried home paychecks a third the size of those of adult males.**

Women had always labored on family farms, but by 1870 one out of every four nonagricultural workers was female. In general they earned one-half of what men did. Nearly all were single and young, anywhere from their midteens to their mid-20s. Most lived in boardinghouses or at home with their parents. Usually they contributed their wages to the family kitty. Once married, they often took on a life of full-time housework and child rearing.

Only 5 percent of married women held jobs outside the home in 1900. Married black women—in need of income because of the low wages paid to their husbands—were four times more likely than married white women to work away from home. Industrialization inevitably pushed women into new jobs. Mainly they worked in industries considered extensions of housework: food processing, textiles and clothing, cigar making, and domestic service.

⌃ Injured boy

New methods of management and marketing opened positions for white-collar women as "typewriters," "telephone girls," bookkeepers, and secretaries. On rare occasions women entered the professions, though law and medical schools were reluctant to admit them. Such discrimination drove ambitious, educated women into nursing, teaching, and library work. Their growing presence soon "feminized" these professions, pushing men upward into managerial slots or out entirely.

Even more than white women, all African Americans faced discrimination in the workplace. They were paid less than whites and given menial jobs. Their greatest opportunities in industry often came as strikebreakers to replace white workers. Once a strike ended, however, black workers were replaced themselves—and hated by the white regulars all the more. The service trades furnished the largest single source of jobs. Craftworkers and a sprinkling of black professionals could usually be found in cities. After the turn of the century, black-owned businesses thrived in the growing black neighborhoods of the North and South.

The American Dream of Success >>

Whatever their separate experiences, working-class Americans did improve their overall lot. Though the gap between the very rich and the very poor widened, most wage earners made some gains. Between 1860 and 1890 real daily wages—pay in terms of buying power—climbed some 50 percent as prices gradually fell. And after 1890 the number of hours on the job began a slow decline.

Yet most unskilled and semiskilled workers in factories continued to receive low pay. In 1890 an unskilled laborer could expect about $1.50 for a 10-hour day; a skilled one, perhaps twice that amount. It took about $600 to make ends meet, but most manufacturing workers made under $500 a year. Native-born white Americans tended to earn more than immigrants, those who spoke English more than those who did not, men more than women, and all others more than African Americans and Asians.

Few workers repeated the rags-to-riches rise of Andrew Carnegie. But some did rise, despite periodic unemployment and ruthless wage cuts. About one-quarter of the manual laborers in one study entered the lower middle class in their own lifetimes. More often such unskilled workers climbed in financial status within their own class. And most workers, seeing some improvement, believed in the American dream of success, even if they did not fully share in it.

 REVIEW

How did industrialization change the working day for people employed in factories?

THE SYSTEMS OF LABOR

For ordinary workers to begin to control industrialization they had to combine, just as businesses did. They needed to join together horizontally—organizing not just locally but on a national scale. They needed to integrate vertically by coordinating action across a wide range of jobs and skills, as Andrew Carnegie coordinated the production of steel. Unions were the workers' systematic response to industrialization.

Early Unions >>

In the United States unions began forming before the Civil War. Skilled craft-workers—carpenters, iron molders, cigar makers—united to counter the growing power of management. Railroad "brotherhoods" also furnished insurance for those hurt or killed on the accident-plagued lines. Largely local and exclusively male, these early craft unions remained weak and unconnected to each other as well as to the growing mass of unskilled workers.

After the war a group of craft unions, brotherhoods, and reformers united skilled and unskilled workers in a nationwide organization. The National Labor Union (NLU) hailed the virtues of a simpler America, when workers controlled their workday, earned a decent living, and had time to be good informed citizens. NLU leaders attacked the wage system as unfair and enslaving and urged workers to manage their own factories. By the early 1870s NLU ranks swelled to more than 600,000.

Among other things, the NLU pressed for the eight-hour workday, the most popular labor demand of the era. Workers saw it as a way not merely of limiting their time on the job but of limiting the power of employers over their lives. "Eight hours for work; eight hours for rest; eight hours for what we will!" proclaimed a banner at one labor rally. Despite the popularity of the issue, the NLU wilted during the depression of 1873.

The Knights of Labor >>

More successful was a national union born in secrecy. In 1869 Uriah Stephens and nine Philadelphia garment cutters founded the Noble and Holy Order of the Knights of Labor. They draped themselves in ritual and regalia to deepen their sense of solidarity and met in secret to evade hostile owners. The Knights remained small and fraternal for a decade. Their strongly Protestant tone repelled Catholics, who made up almost half the workforce in many industries.

In 1879 the Knights elected Terence V. Powderly as their Grand Master Workman. Handsome, dynamic, Irish, and Catholic, Powderly threw off the Knights' secrecy, dropped their rituals, and opened their ranks. He called for "one big union" to embrace the "toiling millions"—skilled and unskilled, men and women, natives and immigrants, all religions, all races. By 1886 membership had leaped to over 700,000, including nearly 30,000 African Americans and 3,000 women.

Like the NLU, the Knights of Labor looked to abolish the wage system and in its place create a cooperative economy of worker-owned businesses. The Knights set up more than 140 cooperative workshops, where workers shared decisions and profits, and sponsored some 200 political candidates. To tame the new industrial order, they supported the eight-hour workday and the regulation of trusts. Underlying this program was a moral vision of society. If only people renounced greed, laziness, and dishonesty, Powderly argued, corruption and class division would disappear. Democracy would flourish. To reform citizens, the Knights promoted the prohibition of child and convict labor and the abolition of liquor.

It was one thing to proclaim a moral vision for his union, quite another to coordinate the activities of so many members. Locals resorted to strikes and violence, actions Powderly condemned. In the mid-1880s such stoppages wrung concessions from the western railroads, but the organization soon became associated with unsuccessful strikes and violent extremists. By 1890 the Knights of Labor teetered near extinction.

The American Federation of Labor >>

The Knights' position as the premier union in the nation was taken by the rival American Federation of Labor (AFL). The AFL reflected the practicality of its leader, Samuel Gompers. Born in a London tenement, the son of a Jewish cigar maker, he had immigrated in 1863 with his family to New York's Lower East Side. Unlike the visionary Powderly, Gompers accepted capitalism and the wage system. What he wanted was "pure and simple union-ism"—higher wages, fewer hours, improved safety, more benefits.

Gompers chose to organize highly skilled craftworkers because they were difficult to replace. He then bargained with employers, using strikes and boycotts only as last resorts. With the Cigar Makers' Union as his base, Gompers helped create the first national federation of craft unions in 1881. In 1886 it was reorganized as the American Federation of Labor. Twenty-five labor groups joined, representing some 150,000 workers. Stressing gradual, concrete gains, he made the AFL the most powerful union in the country. By 1901 it had more than a million members, almost a third of all skilled workers in America.

Gompers was less interested in vertical integration: combining skilled and unskilled workers. For most of his career he preserved the privileges of craftsmen and

Digital Detecting

Eastport, Maine: what adjectives would you use to describe the scene?

At first the view looks somewhat rural, but at least three elements in the photograph suggest otherwise. What are they?

What strikes you about this digitally enlarged portion of the photo?

Photographs can be both revealing and deceptive, but technology can help historians detect what the camera lens actually captured. This print (upper left) of a photo by Lewis Hine, a turn-of-the century photographer, shows 8-year-old Phoebe Thomas returning to her house in Eastport, Maine. The scene seems to be nothing more than a little girl making her way home up a set of stairs. Hine tells us that the young Syrian worked all day in a cannery, shearing the heads off sardines with a butcher's knife. When the Library of Congress scanned the image nearly a century later, a portion of the photo could be digitally enlarged to reveal much more than meets the unaided eye. What appears to be an ordinary homecoming is, in fact, something much worse, as Hine's notes reveal. Phoebe was "running home from the factory all alone, her hand and arm bathed with blood, crying at the top of her voice. She had cut the end of her thumb nearly off, cutting sardines in the factory, and was sent home alone, her mother being busy."

THINKING CRITICALLY

How does the close-up of Phoebe Thomas change the nature of the photograph? What would we make of the photograph without Hine's explanatory notes? Google "Lewis Hine" to learn what he photographed and why.

Credit: Library of Congress Digital Photo ID: nclc 00966.

---

accepted their prejudices against women, blacks, and immigrants. Only two locals—the Cigar Makers' Union and the Typographers' Union—enrolled women. Most affiliates restricted black membership through high entrance fees and other discriminatory practices.

Despite the success of the AFL the laboring classes did not organize themselves as systematically as the barons of industrial America. At the turn of the century union membership included less than 10 percent of industrial workers. Separated by different languages and nationalities, divided by issues of race and gender, workers resisted unionization during the nineteenth century. In fact, a strong strain of individualism often made them regard all collective action as un-American.

The Limits of Industrial Systems >> As

managers sought to increase their control over the workplace, workers often found themselves at the mercy of the new industrial order. Even in boom times, one in three workers was out of a job at least three or four months a year.

In hard times, when a worker's pay dropped and frustration mounted, when a mother worked all night and fell asleep during the day while caring for her children, when food prices suddenly jumped—violence might erupt. "A mob of 1,000 people, with women in the lead, marched through the Jewish quarter of Williamsburg last evening and wrecked half a dozen butcher shops," reported *The New York Times* in 1902.

⌃ In this painting by Robert Koehler, *The Strike* (1886), labor confronts management in a strike that may soon turn bloody. One worker reaches for a stone as an anxious mother and her daughter look on.

In the late nineteenth century a wave of labor activism swept the nation. More often than mob violence, it was strikes and boycotts that challenged the authority of employers and gave evidence of working-class identity and discontent. Most strikes broke out spontaneously, organized by informal leaders in a factory. Thousands of rallies and organized strikes were staged as well, often on behalf of the eight-hour workday, in good times and bad, by union and nonunion workers alike.

In 1877 the country's first nationwide strike opened an era of confrontation between labor and management. When the Baltimore and Ohio Railroad cut wages by 20 percent, a crew in Martinsburg, West Virginia, seized the local depot and blocked the line. Two-thirds of the nation's track shut down in sympathy. When companies hired strikebreakers, striking workers torched rail yards, smashed engines and cars, and tore up track. Local police, state militia, and federal troops finally crushed the strike after 12 bloody days. In its wake, the Great Railroad Strike of 1877 left 100 people dead and $10 million worth of railroad property in rubble. "This may be the beginning of a great civil war . . . between labor and capital," warned one newspaper.

In 1886 tension between labor and capital exploded in the "Great Upheaval"—a series of strikes, boycotts, and rallies. One of the most violent episodes occurred at Haymarket Square in Chicago. A group of anarchists was protesting the recent killing of workers by police at the McCormick Harvesting Company. As rain drenched the small crowd, police moved in and ordered everyone out of the square. Suddenly a bomb exploded. One officer was killed, and 6 others were mortally wounded. When police opened fire, the crowd fired back. Nearly 70 more policemen were injured, and at least 4 civilians died.

Conservatives charged that radicals were responsible for the "Haymarket Massacre." Ordinary citizens who had supported labor grew fearful of its power to spark violence and disorder. Though the bomb thrower was never identified, a trial of questionable legality found eight anarchists guilty of conspiracy to murder. Seven were sentenced to death. Cities enlarged their police forces, and states built more National Guard armories on the borders of working-class neighborhoods.

Management Strikes Again >> The strikes, rallies, and boycotts of 1886 were followed by a second surge of labor activism in 1892. In the silver mines of Coeur d'Alene, Idaho, at the Carnegie steel mill in Homestead, Pennsylvania, in the coal mines near Tracy City, Tennessee, strikes flared. Often state and federal troops joined company guards and Pinkerton detectives to crush these actions.

The broadest confrontation between labor and management took place two years later. A terrible depression had shaken the economy for almost a year when George Pullman, owner of the Palace Car factory and inventor of the plush railroad car, laid off workers, cut wages (but kept rents high on company-owned housing), and refused to discuss grievances. In 1894 workers struck and managed to convince the new American Railway Union (ARU) to support them by boycotting all trains that used

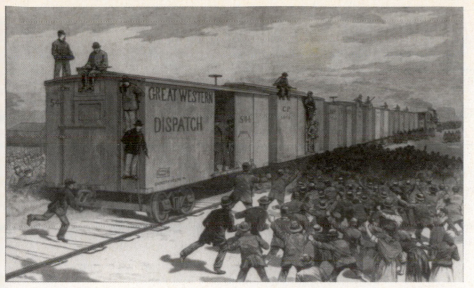

<< The Great Railway Strike of 1877 was the first instance of the massive destruction of machines by workers, who vented their frustrations against the low wages and dangerous working conditions by bringing the nation's rail system to a near standstill. This drawing shows a freight train under the protection of armed U.S. marshals attempting to pull away from an angry mob in East St. Louis, Illinois.

In a matter of only 30 or 40 years, the new industrial order transformed the landscape of America. It left its mark elsewhere in the world, too. British railroad mileage grew to some 20,000 miles by the 1870s, while Germany and France built even larger systems. Japan began constructing its network in the 1870s. Other non-industrial countries followed, especially those rich in raw materials and agricultural commodities. In India the British built the fourth longest railway system in the world. None outstripped the United States. By 1915 its rail network was longer than the next seven largest systems combined.

With remarkable speed, global networks of communication and transportation were set into place. Underwater telegraph cables were laid from the United States to Europe in 1866, to Australia in 1871 and 1872, to Latin America in 1872 and 1873 and to West Africa by 1886. The completion of the Suez Canal in 1869 (the same year a golden spike connected the last link in the transcontinental railroad) hastened the switch from sail-power to steam-driven ships, by slicing thousands of miles from the journey between Europe and Asia. Wheat from the United States and India, wool from Australia, and beef from Argentina poured into Europe, while Europe sent textiles, railroad equipment, coal, and machinery to Asia and the Americas.

Such changes might have seemed effortless to someone like T. S. Hudson, scampering across the rails of America in 1882. But as these networks tied together national economies, swings in the business cycle produced global consequences. When an Austrian bank failed in 1873, depression soon reached the United States. In the mid-1880s and again in the mid-1890s, recessions drove prices down and unemployment up all across the industrialized world.

Industrial workers bore the brunt of the burden, but in Europe they had greater success in unionizing, especially after anticombination laws forbidding strikes were abolished in the decades following 1850. By 1900 British unions had signed up 2 million workers, twice the number of members in either the United States or Germany. As strikes became more common and labor unions more powerful, industrializing nations passed social legislation that included the first social security systems and health insurance. Neither would come to the United States until the Great Depression of the 1930s.

Pullman cars. Quickly the strike spread to 27 states and territories. Anxious railroad owners appealed to President Grover Cleveland for federal help. On the slim pretext that the strike obstructed mail delivery (strikers had actually been willing to handle mail trains without Pullman cars), Cleveland secured a court order halting the strike. He then called several thousand special deputies into Chicago to enforce it. In the rioting that followed, 12 people died and scores were arrested. But the strike was quashed.

In all labor disputes the central issue was the power to shape the new industrial systems. Employers always enjoyed the advantage. They hired and fired workers, set the terms of employment, and ruled the workplace. They fought unions with "yellow dog" contracts that forced workers to refuse to join. Blacklists circulated the names of labor agitators. Lockouts kept protesting workers from plants, and labor spies infiltrated their organizations. With a growing pool of labor, employers could replace strikers and break strikes.

Management could also count on local, state, and federal authorities to send troops to break strikes. In addition, businesses used a powerful new legal weapon, the **injunction**. These court orders prohibited certain actions, including strikes, by barring workers

> **injunction** court order requiring individuals or groups to participate in or refrain from a certain action.

from interfering with their employer's business. It was just such an order that had brought federal deputies into the Pullman strike and put Eugene Debs, head of the railway union, behind bars.

 REVIEW

Through what means, organized and unorganized, did workers respond to industrialization?

CHAPTER SUMMARY

In the last third of the nineteenth century, a new industrial order reshaped the United States.

- New systems—of resource development, technology, invention, transportation, communications, finance, corporate management, and labor—boosted industrial growth and productivity.
- Businesses grew big, expanding vertically and horizontally to curb costs and competition and to increase control and efficiency.
- Industrialization came at a price.
  - Workers found their power, job satisfaction, and free time reduced as their numbers in factories mushroomed.
  - The environment was degraded.
  - A vicious cycle of boom and bust afflicted the economy.
- Workers both resisted and accommodated the new industrial order.
  - Some resisted through informal mechanisms such as slowdowns, absenteeism, and quitting and through spontaneous and more formal ones, including radical unions like the Knights of Labor.
  - Other workers were more accommodating, accepting low-paying jobs and layoffs and creating "pure-and-simple" unions, such as the American Federation of Labor, that accepted the prevailing system of private ownership and wage labor while bargaining for better wages and working conditions.
- The benefits of industrialization were equally undeniable.
  - Life improved materially for many Americans.
  - The real wages of even industrial workers climbed.
- The United States rocketed from fourth place among industrial nations in 1860 to first by 1890.

Significant Events

First oil well drilled near Titusville, Pennsylvania — **1859**

Knights of Labor created

John D. Rockefeller incorporates Standard Oil Company of Ohio — **1869**

1870

Carnegie Steel Company founded; Panic of 1873 — **1873**

Massachusetts enacts first 10-hour workday law for women — **1874**

1876 — Alexander Graham Bell invents the telephone

Additional Reading

For a useful introduction see Edward C. Kirkland, *Industry Comes of Age: Business, Labor, and Public Policy, 1860–1897* (1967). Mechanization and its impact are the focus of Siegfried Giedion's classic *Mechanization Takes Command* (1948). The best overview of American labor is American Social History Project, *Who Built America? Working People and the Nation's Economy, Politics, Culture, & Society, Volume Two: From the Gilded Age to the Present* (1992). Herbert Gutman, *Work, Culture, and Society in Industrializing America: Essays in American Working-Class History* (1976), explores the development of working-class communities in the nineteenth century, while David Montgomery assesses the impact of industrialization on American labor in *The Fall of the House of Labor: The Workplace, the State, and American Labor Activism, 1865–1925* (1987). Leon Fink, *Workingmen's Democracy: The Knights of Labor and American Politics* (1983), examines early efforts of the Knights of Labor to challenge corporate capitalism. Alice Kessler-Harris, *Out to Work: A History of Wage-Earning Women in the United States* (1982), surveys female wage earners and their effect on American culture, family life, and values. Kevin Kenny, *Making Sense of the Molly Maguires* (1998), is a superb study not only of the mysterious Mollys and their tragic end but of immigration, working-class violence, and the history of the Irish in America. Ron Chernow's *Titan: The Life of John D. Rockefeller, Sr.* (1998) and Jean Strouse's definitive *Morgan: American Financier* (1999) help to debunk the image of business leaders as "Robber Barons," without minimizing their ruthlessness. David Nasaw's *Andrew Carnegie* (2006) gives us the most human portrait of the legendary steel baron; for the rise of big railroads, consult T. J. Stiles, *The First Tycoon: The Epic Life of Cornelius Vanderbilt* (2009). Business historian Alfred D. Chandler, Jr.'s *Strategy and Structure: Chapters in the History of American-Industrial Enterprise* (1962) and *The Visible Hand: The Managerial Revolution in American Business* (1977) are seminal accounts of business organization that profile the emergence of a new class of managers. For a comparative view of the rise of big business in the United States, Great Britain, and Germany, see his *Scale and Scope* (1988).

Railroad wage cuts lead to violent strikes; Thomas Edison invents phonograph

American Federation of Labor organized; Haymarket Square bombing

Homestead Steel strike

Pullman strike

U.S. Steel Corporation becomes nation's first billion-dollar company

1877   **1882**   **1886**   **1892**   **1893**   **1894**   **1901**

Rockefeller's Standard Oil Company becomes nation's first trust

Panic of 1893

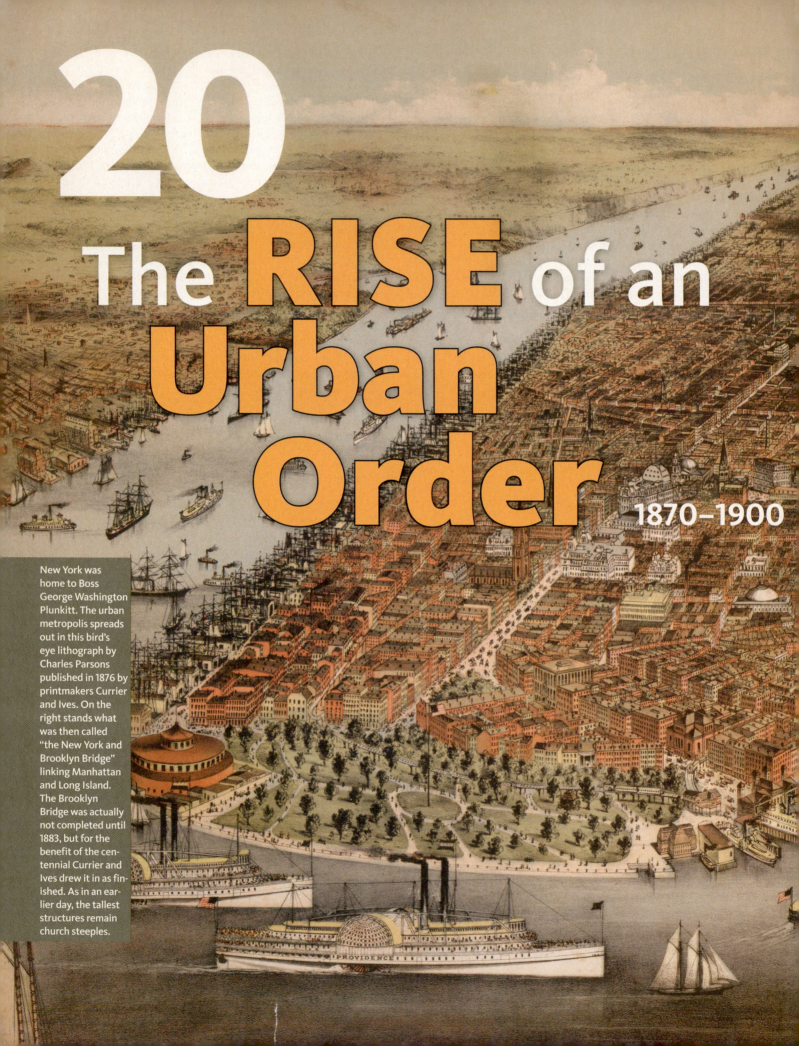

20

The RISE of an Urban Order

1870–1900

New York was home to Boss George Washington Plunkitt. The urban metropolis spreads out in this bird's eye lithograph by Charles Parsons published in 1876 by printmakers Currier and Ives. On the right stands what was then called "the New York and Brooklyn Bridge" linking Manhattan and Long Island. The Brooklyn Bridge was actually not completed until 1883, but for the benefit of the centennial Currier and Ives drew it in as finished. As in an earlier day, the tallest structures remain church steeples.

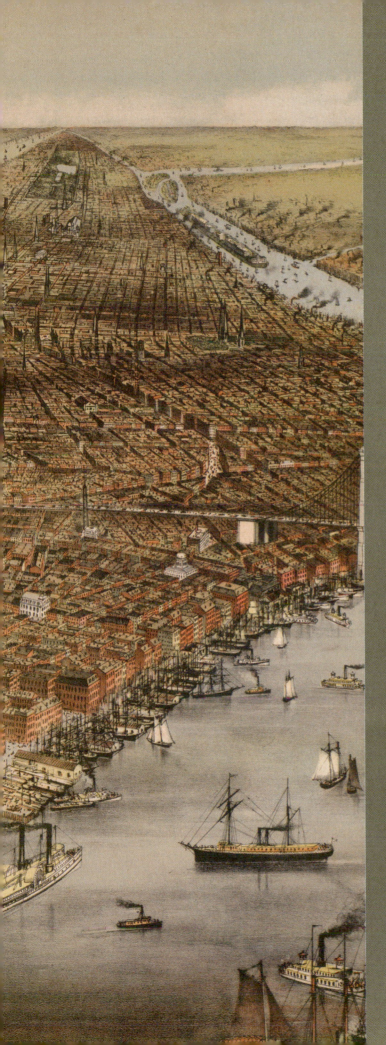

>> **AN AMERICAN STORY**

A DAY IN THE LIFE OF BOSS PLUNKITT

Graziano's bootblack stand was jammed with people, milling about, looking for help. Above the crowd, enthroned like an Irish king, sat George Washington Plunkitt, ward boss of Manhattan's Fifteenth Assembly District. There to help, Plunkitt was a political boss who asked little in return, only votes on Election Day. Plunkitt understood the close relationship between help and votes. "There's got to be in every ward," another boss explained, "somebody that any bloke can come to—no matter what he's done—and get help. Help, you understand; none of your law and justice, but help."

For years Plunkitt had been a leader of Tammany Hall, the Democratic party organization that ruled New York City politics from 1850 to 1930. He spent much of his day helping those in need. A knock on his door might mean a constituent needed a friend plucked from jail; a howling fire engine might herald a family in need of shelter, food, or clothing; men shuffling up to the bootblack stand might need work; a funeral, confirmation, or bar mitzvah might require his presence. Early evening usually found Plunkitt at district headquarters, helping his election captains plot ways of "turning out the vote" in his favor or his cronies'. Then perhaps it was off to a wedding or a birthday party and finally to bed at midnight, exhausted from a day of helping. >>

Such relentless effort helped Plunkitt as well. Born to Irish immigrants, he died a millionaire in 1924. His pluck and practicality would have made him the envy of any industrialist. As with the Carnegies and Rockefellers, fierce ambition fueled his rise from butcher boy to political boss. City politics was his way out of the slums in a world that favored the rich, the educated, and the well established.

Plunkitt's New York was the first great city in history to be ruled by men of the people in an organized and continuing way. Bosses and their henchmen came from the streets and saloons, the slums and tenements, the firehouses and funeral homes. Many of their families had only recently arrived in America.

In an earlier age political leadership had been drawn from the ranks of the wealthy and native-born. America had been an agrarian republic. Most personal relationships were grounded in small communities. By the late nineteenth century, the country was in the midst of an urban explosion. Industrial cities of unparalleled size and diversity were transforming American life. They lured people from all over the country and the globe, created tensions between natives and newcomers, reshaped the social order. For Plunkitt, as for so many Americans, the golden door of opportunity opened onto the city. «

A NEW URBAN AGE

The modern city was the product of industrialization. Cities contained the great investment banks, the smoky mills and dingy sweatshops, the railroad yards, tenements, mansions and new department stores. Opportunity—to work and play—drew people from as near as the countryside and as far away as Italy, Russia, Armenia, and China. By the end of the nineteenth century America had entered a new urban age, with tens of millions of "urbanites," an urban landscape, and a growing urban culture.

The Urban Explosion »
During the 50 years after the Civil War the population of the United States tripled—from 31 million to 92 million. Yet the number of Americans living in cities increased nearly sevenfold. By 1910 nearly half the nation lived in cities large and small.

Cities grew in every region of the country. In the Northeast and upper Midwest early industrialization created more cities than in the West and the South, although a few big cities sprouted there as well. Atlanta, Nashville, and later Dallas and Houston boomed under the influence of railroads. By 1900 Los Angeles with its 100,000 residents was second only to San Francisco on the west coast.

Large urban centers dominated whole regions, tying the country together in a vast urban network. New York, the nation's banker, printer, and chief marketplace, ruled the East. Smaller cities operated within narrower spheres of influence and often specialized. Milwaukee was famous for beer, Tulsa for oil, and Hershey, Pennsylvania, for chocolate.

Cities shaped the natural environment hundreds of miles beyond their limits. Chicago, gateway to the West, became a powerful agent of ecological change. As its lines of commerce and industry radiated outward, the city transformed the rich ecosystems of the West. Wheat to feed Chicago's millions replaced sheltering prairie grasses. Great stands of white pine in Wisconsin vanished, only to reappear in the furniture and frames of Chicago houses, or as fence rails shipped to prairie farms.

The Great Global Migration »
Between 1820 and 1920 some 60 million people across the globe left farms and villages for cities. Beginning in the 1870s new oceangoing, steam-powered ships extended the reach of migrating laborers across continents. In Europe mushrooming populations gave the emigrants a powerful push out, while machinery cut the need for farmworkers.

Surplus farmworkers became a part of a vast international labor force, pulled by industry to cities in Europe and America. The prospect of factory work for better pay and fewer hours especially lured the young. In the United States young farm women spearheaded the urban migration. Mechanization and the rise of commercial agriculture made them less valuable in the fields; mass-produced goods from mail-order houses made them less useful at home.

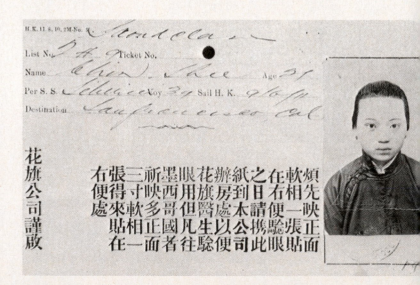

⌃ Chin Shee was 21 years old and bound for San Francisco at the time this boarding pass was issued in Hong Kong in 1911.

Asia sent comparatively fewer newcomers to the United States, Canada, and other industrializing nations hungry for workers. Still, Asian immigrants followed migration patterns similar to those of the workers leaving Europe and for similar reasons. Between 1850 and 1882 rising taxes and rents on land and declining markets drove some 370,000 Chinese across the Pacific to the United States. Nearly 400,000 Japanese arrived between 1885 and 1924.

Immigration from Europe dwarfed all others as new regions of the continent contributed growing numbers. Earlier in the century, European immigrants had come from northern and western Europe. In the 1880s, however, "new" immigrants from southern and eastern Europe began to arrive. Some, like Russian and Polish Jews, were fleeing religious and political persecution. Others left to evade famine and diseases such as cholera, which swept across southern Italy in 1887. But most came for the same reasons that motivated migrants from the countryside: a job, more money, a fresh start.

Ambitious, hardy, and resourceful, immigrants found themselves tested every step of the way to America. It took one to two weeks to cross the Atlantic. Immigrants spent most of the time below decks in cramped, filthy compartments called

"new" immigrants called "new" because they differed from earlier arrivals from Northern and Western Europe; these newcomers came from Eastern and Southern Europe and were largely non-Protestant: Catholics, Jews, and Russian Orthodox Christians.

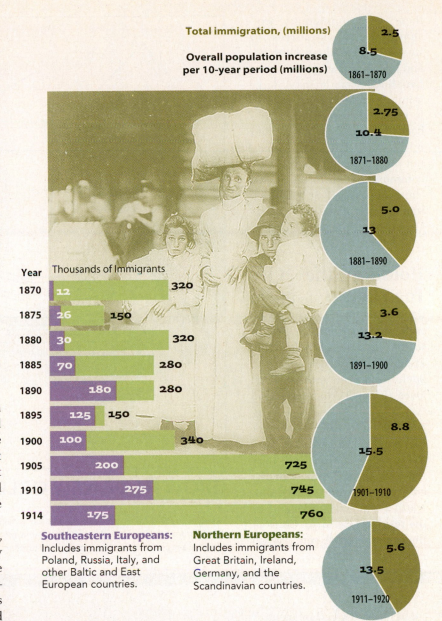

Total immigration, (millions)

Overall population increase per 10-year period (millions)

Period	Overall population increase	Total immigration
1861–1870	8.5	2.5
1871–1880	10.4	2.75
1881–1890	13	5.0
1891–1900	13.2	3.6
1901–1910	15.5	8.8
1911–1920	13.5	5.6

Year	Thousands of Immigrants (Southeastern Europeans)	(Northern Europeans)
1870	12	320
1875	26	150
1880	30	320
1885	70	280
1890	180	280
1895	125	150
1900	100	340
1905	200	725
1910	275	745
1914	175	760

Southeastern Europeans: Includes immigrants from Poland, Russia, Italy, and other Baltic and East European countries.

Northern Europeans: Includes immigrants from Great Britain, Ireland, Germany, and the Scandinavian countries.

IMMIGRATION, 1860–1920

Between 1860 and 1920 immigration increased dramatically as the sources of immigrants shifted from northern Europe to southeastern Europe. Despite fears to the contrary, the proportion of newcomers as a percentage of population increases did not show nearly the same jump.

Opinion

Did massive immigration from eastern and southern Europe help or hinder the United States in the late nineteenth century?

"steerage." Most landed at New York's Castle Garden or the newer facility on nearby Ellis Island, opened in 1892. If arriving from Asia, they landed at Angel Island in San Francisco Bay. They had to pass a medical examination, have their names recorded by customs officials, and pay an entry tax. At any point, they could be detained or shipped home.

Most newcomers were young, between the ages of 15 and 40. Few spoke English or had skills or much education. Unlike earlier arrivals, who were mostly Protestant, these new immigrants worshiped in Catholic, Greek, or Russian Orthodox churches and Jewish synagogues. Almost two-thirds were men. A large number came to make money to buy land or start businesses back home. Some changed their minds and sent for relatives, but those returning home were common enough to be labeled "birds of passage." Still, by 1900 immigrants made up nearly 15 percent of the population.

Holding the City Together >> In colonial days Benjamin Franklin could walk from one end of Boston to the other in an hour. Only Franklin's adopted home, Philadelphia, spilled into suburbs. Over the years these colonial "walking cities" developed ringed patterns of settlement. Merchants, professionals, and the upper classes lived near their shops and offices in the city center. As one walked outward, the income and status of the residents declined. Cities of the late nineteenth century still

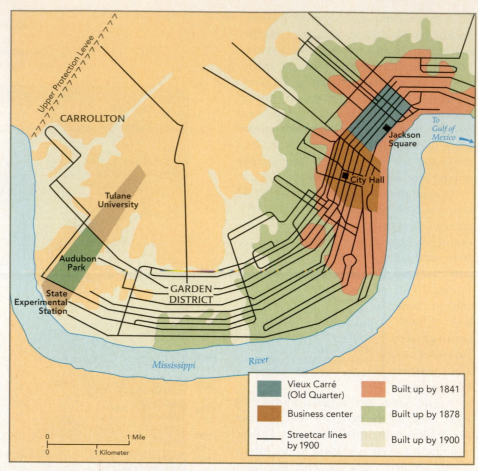

Legend:
- Vieux Carré (Old Quarter)
- Business center
- Streetcar lines by 1900
- Built up by 1841
- Built up by 1878
- Built up by 1900

0 — 1 Mile
0 — 1 Kilometer

GROWTH OF NEW ORLEANS TO 1900

Streetcars helped cities spread beyond business districts while still functioning as organic wholes. By 1900 streetcar lines in New Orleans reached all the way to Audubon Park and Tulane University, bringing these once-distant points within the reach of city dwellers and creating "streetcar suburbs."

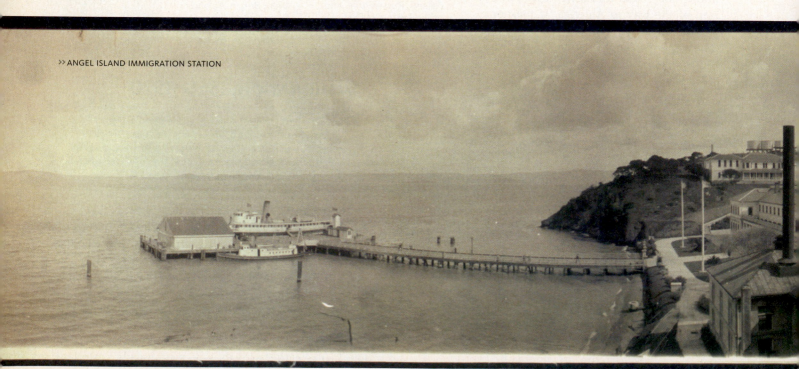

>> ANGEL ISLAND IMMIGRATION STATION

exhibited this ringed pattern, except that industrialization had reversed the order and increased urban sprawl. The wealthy now lived at the outskirts of the city and the poor and working poor at the industrial center.

For all their differences, the circles of settlement held together as a part of an interdependent whole. One reason was an evolving system of urban transportation. By the mid-nineteenth century horse-drawn railways were conveying some 35 million people a year in New York. Their problems were legendary: so slow, a person could walk faster; so crowded (according to Mark Twain), you "had to hang on by your eyelashes and your toenails"; so dirty, tons of horse manure were left daily in the streets.

Civic leaders came to understand that the modern city could not survive, much less grow, without improved transportation. San Francisco installed trolley cars pulled by steam-driven cables. The innovation worked so well in hilly San Francisco that Chicago, Seattle, and other cities installed cable systems in the 1880s. Some cities experimented with elevated trestles, to carry steam locomotives or cable lines high above crowded streets. But none of the breakthroughs quite did the trick. Cables remained slow and unreliable; the elevated railways, or "els," were dirty, ugly, and noisy.

Electricity rescued city travelers. In 1888 Frank Julian Sprague, a naval engineer who had once worked for Thomas Edison, installed the first electric trolley line in Richmond, Virginia. Electrified streetcars were soon speeding along at 12 miles an hour, twice as fast as horses. By 1902 electricity drove nearly all city railways. Sprague's breakthroughs also meant that "subways" could be built without having to worry about tunnels filled with a steam engine's smoke and soot. Between 1895 and 1897 Boston built the first underground electric line. New York followed in 1904 with a subway that ran from the southern tip of Manhattan north to Harlem.

The rich had long been able to keep homes outside city limits, traveling in private carriages. New systems of mass transit freed the middle class and even the poor to live miles from work. For a nickel or two, anyone could ride from central shopping and business districts to the suburban fringes and back. A network of moving vehicles held the segmented and sprawling city together and widened its reach out to "streetcar suburbs."

Bridges and Skyscrapers >> Since cities
often grew along rivers and harbors, their separate parts sometimes had to be joined over water. The principles of building large river bridges had already been worked out by the railroads. It remained for a German immigrant, John Roebling, and his son, Washington, to make the bridge a symbol of urban growth.

Their creation—the legendary Brooklyn Bridge linking Manhattan with Brooklyn—took 13 years to complete, cost $15 million and 20 lives and killed designer John. When it opened in 1883 it stretched more than a mile across the East River, with passage broad enough for a footpath, two double carriage lanes, and two railroad lines. Its arches were cut like giant cathedral windows, and its supporting cables hung, said an awestruck observer, "like divine messages from above." Soon other suspension bridges were spanning the railroad yards in St. Louis and the bay at Galveston, Texas.

Even as late as 1880 church steeples towered over squat factories and office buildings. But growing congestion and the increasing value of land challenged architects to

ALL ELEVATED TRAINS IN CHICAGO
STOP AT THE
Chicago Rock Island AND Pacific Railway Station
ONLY ONE ON THE LOOP

ELEVATED STATION | AT THE "ROCK ISLAND" VAN BUREN ST. STATION.

W. H. TRUESDALE,
Vice-President and General Manager.

JOHN SEBASTIAN,
General Passenger and Ticket Agent.

⌃ This map shows one of Chicago's earliest elevated railway systems. (Note the insert on the lower left, featuring an elevated railway station.) "Els" first appeared in Chicago in 1892 as a way of providing mass transit across the city without disrupting street traffic. The earliest lines did not extend downtown, but by 1897 elevated railways like this one were whisking passengers from the outskirts to the center of the city, known in Chicago as "The Loop."

search for ways to make buildings taller. Thin air became valuable real estate. In place of thick, heavy walls of brick that restricted factory floor space, builders used cast-iron columns. The new "cloudscrapers" were strong, durable, and fire-resistant, ideal for warehouses and also for office buildings and department stores.

Steel, tougher in tension and compression, turned cloudscrapers into skyscrapers. William LeBaron Jenney first used steel in his 10-story Home Life Insurance Building (1885) in Chicago. By the end of the century steel frames and girders raised buildings to 30 stories or more. New York City's triangular Flatiron Building used the new technology to project an angular, yet remarkably delicate elegance. In

Chicago, Daniel Burnham's Reliance Building (1890) made such heavy use of new plate glass windows that contemporaries called it "a glass tower fifteen stories high."

It was no accident that many of the new skyscrapers arose in Chicago. The city had burned nearly to the ground in 1871. The "Chicago school" of architects helped to rebuild it. The young maverick Louis H. Sullivan promised a new urban profile in which the skyscraper would be "every inch a proud and soaring thing." In the Wainwright Building (1890) in St. Louis and the Carson, Pirie, and Scott department store (1889–1904) in Chicago, Sullivan produced towering structures that symbolized the modern industrial city.

Designed by Chicago architect Daniel Burham and completed in 1902, the Fuller Building quickly became known as the "Flatiron Building" for its uniquely triangular shape. With a steel frame, it soared to a height of 22 stories, making it one of the tallest structures in New York City. "I found myself agape," wrote science fiction novelist H. G. Welles when he saw the building, "admiring a sky-scraper, the prow of the Flat-iron Building, to be particular, ploughing up through the traffic of Broadway and Fifth Avenue in the afternoon light."

Slum and Tenement

Slum and Tenement >> Far below the sky-scrapers lay the slums and **tenements** of the inner city. In cramped rooms and sunless hallways, along narrow alleys and in flooded basements, lived the city poor. They often worked there, too. In "sweaters' shops" as many as 18 people labored and slept in foul two-room flats.

> **tenement** building often in disrepair and usually five or six stories in height, in which cheap apartments were rented to tenants.

Slum dwellers often lived on poor diets that left them vulnerable to epidemics. Cholera, typhoid, and an outbreak of yellow fever in Memphis in the 1870s killed tens of thousands. Tuberculosis was deadlier still. Slum children—all city children—were most vulnerable to such diseases. Almost a quarter of the children born in American cities in 1890 never lived to see their first birthday.

The installation of new sewage and water purification systems helped. The modern flush toilet came into use only after the turn of the century. Until then people relied on water closets and communal privies, some of which catered to as many as 800. All too often cities dumped waste into old private vaults or rivers used for drinking water.

Slum housing was often more dangerous than the water. The tubercle bacillus flourished in musty, windowless tenements. In 1879 New York enacted a new housing law requiring a window in all bedrooms of new tenements. Architect James E. Ware won a competition with a creative design that contained an indentation on both sides of the building. When two tenements abutted, the indentations formed a narrow shaft for air and light. From above, the buildings looked like giant dumbbells and packed up to 16 families on a floor.

Originally hailed as an innovation, Ware's dumbbell tenement spread over such cities as Cleveland, Cincinnati, and Boston "like a scab," said an unhappy reformer. The airshafts became giant silos for trash, which blocked what little light had entered and, worse still, carried fires from one story to the next. When the New York housing commission met in 1900, it concluded that conditions were worse than when reformers had started 33 years earlier.

✓ **REVIEW**

How did industrial cities grow and at what costs?

Tenement house yard, photographed by Jacob Riis.

RUNNING AND REFORMING THE CITY

Every new arrival to the city brought dreams and altogether too many needs. Schools and houses had to be built, streets paved, garbage collected, sewers dug, fires fought, utility lines laid. Running the city became a full-time job, and a new breed of full-time politician rose to the task. So, too, did a new breed of reformer, determined to help the needy cope with the ravages of urban life.

The need for change was clear. Many city charters dating from the eighteenth century included a paralyzing system of checks and balances. Mayors vetoed city councils; councils ignored mayors. Jealous state legislatures allowed cities only the most limited and unpopular taxes, such as those on property. At the same time, city governments were often decentralized—fragmented, scattered, at odds with one another. Each branch was a tiny kingdom with its own regulations and taxing authority. As immigrants and rural newcomers flocked to factories and tenements, the structures of urban government strained to adapt.

Boss Rule >>

Why must there be a boss," journalist Lincoln Steffens asked Boss Richard Croker of New York, "when we've got a mayor—and a city council?" "That's why," Croker broke in. "It's because we've got a mayor and a council and judges—and—a hundred other men to deal with." The boss was right. He and his system furnished cities with the centralization, authority, and services they sorely needed.

Bosses ruled through the **political machine.** Often, as with New York's Tammany Hall, machines dated back to the late eighteenth and early nineteenth centuries. They began as fraternal and charitable organizations. Over the years they became centers of political power. In New York the machine was Democratic; in Philadelphia, Republican. Machines could even be found in rural areas such as Duval County, Texas, where the Spanish-speaking Anglo boss Archie Parr molded a powerful alliance with Mexican American landowners.

political machine hierarchical political organization developed in the nineteenth century that controlled the activities of a political party and was usually headed by a political boss.

In an age of enterprise, the boss operated his political machine like a corporation. His office might be a saloon, a funeral home, or, like George Washington Plunkitt's, a shoeshine stand. His managers were party activists, connected in a corporate-like chain of command. Local committeemen reported to district captains, captains to district leaders, district leaders to the boss or bosses who directed the machine.

The goods and services of the machine were basics: a Christmas turkey, a load of coal for the winter, jobs for the unemployed, English-language classes for recent immigrants. Bosses sponsored fun, too: sports teams, glee clubs, balls, and barbecues. In return, citizens expressed their gratitude at the ballot box.

Sometimes the votes of the grateful were not enough. Bosses marshalled the "graveyard vote" by drawing names from tombstones to pad lists of registered voters. They hired "repeaters" to vote under the phony names. When reformers introduced the Australian (secret) ballot in the 1880s to prevent fraud, bosses pulled the "Tasmanian dodge" by premarking election tickets. Failing that, they dumped whole ballot boxes into the river or used hired thugs to scare unpersuaded voters away from the polls.

H. C. WHITE CO., Gen'l Offices N. Bennington, Vt., U.S.A.
Branch Offices: New York, Chicago, London.

<< No city offered bosses more opportunity to build than San Francisco in the wake of the city's greatest natural disaster. Just after 5 A.M. on April 18, 1906, an earthquake estimated at a magnitude of 7.7 on the Richter Scale struck San Francisco. Losses exceeded $235 million ($5.1 billion in 2006 dollars). More than the quake itself, the fires that sprang up in its aftermath helped to destroy half the city. Fires burned for four days. Nearly 28,000 buildings were destroyed. According to one estimate, more than 3,000 people perished in San Francisco and nearby towns, and some 225,000 were left homeless.

Machine-Age Voting

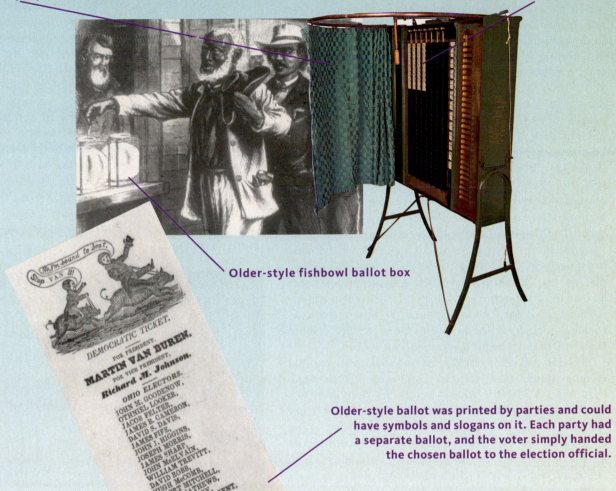

What is the purpose of the curtain?

Levers for mechanically marking ballots.

Older-style fishbowl ballot box

Older-style ballot was printed by parties and could have symbols and slogans on it. Each party had a separate ballot, and the voter simply handed the chosen ballot to the election official.

In the late nineteenth century political corruption often began with voting. Pre-marking ballots, stuffing ballot boxes, paying "repeaters" to vote more than once were all ways to fix the outcome of elections. Reformers fought back. The "Australian" or secret ballot (first used in Victoria, Australia, in 1858 and in the United States in 1888) employed standardized paper ballots, distributed one to a voter at poll places and marked in a booth in secret. Each ballot had the names of candidates printed on them at government expense, as opposed to earlier ballots, which political parties

printed and handed out, often with pictures or symbols on them. Transparent "fishbowl" ballot boxes made it difficult to stuff the boxes beforehand. Taking the process one step further, Jacob A. Myers tested his new "gear-and-lever" voting machine in Lockport, New York, in 1892. He devised the machine, he said, to "protect mechanically the voter from rascaldom, and make the process of casting the ballot perfectly plain, simple and secret." Some called it "the inventive triumph of its age." The voter simply pulled a lever that closed a curtain around him for privacy. Other levers allowed him to vote

for individual candidates or straight-party tickets. The machine recorded and tallied the votes.

THINKING CRITICALLY

What advantages did the voting machine offer over the Australian paper ballot? Over the older style ballots provided by parties? What were the disadvantages of voting machines? Which system was better if voters could not read? What potential for voting fraud exists with today's electronic or optical-scan voting machines?

Rewards, Accomplishments, and Costs »

Why did bosses go to such lengths? Some simply loved the game of politics. More often bosses loved money. Their ability to get it was limited only by their ingenuity or the occasional success of an outraged reformer. The record for brassiness must go to Boss William Tweed. During his reign in the 1860s and 1870s Tweed swindled New York City out of a fortune. His masterpiece of graft was a chunky three-story courthouse in lower Manhattan originally budgeted at $250,000. When Tweed was through, the city had spent more than $13 million, over 60 percent of which lined the pockets of Tweed and his cronies. Tweed died in prison, but with such profits to be made, it was small wonder that bosses nearly matched the emperors of Rome as builders.

In their fashion bosses played a vital role in the industrial city. Rising from the bottom ranks, they guided immigrants into American life and helped some of the underprivileged up from poverty. They changed the urban landscape with a massive construction program. They modernized city government by uniting it and making it perform. Choosing the aldermen, municipal judges, mayors, and administrative officials, bosses exerted new control to provide the contracts and franchises to run cities. Such accomplishments fostered the notion that government could be called on to help the needy. The welfare state, still decades away, had some roots here.

The toll was often outrageous. Inflated taxes, extorted revenue, unpunished vice and crime were only the obvious costs. A woman whose family enjoyed Plunkitt's Christmas turkey might be widowed by an accident to her husband in a sweatshop kept open by timely bribes. Filthy buildings might claim her children as corrupt inspectors ignored serious violations. Buying votes and selling favors, bosses turned democracy into a petty business—as much a "business," said Plunkitt, "as the grocery or dry-goods or the drug business."

Nativism, Revivals, and the Social Gospel »

Urban blight and the condition of the poor inspired social as well as political activism, especially within churches. Not all of it was constructive. The popular Congregationalist minister Josiah Strong concluded that the city was "a menace to society." Along with anxious economists and social workers, he blamed everything from corruption to unemployment on immigrant city dwellers and urged restricting their entry.

In the 1880s and 1890s two depressions sharpened such anxieties. Nativism, a defensive and fearful nationalism, peaked as want ignited prejudice. Organizations such as the new Immigration Restriction League attacked Catholics and foreigners. Already the victims of racial prejudice, the Chinese were easy targets. In 1882 Congress enacted the Chinese Exclusion Act banning the entry of Chinese laborers. It represented an important step in the drive to restrict immigration.

To bridge the gap between the middle class and the poor, some clergy took their missions to the slums. Beginning in 1870 Dwight Lyman Moody, a 300-pound former shoe salesman, won armies of lowly converts with revivals in Boston, Chicago, and other cities. Evangelists helped to found American branches of the British-born Young Men's Christian Association and Salvation Army.

A small group of ministers rejected the traditional notion that weak character explained sin and that society would be perfected only as individual sinners were converted. They spread a new "Social Gospel" that focused on improving the conditions of society to save individuals. In *Applied Christianity* (1886) the influential Washington Gladden preached that the church must be responsible for correcting social injustices, including dangerous working conditions and unfair labor practices. Houses of worship, such as William Rainford's St. George's Episcopal Church in New York, became centers of social activity, with boys' clubs, gymnasiums, libraries, glee clubs, and industrial training programs.

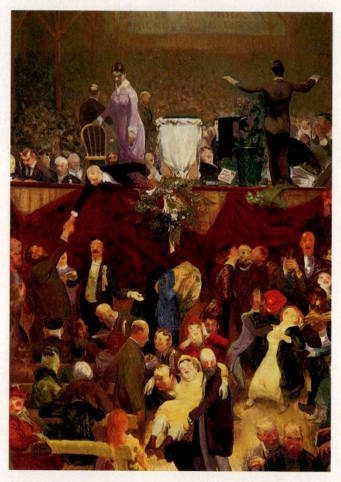

⌃ *The Sawdust Trail*, painted by George Bellows in 1916, depicts one of the revival meetings of William Ashley ("Billy") Sunday in Philadelphia. Sunday, a hard-drinking professional baseball player turned evangelist, began his religious revivals in the 1890s and drew thousands. Here, Sunday leans down from the platform to shake the hand of an admirer. In the foreground, a swooning woman, overcome with a sense of her sins, is carried away.

THE GREAT FEAR OF THE PERIOD
THAT UNCLE SAM MAY BE SWALLOWED BY FOREIGNERS.

⌃ By the 1800s a flood of Southern and Eastern European immigrants were streaming into the new receiving center of Ellis Island in New York Harbor, while the relatively few Asian immigrants who arrived (most were barred from entry by the Chinese Exclusion Act of 1882) came through Angel Island in San Francisco Bay. The rapid rise in immigration ignited nativist fears that immigrants were taking over the country. In the 1870s cartoon pictured here, Irish and Chinese immigrants in their native dress literally gobble up Uncle Sam.

The Social Settlement Movement ⟩⟩

Church-sponsored programs sometimes repelled the immigrant poor, especially when they saw them as thinly disguised missionary efforts. Immigrants and other slum dwellers were more receptive to a bold experiment called the **settlement house.** Situated in the worst slums, often in renovated old houses, these early community centers were run by middle-class women and men to help the poor and foreign-born. At the turn of the century there were more than 100 of them, the most famous being Jane Addams's Hull House in Chicago. In 1898 the Catholic Church sponsored its first settlement house in New York, and in 1900 Bronson House opened its doors to the Latino community in Los Angeles.

> **settlement house** social reform effort that used neighborhood centers in which settlement house workers lived and worked among the poor, often in slum neighborhoods.

High purposes inspired settlement workers, who actually lived in the settlement houses. They left comfortable middle-class homes and dedicated themselves (like the "early Christians," said one) to service and sacrifice. They aimed to teach immigrants American ways and to create a community spirit of "right living through social relations." Immigrants were also encouraged to preserve their heritages through festivals, parades, and museums.

Like political bosses, settlement reformers furnished help, from day nurseries to English-language and cooking classes to playgrounds and libraries. Armed with statistics and personal experiences, they also lobbied for social legislation to improve housing, women's working conditions, and public schools.

✓ **REVIEW**

In what ways did boss rule represent "reform" of city government, and at whose expense did such reform come?

CITY LIFE

City life reflected the stratified nature of American society in the late nineteenth century. Every city had its slums and tenements but also its fashionable avenues, where many-roomed mansions housed the tiny one-percent of city dwellers considered wealthy. In between tenement and mansion lived the broad middle of urban society, which made up nearly a third of the population and owned about half of the nation's wealth. With more money and leisure time, the middle class was increasing its power and influence.

The Immigrant in the City >> When they put into port the first thing immigrants were likely to see was a city. Perhaps it was Boston or New York or Galveston, Texas, where an overflow of Jewish immigrants was directed beginning in 1907. Most immigrants, exhausted physically and financially, settled in cities.

Cities developed a well-defined mosaic of ethnic communities, since immigrants usually clustered together on the basis of their villages or provinces. But these neighborhoods were in constant flux. As many as half the residents moved every 10 years, often because of better-paying jobs or more members of their family working.

Ethnic communities served as havens from the strangeness of American society and springboards to a new life. From the moment they stepped off the boat, newcomers felt pressed to learn English, don American clothes, and drop their "greenhorn" ways. Yet in their neighborhoods they also found comrades who spoke their language, theaters that performed their plays and music, restaurants that served their food. Foreign-language newspapers reported events from both the Old World and the New in a tongue that first-generation immigrants could understand. Meanwhile, immigrant aid societies furnished assistance with housing and jobs and sponsored baseball teams, insurance programs, and English-language classes.

Houses of worship were always at the center of immigrant life. They often catered to the practices of individual towns or provinces. Occasionally they changed their ways under the cultural pressures of American life. Where the Irish dominated the American Catholic Church, other immigrants formed new churches with priests from their homelands. Eastern European Jews began to break the

10413. Washington Street, Boston, showing Old South Church.

⌃ WASHINGTON STREET, BOSTON (1895)

old law against men sitting next to their wives and daughters in synagogues. The Orthodox churches of Armenians, Syrians, Romanians, and Serbians gradually lost their national identifications.

The backgrounds and cultural values of immigrants influenced their choice of jobs. Because Chinese men did not scorn washing or ironing, more than 7,500 of them could be found in San Francisco laundries by 1880. Sewing ladies' garments seemed unmanly to many native-born Americans but not to Russian and Italian tailors. Slavs, who valued steady income over education, often pulled their children from school, sent them to work, and worked themselves in the mines for better pay than in factories.

On the whole, immigrants married later and had more children than did the native-born. Greeks and eastern European Jews prearranged marriages according to tradition. They imported "picture brides," betrothed by mail with a photograph. After marriage men ruled the household, but women managed it. Although child-rearing practices varied, immigrants resisted the relative permissiveness of American parents. Youngsters were expected to contribute like little adults to the welfare of the family.

In these "family economies" of working-class immigrants, key decisions—over whether and whom to marry, over work and education, over when to leave home—were made on the basis of collective rather than

WITNESS

A Chinese Immigrant Names His Children

"He winced at the prospect of saddling his children with names which could be ridiculously distorted into pidgin English. He had had enough, he said, of Sing High, Sing Low, Wun Long Hop, Ching Chong, Long Song. . . . At that time the Governor of California bore the name of Dr. George C. Pardee . . . I was named for a fellow Republican . . . [so we had] to live down . . . the socially forbidding names of George C. Pardee, Alice Roosevelt, Helen Taft, Woodrow Wilson. . . ."

— **Pardee Lowe,** *Father and Glorious Descendant,* 1943

∧ Hester Street, New York City

individual needs. Though immigrant boys were more likely to work outside the home than girls, daughters often went to work at an early age so sons could continue their education. It was customary for one daughter to remain unmarried so she could care for younger siblings or aged parents.

The Chinese were an exception to the pattern. The ban on the immigration of Chinese laborers in the 1880s had frozen the gender ratio of Chinese communities into a curious imbalance. Like other immigrants most Chinese newcomers had been single men. In the wake of the ban, those in the United States could not bring over their wives and families.

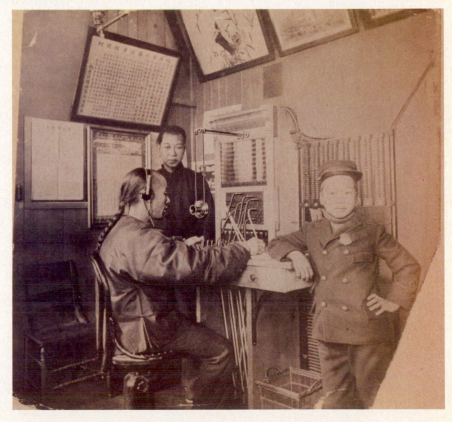

>> The first Chinese telephone operator in San Francisco's Chinatown, the largest community of Chinese outside Asia, is pictured here handling calls from local subscribers. The first switchboard was installed in 1894. Chinese operators had to memorize the names of their users because residents often asked to be connected by name, believing it was impolite to ask by number. This was no easy task. Some subscribers had the same name, so operators also had to learn the occupation and the address of each person on their service. And they had to master the five Chinese dialects spoken by residents.

Nor by law in 13 states could they marry white Americans. With few women, Chinese communities suffered from high rates of prostitution, large numbers of gangs and secret societies, and low birth totals. When the San Francisco earthquake and fire destroyed birth records in 1906, resourceful Chinese immigrants created "paper sons" (and less often "paper daughters") by forging birth certificates and claiming their China-born children as American citizens.

Caught between past and present, pressed to adopt American ways, immigrants nonetheless clung to tradition and assimilated slowly. Their children adjusted more quickly. They soon spoke English like natives, married whomever they pleased, and worked their way out of old neighborhoods. Yet the process was not easy. Children often faced heartrending clashes with parents and rejection from peers.

Urban Middle-Class Life >>
Life for the urban middle class revolved around home and family. By the turn of the century just over a third of middle-class urbanites owned their homes. Often two or three stories, made of brick or brownstone, these houses were a measure of social standing. The plush furniture, heavy drapes, antiques, and curios all signaled the status and refinement of their owners.

> **Baking a loaf of bread required nearly 24 hours, and in 1890 only one in five loaves was made outside the home.**

Such homes, usually on their own lots, also served as havens to protect and nourish the family. Seventeenth-century notions of children as inherently sinful had given way to more modern theories about the shaping influence of environment. Calm and orderly households with nurturing mothers would launch children on the right course. "A clean, fresh, and well-ordered house," stipulated a domestic adviser in 1883, "exercises over its inmates a moral, no less than physical influence, and has a direct tendency to make members of the family sober, peaceable, and considerate of the feelings and happiness of each other."

A woman was judged by the state of her home. The typical homemaker prepared elaborate meals, cleaned, laundered, and sewed. Each task took time. Baking a loaf of bread required nearly 24 hours, and in 1890 four of five loaves were still made at home. Perhaps 25 percent of urban households had live-in servants to help with the work. They were on call about 100 hours a week, were off but one evening and part of Sunday, and averaged $2 to $5 a week in salary.

By the 1890s a wealth of new consumer products eased the burdens of housework. Brand names trumpeted a new age of commercially prepared food—Campbell's soup, Quaker oats, Pillsbury flour, Jell-O, and Cracker Jacks, to name a few. New appliances, such as "self-working" washers, offered mechanical assistance, but shredded shirts and aching arms testified to how far short mechanization still fell.

Toward the end of the century, Saturday became less of a workday and more of a family day. Sunday mornings remained a time for church, still an important center of family life. Afternoons had a more secular flavor. There were shopping trips (city stores often stayed open) and visits to lakes, zoos, and amusement parks (usually built at the end of trolley lines to attract more riders). Outside institutions—fraternal organizations, uplift groups, athletic teams, and church groups—were becoming part of middle-class urban family life.

Victorianism and the Pursuit of Virtue >>
Middle-class life reflected a rigid social code called Victorianism, named for Britain's long-reigning

<< Newly developed "electroplating," which deposited a thin layer of silver or gold over less expensive material, allowed manufacturers to sell to middle-class consumers wares previously reserved for the wealthy. Pictured here are a silver- and gold-plated card receiver and a calling card, once part of the courtly culture of elites and by the 1880s found in more and more middle-class homes. This "downward mobility" of manners and material culture allowed the middle class to ape the conventions of their social superiors, in this case by using calling cards to reinforce social networks and to serve as social barriers should personal contact be unwanted.

Then&Now

FACEBOOK VS. CARTE DE VISITES

Americans of the Victorian era did not have Facebook as a means of presenting a public self, but they had photographs taken that could be given out to friends. Small *cartes de visites* cost over a dollar a dozen, while "cabinets" (larger portraits about 4 by 6 inches) retailed at $2.50 a dozen. Schoolteacher Ida B. Wells, on a tight budget, was very careful about whom she gave—or in some cases, only loaned—her portrait. (For more on Wells, see pages 434–435).

Queen Victoria. It emerged in the 1830s and 1840s as part of an effort to tame the turbulent urban-industrial society developing in Europe.

Victorianism dictated that personal conduct be based on orderly behavior and disciplined moralism. It stressed sobriety, industriousness, self-control, and sexual modesty and taught that demeanor, particularly proper manners, was the backbone of society. According to its sexual precepts, women were "pure vessels," devoid of carnal desire. Their job was to control the "lower natures" of their husbands by withholding sex except for procreation.

Women's fashion mirrored Victorian values. Strenuously laced corsets ("an instrument of torture," according to one woman) pushed breasts up, stomachs in, and rear ends out. The resulting wasplike figure accentuated the breasts and hips, promoting the image of women as child bearers. Ankle-length skirts were draped over bustles, hoops, and petticoats to make hips look even larger and suggest fertility. Such elegant dress set off middle- and upper-class women from those below, whose plain clothes signaled lives of drudgery and want.

When working-class Americans failed to follow Victorian cues, reformers helped them to pursue virtue. In 1879 Frances Willard, fearing the ill effects of alcohol on the family, became the second president of the newly formed Woman's Christian Temperance Union (WCTU; 1874). Under her leadership the WCTU worked relentlessly to stamp out alcohol and promote sexual purity and other middle-class virtues. By the turn of the century it was the largest women's organization in the country, with 500,000 members.

Initially the WCTU focused on **temperance**—the movement, begun in the 1820s, to stamp out the sale of alcoholic beverages and to end drunkenness. For these women the campaign seemed a way not merely to reform society but to protect their homes and families from abuse at the hands of drunken husbands and fathers. And in attacking the saloon, Willard also sought to spread

> **temperance movement** reform movement, begun in the 1820s, to temper or restrain the sale and use of alcohol.

democracy by storming these all-male bastions, where political bosses conducted so much political business and where women were barred from entry. Soon, under the slogan of "Do Everything," the WCTU was also promoting "woman" suffrage, prison reform, better working conditions, and an end to prostitution. Just as important, it offered talented, committed women an opportunity to move out of their homes and churches and into the public arena of lobbying and politics.

Anthony Comstock crusaded with equal vigor against what he saw as moral pollution, ranging from pornography and gambling to the use of nude art models. In 1873 President Ulysses S. Grant signed the so-called Comstock Law, a statute banning from the mails all materials "designed to incite lust." Two days later Comstock went to work as a special agent for the Post Office. In his 41-year career he claimed to have made more than 3,000 arrests and destroyed 160 tons of vice-ridden books and photographs.

Victorian crusaders like Comstock were not simply missionaries of a stuffy morality. They were apostles of a middle-class creed of social control, responding to an increasing incidence of alcoholism, venereal disease, gambling debts, prostitution, and unwanted pregnancies. No doubt they overreacted in warning that the road to ruin lay behind the door of every saloon, gambling parlor, or bedroom. Yet the new urban environment did reflect the disorder of a rapidly industrializing society.

The insistence with which moralists warned against "impropriety" suggests that many people did not heed their advice. Three-quarters of the women surveyed toward the turn of the century reported that they enjoyed sex. The growing variety of contraceptives—including spermicidal douches, sheaths made of animal intestines, rubber condoms, and forerunners of the diaphragm—testified to the desire for pregnancy-free intercourse. Abortion, too, was available. According to one estimate, a third of all pregnancies were aborted, usually with the aid of a midwife. (By the 1880s abortion had been made illegal in most states following the first antiabortion statute in England in 1803.) Despite Victorian marriage manuals, middle-class

Americans became more conscious of sexuality as an emotional dimension of a satisfying union.

Challenges to Convention >>
A few bold men and women challenged conventions of gender and propriety. Victoria Woodhull, publisher of *Woodhull & Claflin's Weekly,* divorced her husband, ran for president in 1872 on the Equal Rights party ticket, and pressed the case for sexual freedom. "I am a free lover!" she shouted to a riotous audience in New York. "I have the inalienable, constitutional, and natural right to love whom I may, to love as long or as short a period as I can, to change that love every day if I please!" Woodhull made a strong public case for sexual freedom. In private, however, she adhered to strict monogamy and romantic love.

The same cosmopolitan conditions that provided protection for Woodhull's unorthodox beliefs also made possible the growth of self-conscious communities of homosexual men and women. Earlier in the century, Americans had idealized romantic friendships among members of the same sex, without necessarily attributing to them sexual overtones. But for friendships with an explicitly sexual dimension, the anonymity of large cities provided new meeting grounds. Single factory workers and clerks, living in furnished rooms rather than with their families in small towns and on farms, were freer to seek others who shared their sexual orientation. Homosexual men and women began forming social networks: on the streets where they regularly met, at specific restaurants and clubs, which, to avoid controversy, sometimes passed themselves off as athletic associations or chess clubs.

Only toward the end of the century did physicians begin to notice homosexual behavior, usually to condemn it as a disease or an inherited infirmity. Not until the turn of the century did the term homosexual even come into existence. Certainly homosexual love was not new. But for the first time in the United States, the conditions of urban life allowed gays and lesbians to define themselves in terms of a larger, self-conscious community, even if they were stoutly condemned by the prevailing Victorian morality.

The Decline of "Manliness" >>
The corrupting influence of city life on manhood troubled some onlookers as much as political or moral corruption distressed reformers. The components of traditional "manliness"—physical vigor, honor and integrity, courage and independence—seemed under assault by life in

> ### I have the inalienable, constitutional, and natural right to love whom I may, to love as long or as short a period as I can, to change that love every day if I please!

the industrial city. White middle- and upper-class men who found themselves working at desks and living in cushy comfort appeared particularly at risk. As early as the 1850s Oliver Wendell Holmes, Sr. (father of the famous Supreme Court Justice), lamented that "such a set of stiff-jointed, soft-muscled, paste-complexioned youth as we can boast in our Atlantic cities never before sprang from the loins of Anglo-Saxon lineage."

The dangers of this decline in "Anglo-Saxon" manliness courted catastrophe according to anxious observers. Soft, listless white men lacked vitality but also the manly discipline and character that came from living what Theodore Roosevelt called "The Strenuous Life" of action and struggle. Debased by the seamy pursuit of business, Roosevelt warned, such "weaklings" left the nation "[trembling] on the brink of doom," its future imperiled by laziness, timidity, and dishonesty. The "virile qualities" essential for achievement and leadership would vanish. Roosevelt, frail and asthmatic as a boy, turned himself into a strapping man through backbreaking workouts. He commanded desk-bound, "civilized" white men to follow his lead, even to reinvigorate their intellects with the "barbarian virtues" of physical strength he saw in darker-hued "primitives." Gender and race were thus being blended into a heady brew of white supremacy.

A frenzy of fitness spread across the nation. Bicycling, rowing, boxing, and what one historian called a college "cult of sports" promised to return middle- and upper-class men to "vigorous and unsullied manhood." Prussian bodybuilder Eugen Sandow ignited a weightlifting craze when he toured the country in the 1890s with feats of strength and poses he

<< Born in 1867, Friedrich Wilhelm Müller fled his native Prussia to evade military service and changed his name to Eugen Sandow. His manly feats of strength impressed audiences less than his rippling physique, seen here (with a strategically placed fig leaf) in this 1893 photograph. American impresarios such as Florenz Ziegfeld had Sandow add posing to his theatrical routine, which later earned him the title of the "Father of Modern Bodybuilding."

dubbed "muscle display performances." In a show of manly courage, a young Roosevelt lit out for the Dakota Badlands, writer Richard Harding Davis for Cuba in the middle of the Spanish-American War, and explorers Robert Peary and Matthew Henson for the North Pole in 1898. Exploration and adventure became exercises in undaunted manliness.

 **REVIEW**

How did class and ethnicity determine life for city dwellers?

CITY CULTURE

"We cannot all live in cities," the reformer Horace Greeley lamented just after the Civil War, "yet nearly all seemed determined to do so." Economic opportunity drew people to the teeming industrial city. But so, too, did a vibrant urban culture.

By the 1890s cities had begun to clean up downtown business districts, pave streets, widen thoroughfares, erect fountains and buildings of marble. This "city beautiful" movement aimed also to elevate public tastes and, like Victorian culture itself, refine the behavior of urbanites. Civic leaders pressed for public education and built museums, libraries, and parks to uplift unruly city masses. Public parks followed the model of New York's Central Park. When it opened in 1858 Central Park was meant to serve as a pastoral retreat from the turbulent industrial city. Its rustic paths, leafy glades, and tranquil lakes, said designer Frederick Law Olmsted, would have "a distinctly harmonizing and refining influence" on even the rudest fellow.

Public Education in an Urban Industrial World >> Those at the bottom and in the middle of city life found in public education one key to success. Although the campaign for public education began in the Jacksonian era, it did not make much headway until after the Civil War, when industrial cities began to mushroom. As late as 1870 half the children in the country received no formal education at all, and one American in five could not read.

Between 1870 and 1900 an educational awakening occurred. As more and more businesses required workers who could read, write, and tally numbers, attendance in public schools more than doubled. The length of the school term rose from 132 to 144 days. Illiteracy fell by half. By the turn of the century, nearly all the states outside the South had enacted mandatory education laws. Almost three of every four school-age children were enrolled. Even so, the average American adult still attended school for only about five years, and less than 10 percent of those eligible continued beyond the eighth grade.

⌃ Educational reformers in the 1870s pushed elementary drawing as a required subject. Their goal was not to turn out gifted artists but to train students in the practical skills needed in an industrial society. Winslow Homer's portrait of a teacher by her blackboard shows the geometric shapes behind practical design.

The average school day started early, but by noon most girls were released under the assumption that they needed less formal education. Curricula stressed the fundamentals of reading, writing, and arithmetic. Courses in manual training, science, and physical education were added as the demand for technical knowledge grew and opportunities to exercise shrank. Students learned by memorization, sitting in silent study with hands clasped or standing erect while they repeated phrases and sums. Few schools encouraged creative thinking. In an age of industrialization, massive immigration, and rapid change, schools taught conformity and values as much as facts and figures. Teachers acted as drillmasters, shaping their charges for the sake of society. "Teachers and books are better security than handcuffs and policemen," wrote a New Jersey college professor in 1879.

As Reconstruction faded, so did the impressive start made in black education. Most of the first generation of former slaves had been illiterate. So eager were they to learn that by the end of the century nearly half of all African

Americans could read. But discrimination soon took its toll. For nearly 100 years after the Civil War, the doctrine of "separate but equal," upheld by the Supreme Court in *Plessy* v. *Ferguson* (1896), kept black and white students apart but scarcely equal. By 1882 public schools in a half dozen southern states were segregated by law, the rest by practice. Underfunded and ill-equipped, black schools served dirt-poor families whose every member had to work.

Like African Americans, immigrants saw education as a way of getting ahead. Some educators saw it as a means of Americanizing newcomers. They assumed that immigrant and native-born children would learn the same lessons in the same language and turn out the same way. Only toward the end of the 1800s, as immigration mounted, did eastern cities begin to offer night classes that taught English, along with civics lessons, for foreigners. When public education proved inadequate, immigrants established their own schools. Catholics, for example, started an elaborate expansion of their parochial schools in 1884.

By the 1880s educational reforms were helping schools respond to the needs of an urban society. Opened first in St. Louis in 1873, American versions of innovative German "kindergartens" put four- to six-year-olds in orderly classrooms while parents went off to work. "**Normal schools**" multiplied to provide teachers with more professional training. And in the new industrial age, science and manual training supplemented more conventional subjects in order to supply industry with educated workers.

> **normal schools** schools that trained teachers, usually for two years and mostly for teaching in the elementary grades.

Higher Learning and the Rise of the Professional >>

Colleges served the urban industrial society, too, not by controlling mass habits but by providing leaders and managers. Early in the nineteenth century, most Americans had regarded higher learning as unmanly and irrelevant. The few who sought it often preferred the superior universities of Europe to those in the United States.

As American society grew more organized, mechanized, and complex, the need for professional, technical, and literary skills brought greater respect for college education. The Morrill Act of 1862 generated a dozen new state colleges and universities, eight mechanical and agricultural colleges, and six black colleges. Private charity added more. Railroad barons such as Johns Hopkins and Leland Stanford used parts of their fortunes to found colleges named after them (Hopkins in 1873, Stanford in 1890). The number of colleges and universities nearly doubled between 1870 and 1910, though less than 5 percent of college-age Americans enrolled in them.

A practical impulse inspired the founding of several black colleges. In the late nineteenth century, few institutions mixed races. Church groups and private foundations, such as the Peabody and Slater funds (supported by white donors from the North), underwrote black colleges after Reconstruction. By 1900, a total of 700 black students were enrolled. About 2,000 had graduated. Through hard work and persistence, some even received degrees from institutions reserved for whites.

In keeping with the new emphasis on practical learning, professional schools multiplied to provide training beyond a college degree. American universities adopted the German model, requiring young scholars to perform research as part of their education. The number of law and medical schools more than doubled between 1870 and 1900; medical students almost tripled. Ten percent of them were women, though their numbers shrank as physicians became more organized and exclusive.

Professionals of all kinds—in law, medicine, engineering, business, academics—swelled the ranks of the middle class. Slowly they were becoming a new force in urban America, replacing the ministers and gentlemen freeholders of an earlier day as community leaders.

Higher Education for Women >>

Before the Civil War women could attend only three private colleges. After the war they had new ones all their own, including Smith (1871), Wellesley (1875), and Bryn Mawr (1885). Such all-women schools, with their mostly female faculties and administrators, deepened an emerging sense of membership in a special community of women. Many land-grant colleges, chartered to serve all people, also admitted women. By 1910 some 40 percent of college students were women, almost double the 1870 figure. Only one college in five refused to accept them.

Potent myths of gender continued to plague women in college. As Dr. Edward Clarke of the Harvard Medical School told thousands of students in *Sex in Education* (1873), the rigors of a

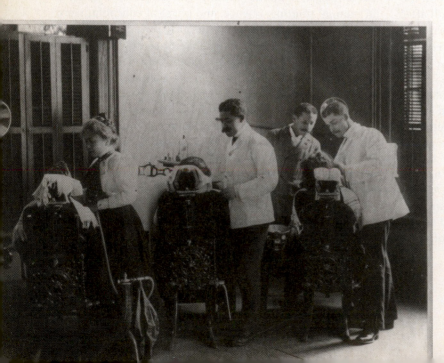

<< DENTISTRY STUDENTS AT HOWARD UNIVERSITY, 1900

ʌ American impressionist Mary Cassatt painted this mural of women picking apples (in entirely unsuitable clothing) for the Women's Building at the Chicago World's Columbian Exposition in 1893. Entitled *Young Women Plucking the Fruits of Knowledge or Science*, it stood the story of Eve and her famous apple on its head. According to the Bible, the fruit was the source of forbidden knowledge: when it was eaten by Eve, who shared it with Adam, the result was humankind's original sin. But Cassatt's mural suggested that the place of women in society was changing. No longer bound by cultural conventions against the dangers of educated women, a new generation of well-schooled females was to be celebrated for its achievements in science, the arts and the professions.

college education could lead the "weaker sex" to physical or mental collapse, infertility, and early death. Women's colleges therefore included a program of physical activity to keep students healthy. Many offered an array of courses in "domestic science"—cooking, sewing, and other such skills—to counter the claim that higher education would be of no value to women.

College students, together with office workers and female athletes, became role models for ambitious young women. These "new women," impatient with custom, cast off Victorian restrictions. Fewer of them married, and more—perhaps 25 percent—were self-supporting. They shed their corsets and bustles and donned lighter, more comfortable clothing, such as "shirtwaist" blouses (styled after men's shirts) and lower-heeled shoes. And they showed that women could move beyond the domestic sphere of home and family.

A Culture of Consumption >> The city
spawned a new material culture built on consumption. As standards of living rose, American industries began providing "ready-made" clothing to replace garments that had once been made at home. Similarly, food and furniture were mass-produced in greater quantities. The city became a giant market for these goods, the place where new patterns of mass consumption took hold. Radiating outward to more rural areas, this urban consumer culture helped to level American society. Increasingly, city businesses sold the same goods to farmer and clerk, rich and poor, native-born and immigrant.

Well-made, inexpensive merchandise in standard sizes and shapes found outlets in new palaces of consumption known as "department stores," so called because they displayed their goods in separate sections or departments. Unlike the small exclusive shops of Europe, department stores were palatial, public, and filled with inviting displays of furniture, housewares, and clothing.

The French writer Emile Zola claimed that department stores "democratized luxury." Anyone could enter free of charge, handle the most elegant and expensive goods, and buy what-ever was affordable. When consumers found goods too pricey, department stores pioneered layaway plans with deferred payments. The department store also educated people by showing them what "proper" families owned and the correct names for such things as women's wear and parlor furniture.

"Chain stores" (a term coined in America) spread the culture of consumption without frills. They catered to the working class, who could not afford department stores, and operated on a cash-and-carry basis. Owners kept their costs down by buying in volume to fill the small stores in growing neighborhood chains. Founded in 1859 the Great Atlantic and Pacific Tea Company (later to become A&P supermarkets) was the first of the chain stores. By 1876 its 76 branch stores had added groceries to the original line of teas.

Far from department and chain stores, rural Americans joined the community of consumers by mail. In 1872 Aaron Montgomery Ward sent his first price sheet to farmers from a livery stable loft in Chicago. Ward avoided the intermediaries and promised savings of 40 percent on fans, needles, trunks, harnesses, and scores of other goods available to city dwellers. By 1884 his catalog boasted 10,000 items, each illustrated by a lavish woodcut. Similarly, Richard W. Sears and Alvah C. Roebuck built a $500 million mail-order business by 1907. Schoolrooms that had no encyclopedia used a Montgomery Ward or Sears catalog instead. When asked the source of the Ten Commandments, one farm boy replied that they came from Sears, Roebuck. Countrywide mass consumption was producing a mass material culture.

Leisure >> As mechanization gradually reduced the
number of hours on the job, factory workers found themselves with more free time. So did the middle class, with

free weekends, evenings, and vacations. A new, stricter division between work and play developed in the more disciplined society of industrial America. City dwellers turned this new leisure time into a consumer item that often reflected differences in class, gender, and ethnicity.

Sports, for example, had been a traditional form of recreation for the rich. They continued to play polo, golf, and the newly imported English game of tennis. Croquet had more middle-class appeal. It required less skill and special equipment. Perhaps as important, it could be enjoyed in mixed company, like the new craze of bicycling. Bicycles evolved from unstable contraptions with large front wheels into "safety" bikes with equal-sized wheels, a dropped middle bar, pneumatic tires, and coaster brakes. On Sunday afternoons city parks became crowded with cyclists, at least those wealthy enough to pay the $100 price tag on such bicycles. Women rode the new safety bikes, too, although social convention prohibited them from riding alone. But cycling broke down conventions too. It required looser garments, freeing women from corsets. And lady cyclists demonstrated that they were hardly too fragile for physical exertion.

Organized spectator sports attracted crowds from every walk of life. Baseball overshadowed all others. For city dwellers with dull work, cramped quarters, and isolated lives, baseball offered the chance to join thousands of others for an exciting outdoor spectacle. The first professional teams appeared in 1869, and slowly the game evolved. Umpires began to call balls and strikes, the overhand replaced the underhand pitch, and fielders put on gloves. Teams from eight cities formed the National League of Professional Baseball Clubs in 1876, followed by the American League in 1901. League players were distinctly working class. At first, teams featured some black players. When African Americans were barred in the 1880s, black professionals formed their own team, the Cuban Giants of Long Island, New York, looking to play anyone they could and taking the name "Cuban" (rather than "Negro") in hopes of being able to play white teams, too.

Horse racing, bicycle tournaments, and other sports of speed and violence helped to break the monotony, frustration, and routine of the industrial city. Perhaps the most violent sport of all, bare-knuckled prizefighting, was illegal in some states, but in others, it gave young men from the streets the chance to stand out from the crowd, win some cash, and prove

their masculinity. In 1869, without pads or helmets, Rutgers beat Princeton in the first intercollegiate football match. College football soon attracted crowds of 50,000 or more.

Arts and Entertainment >>

Other forms of city entertainment also divided along lines of class. For the wealthy and middle class there were symphonies, operas, and theater. High-brow productions of Shakespearean plays catered to the aspirations of American upper classes for culture and European refinement. Popular melodramas gave middle-class audiences the chance to ignore the ambiguities of modern life, booing villains and cheering heroes. By 1900 people were bringing their entertainment home, snapping up some three million new phonograph recordings a year.

Workingmen found a haven from the drudgery of factory, mill, and mine in the saloon. It was an all-male preserve—a workingman's club—where one could drink and talk free from Victorian finger-wagging. Young working women found escape alone or with dates at vaudeville shows, dance halls, and the new amusement parks with their mechanical "thrill rides." In the all-black gaming houses and honky-tonks of St. Louis and New Orleans, the syncopated rhythms of African American composer Scott Joplin's "Maple Leaf Rag" (1899) and other ragtime tunes heralded the coming of jazz.

As much as any form of entertainment, the traveling circus embodied the changes of the new urban, industrial world. Moving outward from their city bases, circuses

>> Artist Edward Shinn's *Sixth Avenue Shoppers* shows a nighttime scene in the city's shopping district. In an era of more flexible gender roles, Shinn nonetheless captures a traditional division of gender with the women (*at left*) crowded around shopping stalls and men (*at right*) hunched over a cockfight.

The Barnum & Bailey Greatest Show on Earth

STRANGE AND SAVAGE TRIBES.

A GLIMPSE OF THE GREAT MENAGERIE TENT, SHOWING THE LOOSE LED ANIMALS AND GRAND ETHNOLOGICAL CONGRESS.

THE WORLD'S GRANDEST, LARGEST, BEST, AMUSEMENT INSTITUTION.

ᐱ This lithograph is from an 1894 poster for the Barnum & Bailey Circus. It depicts a menagerie tent in which exotic animals are displayed side by side with "Strange and Savage Tribes," thus collapsing the boundaries between animals and human beings. Much smaller than the Big Top, menagerie tents allowed Euro-American patrons to examine animals and humans up close. The Barnum show presented its first "ethnological congress" of "native" peoples in 1886, as the United States began its drive for empire abroad. The human specimens were meant to give Americans a glimpse of foreign cultures and to be instructive. "Even the best informed and most intellectual had something to learn," boasted a circus route book.

rode the new rail system across the country (after the first transcontinental tour in 1869) and, with the advent of steamships, crisscrossed the globe. The mammoth New York–based Barnum and Bailey Circus carried dozens of gilded show wagons, scores of animals, tons of equipment, and hundreds of performers, work hands, and animal tenders to the faraway capitals of Europe and Asia. At home the shows drew patrons from every class, ethnicity, and race, sometimes numbering in the tens of thousands. Circus workers erected huge "bigtop" tents with the factory-like precision of modern industry. And, like the city itself, circuses both supported and subverted social conventions. When owners reassured customers that their scantily clad dancers came from respectable families or their muscular lady acrobats prized the Victorian values of motherhood and domesticity, they winked slyly because they knew that the very appearance of these

women, let alone their talents, defied the Victorian ideal of dainty and demure femininity.

 **REVIEW**

How did city culture shape national culture?

Industrialization ignited the growth of cities not just in the United States but all over the world. Great Britain, the birthplace of the Industrial Revolution, became the world's first country with over half its people in towns and cities by 1851. Fifty years later London's population had more than doubled, from 2.7 million to 6.6 million. By 1914, on the eve of the First World War, eight of every ten Britons lived in cities, as did six of ten Germans and nearly five of ten French.

Just as European immigrants poured into cities across the United States, newcomers from Europe, Asia, and the Middle East flowed into South America, Australia, and the Caribbean. Before 1900 two of every three emigrating Italians booked passage not for the United States but for Brazil or Argentina. Chinese immigrants harvested sugar cane in Cuba, built railroads and opened restaurants in Peru, and launched businesses in Trinidad. By 1920 Sao Paulo, the largest city in Brazil, was exploding with Asian immigrants, and Brazil boasted the world's largest Japanese population outside Japan.

The hubbub, the overcrowding, and the corruption of cities like Boss Plunkitt's Manhattan were reflected elsewhere in the world. Before the arrival of mass transit British urban workers were forced to live within walking distance of factories, in dingy row houses beset by the overflow from privies and garbage in the streets. A deadly cholera epidemic in 1848 spurred a campaign to install iron pipes and drains to provide running water and sewers throughout major cities. About the same time Paris underwent a radical renovation in which workers tore down the city's medieval fortress walls, widened major streets into boulevards, and set aside land for green parks. Borrowing innovations from the United States, Europeans adopted horse-drawn streetcars and, later, electric trolleys. With an intracity transportation network in place, the old "walking cities" of Europe, like those in the United States, added suburbs, partially easing the crush of earlier crowding.

The world over, industrial cities transformed both the urban landscape and the daily lives of city dwellers. Critics damned the city's crime and corruption; defenders celebrated its vibrancy and diversity. No matter how they felt, Americans had to search for ways to make that new industrial order work.

CHAPTER SUMMARY

The modern city was the product of industrialization, lying at the center of the new integrated systems of transportation, communications, manufacturing, marketing, and finance.

- Fed by a great global migration of laborers, cities began to grow and to assume their modern shape of ringed residential patterns around central business districts and strict divisions among different classes, races, and ethnic groups.
- The challenge for the political system was to find within its democratic traditions a way to bring order out of the seeming chaos of unchecked urban growth.
- The urban boss and the urban political machine met the needs of cities for centralized authority but at a terrible cost in corruption, while social settlement houses, the Salvation Army, and the Social Gospel churches represented only a start at coping with the problems of poverty and urban blight.

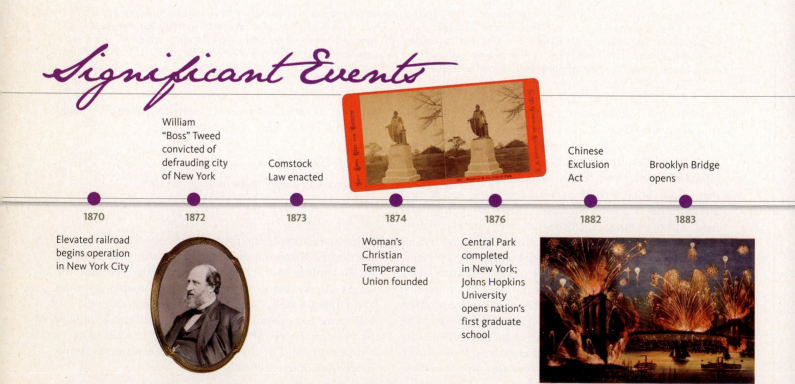

Significant Events

Elevated railroad begins operation in New York City

1870

William "Boss" Tweed convicted of defrauding city of New York

1872

Comstock Law enacted

1873

Woman's Christian Temperance Union founded

1874

Central Park completed in New York; Johns Hopkins University opens nation's first graduate school

1876

Chinese Exclusion Act

1882

Brooklyn Bridge opens

1883

- As cities grew, the middle-class code of behavior—called Victorianism by historians—spread, teaching the values of sobriety, hard work, self-control, and modesty. Such traits served the needs of new industrial society for efficiency and order and the middle-class need for protection against the turbulence of city life.
- Yet for all the emphasis on skills, discipline, and order, the vibrancy of city culture remained attractive. It drew millions in search of education, entertainment, and opportunity, and it radiated outward to almost every corner of the country.

Additional Reading

The best treatment of the rise of cities is Howard B. Chudacoff, *The Evolution of American Urban Society* (rev. ed., 1981). John Stilgoe, *Borderland: The Origins of the American Suburb, 1820–1929* (1988), chronicles the growth of suburban America. William Cronon, *Nature's Metropolis: Chicago and the Great West* (1991), looks at Chicago as part of the ecological landscape. In *Boss Cox's Cincinnati: Urban Politics in the Progressive Era* (1968), Zane Miller reassesses the urban political machine, and Paul Boyer explores efforts at controlling city life in *Urban Masses and Moral Order in America, 1820–1920* (1978). John F. Kasson, *Rudeness & Civility: Manners in Nineteenth-Century Urban America* (1990), and Lawrence Levine, *Highbrow/Lowbrow: The Emergence of Cultural Hierarchy in America* (1988),

investigate the emerging urban culture. For a penetrating examination of traveling circuses as conduits for cultural exchanges, see Janet M. Davis's *The Circus Age: Culture and Society under the American Big Top* (2002).

Marcus Lee Hanson's classic *The Atlantic Migration, 1607–1860* (1940) began the shift in immigration history away from the national and toward a more global perspective. For richly detailed comparative examinations of the immigrant experience, see Roger Daniels, *Coming to America: A History of Immigration and Ethnicity in American Life* (1990), and Ronald Takaki, *A Different Mirror: A History of Multicultural America* (1993). Susan A. Glenn, *Daughters of the Shtetl: Life and Labor in the Immigrant Generation* (1990), throws light on the issue of gender by probing the lives and labor of immigrant women, with particular attention to the shaping effect of Old World Jewish culture. Virginia Yans-McLaughlin, ed., *Immigration Reconsidered: History, Sociology, and Politics* (1990), offers a collection of penetrating essays that places American immigration in its international context. In *New Spirits: Americans in the Gilded Age, 1865–1905* (2006), Rebecca Edwards revises the traditional portrait of the "Gilded Age" by emphasizing the anxieties and optimism of ordinary people, many of them city dwellers, in what she regards as the birth of modern America. Helen Lefkowitz Horowitz's *Rereading Sex: Battles over Sexual Knowledge and Suppression in Nineteenth-Century America* (2002) explores the contradictions of Victorian thinking about all manner of sexual matters, including contraception, abortion, pornography, and free speech.

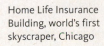

1885

Home Life Insurance Building, world's first skyscraper, Chicago

Nation's first electric trolley line, Richmond, Virginia

1888

Hull House opens in Chicago

1889

1892

Ellis Island opens as receiving station for immigrants

1894

Immigration Restriction League organized

1897

Nation's first subway station, Boston

The Political System

The "Midway Plaisance" was the entertainment district of the Chicago exposition, boasting the world's first ferris wheel (seen in the distance, invented by George Ferris). The exotic buildings, with their domes, minarets, and foreign flags, show how conscious Americans were becoming of the wider world. A woman takes a camel ride (*right*) while many foreigners wander through the plaza.

Under Strain at Home and Abroad

1877–1900

21

>> **AN AMERICAN STORY**

"THE WORLD UNITED AT CHICAGO"

On May 1, 1893, an eager crowd of nearly half a million people jostled into a dramatic plaza fronted on either side by gleaming white buildings. Named the Court of Honor, the plaza was the center of a strange, ornamental city that was at once both awesome and entirely imaginary. >>

At one end stood a building called the Court of Honor, whose magnificent white dome exceeded the height of even the Capitol in Washington. Unlike the marble-built Capitol, however, the Court was all surface: a stucco shell plastered onto a steel frame and then sprayed with white oil paint to make it glisten. Beyond it stretched thoroughfares encompassing over 200 colonnaded buildings, piers, islands, and watercourses. Located five miles south of Chicago's center, this city of the imagination proclaimed itself the "World's Columbian Exposition" to honor the 400th anniversary of Columbus's voyage to America.

President Grover Cleveland opened the world's fair in a way that symbolized the nation's industrial transformation. He pressed a telegrapher's key. Instantly, electric current set 7,000 feet of shafting into motion—motion that in turn unfurled flags, set fountains pumping, and lit 10,000 electric bulbs. The lights played over an array of exhibition buildings soon known as the "White City."

One visitor dismissed the displays within as "the contents of a great dry goods store mixed up with the contents of museums." In a sense he was right. Visitors paraded by an unending stream of typewriters, watches, agricultural machinery, cedar canoes, and refrigerators, to say nothing of a map of the United States fashioned entirely out of pickles. But this riot of mechanical marvels, gewgaws, and bric-a-brac was symbolic, too, of the nation's industrial transformation. The fair resembled nothing so much as a living, breathing version of the new mail-order catalogs whose pages were now introducing the goods of the city to the hinterlands.

The connections made by the fair were international as well. This was the World's Columbian Exposition, with exhibits from 36 nations. Germany's famous manufacturer of armaments, Krupp, had its own separate building. It housed a 120-ton rifled gun 46 feet long and capable of launching a one-ton shell 20 miles. At the fair's amusement park, visitors encountered exotic cultures—and not just temples, huts, and totems, but exhibits in the flesh. The Arabian village featured Saharan camels, veiled ladies, and elders in turbans. Nearby, Irish peasants boiled potatoes over turf fires and Samoan men threw axes.

Like all such fairs the Columbian Exposition created a fantasy. Beyond its boundaries the real world was showing signs of strain. Early in 1893 the Philadelphia and Reading Railroad had gone bankrupt, setting off a financial panic. By the end of the year nearly 500 banks and 15,000 businesses had failed. Although tourists continued to marvel at the fair's wonders, crowds of worried and unemployed workers also gathered in Chicago. On Labor Day Governor John Altgeld of Illinois told one such assemblage that the government was powerless to soften the "suffering and distress" of this latest economic downturn.

In truth the political system was ill equipped to cope with the economic and social revolutions reshaping America. The executive branch remained weak, while Congress and the courts found themselves easily swayed by the financial interests of the industrial class. The crises of the 1890s forced the political order to begin to address such inequities.

The political system also had to take into account developments abroad. Industrialization sent American businesses around the world searching for raw materials and new markets. As that search intensified many influential Americans argued that like European nations, the United States needed to acquire territory overseas. By the end of the century the nation's political system had taken its first steps toward modernization at home and abroad. They included a major political realignment and a growing overseas empire. Both changes and the tensions that accompanied them launched the United States into the twentieth century and an era of prosperity and power. «

THE POLITICS OF PARALYSIS

During the 1880s and 1890s, as the American political system came under strain, Moisei Ostrogorski was traveling across the United States. Like other foreign visitors the Russian political scientist had come to see the new democratic experiment in action. His verdict was as blunt as it was common: "the constituted authorities are unequal to their duty." It seemed that the experiment had fallen victim to greed, indifference, and political mediocrity.

In fact there were deeper problems: a great gulf between rich and poor; a wrenching cycle of boom and bust; the unmet needs of African Americans, women, Indians, and other "others." These problems had scarcely been addressed let alone resolved. Politics was the traditional medium of resolution, but it was grinding into a dangerous stalemate.

Political Stalemate >> From 1877 to 1897 American politics rested on a delicate balance of power that left neither Republicans nor Democrats in control. Republicans inhabited the White House for 12 years; Democrats, for 8. Margins of victory in presidential elections were paper thin. No president could count on having a majority of his party in both houses of Congress for his entire term. Usually Republicans controlled the Senate, Democrats the House of Representatives.

With elections so tight both parties worked hard to bring out the vote. Brass bands, parades, cheering crowds of flag-wavers were "the order of the day and night from end to end of the country," reported a British visitor. When Election Day arrived stores closed and businesses shut down. At political clubs and corner saloons men lined up to get voting orders (along with free drinks) from ward bosses. In the countryside fields went untended as farmers took their families to town, cast their ballots, and bet on the outcome.

An average of nearly 80 percent of eligible voters turned out for presidential elections between 1860 and 1900, a figure higher than at any time since. In that era, however, the electorate made up a smaller percentage of the population. About one American in five actually voted in presidential elections from 1876 to 1892. Virtually all were white males. Women could vote in national elections only in a few western states, and beginning in the 1880s, the South erected barriers that eventually disfranchised many African American voters.

Party loyalty rarely wavered. In every election 16 states could be counted on to vote Republican and 14 Democratic. In only six states—the most important being New York and Ohio—were results ever in doubt.

The Parties >> What inspired such loyalty? Republicans and Democrats did have similarities but also had differences. Both parties supported business and condemned radicalism; neither offered embattled workers and farmers much help. But Democrats believed in states' rights and limited government, while Republicans favored federal activism to foster economic growth. The stronghold of Democrats was the South, where they continually reminded voters that they had led the states of the Old Confederacy, "redeemed" them from Republican Reconstruction, and championed white supremacy. Republicans dominated the North with strong support from industry and business. They, too, invoked memories of the Civil War to secure voters, black

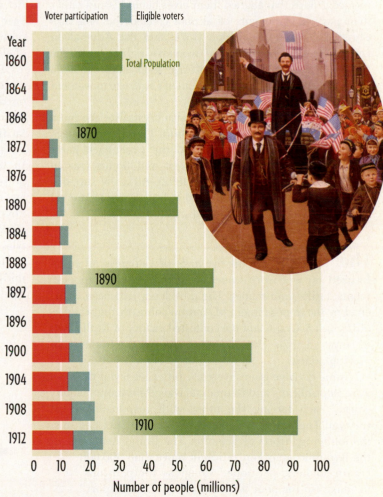

THE VOTING PUBLIC

Between 1860 and 1910 the population and the number of eligible voters increased nearly threefold. As reforms of the early twentieth century reduced the power of political machines and parties, the percentage of voter participation actually declined.

as well as white. "Not every Democrat was a rebel," they chanted, "but every rebel was a Democrat."

Ethnicity and religion also cemented voter loyalty. Republicans drew on old-stock Protestants, who feared new immigrants and put their faith in promoting pious behavior. In the Republican party they found support for immigration restriction, prohibition, and English-only schools. The Democratic party attracted urban political machines, their immigrant voters, and the working poor. Often Catholic, they saw salvation in following religious rituals, not in dictating the conduct of all society. Year after year these cultural loyalties of region, religion, and ethnicity shaped political allegiances.

Outside the two-party system impassioned reformers often fashioned political instruments of their own. Some formed groups that aligned themselves behind issues rather than parties. Opponents of alcohol created the Woman's Christian Temperance Union (1874) and the Anti-Saloon League (1893). Champions of women's rights joined the National American Woman Suffrage Association (1890), a reunion of two branches of the women's suffrage movement that had split in 1869.

Third political parties might also crystallize around a single concern or a particular group. Those who sought inflation of the currency formed the Greenback party (1874). Angry farmers in the West and South created the Populist, or People's, party (1892). All drew supporters from both conventional parties, but as single-interest groups they mobilized minorities, not majorities.

The Issues >>

In the halls of Congress attention focused on well-worn issues: veterans' benefits, appointments, tariffs, and money. The presidency had been weakened by the impeachment of Andrew Johnson, the scandals of Ulysses S. Grant, and the contested victory of Rutherford B. Hayes in 1876. Thus Congress enjoyed the initiative in making policy.

Some divisive issues were the bitter legacy of the Civil War. Republicans and Democrats waved symbolic "bloody shirts," each tarring the other with responsibility for the war. The politics of the Civil War also surfaced in the lobbying efforts of veterans. The Grand Army of the Republic, an organization of more than 400,000 Union soldiers, petitioned Congress for pensions to make up for poor wartime pay and to support the widows and orphans of fallen comrades. By the turn of the century Union army veterans and their families were receiving $157 million annually. It was one of the largest public assistance programs in American history and laid the foundation for the modern welfare state.

By the turn of the century Union army veterans and their families were receiving $157 million annually.

More important than public welfare was the campaign for a new method of staffing federal offices. From barely 53,000 employees at the end of the Civil War, the federal government had mushroomed to 166,000 by the early 1890s, with far more jobs requiring special skills. But dismantling the reigning "spoils system" proved difficult for politicians who rewarded faithful supporters with government jobs regardless of their qualifications. American politics rested on this patronage. Without it, politicians—from presidents to lowly ward captains—feared that they could attract neither workers nor money.

It took the assassination of President James Garfield by a frustrated office seeker in 1881 to move Congress to action. Enacted in 1883 the Civil Service Act, or Pendleton Act, created a bipartisan civil service commission to administer competitive examinations for some federal jobs. Later presidents expanded the jobs covered. By 1896 almost half of all federal workers came under civil service jurisdiction.

The protective tariff also aroused Congress. As promoters of economic growth, Republicans usually championed this tax on manufactured imports. Democrats, with their strength in the agrarian South, generally sought tariff reduction to encourage foreign trade, reduce prices on manufactured goods, and cut the federal surplus. In 1890, when Republicans controlled the House, Congress passed the McKinley Tariff. It raised schedules to an all-time high. The McKinley Tariff also contained a novel twist called "reciprocity" designed to promote freer trade. The president could lower rates if certain countries did the same.

Just as divisive was the issue of currency. Until the mid-1800s money was coined from both gold and silver. The need for more money during the Civil War had led

Opinion

Does government work more effectively when one party controls both the presidency and the congress?

Congress to issue "greenbacks"—currency printed on paper with a green back. For the next decade and a half, Americans argued over whether to print more paper money (not backed by gold or silver) or take it out of circulation. Farmers and other debtors favored greenbacks as a way of inflating prices, which would have the effect of reducing the real cost of their debts. For the opposite reasons, bankers and creditors stood for "sound money" backed by gold. Fear of inflation led Congress first to cut the number of greenbacks and then in 1879 to make all remaining paper money convertible into gold.

A more heated battle was developing over silver-backed money. By the early 1870s so little silver was being used that Congress stopped coining it. A silver mining boom in Nevada soon revived demands for more silver money. In 1878 the Bland-Allison Act inaugurated a limited form of silver coinage. But pressure for unlimited coinage of silver—coining all silver presented at U.S. mints—mounted as silver production quadrupled between 1870 and 1890. In 1890 pressure for silver peaked in the Sherman Silver Purchase Act. It obligated the government to buy 4.5 million ounces of silver every month. Paper tender called "treasury notes," redeemable in either gold or silver, would pay for it. The compromise satisfied both sides only temporarily.

The White House from Hayes to Harrison

>> From the 1870s through the 1890s a string of nearly anonymous presidents presided over the country. Not all were mere caretakers. Some tried to revive the office, but Congress continued to rein in the executive.

Republican Rutherford B. Hayes was the first of the "Ohio dynasty," which included three presidents from 1876 to 1900. Once elected Hayes moved quickly to end Reconstruction and tried unsuccessfully to woo southern Democrats with promises of economic support. His pursuit of civil service reform ended only in splitting his party between "Stalwarts" (who favored the spoils systems) and "Half-Breeds" (who opposed it). Hayes left office after a single term, relieved to be "out of a scrape."

In 1880 Republican James Garfield, another Ohioan, succeeded Hayes by a handful of votes. He spent his first hundred days in the White House besieged by office hunters and failing to placate the rival sections of his party. After Garfield's assassination only six months into his term, Chester A. Arthur, the "spoilsman's spoilsman," became president.

To everyone's surprise the dapper Arthur turned out to be an honest president who broke with machine politicians. He worked to lower the tariff, warmly endorsed the new Civil Service, or Pendleton, Act, and reduced the federal surplus by beginning construction of a modern navy. Such even-handed administration left him little chance for renomination by divided party leaders.

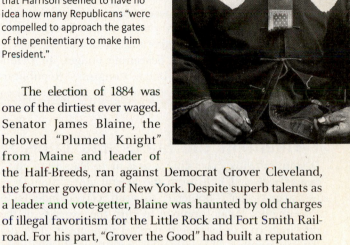

>> A Chinese laborer, holding his queue of long hair, proudly displays patches in support of the 1888 Democratic presidential candidate, Grover Cleveland, and his running mate, Allen B. Thurman. Cleveland and Thurman lost to Benjamin Harrison and Levi P. Morton, a wealthy New York banker. After his victory, Harrison, a pious Presbyterian, grabbed the hand of Senator Matthew Quay and crowed, "Providence has given us the victory." "Providence hadn't a damn thing to do with it," Quay said later, irked that Harrison seemed to have no idea how many Republicans "were compelled to approach the gates of the penitentiary to make him President."

The election of 1884 was one of the dirtiest ever waged. Senator James Blaine, the beloved "Plumed Knight" from Maine and leader of the Half-Breeds, ran against Democrat Grover Cleveland, the former governor of New York. Despite superb talents as a leader and vote-getter, Blaine was haunted by old charges of illegal favoritism for the Little Rock and Fort Smith Railroad. For his part, "Grover the Good" had built a reputation for honesty by fighting corruption and the spoils system in New York. So hard a worker was the portly Cleveland, sighed a reporter, that he "remains within doors constantly, eats and works, eats and works, and works and eats." The bachelor Cleveland spent enough time away from his desk to father an illegitimate child. The campaign rang with Republican taunts of "Ma, ma, where's my pa?"

In the last week of the tight race, the Irish vote in New York swung to the Democrats when a local Protestant minister labeled them the party of "Rum, Romanism, and Rebellion" (alcohol, Catholicism, and the Civil War). New York went to Cleveland, and with it, the election. Democrats crowed with delight over where to find the bachelor "pa": "Gone to the White House, ha, ha, ha!"

Cleveland was the first Democrat elected to the White House since James Buchanan in 1856, and he was more active than many of his predecessors. He pleased reformers by expanding the civil service. His devotion to gold, economy, and efficiency earned him praise from business. He supported the growth of federal power by endorsing the Interstate Commerce Act (1887), new agricultural research, and federal arbitration of labor disputes. Still, his activism remained limited. He vetoed two of every three bills brought to him, more than twice the number vetoed by all his predecessors. Toward the end of his term, embarrassed by the large federal surplus, Cleveland finally reasserted himself by attacking the tariff, but the Republican-controlled Senate blocked his attempt to lower it.

In 1888 Republicans nominated a sturdy defender of tariffs, Benjamin Harrison, the grandson of President William Henry Harrison. Cleveland won a **plurality** of the popular vote but lost in the Electoral College. The "human iceberg" (as Harrison's colleagues called him) worked hard, rarely delegated management, and turned the White House into a well-run office. He helped to shape the Sherman Silver Purchase Act (1890), kept abreast of the McKinley Tariff (1890), and accepted the Sherman Antitrust Act (1890) to limit the size of big businesses.

plurality in elections, a candidate who receives a plurality wins more votes than any other candidate but less than half of all votes cast. Receiving more than half of the votes cast is called a *majority*.

By the end of Harrison's term in 1892 Congress had completed its most productive session of the era, including the first billion-dollar peacetime budget. To Democratic jeers of a "Billion Dollar Congress," Republican House Speaker Thomas Reed shot back, "This is a billion-dollar country!"

Ferment in the States and Cities >>

Despite growing expenditures and more legislation, most people expected little from the federal government. Few newspapers even bothered to send correspondents to Washington. Public pressure to curb the excesses of the new industrial order mounted closer to home, in state and city governments. Experimental and often effective, state programs at least began to grapple with the problems of corporate power, discriminatory railroad rates, political corruption, and urban disorder.

Starting in 1869 with Massachusetts, states established commissions to investigate and regulate industry, especially railroads, America's first big business. By the turn of the century almost two-thirds of the states had them. The first commissions gathered and publicized information on shipping rates and business practices and furnished advice about public policy but had little power.

In the Midwest, on the Great Plains, and in the Far West, merchants and farmers pressed state governments to reduce railroad rates and stop the rebates given to large shippers. On the West Coast and in the Midwest, state legislatures empowered commissions to end rebates and monitor rates. In 1870 Illinois became the first of several states to define railroads as public highways subject to public regulation, including setting maximum rates.

 REVIEW

What factors led to the paralysis of politics in the late nineteenth century?

THE REVOLT OF THE FARMERS

In 1890 the politics of stalemate cracked as the patience of farmers across the South and the western plains finally gave out. Beginning in the 1880s a sharp depression drove down agricultural prices, pushed up surpluses, and forced thousands from their land. Farmers also suffered from a great deal more, including heavy mortgages, widespread poverty, and railroad rates that discriminated against them. In 1890 their resentment boiled over. An agrarian revolt—called **Populism**—swept across the political landscape and broke the stalemate of the previous 20 years.

Populism political outlook that supports the rights and powers of the common people in opposition to the interests of the privileged elite.

The Harvest of Discontent >>

The revolt of the farmers stirred first on the southern frontier, spreading eastward from Texas through the rest of the Old Confederacy, then west across the plains. Farmers blamed their troubles on obvious inequalities: manufacturers protected by the tariff, railroads charging sky-high rates, bankers who held their mounting debts, and expensive intermediaries such as grain elevator operators and millers who stored and processed farm commodities. All seemed to profit at the expense of farmers.

The true picture was more complex. The tariff protected industrial goods but also supported some farm

⌃ Mary Shelley's novel of a man-made creature who turns against its creator strikes the theme for this antirailroad cartoon titled "The American Frankenstein" (1874). "Agriculture, commerce, and manufacture are all in my power," bellows the mechanical monster with the head of a locomotive.

commodities. Railroad rates, however high, actually fell from 1865 to 1890. And although mortgages were heavy, most were short, no more than four years. Farmers often refinanced them, using the money to buy more land and machinery, which only increased their debt. Millers and operators of grain elevators earned handsome profits; yet every year more of them came under state regulation.

In hard times, when debts mounted and children went hungry, complexity mattered little. And in the South many poor farmers seemed condemned to hard times forever. A credit crunch lay at the root of the problem, since most southern farmers had to borrow money to plant and harvest their crops. The inequities of sharecropping and the crop-lien system (page 356) forced them deeper into debt. When crop prices fell, farmers borrowed still more, stretching the financial resources of the South beyond their meager limits. Within a few years after the Civil War, Massachusetts' banks had five times as much money as all the banks of the Old Confederacy.

Beginning in the 1870s, nearly 100,000 debt-ridden farmers a year picked up stakes across the Deep South and fled to Texas to escape the system, only to find it waiting for them. Others stood and fought, as one pamphlet exhorted in 1889, "not with glittering musket, flaming sword and deadly cannon, but with the silent, potent and all-powerful ballot."

The Origins of the Farmers' Alliance »

Before farmers could vote together, they had to get together. Life on the farm was harsh, drab, and isolated. Such conditions shocked Oliver Hudson Kelley as he traveled across the South after the Civil War. In 1867 the young government clerk founded the Patrons of Husbandry to brighten the lives of farmers and broaden their horizons. Local chapters, called granges, brought a dozen or so farmers and their families together to pray, sing, and learn new farming techniques. The Grangers sponsored fairs, picnics, dances, lectures—anything to break the bleakness of farm life. After a slow start the Patrons of Husbandry grew quickly. By 1875 there were 800,000 members in 20,000 locales, most in the Midwest, South, and Southwest.

At first the Grangers swore off politics. But in a pattern often repeated, socializing led to a recognition of common problems and recognition to economic and then political solutions. By pooling their money for supplies and equipment to store and market their crops, for example, Grangers sought to avoid the high charges of intermediaries. By the early 1870s they also were lobbying midwestern legislatures to adopt "Granger laws" regulating rates charged by railroads, grain elevator operators, and other intermediaries.

Eight "Granger cases" came before the Supreme Court in the 1870s to test the new regulatory measures. The most important of them, *Munn v. Illinois* (1877), upheld the right of Illinois to regulate private property (in this case, giant elevators used for storing grain) "devoted to a public use." Later decisions allowed state regulation of railroads but only within state lines. Congress responded in 1887 by creating the Interstate Commerce Commission, a federal agency to regulate commerce across state boundaries. In practice, it had little power, but it was a key step toward establishing the public right to regulate private corporations.

Slumping prices in the 1870s and 1880s bred new farm organizations. Slowly they blended into what the press called the "Alliance Movement." The Southern Alliance, formed in Texas in 1875, spread rapidly after Dr. Charles W. Macune took command in 1886. A doctor and lawyer as well as a farmer, Macune planned to expand the state's network of local chapters, or sub-alliances, into a national network of state Alliance exchanges. Like the Grangers the exchanges pooled their resources in cooperatively owned enterprises for buying and selling, milling and storing, banking and manufacturing.

Soon the Southern Alliance was publicizing its activities in local newspapers, publishing a journal, and sending lecturers across the country. For a brief period, between 1886 and 1892, the Alliance cooperatives multiplied throughout the South, grew to more than a million members, and challenged accepted ways of doing business. Macune claimed that his new Texas Exchange saved members 40 percent on plows and 30 percent on wagons. But most Alliance cooperatives were managed by farmers without the time or experience to succeed. Usually opposed by irate local merchants, the ventures eventually failed.

Although the Southern Alliance admitted no African Americans, it encouraged them to organize. A small group

WITNESS
A Nebraska Farmer Bled Dry

"The hot winds burned up the entire crop, leaving thousands of families wholly destitute . . . [But we are even more cursed] by the swindling games of the bankers and money loaners, who have taken the money and now are after the property, leaving the farmer moneyless and homeless . . . The time comes to pay, I ask for a few days. No I can't wait; must have the money: If I can't get the money, I have the extreme pleasure of seeing my property taken and sold by this iron handed money loaner while my family and I suffer."

— W. M. Taylor to editor, *Farmer's Alliance*, **January 10, 1891**

of black and white Texans founded the Colored Farmers' National Alliance and Cooperative Union in 1886. By 1891 a quarter of a million black farmers had joined. Its operations were largely secret, since public action often brought swift retaliation from white supremacists. When the Colored Farmers' Alliance organized a strike of black cotton pickers near Memphis in 1891, white mobs hunted down and lynched 15 strikers. The murders went unpunished, and the Colored Alliance began to founder.

The Alliance Peaks >>

The key to success for what soon became known as the National Farmers' Alliance lay not in organization but leadership. Alliance lecturers fanned out across the South and the Great Plains, organizing suballiances and teaching new members about finance and cooperative businesses. Women were often as active as men, sometimes more active. In the summer of 1890 alone, Alliance organizer Mary Elizabeth Lease, the "Kansas Pythoness" known for her biting attacks on big business, gave 160 speeches.

In 1890 members of the Alliance met in Ocala, Florida, and issued the "Ocala Demands." The manifesto reflected their deep distrust of "the money power"— large corporations and banks whose financial power gave them the ability to manipulate the "free" market. The Ocala Demands called on government to correct such abuses by reducing tariffs, abolishing national banks, regulating railroads, and coining silver money freely. The platform also demanded a federal income tax and the popular election of senators, to make government more responsive to the public. The most innovative feature came from Charles Macune. His "subtreasury system" would have required the federal government to furnish warehouses for harvested crops and low-interest loans to tide farmers over until prices rose. Under such a system farmers would no longer have had to sell in a glutted market, as they did under the crop-lien system. And they could expand the money supply simply by borrowing at harvest time.

In the off-year elections of 1890 the old parties faced hostile farmers across the nation. In the South, the Alliance worked within the Democratic party and elected 4 governors, won 8 legislatures, and sent 44 members of the House and 3 senators to Washington. Newly created farmer parties elected 5 representatives and 2 senators in Kansas and South Dakota and took over both houses of the Nebraska legislature.

In February 1892, as the presidential election year opened, a convention of 900 labor, feminist, farm, and other reform delegates (100 of them black) met in St. Louis. They founded the People's, or Populist, party and called for another convention to nominate a presidential ticket. Initially southern Populists held back, clinging to their strategy of working within the Democratic party. But when newly elected Democrats failed to support Alliance programs, southern leaders such as Tom Watson of Georgia abandoned the Democrats and began recruiting black and white farmers for the Populists. Although a wealthy farmer, Watson sympathized with the poor of both races.

The national convention of Populists met in Omaha, Nebraska, on Independence Day, 1892. Their impassioned platform promised to return government "to the hands of 'the plain people.'" Planks advocated the subtreasury plan, unlimited coinage of silver and an increase in the money supply, direct election of senators, an income tax, and government ownership of railroads, telegraph, and telephone. To attract wage earners the party endorsed the eight-hour workday, restriction of immigration, and a ban on the use of Pinkerton detectives in labor disputes—for the Pinkertons had engaged in a savage gun battle with strikers that year at Andrew Carnegie's Homestead steel plant. Delegates rallied behind the old greenbacker and Union general James B. Weaver, carefully balancing their presidential nomination with a one-legged Confederate veteran as his running mate.

The Election of 1892 >>

The Populists enlivened the otherwise dull campaign, as Democrat Grover Cleveland and Republican incumbent Benjamin Harrison refought the election of 1888. This time, however,

>> This illustration by artist W. W. Denslow, entitled "You Ought to Be Ashamed of Yourself," is from *The Wonderful Wizard of OZ*, published in 1900 by L. Frank Baum. It was the first of 14 best-selling books on the mythical land. Although Baum claimed only to be telling children's stories, some readers have found a symbolic resemblance to the Populist politics of the day. The "yellow brick road" is the gold standard, they say, leading to a place of false promises (the Emerald City of Oz) under the spell of a bellowing politician (the Wizard), who is exposed by the Scarecrow (farmers), the Tin Man (laborers), and the Lion (the Populists).

" You ought to be ashamed of yourself!"

Cleveland won, and for the first time since the Civil War, Democrats gained control of both houses of Congress. The Populists, too, enjoyed success. Weaver polled over a million votes, the first third-party candidate to do so. Populists elected 3 governors, 5 senators, 10 representatives, and nearly 1,500 members of state legislatures.

Despite these victories the election revealed dangerous weaknesses in the People's party. No doubt a campaign of intimidation and repression hurt the People's party in the South, where white conservatives had been appalled by Tom Watson's open courtship of black southerners. In the North Populists failed to win over labor and most city dwellers. Both were more concerned with family budgets than with the problems of farmers and the downtrodden.

The darker side of Populism also put off many Americans. Its rhetoric was often violent and laced with anti-immigrant, nativist slurs; it spoke ominously of conspiracies and stridently in favor of immigration restriction. In fact the Alliance lost members, an omen of defeats to come. But for the present the People's party had demonstrated two conflicting truths: how far from the needs of many ordinary Americans the two parties had drifted, and how difficult it would be to break their power.

 **REVIEW**

How did the Farmers' Alliance and the People's Party attempt to resolve the problems faced by farmers?

THE NEW REALIGNMENT

On May 1, 1893, President Cleveland was in Chicago to throw the switch that set ablaze 10,000 electric bulbs and opened the World's Columbian Exposition (page 394). Four days later a wave of bankruptcies destroyed major firms across the country, and stock prices sank to all-time lows, setting off the depression of 1893.

At first Chicago staved off the worst, thanks to the business generated by the exposition. But when its doors closed in October, thousands of laborers found themselves out of work. Chicago's mayor estimated the number of unemployed in the city to be near 200,000. He had some firsthand experience on which to base his calculations. Every night desperate men slept on the floors and stairways of City Hall and every police station in the city put up 60 to 100 additional homeless.

The sharp contrast between the exposition's White City and the nation's economic misery demonstrated the inability of the political system to smooth out the economy's cycle of boom and bust. The new industrial order had brought prosperity by increasing production, opening markets, and tying Americans closer together. But in 1893

⌃ The political and social turbulence of the era is reflected in this cartoon of a businessman being tossed and buffeted by agrarian Populists and "Silverites" as well as Republicans and Democrats.

the cost of interdependence came due. A major downturn in one area affected the other sectors of the economy. And with no way to control swings in the business cycle, depression came on a scale as large as that of the booming prosperity. Out of the crisis emerged a new realignment that left the Republican party in control of national politics for decades to come.

The Depression of 1893 ≫ The depression of 1893, the deepest the nation had yet experienced, lasted until 1897. Railroad baron and descendant of two presidents Charles Francis Adams Jr. called it a "convulsion," but the country experienced it as crushing idleness. By the end of 1894 nearly one worker in five was out of a job.

The federal government had no program at all. "While the people should patriotically and cheerfully support their Government," President Cleveland declared, "its functions do not include the support of the people." The states offered little more. Relief, like poverty, was considered a private matter. The burden fell on local charities, benevolent societies, churches, labor unions, and ward bosses.

Others were less charitable. As the popular preacher Henry Ward Beecher told his congregation what most Americans believed: "No man in this land suffers from poverty unless it be more than his fault—unless it be his sin." But the scale of hardship was so great, its targets so random, that anyone could be thrown out of work—an industrious neighbor, a factory foreman with 20 years on the job, a bank president. Older attitudes about personal responsibility for poverty began to give way to new ideas about its social origins and the obligation of public agencies to help.

The Rumblings of Unrest >>

Even before the depression, rumblings of unrest had begun to roll across the country. The Great Railroad Strike of 1877 ignited nearly two decades of labor strife (page 395). After 1893 discontent mounted as wages were cut, employees laid off, and factories closed. During the first year of the depression, 1400 strikes sent more than half a million workers from their jobs.

Uneasy business executives and politicians saw radicalism and the possibility of revolution in every strike. But the depression of 1893 unleashed another force: simple discontent. In the spring of 1894 government inaction came under fire. On Easter Sunday "General" Jacob Coxey, a 39-year-old Populist and factory owner, launched the "Tramps' March on Washington" from Massillon, Ohio. His "Commonweal Army of Christ"—some 500 men, women, and children—descended on Washington to offer "a petition with boots on" for a federal program of public works. Cleveland's staff tightened security around the White House as other "armies" of unemployed mobilized. On May 1, Coxey's troops, armed with "clubs of peace," massed at the foot of the Capitol. When Coxey entered the Capitol grounds 100 mounted police routed the demonstrators and arrested the general for trespassing on the grass. Nothing came of the protest, other than to signal a growing demand for federal action.

Federal help was not to be found. President Cleveland had barely moved into the White House when the depression struck. The country blamed him; he blamed silver. In his view the Sherman Silver Purchase Act of 1890 had shaken business confidence by forcing the government to use its shrinking reserves of gold to purchase (though not coin) silver. Repeal of the act, Cleveland believed, was the way to build gold reserves and restore confidence. After bitter debate, Congress complied. But this economic tinkering only strengthened the resolve of "silverites" in the Democratic party to overwhelm Cleveland's conservative "gold" wing.

Worse for the president, repeal of silver purchases brought no economic revival. In the short run abandoning silver hurt the economy by contracting the money supply just when expansion might have stimulated it by providing needed credit. As panic and unemployment spread across the country, Cleveland's popularity wilted. Democrats were buried in the congressional elections of 1894. Dropping moralistic reforms and stressing national activism, Republicans won control of both the House and the Senate.

With the Democrats confined to the South, the politics of stalemate was over. All that remained for the Republican party was to capture the White House in 1896.

The Battle of the Standards >>

The campaign of 1896 quickly became a "battle of the standards." Both major parties obsessed over whether gold alone or gold and silver should become the monetary standard. Most Republicans saw gold as the stable base for building business confidence and economic prosperity. They adopted a platform calling for "sound money" supported by gold. Their candidate, Governor William McKinley of Ohio, cautiously supported the gold plank and firmly believed in high tariffs to protect American industry.

Silverites campaigned for "free and independent" coinage of silver, in which the Treasury freely minted all the silver presented to it, independent of other nations. The supply of money would increase, prices would rise, and the economy would revive—or so their theory said. The free silver movement was more than a monetary theory. It was a symbolic protest of region and class—of the agricultural South and West against the commercial Northeast, of debt-ridden farm folk against industrialists and financiers, of

⌃ William Jennings Bryan made the first of his three presidential bids in 1896, when he ran on both the Democratic and Populist tickets. Passionate in his convictions and devoted to the plain people, the "Great Commoner" is depicted in this hostile cartoon as a Populist snake devouring the Democratic party.

have-nots against haves. Silverites pressed their case like preachers exhorting their flocks, nowhere more effectively than in William Harvey's best-selling pamphlet, *Coin's Financial School* (1894). It reached tens of thousands of readers with the common sense of Coin, its young hero, fighting for silver.

At the Democratic convention in Chicago, William Jennings Bryan of Nebraska was ready to fight as well. Just 36 years old, Bryan looked "like a young divine"—"tall, slender, handsome," with a rich melodic voice that reached the back rows of the largest halls (no small asset in the days before electric amplification). He had served two terms in Congress and worked as a journalist. He favored low tariffs, opposed Cleveland, and came out belatedly for free silver. Systematically, he coordinated a quiet fight for his nomination.

Silverites controlled the convention from the start. They paraded with silver banners, wore silver buttons, and wrote a plank into the anti-Cleveland platform calling for free and unlimited coinage of the metal. The high point came when Bryan stepped to the lectern and offered himself to "a cause as holy as the cause of liberty—the cause of humanity." The crowd was in a near frenzy as he reached the dramatic climax and spread his arms in mock crucifixion: "You shall not crucify mankind upon a cross of gold." The next day the convention nominated him for the presidency.

Populists were in a quandary. They expected the Democrats to stick with Cleveland and gold, sending unhappy silverites headlong into their camp. Instead, the Democrats stole their thunder by endorsing silver and nominating Bryan. "If we fuse [with the Democrats] we are sunk," complained one Populist. "If we don't fuse, all the silver men we have will leave us for the more powerful Democrats." At a bitter convention fusionists nominated Bryan for president. The best anti-fusionists could do was drop the Democrats' vice presidential candidate in favor of the fiery agrarian rebel from Georgia, Tom Watson.

Campaign and Election >>

Bryan knew he faced an uphill battle. Mounting an aggressive campaign that would be imitated in the future, he traveled 18,000 miles by train, gave as many as 30 speeches a day, and reached perhaps 3 million people in 27 states. The nomination of the People's party actually did more harm than good by labeling Bryan a Populist (which he was not) and a radical (which he definitely was not). Devoted to the "plain people," the Great Commoner spoke for rural America and Jeffersonian values: small farmers, small towns, small government.

McKinley knew he could not compete with Bryan's barnstorming. He contented himself with sedate speeches from his front porch in Canton, Ohio. The folksy appearance of the campaign belied its reality. From the

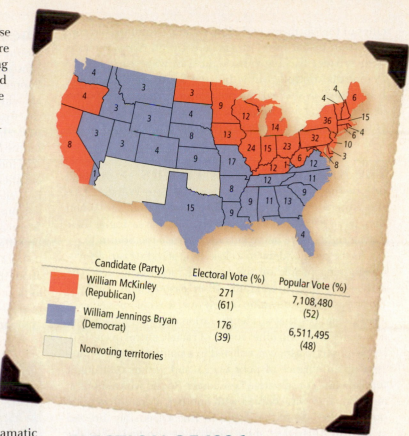

Candidate (Party)	Electoral Vote (%)	Popular Vote (%)
William McKinley (Republican)	271 (61)	7,108,480 (52)
William Jennings Bryan (Democrat)	176 (39)	6,511,495 (48)
Nonvoting territories		

ELECTION OF 1896

The critical election of 1896 established the Republicans as the majority party, ending two decades of political gridlock with a new political realignment. Republican victor William McKinley dominated the large industrial cities and states, as the returns of the Electoral College show.

beginning, campaign strategist Marcus Alonzo Hanna, a talented Ohio industrialist, relied on modern techniques of organization and marketing. He advertised McKinley, said Theodore Roosevelt, "as if he were patent medicine." The well-financed campaign brought to Canton tens of thousands, who cheered the candidate's promises of a "full dinner pail." Hanna also saturated the country with millions of leaflets, along with 1,400 speakers attacking free trade and free silver. McKinley won in a walk, amassing the first majority of the popular vote since Ulysses S. Grant in 1872.

The election proved to be one of the most critical in the republic's history.[1] Over the previous three decades, political life had been characterized by vibrant campaigns, slim party margins, high voter turnout, and low-profile presidents. The election of 1896 signaled a new era of dwindling party loyalties and voter turnout, stronger presidents, and Republican rule. McKinley's victory broke the political stalemate and forged a powerful coalition that dominated politics for the next 30 years. It rested on the industrial

[1] Five elections, in addition to the contest of 1896, are often cited as critical shifts in voter allegiance and party alignments: the Federalist defeat of 1800, Andrew Jackson's rise in 1828, Lincoln's Republican triumph of 1860, Al Smith's Democratic loss in 1928, and—perhaps—Ronald Reagan's conservative tide of 1980.

cities of the Northeast and Midwest and combined old support from businesses, farmers, and Union Army veterans with broader backing from industrial wage earners. The Democrats controlled little but the South. And the Populists virtually vanished, but not before leaving a compound legacy: as a catalyst for political realignment, a cry for federal action, and a prelude to a new age of reform.

The Rise of Jim Crow Politics >>

In 1892, despite the stumping of Populists like Tom Watson, African Americans cast their ballots for Republicans, when they were permitted to vote freely. But increasingly, their voting rights were being curtailed across the South.

As the century drew to a close, long-standing racialism—categorizing people on the basis of race—deepened. The arrival of "new" immigrants from eastern and southern Europe and the acquisition of new overseas colonies encouraged prejudices that stridently rationalized white supremacy, segregation and other forms of racial control (page 361). In the South racism was enlisted in a political purpose: preventing an alliance of poor blacks and whites that might topple white conservative Democrats. So the white supremacy campaign was coupled with another, a drive to deprive poor southerners of their right to vote. Ostensibly directed at African Americans, these campaigns also had a broader target in the world of politics: rebellion from below, whether black or white.

Mississippi, where Democrats had led the move to "redeem" their state from Republican Reconstruction, in 1890 took the lead in disfranchising African Americans. A new state constitution required voters to pay a poll tax and pass a literacy test, requirements that eliminated the great majority of black voters. Conservative Democrats favored the plan, because it also reduced the voting of poor whites, who were most likely to join opposition parties. Before the new constitution went into effect, Mississippi contained more than 250,000 eligible voters. By 1892, after its adoption, there were fewer than 77,000. Between 1895 and 1908, disfranchisement campaigns won out in every southern state, barring many poor whites from the polls as well.

The disfranchisement campaign had one final consequence: splitting rebellious whites from blacks, as the fate of Tom Watson demonstrated. Only a dozen years after his biracial campaign of 1892, Watson was promoting black disfranchisement in Georgia. Like other southern Populists, Watson returned to the Democratic party still hoping to help poor whites. But he turned against black southerners. Only by playing a powerful race card could he hope to win election. "What does civilization owe the negro?" he asked bitterly. "Nothing! Nothing!! NOTHING!!!" In 1920, after a decade of baiting blacks (as well as Catholics and Jews), the Georgia firebrand was elected to the Senate. Watson, who began with such high racial ideals, gained power only by abandoning them.

The African American Response >>

To mount a successful crusade for disfranchisement, white conservatives inflamed racial passions. They staged "White Supremacy Jubilees" and peppered newspaper editorials with complaints of "bumptious" and "impudent" African Americans. The number of black lynchings by whites peaked during the 1890s, averaging over a hundred a year for the decade. Most took place in the South.

Under such circumstances African Americans worked out their own responses to the climate of intolerance. Ida B. Wells, a black woman born into slavery, turned her talents into a nationwide campaign against lynching when a friend and two of his partners in the People's Grocery were brutally murdered after a fight with a white competitor in 1892. She spent much of her time educating Americans about the use of lynching and other forms of mob violence as devices for terrorizing African Americans in the absence of slavery. Though her lobbying failed to produce a federal antilynching law, Wells did help organize black women,

↗ This black-and-white photo of the charismatic African American activist and educator Booker T. Washington highlights his piercing gray eyes nearly luminous against what one observer described as his "reddish" complexion. Born into slavery, Washington sits here with his legs casually crossed, a literate, well-to-do free man in a suit and tie. (Note the reading material in his lap.) "He wasn't dark and he wasn't light," wrote the composer Zenobia Powell Perry. "I'll never forget those eyes." In many ways Washington served as a bridge between white and black worlds and his "in between" complexion may have advanced that role.

eventually into the National Association of Colored Women in 1896. It supported wide-ranging reforms, including education, housing, health care, and, of course, antilynching.

Wells's campaign focused on mob violence, but another former slave, Booker T. Washington, stressed instead the need for accepting the prevailing framework for race relations and working within it. "I love the South," he reassured an audience of white and black southerners in Atlanta in 1895. He conceded that white prejudice existed throughout the region but nonetheless counseled African Americans to work for their economic betterment through manual labor. Every laborer who learned a trade, every farmer who tilled the land could increase his or her savings. Those earnings amounted to "a little green ballot" that "no one will throw out or refuse to count." Toward that end, Washington founded the Tuskegee Institute in Alabama in 1881. It stressed vocational skills for farming, manual trades, and industrial work.

Many white Americans hailed what one black critic called Washington's "Atlanta Compromise," for it struck the note of patient humility they were eager to hear. For African Americans, it made the best of a bad situation. Washington, an astute politician, discovered that philanthropists across the nation hoped to make Tuskegee an example of their generosity. He was the honored guest of Andrew Carnegie at his imposing Skibo Castle. California railroad magnate Collis Huntington became his friend, as did other business executives eager to discuss "public and social questions."

Throughout, Washington preached accommodation to the racial caste system. He accepted segregation (as long as separate facilities were equal) and qualifications on voting (if they applied to white citizens as well). Above all Washington sought economic self-improvement for common black folk in fields and factories. In 1900 he organized the National Negro Business League to help establish black businessmen as the leaders of their people. The rapid growth of local chapters (320 by 1907) extended his influence across the country.

In the "Solid South" (as well as an openly racialized North) it was Washington's restrained approach that articulated an agenda for most African Americans. The ferment of the early 1890s among black Populists and white was replaced by an all-white Democratic party that dominated the region for decades to come but remained in the minority on the national level.

McKinley in the White House ›› In William McKinley, Republicans found a skillful chief with a national agenda and personal charm. He cultivated news reporters, openly walked the streets of Washington, and

> ## Above all Washington sought economic self-improvement for common black folk in fields and factories.

courted the public with handshakes and flowers plucked from his lapel. Firmly but delicately, he curbed the power of state bosses. When necessary, he prodded Congress to action. In all these ways, he foreshadowed "modern" presidents, who would act as party leaders rather than as executive caretakers.

Fortune at first smiled on McKinley. When he entered the White House, the economy had already begun its recovery. Factory orders were slowly increasing, and unemployment dropped. Farm prices climbed. New discoveries of gold in Alaska and South Africa expanded the supply of money without causing "gold bugs" to panic that it was being destabilized by silver.

Freed from the burdens of the economic crisis, McKinley called a special session of Congress to revise the tariff. In 1897 the Dingley Tariff raised protective rates still higher but followed the strategy of reciprocity by allowing U.S. tariffs to come down if other nations lowered theirs. McKinley also sought a solution for resolving railroad strikes before they turned violent. The Erdman Act of 1898 set up machinery for government mediation. McKinley even began laying plans for stronger regulation of trusts.

The same expansiveness that had pushed an industrial nation across the continent and shipped grain and cotton abroad was also drawing the country into a race for empire and a war with Spain. Regulation—and an age of reform—would have to await the next century.

 REVIEW

How did the election of 1896 resolve the "Politics of Stalemate" of the late nineteenth century?

VISIONS OF EMPIRE

The war with Spain was only the affair of the moment that turned American attention abroad. Underlying the conflict were larger forces linking the United States to the world economy and international events. By the 1890s, southern farmers were exporting half their cotton crop to factories worldwide. Western wheat farmers earned some 30 to 40 percent of their income from foreign markets. John D. Rockefeller's Standard Oil Company shipped about two-thirds of its refined products overseas, and Cyrus McCormick supplied Russian farmers with the reaper.

More than commerce turned American eyes overseas. Since the 1840s expansionists had spoken of a divine destiny to overspread the North American continent. Some Americans still cast covetous glances at Canada to the north

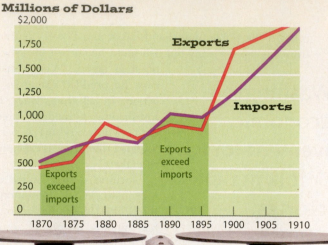

Millions of Dollars

Exports

Imports

Exports exceed imports

Exports exceed imports

Year

BALANCE OF U.S. IMPORTS AND EXPORTS, 1870–1910

After the depression of 1893 both imports and exports rose sharply, suggesting one reason why the age of imperialism was so closely linked with the emerging global industrial economy.

and Mexico and Cuba to the south. And they dreamed of empire in more distant lands.

Imperialism, European-Style and American >>

The scramble for empire was well under way by the time the Americans, Japanese, and Germans entered it in the late nineteenth century. Spain and Portugal still clung to the remnants of their colonial empires. Meanwhile, England, France, and Russia accelerated their drive to control foreign peoples and lands.

imperialism acquisition of control over the government and the economy of another nation, usually by conquest.

The late nineteenth century became the new age of **imperialism** because weapons technology and new networks of communication, transportation, and commerce brought the prospect of effective, truly global empires within reach.

The speed and efficiency with which Europeans took over in the Niger and Congo basins of Africa in the 1880s prompted many Americans to argue for this European-style imperialism of conquest and possession. Germany, Japan, and Belgium were eagerly joining the hunt for colonies. But other Americans preferred a more indirect

imperialism: one that exported products, ideas, and influence. To them, this American-style imperialism seemed somehow purer, for they could portray themselves as bearers of long-cherished values: democracy, free-enterprise capitalism, and Christianity.

While Americans tried to justify imperial control in the name of such values, social, economic, and political forces were drawing them rapidly into the imperial race. The growth of industrial networks linked them to international markets as never before. With economic systems more tightly knit and political systems more responsive to industrialists and financiers, a rush for markets and distant lands was perhaps unavoidable.

The Shapers of American Imperialism >>

Although the climate for expansion and imperialism was present at the end of the nineteenth century, the small farmer or steelworker was little concerned with how the United States advanced its goals abroad. An elite group—Christian missionaries, intellectuals, business leaders, and commercial farmers—joined navy careerists to shape American imperialism. In doing so, they lobbied the White House and Congress, where foreign policy was made, and the State and War departments, where it was carried out.

The success of imperial ventures depended on a strong navy, whether to project American might abroad or to guard the sea lanes of commerce. But by 1880 the once-proud Civil War fleet of more than 600 warships was rotting from neglect. The U.S. Navy ranked twelfth in the world, behind Denmark and Chile. The United States had a coastal fleet but no functional fleet to protect its interests overseas. Discontented navy officers combined with trade-hungry business leaders to lobby Congress for a modern navy.

Alfred Thayer Mahan, a navy captain and later admiral, formulated their ideas into a widely accepted theory of **navalism.** In *The Influence of Sea Power Upon History* (1890), Mahan argued that great nations were seafaring powers that relied on foreign trade for wealth and might. The only way to protect foreign markets, Mahan reasoned, was with large cruisers and battleships. These ships, operating far from American shores, would need coaling stations and other facilities to resupply them throughout the world.

navalism theories of warfare and trade that rely on a nation's navy as a principal instrument of policy.

Mahan's logic was so persuasive and the profits to be reaped by American factories so great that in the 1880s Congress launched a program to rebuild the old wood-and-sail navy with steam vessels made of steel. By 1900 the U.S. Navy ranked third in the world. With a modern navy the country had the means to become an imperial power.

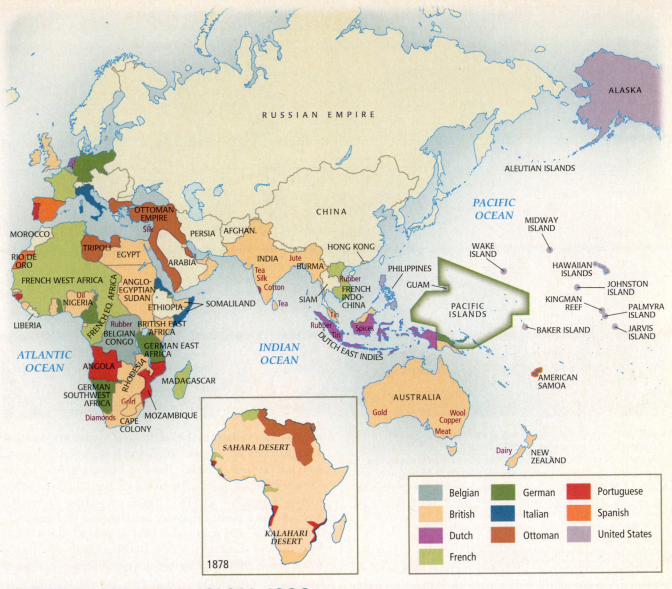

IMPERIALIST EXPANSION, 1900

Often resource-poor countries such as Great Britain sought colonies for their raw materials—for example, South African diamonds and tin from Southeast Asia. While China appears to be undivided, the major powers were busy establishing spheres of influence there.

Protestant missionaries provided a spiritual rationale that complemented Mahan's navalism. Because missionaries often encountered people whose cultural differences made them unreceptive to the Christian message, many believed that the natives first had to become Western in culture before becoming Christian in belief. They introduced Western goods, education, and systems of government administration—any "civilizing medium," as one minister remarked. Yet most American missionaries were not territorial imperialists. They eagerly took up what they called the "White Man's Burden" of introducing civilization to the "colored" races of the world but opposed direct military or political intervention.

From scholars, academics, and scientists came racial theories to justify European and American expansion. Charles Darwin's *On the Origin of Species* (1859) had popularized the notion that among animal species, the fittest survived through a process of natural selection. Social Darwinists (page 389) argued that the same laws of survival governed the social order. When applied aggressively, social Darwinism was used to justify theories of white supremacy as well as the slaughter and enslavement of nonwhite native peoples who resisted conquest. When combined with the somewhat more humane "White Man's Burden" of Christian missionaries, American imperialism included uplifting natives by spreading Western ideas, religion, and government.

Perhaps more compelling than either racial or religious motives for American expansion was the need for trade. The business cycle of boom and bust reminded Americans of the unpredictability of their economy. In hard times people sought salvation wherever they could, and one obvious

↟ Missionaries often viewed the Chinese as uncivilized "heathen," whose souls needed saving and whose culture needed civilizing. This cartoon, published around 1900, pokes fun at the common stereotype by suggesting what the Chinese must think of the American "heathen." "Contributions Received Here to Save the Foreign Devils," reads the sign of the Chinese "preacher," who laments the uncivilized behavior of corrupt American city governments, feuding backwoodsmen, rioting laborers, and mobs tormenting Chinese and black Americans.

road to redemption lay in markets abroad. With American companies outgrowing the home market, explained the National Association of Manufacturers, "expansion of our foreign trade is [the] only promise of relief."

Dreams of a Commercial Empire ≫

No one did more to initiate the idea of a "New Empire" of commerce for the United States than William Henry Seward, secretary of state under Abraham Lincoln and Andrew Johnson. Seward believed that "empire has . . . made its way constantly westward . . . until the tides of the renewed and decaying civilizations of the world meet on the shores of the Pacific Ocean." The United States must thus be prepared to win supremacy in the Far East—not by planting colonies or sending troops but by pursuing commerce. Equal access to foreign markets, often called the "open door," guided American policy in Asia and made Seward's strategy truly revolutionary.

While he pursued ties to Japan, Korea, and China, Seward promoted a transcontinental railroad at home and a canal across the Central American isthmus. Link by link, he was trying to connect eastern factories to western ports in the United States and, from there, to markets in the Far East. In pursuit of these goals Seward made two acquisitions in

1867: Midway Island in the Pacific, and Alaska. Midway was unimportant by itself; its value lay in being a way station to Asia not far from Hawaii, where missionary planters were already establishing an American presence. Critics called Alaska "Seward's Folly," but he paid only about 2 cents an acre for a mineral-rich territory twice the size of Texas.

Seward's conviction that the future of the United States lay in the Pacific and Asia flourished only in the 1890s, when Mahan provided the naval theory necessary to make the leap and the vanishing American frontier supplied an economic rationale for extending Manifest Destiny beyond continental borders of the nation. But in the 1880s Secretary of State James G. Blaine began to look for ways to expand American trade and influence southward into Central and South America, where Great Britain had interests of its own to protect.

Blaine launched a campaign to cancel the Clayton-Bulwer Treaty (1850), which shared rights with Great Britain to any canal built in Central America. In 1901 Great Britain finally ceded its interest in building a canal across the Central American isthmus in return for a U.S. promise to leave such a canal open to ships of all nations. Blaine also tried to shift Central American imports from British to U.S. goods by proposing that a "customs union" be created to reduce trade barriers in the Americas. His efforts resulted only in a weak Pan-American Union to foster peaceful understanding in the region.

If American expansionists wanted to extend trade across the Pacific to China, Hawaii was the crucial link. It afforded a fine naval base and a refueling station along the route to Asia. In 1893, American sugar planters overthrew the recently enthroned Queen Liliuokalani, a

Hawaiian nationalist eager to rid the island of American influence. Their success was ensured when a contingent of U.S. marines arrived ashore on the pretext of protecting American lives. Eager to avoid the McKinley Tariff's new tax on sugar imported into the United States, planters lobbied for the annexation of Hawaii, but President Cleveland refused. He was no foe of expansion but was, as his secretary of state noted, "unalterably opposed to stealing territory, or of annexing people against their consent, and the people of Hawaii do not favor annexation." The idea of incorporating the nonwhite population also troubled Cleveland. For a time, matters stood at a stalemate.

 REVIEW

What social, economic, and cultural factors drew the United States into the race for empire?

THE IMPERIAL MOMENT

In 1895, after almost 15 years of planning from exile in the United States, José Martí returned to Cuba to renew the struggle for independence from Spain. With cries of *Cuba libre* ("free Cuba"), Martí and his rebels cut railroad lines, destroyed sugar mills, and set fire to cane fields. Within a year rebel forces controlled more than half the island. But even as they fought the Spanish, the rebels worried about the United States. Their island, just 90 miles off the coast of Florida, had long been a target of American expansionists and business interests. "I have lived in the bowels of the monster," Martí said in reference to the United States, "and I know it."

The Spanish overlords struck back at Martí and his followers with brutal violence. Governor-General Valeriano Weyler herded a half million Cubans from their homes into fortified camps where filth, disease, and starvation killed perhaps 200,000. Outside these "reconcentration" camps, Weyler chased the rebels across the countryside, polluting drinking water, killing farm animals, burning crops. By 1898 U. S. soldiers were fighting Spaniards in Cuba and the Philippines in what Secretary of State John Hay called "the splendid little war." Neither the Cubans nor the Filipinos emerged from the conflict as free as they hoped.

Mounting Tensions >> President Cleveland had little sympathy for the Cuban revolt. He doubted that the mostly black population was capable of self-government and feared that independence from Spain might lead to chaos on the island. Already the revolution had caused widespread destruction of American-owned property. The president settled on a policy that favored neither the Spanish nor the rebels: opposing the rebellion, but pressing Spain to grant Cuba some freedoms.

In the Republican party expansionists such as Theodore Roosevelt and Massachusetts senator Henry Cabot Lodge urged a more forceful policy. In 1896 they succeeded in writing an imperial wish list into the Republican national platform: annexation of Hawai'i, the construction of a Nicaraguan canal, purchase of the Virgin Islands, and more naval expansion. They also called for recognition of Cuban independence, a step that, if taken, would likely provoke war with Spain. When William McKinley entered the White House, however, his Republican supporters found only a moderate expansionist. Cautiously, privately, he lobbied Spain to stop cracking down on the rebels and destroying American property.

In 1897 Spain promised to remove the much-despised Weyler, end the reconcentration policy, and offer Cuba greater autonomy. The shift encouraged McKinley to resist pressure at home for more hostile action. But leaders of the Spanish army in Cuba had no desire to compromise. Although Weyler was removed the military renewed efforts to crush the rebels and stirred pro-army riots in the streets of Havana. Early in 1898 McKinley dispatched the battleship *Maine* to show that the United States meant to protect its interests and its citizens.

Then in February 1898 the State Department received a stolen copy of a letter to Cuba sent by the Spanish minister in Washington, Enrique Dupuy de Lôme. So did William Randolph Hearst, a pioneer of sensationalist, or **"yellow," journalism** who was eager for war with Spain. "WORST INSULT TO THE UNITED STATES IN ITS HISTORY," screamed the headline of Hearst's New York *Journal*. What had de Lôme actually written? After referring to McKinley as a mere "would-be politician," the letter admitted that Spain had no

yellow journalism brand of newspaper reporting that stresses excitement and shock over even-handedness and dull fact.

Point of View

Gender and the Spanish-American War

"If we shift from economic, annexationist, and strategic arguments (that is, from what appear to be national self-interest arguments) to political explanations [for the Spanish-American War], gender appears even more germane. The late-nineteenth-century belief that 'manly' character was a prerequisite for full citizenship and political leadership can explain why support for bellicose policies seemed politically astute."

KRISTIN HOGANSON *Fighting for American Manhood: How Gender Politics Provoked the Spanish-American and Philippine-American Wars*

↟ The grisly depiction of the explosion that sank the battleship *Maine* in Havana harbor in 1898, complete with a panel titled "Recovering the Dead Bodies" (*upper right*). Illustrations such as this one helped jingoists turn the event into a battle cry, "Remember the Maine."

intention of changing its policy of crushing the rebels. Red-faced Spanish officials immediately recalled de Lôme, but most Americans now believed that Spain had deceived the United States.

On February 15, 1898, as the Maine lay at anchor in the Havana harbor, explosions ripped through the hull. Within minutes the ship sank to the bottom, killing some 260 American sailors. Much later an official investigation concluded that the explosion was the result of spontaneous combustion in a coal bunker aboard ship. Most Americans at the time, inflamed by hysterical news accounts, concluded that Spanish agents had sabotaged the ship.

Pressures for war proved too great to resist, and on April 11, McKinley asked Congress to authorize "forceful intervention" in Cuba. Nine days later Congress recognized Cuban independence, insisted on the withdrawal of Spanish forces, and gave the president authority to use military force. In a flush of idealism, Congress also adopted the Teller Amendment, renouncing any aim to annex Cuba.

Certainly both idealism and moral outrage led many Americans down the path to war. But in the end, the "splendid little war" came as a result of less lofty ambitions: empire, trade, glory.

The Imperial War >> For the 5,462 men who died there was little splendid about the Spanish-American War. Only 379 gave their lives in battle. The rest succumbed to accidents, disease, and the mismanagement of an unprepared army. Rather than tropical uniforms troops were issued winter woolens and sometimes fed on rations that were diseased, rotten, or poisoned. Some soldiers found themselves fighting with weapons from the Civil War.

The navy fared better. Decisions in the 1880s to modernize the fleet paid handsome dividends. Naval battles largely determined the outcome of the war. As soon as war was declared, Admiral George Dewey ordered his Asiatic battle squadron from China to the Philippines. Just before dawn on May 1, he opened fire on the Spanish ships in Manila Bay. Five hours later the entire Spanish squadron lay at the bottom of the bay. Dewey had no plans to follow up his stunning victory with an invasion. His fleet carried no marines with which to take Manila. So ill prepared was President McKinley for war, let alone victory, that only after learning of Dewey's success did he order 11,000 American troops to the Philippines.

Halfway around the globe, another Spanish fleet had slipped into Santiago harbor in Cuba just before the arrival of the U.S. Navy. The navy blockaded the island, expecting the Spanish to flee under the cover of darkness. Instead, in broad daylight on July 3, the Spanish fleet made a desperate dash for the open seas. So startled were

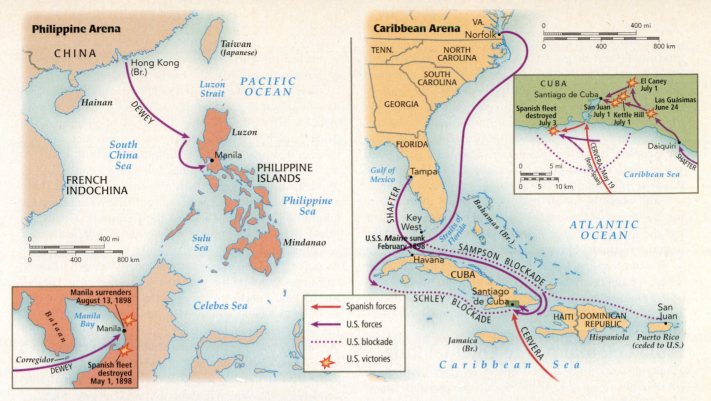

THE SPANISH-AMERICAN WAR

Had the Spanish-American war depended largely on ground forces, the ill-prepared U.S. Army might have fared poorly. But the key to success, in both Cuba and the Philippines, was naval warfare, in which the recently modernized American fleet had a critical edge. Proximity to Cuba also gave the United States an advantage in delivering troops and supplies and in maintaining a naval blockade that isolated Spanish forces.

the Americans that several of their ships nearly collided as they rushed to attack their exposed foes. All seven Spanish ships were sunk. With Cuba now cut off from Spain, the war was virtually won.

Without a fleet for cover or any way to escape, the Spanish garrison surrendered on July 17. In the Philippines, a similar brief battle preceded the American taking of Manila on August 13. The "splendid little war" had ended in less than four months.

Peace and the Debate over Empire ≫

Conquering Cuba and the Philippines proved easier than deciding what to do with them. The Teller Amendment had renounced any American claim to Cuba. But clearly the United States had not freed the island to see chaos reign or American business and military interests excluded. And what of the Philippines—and Spanish Puerto Rico, which American forces had taken without a struggle? Powerful public and congressional sentiment pushed McKinley to claim empire as the fruits of victory.

Even the president favored such a course. The battle in the Pacific highlighted the need for naval bases and coaling stations. "To maintain our flag in the Philippines, we must raise our flag in Hawaii," the New York *Sun* insisted. On July 7 McKinley signed a joint congressional resolution annexing Hawaii, as planters had wanted for nearly a decade.

The Philippines presented a more difficult problem. Filipinos had greeted the American forces as liberators, not new colonizers. The popular leader of the rebel forces fighting Spain, Emilio Aguinaldo, had returned to the islands on an American ship. To the rebels' dismay, McKinley insisted that the islands were under American authority until the peace treaty settled matters.

Many influential Americans—former president Grover Cleveland, steel baron Andrew Carnegie, novelist Mark Twain—opposed annexation of the Philippines. Yet even these anti-imperialists favored expansion, if only in the form of trade. Business leaders especially believed that the country could enjoy the economic benefits of the Philippines without the costs of maintaining it as a colony. Annexation would mire the United States too deeply in the quicksands of Asian politics, they argued. More important, a large, costly fleet would be necessary to defend the islands. To the imperialists that was precisely the point: a large fleet was crucial to the interests of a powerful commercial nation.

Racist ideas shaped both sides of the argument. Imperialists believed that the racial inferiority of nonwhites made occupation of the Philippines necessary, and they were ready to assume the "White Man's Burden" and govern. Gradually, they argued, Filipinos would be taught the virtues of Western civilization, Christianity,[2] democracy,

[2] In point of fact, most Filipinos were already Catholic after many years under Spanish rule.

and self-rule. Anti-imperialists, however, feared racial intermixing and the possibility that Asian workers would flood the American labor market. They also maintained that dark-skinned people would never develop the capacity for self-government. An American government in the Philippines could be sustained only at the point of bayonets—yet the U.S. Constitution made no provision for governing people without representation or equal rights. Such a precedent, the anti-imperialists warned, might one day threaten American liberties at home.

Still, when the Senate debated the Treaty of Paris ending the Spanish-American War in 1898, the imperialists had the support of the president, most of Congress, and the majority of public opinion. Even such an anti-imperialist as William Jennings Bryan, defeated by McKinley in 1896, supported the treaty. In it Spain surrendered title to Cuba, ceded Puerto Rico and Guam to the United States, and in return for $20 million turned over the Philippines as well.

From Colonial War to Colonial Rule >>

Managing an empire turned out to be even more devilish than acquiring one. As the Senate debated annexation of the Philippines in Washington in 1899, rebels clashed with an American patrol outside Manila, igniting a guerrilla war. The few Americans who paid attention called it the "Filipino insurrection," but to those who fought, it was the Philippine-American War. When it ended more than three years later, nearly 5,000 Americans, 25,000 rebels, and perhaps as many as 200,000 civilians lay dead.

After a series of conventional battles ended in their defeat, Filipino *insurrectos* quickly learned to take advantage of the mountainous, jungle terrain of the Philippine archipelago. From his hideaway in the mountains of Bayombong, Aguinaldo ordered his men to employ *guerilla* (literally "little war" in Spanish) tactics. Hit-and-run ambushes by lightly armed rebels were perfectly suited to the dense landscape. As *insurrectos* melted into tropical forests and friendly villages, Americans could barely distinguish between enemies and friends. It was the first instance of jungle warfare the United States had ever encountered.

Jungle warfare aggravated racial antagonisms and spurred savage fighting on both sides. Rebel resistance to foreign occupation was accompanied by reports of *insurrectos* treating American prisoners in "fiendish fashion," burying some alive, dismembering others, and slaughtering even Filipinos who opposed them. For their part American soldiers dismissed Filipinos as nearly subhuman. "The only good Filipino is a dead one," declared one U.S. soldier, echoing the infamous anti-Indian cry of the American West.

To combat the insurgents General Arthur MacArthur imposed a brutal campaign of "pacification" late in 1899. Filipinos were herded into concentration camps for their protection, and food and crops were seized or torched to starve the rebels into surrender. The strategy was embarrassingly reminiscent of "Butcher" Weyler in Cuba. Only after the capture of Aguinaldo and the last gasps of rebel resistance did the war finally come to a close in 1902. It marked the end of the westward march of American empire that began with the Louisiana Purchase in 1803.

Despite the bitter guerrilla war, the United States ruled its new island territory with relative benevolence. Under William Howard Taft, the first civilian governor, the Americans built schools, roads, sewers, and factories and inaugurated new farming techniques. The aim, said Taft, was to prepare the Philippines for independence, and to prove it, he granted great authority to local officials. These advances—social, economic, and political—benefited the Filipino elite and thus earned their support. Finally, on July 4, 1946, the Philippines were granted independence.

The United States played a similar role in Puerto Rico. As in the Philippines, executive authority resided in a governor appointed by the U.S. president. Under the Foraker Act of 1900 Puerto Ricans received a voice in their government as well as a nonvoting representative in the U.S. House of Representatives and certain tariff advantages. All the same, many Puerto Ricans chafed at the idea of such second-class citizenship. Some favored eventual admission to the United States as a state while others advocated independence, a division of opinion that persists even today.

An Open Door in China >>

Interest in Asia drove the United States to annex the Philippines; and annexation of the Philippines established the United States as a Pacific power with an eye on Asia. As ever, the possibility of markets in China—whether for Christian souls or consumer goods—proved an irresistible lure.

Both the British, who dominated China's export trade, and the Americans, who wanted to, worried that China might soon be carved up by other powers. Japan had defeated China in 1895, encouraging Russia, Germany, and France to join in demanding trade concessions. Each nation sought to establish an Asian "**sphere of influence**" in which its commercial and military interests reigned. Such spheres often ended in commercial and other restrictions against rival powers. Since Britain and the United States wanted the benefits of trade rather than actual colonies, they tried to limit foreign demands while leaving China open to all commerce.

sphere of influence geographic region beyond its border over which a nation exerts political or economic control.

In 1899, at the urging of the British, Secretary of State John Hay circulated the first of two "open door" notes among the imperial powers. He did not ask them to relinquish their spheres of influence in China, only to keep them open to free trade with other nations. Japan and most of the European powers agreed in broad outline with Hay's policy, out of fear that the Americans might tip the delicate balance by siding with a rival. Hay seized on the tepid response and brashly announced that the open door in China was international policy.

Unrest soon threatened to close the door. Chinese nationalists, known to Westerners as Boxers for their clenched-fist

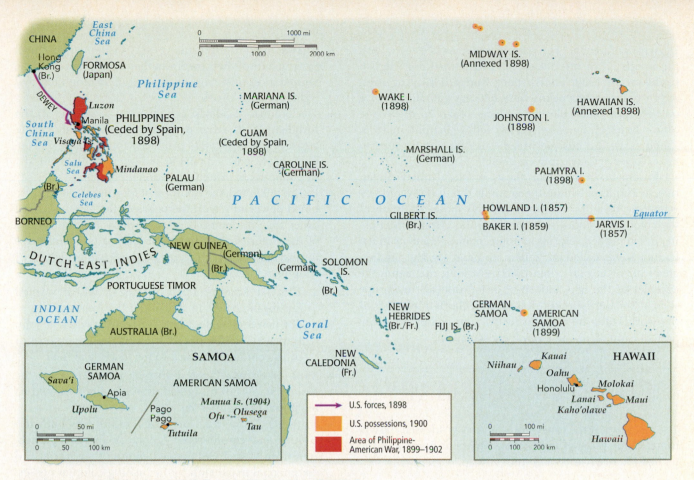

THE UNITED STATES IN THE PACIFIC

In the late nineteenth century Germany and the United States emerged as Pacific naval powers and contestants for influence and trade in China. The island groups of the Central and Southwest Pacific were of little economic value but had great strategic worth as bases and coaling stations along the route to Asia.

symbol, formed secret societies to drive out the *fon kwei,* or foreign devils. Encouraged by the Chinese empress, Boxers murdered hundreds of Christian missionaries and their followers and besieged foreign diplomats and citizens at the British Embassy in Beijing. European nations quickly dispatched troops to quell the uprising and free the diplomats, while President McKinley sent 2,500 Americans to join the march to the capital city. Along the way, the angry foreign armies plundered the countryside and killed civilians before reaching Beijing and breaking the siege.

Hay feared that once in control of Beijing the conquerors might never leave, so he sent a second open-door note in 1900, this time asking foreign powers to respect China's territorial and administrative integrity. They endorsed the proposal in principle only. In fact the open-door notes together amounted to little more than an announcement of American desires to maintain stability and trade in Asia. Yet they reflected a fundamental purpose to which the United States dedicated itself across the globe: to open closed markets and to keep open those markets that other empires had yet to close. The new American empire would have its share of colonies, but in Asia as elsewhere it would be built primarily on trade.

REVIEW

Why did imperialists launch their quest for empire, and why did anti-imperialists oppose them?

In the end, the Chicago World's Fair of 1893 proved an apt reflection of the world at home and abroad. Though the fair showed off its exhibits within gleaming white buildings, at the same time the political system cracked under the strain of a depression. As the Fair gathered exhibits from all over the globe, the scramble for resources and markets culminated in an age of imperialism. National greatness walked hand in hand with empire, it seemed—whether reflected in the gleaming plaster buildings of the White City or the German guns on exhibit. Employing the gendered language of the day, one German historian proclaimed: "Every virile people has established colonial power." The United States joined the rush somewhat late, trailing behind the French, British, Germans, and Dutch in part because it was still extracting raw materials from its own "colonial" regions in the defeated South and the booming West.

As in the United States, European imperialists sometimes justified their rule over nonwhite peoples in

Darwinian fashion. "The path of progress is strewn with the wreck . . . of inferior races," proclaimed one English professor in 1900. British poet Rudyard Kipling even suggested that Europeans were making a noble sacrifice on behalf of their colonial subjects. "Take up the White Man's Burden," he exhorted his fellow Britons in 1899. "Send forth the best ye breed—/Go bind your sons to exile/To serve your captives' need."

European critics, like those in the United States, rejected imperialism on the grounds that it delivered few economic benefits, compromised the moral standing of the colonizers, and distracted the public from undertaking much needed reforms at home. Just as Populists in the United States called on "toilers" to band together and on government to play a more active role in managing the excesses of the new industrial order, radicals in Europe such as the German-born Karl Marx exhorted "workers of the world" to unite and "throw off your chains" by abandoning capitalism and embracing socialism.

CHAPTER SUMMARY

The last third of the nineteenth century witnessed the culmination of years of political stalemate at home and the realization of dreams of empire abroad.

- Republicans and Democrats ground politics into near gridlock over the well-worn issues of regional conflict, tariff, and monetary reform.

- Discontented Americans often fashioned political instruments of their own, whether for woman suffrage, temperance, monetary change, antilynching and civil rights, or farm issues.
- The political deadlock came finally to an end in the turbulent 1890s, when depression-spawned labor strife and a revolt of farmers produced the People's, or Populist, party and a political realignment that left the Republicans in control of national politics.
- By the 1890s, too, the tradition of Manifest Destiny combined powerfully with the needs of the new industrial order for raw materials and markets and the closing of the American frontier to produce a powerful drive toward empire, which rested on these two principles of American foreign policy:
  - The old Monroe Doctrine (1823), which warned European powers to stay out of the Americas.
  - The newer open-door notes of Secretary of State John Hay (1899–1900), which stressed the importance of equal commercial access to the markets of Asia.
- Most Americans favored an overseas empire for the United States but disagreed over whether it should be territorial or commercial.
- In the end America's overseas empire was both territorial and commercial. A victory in the Spanish-American War (1898) capped an era of territorial and commercial expansion by furnishing colonial possessions in the Caribbean and the Pacific and at the same time providing more stepping-stones to the markets of Asia.

Significant Events

1867	1869	1874	1877	1881	1887	1890
Patrons of Husbandry ("Grange") founded; Alaska acquired	Massachusetts establishes first state regulatory commission				Interstate Commerce created	Sherman Antitrust Act; Ocala Demands
	Woman's Christian Temperance Union formed	*Munn v. Illinois*	Garfield assassinated; Booker T. Washington founds Tuskegee Normal and Industrial Institute			

Additional Reading

Heather Richardson, *West from Appomattox: The Reconstruction of America after the Civil War* (2007), is a good overview. Republican Party politics from Lincoln to the election of George W. Bush is covered in Lewis L. Gould's *Grand Old Party: A History of the Republicans* (2003). John Hicks's classic *The Populist Revolt* (1931) emphasizes poverty as the driving force behind Populism, while Lawrence Goodwyn portrays Populists as crusaders for radical democratic change in *Democratic Promise: The Populist Movement in America* (1976). Also useful is Robert C. McMath, Jr., *American Populism: A Social History, 1877–1898* (1993) and Charles Postel, *The Populist Vision* (2007). Michael Kazin stresses William Jennings Bryan's religious moorings and liberal instincts in *A Godly Hero: The Life of William Jennings Bryan* (2006). Charles Hoffman, *The Depression of the Nineties: An Economic History* (1970), provides a lucid profile of the crisis. Theda Skocpol's *Protecting Soldiers and Mothers: The Political Origins of Social Policy in the United States* (1994), stresses the nineteenth-century origins of the welfare state and the interplay between the state and nongovernmental political groups.

On the spread of segregation, see C. Vann Woodward's classic *The Strange Career of Jim Crow* (4th ed., 2002).

Woodward focuses on changes in the law, while John Cell, *The Highest Stage of White Supremacy* (1982), points to the role of the city. Contrasting approaches to race relations can be seen in Louis Harlan's two-volume *Booker T. Washington* (1972 and 1983) and David Levering Lewis's *W.E.B. DuBois: Biography of a Race* (1993). James West Davidson uses Ida B. Wells to provide a cultural portrait of the first generation of freed African Americans in *"They Say": Ida B. Wells and the Reconstruction of Race* (2007).

For broad interpretive views of American foreign policy, see Michael Hunt, *Ideology and American Foreign Policy* (1984); John Dobson, *America's Ascent: The United States Becomes a Great Power, 1880–1914* (1978); and Walter LaFeber, *The American Age* (1989). A. G. Hopkins, ed., *Global History: Interactions Between the Universal and the Local* (2006), provides useful cultural perspectives. For regional approaches, see LaFeber's *Inevitable Revolutions* (3rd ed., 1993) on Central America and Hunt's *The Making of a Special Relationship* (1983) on China. On the role of missionaries, see Jane Hunter's *The Gospel of Gentility: American Women Missionaries in Turn-of-the-Century China* (1984). Ivan Musicant, *Empire by Default* (1998) covers the Spanish-American War and its consequences. For the Philippines, see Stanley Karnow's *In Our Image* (1989) and Brian McAlister Linn's thorough study of *The Philippine War* (2000).

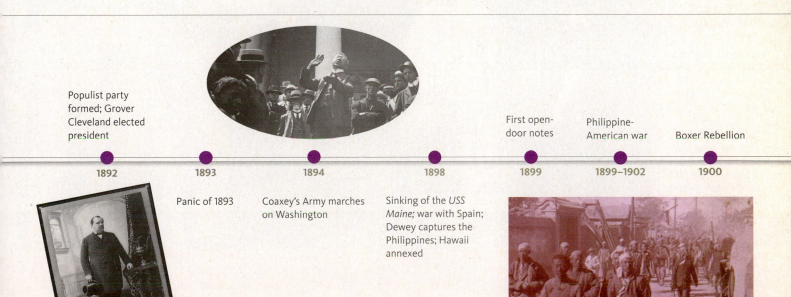

1892 — Populist party formed; Grover Cleveland elected president

1893 — Panic of 1893

1894 — Coaxey's Army marches on Washington

1898 — Sinking of the *USS Maine;* war with Spain; Dewey captures the Philippines; Hawaii annexed

1899 — First open-door notes

1899–1902 — Philippine-American war

1900 — Boxer Rebellion

WOMAN SUFFRAGE HEADQUARTERS.
MEN OF OHIO!
GIVE THE WOMEN A SQUARE DEAL
Vote For Amendment Nº 23 On September 3 – 191

COME IN AND LEARN
WHY WOMEN
OUGHT to Vote.

Women in Cleveland, Ohio, organize to turn out the vote in 1912, borrowing Theodore Roosevelt's demand for a "Square Deal." They lost this particular fight: the Nineteenth Amendment, accomplishing their goal nationally, was not ratified until 1920.

THE Progressive

22

>> **AN AMERICAN STORY**

BURNED ALIVE IN THE CITY

Quitting time, March 25, 1911. The fire started in the lofts as the workers were leaving their sewing machines at the Triangle Shirtwaist Company in New York City. In minutes the top stories of the Asch building were ablaze. Terrified seamstresses groped through the black smoke, only to find exits locked or clogged with bodies. All but one of the few working fire escapes collapsed. >>

Era 1890–1920

When the fire trucks arrived fire-fighters discovered that their ladders could not reach the top stories. "Spectators saw again and again pitiable companionships formed in the instant of death—girls who placed their arms around each other as they leaped," read one news story. Their bodies hit the sidewalk with a sickening thud or were spiked on the iron guard rails. One hundred forty-six people died, most of them young immigrant women.

A few days later a silent funeral procession of 80,000 New Yorkers marched up Fifth Avenue in the rain. At the Metropolitan Opera House union leader Rose Schneiderman told a rally: "This is not the first time that girls have been burned alive in the city." Over the next four years the recommendations of a special state commission produced 56 state laws regulating fire safety, hours, machinery, and homework. They amounted to the most far-reaching labor code in the country.

The Triangle fire shocked the nation and underscored a growing crisis: modern industrial society had created profound strains, widespread misery, and deep class divisions. Corporations grew to unimagined size, bought and sold legislators, dictated the terms of their own profit. Men, women, and children worked around the clock in dangerous factories for barely living wages. In cities across America, tenement-bred disease took innocent lives, criminals threatened people and property, saloons tied the working poor to dishonest political bosses. Even among the middle class, mild but persistent inflation was shrinking their wallets. "It was a world of greed," concluded one worker; "the human being didn't mean anything."

Human beings did mean something to followers of an influential drive for reform sweeping the country. Progressivism had emerged in the mid-1890s and lasted through World War I. The campaign sprang from many impulses, mixing a liberal concern for the poor and working class with conservative efforts to stabilize business and avoid social chaos. Above all, progressives wanted to soften the harsh impact of industrialization, urbanization, and immigration.

Progressivism began in the cities, where those forces converged. It was organized by an angry, idealistic middle class and percolated up from neighborhoods to city halls, state capitals, and, finally, Washington. Though usually pursued through politics, the goals of progressives were broadly social—to create a "good society" where people could live decently, harmoniously, and prosperously, along middle-class guidelines.

Unlike earlier reformers, progressives saw government as a protector, not an oppressor. Only government possessed the resources for the broad-based reforms they sought. Progressivism spawned the modern activist state, with its capacity to regulate the economy and manage society. And because American society had become so interdependent, progressivism became the first nationwide reform campaign. No political party monopolized it; no single group controlled it. It flowered in the presidencies of Republican Theodore Roosevelt and Democrat Woodrow Wilson. In 1912 It even spawned its own party, the Progressive, or "Bull Moose," party. By then progressivism had filtered well beyond politics into every realm of American life. ◀◀

⌃ In 1911 the fiery deaths of 146 people at the Triangle Shirtwaist Company shocked the nation. Fire fighters arrived within minutes, but their ladders could not reach the top stories. Trapped by locked doors, those who failed to escape perished within or leaped to their deaths on the streets below. Following the horrifying episode, New York enacted the most ambitious labor code in the country.

THE ROOTS OF PROGRESSIVE REFORM

Families turned from their homes; an army of unemployed on the roads; hunger, strikes, and bloody violence across the country—the wrenching depression of 1893 forced Americans to take stock of their new industrial order. They found common complaints that cut across region, class, religion, and ethnicity. If streetcar companies raised fares while service deteriorated, if food processors doctored their canned goods with harmful additives, if politicians skimmed money from the public till, everyone suffered.

The result was not a coherent progressive movement but a set of loosely connected reforms: efficient government and honest politics; greater regulation of business and a more orderly economy; social justice for the urban poor and social welfare to protect children, women, workers, and consumers. Some progressives looked to purify society by outlawing alcohol and drugs, stamping out prostitution and slums, and restricting the flood of new immigrants. All tried to make business and government more responsive to the democratic will of the people.

Paternalistic by nature, progressives often imposed their solutions no matter what the poor or oppressed saw as their own best interests. Progressives acted partly out of nostalgia. They wanted to redeem such traditional American values as democracy, individual opportunity, and public service. Yet if their ends were traditional, their means were modern. They used the systems and methods of the new industrial order—the latest techniques of organization, management, and science—to fight its excesses.

Progressive Beliefs >>
Progressives were moderate modernizers. They accepted the American system as sound, in need of only adjustment. Many drew on Darwinian theories of evolution to buttress this gradual approach to change. With its notion of slowly changing species, evolution undermined the acceptance of fixed principles that guided social thought in the Victorian era. Progressives saw an evolving landscape of shifting values. They denied the commonly held doctrine of inborn sinfulness and instead saw people as having a greater potential for good than evil.

Progressives still had to explain the existence of evil and wrongdoing. Most agreed that they were "largely, if not wholly, products of society or environment." People went wrong, wrote one progressive, because of "what happens to them." If what happened to "bad people" could be changed, the human potential for good could be released.

With an eye to results, progressives asked not "Is it true?" but "Does it work?" Philosopher Charles Peirce called this new way of thinking "**pragmatism.**" William James, the Harvard psychologist, became its most famous popularizer. For James, pragmatism meant "looking towards last things, fruits, consequences, facts."

> **pragmatism** philosophical movement that stressed the visible, real-world results of ideas.

The Pragmatic Approach >>
Pragmatism led educators, social scientists, and lawyers to adopt new approaches to reform. John Dewey, the master educator of the progressive era, believed that environment shaped the patterns of human thought. Instead of demanding mindless memorization of abstract and unconnected facts, Dewey tried to "make each one of our schools an embryonic community life." At his School of Pedagogy, founded in 1896, he let students unbolt their desks from the floor, move about, and learn by doing in cooperation with others so that they could train for real life.

Psychologist John B. Watson believed that human behavior could be shaped at will. Give him control of an infant's world from birth, Watson boasted, "and I'll guarantee to take any one at random and train him to become any specialist I might select, doctor, lawyer, artist, merchant, chief, and yes, even beggarman and thief." "Behaviorism" swept the social sciences and, later, advertising, where Watson himself eventually landed.

> **behaviorism** school of psychology, founded by John Watson, that measures human behavior, believes it can be shaped, and discounts emotion as subjective.

Lawyers and legal theorists applied their own blend of pragmatism and behaviorism. Justice Oliver Wendell Holmes, Jr., appointed to the Supreme Court in 1902, rejected the idea that the traditions of law were constant and universal. Law was a living organism to be interpreted according to experience and the needs of a changing society.

Opinion

Progressives claimed that their reforms protected "good people" from "bad interests." Did they?

sociological jurisprudence legal theory that emphasizes the importance not merely of precedent but of contemporary social context in interpreting the law.

This environmental view of the law, known as "**sociological jurisprudence**," found a skilled practitioner in Louis Brandeis. Shaken by the brutal suppression of the Homestead steel strike of 1892, Brandeis quit his corporate practice and proclaimed himself the "people's lawyer." The law must "guide by the light of reason," he wrote, which meant bringing everyday life to bear in any court case. When laundry owner Curt Muller challenged an Oregon law limiting his laundresses to a 10-hour workday, Brandeis defended the statute before the Supreme Court in 1908. His famous brief contained 102 pages describing the damaging effects of long hours on working women and only 15 pages of legal precedents. In *Muller v. Oregon,* the Supreme Court upheld Oregon's right to limit the working hours of laborers and thus legitimized the "Brandeis Brief."

The Progressive Method

>> Seeing the nation torn by conflict, progressives tried to restore a sense of community through the ideal of a single public interest. Christian ethics were their guide, applied after using the latest scientific methods to gather and analyze data about a social problem. The modern corporation furnished an appealing model for organization. Like corporate executives, progressives relied on careful management, coordinated systems, and specialized bureaucracies to carry out reforms.

Between 1902 and 1912 a new breed of journalists provided the necessary evidence and fired public indignation. They investigated wrongdoers, named them in print, and described their misdeeds in vivid detail. Most exposés began as articles in mass-circulation magazines such as *McClure's.* The magazine stirred controversy (and boosted circulation) when publisher Samuel McClure sent reporter Lincoln Steffens to uncover the crooked ties between business and politics. *McClure's* published "Tweed Days in St. Louis," the first of a series of investigative articles, in October 1902. Soon a full-blown literature of exposure was covering every ill from unsafe food to child labor.

A disgusted Theodore Roosevelt thought the new reporters had gone too far and called them "muckrakers," after the man who raked up filth in the seventeenth-century classic *Pilgrim's Progress.* But by documenting dishonesty and blight, muckrakers not only aroused people but also educated them. No broad reform movement of American institutions would have taken place without them.

To move beyond exposure to solutions, progressives stressed volunteerism and collective action. They drew on the organizational impulse that seemed everywhere to be bringing people together in new interest groups. Between 1890 and 1920 nearly 400 organizations were founded, many to combat the ills of industrial society. Some, like the National Consumers' League, grew out of efforts to promote general causes—in this case protecting consumers and workers from exploitation. Others, such as the National Tuberculosis Association, aimed at a specific problem.

When voluntary action failed, progressives looked to government to protect the public welfare. They mistrusted legislators, who might be controlled by corporate interests or political machines and were in any case too numerous to monitor. So they strengthened the executive branch by increasing the power of individual mayors, governors, and presidents. Then they watched those executives carefully.

Progressives also drew on the expertise of the newly professionalized middle class. Doctors, engineers, psychiatrists, and city planners mounted campaigns to stamp out venereal disease and dysentery, to reform prisons and asylums, and to beautify cities. At local, state, and federal levels, new agencies and commissions staffed by experts began to investigate and regulate lobbyists, insurance and railroad companies, public health, even government itself.

 REVIEW

What ills did progressives see in society, what solutions did they propose, and what ideas shaped those solutions?

THE SEARCH FOR THE GOOD SOCIETY

If progressivism ended in politics, it began with social reform: the need to reach out, to do something to bring the "good society" a step closer. Ellen Richards had just such ends in mind in 1890 when she opened the New England Kitchen in downtown Boston. Richards, a chemist and home economist, designed the kitchen to sell cheap, wholesome food to the working poor. For a few pennies, customers could choose from a nutritious menu, every dish of which had been tested in Richards's laboratory at the Massachusetts Institute of Technology.

The New England Kitchen promoted social as well as nutritional reform. Women freed from the drudgery of cooking could seek gainful employment. And as a "household experiment station" and center for dietary information, the kitchen tried to educate the poor and Americanize immigrants by showing them how the middle class prepared meals.

In the end the New England Kitchen served more as an inexpensive eatery for middle-class working women and students than as a resource for the poor or an agency of Americanization. Still, Ellen Richards's experiment reflected a pattern typical of progressive social reform: the mix of professionalism with uplift; socially conscious women entering the public arena; the hope of creating a better world along middle-class lines.

Poverty in a New Light »

During the 1890s crime reporter and photographer Jacob Riis introduced middle-class audiences to urban poverty. Writing in vivid detail in *How the Other Half Lives* (1890), he brought readers into the teeming tenement. Accompanying his text were shocking photos of poverty-stricken Americans—Riis's "other half." He used them to tell a moralistic story, as the earlier English novelist Charles Dickens had used his melodramatic tales to attack the abuses of industrialism. People began to see poverty in a new, more sympathetic light—the fault less of the individual than of social conditions.

A haunting naturalism in fiction and painting followed Riis's gritty photographic essays. In *McTeague* (1899) and *Sister Carrie* (1900), novelists Frank Norris and Theodore Dreiser spun dark tales of city dwellers struggling to keep body and soul intact. The "Ashcan school" painted urban life in all its grimy realism. Photographer Alfred Stieglitz and painters John Sloan and George Bellows chose slums, tenements, and dirty streets as subjects. Poverty began to look less ominous and more heartrending.

A new profession—social work—proceeded from this new view of poverty. Social work developed out of the old settlement house movement (page 409). Like the physicians from whom they drew inspiration, social workers studied hard data to diagnose the problems of their "clients" and worked with them to solve their problems. A social worker's "differential casework" attempted to treat individuals case by case, each according to the way environment shaped the client.

⌃ Jacob Riis, the Danish-born reporter and photographer, stalked the streets of New York, meticulously recording the squalor in which many slum-dwellers lived. Here one photograph exposes a cramped tenement room "not thirteen feet either way," housing "twelve men and women" for a night's lodging at "5 cents a spot." The first edition of *How the Other Half Lives* used only engravings made from photographs; later editions added the detail and poignancy of the actual photos.

Expanding the "Woman's Sphere" »

Progressive social reform attracted a great many women seeking what Jane Addams called "the larger life" of public affairs. In the late nineteenth century women found that protecting their traditional sphere of home and family forced them to move beyond it. Bringing up children, making meals, keeping house, and caring for the sick now involved community decisions about schools, the food supply, public health, and countless other matters.

Many middle- and upper-middle-class women received their first taste of public life from women's organizations, including mothers' clubs, temperance societies, and church groups. By the turn of the century some 500 women's clubs boasted over 160,000 members. Through the General Federation of Women's Clubs, they funded libraries and hospitals and supported schools, settlement houses, compulsory education, and child labor laws. Eventually they reached outside the home and family to endorse such controversial causes as woman suffrage and unionization. To that list the National Association of Colored Women added the special concerns of African Americans, none more urgent than the fight against lynching.

The dawn of the century saw the rise of a new generation of women. Longer lived, better educated, and less often married than their mothers, they were also willing to pursue professional careers for fulfillment. Usually they turned to professions that involved the traditional female role of nurturer—nursing, library work, teaching, and settlement house work. Custom and prejudice still restricted these new women. The faculty at the Massachusetts Institute of Technology, for example, refused to allow Ellen Richards to pursue a doctorate. Instead they hired her to run the gender-segregated "Woman's Laboratory" for training public school teachers. At the turn of the century only about 1,500 female lawyers practiced in the United States, and in 1910 women made up barely 6 percent of licensed physicians.

Despite the often bitter opposition of families, some feminists tried to destroy the boundaries of the woman's sphere. In *Women and Economics* (1898) Charlotte Perkins Gilman condemned the conventions of womanhood—femininity, marriage, maternity, domesticity—as enslaving

⌃ Middle-class women found a productive vehicle for social and political action in the General Federated Women's Clubs. The clubs also gave many women the opportunity to organize and lead and served as a launch pad for female reformers such as Jane Addams, Julia Ward Howe, and Julia Lathrop. "When I want anything in Boston remedied," said reformer Edward Everett Hale, "I go down to the New England Women's Club." Here a group of women proudly displays the banner of the Washington, DC, branch.

more middle-class urban women thus became "social housekeepers." From their own homes they turned to the homes of their neighbors and from there to all of society.

Social Welfare >>

In the "bigger family of the city," as one woman reformer called it, settlement house workers found that they alone could not care for the welfare of the poor. If industrial America, with its sooty factories and overcrowded slums, was to be transformed into the good society, individual acts of charity would have to be supplemented by government. Laws had to be passed and agencies created to promote social welfare, including improved housing, workplaces, parks, and playgrounds, the abolition of child labor, and the enactment of eight-hour-day laws for working women.

By 1910 the more than 400 settlement houses across the nation had organized into a loose affiliation ready to help fashion government policy. With greater experience than men in the field, women led the way. Julia Lathrop, a Vassar College graduate, spent 20 years at Jane Addams's Hull House before becoming the first head of the new federal Children's Bureau in 1912. By then two-thirds of the states had adopted some child labor legislation, although loopholes exempted countless youngsters from coverage. Under Lathrop's leadership, Congress passed the Keating-Owen Act (1916), forbidding goods manufactured by children to cross state lines.[1]

Florence Kelley, who had also worked at Hull House, spearheaded a similar campaign in Illinois to protect women workers by limiting their workday to eight hours. As general secretary of the National Consumers' League, she also organized boycotts of companies that treated employees inhumanely. Eventually most states enacted laws restricting the number of hours women could work.

[1] The Supreme Court struck down the law in 1918 as an improper regulation of local labor; nonetheless, it focused greater attention on the abuses of child labor.

and obsolete. She argued for a radically restructured society with large apartment houses, communal arrangements for child rearing and housekeeping, and cooperative kitchens to free women from economic dependence on men.

Margaret Sanger sought to free women from chronic pregnancy. Sanger, a visiting nurse on the Lower East Side of New York, had seen too many poor women overburdened with children, pregnant year after year and sometimes dying through self-induced abortions. The consequences were crippling. "Women cannot be on equal footing with men until they have complete control over their reproductive functions," she argued. She became a crusader for what she called "birth control." By distributing information on contraception, she hoped to free women from unwanted pregnancies.

Single or married, militant or moderate, professional or lay, white or black, more and

WITNESS

Jane Addams Finds a Child Sick of Candy

"Our very first Christmas at Hull-House, when we as yet knew nothing of child labor, a number of little girls refused the candy which was offered them as part of the Christmas good cheer, saying simply that they 'worked in a candy factory and could not bear the sight of it.' We discovered that for six weeks they had worked from seven in the morning until nine at night, and they were exhausted as well as satiated."

— Jane Addams, *Twenty Years at Hull-House*, 1910

Woman Suffrage >>

Ever since the conference for women's rights held at Seneca Falls in 1848, women reformers had pressed for the right to vote on the grounds of simple justice and equal opportunity. They adopted the slogan "woman suffrage" to emphasize the solidarity of women. Progressives embraced woman suffrage by stressing what they saw as the practical results of protecting the home and increasing the voting power of native-born whites. The "purer sensibilities" of women—an ideal held by Victorians and progressives alike—also would help cleanse the political process of selfishness and corruption.

The suffrage movement benefited, too, from new leadership. In 1900 Carrie Chapman Catt became president of the National American Woman Suffrage Association, founded by Susan B. Anthony in 1890. Politically astute and a skilled organizer, Catt mapped a grassroots strategy of education and persuasion from state to state. She called it "the winning plan." As the map (page 454) shows, victories came first in the West, where women and men had already forged a more equal partnership to overcome the hardships of frontier life. By 1914, 10 western states (and Kansas) had granted women the vote in state elections, as Illinois had in presidential elections.

The slow pace of progress drove some suffragists to militancy. The shift in tactics had its origins abroad. In England the campaign for woman suffrage had peaked after 1900, when Emmeline Pankhurst and her daughters Christabel and Sylvia turned to violence to make their point that women should be given the right to vote. They and their followers chained themselves to the visitors'

gallery in the House of Commons and slashed paintings in museums. They smashed the windows of department stores, broke up political meetings, even burned the houses of members of Parliament.

British authorities arrested the suffragists and threw them in jail, Emmeline Pankhurst included. When the women went on hunger strikes in prison, wardens tied them down, held their mouths open with wooden clamps, and fed them by force through tubes placed down their throats and noses. Rather than permit the protesters to die as martyrs, Parliament passed the Cat and Mouse Act, a statute of doubtful legality that allowed officials to release starving prisoners, then rearrest them once they returned to health.

Among the British suffragists was a small American with large, determined eyes. In 1907, barely out of her teens, Alice Paul had gone to England to join the suffrage crusade. When asked why she had enlisted, she recalled her Quaker upbringing. "One of their principles . . . is equality of the sexes," she explained. Paul marched arm in arm with British suffragists through the streets of London and more than once was imprisoned and refused to eat.

Three years later, in 1913, Paul organized 5,000 women to parade in protest at President Woodrow Wilson's inauguration. Wilson himself was skeptical of women voting and favored a state-by-state approach to the issue. Half a million people watched as a near-riot ensued. Paul and other suffragists were hauled to jail, stripped naked, and thrown into cells with prostitutes.

In 1914 Paul broke with the more moderate National American Woman Suffrage Association and formed the Congressional Union, dedicated to enacting national woman suffrage through a constitutional amendment. She soon allied her organization with western women voters in the militant National Woman's party in 1917. On October 20, 1917, Paul was arrested for protesting in favor of a constitutional amendment at the gates of the White House. She received a seven-month sentence. Guards dragged her off to a cell block in the Washington jail, where she and others refused to eat. Prison officials declared her insane, but a public outcry over her treatment soon led to her release.

Such repression only widened public support for woman suffrage in the United States and elsewhere. So did the contributions of

THE AWAKENING

⌃ "The Awakening," a 1915 cartoon, offers a graphic and emotion-laden map of woman suffrage. Here, a torch-bearing woman in classical dress carries the franchise to the eastern states, where desperate women eagerly reach out.

women to the First World War at home and abroad (see Chapter 23). In the wake of the war, Great Britain granted women (over age 30) the right to vote in 1918, Germany and Austria in 1919, and the United States in 1920 through the Nineteenth Amendment. Overnight the number of eligible voters in the country doubled.

 REVIEW

Why were women so deeply involved in the "Search for the Good Society," and what were some of their chief accomplishments?

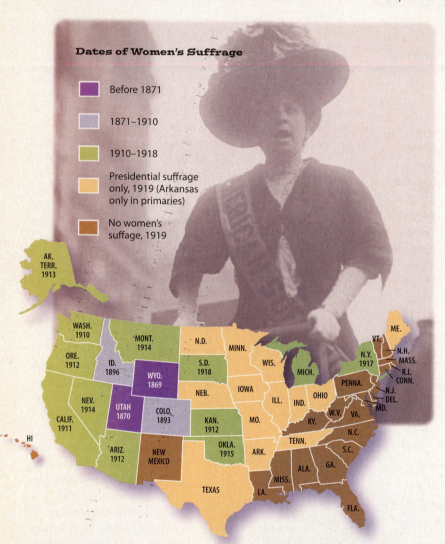

Dates of Women's Suffrage

- ■ Before 1871
- ■ 1871–1910
- ■ 1910–1918
- ■ Presidential suffrage only, 1919 (Arkansas only in primaries)
- ■ No women's suffrage, 1919

AK. TERR. 1913

WASH. 1910
ORE. 1912
ID. 1896
MONT. 1914
N.D.
MINN.
ME.
VT.
N.H.
MASS.
N.Y. 1917
R.I.
CONN.
NEV. 1914
CALIF. 1911
UTAH 1870
WYO. 1869
COLO. 1893
S.D. 1918
WIS.
MICH.
PENNA.
N.J.
DEL.
MD.
NEB.
IOWA
ILL.
IND.
OHIO
W.V.
VA.
KY.
HI
ARIZ. 1912
NEW MEXICO
KAN. 1912
MO.
OKLA. 1915
ARK.
TENN.
N.C.
S.C.
GA.
MISS.
ALA.
TEXAS
LA.
FLA.

WOMEN'S SUFFRAGE

Western states were the first to grant women the right to vote. Sparsely populated and more egalitarian than the rest of the nation, the West was used to women participating fully in settlement and work. Other sections of the country, notably the Midwest, granted women partial suffrage, which included voting for school boards and taxes. Suffragists encountered the most intractable resistance in the South, where rigid codes of social conduct elevated women symbolically but shackled them practically.

CONTROLLING THE MASSES

"Observe immigrants," wrote one American in 1912. "You are struck by the fact that from ten to twenty percent are hirsute, low-browed, big-faced persons of obviously low mentality." The writer was neither an uneducated fanatic nor a stern opponent of change. He was Professor Edward A. Ross, a progressive who prided himself on his scientific study of sociology.

Faced with the chaos of urban life, more than a few progressives feared they were losing control of their country. Saloons and dance halls lured youngsters and impoverished laborers; prostitutes walked the streets; vulgar amusements pandered to the uneducated. And worse—strange Old World cultures clashed with "all-American" customs, and races jostled uneasily. The city challenged middle-class reformers to convert this riot of diversity into a more uniform society. To maintain control they sometimes moved beyond education and regulation and sought restrictive laws to control the new masses.

Stemming the Immigrant Tide >>
A rising tide of new immigrants with darker complexions and non-Protestant religions from southern and eastern Europe especially chilled native-born Americans, including progressive reformers anxious over the changing ethnic make-up of the country. In northern cities progressives often succeeded in reducing the voting power of these new immigrants by increasing residency requirements.

The now-discredited science of "eugenics" lent respectability to the idea that the newcomers were biologically inferior. Eugenicists believed that heredity determined everything and advocated selective breeding for human improvement. By 1914 magazine articles discussed eugenics more than slums, tenements, and living standards combined. In *The Passing of the Great Race* (1916), amateur zoologist Madison Grant helped to popularize the notion that the "lesser breeds" threatened to "mongrelize" America. So powerful was the pull of eugenics that it captured the support of some progressives, including birth control advocate Margaret Sanger.

Most progressives believed in the shaping power of environment and so favored either assimilating immigrants into American society or restricting their entry into the country. Jane Addams, for one, stressed the "gifts" immigrants brought: folk rituals, dances, music, and handicrafts. With characteristic paternalism, she and other reformers hoped to "Americanize" the foreign-born (the term had been newly coined) by teaching them middle-class ways. Education was one key. Progressive educator Peter Roberts, for example, developed a lesson plan for the Young Men's Christian Association that taught immigrants how to dress, tip, buy groceries, and vote.

Less tolerant citizens (often native-born and white) sought to restrict immigration as a way of reasserting control and achieving social harmony. Usually not progressives themselves, they employed progressive methods of organization, investigation, education, and legislation. Active since the 1890s, the Immigration Restriction League pressed Congress in 1907 to require a literacy test for admission into the United States. Presidents Taft and Wilson vetoed it, but Congress overrode Wilson's second veto in 1917 as war fever raised fears of foreigners to a new peak.

The Curse of Demon Rum >> Tied closely to

concern over immigrants, many of whom came from drinking cultures, was an attack on saloons. Part of a broader crusade to clean up cities, the antisaloon campaign drew strength from the century-old drive to lessen the consumption of alcohol. Women made up a disproportionate number of alcohol reformers. In some ways the temperance movement reflected their growing campaign to storm male domains, in this case the saloon, and to contain male violence, particularly the wife and child abuse associated with drinking.

Reformers considered a national ban on drinking unrealistic and intrusive. Instead they concentrated on prohibiting the sale of alcohol at local and state levels. Led by the Anti-Saloon League (1893), a massive publicity campaign bombarded citizens with pamphlets and advertisements. Doctors cited scientific evidence linking alcohol to cirrhosis, heart disease, and insanity. Social workers connected drink to the deterioration of the family; employers, to accidents on the job

and lost efficiency; and political reformers to corrupt political machines that were often housed in saloons.

By 1917 three out of four Americans lived in dry counties. Nearly two-thirds of the states had adopted laws outlawing the manufacture and sale of alcohol. Not all progressives were prohibitionists, but by curtailing the liquor business those who were breathed a sigh of relief at having taken some of the profit out of human pain and corruption.

Prostitution >> No urban vice worried reformers

more than prostitution. In their eyes it was a "social evil" that threatened young city women. The Chicago Vice Commission of 1910 estimated that 5,000 full-time and 10,000 occasional prostitutes plied their trade in the city. Other cities, small and large, reported similar findings.

An unlikely group of reformers united to fight the vice: feminists who wanted husbands to be as chaste as their wives, social hygienists worried about the spread of venereal disease, immigration restrictionists who regarded the growth of prostitution as yet another sign of corrupt newcomers. Progressives condemned prostitution but saw the problem in economic and environmental terms. "Poverty causes prostitution," concluded the Illinois Vice Commission in 1916.

Some reformers saw more active agents at work. Rumors spread of a vast and profitable "white slave trade." Men armed with hypodermic needles were said to be drugging and kidnapping young women. Although the average female rider of the streetcar was hardly in danger of villainous abduction, every city had locked pens where women were held captive and forced into prostitution. By conservative estimates they constituted some 10 percent of all prostitutes.

As real abuses blended with sensationalism, Congress passed the Mann Act (1910), prohibiting the interstate transport of women for immoral purposes. By 1918 reformers succeeded in banning previously tolerated "red-light" districts in most cities.

red-light district area in cities reserved for prostitutes. The term, first employed in the United States, resulted from the use of red lights to show that prostitutes were open for business.

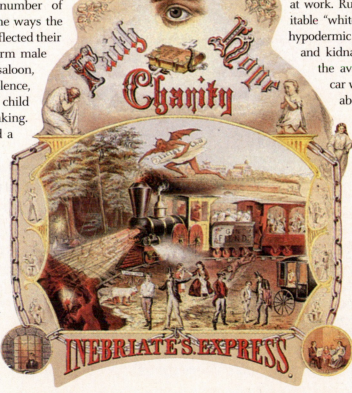

⌃ The "Inebriate's Express," loaded with drunken riders, is heading straight for hell. This detail from a chromolithograph, published around 1900, was typical of Victorian-era responses to the problems posed by alcohol. To the all-seeing eye of the omnipotent God, faith, hope, charity, and the Bible are sufficient to cure the problems of drinking.

As with the liquor trade, progressives went after those who made money from misery.

Historian's TOOLBOX

Mementos of Murder

Jesse Washington
Could this be "Joe"?
Men face the camera without making any effort to mask their faces
Young boys present
Katy Electric Studio Temple Texas H. Lippe Prop.
No stamp or postmark indicating that the card was sent. Did "Joe" keep it?
"This is the Barbecue we had last night[.] My picture is to the left with a cross over it[.] your son, Joe."
POST CARD
PLACE STAMP HERE
KATY ELECTRIC STUDIO
TEMPLE TEXAS.
H. LIPPE PROP.
This is The Barbecue we had last night my picture is to the left with a cross over it your son, Joe.

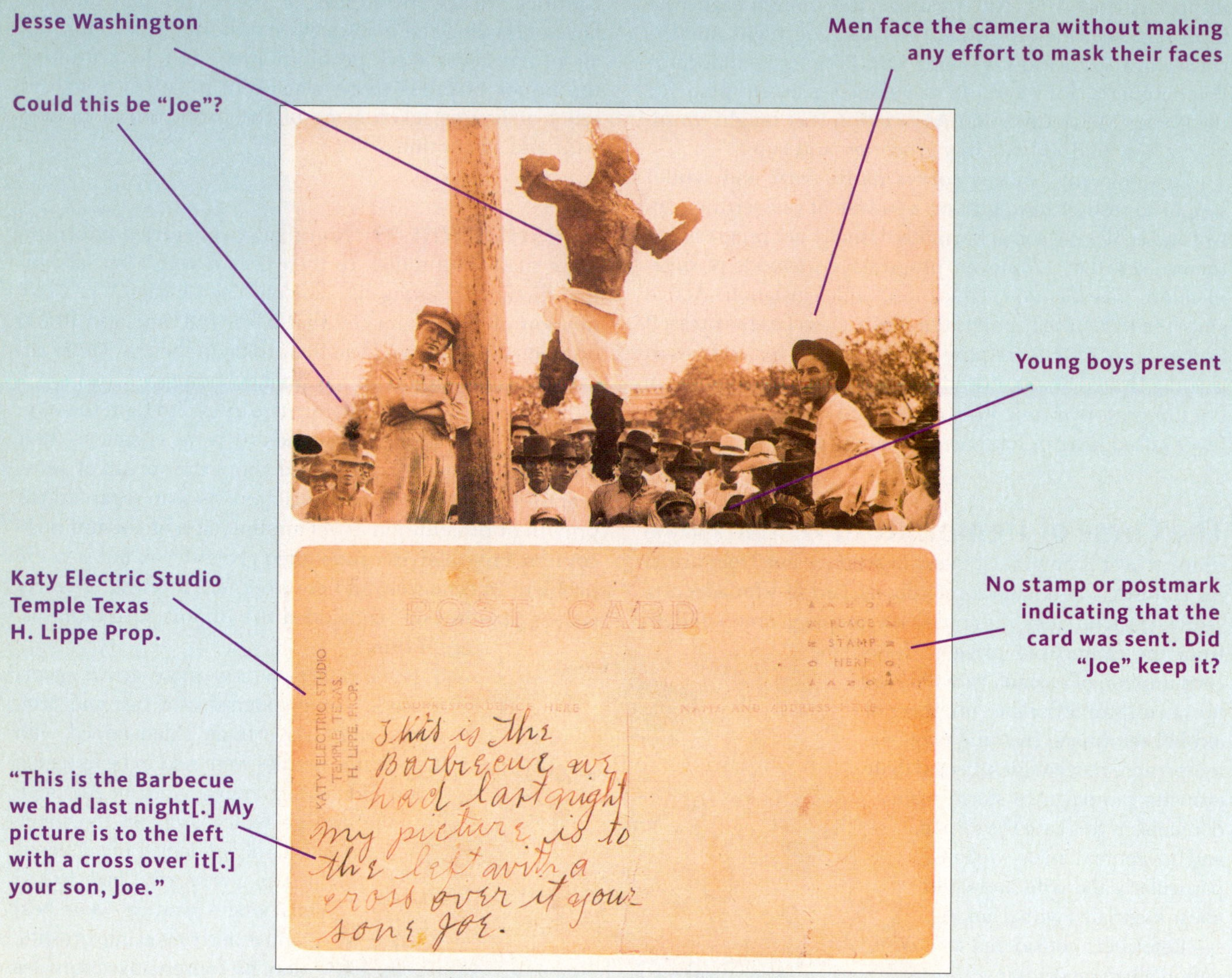

Not all historians need be professionals. Even amateurs can help us see the past in a new light. James Allen described himself as a "picker," rummaging through other people's junk for things he might sell. Postcards hadn't much interested him until he came on one that bore the photograph of a lynching. "It wasn't the corpse that bewildered me but the canine-thin faces of pack," he recalled. Collected and later published by Allen, such postcards memorializing lynchings were one segment of a larger industry that flourished in the late nineteenth and early twentieth centuries. For a penny in postage the cards might be of hotels or city streets or even just photos of individuals taken by photographers, which could be sent to friends and relatives as souvenirs. But the cards Allen came across over the years were of a different order: grisly mementos of a ritualized murder. The one above—of the lynching and burning of an African American named Jesse Washington in 1916—appears not to have been mailed.

THINKING CRITICALLY

Why might people have their photographs taken for postcards at a lynching and then send the cards to parents and other relatives? What does that tell us about the racial environment in which such events occurred?

Source: James Allen, *Without Sanctuary: Lynching Photography in America* (2000).

"For Whites Only" >> Most progressives paid little attention to the suffering of African Americans. The 1890s had been a low point for black citizens, most of whom still lived in the rural South. Across the region, the lynching of African Americans increased, as did restrictions on black voting and the use of segregated facilities. Signs decreeing "For Whites Only" appeared on drinking fountains and rest rooms and in other public places.

A few progressives condemned racial discrimination, but most ignored it—or used it to political advantage. Throughout the South, white progressives and old-guard politicians used the rhetoric of reform to support white supremacy. Such "reformers" won office by promising to disfranchise African Americans to break the power of corrupt political machines that marshaled the black vote in the South, much as northern machines did with immigrant voters.

In the face of such discrimination African Americans fought back. After the turn of the century some black critics rejected the accommodation of Booker T. Washington's "Atlanta Compromise." Washington's cautious approach counseled African Americans to accept segregation and work their way up the economic ladder by learning a vocational trade such as carpentry or mechanics (page 435). W. E. B. Du Bois, a professor at Atlanta University, leveled the most stinging attack in *The Souls of Black Folk* (1903). He saw no benefit for African Americans in sacrificing intellectual growth for narrow vocational training. Nor was he willing to abide the humiliating stigma that came from the discriminatory caste system of the South. A better future would come only if black citizens struggled politically to achieve suffrage and equal rights.

Instead of exhorting African Americans to pull themselves up slowly from the bottom, Du Bois called on the "talented tenth," a cultured black vanguard, to blaze a trail of protest against segregation, disfranchisement, and discrimination. In 1905 he founded the Niagara movement for political and economic equality. Four years later, in 1909, a coalition of blacks and white reformers transformed the Niagara movement into the National Association for the Advancement of Colored People (NAACP). As with other progressive organizations, its membership was largely limited to the middle class. It worked to extend the principles of tolerance and equal opportunity in a color-blind fashion by mounting legal challenges to segregation and bigotry and pressing for protective legislation. By 1914 the NAACP had some 6,000 members in 50 branches across the country. Accommodation was giving way to new combative organizations and new forms of protest.

 REVIEW

Which "masses" did progressives want to control, why did they want to control them, and what instruments did they employ?

THE POLITICS OF MUNICIPAL AND STATE REFORM

Reform the system. In the end, so many urban problems came back to overhauling government. Jane Addams learned as much outside the doors of her beloved Hull House in Chicago. For months during the early 1890s, garbage had piled up in the streets. The filth and stench drove Addams and her fellow workers to city hall in protest—700 times in one summer—but to no avail. In Chicago, as elsewhere, a corrupt band of city bosses made garbage collection a plum to be awarded to the company that paid the most for it.

In desperation Addams submitted a bid for garbage removal in the ward. When it was thrown out on a technicality, she won an appointment as garbage inspector. For almost a year she dogged collection carts, but boss politics kept things dirty. So Addams ran candidates in 1896 and 1898 against the local ward boss. They lost, but Addams kept up the fight for honest government and social reform—at city hall, in the Illinois legislature, and finally in Washington. Politics turned out to be the only way to clean things up.

The Reformation of the Cities >> In the smokestack cities of the Midwest, where the frustrations of industrial and agricultural America fed each other, the urban battleground furnished the middle class with the first test of political reform. A series of colorful and independent mayors demonstrated that cities could be run cleanly and humanely without changing the structure of government. Other cities across the country experimented with new forms of governing.

In Detroit shoe magnate Hazen Pingree turned the mayor's office into an agency of reform when elected in 1889. By the end of his fourth term, Detroit had new parks and public baths, fairer taxes, ownership of the local light plant, and a work-relief program for victims of the depression of 1893. In 1901 Cleveland mayor Tom Johnson launched a similar reform campaign. Before he was through, municipal franchises had been limited to a fraction of their previous 99-year terms, and the city ran the utility company. By 1915 nearly two out of every three cities had copied some form of this "gas and water socialism" to control the runaway prices of utility companies.

Tragedy sometimes dramatized the need to alter the very structure of government. On a hot September night in 1900 a tidal wave from the Gulf of Mexico smashed the port city of Galveston, Texas. The city sank into confusion. Business leaders stepped in with a new charter that replaced the mayor and city council with a powerful commission. Each of five commissioners controlled a municipal department, and together they ran the city. Nearly 400 cities had adopted the plan by 1920. Expert commissioners enhanced efficiency and helped to check party rule in municipal government.

In still other cities elected officials appointed an outside expert or "city manager" to run things, the first in Staunton, Virginia, in 1908. Within a decade 45 cities had them. At lower levels experts took charge of services: engineers oversaw utilities; accountants, finances; doctors and nurses, public health; specially trained firefighters and police, the safety of citizens.

Progressivism in the States >> "Whenever we try to do anything, we run up against the charter," complained one reform-minded mayor. Charters granted by state governments defined the powers of cities. The rural interests that generally dominated state legislatures rarely gave cities adequate authority to levy taxes, set voting requirements, draw up budgets, or legislate reforms. State legislatures, too, found themselves under the influence of business interests, party machines, and county courthouse rings. Reformers therefore tried to place their candidates where they could do some good: in the governors' mansions.

State progressivism, like urban reform, enjoyed its earliest success in the Midwest, under the leadership of Robert La Follette of Wisconsin. La Follette first won election to Congress in 1885 by toeing the Republican line of high tariffs and the gold standard. When a Republican boss offered him a bribe in a railroad case, La Follette pledged to break "the power of this corrupt influence." In 1900 he won the governorship of Wisconsin as an uncommonly independent Republican.

Over the next six years "Battle Bob" La Follette made Wisconsin, in the words of Theodore Roosevelt, "the laboratory of democracy." La Follette's "**Wisconsin idea**" produced the most comprehensive set of state reforms in American history. There were new laws regulating railroads, controlling corruption, and expanding the civil service. His direct primary weakened the hold of party bosses by transferring nominations from the party to the voters. La Follette's Wisconsin created the first state income tax, the first state commission to oversee factory safety and sanitation, and the first Legislative Reference Bureau—at the University of Wisconsin. University-trained experts poured into state government.

Wisconsin idea series of progressive reforms at the state level promoted by Robert LaFollette during his governorship of Wisconsin (1901–1906). They included primary elections, corporate property taxes, regulation of railroads and public utilities, and supervision of public resources in the public interest.

> ## La Follette's 'Wisconsin idea' produced the most comprehensive set of state reforms in American history.

Other states copied the Wisconsin idea or hatched their own. All but three had direct primary laws by 1916. To cut the power of party organizations and make office holders directly responsible to the public, progressives worked for three additional reforms: initiative (voter introduction of legislation), referendum (voter enactment or repeal of laws), and recall (voter-initiated removal of elected officials). In 1913 the Seventeenth Amendment to the Constitution permitted the direct election of senators. Previously they had been chosen by state legislatures, where political machines and corporate lobbyists controlled the selections.

Almost every state established regulatory commissions with the power to hold public hearings, examine company books, and question officials. Some could set maximum prices and rates. Yet it was not always easy to define, let alone serve, the "public good." All too often commissioners found themselves refereeing battles within industries rather than between what progressives called "the bad interests" and "the good people." Regulators also had to rely on the advice of experts drawn from the business community itself. Many commissions thus became captured by the industries they regulated.

Social welfare received special attention from the states. The lack of workers' compensation for injury, illness, or death on the job had long drawn fire from reformers and labor leaders. American courts still operated on the common-law assumption that employees accepted the risks of work. Workers or their families could collect damages only if they proved employer negligence. Most accident victims received nothing. In 1902 Maryland finally adopted the first workers' compensation act. By 1916 most states required insurance for factory accidents, and over half had employer liability laws. Thirteen states also provided pensions for widows with dependent children.

Often such working-class reforms found advocates among women's associations, especially those concerned with mothers, children, and working women. The Federation of Women's Clubs opened a crusade for mothers' pensions (a forerunner of Aid to Mothers with Dependent Children). When in 1912 the National Consumers' League and other women's groups succeeded in establishing the Children's Bureau, it was the first federal welfare agency and the only female-run national bureau in the world. At a time when women lacked the vote, they nonetheless sowed the seeds of the welfare state.

 REVIEW

What reforms did cities and states enact, and how did those reforms address the problems they faced?

PROGRESSIVISM GOES TO WASHINGTON

On September 6, 1901, at the Pan-American Exposition in Buffalo, New York, Leon Czolgosz stood nervously in line. He was waiting among well-wishers to meet President William McKinley. Unemployed and bent on murder, Czolgosz shuffled toward McKinley. As the president reached out, Czolgosz fired two bullets into his chest. McKinley slumped into a chair. Eight days later the president was dead. The mantle of power passed to Theodore Roosevelt. At 42 he was the youngest president ever to hold the office.

Roosevelt's succession was a political accident. Party leaders had seen the weak office of vice president as a way of removing him from power, but the tragedy in Buffalo foiled their plans. Surely progressivism would have come to Washington without him, and while there, he was never its most daring advocate. In many ways he was quite conservative. He saw reform as a way to avoid more radical change. Yet without Theodore Roosevelt, progressivism would have had neither the broad popular appeal nor the buoyancy he gave it.

TR ›› TR, as so many Americans called him, was the scion of seven generations of wealthy, aristocratic New Yorkers. A sickly boy, he built his body through rigorous exercise, sharpened his mind through constant study, and pursued a life so strenuous that few could keep up. He learned to ride and shoot, roped cattle in the Dakota Badlands, mastered judo, and later in life climbed the Matterhorn, hunted African game, and explored the Amazon.

In 1880, driven by an urge to lead and serve, Roosevelt won election to the New York State Assembly. In rapid succession he became a civil service commissioner in Washington, New York City police commissioner, assistant secretary of the navy, and the Rough Rider hero of the Spanish-American War. At the age of 40 he won election as reform governor of New York and two years later as vice president.

As president Roosevelt brought to the Executive Mansion (he renamed it the "White House") a passion for order, a commitment to the public, and a sense of presidential possibilities. Most presidents believed that the Constitution set limits on their power. Roosevelt thought that the president could do anything not expressly forbidden in the document. Recognizing the value of publicity, he gave reporters the first press room in the White House and a chief executive worthy of near-constant coverage. He was the first president to ride in an automobile, fly in an airplane, and dive in a submarine—and everyone knew it.

To dramatize racial injustice Roosevelt invited black educator Booker T. Washington to lunch at the White House in 1901. White southern journalists called such race mingling treason, but for Roosevelt the gesture served both principle and politics. His lunch with Washington was part of a "black and tan" strategy to build a biracial coalition among southern Republicans. He denounced lynching and appointed black southerners to important federal offices in Mississippi and South Carolina.

Sensing the limits of political feasibility, Roosevelt went no further. Perhaps his own racial narrowness stopped him, too. In 1906, when Atlanta exploded in a race riot that left 12 people dead, he said nothing. Later that year he discharged "without honor" three entire companies of African American troops because some of the soldiers were unjustly charged with having "shot up" Brownsville, Texas. All lost their pensions, including six winners of the Medal of Honor. The act stained Roosevelt's record. Congress acknowledged the wrong in 1972 by granting the soldiers honorable discharges.

‹‹ Bullnecked and barrel-chested, Theodore Roosevelt was "pure act," said one admirer. Critics, less enthused with his perpetual motion, charged him with having the attention span of a golden retriever.

⚐ Beef Industry of the 1900s, Chicago

A Square Deal >>

Roosevelt could not long follow the cautious course McKinley had charted. He had more energetic plans in mind for the country. He accepted growth—whether of business, labor, or agriculture—as natural. In his pluralistic system, big labor would counterbalance big capital, big farm organizations would offset big food processors, and so on. Standing astride them all, mediating when needed, was a big government that could ensure fairness. Later, as he campaigned for a second term in 1904, Roosevelt named his program the "Square Deal."

In a startling display of presidential initiative, Roosevelt in 1902 intervened in a strike that idled 140,000 miners and paralyzed the anthracite (hard) coal industry. As winter approached, public resentment with the operators mounted when they refused even to recognize the miners' union, let alone negotiate. Roosevelt summoned both sides to the White House. John A. Mitchell, the young president of the United Mine Workers, agreed to arbitration, but mine owners balked. Roosevelt leaked word to Wall Street that the army would take over the mines if management did not yield.

Seldom had a recent president acted so decisively, and never on behalf of strikers. In late October 1902 the owners settled by granting miners a 10 percent wage hike and a nine-hour day in return for increases in coal prices and no recognition of the union. Roosevelt was equally prepared to intervene on the side of management, as he did when he sent federal troops to end strikes in Arizona in 1903 and Colorado in 1904. His aim was to establish a vigorous presidency ready to deal squarely with both sides.

Roosevelt especially needed to face the issue of economic concentration. Financial power had become consolidated in giant trusts following a wave of mergers at the end of the century. Government investigations revealed rampant corporate abuses: rebates, collusion, **"watered" stock,** payoffs to government officials. The conservative courts showed little willingness to break up the giants or blunt their power. In *United States v. E. C. Knight* (1895), the Supreme Court had crippled the Sherman Antitrust Act by ruling that the law applied only to commerce that crossed state lines and not to manufacturing even when products were sold in another state. The decision left the American Sugar Refining Company in control of 98 percent of the nation's sugar factories.

"watered" stock stock issued in excess of the assets of a company. The term derived from the practice of some ranchers who made their cattle drink large amounts of water before weighing them for sale.

In his first State of the Union message, Roosevelt told Congress that he did not oppose business concentration. As he saw it, large corporations were not only inevitable but more productive than smaller operations. He wanted to regulate them to make them fairer and more efficient. Only then would the economic order be humanized, its victims protected, and class violence avoided. Like individuals, trusts had to be held to strict standards of morality. Conduct, not size, was the yardstick TR used to measure "good" and "bad" trusts.

With a progressive's faith in the power of publicity and a regulator's need for the facts, Roosevelt moved immediately to strengthen the federal power of investigation. He called for the creation of a Department of Labor and Commerce with a Bureau of Corporations that could force companies to hand over their records. Congressional conservatives shuddered at the prospect of putting corporate books on display. Finally, after Roosevelt charged that John D. Rockefeller was orchestrating the opposition, Congress enacted the legislation and provided the Justice Department with additional staff to prosecute antitrust cases.

In 1902, to demonstrate the power of government, Roosevelt had his attorney general file an antitrust suit against the Northern Securities Company. The mammoth holding company virtually monopolized railroads in the Northwest, setting its high freight rates and ignoring local protests. Here was a symbol of the "bad" trust. A trust-conscious nation cheered as the Supreme Court ordered the company to dissolve in 1904. Ultimately the Roosevelt administration brought suit against 44 giants, including Standard Oil Company, American Tobacco Company, and Du Pont Corporation.

Despite his reputation for trust-busting, Roosevelt always preferred regulation. The problems of the railroads, for example, were newly underscored by a recent round of consolidation that contributed to higher freight rates. In 1903 Roosevelt pressed Congress to passed the Elkins Act, which gave the ineffective **Interstate Commerce** Commission (ICC)

interstate commerce trade in goods that crosses state lines.

power to end rebates. Even the railroads cheered because the act saved them from the costly practice of granting special reductions to large shippers.

By the election of 1904 the president's initiatives had won him broad popular support. He trounced his two rivals, Democrat Alton B. Parker, a jurist from New York, and Eugene V. Debs of the Socialist party. No longer was he a "political accident," Roosevelt boasted.

Conservatives in his own party opposed Roosevelt's meddling in the private sector. But progressives demanded still more regulation of the railroads. In 1906 the president finally reached a compromise typical of his restrained approach to reform. The Hepburn Railway Act allowed the ICC to set maximum rates and to regulate sleeping car companies, ferries, bridges, and terminals. Progressives did not gain the provision for disclosure of company value or service costs they sought, but the Hepburn Act drew Roosevelt nearer to his goal of continuous regulation of business.

Bad Food and Pristine Wilds >> Extending the umbrella of federal protection to consumers, Roosevelt belatedly threw his weight behind two campaigns for healthy foods and drugs. Several pure food and drug bills had already died at the hands of lobbyists, despite a presidential endorsement. The appearance of Upton Sinclair's *The Jungle* in 1906 spurred Congress to act. The novel contained a brief but dramatic description of the slaughter of cattle infected with tuberculosis, of meat covered with rat dung, and of men falling into cooking vats. Readers paid scant attention to the workers, the true target of Sinclair's sympathy, but their stomachs turned at what they might be eating for breakfast. The Pure Food and Drug Act of 1906 sailed through Congress, and the Meat Inspection Act soon followed.

Roosevelt came late to the consumer cause, but on conservation he led the nation. An outdoors enthusiast, he galvanized public concern over the reckless use of natural resources. His chief forester, Gifford Pinchot, persuaded him that planned management under federal guidance was needed to protect the natural domain. Cutting trees must be synchronized with tree plantings, oil pumped from the ground under controlled conditions, and so on.

In the western states water was the problem. Economic growth, even survival, depended on it. As uneven local and state water policies sparked controversy, violence, and waste, many progressives campaigned for a federal program to replace the chaotic web of rules. The Reclamation Act of 1902 set aside proceeds from the sale of public lands for irrigation projects. Its passage signaled a progressive step toward the conservationist goal of rational resource development.

Conservation often came into conflict with the more radical vision of preservationists. As early as 1864 naturalist George Perkins Marsh sounded an alarm. In *Man and Nature; or Physical Geography as Modified by Human Action,* Marsh warned that human action enhanced by

technology could damage the planet. Already, he wrote, the agricultural and industrial revolutions had begun to erode land, deforest timberland, dry up watersheds, and endanger plants and animals.

Another naturalist, the wilderness philosopher John Muir, took Marsh a step further. As a boy, the Scottish-born Muir had immigrated to the United States with his family. Trained as an engineer, he nearly lost his sight when a sharp file punctured his right eye. His sight miraculously returned, and he vowed to be "true to myself" by following his passion: the study of the wild world. Study turned to activism in 1892 when Muir cofounded the Sierra Club. He hoped to maintain such natural wonders as the

⌃ Long a target of reformers, patent medicines made wild curative claims, ranging from restoring hair and cleaning the blood to ridding an invalid of worms, as with this "Tonic Vermifuge" advertised in 1889. The Pure Food and Drug Act finally placed them under federal regulation.

⌃ The Sierra Club, founded by naturalist John Muir, believed in the importance of preserving wilderness in its natural state. "In God's wilderness," Muir wrote in 1890, "lies the hope of the world—the great fresh unblighted, unredeemed wilderness." Muir helped persuade President Theodore Roosevelt to double the number of national parks. Here, some Sierra Club members lounge at the base of a giant redwood in Big Basin in 1905.

Hetch-Hetchy valley in his beloved Yosemite National Park in a state of "forever wild" to benefit future generations. Many conservationists saw these valleys only as sites for dams and reservoirs to manage and control water. "When we try to pick out anything by itself," Muir wrote, "we find it hitched to everything else in the universe."

Controversy flared after 1900, when San Francisco announced plans to create a city reservoir by flooding the Hetch-Hetchy valley. For 13 years Muir waged a publicity campaign against the reservoir. Pinchot enthusiastically backed San Francisco's claim. Roosevelt, torn by his friendship with Muir, did so less loudly. Not until 1913 did President Woodrow Wilson finally decide the issue in favor of San Francisco. Conservation had won over preservation.

Over the protests of cattle and timber interests, Roosevelt added nearly 200 million acres to government forest reserves, placed coal and mineral lands, oil reserves, and water-power sites in the public domain, and enlarged the national park system. When Congress balked, Roosevelt

appropriated another 17 million acres of forest before the legislators could pass a bill limiting him. Roosevelt also set in motion national congresses and commissions on conservation and mobilized governors across the country. Like a good progressive, he sent hundreds of experts to work applying science, education, and technology to environmental problems.

The Troubled Taft >>
On March 4, 1909, as snow swirled outside the White House, William Howard Taft readied himself for his inauguration. Over breakfast with Roosevelt, he basked in the glow of recent Republican victories. As Roosevelt's hand-picked successor, Taft had beaten Democrat William Jennings Bryan in the "Great Commoner's" third and last bid for the presidency. Republicans had retained control of Congress as well as a host of northern legislatures. Reform was at high tide, and Taft was eager to continue the Roosevelt program.

"Will," as Roosevelt liked to call him, was a distinguished jurist and public servant, the first American governor-general of the Philippines, and Roosevelt's secretary of war. Taft had great administrative skill and personal charm but disliked political maneuvering. He preferred conciliation to confrontation.

Trouble began early when progressives in the House moved to curb the near-dictatorial power of conservative Speaker Joseph Cannon. Taft waffled, first supporting then abandoning them to preserve the tariff reductions he was seeking. When progressives later broke Cannon's power without Taft's help, they scorned the president. And Taft's compromise was wasted. Senate protectionists peppered the tariff bill with so many amendments that rates jumped nearly to their old levels.

Late in 1909 the rift between Taft and progressives reached the breaking point in a dispute over conservation. Taft had appointed Richard Ballinger secretary of the interior over the objections of Roosevelt's old friend and mentor, Chief Forester Pinchot. When Ballinger opened a million acres of public lands for sale, Pinchot charged that shady dealings led Ballinger to transfer Alaskan public coal lands to a syndicate that included J. P. Morgan. Early in 1910 Taft fired Pinchot for insubordination. Angry progressives saw the Ballinger-Pinchot controversy as another betrayal by Taft. They began to look longingly across the Atlantic, where TR was stalking big game in Africa.

Despite his failures Taft was no conservative pawn. For the next two years he pushed Congress to enact a progressive program regulating safety standards for mines and railroads, creating a federal children's bureau, and setting an eight-hour workday for federal employees. Taft's support of a graduated income tax—sometimes heated, sometimes lukewarm—was finally decisive. Early in 1913 it became the Sixteenth Amendment. Historians view it as one of the most important reforms of the century, for it eventually generated the revenue for many new social programs.

The Election of 1912 >>

In June 1910 Roosevelt came home, laden with hunting trophies and exuberant as ever. He found Taft unhappy and progressive Republicans threatening to defect. Party loyalty kept Roosevelt quiet through most of 1911, but in October, Taft pricked him personally on the sensitive matter of busting trusts. Like TR, Taft accepted trusts as natural, but he failed to make Roosevelt's distinction between "good" and "bad" ones. He demanded, more impartially, that all trusts be prevented from restraining trade. In four years as president, Taft had brought nearly twice the antitrust suits Roosevelt had in seven years.

In October 1911 the Justice Department charged U.S. Steel with having violated the Sherman Antitrust Act by acquiring the Tennessee Coal and Iron Company. Roosevelt regarded the action as a personal rebuke, since he himself had allowed U.S. Steel to proceed with the acquisition. Taft, complained TR, "was playing small, mean, and foolish politics."

Roosevelt decided to play big, high-minded, and presidential. Already, in a speech at Osawatomie, Kansas, in 1910, he had outlined a program of sweeping national reform. His "New Nationalism" recognized the value of consolidation in the economy—whether big business or big labor—but insisted on protecting the interests of individuals through big government. The New Nationalism went further, stressing planning and efficiency under a powerful executive as "steward of the public welfare." It promised taxes on incomes and inheritances and greater regulation of industry. And it embraced social justice, specifically workers' compensation for accidents, minimum wages and maximum hours, child labor laws, and "equal suffrage"—a nod to women and loyal black Republicans. Roosevelt, a cautious reformer as president, grew daring as he campaigned for the White House.

"My hat is in the ring!" Roosevelt announced in February 1912. The enormously popular Roosevelt won most of the primaries; but by the time Republicans met in Chicago in June 1912, Taft had used presidential patronage and promises to secure the nomination. A frustrated Roosevelt bolted and took progressive Republicans with him.

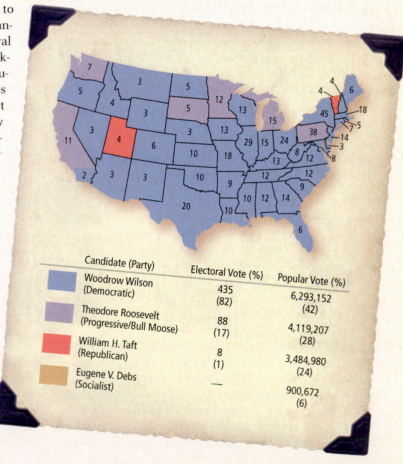

Candidate (Party)	Electoral Vote (%)	Popular Vote (%)
Woodrow Wilson (Democratic)	435 (82)	6,293,152 (42)
Theodore Roosevelt (Progressive/Bull Moose)	88 (17)	4,119,207 (28)
William H. Taft (Republican)	8 (1)	3,484,980 (24)
Eugene V. Debs (Socialist)	—	900,672 (6)

Two months later, amid choruses of "Onward Christian Soldiers," delegates to the newly formed Progressive party nominated Roosevelt for the presidency. "I'm feeling like a bull moose!" he bellowed. Progressives suddenly had a symbol for their new party.

The Democrats met in Baltimore, jubilant over the prospect of a divided Republican party. Delegates chose as their candidate Woodrow Wilson, the progressive governor of New Jersey. Wilson wisely concentrated his fire on Roosevelt. He countered the New Nationalism with his "New Freedom." It rejected the economic consolidation that Roosevelt embraced. Bigness was a sin, crowding out competition, promoting inefficiency, and reducing opportunity. Only by strictly limiting the size of businesses could the free market be preserved. And only by keeping government small could individual freedom be preserved. "Liberty," Wilson cautioned," has never come from government," only from the "limitation of governmental power."

Increasingly voters found Taft beside the point. In an age of reform, even the Socialists looked good. Better led, financed, and organized than ever, the Socialist party had increased its membership to nearly 135,000 by 1912. The party also had an appealing candidate in Eugene V. Debs, a homegrown Indiana radical. He had won 400,000 votes for president in 1904. Now, in 1912, he summoned voters to make "the working class the ruling class."

On Election Day voters gave progressivism a resounding endorsement. Wilson won 6.3 million votes; Roosevelt, 4.1 million; Taft, just 3.6 million. Debs received almost a million votes. Together the two progressive candidates amassed a three-to-one margin. But the Republican split had broken the party's hold on national politics. For the first time since 1896, a Democrat would sit in the White House—and with his party in control of Congress.

 REVIEW

How did President Roosevelt's reform agenda reflect his promise of a "Square Deal" for Americans?

WOODROW WILSON AND THE POLITICS OF MORALITY

Soon after the election Woodrow Wilson made a proud if startling confession to the chairman of the Democratic National Committee: "God ordained that I should be the next President of the United States." To the White House Wilson brought a sense of destiny and a passion for reform. All his life he believed he was meant to accomplish great things, and he did. Under him, progressivism peaked.

Early Career >>
From the moment of his birth in 1856 Woodrow Wilson felt he could not escape destiny. It was all around him. In his family's Presbyterian faith, in the sermons of his minister father, in dinnertime talk ran the unbending belief in a world predetermined by God and ruled by saved souls, an "elect." Wilson ached to be one of them and behaved as though he were.

Like most southerners, he loved the Democratic party, hated the tariff, and accepted racial separation. (Under his presidency, segregation returned to Washington for the first time since Reconstruction.) An early career in law bored him, so he turned to history and political science and became a professor. His studies persuaded him that a modern president must act as a "prime minister," directing and uniting his party, molding legislation and public opinion, exerting continuous leadership. In 1910, after a stormy tenure as head of Princeton University, Wilson was helped by Democratic party bosses to win the governorship of New Jersey. In 1912 they helped him again, this time to the presidency of the country.

The Reforms of the New Freedom >>
As governor Wilson led New Jersey on the path of progressive reform. As president he was a model of progressive leadership. More than Roosevelt he shaped policy and legislation. He went to Congress to let members know he intended to work personally with them. He kept party discipline tight and mobilized public opinion when Congress refused to act.

Lowering the high tariff was Wilson's first order of business. Progressives had long attacked the tariff as another example of the power of trusts. By protecting American manufacturers, Wilson argued, such barriers weakened the competition he cherished. When the Senate threatened to raise rates, the new president appealed directly to the public. "Industrious" and "insidious" lobbyists were blocking reform, he cried to reporters.

The Underwood-Simmons Tariff of 1913 marked the first downward revision in 19 years and the biggest since before the Civil War. To compensate for lost revenue, Congress enacted a graduated income tax under the newly adopted Sixteenth Amendment. It applied solely to corporations and the tiny fraction of Americans who earned more than $4,000 a year. It nonetheless began a momentous shift in government revenue from its nineteenth-century base—public lands, alcohol taxes, and customs duties—to its twentieth-century base: personal and corporate incomes.

Wilson turned next to the perennial problems of money and banking. Early in 1913 a congressional committee under Arsène Pujo revealed that a few powerful banks controlled the nation's credit system. They could choke Wilson's free market by raising interest rates or tightening the supply of money. As a banking reform bill moved through Congress in 1913, opinion was divided among conservatives, who wanted centralized and private control,

the **United States**

23 and the Collapse *of the* Old World Order

1901–1920

The horror of battle in World War I is graphically captured in this detail from a painting by Georges Leroux titled *L'Enfer* (*"Hell"*). The figures on the right, with helmets and gas masks, crouch in what looks like a muddy shell hole as they try to escape artillery fire and poison gas.

- Moralistic urges to rid society of industries such as the liquor trade and prostitution, to bridge the gap between immigrants and native-born Americans, and to soften the consequences of industrialization through social justice and social welfare.
- Led by members of the urban middle class, progressives were moderate modernizers, embracing such traditional American values as democracy, Judeo-Christian ethics, individualism, and the spirit of public service while employing new techniques of management and planning, coordinated systems, and bureaucracies of experts.
- Progressive women extended their traditional sphere of home and family to become "social housekeepers" and crusaders for women's rights, especially the right to vote.
- Progressivism animated politics, first at the local and state levels, then in the presidencies of Theodore Roosevelt and Woodrow Wilson.
- In the end, the weaknesses of progressivism—its fuzzy conception of the public interest, its exclusion of minorities, and the ease with which its regulatory mechanisms were "captured" by those being regulated—were matched by its accomplishments in establishing the modern, activist state.

Additional Reading

The long debate over progressivism is traced in Arthur S. Link and Richard L. McCormick, *Progressivism* (1983). Benchmarks include George Mowry, *The California Progressives* (1951), and Richard Hofstadter, *The Age of Reform* (1955), both of which see progressives as a small elite seeking to recapture its fading status. Gabriel Kolko's controversial *Triumph of Conservatism* (1963) asserts that business "captured" reform to control competition and stave off stricter federal regulation. Michael McGerr's *A Fierce Discontent: The Rise and Fall of the Progressive Movement* (2003) sees progressivism as a daring middle-class movement to transform society. David Traxel sees both reforming Progressives and the First World War as spawning a *Crusader Nation* (2006). Finally, Jackson Lears, *Rebirth of a Nation* (2009), places progressivism in the context of an enduring search for regeneration in the decades after the Civil War.

The social history of progressivism is the focus of Steven J. Diner's *A Very Different Age* (1998). Eric Rauchway's *Murdering McKinley: The Making of Theodore Roosevelt's America* (2003) presents a fresh account of the era, while James Chace recounts its turning point in *1912: Wilson, Roosevelt, Taft, and Debs and the Election that Changed the Country* (2004).

John M. Blum, *The Republican Roosevelt* (1954), remains the most incisive rendering of TR, and Lewis L. Gould, *The Presidency of Theodore Roosevelt* (1991), is the best single-volume study of the White House years. In *The Wilderness Warrior: Theodore Roosevelt and the Crusade for America* (2009), Douglas Brinkley puts TR in the thick of the conservation movement and examines his environmental legacy. Unsurpassed in detail and depth is Arthur Link, *Woodrow Wilson*, 5 vols. (1947–1965). Robert Crunden, *Ministers of Reform* (1982), emphasizes the cultural aspects of progressivism, and Ellen Chesler, *Woman of Valor* (1992), offers a feminist perspective on Margaret Sanger. Melvyn Urofsky's *Louis D. Brandeis* (2009) is admiring and authoritative. In *Triangle: The Fire That Changed America* (2004), David Von Drehle offers the fullest account yet of that calamity.

W. E. B. DU BOIS

1909
Ballinger-Pinchot controversy; NAACP founded

1911
Triangle Shirtwaist fire

1912
Woodrow Wilson elected president

1913
Sixteenth and Seventeenth amendments; Federal Reserve Act passed

1914
Clayton Antitrust Act passed; Federal Trade Commission created

1917
Congress enacts literacy test for new immigrants

1920
Nineteenth Amendment grants women the right to vote

PRESIDENT'S SIGNATURE ENACTS CURRENCY LAW
Wilson Declares It the First of Series of Constructive Acts to Aid Business.
Makes Speech to Group of Democratic Leaders.
Conference Report Adopted in Senate by Vote of 43 to 25.
Banks All Over the Country Hasten to Enter Federal Reserve System.
WILSON SEES DAWN OF NEW ERA IN BUSINESS
Aims to Make Prosperity Free to Have Unimpeded Momentum.

setting an eight-hour day for workers on interstate railroads. He supported the Keating-Owen Child Labor Act (page 452). Farmers benefited from legislation providing them with low-interest loans. And just before the election of 1916 Wilson intervened to avert a nationwide strike of rail workers.

Woodrow Wilson's administration capped a decade and a half of heady reform. Seeing chaos in the modern industrial city, progressive reformers worked to reduce the damage of poverty and the hazards of industrial work, control rising immigration, and spread a middle-class ideal of morality. In city halls and state legislatures, they tried to break the power of corporate interests and entrenched political machines. In Washington, they enlarged government and broadened its mission from caretaker to promoter of public welfare.

 REVIEW

Compare and contrast Theodore Roosevelt's approach to reform with that of Woodrow Wilson.

The United States was not alone in these efforts. The Machine Age triggered a wave of progressive reform across the industrialized world. Movements for social justice and social welfare sprang up first in Great Britain, where the industrial revolution began. There, reformers publicized the plight of women and children in factories and mines as early as the 1820s. The resulting Factory Act of 1833 outlawed child labor in textile mills for those under the age of nine. The Mines Act of 1842 made it illegal to employ all women as well as children younger than ten in work underground. In 1884 Toynbee Hall, the world's first social settlement house, opened in London's East End to minister to the needs of the poor. It became the model for Jane Addams's Hull House in Chicago.

In political reforms the world sometimes lagged behind the United States, particularly on the issue of woman suffrage. Except in Scandinavia, most European women did not receive the vote until after World War I. Despite the democratic revolutions that swept across Latin America in the nineteenth century, national women's suffrage was opposed by the Catholic Church and did not come to Ecuador until 1929 and El Salvador until 1939. Asia was slower still, often because colonial rulers denied or limited suffrage or because patriarchal Asian societies looked on women as subordinate to men. Only in 1950, for example, after India achieved independence did women receive the right to vote.

CHAPTER SUMMARY

Progressivism embraced a broad-based set of reforms and became the first truly national reform movement in American history.

- Progressive reform sprang from many impulses:
  - Desires to curb the advancing power of big business and to end political corruption.
  - Efforts to bring order and efficiency to economic and political life.
  - Attempts by new interest groups to make business and government more responsive to the needs of ordinary citizens.

Significant Events

Illinois legislature enacts eight-hour workday law for women

United States v. E. C. Knight

President McKinley assassinated; Theodore Roosevelt becomes president

Elkins Act ends railroad rebates; Wisconsin first state to enact direct primary

William Howard Taft elected president

1893 · 1895 · 1901 · 1902 · 1903 · 1906 · 1908

Northern Securities Company dissolved under Sherman Antitrust Act; anthracite coal miners strike in Pennsylvania

Hepburn Act strengthens Interstate Commerce Commission; Meat Inspection and Pure Food and Drug acts passed

E. C. KNIGHT

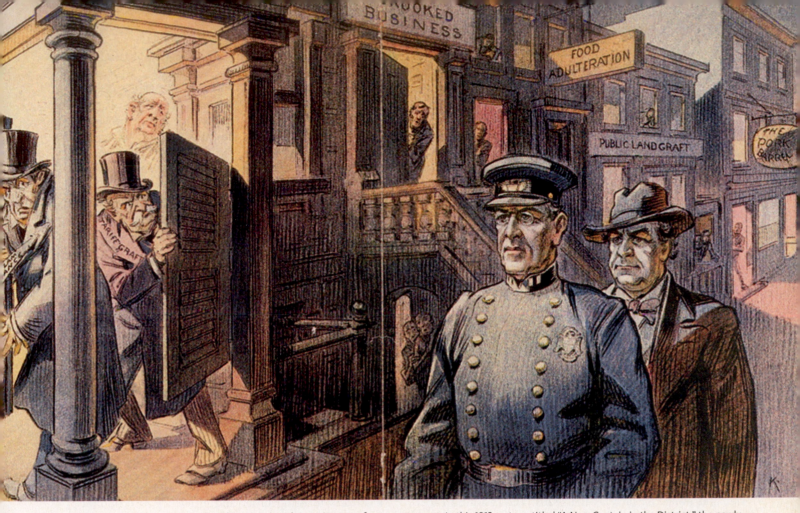

▲ Woodrow Wilson came to the White House with promises to reform government. In this 1913 cartoon titled "A New Captain in the District," the newly elected president strides through corrupt Washington, ready to police such abuses as easy land grants and pork barreling, the much-criticized congressional practice of voting for projects that benefit home districts and constituents.

rural Democrats, who wanted regional banks under local bankers, and Populists and progressives—including Bryan and La Follette—who wanted government control.

Wilson split their differences in the Federal Reserve Act of 1913. The new Federal Reserve System contained 12 regional banks scattered across the country. But it also created a central Federal Reserve Board in Washington, appointed by the president, to supervise the system. The board could regulate credit and the money supply by setting the interest rate it charged member banks, by buying or selling government bonds, and by issuing paper currency called Federal Reserve notes.

When Wilson finally took on the trusts, he inched toward the New Nationalism of Theodore Roosevelt. The Federal Trade Commission Act of 1914 created a bipartisan executive agency to oversee business activity. The end—to enforce orderly competition—was distinctly Wilsonian, but the means—an executive commission to regulate commerce—were pure Roosevelt.

Roosevelt would have stopped there, but Wilson made good on his campaign pledge to attack trusts. The Clayton Antitrust Act (1914) barred some of the worst corporate practices: price discrimination, holding companies, and interlocking directorates (directors of one corporate board sitting on others). Despite Wilson's bias against size, the advantages of large-scale production and distribution were inescapable. In practice his administration chose to regulate rather than breakup bigness. The Justice Department filed fewer antitrust suits than it had under the Taft administration.

Labor and Social Reform >> For all of Wilson's impressive accomplishments, voters seemed uninspired by the New Freedom. Off-year election losses in 1914 pushed Wilson toward the social reforms of the New Nationalism he had once criticized as paternalistic and unconstitutional. He signaled the change early in 1916 when he nominated his close adviser Louis D. Brandeis to the Supreme Court. The progressive Brandeis had fought for the social reforms lacking from Wilson's agenda. His appointment also broke the tradition of anti-Semitism that had previously kept Jews such as Brandies off the Court.

In other ways, Wilson showed a new willingness to intervene more actively in the economy. He pressed for laws improving the working conditions of merchant seamen and

PANAMA CANAL—OLD AND NEW TRANSOCEANIC ROUTES

Tropical forests cover three-fourths of Panama, including the Canal Zone. Vegetation is denser at high elevations but tightly packed even below 1,000 feet. The terrain is rugged, but the distance saved by the canal (nearly 8,000 miles) convinced Roosevelt and other American leaders that the ordeal of construction and the loss of lives were worthwhile in the long run.

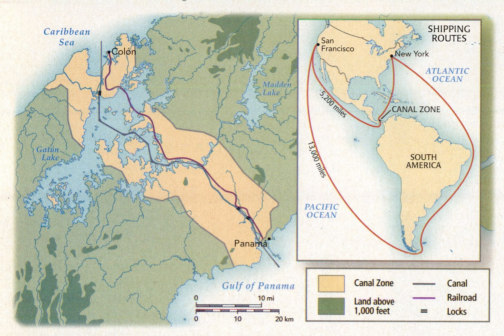

modernized the army and tripled its size, created a general staff for planning and mobilization, and established the Army War College. As a pivot point between the two hemispheres, his canal allowed the United States to flex its strength across the globe.

These expanding horizons came about largely as an outgrowth of American commercial and industrial expansion, just as the imperialist empires of Great Britain, France, Germany, Russia, and Japan reflected the spread of their own industrial and commercial might. The Americans, steeped in democratic ideals, frequently seemed uncomfortable with the naked ambitions of European empire-builders. Roosevelt's embrace of the canal, however, showed how far some Americans would go to shape the world in their interests.

Expansionist diplomats at home and abroad assured each other that global order could be maintained by balancing power through a set of carefully crafted alliances. That system of alliances did not hold. In 1914, the year the Panama Canal opened, the old world order shattered in a terrible war. **≪**

"I took the isthmus," President Theodore Roosevelt later told a cheering crowd. In a way he did. In 1903 he reached an agreement with Colombia to lease the needed strip of land. Hoping for more money and greater control over the canal, the Colombian senate refused to ratify the agreement.

Privately TR talked of seizing Panama. But when he learned of a budding independence movement there, he let it be known that he would welcome a revolt. On schedule and without bloodshed, the Panamanians rebelled late in 1903. The next day a U.S. cruiser dropped anchor offshore to prevent Colombia from landing troops. The United States quickly recognized the new Republic of Panama and concluded a treaty for a renewable lease on a canal zone 10 miles wide. Panama received $10 million plus an annual rent of $250,000, the same terms offered to Colombia. Critics called it "a rough-riding assault upon another republic."

The Panama Canal embodied Roosevelt's muscular policy of respect through military strength. TR

>> AN AMERICAN STORY

"A PATH BETWEEN THE SEAS"

I n 1898, as eager young men signed up to kill Spaniards in Cuba, the USS *Oregon* left San Francisco Bay on a roundabout route toward its battle station in the Caribbean. It first headed south through the Pacific, passing Central America and leaving it thousands of miles behind. Then in the narrow Strait of Magellan at South America's tip, the ship encountered a gale so ferocious that the shore could not be seen. But the *Oregon* passed into the Atlantic and steamed north. Finally, after 68 days and 13,000 miles at sea, it helped win the Battle of Santiago Bay and the Spanish-American War.

The daring voyage electrified the nation but worried its leaders. Since the defeat of Mexico in 1848, the United States had stretched from the Atlantic to the Pacific without enough navy to go around. As an emerging power, the country needed a "path between the seas," a canal across the narrow isthmus of Colombia's Panamanian province in Central America, to defend itself and to promote its growing trade. >>

PROGRESSIVE DIPLOMACY

As the Panama Canal was being built, progressive diplomacy was taking shape. Like progressive politics, it stressed moralism and order as it stretched executive power to new limits in an attempt to mold and remake the international environment. At the core of this mission lay a belief in the superiority of Anglo-American institutions and the need to spread them across the world. Every Western leader assumed that northern Europeans were racially superior, too, with a responsibility to uplift the "lesser peoples" of the tropical zones.

Economic expansion underlay the commitment to a civilizing mission. The depression of 1893 encouraged American manufacturers and farmers to look overseas for markets, and that expansion continued after 1900. Every administration committed itself to opening doors of trade and keeping them open.

Big Stick in the Caribbean >>

Theodore Roosevelt liked to invoke the old African proverb "Walk softly and carry a big stick." In the Caribbean, however, he moved both loudly and mightily. The Panama Canal gave the United States a commanding position in the Western Hemisphere. Its importance required the country to "police the surrounding premises," explained Secretary of State Elihu Root. Before granting Cuba independence in 1902, the United States reorganized its finances and wrote into the Cuban constitution the Platt Amendment. It gave American authorities the right to intervene if Cuban independence or internal order were threatened. Claiming that power, U.S. troops occupied the island twice between 1906 and 1923.

In looking to enforce a favorable environment for trade in the Caribbean, Roosevelt also worried about European intentions. The Monroe Doctrine of 1823 had declared against further European colonization of the Western Hemisphere, but in the early twentieth century the rising debts of Latin Americans to Europeans invited intrusion. "If we intend to say hands off to the power of Europe, then sooner or later we must keep order ourselves," Roosevelt warned.

Going well beyond Monroe's concept of resisting foreign penetration, Roosevelt asserted American command of the Caribbean. In 1904, when the Dominican Republic defaulted on its debts, he added the "Roosevelt Corollary" to the Monroe Doctrine by claiming the right to police the Americas. Under it, the United States assumed responsibility for several Caribbean states, including the Dominican Republic, Cuba, and Panama.

A "Diplomatist of the Highest Rank" >>

In the Far East Roosevelt exercised ingenuity rather than force, since he considered Asia beyond the American sphere of influence. Like President McKinley, TR committed himself only to maintaining an "open door" of equal access to trade in China and to protecting the Philippines, "our heel of Achilles."

The key lay in offsetting Russian and Japanese ambitions in the region. When Japan attacked Russian holdings in the Chinese province of Manchuria in 1904, Roosevelt offered to mediate. Both sides met at the U.S. Naval Base near Portsmouth, New Hampshire, and, under Roosevelt's guidance, produced the Treaty of Portsmouth in 1905. It recognized the Japanese victory (the first by an Asian power over a European country) and ceded territory on the Asian mainland to Japan. Japan promised to leave Manchuria as part of China and keep trade open to all foreign nations. Both the balance of power in Asia and the open door in China had been preserved. Roosevelt's diplomacy earned him the Nobel Peace Prize in 1906.

⤊ As its global involvement in international affairs increased, the United States helped bring about an end to the Russo-Japanese War in 1905. This Japanese postcard shows newsrunners bringing the latest word on the war to interested readers.

Some Japanese nationalists resented the peace treaty for curbing Japan's ambitions in Asia. Their anger surfaced in a protest lodged, of all places, against the San Francisco school board. In 1906 rising Japanese immigration led San Francisco school authorities to place the city's 93 Asian students in a separate school. Roosevelt, fuming at the "infernal fools in California," summoned the mayor of San Francisco to the White House. In exchange for an end to the segregation order, Roosevelt offered to arrange a mutual restriction of immigration between Japan and the United States. In 1907 all sides accepted his "gentlemen's agreement."

The San Francisco school crisis sparked wild rumors that Japan was bent on taking Hawai'i, the Philippines, or the Panama Canal. In case Japan or any other nation thought of upsetting the Pacific balance, Roosevelt sent 16 gleaming white battleships on a world tour in 1907. The show of force heralded a new age of American naval might but had an unintended consequence that haunted Americans for decades: it spurred Japanese admirals to expand their own navy.

Watching Roosevelt in his second term, an amazed London *Morning Post* dubbed him a "diplomatist of the highest rank." Abroad as at home, his brand of progressivism was grounded in an enthusiastic nationalism that mixed force with finesse to achieve balance and order.

Dollar Diplomacy >> Instead of force or finesse William Howard Taft relied on private investment to promote economic stability, keep peace, and tie debt-ridden nations to the United States. His "dollar diplomacy" simply amounted to "substituting dollars for bullets," Taft explained. He and Philander Knox, his prickly secretary of state, treated the restless nations of Latin America like ailing corporations, injecting capital and reorganizing management. By the time Taft left office in 1913, half of all American investments abroad were in Latin America.

Failure dogged Taft overseas as it did at home. In the Caribbean his dollar diplomacy was linked so closely with unpopular regimes, corporations, and banks that Woodrow Wilson scrapped it as soon as he entered the White House. In 1912 a revolution in Nicaragua led Taft to dispatch 2,000 marines to protect American lives and property. Sporadic American intrusions lasted more than a dozen years.

Taft's efforts to strengthen China with investments and trade only intensified rivalry with Japan and made China more suspicious of all foreigners, including Americans. In 1911 the southern Chinese provinces rebelled against foreign intrusion and overthrew the monarchy. Only persistent pressure from the White House kept dollar diplomacy in Asia alive at all.

REVIEW

How did Theodore Roosevelt's policies in Latin America and Asia differ from William Howard Taft's?

WOODROW WILSON AND MORAL DIPLOMACY

The Lightfoot Club had been meeting in Reverend Wilson's hayloft for months when the question of whether the pen was mightier than the sword came up. Young Tommy Wilson, who had organized the debating society, jumped at the chance to argue that written words were more powerful than armies. When the boys drew lots, Tommy ended up on the other side. "I can't argue for something I don't

believe in," he protested. Thomas Woodrow Wilson eventually dropped his first name, but he never gave up his boyhood conviction that morality, at least as he defined it, should guide conduct. To the diplomacy of order, force, and finance, Wilson added a missionary zeal for spreading capitalism, democracy, and the progressive values of harmony and cooperation.

Missionary Diplomacy >> As president, Woodrow Wilson revived and enlarged Jefferson's notion of the United States as a beacon of freedom. "We are chosen, and prominently chosen, to show the way to the nations of the world how they shall walk in the paths of liberty," he said. Such paternalism only thinly masked Wilson's assumption of Anglo-American superiority and his willingness to spread Western-style democracy, capitalism, and morality through force.

Wilson's missionary diplomacy had a practical side. In the twentieth century foreign markets would serve as America's new frontier. American industries "will burst their jackets if they cannot find free outlets in the markets of the world," he cautioned in 1912. Wilson's genius lay in reconciling this commercial self-interest with a global idealism. In his eyes, exporting American democracy and capitalism would promote stability and progress throughout the world.

In Asia and the Pacific, Wilson moved to put "moral and public considerations" ahead of the "material interests of individuals." He pulled American bankers out of a six-nation railroad project in China backed by President Taft. The scheme encouraged foreign intervention and undermined Chinese sovereignty, Wilson said. The United States became the first major power to recognize the new democratic Republic of China after a revolution in 1911 and in 1915 strongly opposed Japan's "21 Demands" for territorial and commercial privileges in the country.

In the Caribbean and Latin America Wilson discovered that interests closer to home could not be pursued through principles alone. In August 1914 he convinced Nicaragua, already occupied by American troops, to yield control of a naval base and grant the United States an alternative canal route. Upheavals in Haiti and the Dominican Republic brought in the U.S. Marines. By the end of his administration American troops were still stationed there and also in Cuba. Missionary diplomacy, it turned out, could spread its gospel with steel as well as cash.

Intervention in Mexico >> In Mexico a lingering crisis turned Wilson's "moral diplomacy" into a mockery. A common border, 400 years of shared history, and millions of dollars in investments made what happened in Mexico of urgent importance to the United States. In 1910 a revolution plunged Mexico into turmoil. Just as Wilson was entering the White House in 1913, the ruthless general Victoriano Huerta emerged as head of the

AMERICAN INTERVENTIONS IN THE CARIBBEAN, 1898–1930

In the first three decades of the twentieth century, armed and unarmed interventions by the United States virtually transformed the Caribbean into an American lake.

UNITED STATES

Columbus

VILLA, 1916

PERSHING, 1916–1917

Parral

CARRANZA'S TROOPS, 1916

MEXICO

FLETCHER, 1914

Tampico **U.S. sailors arrested, 1914**

Veracruz **U.S. Navy seizes, 1914**

PACIFIC OCEAN

GUATEMALA 1920

EL SALVADOR **U.S. naval action, 1932**

Gulf of Fonseca 1914–1933

Gulf of Mexico

Bahía Honda 1903–1912

Havana

CUBA 1898–1902, 1906–1909, 1912, 1917–1933

Guantánamo Bay 1903–

JAMAICA (Br.)

BR. HONDURAS

HONDURAS 1903, 1907, 1911, 1912, 1919, 1924–1925

NICARAGUA 1898, 1899, 1910, 1912–1925, 1926–1933

COSTA RICA

PANAMA **Seceded from Colombia, 1903** 1903, 1908, 1912, 1918–1920

CANAL ZONE **Leased** 1903–1999

BAHAMAS (Br.)

ATLANTIC OCEAN

HAITI 1915–1934

San Juan

VIRGIN IS. **Purchased from Denmark, 1917**

DOMINICAN REP. 1903–1904, 1914, 1916–1924

PUERTO RICO **Annexed 1898**

Caribbean Sea

VENEZUELA

COLOMBIA **U.S. naval action, 1901–1903**

Legend:

U.S. territory, 1900	U.S. forces →
U.S. protectorate	Mexican forces →
1914 — Period of U.S. occupation	▲ Naval base leased to U.S.

government. Wealthy landowners and foreign investors endorsed Huerta, who was likely to protect their holdings. Soon a bloody civil war was raging.

Unlike most European leaders, Wilson refused to recognize Huerta and his "government of butchers." (Huerta had murdered the popular leader Francisco Madero.) Instead, he backed rebel leader Venustiano Carranza. When a bankrupt Huerta resigned in 1914, Carranza formed a new constitutionalist government but refused to follow Wilson's guidelines. Wilson threw his support to Francisco "Pancho" Villa, a wily, peasant-born general who had broken from Carranza. Together with Emiliano Zapata, another peasant leader, Villa kept rebellion flickering.

A year later, when Wilson finally recognized the Carranza regime, Villa turned against the United States. In January 1916 he abducted 18 Americans from a train in Mexico and slaughtered them. In March he galloped into Columbus, New Mexico, killed 19 people, and left the town in flames. Wilson ordered 6,000 troops into Mexico to capture Villa. A reluctant Carranza agreed to the American invasion.

For nearly two years, General John "Black Jack" Pershing (nicknamed for the all-black unit he commanded in the Spanish-American War) chased Villa on horseback, in

⚔ General John J. "Black Jack" Pershing led U.S. forces into Mexico to catch rebel leader Pancho Villa "dead or alive." Villa (pictured here on horseback leading a band of his rebels) eluded the Americans for several months before they abandoned the expedition. Audacious and ruthless, he was worshipped by Mexican peasants, who extolled his exploits in folktales and ballads after his assassination in 1923 by Mexican political rivals.

automobiles, and with airplanes. There were bloody skirmishes with government troops but not a single one with Villa and his rebels. As the chase turned wilder and wilder, Carranza withdrew his consent for U.S. troops on Mexican soil. Early in 1917 Wilson pulled Pershing home. The "punitive expedition," as the president called it, poisoned Mexican-American relations for the next 30 years.

 REVIEW

What was "missionary" about Woodrow Wilson's diplomacy, and how successfully did he pursue it?

THE ROAD TO WAR

In early 1917, around the time that Wilson recalled Pershing, the British liner *Laconia* was making its way home across the Atlantic. Passengers below decks talked almost casually of the war raging in Europe since 1914. "What do you think are our chances of being torpedoed?" asked Floyd Gibbons, an American reporter. Since Germany had stepped up its submarine attacks, the question was unavoidable. The answer came moments later when a torpedo hit the vessel. As warning whistles blasted, the passengers abandoned ship. From lifeboats they watched a second torpedo send the *Laconia* to a watery grave. After a miserable night spent bobbing in the waves, Gibbons was rescued. But by 1917 other citizens of the neutral United States had already lost their lives at sea. Despite its best efforts, the country soon found itself at war.

The Guns of August >> For a century profound strains had been pushing Europe toward war. Its population tripled, its middle and working classes swelled, and discontent with industrial society grew. Nationalism surged and with it, militarism and imperialism. Led by Kaiser Wilhelm II and eager for empire, Germany aligned itself with Turkey and Austria-Hungary. The established imperial powers of England and France looked to contain Germany by supporting its foe, Russia. By the summer of 1914 Europe bristled with weapons, troops, and armor-plated navies. And these war machines were linked to

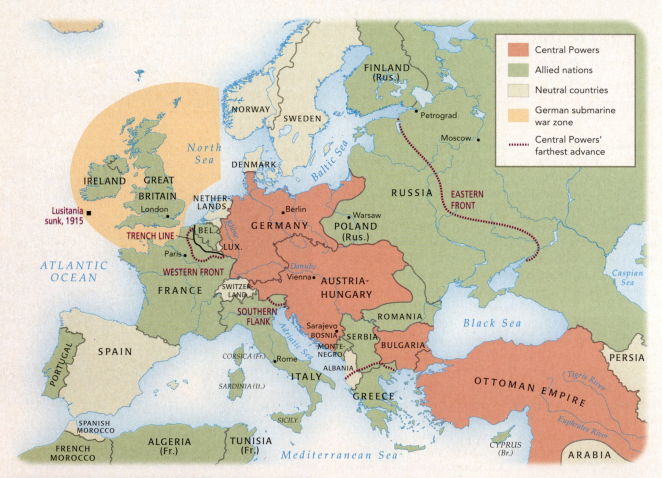

THE WAR IN EUROPE, 1914–1917

When World War I erupted, few countries in Europe remained neutral. The armies of the Central Powers penetrated as far west as France and as far east as Russia. By 1917 the war in Europe had settled into a hideous standoff along a deadly line of trenches on the western front.

one another through a web of diplomatic and military alliances—all of them committed to war, should someone or some nation set chaos in motion.

That moment came on June 28, 1914, in the streets of Sarajevo, the provincial capital of Bosnia in southwest Austria-Hungary. There, the heir to the Austro-Hungarian throne, Archduke Franz Ferdinand, was gunned down with his wife. The young assassin who carried out the deed belonged to the Black Hand, a terrorist group that had vowed to reunite Bosnia with Serbia to create another Slavic nation on Austria-Hungary's border.

Austria-Hungary mobilized to punish all of Serbia. In response, rival Russia called up its 6-million-man army to help the Serbs. Germany joined with Austria-Hungary; France, with Russia. On July 28, after a month of insincere demands for apologies, Austria-Hungary attacked Serbia. Germany declared war on Russia on August 1 and, two days later, on France.

The guns of August heralded the first global war. Like so many dominoes, nations fell into line. Britain, Japan, Romania, and later Italy rushed to the side of "Allies" France and Russia; Bulgaria and Turkey to the "Central Powers" of Germany and Austria-Hungary. Armies fought from the deserts of North Africa to the plains of Flanders. Fleets battled off the coasts of Chile and Sumatra.

Neutral But Not Impartial ▸▸

The outbreak of war in Europe shocked most Americans. Few knew Serbia as anything but a tiny splotch on a map. Fewer still were prepared to go to war in its defense. President Wilson issued a declaration of neutrality and approved a plan for evacuating Americans stranded in Belgium.

Wilson soon came to see the calamity as an opportunity. In his mind a neutral America could lead warring nations to "a peace without victory"—without territorial concessions or monetary reparations—and a new world order. Selfish nationalism would give way to cooperative internationalism; power politics, to collective security in which nations joined together to ensure the safety of all and to isolate aggressors. Progressive faith in reason would triumph over irrational violence. Everything hinged on maintaining neutrality. Only if America remained "impartial in thought as well as action" could it lead the way to a higher peace.

True impartiality was impossible. Americans of German and Austrian descent naturally sympathized with the Central Powers, as did Irish Americans, on the grounds of England's centuries-old domination of Ireland. The bonds of language, culture, and history tied most Americans to Great Britain. And gratitude for French aid during the American Revolution still lived.

> **The guns of August heralded the first global war. Like so many dominoes, nations fell into line, either as "Allies" or as "Central Powers."**

Germany aroused different sentiments. Although some progressives admired German social reforms, Americans generally saw Germany as an iron military power bent on conquest. Americans read British propaganda of spike-helmeted "Huns" raping Belgian women, bayoneting their children, pillaging their towns. Some of the stories were true, some embellished, some manufactured, but all worked against Germany in the United States.

American economic ties to Britain and France also created a financial investment in Allied victory. The American economy boomed with the flood of war orders. Between 1914 and 1916 trade with the Allies rocketed from $800 million to $3 billion. The Allies eventually borrowed more than $2 billion from American banks to finance their purchases. In contrast, a British blockade reduced American war goods trade with the Central Powers to a trickle.

The Diplomacy of Neutrality ▸▸

Wilson had admired Great Britain all his life. Try as he might he could not contain his British sympathies. Although he insisted that all warring powers respect the right of neutrals to trade with any nation, he hesitated to retaliate against Great Britain's blockade of Germany. Britain's powerful navy was its key to victory over Germany, a land power. By the end of 1915 the United States had all but accepted the British blockade, while American supplies continued to flow to England. True neutrality was dead.

Early in 1915 Germany turned to a dreadful new weapon to even the odds at sea. It mounted a counterblockade of Great Britain with two dozen submarines, or *Unterseeboote,* called U-boats. Before submarines, sea raiders usually gave crews and passengers the chance to escape. But if thin-skinned U-boats surfaced to obey these conventions, they risked being rammed or blown from the water. So submarines attacked without warning and spared no lives. Invoking international law and national honor, Wilson threatened to hold Germany to "strict accountability" for any American losses. Germany promised not to sink any American ships, but soon a new issue grabbed the headlines: the safety of American passengers on vessels of nations at war.

On the morning of May 7, 1915, the British passenger liner *Lusitania* appeared out of a fog bank off the coast of Ireland on its way from New York to Southampton. The commander of the German U-20 could hardly believe his eyes: the giant ship filled the viewfinder of his periscope. He fired a single torpedo. A tremendous roar followed as one of the *Lusitania*'s main boilers exploded. The ship listed so badly that lifeboats could barely be launched before the vessel sank. Nearly 1,200 men, women, and children perished, including 128 Americans.

Wilson, though horrified, did little more than send notes of protest to Germany. Secretary of State William Jennings Bryan, an advocate of what he called "real neutrality," wanted equal protests lodged against both German submarines and British blockaders. He suspected that the *Lusitania* carried munitions and was thus a legitimate target. (Much later, evidence proved him right.) Relying on passengers for protection against attack, Bryan argued, was "like putting women and children in front of an army." Rather than endorse Wilson's policy, Bryan resigned.

Battling on two fronts in Europe, Germany wanted to keep the United States out of the war. But in February 1916 a desperate Germany declared submarine warfare on all armed vessels, belligerent or neutral. A month later a U-boat commander mistook the French steamer *Sussex* for a mine layer and torpedoed the unarmed vessel. Several Americans were injured.

In mid-April Wilson issued an ultimatum. If Germany refused to stop sinking nonmilitary vessels, the United States would break off diplomatic relations. War would surely follow. Without enough U-boats to control the seas, Germany agreed to Wilson's terms, all but abandoning its counterblockade. This *Sussex* pledge gave Wilson a major victory but carried a grave risk. If German submarines resumed unrestricted attacks, the United States would have to go to war.

Peace, Preparedness, and the Election of 1916 >>

While hundreds of young Yanks slipped across the border to enlist in the Canadian army, most Americans agreed that neutrality was the wisest course. Pacifists condemned the war, but Republicans and corporate leaders argued that keeping the nation at peace required military strength. The army numbered only 80,000 men in 1914; the navy, just 37 battleships and a handful of new "dreadnoughts," or supercruisers. Advocates of "preparedness" called for a navy larger than Great Britain's, an army of millions of reservists, and universal military training.

By the end of 1915 frustration with German submarines led Wilson to join the cause. He toured the country promoting preparedness and promising a "navy second to none." In Washington he pressed Congress to double the army, increase

^ J. H. Cassel's 1915 cartoon "Without Warning!" captures the horror of the marine attack on the *Lusitania*. A bloody saber in the hand of a spike helmeted German knifes through the ship from beneath the waves. Flag-waving Americans fall helplessly into the sea and drown.

the National Guard, and begin construction of the largest navy in the world. Preparedness had political power, too, as the Democrats discovered early in the presidential campaign of 1916.

As the Democratic convention opened in June, the keynote speaker began what he expected to be a dull description of Wilson's recent diplomatic maneuvers—only to have the crowd roar back in each case, "What did we do?" The speaker knew the answer and shouted it back: "We didn't go to war!" The next day Wilson was renominated by acclamation. "He Kept Us Out of War" became his campaign slogan.

The Republicans had already nominated Charles Evans Hughes, the former governor of New York. He endorsed "straight and honest" neutrality and peace. Despite his moderate stand, Democrats succeeded in painting him as a warmonger. By the time the polls closed, Wilson had squeaked out

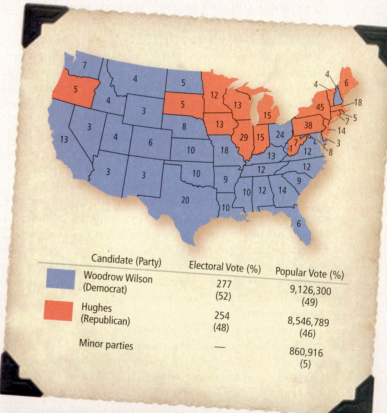

Candidate (Party)	Electoral Vote (%)	Popular Vote (%)
Woodrow Wilson (Democrat)	277 (52)	9,126,300 (49)
Hughes (Republican)	254 (48)	8,546,789 (46)
Minor parties	—	860,916 (5)

ELECTION OF 1916

a victory, carried again to the presidency on a tide of prosperity, progressive reform, and, most of all, promises of peace.

Wilson's Final Peace Offensive >>
Twice since 1915 Wilson had sent his trusted advisor Edward House to Europe to negotiate a peace among the warring powers, and twice House had failed. With the election over, Wilson opened his final peace offensive. When he asked the belligerents to state their terms for a cease-fire, neither side responded. Frustrated, fearful, and genuinely agonized, Wilson called for "a peace among equals" in January 1917.

As Wilson spoke, a fleet of U-boats was cruising toward the British Isles. Weeks earlier German military leaders had persuaded the Kaiser to take one last gamble to starve the Allies into submission. On January 31, 1917, the German ambassador in Washington announced that unrestricted submarine warfare would resume the next day.

Wilson's dream of keeping the country from war collapsed. He asked Congress for authority to arm merchant ships and severed relations with Germany. Then British authorities handed him a bombshell—an intercepted telegram from the German foreign secretary, Arthur Zimmermann, to the Kaiser's ambassador in Mexico. In the event of war the ambassador was instructed to offer Mexico guns, money, and its "lost territory in Texas, New Mexico, and Arizona" to attack the United States. Wilson angrily released the Zimmermann telegram to the press. Soon after, he ordered gun crews aboard merchant ships and directed them to shoot U-boats on sight.

The momentum of events now propelled a reluctant Wilson toward war. On March 12, U-boats torpedoed the American merchant vessel *Algonquin.* On March 15 a revolution in Russia toppled Czar Nicholas II. A key ally was crumbling from within. By the end of the month U-boats had sunk nearly 600,000 tons of Allied and neutral shipping. For the first time reports came to Washington of cracking morale in the Allied ranks.

On April 2 Wilson trudged up the steps of the capitol and delivered to Congress a stirring war message, calling "for democracy, for the right of those who submit to authority to have a voice in their own governments, for the rights and liberties of small nations." Six senators and 50 House members opposed the war resolution, including the first woman in Congress, Jeannette Rankin of Wyoming. Cultural, economic, and historical ties to the Allies, along with the German campaign of submarine warfare, had tipped the country toward war. Wilson had not wanted it, but now the battlefield seemed the only path to a higher peace.

> ✅ **REVIEW**
>
> What steps did Woodrow Wilson take to avoid World War I, and why did they fail?

WAR AND SOCIETY

In 1915 the German zeppelin LZ-38, hovering at 8,000 feet, dropped a load of bombs that killed seven Londoners. For the first time in history, civilians died in an air attack. Few aerial bombardments occurred during the First World War, but they signaled the growing importance of the home front in modern combat. Governments not only fielded armies but also mobilized industry, controlled labor, even rationed food. In the United States, traditions of cooperation and volunteerism helped to organize the home front and the battle front, often in ways that were peculiarly progressive.

The Slaughter of Stalemate >>
While the United States debated entry into the Great War, the Allies were coming perilously close to losing it. Following the initial German assault in 1914, the war had settled into a grisly stalemate. A continuous, immovable front stretched south from Flanders to the border of Switzerland. Troops dug ditches, six to eight feet deep and four to five feet wide, to escape bullets, grenades, and artillery. Twenty-five thousand miles of these "trenches" slashed a muddy scar across Europe. Men lived in them for years, prey to disease, lice, and a plague of rats.

War in the machine age gave the advantage to the defense. When soldiers bravely charged "over the top" of the trenches, they were shredded by machine guns that fired 600 rounds a minute. Poison gas choked them in their tracks. Giant howitzers lobbed shells on them from positions too distant to see. In the Battle of the Somme River in 1916 a million men were killed in just four months of fighting. Only late in the war did new armored

Opinion

Should the United States have fought in World War I?

↑ Trench warfare, wrote one general, was "marked by uniform formations, the regulation of space and time by higher commands down to the smallest details . . . fixed distances between units and individuals." The reality was something else again.

"landships"—code-named "tanks"—return the advantage to the offense by surmounting the trench barriers with their caterpillar treads.

By then Vladimir Lenin was speeding home to Russia, where food riots, coal shortages, and protests against the government had led to revolution. Lenin had been exiled to Switzerland during the early stages of the Russian Revolution but returned to lead his Bolshevik party to power in November 1917. Soon the Russians negotiated a separate peace with Germany, which then transferred a million German soldiers to the western front for the coming spring offensive.

"You're in the Army Now" >> The Allies'
plight drove the army into a crash program to send a million soldiers to Europe by the spring of 1918. The United States had barely 180,000 men in uniform. To raise the force, Congress passed the Selective Service Act in May 1917. Feelings against the draft ran high, but progressives were more inclined to see military service as an opportunity to unite America and promote democracy. "Universal [military] training will jumble the boys of America all together, . . . smashing all the petty class distinctions that now divide, and prompting a brand of real democracy," said one of them.

On July 20, 1917, Secretary of War Newton Baker tied a blindfold over his eyes, reached into a huge glass bowl, and drew the first number in the new draft lottery. Some 24 million men were registered. Almost 3 million were drafted; another 2 million volunteered. Most were white, and all were young, between the ages of 21 and 31. Several thousand women served as military clerks, telephone operators, and nurses. In a nation of immigrants, nearly one draftee in five was born in another country. Training often aimed at educating and Americanizing these ethnic recruits. In special "development battalions" drill sergeants barked out orders while volunteers from the YMCA taught American history and English.

Mexican Americans and African Americans volunteered in disproportionately high numbers. While Mexican Americans were integrated into regular Army units, African Americans remained segregated. They quickly filled the four all-black army and eight National Guard units already in existence. Abroad, where 200,000 black troops served in France, only about a quarter were permitted in combat. Southern Democrats in Congress had opposed training African Americans to arms, fearful of putting "arrogant, strutting representatives of black soldiery in every community." Four regiments of the all-black Ninety-third Division, brigaded with the French army, were nonetheless among the first Americans in the trenches and among the most decorated units in the U.S. Army.

Racial violence sometimes flared among the troops. The worst episode occurred in Houston in the summer of 1917. Harassed by white soldiers and by the city's Jim Crow laws, seasoned black regulars rioted and killed 17 white civilians. Their whole battalion was disarmed and sent under arrest to New Mexico. Thirteen troopers were condemned to death and hanged within days, too quickly for appeals even to be filed.

Progressive reformers did not miss the opportunity to put the social sciences to work in the army. Most recruits had fewer than seven years of education, yet they had to be classified and assigned quickly to units. Psychologists saw the chance to use new intelligence tests to help the army and prove their own theories about the value of "IQ" (intelligence quotient) in measuring brainpower. In fact, these new "scientific" IQ tests often measured little more than class origins. Questions such as "Who wrote 'The Raven'?" exposed background rather than intelligence. The army stopped the testing program in January 1919, but schools across the country adopted it after the war, reinforcing many ethnic and racial prejudices.

Mobilizing the Economy >> Armed, clothed
and drilled, the doughboys sailed off aboard the "Atlantic Ferry"—the ships that conveyed them to Europe. (Infantrymen were called "doughboys," most likely because of the clay dough used by soldiers in the 1850s to clean brass belt buckles.) To equip, feed, and transport an army of nearly 5 million required a national effort.

At the Treasury Department, Secretary William Gibbs McAdoo fretted over how to finance the war, which cost, finally, $32 billion. At the time the entire **national debt**

Historian's TOOLBOX

Sounding the Times: *Over There*

William J. Reilly was a popular sailor who performed this song and others.

What language is this? Why include this version of the lyrics?

Leo Feist paid the original publisher of the music $25,000 for the rights to the song, a record at that time. What other ways does the sheet music show that Feist was hoping to make money?

Music has always sounded the times and given historians a feel for the emotional temper of the moment. When George M. Cohan set out to put the martial spirit of the country to music in 1917, the United States had just entered the First World War. Cohan, the son of Irish Catholics, claimed to have written the song on a train ride from New Rochelle to New York City. "I read those war headlines," he later recalled, "and I got to thinking and humming to myself and for a minute, I thought I was going to dance." The song became a popular hit, a powerful recruiting tool for the armed services, and a measure of the innocence of Americans who blithely marched "over there" to save war-torn Europe, only to enter the inferno of industrialized warfare. The song begins with a rhythmic drumbeat and a call to arms: "Johnnie get your gun / Get your gun, get your gun," and builds to its famous chorus, "Over there, over there / Send the word, send the word, over there / That the Yanks are coming / The Yanks are coming / The drums rum-tumming / Ev'rywhere." (To read the entire text of the song and to hear recordings from 1917, see www.firstworldwar.com/audio/overthere.htm).

THINKING CRITICALLY

What is the message of the lyrics of the song? How does the music affect the message? How does it help to have so many of the lines repeated? During the Second World War, songs of nostalgia for the home front such as "White Christmas" replaced martial songs such as "Over There." Why might that have been the case?

The preceding image and text come from the Duke University Library. (Accessed on July 27, 2009 at http://scriptorium.lib.duke.edu/sheetmusic/n/n09/n0967/).

---

ran to only $2 billion. New taxes paid about a third of the war costs. The rest came from loans financed through "Liberty" and "Victory" bonds and war savings certificates. By 1920 the national debt had climbed to $20 billion.

[**national debt** cumulative total of all previous annual federal deficits or budget shortfalls incurred each year and owed by the federal government.

With sweeping grants of authority provided by Congress, President Wilson constructed a massive bureaucracy to mobilize the home front. What emerged was a **managed economy** similar to the New Nationalism envisioned by Theodore Roosevelt. A War

[**managed economy** economy directed by the government with power over prices, allocation of resources, and marketing of goods.

Then&Now

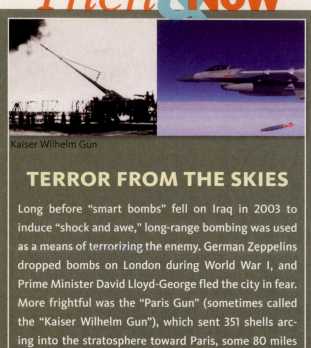

Kaiser Wilhelm Gun

TERROR FROM THE SKIES

Long before "smart bombs" fell on Iraq in 2003 to induce "shock and awe," long-range bombing was used as a means of terrorizing the enemy. German Zeppelins dropped bombs on London during World War I, and Prime Minister David Lloyd-George fled the city in fear. More frightful was the "Paris Gun" (sometimes called the "Kaiser Wilhelm Gun"), which sent 351 shells arcing into the stratosphere toward Paris, some 80 miles away. At least 256 Parisians died, and another 620 were wounded. Although the gun's 92-foot barrel had to be replaced after 65 rounds, the Paris gun still succeeded as a weapon of terror.

trade association organization of individuals and firms in a given industry that provides lobbying and other services to members.

Industries Board (WIB) coordinated production through networks of industrial and **trade associations**. Rather than order firms to comply and risk law suits against the government, the WIB relied on persuasion through publicity and "cost-plus" contracts that covered all production costs, plus a guaranteed profit. Antitrust suits, which might have prevented corporate cooperation, were simply put "to sleep," recalled one official. Corporate profits tripled, and production soared.

The Food Administration encouraged farmers to grow more and citizens to eat less wastefully. Publicity campaigns promoted "wheatless" and "meatless" days and exhorted families to plant "victory" vegetable gardens. Spurred by rising prices, farmers brought more marginal lands into cultivation as their real income jumped 25 percent.

A Fuel Administration met the army's energy needs by increasing production and limiting domestic consumption. The U.S. Railroad Administration simply took over rail lines for the duration of the war. Government coordination, together with a new system of permits, got freight moving and kept workers happy. Rail workers saw their wages grow by $300 million. Railroad unions won recognition, an eight-hour day, and a grievance procedure. For the first time in decades labor unrest on the rail lines subsided, and the trains ran on schedule.

The modern **bureaucratic state** received a big boost during the 18 months of American participation in the war. Speeding trends already under way, some 5,000 new federal agencies centralized authority and cooperated with business and labor. The number of federal employees more than doubled between 1916 and 1918 to over 850,000. The wartime bureaucracy was dismantled at the end of the war, but it set an important precedent for the future.

bureaucratic state government run by administrative bureaus and staffed by non-elected officials.

War Work >>

The war benefited working men and women, though not as much as their employers. Government contracts guaranteed high wages, an eight-hour day, and equal pay to men and women for comparable work. To encourage people to stay on the job federal contracting agencies set up special classes to teach employers the new science of personnel management in order to supervise workers more efficiently and humanely. American industry moved one step closer to the "**welfare capitalism**" of the 1920s, with its profit sharing, company unions, and personnel departments to forestall worker discontent.

welfare capitalism business practice of providing welfare—in the form of pension and profit-sharing programs, subsidized housing, personnel management, paid vacations, and other services and benefits—for workers.

Personnel management was not always enough to guarantee industrial peace. In 1917 American workers called over 4,000 strikes, the most in American history. To keep factories running smoothly, President Wilson created the National War Labor Board (NWLB) early in 1918. The NWLB arbitrated more than 1,000 labor disputes, helped to increase wages, and established overtime pay. In return for pledges not to strike, the board guaranteed the rights of unions to organize and bargain collectively. Membership in the American Federation of Labor almost doubled by 1919.

The wartime demand for workers brought nearly a million new women into the labor force. Most were young and single. Some took over jobs once held by men as railroad engineers, drill press operators, and electric lift truck drivers. The prewar trend toward higher-paying jobs intensified, though most women still earned less than the men they replaced. And some of the most spectacular gains in defense and government work evaporated after the war as male veterans returned and the country demobilized.

Women in war work nonetheless helped to energize several women's causes and organizations. Radical suffragist Alice Paul and others who had protested against the war now argued for women's rights, including the right to vote, on the basis of it. As women worked beside men in wartime factories and offices, in nursing stations at home or on the front, and in patriotic and other volunteer organizations, they could argue more convincingly for both economic and political equality. One step in that direction came after the war with the ratification of the Nineteenth Amendment in 1920 granting women the right to vote.

Great Migrations ➤➤

War work sparked massive migrations of laborers. As the fighting abroad choked off immigration and the draft depleted the workforce, factory owners scoured the country for workers. Industrial cities, no matter how small, soon swelled with newcomers. Between 1917 and 1920 some 150,000 Mexicans crossed the border into Texas, California, New Mexico, and Arizona. Some Mexican Americans left segregated barrios of western cities for war plants in Chicago, Omaha, and other northern cities, pushed out by the cheaper labor from Mexico and seeking higher-paying jobs. But most worked on farms and ranches, freed from military service by the deferment granted to agricultural labor.

Northern labor agents fanned out across the rural South to recruit young African Americans, while black newspapers like the Chicago *Defender* summoned them up to the "Land of Hope." During the war more than 400,000 moved to the booming industries of the North. Largely unskilled and semiskilled, they worked in the steel mills of Pennsylvania, the war plants of Massachusetts, the brickyards

↑ The constraints of war brought more women than ever into the job market. These women work on a production line manufacturing bullets. The novelty of the situation seems evident from the fashionable high-heeled high-button shoes that they wear—ill suited to the conditions in an armaments plant.

of New Jersey. Southern towns were decimated by the drain.

These migrations of African Americans—into the army as well as into the city—aggravated racial tensions. Lynching parties murdered 38 black southerners in 1917 and 58 in 1918. In 1919, after the war ended, more than 70 were hanged, some still in uniform. Housing shortages and job competition helped to ignite race riots across the North. In almost every city black citizens, stirred by war rhetoric of freedom and democracy, showed new militancy. During the bloody "red summer" of 1919 race wars broke out in Washington, D.C., Omaha, Nebraska, New York City, and Chicago, where thousands of African Americans were burned out of their homes and hundreds injured as they fought white mobs.

Propaganda and Civil Liberties ➤➤

"Once lead this people into war," President Wilson warned before American entry into the conflict, "and they'll forget there ever was such a thing as tolerance." Americans succumbed to a ruthless hysteria during World War I, but they had help. Wilson knew how reluctant Americans had been to enter the war. In 1917 he created the Committee on Public Information (CPI) to cement American commitment to the war.

Under George Creel, a California journalist, the CPI launched a vigorous publicity campaign that produced colorful war posters, 75 million pamphlets, and patriotic "war expositions" in two dozen cities across the country. An army of 75,000 fast-talking "Four-Minute Men" invaded theaters, schools, and churches to keep patriotism at "white heat" with four minutes of war tirades. The CPI organized "Loyalty Leagues" in ethnic communities and sponsored rallies, including a much-publicized immigrant "pilgrimage" to the birthplace of George Washington.

As war fever mounted voluntary patriotism blossomed into an orgy of "100 percent Americanism" that bred distrust of all aliens, radicals, pacifists, and dissenters. German Americans became special targets. In Iowa the governor made it a crime to speak German in public. When a mob outside St. Louis lynched a naturalized German American who had tried to enlist in the navy, a jury found the leaders not guilty.

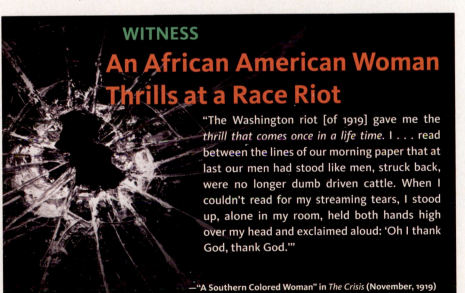

WITNESS

An African American Woman Thrills at a Race Riot

"The Washington riot [of 1919] gave me the *thrill that comes once in a life time.* I . . . read between the lines of our morning paper that at last our men had stood like men, struck back, were no longer dumb driven cattle. When I couldn't read for my streaming tears, I stood up, alone in my room, held both hands high over my head and exclaimed aloud: 'Oh I thank God, thank God.'"

—"A Southern Colored Woman" in *The Crisis* (November, 1919)

sedition words or actions that incite revolt against the law or duly constituted government.

Congress gave hysteria more legal bite by passing the Espionage and the **Sedition** acts of 1917 and 1918. Both set harsh penalties for any actions that hindered the war effort or that could be viewed as even remotely unpatriotic. Following passage, 1,500 citizens were arrested for offenses that included denouncing the draft, criticizing the Red Cross, and complaining about wartime taxes.

Radical groups received especially severe treatment. The Industrial Workers of the World (IWW), a militant union centered in western states, saw the war as a battle among capitalists and threatened to strike mining and lumber companies in protest. Federal agents raided IWW headquarters in Chicago and arrested 113 members. The crusade destroyed the union. Similarly, the Socialist party opposed the "capitalist" war. In response the postmaster general banned a dozen Socialist publications from the mail, though the party was a legal organization that had elected mayors, municipal officials, and members of Congress. In 1918 government agents arrested Eugene V. Debs, the Socialist candidate for president in 1912, for an antiwar speech. A jury found him guilty of sedition and sentenced him to 10 years in jail.

The Supreme Court endorsed such actions. In *Schenck v. United States* (1919) the Court unanimously affirmed the conviction of a Socialist party officer who had mailed pamphlets urging resistance to the draft. The pamphlets, wrote Justice Oliver Wendell Holmes, created "a clear and present danger" to a nation at war.

Over There >> The first American doughboys landed in France in June 1917, but few saw battle. General John Pershing held back his raw troops until they received more training. He also separated them in a distinct American Expeditionary Force to preserve their identity and avoid Allied disagreements over strategy.

In the spring of 1918, as the Germans pushed toward Paris, Pershing rushed 70,000 American troops to the front. American units helped block the Germans at the town of Château-Thierry and at Belleau Wood. Two more German attacks, one at Amiens and the other just east of the Marne River, ended in costly German retreats. In September 1918, half a million American soldiers and a smaller number of French troops overran the German stronghold at Saint-Mihiel in four days.

With their army in retreat and civilian morale low, Germany's leaders sought an **armistice.** They hoped to negotiate terms along the lines laid out by Woodrow Wilson in a speech to Congress in January 1918. Wilson's bright vision of peace had encompassed 14 points. The key provisions called for open diplomacy, free seas and free trade, disarmament, democratic self-rule, and an "association of nations" to guarantee collective security. It was nothing less than a new world order to end selfish nationalism, imperialism, and war.

armistice mutually agreed-on truce or temporary halt in the fighting of a war so that the combatants may discuss peace.

Allied leaders were not impressed. "President Wilson and his Fourteen Points bore me," French premier Georges Clemenceau said. "Even God Almighty has only ten!" Wilson's idealistic platform was also designed to save the Allies deeper embarrassment. Almost as soon as it came to power in 1917, the new Bolshevik government in Moscow began publishing secret treaties from the czar's archives. They revealed that the Allies had gone to war for territory and colonies, not for high principles. Wilson's Fourteen Points had given their cause a nobler purpose.

THE FINAL GERMAN OFFENSIVE AND ALLIED COUNTERATTACK, 1918

On the morning of March 21, 1918, over 60 German divisions sliced through Allied lines. They then plunged within 50 miles of Paris before being stopped at the Marne River in July. The Allied counterattack was marked by notable American victories at Château-Thierry, Belleau Wood, Saint-Mihiel, and Meuse-Argonne.

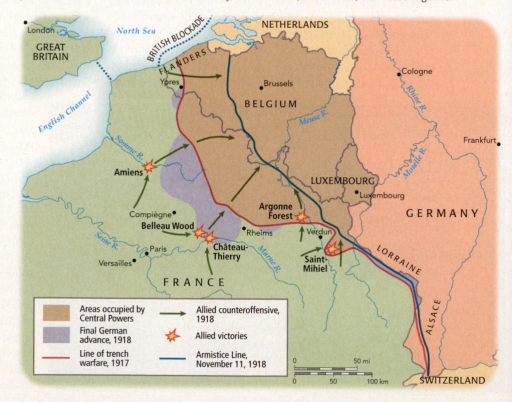

24

>> AN AMERICAN STORY

YESTERDAY MEETS TODAY IN THE NEW ERA

Just before Christmas 1918 the "Gospel Car" pulled into Los Angeles. Bold letters on the side announced: "JESUS IS COMING—GET READY." Aimee Semple McPherson, the ravishing redheaded driver, had just completed a cross-country trip to seek her evangelical destiny. At first Sister Aimee found destiny elusive. Three years of wandering across California finally landed her in San Diego, a city with the state's highest rates of illness and suicide. It was the perfect place to preach her healing message of the "Foursquare Gospel." Sister Aimee's revival attracted 30,000 people, who witnessed her first miracle: a paralytic walked. **>>**

⌃ Sister Aimee Semple McPherson, billed as the "world's most pulchritudinous evangelist," in her robes.

On New Year's Day 1923, to the blare of trumpets, Sister Aimee unveiled the $1.5 million Angelus Temple, graced by a 75-foot rotating electronic cross and a 5,000-seat auditorium. Her lively sermons, broadcast over her own radio station, carried the spirit of what people were calling the "New Era" of productivity and consumerism. Country preachers menaced their congregations with visions of eternal damnation. Sister Aimee, wrote a reporter, offered "flowers, music, golden trumpets, red robes, angels, incense, nonsense, and sex appeal."

Modernizing the gospel was only one symptom of the New Era. Writing in 1931 journalist Frederick Lewis Allen found the changes of the preceding decade so overwhelming that it hardly seemed possible 1919 was "only yesterday," as he titled his best-selling book. To demonstrate the transformation, Allen followed an average American couple, the fictitious "Mr. and Mrs. Smith," through the decade.

Among the most striking changes was the revolution in women's fashions and behavior. Mrs. Smith's hemline jumped from her ankle to her knee.

With Prohibition in full force, she and other women of her day walked into illegal "speakeasy" saloons as readily as men. The Smiths danced to jazz and sprinkled their conversations with references to "repressed sexual drives" and the best methods of contraception. Perhaps the most striking change was these "average" Americans lived in a city. The census of 1920 showed that for the first time just over half the population were urbanites.

Yet the city-dwelling Smiths of Frederick Allen's imagination were hardly average. Nearly as many Americans lived on isolated farms and in villages and clung to the small-town values of an earlier America. In tiny Hyden, Kentucky, along the Cumberland Plateau, Main Street remained unpaved. By 1930 there were only 10 automobiles in the whole county. God-fearing Baptists still repaired to the Middle Fork of the Kentucky River for an open-air baptism when they declared their new birth in Christ. They would have nothing to do with jazz or the showy miracles of Aimee McPherson.

As much as some Americans resisted the transforming forces of modern life, the New Era could not be walled out. New industrial technologies produced a host of consumer goods, while large corporations developed more "modern" bureaucracies to make workers and production lines more efficient. Whether Americans embraced the New Era or condemned it, change came nonetheless, in the form of a mass-produced consumer economy, a culture shaped by mass media, and a more materialistic society. ≪

THE ROARING ECONOMY

In the 1920s the United States was in the midst of a production boom. Manufacturing rose 64 percent; output per work hour, 40 percent. The sale of electricity doubled; fuel oil purchases more than doubled. Between 1922 and 1927 the economy grew by 7 percent a year—the largest peacetime rate ever. If anything roared in the "Roaring Twenties," it was production and consumption.

Technology, Consumer Spending, and the Boom in Construction
>> Technology was partly responsible for the upsurge. Steam turbines and shovels, electric motors, belt and bucket conveyors, and countless other new machines became commonplace at work sites. Machines replaced 200,000 workers each year, and a new phrase—"technological unemployment"—entered the vocabulary. Even so, demand kept the labor force growing at a rate faster than that of the population. And pay improved. Between 1919 and 1927, average income climbed nearly $150 for each American.

Consumer goods, the product of a maturing industrial economy, fueled rising demand. Cigarette lighters, wristwatches, radios, and other new products disappeared from store shelves almost as quickly as they appeared. The improvement in productivity helped to keep prices down. Meanwhile, the purchasing power of wage earners jumped by 20 percent. But for all the prosperity, a dangerous imbalance was developing. Most Americans saved little. Personal debt rose two and a half times faster than personal income, an unhealthy sign of consumers scrambling to spend.

Along with technology and consumer spending, new "boom industries" promoted economic growth. Construction was one. In a rebound after the war years, residential construction doubled as suburb populations soared. Beverly Hills on the edge of Los Angeles grew by 2,500 percent. New roads made suburban life possible and pumped millions of dollars into the economy. In 1919 Oregon, New Mexico, and Colorado hit on a novel idea for financing roads: a tax on gasoline. Within a decade every state had one.

Construction stimulated other businesses: steel, concrete, lumber, home mortgages, and insurance. It even helped change the nation's eating habits. The limited storage space of small "kitchenettes" in new apartments boosted supermarket chains and the canning industry. And as shipments of fresh fruits and vegetables sped across new roads, interest in nutrition grew. Vitamins, publicized with new zeal, appeared on breakfast tables.

The Automobile
>> No industry boomed more than auto manufacturing. Although cars first appeared at the turn of the century, for many years they remained expensive toys. By 1920 there were 10 million in America. By 1929 the total jumped to 26 million, one for every 5 people (compared with one for every 43 in Britain). Automakers bought more rubber, plate glass, nickel, and lead than any other industry. By the end of the decade one American in four somehow earned a living from automobiles.

Henry Ford made it possible by pushing standardization and mass production to such ruthless extremes that the automobile became affordable. Trading on his fame as a race-car manufacturer, he founded the Ford Motor

The East Coryell Company marketed ethyl alcohol gasoline as an alternative to hydrocarbon-based fuels. In Lincoln, Nebraska, this gas station touted the virtue of "corn alcohol gasoline" using an eye-catching pump with an ear of corn painted on each of its four sides.

ONLY PACKARD CAN BUILD A PACKARD

« In the 1920s automobile advertising shifted gears by broadening its audience and making the automobile a symbol of social success. Earlier advertisements had stressed the technical advantages of automobiles and were aimed strictly at men. Here an automobile advertisement from 1925 emphasizes the subliminal rewards of owning a luxury car. Prestige, power, wealth, and romantic love belong to a man who owns a Packard automobile. And women are not ignored. The advertisement points out to women that owning a Packard is not only "evidence of discriminating taste" but also a sign of cost-consciousness for family-minded females.

FRANK QUAIL

A MAN IS KNOWN BY THE CAR HE KEEPS

In the old days men were rated by the homes in which they lived

and few but their friends saw them.

Today, men are rated by the cars they drive

and everybody sees them—

for the car is mobile and the home is not.

To own a Packard is an evidence of discriminating taste.

Woman, with her observing eye, has known this for twenty-five years.

And woman, proverbial for her greater thrift, will insist upon the family motor car being a Packard once she learns that the Packard Six costs less to own, operate and maintain than the ordinary car the family has been buying every year or two.

Packard Six and Packard Eight both furnished in ten body types, open and enclosed. Packard's extremely liberal monthly payment plan makes possible the immediate enjoyment of a Packard, purchasing out of income instead of capital.

A S K   T H E   M A N   W H O   O W N S   O N E

Company in 1903 with the dream of building a "motor car for the multitude." The way to succeed was to reduce manufacturing costs by making all the cars alike, "just like one pin is like another pin." In 1908 Ford perfected the Model T with a 20-horsepower engine and a body of steel. It was high enough to ride the worst roads, and it came in only one color: black.

Priced at $845, the Model T was cheap by industry standards but still too costly and too time-consuming to build. To hold down costs and increase efficiency, Ford engineers copied a practice of Chicago meatpacking houses, where beef carcasses were carried on moving chains past meat dressers. In 1914 Ford introduced the moving assembly line. A conveyor belt, positioned waist high to eliminate bending or walking, propelled the chassis past stationary workers who put the cars together. The process cut assembly time in half. In 1925 new Model Ts were rolling off the lines every 10 seconds. At $290, almost anybody could buy one. By 1927 Ford had sold 15 million of his "tin lizzies."

Ford was also a social prophet. Breaking with other manufacturers, he preached a "doctrine of high wages." According to it, workers with extra money in their pockets would buy enough to sustain a booming prosperity. In 1915 Ford's plants in Dearborn established the "Five-Dollar Day," twice the wage rate in Detroit. He reduced working hours from 48 to 40 a week and cut the workweek to five days.

Yet many Ford workers were unhappy. Ford admitted that the repetitive operations on his assembly line made it almost impossible for a worker "to continue long at the same job." The Five-Dollar Day was designed, in part, to reduce turnover rates of 300 percent a year at Ford plants. Ford recouped his profits by speeding up the assembly line and enforcing stringent work practices. Ford workers could not sit or talk on the job, communicating only in the "Ford Whisper" without moving their lips. A "Sociological Department" spied on workers at home.

By making automobiles available to nearly everyone, the industry changed the face of America. The spreading web of paved roads fueled urban sprawl, real estate booms in California and Florida, and a new roadside economy of restaurants, service stations, and motels. Thousands of "auto camps" opened to provide tourists with tents and crude toilets. Automobile travel broke down rural isolation and advanced common dialects and manners.

Across the country the automobile gave the young unprecedented freedom from parental control. After hearing 30 cases of "sex crimes" (19 had occurred in cars), an exasperated juvenile court judge labeled the automobile "a house of prostitution on wheels." It was, of course, much more: a catalyst for economic growth, a transportation revolution, and a symbol of modernization.

The Future of Energy >> The automobile also helped to ensure that the future of energy would be written in oil. It was never foreordained but the result of several factors, some natural, others economic, and still others corporate-made.

One factor was abundance. Beginning with the great oil strike at Titusville, Pennsylvania, in 1859, drillers tapped into huge pools of petroleum in Ohio, Indiana, Illinois, and other states in the South and the West. Following the mammoth discovery in southeast Texas in 1901 at Spindletop, crude or unrefined oil from the field dropped to 3 cents a barrel. Coal-driven railroad and steamship companies jumped at the chance to buy new energy at cut-rate costs.

Chemistry abetted abundance. Over the next 20 years, chemists found that "cracking" or breaking the string of carbon molecules in oil more than doubled the gasoline squeezed from a barrel of unrefined petroleum. In the early 1920s engineers at General Motors figured out that creating more complex hydrocarbon molecules could prevent a serious problem: the premature ignition of fuel, which siphoned off energy and produced a familiar "knocking" sound upon acceleration. They also discovered that adding certain compounds, including tetraethyl lead, could raise the energy level of this "high-octane" gasoline without knocking.

Among the other antiknock additives was alcohol. Alcohol from fermented plants could also power engines. Peanut oil drove the first Diesel engines. By 1925 Henry Ford was calling alcohol "the fuel of the future." Hydrocarbons were bound to run out, leaving the United States dependent on foreign reserves and eventually the planet without its most precious source of fuel. But as long as plants grew, alcohol was endlessly renewable and thus to Ford the energy of tomorrow.

For a time in the 1920s other automobile manufacturers as well as engineers and chemists agreed, but in the end alcohol lost out. For one thing, alcohol provided 30 percent less energy than gasoline did. For another, alcohol was more expensive to produce when growing, harvesting, distilling, and transporting were taken into account. Also important, new oil discoveries on the eve of the Great Depression drove down crude oil prices to

> To hold down costs and increase efficiency, Ford engineers copied a practice of Chicago meatpacking houses, where beef carcasses were carried on moving chains past meat dressers.

2 cents a barrel by 1931. Finally, GM and its Ethyl Corporation, which stood to profit from leaded gasoline, waged a relentless campaign against alcohol as a fuel or an additive.

The long-term price paid for energy dependence on oil and leaded gasoline told over time. Half a century later long lines at gas stations and high prices at the pump testified to the power of foreign producers to vex American consumers and threaten national security by reducing the flow of oil into the country. Even earlier, minute flecks of lead in oil refineries were poisoning workers, while lead-laden emissions from automobiles contaminated soil and water until federal regulations began to phase out the metal from gasoline and other products in the 1970s. Smog thickened by emissions from gasoline-driven automobiles engulfed cities such as Los Angeles in a choking haze. Led by California, new regulations set limits on harmful auto emissions in the 1960s and 1970s.

The Business of America >>
"The chief business of the American people," President Calvin Coolidge declared in 1925, "is business." A generation earlier, progressives had criticized business for its social irresponsibility. But the wartime contributions of business managers and the return of prosperity in 1922 from a short-lived recession gained them renewed respect.

Encouraged by federal permissiveness, a wave of mergers swept the economy. Between 1919 and 1930 some 8,000 firms disappeared as large gobbled small. Oligopolies (where a few firms dominated whole industries) grew in steel, meatpacking, cigarettes, and other businesses. National chains began to replace local "mom-and-pop" stores. By 1929 one bag of groceries in 10 came from the 15,000 red-and-gold markets of the Great Atlantic and Pacific Tea Company, commonly known as A&P.

This expansion and consolidation meant that national wealth was being controlled not by affluent individuals but by corporations. The model of modern business was the large corporation, in which those who actually managed the company had little to do with those who owned it, the shareholders. A salaried bureaucracy of executives and plant managers formed an elite class. They learned the techniques of **scientific management** through new schools of business as well as new professional societies and consulting firms. They channeled earnings back into their companies to expand factories and carry on research. By the end of the decade more than a thousand firms

scientific management system of factory production that stresses efficiency, pioneered by American engineer Frederick Winslow Taylor.

had research laboratories and no shareholder owned more than 1 or 2 percent of company stock.

Welfare Capitalism >>
The new scientific management also stressed good relations between managers and employees. There was reason to, for a rash of postwar strikes had left business leaders suspicious as ever of labor unions and determined to find ways to limit their influence.

Some tactics were more strong-armed than scientific. In 1921 the National Association of Manufacturers, the Chamber of Commerce, and other employer groups launched the "American Plan," aimed at ending "closed shops," factories where only union members could work. Employers made workers sign agreements disavowing union membership. Companies infiltrated unions with spies, locked union members out of factories, and boycotted firms that hired union labor.

The benevolent side of the American Plan involved a social innovation called "welfare capitalism." Companies such as General Electric and Bethlehem Steel pledged to care for their employees and give them incentives for working hard. They built clean, safe factories, installed cafeterias, hired trained dietitians, formed baseball teams and glee clubs. Several hundred firms encouraged perhaps a million workers to buy company stock and even more to enroll in company unions. Called "Kiss-Me Clubs" for their lack of power, they nonetheless offered what few independent unions could match: health and safety insurance; a grievance procedure; and representation for minorities and women.

Most companies cared more for production than for contented employees. Welfare capitalism affected barely 5 percent of the workforce and often gave benefits only to

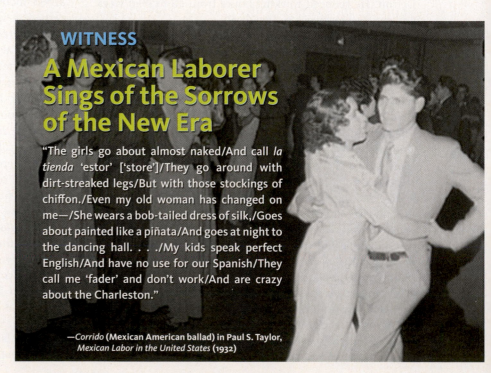

WITNESS

A Mexican Laborer Sings of the Sorrows of the New Era

"The girls go about almost naked/And call *la tienda* 'estor' ['store']/They go around with dirt-streaked legs/But with those stockings of chiffon./Even my old woman has changed on me—/She wears a bob-tailed dress of silk,/Goes about painted like a piñata/And goes at night to the dancing hall. . . ./My kids speak perfect English/And have no use for our Spanish/They call me 'fader' and don't work/And are crazy about the Charleston."

—*Corrido* (Mexican American ballad) in Paul S. Taylor, *Mexican Labor in the United States* (1932)

skilled laborers, the hardest to replace. In the 1920s a family of four could live in "minimum health and decency" on $2,000 a year. The average industrial wage was $1,304. Thus working-class families often needed more than one wage earner just to get by. Over a million children, ages 10 to 15, still worked full-time in 1920.

In 1927, in the most famous strike of the decade, 2,500 mill hands in the textile town of Gastonia, North Carolina, left their jobs. Even strikebreakers walked out. Eventually, authorities broke the strike, foreshadowing a national trend. A year later there were only 629 strikes, a record low for the nation. Union membership sank from almost 5 million in 1921 to less than 3.5 million in 1929.

The Consumer Culture >> During the late nineteenth century the economy had boomed, too, but much of its growth went into nonconsumer goods: steel factories and rails, telephone and electric networks. By World War I these industrial networks penetrated enough of the country to create mass markets. As a greater percentage of the nation's industries turned out consumer goods, prosperity hinged increasingly on consumption. If consumers purchased more goods, production would rise and high volume sales would bring down costs, lifting sales still higher, increasing employment, and repeating the cycle again.

Consumption was the key, and increased consumption rested on two innovations: advertising to encourage people to buy and credit to help them pay. Around the turn of the century, advertisers began a critical shift from emphasizing products to stressing the desires of consumers for health, popularity, and social prestige. Albert Lasker, the owner of Chicago's largest advertising firm, Lord and Thomas, created modern advertising in America. His eye-catching ads were hard-hitting, positive, and often preposterous. To expand the sales of Lucky Strike cigarettes, Lord and Thomas advertisements claimed that smoking made people slimmer and more courageous. "Lucky's" became one of the most popular brands in America.

Advertisers encouraged Americans to borrow against tomorrow so they could purchase what advertising convinced them they wanted today. Installment buying had once been confined to sewing machines and pianos. In the 1920s it grew into the tenth biggest business in the country. In 1919 automaker Alfred Sloan created millions of new customers by establishing the General Motors Acceptance Corporation, the nation's first consumer credit organization. By 1929 Americans were buying most of their cars, radios, and furniture on the installment plan. Consumer debt had jumped 250 percent to $7 billion, almost twice the federal budget.

REVIEW

What factors produced unprecedented economic growth in the 1920s?

A MASS SOCIETY

In the evening after a day's work in the fields—perhaps in front of an adobe house built by one of the western sugar beet companies—Mexican American workers might gather to chat or sing a *corrido* or two. The *corrido,* or ballad, was a Mexican folk tradition. But the subjects changed over time to match the concerns of composers. One *corrido* during the 1920s told of a field laborer distressed over his family's rejection of Mexican customs in favor of new American fashions (see "Witness box"). His wife, he sang, wore makeup and went about "painted like a piñata." His children spoke English, not Spanish, and loved the latest dance crazes.

For Americans from all backgrounds the New Era was witness to "a vast dissolution of ancient habits," commented columnist Walter Lippmann. Mass marketing and mass distribution led not simply to a higher standard of living but to a life less regional and diverse. In place of moral standards set by local communities and churches came "modern" styles and attitudes, spread by the new mass media of movies, radio, and magazines. In the place of "ancient habits" came the forces of mass society: independent women, freer love, standardized culture, urban energy and impersonality, and growing alienation.

A "New Woman" >>

During the tumultuous 1890s a "New Woman" appeared, one more assertive, athletic, and independent than her Victorian peers. By the 1920s more modern versions of this New Woman were being charged with leading what Frederick Lewis Allen called the "revolution in manners and morals." The most flamboyant of them wore makeup, close-fitting felt hats, long-waisted dresses, and strings of beads. Cocktail in hand, footloose and economically free, they called themselves

>> Not all women conformed to the rambunctious image of the flapper. Pictured here is Margaret Gorman of Washington, D.C, crowned in 1921 as the first Miss America. She represented the wholesome and athletic aspects of the New Woman.

"flappers." They became a symbol of liberation to some, of decadence to others.

World War I served as a powerful social catalyst, continuing the prewar trend toward increasing the percentage of women in the workforce and changing many attitudes. Before the war women could be arrested for smoking cigarettes openly, using profanity, and driving automobiles without men beside them. Wartime America ended many of these restrictions. With women bagging explosives and running locomotives, the old taboos often seemed silly.

Disseminating birth control information by mail had also been a crime before the war. By the armistice there was a birth control clinic in Brooklyn, a National Birth Control League, and later an American Birth Control League led by Margaret Sanger. Sanger's crusade began as an attempt to save poor women from the burdens of unwanted pregnancies. By the 1920s her message had found a receptive middle-class audience. Surveys showed that by the 1930s nearly 90 percent of college-educated couples practiced contraception.

Being able to a degree to control pregnancy, women felt less guilt about enjoying sex. In 1909 Sigmund Freud had come to America to lecture on his theories of coping with the unconscious and overcoming harmful repressions. Some of Freud's ideas, specifically his emphasis on childhood sexuality, shocked Americans, while most of his complex theories sailed over their heads. As popularized in the 1920s Freudian psychology stamped sexuality as a key to health.

Such changes in the social climate were real enough, but the life of a flapper girl hardly mirrored the experiences of most American women. Over the decade the female labor force grew by only 1 percent. As late as 1930 nearly 60 percent of all working women were African American or foreign-born and generally held low-paying jobs in domestic service or the garment industry.

The New Era did spawn new careers for women. The consumer culture capitalized on a preoccupation with appearance and led to the opening of some 40,000 beauty parlors staffed by hairdressers, manicurists, and cosmeticians. "Women's fields" carved out by progressive reformers expanded opportunities in education, libraries, and social welfare. Women earned a higher percentage of doctoral degrees (from 10 percent in 1910 to 15.4 percent in 1930) and held more college teaching posts than ever (32 percent). But in most areas professional men resisted the "feminization" of the workforce. The number of female doctors dropped by half. Medical

⌃ "Street selling was torture for me," Margaret Sanger recalled of her efforts to promote the Birth Control Review. A heckler once shouted: "Have you ever heard God's word to be fruitful and multiply?" Sanger shot back, "They've done that already."

schools imposed restrictive quotas, and 90 percent of all hospitals rejected female interns.

In 1924 two women—Nellie Ross in Wyoming and Miriam ("Ma") Ferguson in Texas—were elected governors, the first female chief executives. For the most part, though, women continued to be marginalized in party politics while remaining widely involved in educational and welfare programs. Operating outside male-dominated political parties, women activists succeeded in winning passage of the Sheppard-Towner Federal Maternity and Infancy Act in 1921 to fight high rates of infant mortality with rural prenatal and baby care centers. It was the first federal welfare statute. Yet by the end of the decade the Sheppard-Towner Act had lapsed.

In the wake of their greatest success the hard-won vote for women, feminists splintered. The National Woman Suffrage Association disbanded in 1920. In its place the new League of Women Voters campaigned to encourage informed voting. For the more militant Alice Paul and her allies, that was not enough. Their National Woman's party pressed for a constitutional Equal Rights Amendment (ERA). Social workers and others familiar with the conditions under which women labored opposed it. Death and injury rates for women were nearly double those for men. To them the ERA meant losing the protection as well as the benefits women derived from mothers' pensions and maternity insurance. Joined by most men and a majority of Congress, they fought the amendment to a standstill.

Mass Media ≫

In balmy California, where movies could be made year-round, Hollywood helped give the New Woman notoriety as a temptress and trendsetter. When sexy actress Theda Bara appeared in *The Blue Flame* in 1920, crowds mobbed theaters. And just as Hollywood dictated standards of physical attractiveness, it became the judge of taste and fashion in countless other ways because motion pictures were a virtually universal medium. There was no need for literacy or fluency, no need even for sound, given the power of the pictures parading across the screen.

Motion pictures, invented in 1889, had first been shown in tiny neighborhood theaters called "nickelodeons." For only a nickel patrons watched a silent screen flicker with moving images as an accompanist played music on a tinny piano. Often children read the subtitles aloud to their immigrant parents, translating into Italian, Yiddish, or German. After the first feature-length film, *The Great Train Robbery* (1903), productions became rich in spectacle, attracted middle-class audiences, and turned into America's favorite form of entertainment. By 1926 more than 20,000 movie houses offered customers lavish theaters with overstuffed seats, live music, and a celluloid dream world. At the end of the decade they were drawing over 100 million people a week, roughly the equivalent of the national population.

In the spring of 1920 Frank Conrad of the Westinghouse Company in East Pittsburgh rigged up a research station in his barn and started transmitting phonograph music and baseball scores to local wireless operators. Six months later Westinghouse officials opened the first licensed broadcasting station in history, KDKA, to stimulate sales of their supplies. By 1922 the number of licensed stations had jumped to 430, and by the end of the decade nearly one home in three had a radio ("furniture that talks," comedian Fred Allen called it).

At first radio was seen as a civilizing force. "The air is your theater, your college, your newspaper, your library," exalted one ad in 1924. But with the growing number of sets came commercial broadcasting, catering to more common tastes. Almost the entire nation listened to *Amos 'n' Andy*, a comedy about African Americans created by two white vaudevillians in 1929. At night families gathered around the radio instead of the fireplace, listening to a concert, perhaps, rather than going out to hear music. Linked by nothing but airwaves, Americans were finding themselves part of a vast new community of listeners.

Print journalism also broadened its audience during the 1920s. In 1923 Yale classmates Henry R. Luce and Briton Hadden rewrote news stories in a snappy style, mixed them with photographs, and created the country's first national weekly, *Time* magazine. Fifty-five giant newspaper chains distributed 230 newspapers with a combined circulation of 13 million by 1927. Though they controlled less than 10 percent of all papers, the chains pioneered modern mass news techniques. Editors relied on central offices and syndicates to prepare editorials, sports, gossip, and Sunday features for a national readership.

The Cult of Celebrity >>

In a world where Americans were rapidly being reduced to anonymous parts of a mass industrialized society, media offered them a chance to identify with achievements of individuals by creating a world of celebrities and heroes. Sports figures such as Babe Ruth, business executives like Henry Ford, and movie stars led by Latin heartthrob Rudolf Valentino found their exploits splashed across front pages and followed on radio by millions hungry for excitement and eager to project their own dreams onto others.

No celebrity attracted more attention than a shy, reed-thin youth named Charles Lindbergh. Early on May 20, 1927, "Lucky Lindy" streaked into the skies above Long

⌃ Charles A. Lindbergh, with *Spirit of St. Louis* in background, May 31, 1927

Island aboard a silver-winged monoplane called the *Spirit of St. Louis* and headed east. Thirty-three hours and 30 minutes later he landed just outside Paris, the first flier to cross the Atlantic alone. An ecstatic mob nearly tore his plane to pieces in search of souvenirs.

Lindbergh returned with his plane aboard the warship USS *Memphis*. In New York City alone nearly four million cheering fans greeted him. Lindbergh had "fired the imagination of mankind," observed one newspaper. Never before had an individual mastered a machine so completely or conquered nature so courageously. To Americans ambivalent about mass society and anxious over being subordinated to bureaucracy and technology, here was a sign. Perhaps like Lindbergh they could control their New Era without surrendering their cherished individualism.

"Ain't We Got Fun?" >>

"Ev'ry morning, ev'ry evening, ain't we got fun?" ran the 1921 hit song. As the average hours on the job each week decreased from 47.2 in 1920 to 42 by 1930, spending on amusement and recreation shot up 300 percent. Spectator sports came of age. In 1921, 60,000 fans paid $1.8 million to see Jack Dempsey, the "Manassas Mauler," knock out French champion Georges Carpentier. Millions more listened as radio took them ringside for the first time in sports history. Universities constructed huge stadiums for football, such as Ohio State's 64,000-seater. By 1930 college football games were outdrawing major league baseball.

Baseball remained the national pastime but became a bigger business. An ugly World Series scandal in 1919 led owners to appoint Judge Kenesaw Mountain Landis "czar" of the sport early in the decade. His strict rule reformed the game. In 1920 the son of immigrants revolutionized it. George Herman "Babe" Ruth hit 54 home runs and made the New York Yankees the first club to attract a million fans in one season. His legendary drinking and womanizing also made him baseball's bad boy. But under the guidance of the first modern sports agent, Christy Walsh, Ruth became the highest-paid player in the game and made a fortune endorsing everything from automobiles to clothing.

At parties old diversions—charades, card tricks, recitations—faded in popularity as dancing took over. The ungainly camel walk, the sultry tango, and in 1924 the frantic Charleston were the urban standards. Country barns featured a revival of square dancing with music from Detroit's WBZ and sponsored by Henry Ford. From turn-of-the-century brothels and gaming houses in New Orleans, Memphis, and St. Louis came a rhythmic, compelling music that swept into nightclubs and over the airwaves and soon stamped the age with its name: jazz.

Jazz was a remarkably complex blend of several older African American musical traditions, combining the soulfulness of the blues with the syncopated rhythms of ragtime music. The distinctive style of jazz bands came from a marvelous improvising as the musicians embellished melodies and played off one another. The style spread when the "Original Dixieland Jazz Band" (hardly original but possessed of the commercial advantage of being white) recorded a few numbers for the phonograph. Black New Orleans stalwarts like Joe "King" Oliver's Creole Jazz Band began touring, and in 1924 Paul Whiteman inaugurated respectable "white" jazz in a concert at Carnegie Hall. When self-appointed guardians of good taste denounced such music as "intellectual and spiritual debauchery," Whiteman disagreed: "Jazz is the folk music of the machine age."

The Art of Alienation

>> Before World War I a generation of young writers began rebelling against Victorian purity. The savagery of the war drove many of them even farther from faith in reason or progress. Instead they embraced a "nihilism" that denied all meaning in life. When the war ended they turned their resentment against American life, especially its small towns, big businesses, conformity, and materialism. Some led unconventional lives in New York City's Greenwich Village. Others, called **expatriates**, left the country altogether for the artistic freedom of London and Paris. Their alienation helped produce a literary outpouring unmatched in American history.

At home Minnesota-born Sinclair Lewis, the first American to win a Nobel Prize in

expatriate one who leaves the country of one's birth or citizenship to live in another, often out of a sense of alienation.

<< *Blues*, painted in 1929 by African American artist Archibald Motley Jr., evokes the improvised rhythms of the Jazz Age—and a sense of modernity that transformed American music just as Aimee Semple McPherson was modernizing and transforming American religion. New Orleans–born Motley was one of a group of black genre painters in the 1920s that became part of the Harlem Renaissance.

Literature, sketched a scathing vision of midwestern small-town life in *Main Street* (1920). The book described "savorless people . . . saying mechanical things about the excellence of Ford automobiles, and viewing themselves as the greatest race in the world." His next novel, *Babbitt* (1922), dissected small-town businessman George Follansbee Babbitt, a peppy realtor from the fictional city of Zenith. Faintly absurd and supremely dull, Babbitt was the epitome of the average.

A "New Negro" »

As World War I seared white intellectuals, it also galvanized black Americans. Wartime labor shortages spurred a migration of half a million African Americans from the rural South into urban industrial North. Postwar unemployment and racial violence quickly dashed black hopes for equality. Common folk in these urban enclaves found an outlet for their alienation in a charismatic nationalist from Jamaica named Marcus Garvey.

Garvey brought his organization, the Universal Negro Improvement Association (UNIA), to the United States in 1916 in hopes of restoring black pride by returning Africans to Africa and Africa to Africans. "Up you mighty race," he told his followers, "you can accomplish what you will." When Garvey spoke at the first national UNIA

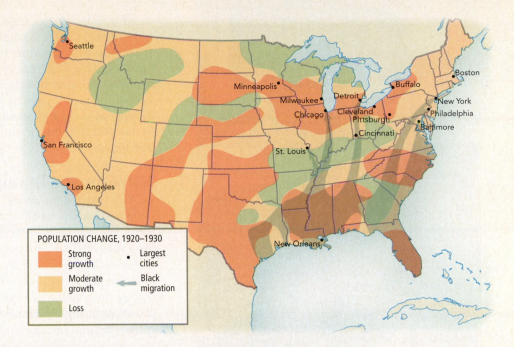

POPULATION CHANGE, 1920–1930

- Strong growth
- Moderate growth
- Loss
- Largest cities
- Black migration

AREAS OF POPULATION GROWTH

In the 1920s the population of urban America grew by some 15 million people, at the time the greatest 10-year jump in American history. Cities grew largely by depopulating rural areas. In the most dramatic manifestation of the overall trend, more than a million African Americans migrated from the rural South to the urban North.

convention in 1920, over 25,000 supporters jammed into Madison Square Garden in New York. Even his harshest critics admitted there were at least half a million members in more than 30 branches of his organization. It was the first mass movement of African Americans in history. But in 1925 Garvey was convicted of mail fraud for having oversold stock in his Black Star Line, the steamship company founded to return African Americans to Africa. His dream shattered.

As Garvey rose to prominence a renaissance of black literature, painting, and sculpture was brewing in Harlem. The first inklings came in 1922 when Claude McKay, another Jamaican immigrant, published a book of poems titled *White Shadows*. In his most famous poem, "If We Must Die," McKay mixed defiance and dignity: "Like men we'll face the murderous, cowardly pack / Pressed to the wall, dying but fighting back!"

Often supported by white patrons, or "angels," young black writers and artists found their subjects in the street life of cities, the folkways of the rural South, and the primitivism of preindustrial cultures. Poet Langston Hughes reminded his readers of the ancient heritage of African Americans in "The Negro Speaks of Rivers," and Zora Neale Hurston collected folktales, songs, and prayers of black southerners.

Opinion

Had Martin Luther King been active during the 1920s, could the modern civil rights movement have begun decades earlier than the 1950s?

^ MARCUS GARVEY

Though generally not a racial protest, the Harlem Renaissance drew on the growing assertiveness of African Americans as well as on the alienation of white intellectuals. In 1925 Alain Locke, a black professor from Howard University, collected a sampling of their works in *The New Negro.* The title reflected not only an artistic movement but also a new racial consciousness.

 REVIEW

How did mass media and mass culture reshape American life in the 1920s?

DEFENDERS OF THE FAITH

As mass society pushed the country into a future of machines, organization, middle-class living, and cosmopolitan diversity, not everyone approved. Dr. and Mrs. Wilbur Crafts, the authors of *Intoxicating Drinks and Drugs in All Lands and Times,* set forth a litany of modern sins that tempted young people in this "age of cities." "Foul pictures, corrupt literature, leprous shows, gambling slot machines, saloons, and Sabbath breaking. . . . We are trying to raise saints in hell."

The changing values of the New Era seemed especially threatening to traditionalists like the Crafts. Their deeply held beliefs reflected the rural roots of so many Americans:

an ethic that valued neighborliness, small communities, and sameness in race, religion, and ethnicity. Opponents of the new ways could be found among country folk and rural migrants to cities as well as an embattled Protestant elite. All were determined to defend the older faiths against the modern age of urban anonymity, moral fluidity, diverse races and ethnicities, and religious pluralism. In the 1920s a full-scale culture war erupted pitting these traditionalists against the forces of modern life.

Nativism and Immigration Restriction >>

In 1921 two Italian aliens and admitted anarchists presented a dramatic challenge to those older faiths. Nicola Sacco and Bartolomeo Vanzetti were sentenced to death for a shoe company robbery and murder in South Braintree, Massachusetts. Critics charged that they were innocent and convicted only of being foreign-born radicals. During the trial the presiding judge had scorned them in private as "anarchist bastards," and in 1927 they were executed. For protesters around the world, the execution was a symbol of American bigotry and prejudice.

By then, nativism—a rabid hostility to foreigners—had produced the most restrictive immigration laws in American history. In the aftermath of World War I immigration was running close to one million a year, almost as high as prewar levels. Most immigrants came from eastern and southern Europe and from Mexico; the majority were Catholics and Jews. Alarmed native-born Protestants warned that if the flood continued, Americans might become "a hybrid race of people as worthless and futile as the good-for-nothing mongrels of Central America and Southeastern Europe." Appreciating the

^ Sacco and Vanzetti, dressed in suits and handcuffed for their court appearance.

benefits of a shrunken labor pool, the American Federation of Labor also supported restriction.

In the Southwest, Mexicans and Mexican Americans became a special target of concern. The Spanish had inhabited the region for nearly 400 years, producing a rich blend of European and Indian cultures. By 1900 about 300,000 Mexican Americans lived in the United States. In the following decade Mexicans fleeing poverty and a revolution in 1910 almost doubled the Latino population of Texas and New Mexico. In California it quadrupled. During World War I, labor shortages led authorities to relax immigration laws, and in the 1920s American farmers in search of cheap labor opened a campaign to attract Mexican farm workers.

Pushed out by the new arrivals, tens of thousands of Mexican Americans moved north. By the end of the 1920s northern industrial cities had thriving communities of Mexicans. In these neighborhoods or *barrios* Spanish-speaking newcomers settled into an immigrant life of family and festivals, churchgoing, hard work, and slow adaptation. The census of 1930 listed nearly 1.5 million Mexicans living in the United States, not including an untold number who entered the country illegally.

Mexicans were just one target of the National Origins Act, first enacted in 1921. It capped all immigration at 350,000 and parceled out the slots by admitting a quota of up to 3 percent of each nationality living in the United States as of the census of 1910. The system of quotas favored "races" commonly believed to be superior—"Nordics"—over those considered inferior—"Alpines" and "Mediterraneans." In 1924 a new National Origins Act reduced the total admitted to 150,000, reduced the percentage to 2, and pushed the base year back to 1890, before the bulk of southern and eastern Europeans arrived.

The National Origins acts fixed the pattern of immigration for the next four decades. Immigration from southern and eastern Europe was reduced to a trickle. The free flow of Europeans to America, a migration of classes and nationalities that had been unimpeded for 300 years, came to an end.

The "Noble Experiment" >> For nearly a hundred years reformers tried with sporadic success to reduce the consumption of alcohol. Their most ambitious campaign climaxed in January 1920, when the Eighteenth Amendment went into effect. Its ban on liquor was not total: private citizens could still drink. They simply could not manufacture, sell, transport, or import any

"intoxicating beverage" containing more than 0.5 percent alcohol. Despite being underfunded and understaffed, the effort reduced alcohol consumption by as much as half.

The consequences of so vast a social experiment were significant and often unexpected. Prohibition reversed the prewar trend toward beer and wine, since hard liquor brought greater profits to bootleggers or manufacturers of illegal alcohol. Prohibition helped to line the pockets and boost the fame of gangsters, including "Scarface" Al Capone. It also advanced women's rights. While saloons had discriminated against "ladies" by having them enter through a separate door or barring them entirely, "speakeasies"—taverns operating undercover—welcomed them.

For all its unhappy consequences, Prohibition enjoyed wide backing. The best science taught that alcohol was bad for health; the best social science, that it corroded family life and weakened society. Corporate executives and labor leaders supported Prohibition to promote a sober, efficient workforce. Many Catholics favored it because they saw the road to perdition lined with liquor bottles. Finally, the liquor industry hurt itself with a terrible record of corrupting legislatures and minors, who were targets of its campaign to recruit young drinkers in the competitive saloon business.

Prohibition can also be understood as cultural and class legislation. Support ran deepest in Protestant churches, especially the evangelical Baptists and Methodists. And there had always been a strong antiurban and anti-immigrant bias among reformers. As it turned out, the steepest decline in drinking occurred among these working-class ethnics. Traditionalists might celebrate the triumph of the "noble experiment," but modern urbanites either ignored or resented it.

KKK >> On Thanksgiving Day 1915, just outside Atlanta, 16 men trudged up a rocky trail to the crest of Stone Mountain. There, as night fell, they set ablaze a huge wooden cross and swore allegiance to the Invisible Empire, Knights of the Ku Klux Klan.

>> As the Ku Klux Klan grew in influence after World War I, race riots erupted in over 25 cities beginning in 1919, including Chicago; Longview, Texas; Knoxville, Tennessee; and Omaha, Nebraska. More than 70 African Americans were lynched in the first year after the end of the war, and 11 were burned alive. Many blacks fought back, their experience in World War I having made them determined to resist repression. In June 1921 rioting in Tulsa, Oklahoma, left 21 African Americans as well as 11 whites dead. As the billowing smoke in this photograph indicates, white mobs burned down entire neighborhoods belonging to the black community. The National Guard was called out to reestablish order.

The modern Klan, a throwback to the hooded order of Reconstruction days (page 349), reflected the insecurities of the New Era. Klansmen worried about the changes and conflicts in American society, which they attributed to the rising tide of immigrants, "uppity women," and African Americans who refused to "recognize their place." Whereas any white man could join the old Klan, the new one admitted only "native born, white, gentile [Protestant] Americans." Unlike the hooded night riders of old, the reborn Klan was not confined to the South. By the 1920s its capital was Indianapolis, Indiana. More than half of its leadership and over a third of its members came from cities of more than 100,000 people.

The new Klan drew on the culture of small-town America. It was patriotic, gave to local charities, and boasted the kind of outfits and rituals adopted by many fraternal lodges. Klansmen wore white hooded sheets and satin robes. A typical gathering brought the whole family to a barbecue with fireworks and hymn singing, capped by the burning of a giant cross. Members came mostly from the middle and working classes: small businesspeople, clerical workers, independent professionals, farmers, and laborers with few skills. The Klan offered them status, security, and the promise of restoring an older America where white supremacy, chastity, and Protestantism reigned. When boycotts and whispering campaigns failed to cleanse communities of Jews, Mexicans, Japanese, or others who offended their social code, the Klan resorted to floggings, kidnappings, acid mutilations, and murder.

Using modern methods of promotion, two professional fund-raisers, and an army of 1,000 salesmen, the Klan enrolled perhaps 3 million dues-paying members by the early 1920s. Moving into politics, its candidates captured legislatures in Indiana, Texas, Oklahoma, and Oregon. The organization was instrumental in electing six governors, three senators, and thousands of local officials. In the end, however, the Klan was undone by sex scandals and financial corruption. Its political power waned after 1925, when the grand dragon of the Indiana Klan was sentenced to life imprisonment for rape and second-degree murder.

Fundamentalism versus Darwinism »

Although Aimee Semple McPherson embraced the fashions of the New Era, many Protestants, especially in rural areas, felt threatened by the secular aspects of modern life. Beginning in the late nineteenth century, scientists and intellectuals spoke openly about the relativity of moral values, questioned the possibility of biblical miracles, and depicted religiosity as the result of hidden psychological needs and the Bible as mere literature. Darwinism, pragmatism, and other scientific and philosophical theories left traditional religious teachings open to skepticism and scorn.

As early as the 1870s liberal Protestants sought to make Christianity more relevant to contemporary life through a movement known as Modernism. One leader defined it as "the use of scientific, historical and social methods in understanding and applying evangelical Christianity to the needs of living persons." Conservative Protestants disagreed with this updating of orthodoxy. Between 1910 and 1915 two wealthy oilmen from Los Angeles subsidized the publication of some three million copies of a series of pamphlets called *The Fundamentals.* They advocated a return to what some conservatives considered the fundamentals of Christian faith, among them the virgin birth, the resurrection of Jesus, and a literal reading of Scripture. After 1920 a variety of conservative Protestants began referring to themselves as "Fundamentalists."

The Fundamentalist movement grew dramatically in the first two decades of the twentieth century, fed by fears of Protestant Modernism as well as of Catholic and Jewish immigrants flooding the country. Nothing disturbed Fundamentalists more than Darwinian theories of evolution that challenged the divine origins of humankind. In 1925 what began as an in-house fight among Protestants became a national brawl when the Tennessee legislature made it illegal to teach that "man has descended from a lower order of animals."

In 1925, encouraged by the newly formed American Civil Liberties Union, skeptics in the town of Dayton, Tennessee, decided to test the law by putting a bespectacled biology teacher named John T. Scopes on trial for teaching evolution. Behind the scenes Scopes's sponsors were preoccupied as much with the commercial boost a sensational trial could give their town as with the defense of academic freedom.

When the Scopes trial opened in July, millions listened over the radio to the first trial ever broadcast. Inside the

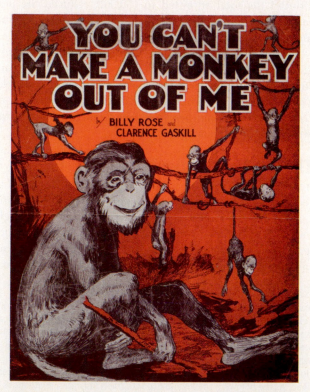

⌃ The sheet-music cover for a song satirizing the Scopes "Monkey" Trial over the teaching of evolution.

courtroom Clarence Darrow, the renowned defense lawyer from Chicago and a professed agnostic, acted as co-counsel for Scopes. Serving as co-prosecutor was William Jennings Bryan, the three-time presidential candidate who had recently joined the antievolution crusade. It was urban Darrow against rural Bryan in what Bryan described as a "duel to the death" between Christianity and evolution.

The presiding judge ruled that scientists could not be used to defend evolution. He considered their testimony "hearsay" because they had not been present at the Creation. The defense virtually collapsed, until Darrow called Bryan to the stand as an "expert on the Bible." Under withering examination Bryan admitted that the Earth might not have been made "in six days of 24-hours." Even so, the Dayton jury took only eight minutes to find Scopes guilty and fine him $100.

By then the excesses of the Scopes trial had transformed it into more of a national joke than a confrontation between darkness and light. But the debate over evolution raised a larger question that continued to reverberate throughout the twentieth century. As scientific, religious, and cultural standards clashed, how much should religious beliefs and local standards influence public education?

> **But the debate over evolution raised a larger question . . . how much should religious beliefs and local standards influence public education?**

✓ **REVIEW**

Along what fronts did traditionalists fight the culture war of the 1920s and with what weapons?

REPUBLICANS ASCENDANT

"The change is amazing," wrote a Washington reporter after the inauguration of Warren G. Harding in March 1921. Sentries disappeared from the gates of the White House, tourists again walked the halls, and reporters freely questioned the president for the first time in years. The reign of "normalcy," as Harding called it, had begun. "By 'normalcy,'" he explained, ". . . I mean normal procedure, the natural way, without excess."

The Politics of "Normalcy" >>   "Normalcy" turned out to be anything but normality. After eight years of Democratic rule, Republicans gained control of the White House and both houses of Congress. Fifteen years of reform gave way to eight years of cautious governing. The

presidency, strengthened by Wilson, fell into weak hands. The cabinet and the Congress set the course of the nation.

Harding and his successor, Calvin Coolidge, were content with delegating power, in Harding's case to a cabinet of what he called "the best minds." Harding appointed some men of quality: Charles Evans Hughes as secretary of state, Henry C. Wallace as secretary of agriculture, and Herbert Hoover as secretary of commerce. He also made, as one critic put it, "unspeakably bad appointments": his old crony Harry Daugherty as attorney general and New Mexico senator Albert Fall as interior secretary. Daugherty sold influence for cash and resigned in 1923. In 1929 Albert Fall became the first cabinet member to be convicted of a felony. In 1922 he had accepted bribes of more than $400,000 for secretly leasing naval oil reserves at Elk Hill, California, and Teapot Dome, Wyoming, to private oil companies.

Harding died suddenly in August 1923, before most of the scandals came to light. Although he would be remembered as passive and weak-kneed, his tolerance and moderation had a calming influence on the strife-ridden nation in the aftermath of World War I. Slowly he had even begun to lead. In 1921 he created a Bureau of the Budget that brought modern accounting techniques to the management of federal revenues. Toward the end of his administration he cleared an early scandal from the Veterans' Bureau and set an agenda for Congress that included expanding the merchant marine.

To his credit Calvin Coolidge handled Harding's sordid legacy with skill and dispatch. He created a special investigatory commission, prosecuted wrongdoers, and restored the confidence of the nation. Decisiveness, when he chose to exercise it, was one of Coolidge's hallmarks. He believed in small-town democracy and minimalist government. "One of the most important accomplishments of my administration has been minding my own business," he boasted. Above all Coolidge worshiped wealth. "Civilization and profits," he once said, "go hand in hand."

The Policies of Mellon and Hoover >>
Coolidge retained most of Harding's cabinet, including his powerful treasury secretary, Andrew Mellon. The former head of aluminum giant Alcoa, Mellon believed that prosperity "trickled down" from rich to poor through investment, which raised production, employment, and wages. In 1921 Mellon persuaded Congress to repeal the excess-profits tax on corporations; under Coolidge he convinced legislators to end all gift taxes, to halve estate and income taxes, and to reduce corporation and consumption taxes even further. In 1922 he endorsed the protective Fordney-McCumber Tariff, raising rates on manufactured and farm goods.

Unlike Mellon, Commerce Secretary Herbert Hoover (also a Harding holdover) was not a traditional conservative who sought only to create a healthy environment for business. Instead, he promoted a progressive brand of capitalism called "associationalism." It aimed at aiding businesses directly by spreading a new gospel of efficiency and productivity through trade associations, groups of private companies organized industry by industry. The role of government, as Hoover saw it, was to encourage voluntary cooperation among businesses. In his view government agencies should provide advice, statistics, and forums where business leaders could exchange ideas, set industry standards, and develop markets.

In these ways, Hoover hoped to eliminate waste, cut costs, and end the boom-and-bust business cycle of ruthless competition. Lower costs would be passed on to consumers in the form of lower prices and so would serve the public interest, as would the principles of welfare capitalism. These ideals Hoover promoted by prodding firms to sponsor company unions, pay workers decent wages, and protect them from factory hazards and unemployment. Meanwhile, the Commerce Department worked to expand foreign markets and fight international cartels.

Both Hoover and Mellon, each in his own way, placed government in the service of business. As a result the impact of government on the economy grew. So did its size, by more than 40,000 employees between 1921 and 1930. Building on their wartime partnership, government and business dropped all pretense of a laissez-faire economy. Efficiency increased, production soared, and prosperity reigned. At the same time, however, Mellon's tax policies helped to concentrate wealth in the hands of fewer individuals and corporations, while Hoover's associationalism helped them to consolidate their power. By the end of the decade, 200 giant corporations controlled almost half the corporate assets in America.

Distress Signals >> Some economic groups remained outside the magic circle of Republican prosperity. Ironically, they included those people who made up the biggest business in America: farmers. In 1920 agriculture still had an investment value greater than manufacturing, all utilities, and all railroads combined. Yet the farmers' portion of the national income shrank by almost half during the 1920s. The government withdrew wartime price supports for wheat and ended its practice of feeding refugees with American surpluses. As postwar European agriculture revived, the demand for American exports dropped. New dietary habits meant that Americans were eating 75 fewer pounds of food annually than they had 10 years earlier. New synthetic fibers drove down demand for natural wool and cotton.

For the five years that Coolidge ran a "businessman's government," workers reaped few gains. Wages, purchasing power, and bargaining rights stagnated. Although welfare capitalism promised benefits to workers, only a handful of companies put it into practice. Those that did often used it to weaken independent unions. As dangerous imbalances in the economy developed, Coolidge ignored them.

One sign of distress no one could ignore: the great Mississippi flood of 1927. After years of deforestation and months of heavy rain, the Mississippi River burst through its levees, rampaging from southern Missouri to Louisiana, an area roughly the size of New England. Floodwaters reached 100 feet in some places and did not recede for three months.

A network of private agencies was quickly knit together and placed under the control of Commerce secretary Herbert Hoover. An army of local citizens, many of them black and some conscripted at

THE GREAT FLOOD OF 1927

Hurricane Katrina (2005), the costliest storm in U.S. history, devastated parts of four states. By comparison the Great Mississippi Flood of 1927 swamped parts of 11 states and covered some 27,000 square miles. It sparked a massive migration of tens of thousands of African Americas from the affected areas to northern cities, such as Chicago.

gunpoint, erected refugee camps to cope with the 700,000 people displaced by the flood. Relief efforts were hardly equal to the task. Nearly 250 people died, and 130,000 homes were destroyed. Property damage ran to $350 million ($5 billion in today's dollars). Before the end of 1928 half the African American population of the Mississippi Delta's black belt had fled the region. For the rest of the decade commerce throughout the central United States suffered. Still, federal legislation had been passed—for the first time—giving the government responsibility for controlling such disasters along the Mississippi.

If most Americans disregarded most distress signals at home, they paid almost no heed to economic unrest abroad. At the end of World War I Europe's victors had forced Germany to take on $33 billion in war costs or reparations, partly to repay their own war debts to the United States. When Germany defaulted in 1923 French forces occupied the Ruhr valley in Germany's industrial heartland. Germany struck back by printing more money, a move that dramatized the crushing burden of its debt. Runaway inflation wiped out the savings of the German middle class, shook confidence in the new Weimar Republic, and soon threatened the economic structure of all Europe.

In 1924 American business leader Charles G. Dawes persuaded the victorious Europeans to scale down reparations. In return the United States promised to help stabilize the German economy. Encouraged by the State Department, American bankers made large loans to Germany, with which the Germans paid their reparations. The European victors then used those funds to repay their war debts to the United States. It amounted to taking money from one American pocket and placing it in another. In 1926 the United States also reduced European war debts. Canceling them altogether would have made more sense, but few Americans were so forgiving.

Despite Europe's debt problems a costly arms race continued among the great powers, despite popular calls for peace and frugality. Two grand diplomatic gestures reflected the twin desires for peace and economy. In 1921, following the lead of the United States, the world's sea powers agreed to freeze battleship construction for 10 years and set ratios on the tonnage of each navy. The Five-Power Agreement was the first disarmament treaty in modern history. A more extravagant gesture came seven years later, in 1928, when the major nations of the world (except the Soviet Union) signed an agreement outlawing war, the Kellogg-Briand Pact. "Peace is proclaimed," announced Secretary of State Frank Kellogg as he signed the document with a foot-long pen of gold.

What seemed so bold on paper proved to be ineffective in practice. The French, for example, resented the lower limits set on their battleships under the Five-Power Agreement and began building smaller warships such as submarines, cruisers, and destroyers. The arms race now concentrated on these vessels.

And the Kellogg-Briand Pact remained a toothless proclamation with no means of enforcement.

The Election of 1928 >>

On August 2, 1927, in a small classroom in Rapid City, South Dakota, Calvin Coolidge handed a terse typewritten message to reporters: "I do not choose to run for President in nineteen twenty-eight." Republicans honored the request and nominated Herbert Hoover. Hoover was not a politician but an administrator and had never once campaigned for public office. It didn't matter. Republican prosperity made it difficult for any Democrat to win. Hoover, perhaps the most admired public official in America, made it impossible.

The Democratic party continued to fracture between its rural supporters in the South and West and urban laborers in the Northeast. By 1928 the shift in population toward cities had given an edge to the party's urban wing. Former New York governor Al Smith won the nomination on the first ballot, even though his handicaps were evident. When the New York City–bred Smith spoke "poisonally" on the "rhadio," his accent made voters across America wince. Though he pledged to enforce Prohibition, he campaigned against it and even took an occasional drink (which produced the false rumor that Smith was a hopeless alcoholic). Most damaging of all, he was Catholic, at a time when anti-Catholicism remained strong in many areas of the country.

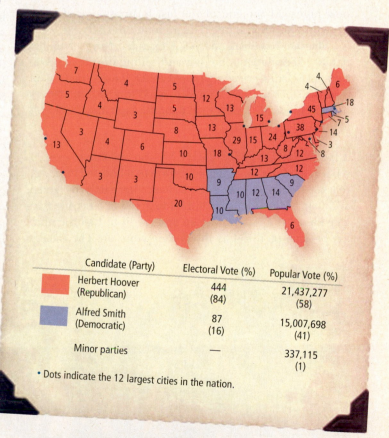

Candidate (Party)	Electoral Vote (%)	Popular Vote (%)
Herbert Hoover (Republican)	444 (84)	21,437,277 (58)
Alfred Smith (Democratic)	87 (16)	15,007,698 (41)
Minor parties	—	337,115 (1)

• Dots indicate the 12 largest cities in the nation.

ELECTION OF 1928

In the election of 1928 nearly 60 percent of eligible voters turned out to give all but eight states to Hoover. The solidly Democratic South cracked for the first time. Still, the stirrings of a major political realignment were buried in the returns. The 12 largest cities in the country had gone to the Republicans in their victorious 1924 campaign. In 1928 the Democrats won them. The Democrats were becoming the party of the cities and of immigrants. Around this core they would build the most powerful vote-getting coalition of the twentieth century.

 REVIEW

What public policies did Presidents Harding and Coolidge pursue during the 1920s?

THE GREAT BULL MARKET

Strolling across the felt-padded floor of the New York Stock Exchange, Superintendent William Crawford greeted the New Year with swaggering confidence. The rampaging "bulls," or buyers of stock, had routed the hibernating "bears," those who sell. It was the greatest bull market in history, as eager purchasers drove prices to new highs. At the end of the last business day of 1928, Crawford declared flatly, "The millennium's arrived."

Veteran financial analyst Alexander Noyes had his doubts. Speculation—buying and selling on the expectation that rising prices will yield quick gains—had taken over the stock market. "Something has to give," said Noyes in September 1929. Less than a month later, the Great Bull Market fell in a heap.

The Rampaging Bull >> No one knows exactly what caused the wave of speculation that boosted the stock market to dizzying heights. Driven alternately by greed and fear, the market succumbed to greed in a decade that considered it a virtue. Money and credit to fuel the market became plentiful as the decade wore on. The money

supply expanded by $6 billion, fed by nearly $900 million worth of gold from overseas. Corporate profits grew by 80 percent. At interest rates as high as 25 percent, more could be made from lending money to brokers (who then made "brokers' loans" to clients for stock purchases) than from constructing new factories. By 1929 brokers' loans had almost tripled from two years earlier.

"Margin requirements," the cash actually put down to purchase stock, hovered around 50 percent for most of the decade. Thus buyers had to come up with only half the price of a share. The rest came from credit furnished by brokers' loans. As trading reached record heights in August 1929, the Federal Reserve Board tried to dampen speculation by raising the interest rates. Higher interest rates made borrowing more expensive and, authorities hoped, would rein in the galloping bull market. They were wrong. It was already too late.

The Great Crash >> At the opening bell on Thursday, October 24, 1929, a torrent of orders to sell flooded the exchange, triggered by nervous speculators worried about a decline. Prices plunged as panic set in. By the end of "Black Thursday" nearly 13 million shares had been traded—a record. Losses stood at $3 billion, another record. Thirty-five of the largest brokerage houses on Wall Street issued a joint statement of reassurance: "The worst has passed."

The worst had just begun. Prices rallied for the rest of the week, buoyed by a bankers' buying pool. The following Tuesday, October 29, 1929, the bubble burst. Stockholders lost $10 billion in a single day. Within a month industrial stocks lost half of what they had been worth in September. And the downward slide continued for almost four years. At their peak in 1929 stocks had been worth $87 billion. In 1933 they bottomed out at $18 billion.

The Great Crash did not cause the Great Depression, but it did damage the economy and broke the unbounded optimism upon which the New Era rested. Although only about 500,000 people were actually trading stocks by the end of the decade, their investments helped to sustain prosperity. Thousands of middle-class investors lost their savings and their futures. Commercial banks—some loaded with corporate stocks, others financing brokers' loans—reeled in the wake of the crash.

ON THE FLOOR — N.Y. STOCK EXCHANGE   REGINALD MARSH

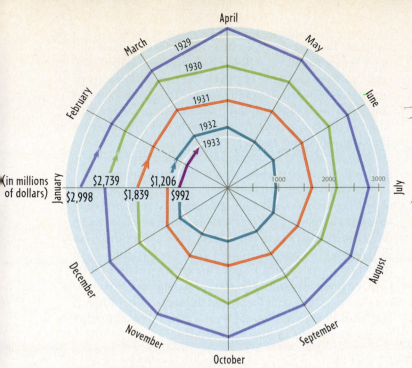

April 1929
March 1930
May 1931
February 1932
1933
June
January (in millions of dollars)
$2,739 $1,206
$2,998 $1,839 $992
1000 2000 3000
July
December
August
November
September
October

DECLINING WORLD TRADE, 1929–1933

As the Great Depression deepened, world trade spiraled downward. Here the imports of 75 countries are tracked from 1929 to 1933. (The amounts are measured in millions of U.S. gold dollars.) The greatest annual decline occurred between 1930 and 1931 as production plummeted and nation after nation began to erect high tariff barriers to protect their domestic markets from cheaper imports. Over the four-year period, world import trade fell by almost two-thirds, only underscoring the growing interdependence of the global economy.

The Great Crash signaled the start of the greatest depression in the history of the modern world. In the United States, the gains of the 1920s were wiped out in a few years. In the first three years after the crash, national income fell by half, factory wages by almost half. By some estimates 85,000 businesses failed.

Although the Great Depression was less deep and less prolonged in other countries, the shock waves from the United States rippled around the globe, helping to topple already-fragile economies in Europe. American loans, investments, and purchases had propped up Europe since the end of World War I. When those resources dried up in the wake of the crash, European governments defaulted on war debts. More European banks failed; more businesses collapsed; unemployment surged to at least 30 million worldwide by 1932.

Europeans scrambled to protect themselves. Led by Great Britain in 1931, 41 nations abandoned the gold standard to give themselves more monetary flexibility. Foreign governments hoped to devalue their currencies by expanding their supplies of money. Conventional wisdom taught that exports would be cheaper and foreign trade would increase. But several countries did so at once, while each country raised tariffs to protect itself from foreign

competition. Devaluation failed, and the resulting trade barriers only deepened the crisis.

In the United States declining sales abroad sent crop prices to new lows. Farm income dropped by more than half. Spurred by defaults on farm mortgages, an epidemic of rural bank failures spread to the cities. Nervous depositors rushed to withdraw their cash. Even healthy banks could not bear the strain. In August 1930 every bank in Toledo but one closed its doors. Between 1929 and 1933 collapsing banks took more than $20 billion in assets with them. The economy was spiraling downward, and no one could stop it.

The Causes of the Great Depression »

What, then, caused the Great Depression in the United States? In the months before the crash, with national attention riveted on the booming stock market, hardly anyone paid attention to existing defects in the American economy. But by 1928 the booming construction and automobile industries began to lose vitality as demand sagged. In fact increases in consumer spending for all goods and services slowed to a lethargic 1.5 percent for 1928–1929. Warehouses began to fill as sales fell and inventories climbed.

In one sense businesses had done too well. Corporations had boosted their profits by keeping the cost of labor and raw materials low as well as by increasing productivity (producing more, using fewer workers). But businesses used their profits to expand factories rather than to pay workers higher wages. Without strong labor unions or government support, real wages never kept pace with productivity, which led to a paradox. As consumers, workers did not have enough money to buy the products they were making more efficiently and at lower cost.

People made up the difference between earnings and purchases by borrowing. Consumers bought "on time," paying for merchandise a little each month. During the decade consumer debt rose by 250 percent. Few could afford to keep spending at that rate. Nor could the distribution of wealth sustain prosperity. By 1929, 1 percent of the population owned 36 percent of all personal wealth. The wealthy had more money than they could possibly spend, and they saved too much. The working and middle classes had not nearly enough to keep the economy growing, spend though they might.

Another problem lay with the banking system. Mismanagement, greed, and the emergence of a new type of executive—half banker, half broker—led banks to divert more funds into speculative investments. The uniquely decentralized American banking system left no way to set things right if a bank failed. At the end of the decade half of the 25,000 banks in America lay outside the Federal Reserve System. Its controls even over member banks were weak. During the decade, 6,000 banks had already failed.

A shaky corporate structure only made matters worse. No government agency at all monitored the stock exchanges, while big business operated largely unchecked. Insider stock trading, shady stock deals, and outright stock fraud ran rampant. Meanwhile, public policy encouraged corporate consolidation and control by filing fewer anti-trust suits. High profits and the Mellon tax program under Coolidge helped to make many corporations wealthy enough to avoid borrowing. Thus changes in interest rates—over which the Federal Reserve exercised some control—had little influence on them. Free from government regulation, fluctuating prices, and the need for loans, huge corporations ruled the economy. And they ruled badly.

Unemployment began to increase as early as 1927, a sign of growing softness in the economy. By the fall of 1929 some 2 million people were out of work. Many of them were in textiles, coal mining, lumbering, and railroads. All were "sick" industries during the decade, suffering from overexpansion, reduced demand, and weak management.

Finally, plain economic ignorance contributed to the calamity. High tariffs protected American industries but discouraged European businesses from selling to the world's most profitable market. Only American loans and investments supported demand abroad. When the American economy collapsed, those vanished and with them went American foreign trade. Furthermore, the Federal Reserve had been stimulating the economy both by expanding the money supply and by lowering interest rates. Those moves only fed the speculative fever by furnishing investors with more money at lower costs. A decision finally to raise interest rates in 1929 to stem speculation ended up speeding the slide by making it more expensive to borrow when borrowing might have slowed the decline.

 REVIEW

What caused the Great Depression, and what role did the Great Stock Market crash play in the downturn?

The American mix of exuberance, hedonism, and anxiety was mirrored in other nations. As postwar peace unfolded, many of the world's political systems seemed to sustain Woodrow Wilson's dream of a world made safe for democracy. Hapsburg Germany transformed itself into the Weimar Republic, whose constitution provided universal suffrage and a bill of rights. The new nations carved out of the old Russian and Austro-Hungarian empires attempted to create similarly democratic governments, while in Turkey, Kemal Ataturk abolished the sultanate and established the Turkish Republic. In India, the Congress party formed by Mohandas K. Gandhi pressed the British to grant them greater political representation.

The Great Crash and the Great Depression rocked these fragile beginnings. A fledgling democracy in depression-wracked Germany gave way to a totalitarian state, while dire economic straits strengthened the hands of dictators in Italy and the Soviet Union. Japan, too, departed from its peaceful parliamentary path toward aggressive militarism, emperor worship, and foreign expansion. No one—not the brokers of Wall Street, not the captains of industry, not the diplomats at the League of Nations—could predict the future in such an unstable world.

CHAPTER SUMMARY

The New Era of the 1920s brought a booming economy and modern times to America, vastly accelerating the forces of change—bureaucracy, productivity, technology, advertising and consumerism, mass media, and suburbanization. Urban-rural tensions peaked with shifts in population that gave cities new power, but as the decade wore on, weaknesses in the economy and a new ethos of getting and spending proved to be the New Era's undoing.

- Technology, advertising and consumer spending, and such boom industries as automobile manufacturing and construction fueled the largest peacetime economic growth in American history to that date.
- Key features of modern life—mass society, mass culture, and mass consumption—took hold, fed by mass

Significant Events

AWAITING EXAMINATION, ELLIS ISLAND

Henry Ford introduces moving assembly line

Marcus Garvey brings Universal Negro Improvement Association to America

First commercial radio broadcast; Warren Harding elected president

| 1914 | 1915 | 1916 | 1919 | 1920 | 1921 | 1921–1922 |

Modern Ku Klux Klan founded

Eighteenth Amendment outlawing alcohol use ratified

Congress enacts quotas on immigration

Washington Naval Disarmament Conference

media in the form of radio, movies, and mass-circulation newspapers and magazines.

- Modern life unsettled old ways and eroded social conventions that had limited life, especially for women and children, leading to the emergence of a New Woman.
- Great migrations of African Americans from the rural South to the urban North and of Latinos from Mexico to the United States reshaped the social landscape.
- Traditional culture, centered in rural America, hardened and defended itself against change through immigration restriction, Prohibition, Fundamentalism, and a reborn Ku Klux Klan.
- A galloping bull market in stocks reflected the commitment of government to big business and economic growth.
- When the stock market crashed in 1929, weaknesses in the economy—overexpansion, declining purchasing power, uneven distribution of wealth, weak banking and corporate structures, "sick" industries, and economic ignorance—finally brought the economy down, and with it the New Era came to a close.

Additional Reading

For years, Frederick Lewis Allen, *Only Yesterday: An Informal History of the 1920s* (1931), shaped the stereotyped view of the decade as a frivolous interlude between World War I and the Great Depression. William Leuchtenburg, *The Perils of Prosperity, 1914–1932* (1958), began an important reconsideration by stressing the serious conflict between urban and rural America and the emergence of modern mass society. Lynn Dumenil updates Leuchtenburg in her excellent *The Modern Temper: American Culture and Society in the 1920s* (1995). Ann Douglas, *Terrible Honesty: Mongrel Manhattan in the 1920s* (1995), puts Manhattan at the core of the cultural transformation in the 1920s. On immigration restriction beginning in 1882 and ending with debates sparked by 9/11, see Roger Daniels, *Guarding the Golden Door: American Immigration Policy and Immigrants Since 1882* (2004). On the Scopes trial, see Edward J. Larson, *Summer for the Gods: The Scopes Trial and America's Continuing Debate over Science and Religion* (1997).

Roland Marchand, *Advertising the American Dream: Making Way for Modernity, 1920–1940* (1985), analyzes the role of advertising in shaping mass consumption, values, and culture, and Ellis Hawley, *The Great War and the Search for a Modern Order* (1979), emphasizes economic institutions. For women in the 1920s, see: Kathleen M. Blee, *Women of the Klan: Racism and Gender in the 1920s* (1991) and Virginia Scharff, *Taking the Wheel: Women and the Coming of the Motor Age* (1991). In a penetrating and gendered discussion of Garveyism and of the Harlem Renaissance, Martin Summers profiles evolving notions of what it meant to be a black man in *Manliness and Its Discontents: The Black Middle Class & the Transformation of Masculinity, 1900–1930* (2004).

The most thorough and readable examination of the stock market and its relation to the economy and public policy in the 1920s is still Robert Sobel, *The Great Bull Market: Wall Street in the 1920s* (1968). For the run-up to the crash, see Maury Klein, *Rainbow's End: The Crash of 1929* (2001). The best books on the disintegration of the American economy remain Lester Chandler, *America's Greatest Depression, 1929–1941* (1970), and, from a global standpoint, Charles Kindleberger, *The World in Depression, 1929–1939* (1973). For an analysis of the Great Depression from the perspective of Keynesian economics, see John Kenneth Galbraith, *The Great Crash* (rev. ed., 1988). For the argument of monetarists, who see the roots of the depression in the shrinking money supply, see Milton Friedman and Anna Jacobson Schwartz, *Monetary History of the United States* (1963), and Peter Temin, *Did Monetary Forces Cause the Great Depression?* (1976). John M. Barry, *Rising Tide: The Great Mississippi Flood of 1927 and How It Changed America* (1997), is especially good in describing the fate of African Americans and the failure of government and private aid organizations.

Harding dies; Calvin Coolidge becomes president; Harding scandals break

Dawes plan to stabilize German inflation; Coolidge elected president

1923

1924

1925

Scopes convicted of teaching evolution in Tennessee

Herbert Hoover elected president; Kellogg-Briand Pact signed

Stock market crashes

1927

1928

1929

Charles Lindbergh's solo flight across the Atlantic; Sacco and Vanzetti executed

PRESIDENT COOLIDGE & "MOTHER" JONES

COOLIDGE, HOOVER, & KELLOGG

25

Homesteaders Jack and Edith Whinery lived with their five children in Pie Town, New Mexico, where the effects of the Great Depression lingered past the end of the depression decade. In October 1940 photographer Russell Lee took this color slide of the Whinerys in their Pie Town home. Pie Town had been founded in the boom years of the 1920s as the headquarters of Clyde Norman's apple pie business. The town foundered in the 1930s, despite efforts to run it as a collective. This slide is part of a larger series of color images taken by Lee and other government photographers at sites across the country. Does the use of color change our view of the past captured in the photograph?

The
Great Depression

In 1933 and 1934 Hickok found that Roosevelt's relief program was falling short. Its half-billion-dollar subsidy to states, localities, and charities was still leaving out too many Americans, like the sharecropper Hickok discovered near Raleigh, North Carolina. He and his daughters had been living in a tobacco barn for two weeks on little more than weeds and table scraps. "Seems like we just keep goin' lower and lower," said the 16-year-old.

To Hickok's surprise, hope still flickered in her eyes. Hickok couldn't explain it until she noticed a pin on the girl's chest. It was a campaign button from the 1932 election—"a profile of the President." Hope sprang from the man in the White House.

Before Franklin D. Roosevelt and the New Deal, the White House was far removed from ordinary citizens. The only federal agency with which they had any contact was the post office.

And these days it usually delivered bad news. But as Hickok traveled across the country in 1933, she detected a change. People were talking about government programs. Perhaps it was long-awaited contributions to relief or maybe reforms in securities and banking or the new recovery programs for industry and agriculture. Just as likely it was Franklin Roosevelt. People, she wrote, were "for the President."

The message was clear: Franklin Roosevelt and the New Deal had begun to restore national confidence. Though it never brought full recovery, the New Deal did improve economic conditions and provided relief to millions of Americans. It reformed the economic system and committed the federal government to managing its ups and downs. In doing so it extended the progressive drive to soften industrialization and translated decades of growing concern for the disadvantaged into a federal aid program. For the first time, Americans believed Washington would help them through a terrible crisis. The liberal state came of age: active, interventionist, and committed to social welfare.

⌃ Shantytowns (called "Hoovervilles" after President Herbert Hoover) sprang up around most cities as the Depression deepened. Sometimes the down-and-out turned to desperate action. In 1931 a hunger riot broke out when the unemployed stormed a grocery store in Oklahoma City. Two years later in Chicago 55 citizens were arrested when they were found tearing down a four-story building and taking it away brick by brick.

THE HUMAN IMPACT OF THE GREAT DEPRESSION

Long breadlines snaked around corners. Vacant-eyed apple-sellers stood shivering in the wind. A man with his hat in his hand came to the back door asking for food in exchange for work. Between 1929 and 1932 an average of 100,000 people lost their jobs every week until some 13 million Americans were jobless. At least one worker in four could find no work at all.

The Great Depression was a great leveler that reduced differences in the face of common want. The New York seamstress without enough piecework to pay her rent felt the same pinch of frustration and anger as the Berkeley student whose college education was cut short when the bank let her father go. Not everyone was devastated. Most Americans survived by cooperating with one another and scrimping to make ends meet. As one Depression victim recalled, "We lived lean."

Hard Times ⟫ Hard times lasted for a decade. Even before the Great Crash many Americans were having trouble making a living. In 1929 a family of four

>>   **AN AMERICAN STORY**

LETTERS FROM THE EDGE

Winner, South Dakota, November 10, 1933. "Dammit, I don't WANT to write to you again tonight. It's been a long, long day, and I'm tired." All the days had been long since Lorena Hickok began her cross-country trek. Four months earlier Harry Hopkins, the new federal relief administrator, hired the journalist to report on the relief efforts of the New Deal. "Talk with the unemployed," he told her, ". . . and when you talk to them, don't ever forget that but for the grace of God you, I, any of our friends might be in their shoes." >>

1929–1939

and the New Deal

⌃ The unemployed, New York City, 1930

required $2,000 a year for the barest necessities—more money than 60 percent of American families earned.

Unable to pay mortgages or rent, many families lived off the generosity of forgiving landlords. Some traded down to smaller quarters or simply lost their homes. By 1932 between 1 million and 2 million Americans were homeless wanderers, among them an estimated 25,000 nomadic families. For the first time, emigration out of the United States exceeded immigration into it because Americans could find no work in their own country. Despite official claims that no one starved, the New York City Welfare Council reported 29 victims of starvation and 110 dead of malnutrition in 1932.

Marriages and births, symbols of faith in the future, decreased. For the first time in three centuries the curve of population growth began to level, as many young couples postponed having children. Experts worried about an impending "baby crop shortage." Strong families hung together and grew closer; weak ones languished or fell apart. Although divorce declined, desertion—the "poor man's divorce"—mushroomed. Under the strain, rates of mental illness and suicide rose as well.

Many fathers, whose lives had been defined by work, suddenly had nothing to do. They grew listless and depressed. Most mothers stayed home and found their traditional roles as nurturer and household manager less disrupted than the bread-winning roles of their husbands. Between 1929 and 1933 living costs dropped 25 percent, but family incomes tumbled by 40 percent.

Homemakers watched household budgets with a closer eye than ever. They canned more food and substituted less expensive fish for meat. When they earned extra money they often did so within the confines of the "woman's sphere" by taking in boarders, laundry, and sewing, opening beauty parlors in their kitchens, and selling baked goods.

For those women who worked outside the home, prejudice still relegated them to so-called women's work. Over half the female labor force continued to work in domestic service or the garment trades, while others found traditional employment as schoolteachers, social workers, and secretaries. Only slowly did the female proportion of the workforce reach pre-Depression levels, until it rose finally to 25 percent by 1940, largely because women were willing to take almost any job.

Whether in the renewed importance of homemaking or the reemergence of home industries, the Great Depression sent ordinary Americans scurrying for the reassuring shelter of past practices and left many of them badly shaken. Shame, self-doubt, and pessimism became epidemic as people blamed themselves for their circumstances. "I would go stand on the relief line [and] bend my head low so nobody would recognize me," recalled one man. The lasting legacy of humiliation and fear—that you had caused your own downfall; that the bottom would drop out again—was what one writer called an "invisible scar."

The Golden Age of Radio and Film »

By the end of the decade almost 9 out of 10 families owned radios. People depended on radios for nearly everything—news, sports, and weather; music and entertainment; advice on how to bake a cake or find God. Some programming helped change national habits. When *The Sporting News* conducted a baseball poll in 1932, editors were surprised to discover that a "new crop of fans has been created by radio . . . the women." Many women were at home during the day when most games were played, and broadcasters went out of their way to educate these new listeners. Night games soon outran day games in attendance, in part because husbands began taking wives and daughters, whose interest was sparked by radio.

Radio entered a golden age of commercialism. Advertisers hawked their products on variety programs like Major Bowes' *Amateur Hour* and comedy shows with entertainers such as George Burns and Gracie Allen. Daytime melodramas (called "soap operas" because they were sponsored by soap companies) aimed at women with stories of the personal struggles of ordinary folk.

Radio continued to bind the country together. A teenager in Splendora, Texas, could listen to the same wisecracks from Jack Benny, the same music from Guy Lombardo, as kids in New York and Los Angeles. In 1938 Orson Welles broadcast H. G. Wells's classic science fiction tale *The War of the Worlds.* Americans everywhere listened to breathless reports of an "invasion from Mars," and many believed it. In Newark, New Jersey, cars jammed roads as families rushed to evacuate the city. The nation, bombarded with reports of impending war in Europe and used to responding to radio advertising, was prepared to believe almost anything, even reports of invaders from Mars.

⌃ Art Deco Radio, 1930. Art Deco, popularized in the 1920s, relied on the geometrical patterns of machines arranged in decorative designs.

In Hollywood an efficient but autocratic studio system churned out a record number of feature films. Eight motion picture companies produced more than two-thirds of them. Color, first introduced to feature films in *Becky Sharp* (1935), soon complemented sound, which had debuted in the 1927 version of *The Jazz Singer.* Neither alone could keep movie theaters full. As attendance dropped early in the Depression, big studios such as Metro-Goldwyn-Mayer and Universal lured audiences back with films that shocked, titillated, and just plain entertained.

By the mid-1930s more than 60 percent of Americans were going to the movies at least once a week. They saw tamer films as the industry began regulating movie content in the face of growing criticism. In 1933 the Catholic Church created the Legion of Decency to monitor features. To avoid censorship and boycotts, studios stiffened their own regulations. Producers could not depict homosexuality, abortion, drug use, or sex. (Even the word "sex" was banned, as was all profanity.) Middle-class morality reigned on the screen, and most Depression movies, like most of popular culture, preserved traditional values.

In Europe the "mass aspects" of media could cut more than one way politically and culturally. While Hollywood produced films that affirmed popular faith in democratic government, a capitalist economy, and the success ethic, totalitarian Nazi Germany broadcast the fiery rallies and speeches of Adolf Hitler, which seemed bent on encouraging racist fears and inflaming public hysteria. German director Leni Riefehstahl used her cinematic gifts to combine myth, symbol, and documentary into an image of Hitler as the Führer, a national savior with the power of a pagan god and the charisma of cult leader.

"Dirty Thirties": An Ecological Disaster »

Each year between 1932 and 1939 an average of nearly 50 dust storms, or "black blizzards," turned 1,500 square miles between the Oklahoma panhandle and western Kansas into a gigantic "Dust Bowl," whose baleful effects were felt as far north as the Dakotas and as far south as Texas. It was one of the worst ecological disasters in modern history. Nature played its part, scorching the earth and whipping the winds. But the "dirty thirties" were mostly made by human beings. The semiarid lands west of the 98th meridian were not suitable for agriculture or livestock. Sixty years of intensive farming and grazing had stripped the prairie of its natural vegetation and rendered it defenseless against the elements. When the dry winds came, one-third of the Great Plains simply vanished into thin air.

Some 3.5 million plains people abandoned their farms. Landowners or corporations forced off about half of them as large-scale commercial farming slowly spread into the heartland of America. Commercial farms were more common in California, where 10 percent of the farms grew more than 50 percent of the crops. As in industrial

"Black blizzards" dwarfed the landscape and everything human in it. The drought that helped bring them about lasted from 1932 to 1936. In a single day in 1934 dust storms dumped 12 million tons of western dirt on Chicago. This automobile flees the approaching clouds on a road stretching across the Texas panhandle.

Immigration station near U.S. border, 1938

America, the strategy in agricultural America was to consolidate and mechanize. In most Dust Bowl counties people owned less than half the land they farmed. American agriculture was turning from a way of life into an industry. And as the economy contracted, owners cut costs by cutting workers.

Relief offices around the country reported a change in migrant families. Rather than black or brown, more and more were white and native-born, typically a young married couple with one child. Long-distance migrants from Oklahoma, Arizona, and Texas usually set their sights on California. If they were like the Joad family in John Steinbeck's classic novel *The Grapes of Wrath* (1939), they drove west along Route 66 through Arizona and New Mexico, their belongings piled high atop rickety jalopies, heading for the West Coast and the promise of jobs picking fruit and harvesting vegetables.

More than 350,000 Oklahomans migrated to California—so many that "Okie" came to mean any Dust Bowler, even though most of Oklahoma lay outside the Dust Bowl. Only one in two or three migrants actually found work. The labor surplus allowed growers to cut wages to less than a third the subsistence level. Families that did not work formed wretched enclaves called "little Oklahomas." The worst were located in the fertile Imperial Valley. There, at the end of the decade, relief officials discovered a family of 10 living in a 1921 Ford.

Mexican Americans and Repatriation >>

The Chávez family lost their family farm in Arizona in 1934. César, barely six years old at the time, remembered only images of their departure: a "giant tractor" leveling the corral; the loss of his room and bed; a beat-up Chevy hauling the family west; his father promising to buy

another farm. But the elder Chávez could never keep his promise. Instead, he and his family "followed the crops" in California. In eight years César went to 37 schools. When they found work, his family earned less than $10 a week. His father joined strikers in the Imperial Valley in the mid-1930s, only to have the strikes crushed. "Some people put this out of their minds," said César Chávez years later. "I don't." Thirty years later he founded the United Farm Workers of America, the first union of migratory workers in the country.

A deep ambivalence had always characterized American attitudes toward Mexicans, but the Great Depression turned most Anglo communities against them. Cities such as Los Angeles, fearing the burden of relief, found it cheaper to ship Mexicans home. Some migrants left voluntarily. Frustrated officials or angry neighbors drove out others. Beginning in 1931 the federal government launched a series of deportations, or **repatriations**, of Mexicans back to Mexico. These deportations included the Mexicans' American-born children, who by law were citizens of the United States.

repatriation act of returning people to their nation of origin. The term often refers to the act of returning soldiers or refugees to their birth country.

During the decade the Latino population of the Southwest dropped by 500,000. In Chicago, the Mexican community shrank by almost half. Staying in the United States often turned out to be as difficult as leaving. The average income of Mexican American families in the Rio Grande valley of Texas was $506 a year. Following the harvest made schooling particularly difficult: fewer than two Mexican American children in ten completed five years of school.

For Americans of Mexican descent, the Great Depression only deepened anxiety over identity. Were they

Mexicans, as many Anglos regarded them, or were they Americans, as they regarded themselves? In the 1920s, such questions produced several organizations founded to assert the American identity of native-born and naturalized Mexican Americans and to pursue their civil rights. In 1929, on the eve of the Depression, many of these organizations were consolidated into the League of United Latin American Citizens (LULAC). By the early 1940s, "Flying Squadrons" of LULAC organizers had founded some 80 chapters nationwide, making it the largest Mexican American civil rights association in the country.

LULAC permitted only those Latinos who were American citizens to join, thus excluding hundreds of thousands of ethnic Mexicans who nonetheless regarded the United States as their home. It pointedly conducted meetings in English. An assimilated middle class provided its leadership and stressed desegregation of public schools, voter registration, and an end to discrimination in public facilities and on juries.

African Americans in the Depression ▸▸

Hard times were nothing new to African Americans. "The Negro was born in depression," opined one black man. "It only became official when it hit the white man." Still, when the Depression struck, black unemployment surged. By 1932 it reached 50 percent, twice the national level. By 1933 several cities reported between 25 and 40 percent of their black residents with no support except relief payments.

Migration out of the rural South, up 800,000 during the 1920s, dropped by 50 percent in the 1930s. As late as 1940 three of four African Americans still lived in rural areas; yet conditions there were just as bad as in cities. In 1934 one study estimated the average income for black cotton farmers at under $200 a year. Millions of African Americans made do by stretching meager incomes, as they had for years.

Like many African Americans, George Baker refused to be victimized by the Depression. Baker had moved from Georgia to Harlem in 1915. He changed his name to M. J. Divine and founded a religious cult that promised followers an afterlife of full equality. In the 1930s "Father Divine" preached economic cooperation and opened shelters, or "heavens," for regenerate "angels," black and white. In Detroit Elijah Poole began calling himself Elijah Muhammad and in 1931 established the Black Muslims, a blend of Islamic faith and black nationalism. He exhorted African Americans to celebrate their African heritage, to live a life of self-discipline and self-help, and to strive for a separate all-black nation.

The Depression inflamed racial prejudice. Lynchings tripled between 1932 and 1933. In 1932 the Supreme Court ordered a retrial in the most celebrated racial case of the decade. A year earlier nine black teenagers had been accused of raping two white women on a train bound for Scottsboro, Alabama. Within weeks all-white juries had sentenced eight of them to death. The convictions rested on the testimony of the women, one of whom later admitted that the boys had been framed. Appeals kept the case alive for almost a decade. In the end charges against four of the "Scottsboro boys" were dropped. The other five received substantial prison sentences.

 REVIEW

What were the human costs of the Great Depression for Anglos, Latinos, and African Americans?

THE TRAGEDY OF HERBERT HOOVER

The presidency of Herbert Hoover began with great promise but soon became a nightmare both personal and professional. "I have no fears for the future of our country," he announced at his inauguration in March 1929. But within seven months a "depression" struck. (Hoover used the word instead of the traditional "panic" to downplay the emergency.) Despite more effort than any of his predecessors to restore a damaged economy, he failed to turn the economic tide. For all of Hoover's promise and innovative intelligence, he was a transitional figure, important as a break from the do-nothing policies of past depression presidents and a herald of more active presidents to come.

The Failure of Relief ▸▸

By the winter of 1931–1932 the picture was bleak: relief organizations with too little money and too few resources to make much headway against the Depression. Once-mighty private charity dwindled to 6 percent of all relief funds.

Ethnic charities tried to stave off disaster for their own. Over the years Mexican Americans and Puerto Ricans turned to *mutualistas,* traditional societies that provided members with social support, life insurance, and sickness benefits. In San Francisco, the Chinese Six Companies offered food and clothing to needy Chinese Americans. But as the head of the Federation of Jewish Charities warned, private efforts were failing. The government would be "compelled, by the cruel events ahead of us, to step into the situation and bring relief on a large scale."

An estimated 30 million needy people nationwide quickly depleted city treasuries, already pressed because nearly 30 percent of city taxpayers had fallen behind in paying the taxes they owed. In Philadelphia relief payments to a family of four totaled $5.50 a week, the highest

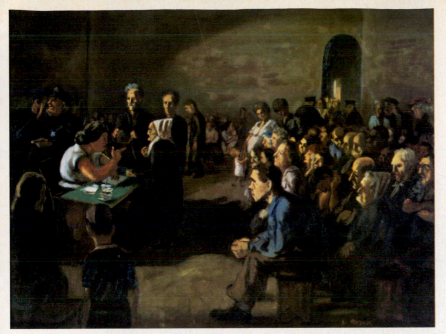

⌃ Louis Ribak's *Home Relief Station* grimly portrays the failing relief efforts of private charities and the humiliation of applying for relief. A crowd of broken men and women sits anxiously as a burly administrator interrogates a frail relief applicant. To go on relief, said one man, was to endure a "crucifixion."

in the country. Some cities gave nothing to unmarried people or childless couples, no matter how impoverished they were.

Cities clamored for help from state capitals, but after a decade of extravagant spending and sloppy bookkeeping, many states were already running in the red. As businesses and property values collapsed, tax bases shrank and with them state revenues. Until New York established its Temporary Emergency Relief Administration (TERA) in 1931, no state had any agency at all to handle the problem of unemployment.

The Hoover Depression Program ≫

Beginning in 1930 President Hoover assumed leadership in combating the depression with more vigor and compassion than any other executive. It was a mark of his character. Orphaned at nine, he became one of Stanford University's first graduates and, before the age of 40, the millionaire head of one of the most successful mine engineering firms in the world. As a good Quaker, he balanced private gain with public service, saving starving Belgian refugees in 1915 after war broke out in Europe. He worked 14 hours a day, paid his own salary, and convinced private organizations and businesses to donate food, clothing, and other necessities. In his honor, Finns coined a new word: to "hoover" meant to help.

When the Depression struck, Hoover was no passive president. Past presidents feared that any intervention at all by government would upset the natural workings of the economy and that their sole responsibility was to keep the budget balanced. But Hoover understood the vicious cycle in which rising unemployment drove down

consumer demand, and he appreciated the need for stimulating investment. Thus he set in motion an unprecedented program of government activism.

Despite all his work, Hoover's program failed. At first, he rallied business leaders, who pledged to maintain employment, wages, and prices—only to back down as the economy sputtered. He pushed a tax cut through Congress in 1930 in order to increase the purchasing power of consumers. But when the cuts produced an unbalanced federal budget, Hoover reversed course. At bottom he firmly believed that capitalism would generate its own recovery and that a balanced federal budget was required in order to restore the confidence of business. So he agreed to tax increases in 1932, further undermining investment and consumption.

Equally disastrous, the president endorsed the Smoot-Hawley Tariff (1930) to protect the United States from cheap foreign goods. That bill brought a wave of retaliation from countries abroad, which choked world trade and reduced American sales overseas. Even the $1 billion that Hoover spent on **public works**—more than the total spent by all his predecessors combined—did not approach the $10 billion needed to employ only half the jobless. Spending such huge sums seemed unthinkable when the entire federal budget was only $3.2 billion.

> **public works** government-financed construction projects, such as highways and bridges, for use by the public.

Under pressure from Congress Hoover took his boldest action to save the banks. Between 1930 and 1932 some 5,100 banks failed as panicky depositors withdrew their funds. Hoover agreed to permit the creation of the Reconstruction Finance Corporation (RFC) in 1932, an agency that could lend money to banks. Modeled on a similar agency created during World War I, the RFC had a capital stock of $500 million and the power to borrow four times that amount. Within three months bank failures dropped from 70 a week to 1 every two weeks.

In spite of this success, Hoover drew criticism for rescuing banks and not people. From the start he rejected the idea of federal relief for the unemployed for fear that a "dole," or giveaway program, would damage the initiative of recipients, perhaps even produce a permanent underclass. The bureaucracy that would be needed to police recipients would inevitably meddle in the private lives of citizens and bring a "train of corruption and waste," Hoover said. He assumed that neighborliness and cooperation would be enough.

As unemployment worsened Hoover softened his stand on federal relief. In 1932 he allowed Congress to pass the Emergency Relief and Construction Act. It authorized the RFC to lend up to $1.5 billion for "reproductive" public works that paid for themselves—like toll bridges and slum clearance. Another $300 million went to states as loans for the direct relief of the unemployed. Yet in

In the early years of the Depression demonstrations by the unemployed, some organized by Communists and other radicals, broke out all over the country. On March 6, 1930, a Communist-led protest at Union Square in New York turned into an ugly riot. In 1935 Communist parties, under orders from Moscow, allied with democratic and socialist groups against fascism, proclaiming in the United States that "Communism is twentieth-century Americanism."

this Depression, $300 million was a pittance. When the governor of Pennsylvania requested loans to furnish the destitute with 13 cents a day for a year, the RFC sent only enough for 3 cents a day.

Stirrings of Discontent >>

Despite unprecedented action, Hoover could not stem rising discontent. "The word revolution is heard at every hand," one writer warned in 1932. Some wondered if capitalism itself had gone bankrupt.

In 1932 anger erupted into violence. Wisconsin dairy farmers overturned tens of thousands of milk cans in a fruitless effort to increase prices. A 48-mile long "Coal Caravan" of striking miners drove through southern Illinois in protest. Three thousand marchers stormed Henry Ford's plant in Dearborn, only to have Ford police turn power water hoses and guns on them. When it was over, four marchers lay dead and more than 20 more wounded.

For all the stirrings of discontent, revolution was never a danger. In 1932 the Communist party of the United States had 20,000 members—up from 6,500 only three years earlier but hardly enough to constitute a political force. Deeply suspicious of Marxist doctrine, most Americans were unsympathetic to their cries for collectivism and an end to capitalism. Fewer than 1,000 African

Americans joined the party in the early 1930s, despite its strong support for civil rights.

At first hostile to established politics, the Communists adopted a more cooperative strategy to contain Adolf Hitler when his Nazi party won control of Germany in 1933. The Soviet Union ordered Communist parties in Europe and the United States to join with liberal politicians in a "popular front" against Nazism. Thereafter party membership peaked in the mid-1930s at about 80,000.

The Bonus Army >>

Hoover sympathized with the discontented but as the "Bonus Army" learned in the summer of 1932, his compassion had limits. The army, a scruffy collection of World War I veterans, was hungry and looking to cash in the bonus certificates they had received from Congress in 1924 as a reward for wartime service. By the time they reached Washington, D.C., in June 1932, their numbers had swelled to nearly 20,000, the largest protest in the city's history. Hoover dismissed them as a special-interest lobby and refused to see their leaders. When the Senate blocked the bonus bill, most veterans left.

About 2,000 stayed to dramatize their plight, camping with their families and parading peaceably. Despite the efforts of the Washington police to evict them, the protesters refused to leave. By the end of July, the president had had enough. He called in the U.S. Army under the command of Chief of Staff General Douglas MacArthur. MacArthur arrived with four troops of saber-brandishing cavalry, six tanks, and a column of infantry with bayonets ready for action. By the time the smoke cleared the next morning, the Bonus marchers had vanished except for 300 wounded veterans.

Though he had intended that the army only assist the police, Hoover accepted responsibility for the action. And the sight of unarmed and unemployed veterans under attack by American troops soured most Americans. In Albany, New York, Governor Franklin D. Roosevelt exploded at the president's failure: "There is nothing inside the man but jelly."

The Election of 1932 »

In 1932 Republicans stuck with Hoover and endorsed his Depression program. Democrats countered with Franklin D. Roosevelt, the charismatic New York governor. As a sign of change, Roosevelt broke precedent by flying to Chicago and addressing the delegates in person. "I pledge you, I pledge myself to a new deal for the American people," he told them.

Without a national following, Roosevelt zigged and zagged in an effort to appeal to the broadest possible bloc of voters. One minute he called for a balanced budget, the next for costly public works and aid to the unemployed. He promised to

help business, then spoke of remembering the "forgotten man" and "distributing wealth and products more equitably." For his part, Hoover denounced Roosevelt's New Deal as a "dangerous departure" from time-honored traditions, one that would destroy American values and institutions and "build a bureaucracy such as we have never seen in our history."

On Election Day, Roosevelt captured a thundering 58 percent of the popular vote and carried with him large Democratic majorities in the Congress. Just as telling as the margin of victory were its sources. Industrial workers in the North, poor farmers in the South and West, immigrants and big-city dwellers everywhere were being galvanized into a broad new coalition. These people had experienced firsthand the savage effects of the boom-and-bust business cycle and wanted change. They turned to Roosevelt and the Democrats, who recognized that in a modern industrial state it was not enough to rally round business and hope that capitalism would right itself. Over 30 years of nearly unbroken Republican rule came to an end.

✓ REVIEW

What were the shortcomings of Herbert Hoover's depression program?

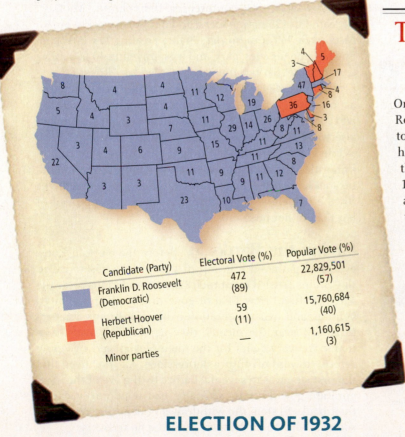

Candidate (Party)	Electoral Vote (%)	Popular Vote (%)
Franklin D. Roosevelt (Democratic)	472 (89)	22,829,501 (57)
Herbert Hoover (Republican)	59 (11)	15,760,684 (40)
Minor parties	—	1,160,615 (3)

ELECTION OF 1932

THE EARLY NEW DEAL (1933–1935)

On March 4, 1933, as the clocks struck noon, Eleanor Roosevelt wondered if it were possible to "do anything to save America now." She looked at her husband, who had just been sworn in as thirty-second president of the United States. Franklin faced the audience of over 100,000. Heeding the nation's call for "action, and action now," he promised to exercise "broad Executive power to wage a war against the emergency." The crowd cheered. Eleanor was terrified: "One has the feeling of going it blindly because we're in a tremendous stream, and none of us know where we're going to land."

The early New Deal unfolded in the spring of 1933 with a chaotic 100-day burst of legislation. It stressed recovery through planning and cooperation with business but also tried to aid the unemployed and reform the economic system. Above all, the early New Deal broke the cycle of despair. With Roosevelt in the White House, most Americans believed that they were in good hands, wherever they landed.

The Democratic Roosevelts

The Democratic Roosevelts >> From the moment they entered it in 1933, Franklin and Eleanor—the Democratic Roosevelts—transformed the White House. No more seven-course meals as Hoover had served in an effort to show that nothing was really wrong. Instead, visitors got fare fit for a boarding-house. The gesture was symbolic, but it made the president's point of ending business as usual.

Such belt-tightening was new to Franklin Roosevelt. Born of an old Dutch family in New York, he grew up rich and pampered. He idolized his Republican cousin Theodore Roosevelt and mimicked his career, except as a Democrat. Like Theodore, Franklin graduated from Harvard University (in 1904), won a seat in the New York State legislature (in 1910), secured an appointment as assistant secretary of the navy (in 1913), and ran for the vice presidency (in 1920). Then disaster struck. On vacation in the summer of 1921, Roosevelt fell ill with poliomyelitis. The disease paralyzed him from the waist down.

Roosevelt emerged from the ordeal to win the governorship of New York in 1928. When the Depression struck, he created the first state relief agency in 1931, the Temporary Emergency Relief Administration. Aid to the

WITNESS

"My Day": The First Lady in Tennessee

"Johnson City, Tennessee, May 31, 1939—I looked out of the window of the train this morning . . . and saw a little girl, slim and bent over, carrying two heavy pails of water across a field to an unpainted house. How far that water had to be carried, I do not know, but it is one thing to carry it on a camping trip for fun during a summer's holiday, and it is another thing to carry it day in and day out as part of the routine of living."

—Eleanor Roosevelt, "My Day" newspaper column (1939)

jobless "must be extended by Government, not as a matter of charity, but as a matter of social duty," he explained. He considered himself a progressive but moved well beyond the cautious federal activism of most progressives. He adopted no single ideology. He cared little about economic principles. What he wanted were results. Experimentation became a hallmark of the New Deal.

Eleanor Roosevelt redefined what it meant to be first lady. Never had a president's wife been so visible, so much of a crusader, so cool under fire. She was the first first lady to hold weekly press conferences. Her column, "My Day," appeared in 135 newspapers, and her twice-weekly broadcasts made her a radio personality rivaling her husband. She became his eyes, ears, and legs, traveling 40,000 miles a year. Secret Service men code-named her "Rover."

Eleanor believed she was only a spur to presidential action. But she was active in her own right, as a teacher and social reformer before Franklin became president and afterward as a tireless advocate of the underdog. In the White House, she pressed him to hire more women and minorities but also supported antilynching and anti-poll-tax measures, when he would not, and experimental towns for the homeless. By 1939 more Americans approved of her than of her husband.

Saving the Banks >> Before the election Roosevelt had gathered a group of economic advisers called the "Brains Trust." Out of their recommendations came the early, or "first," New Deal of government planning, intervention, and experimentation. Although Brains Trusters disagreed over the means, they agreed over ends: economic recovery, relief for the unemployed, and sweeping reform to ward off future depressions. All concurred that the first step was to save the banks. By the eve of the inauguration governors in 38 states had temporarily closed their banks to stem the withdrawal of deposits. Without a sound credit structure, there could be no recovery.

↑ Franklin Roosevelt contracted polio in 1921 and remained paralyzed from the waist down for the rest of his life. Out of respect for his politically motivated wishes, photographers rarely showed him wearing heavy leg braces or sitting in a wheelchair. This photograph, snapped outside his New York City brownstone in September 1933 during his first year as president, is one of the few in which Roosevelt's braces are visible (just below the cuffs of his trousers). Note the wooden ramp constructed especially to help hold him up.

On March 5, the day after his inauguration, Roosevelt ordered every bank in the country closed for four days. He shrewdly called it a "bank holiday." On March 9, the president introduced emergency banking legislation. The House passed the measure, sight unseen, and the Senate endorsed it later in the day. Roosevelt signed it that night.

Rather than nationalizing the banks as radicals wanted, the Emergency Banking Act followed the modest course of extending federal assistance to them. Sound banks would reopen immediately with government support. Troubled banks would be handed over to federal "conservators," who would guide them to solvency. In plain and simple language, Roosevelt explained what was happening in the first of his many informal "fireside chat" radio broadcasts. When banks reopened the next day, deposits exceeded withdrawals.

To guard against another stock crash, financial reforms gave government greater authority to manage the currency and regulate stock transactions. In April 1933 Roosevelt dropped the gold standard and began experimenting with the value of the dollar to boost prices. Later that spring the Glass-Steagall Banking Act restricted speculation by banks and, more important, created federal insurance for bank deposits of up to $2,500. Despite

Roosevelt's objections that the Federal Deposit Insurance Corporation would preserve weak banks at the expense of strong ones, fewer banks failed for the rest of the decade than in the best year of the 1920s. The Securities Exchange Act (1934) established a new federal agency, the Securities and Exchange Commission, to oversee the stock market.

Relief for the Unemployed >>

Saving the banks and financial markets meant little if human suffering continued. Mortgage relief for the millions who had lost their homes came eventually in 1934 in the Home Owners' Loan Act. The need to alleviate starvation led Roosevelt to propose a bold new giveaway program. The Federal Emergency Relief Administration (FERA) opened its door in May 1933. Sitting amid unpacked boxes, gulping coffee and chain-smoking, former social worker Harry Hopkins spent $5 million in his first two hours as head of the new agency. In its two-year existence FERA furnished more than $1 billion in grants to states, local areas, and private charities.

Hopkins persuaded Roosevelt to expand relief with an innovative shift from government giveaways to a work program to see workers through the winter of 1933–1934.

UNEMPLOYMENT RELIEF, 1934

The percentage of those receiving unemployment relief differed markedly throughout the nation. The farm belt of the plains was especially hard-hit, with 41 percent of South Dakota's citizens receiving federal benefits. In the East, the percentage dropped as low as 8 percent in some states.

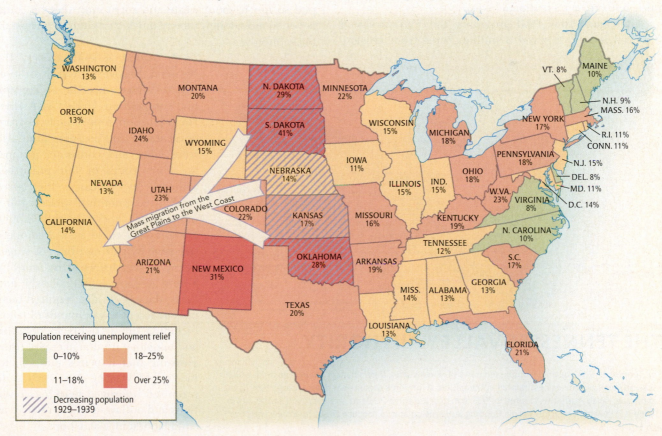

Paying someone "to do something socially useful," Hopkins explained, "preserves a man's morale." The Civil Works Administration (CWA) employed 4 million Americans. Alarmed at the high cost of the program, Roosevelt disbanded the CWA in the spring of 1934. It nonetheless furnished a new weapon against unemployment and an important precedent for future aid programs.

Another work relief program established in 1933 proved even more creative. The Civilian Conservation Corps (CCC) was Roosevelt's pet project. It combined his concern for conservation with compassion for youth. The CCC took unmarried 18- to 25-year-olds from relief rolls and sent them into the woods and fields to plant trees, build parks, and fight soil erosion. During its 10 years, the CCC provided 2.5 million young men with jobs (which prompted some critics to chant, "Where's the she, she, she?").

New Dealers intended relief programs to last only through the crisis. But the Tennessee Valley Authority (TVA)—a massive public works project created in 1933—helped to relieve unemployment but also made a continuing contribution to regional planning. For a decade, planners had dreamed of transforming the flood-ridden basin of the Tennessee River, one of the poorest areas of the country, with a program of regional development and social engineering. The TVA constructed a series of dams along the seven-state basin to control flooding, improve navigation, and generate cheap electric power. In cooperation with state and local officials, it also launched social programs to stamp out malaria, provide library bookmobiles, and create recreational lakes.

Like many New Deal programs, the TVA produced a mixed legacy. It saved 3 million acres from erosion, multiplied the average income in the valley tenfold, and repaid its original investment in federal taxes. Its cheap electricity helped to bring down the rates of private utility companies. But the experiment in regional planning also pushed thousands of families from their land, failed to end poverty, and created an agency that became one of the worst polluters in the country.

Planning for Industrial Recovery »

Planning, not just for regions but for the whole economy, seemed to many New Dealers the key to recovery. Some held that if businesses were allowed to plan and cooperate with one another, the ruthless competition that was driving down prices, wages, and employment could be controlled and the riddle of recovery solved. Business leaders had been urging such a course since 1931. In June 1933, under the National Industrial Recovery Act (NIRA), Roosevelt put planning to work for industry.

The legislation created two new agencies. The Public Works Administration (PWA) was designed to boost industrial activity and consumer spending with a $3.3 billion public works program. The companies put under contract and unemployed workers hired would help stimulate the economy through their purchases and leave a legacy of capital improvement. Harold Ickes, the prickly interior secretary who headed PWA, built the Triborough Bridge and Lincoln Tunnel in New York, the port city of Brownsville, Texas, and two aircraft carriers. But he worried so much about waste and corruption that he could never spend enough money quickly enough to jumpstart the economy.

A second federal agency, the National Recovery Administration (NRA), aimed directly at controlling competition. Under NRA chief Hugh Johnson, representatives from government and business (and also from labor and consumer groups) drew up "codes of fair practices." Industry by industry, the codes established minimum prices, minimum wages, and maximum hours. No company could seek a competitive edge by cutting prices or wages below certain levels or by working a few employees mercilessly and firing the rest. It also required business to accept key demands of labor, including union rights to organize and bargain with management (thus ensuring that if prices jumped, so, too, might wages). And each code promised improved working conditions and outlawed such practices as child labor and sweatshops.

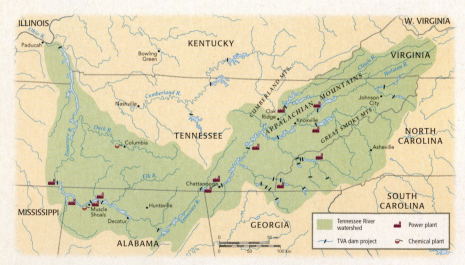

THE TENNESSEE VALLEY AUTHORITY

The Tennessee River basin encompassed parts of seven states. Rivers honeycombed the area, which received some of the heaviest rainfall in the nation. A longtime dream of Senator George Norris, the Tennessee Valley Authority, created in 1933, constructed some 20 dams and improved 5 others over the next 20 years to control chronic flooding and erosion and to produce cheap hydroelectric power and fertilizers.

No business was forced to comply because New Dealers feared that government coercion might be ruled unconstitutional. The NRA relied on voluntary participation. A publicity campaign of parades, posters, and public pledges exhorted businesses to join the NRA and consumers to buy only NRA-sanctioned products. More than two million employers eventually signed up. In store windows and on merchandise, shiny decals with blue-eagle crests alerted customers that "We Do Our Part."

For all the hoopla, the NRA failed to bring recovery. Big businesses shaped the codes to their advantage and frequently limited production to maintain or even raise prices. Not all businesses joined, and those that did often found the codes too complicated or costly to follow. Even NRA support for labor tottered, After all, it had no means of enforcing its guarantee of union rights. Business survived under the NRA, but without increasing production there was no incentive for the expansion and new investment needed to end hard times. The NRA was soon spawning little but evasion and criticism.

On May 27, 1935, the Supreme Court struck down the floundering NRA in *Schecter Poultry Corp. v. United States*. The justices unanimously ruled that the NRA had exceeded federal power over commerce among the states by regulating the Schecter brothers' poultry business in a single state, New York. Privately Roosevelt was relieved to be rid of the NRA. But he and other New Dealers were plainly shaken by the grounds of the decision. Their broad view of the commerce clause to fight the Depression suffered a grave blow. Distress inside the adminstration only grew when Justice Benjamin Cardozo added a chilling afterthought:

the NRA's code making represented "an unconstitutional delegation of legislative power" to the executive branch. Without the ability to make rules and regulations, all the executive agencies of the New Deal might flounder.

Planning for Agriculture >>

Like planning for industry, New Deal planning for agriculture relied on private interests—the farmers—to act as the principal planners. Under the Agricultural Adjustment Act of 1933, farmers limited their own production. The government, in turn, paid them for leaving their fields fallow, while a tax on millers, cotton ginners, and other processors financed the payments. In theory, production limits would reduce surpluses, demand for farm commodities would rise (as would prices), and agriculture would recover.

In practice, the Agricultural Adjustment Administration (AAA) did help to increase prices. Unlike the code-ridden NRA, the AAA wisely confined coverage to seven basic commodities. As a way to push prices even higher, the new Commodity Credit Corporation gave loans to farmers who stored their crops rather than sold them—a revival of the Populists' old subtreasury plan (see page 430). Farm income rose from $5.5 billion in 1932 to $8.7 billion in 1935.

Not all the gains in farm income were the result of government actions or free from problems. In the mid-1930s dust storms, droughts, and floods helped reduce harvests and push up prices. The AAA, moreover, failed to distribute its benefits equally. Large landowners controlled decisions over which plots would be left fallow. In the South these decisions frequently meant cutting the acreage of tenants and sharecroppers or forcing them out.

⌃ "Look in her eyes" read the caption of the photograph on the left, snapped by photojournalist Dorothea Lange in 1936. Titled "Migrant Mother," the photo became an icon of the era, depicting the anxiety and desperation of so many Americans as well as the perseverance of 32-year-old peapicker Florence Thompson. Her worry-worn face is framed by her children as they turn away from the camera and lean on their mother for support. Lange took at last six photographs of Thompson and her family for the Farm Security Administration. Other poses were less haunting, as can be seen from the photo on the right where the little girl smiles almost reflexively into the camera. FSA administrators chose the more moving photograph to show the human costs of the depression and to justify the cost of government programs to help the dispossessed.

Even when they reduced the acreage that they themselves plowed, big farmers could increase yields through intensive cultivation.

In 1936 the Supreme Court voided the Agricultural Adjustment Act. In *Butler v. U.S.,* the six-justice majority concluded that the government had no right to regulate agriculture, either by limiting production or by taxing processors. A hastily drawn replacement, the Soil Conservation and Domestic Allotment Act (1936), addressed the complaints. Farmers were now subsidized for practicing "conservation"—taking soil-depleting crops off the land—and paid from general revenues instead of a special tax. A second Agricultural Adjustment Act in 1938 returned production quotas.

Other agencies tried to help impoverished farmers. The Farm Credit Administration refinanced about a fifth of all farm mortgages. In 1935 the Resettlement Administration gave marginal farmers a fresh start by moving them to better land. Beginning in 1937 the Farm Security Administration furnished low-interest loans to help tenants buy family farms. In no case, however, did the rural poor have enough political clout to obtain sufficient funds from Congress. Fewer than 5000 families of a projected 500,000 were resettled, and less than 2 percent of tenant farmers received loans.

> **In California discontented voters took over the Democratic party and turned sharply to the left by nominating novelist Upton Sinclair, a Socialist, for governor.**

 REVIEW

What measures did the early New Deal take to relieve the Depression, and how successful were they?

A SECOND NEW DEAL (1935–1936)

"Boys—this is our hour," crowed the president's closest adviser, Harry Hopkins, in the spring of 1935. A year earlier voters broke precedent by returning the party in power to Congress, giving the Democrats their largest majorities in decades. With the presidential election only a year away, time was short and Hopkins knew it: "We've got to get everything we want—a works program, social security, wages and hours, everything—now or never."

Hopkins calculated correctly. In 1935 politics, swept along by a torrent of protest, led to a "second hundred days" of lawmaking and a "Second New Deal." The emphasis shifted from planning and cooperation with business to greater regulation of business, broader relief, and bolder reform. A limited welfare state emerged in which the government was finally committed, at least symbolically, to guaranteeing the material well-being of needy Americans.

Dissent from the Deal >>

In 1934 a mob of 6,000 stormed the Minneapolis city hall, demanding more relief and higher pay for government jobs. In San Francisco longshoremen walked off the job, setting off a citywide strike. By year's end, 1.5 million workers had joined in 1,800 strikes. Conditions were improving but not quickly enough, and across the country dissenters gathered strength.

From the right came the charges of a few wealthy business executives and conservatives that Roosevelt was an enemy of private property and a dictator in the making. In August 1934 they founded the American Liberty League. Despite spending $1 million in anti–New Deal advertising, the league won little support and only helped to convince the president that cooperation with business was failing.

In California discontented voters took over the Democratic party and turned sharply to the left by nominating novelist Upton Sinclair, a Socialist, for governor. Running under the slogan "End Poverty in California" (EPIC), Sinclair proposed to confiscate idle factories and land and permit the unemployed to produce for their own use. Republicans mounted a no-holds-barred counterattack, including fake newsreels depicting Sinclair as a Bolshevik, atheist, and free-lover. Sinclair lost the election but won nearly 1 million votes.

Huey P. Long, the flamboyant senator from Louisiana, had ridden to power on a wave of rural discontent against banks, corporations, and political machines. As governor of Louisiana he pushed through reforms regulating utilities, building roads and schools, even distributing free schoolbooks. Opponents called him a "dictator"; most Louisianans simply called him the "Kingfish." Breaking with Roosevelt in 1933, Long pledged to bring about recovery by making "every man a king." "Share Our Wealth" was a drastic but simple plan: the government would limit the size of all fortunes and confiscate the rest. Every family would then be guaranteed an annual income of $2,500 and an estate of $5,000, enough to buy a house, an automobile, and a radio (over which Long had already built a national following).

By 1935, one year after its founding, Long's Share Our Wealth organization boasted 27,000 clubs with files containing nearly 8 million names. Democratic National Committee members shuddered at polls showing that Long might capture up to 4 million votes in 1936, enough to put a Republican in the White House. But late in 1935, in the corridors of the Louisiana capitol, Long was shot to death by a disgruntled constituent whose family had been wronged by the Long political machine.

Father Charles Coughlin was Long's urban counterpart. Where Long explained the Depression as the result of bloated fortunes, Coughlin blamed the banks. In weekly broadcasts from the Shrine of the Little Flower in suburban Detroit, the "Radio Priest" told his working-class, largely Catholic audience of the international bankers who had toppled the world economy by manipulating gold-backed currencies.

Coughlin promised to end the Depression with simple strokes: nationalizing banks, inflating the currency with silver, spreading work. (None would have worked, because each would have dampened investment, the key to recovery.) Across the urban North, 30 to 40 million Americans—the largest audience in the world—huddled around their radios to listen. In 1934 Coughlin organized the National Union for Social Justice to pressure both parties. As the election of 1936 approached, the union loomed on the political horizon.

A less ominous challenge came from Dr. Francis Townsend. The 67-year-old physician had recently retired in California from the public health service. Moved by the plight of elderly Americans without pension plans or medical insurance, Townsend set up Old Age Revolving Pensions, Limited, in 1934. He proposed to have the government pay $200 a month to those 60 years or older who quit their jobs and spent the money within 30 days. By 1936 Townsend clubs counted 3.5 million members, most of them small businesspeople and farmers at or beyond retirement age.

For all their differences, Sinclair, Long, Coughlin, Townsend, and other critics struck similar chords. Although the solutions they proposed were simplistic, the problems they addressed were serious: a maldistribution of goods and wealth, inadequacies in the money supply, the plight of the elderly. They attacked the growing control of corporations, banks, and government over individuals and communities. And they created mass political movements based on social as well as economic dissatisfaction. When Sinclair supporters pledged to produce for their own use and Long's followers swore to "share our wealth," when Coughlinites damned the "monied interests" and elderly Townsendites bemoaned foul-ups in Washington,

they were also trying to protect their freedom and their communities from the intrusion of big business and big government.

The Second Hundred Days >> By the spring of 1935, the forces of discontent were pushing Roosevelt to more action. So was Congress. With Democrats accounting for more than two-thirds of both houses, they were prepared to outspend the president in extending the New Deal. A "second hundred days" produced a legislative barrage that moved the New Deal toward Roosevelt's ultimate destination—"a little to the left of center," where government could soften the impact of industrialism, protect the needy, and compensate for the boom-and-bust business cycle.

To help the many Americans who were still jobless Roosevelt proposed the Emergency Relief Appropriation Act of 1935, with a record $4.8 billion for relief and employment. Some of the money went to the new National Youth Administration (NYA) for more than 4.5 million jobs for young people. But the lion's share went to the new Works Progress Administration (WPA), where Harry Hopkins mounted the largest work relief program in history. Before its end in 1943, the WPA employed at least 8.5 million people. Constrained from competing with private industry and committed to spending 80 percent of his budget on wages, Hopkins showed remarkable

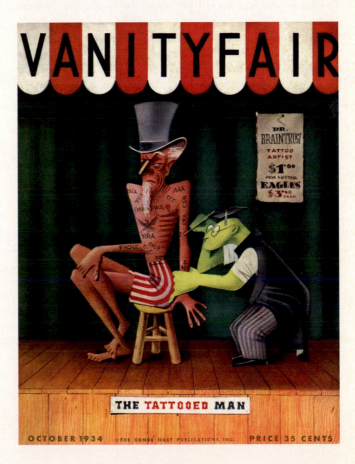

VANITYFAIR

DR. BRAINTRUST
TATTOO ARTIST
$1.00 PER LETTER
EAGLES $3.00 EACH

THE TATTOOED MAN

OCTOBER 1934   © THE CONDÉ NAST PUBLICATIONS, INC.   PRICE 35 CENTS

>> Despite the popularity of Roosevelt and the New Deal, there were critics. New federal agencies, designated by their initials, became easy targets of satirists and cartoonists. In this 1934 cartoon, a wincing Uncle Sam receives an unwelcome set of tattoos, each signifying a New Deal agency.

ingenuity. WPA workers taught women to sew in West Virginia and psychiatric patients to draw in Cincinnati. They built the Griffith Observatory in California and near the peak of Mount Hood in Oregon erected the spectacular Timberline Lodge, log by log.

The ambitious Social Security Act, passed in 1935, sought to help those who could not help themselves: the aged poor, the infirm, dependent children. In this commitment to the destitute it laid the groundwork for the modern welfare state. But Social Security also acted as an economic stabilizer by furnishing pensions for retirees and insurance for those who lost their jobs. A payroll tax on both employer and employee underwrote pensions after age 65, while an employer-financed system of insurance made possible government payments to unemployed workers.

Social Security marked a historic reversal in American political values. A new social contract between the government and the people replaced the gospel of self-help and the older policies of laissez faire. At last government acknowledged a broad responsibility to protect the social rights of citizens. The welfare state, foreshadowed in the aid given veterans and their families after the Civil War, was institutionalized, though its coverage was limited. To win the votes of southern congressmen hostile to African Americans, the legislation excluded farmworkers and domestic servants, doubtless among the neediest Americans but often black and disproportionately southern.

Roosevelt had hoped for social insurance that would cover Americans "from cradle to grave." Congress whittled down his plan, but its labor legislation pushed the president well beyond his goal of providing paternalistic aid for workers, such as establishing pension plans and unemployment insurance. New York senator Robert Wagner, the son of a janitor, wanted workers to fight their own battles. In 1933 he had included union recognition in the

⌃ Social Security poster, 1935

NRA. When the Supreme Court killed the NRA in 1935, Wagner introduced what became the National Labor Relations Act. (So important had labor support become to Roosevelt that he gave the bill his belated blessing.) The "Wagner Act" created a National Labor Relations Board (NLRB) to supervise the election of unions and ensure union rights to bargain. Most vital, the NLRB had the power to enforce these policies. By 1941 the number of unionized workers had doubled.

Roosevelt responded to the growing hostility of business by turning against the wealthy and powerful in 1935. The popularity of Long's tirades against the rich and Coughlin's against banks sharpened his points of attack. The Revenue Act of 1935 (called the "Wealth Tax Act") threatened to "soak the rich." By the time it worked its way through Congress, however, it levied only moderate taxes on high incomes and inheritances. The Banking Act of 1935

Point of View

Congress Passes the Buck

"At the beginning of the same month [March 1933, when Adolf Hitler became dictator of Germany], Franklin Delano Roosevelt was inaugurated as president of the United States—a milestone that was seen alternately as American democracy's vigorous reaction to global political and economic developments and as its tacit surrender to them. The broad-ranging powers granted to Roosevelt by Congress, before that body went into recess, were unprecedented in time of peace. Through this 'delegation of powers,' Congress had, in effect, temporarily done away with itself as the legislative branch of government."

WOLFGANG SCHIVELBUSCH *Three New Deals: Reflections on Roosevelt's America, Mussolini's Italy, and Hitler's Germany, 1933–1939*

centralized authority over the money market in the Federal Reserve Board. By controlling interest rates and the money supply, government increased its ability to compensate for swings in the economy. The Public Utilities Holding Company Act (1935) limited the size of utility empires. Long the target of progressive reformers, the giant holding companies produced nothing but higher profits for speculators and higher prices for consumers. Diluted like the wealth tax, the utility law was still a political victory for New Dealers.

The Election of 1936 >> In June 1936 Roosevelt traveled to Philadelphia to accept the Democratic nomination for a second term as president. "This generation of Americans has a rendezvous with destiny," he told a crowd of 100,000. Whatever destiny had in store for his generation, Roosevelt knew that the coming election would turn on a single issue: "It's myself, and people must be either for me or against me."

Roosevelt ignored his Republican opponent, Governor Alfred Landon of Kansas. Despite a bulging campaign chest of $14 million, Landon lacked luster as well as issues. He favored the regulation of business, a balanced budget, and much of the New Deal. For his part Roosevelt turned the election into a contest between haves and have-nots. The forces of "organized money are unanimous in their hate for me," he told a roaring crowd at New York's Madison Square Garden, "and I welcome their hatred."

The strategy deflated Republicans, discredited conservatives, and stole the thunder of the newly formed Union Party of Townsendites, Coughlinites, and old Long supporters. The election returns shocked even experienced observers. Roosevelt won the largest electoral victory ever—523 to 8—and a whopping 60.8 percent of the popular vote. The margin of victory came from those at the bottom of the economic ladder, grateful for help furnished by the New Deal.

A dramatic political realignment was now clearly in place, as important as the Republican rise to power in 1896. The Democrats reigned as the new majority party for the next 30 years. The "Roosevelt coalition" rested on three pillars: traditional Democratic support in the South; citizens of the big cities, particularly ethnics and African Americans; and labor, both organized and unorganized. The minority Republicans became the party of big business and small towns.

 REVIEW

What were the differences between the "first" and "second" New Deals?

THE NEW DEAL AND THE AMERICAN PEOPLE

Before 1939 farmers in the Hill Country of Texas spent their evenings in the light of 25-watt kerosene lamps. Their wives washed eight loads of laundry a week, all by hand. Everyday they hauled home 200 gallons—about 1,500 pounds—of water from nearby wells. Farms had no milking machines, no washers, no automatic pumps or water heaters, no refrigerators, and no radios.

The reason for this limited life was simple: the Hill Country had no electricity. Thus no agency of the Roosevelt administration changed the way people lived more

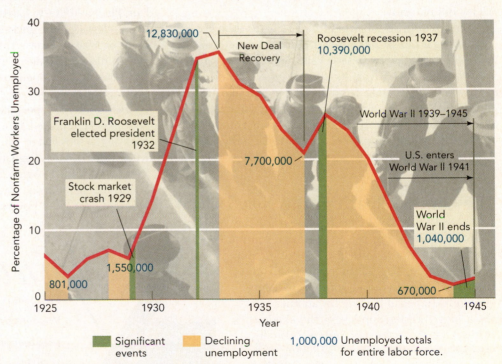

UNEMPLOYMENT, 1925–1945

Unemployment mushroomed in the wake of the stock market crash of 1929. It did not drop to 1929 levels until American entry into the Second World War in 1941. The yellow bands indicate periods of declining unemployment. Note that unemployment begins to rise in 1945 as the military services begin to stand down, wartime industries begin the slow shift to peacetime production, and returning veterans begin to flood the labor force.

dramatically than the Rural Electrification Administration (REA), created in 1935. At the time less than 10 percent of American farms had electricity. Six years later 40 percent did, and by 1950, 90 percent. The New Deal did not always have such a marked impact, and its overall record was mixed. But time and again it changed the lives of ordinary people as government never had before.

The New Deal and Western Water ➤➤

In September 1936 President Roosevelt pushed a button in Washington, D.C., and sent electricity pulsing westward from the towering Hoover Dam in Colorado (begun under the Hoover Administration) to cities as far away as Los Angeles. The waters thus diverted irrigated 2.5 million acres, while the dam's floodgates protected millions of people in southern California, Nevada, and Arizona. In its water management programs, the New Deal further extended federal power, literally across the country.

Hoover Dam was one of several multipurpose dams completed under the New Deal in the arid West. The aim was simple: to control whole river systems for regional use. Buchanan Dam on the lower Colorado River, the Bonneville and Grand Coulee dams on the Columbia, and many smaller versions curbed floods, generated cheap electricity, and developed river basins from Texas to Washington State. Beginning in 1938, the All-American Canal diverted the Colorado River to irrigate the Imperial Valley in California.

The environmental price of such rewards soon became evident, as it did with the New Deal's experiment in eastern water use, the Tennessee Valley Authority. The once mighty Columbia River, its surging waters checked by dams, flowed sedately from human-made lake to lake, but without the salmon whose spawning runs were also checked. Blocked by the All-American Canal from its path to the sea, the Colorado River slowly turned salty, until by 1950 its waters were unfit for drinking or irrigation.

The Limited Reach of the New Deal ➤➤

In the spring of 1939 the Daughters of the American Revolution refused to permit the black contralto Marian Anderson to sing at Constitution Hall in Washington, D.C. Eleanor Roosevelt quit the DAR in protest, and Interior secretary Harold Ickes began looking for another site. On a nippy Easter Sunday, in the shadow of the Lincoln Memorial, Anderson finally stepped to the microphone and sang to a crowd of 7,500. Lincoln himself would not have missed the irony.

In 1932 most African Americans cast their ballots as they had since Reconstruction— for Republicans, the party of Abraham Lincoln and emancipation. But disenchantment with decades of broken promises was spreading, and by 1934 African Americans were voting for Democrats. "Let Jesus lead you and Roosevelt feed you," a black preacher told his congregation on the eve of the 1936 election. When the returns were counted, three of four black voters had cast their ballots for Roosevelt.

The New Deal accounted for this voting revolution. Sympathetic but never a champion, Roosevelt regarded African Americans as one of many groups whose interests he brokered. Even that was an improvement. Federal offices had been segregated since Woodrow Wilson's day, and in the 1920s black leaders called Hoover "the man in the lily-White House." Under Roosevelt racial integration slowly returned to government. Supporters of civil rights such as Eleanor Roosevelt and Harold Ickes brought economist Robert C. Weaver and other black advisers into the administration, forming a "Black Cabinet" to help design federal policy. Mary McLeod Bethune, a sharecropper's daughter and founder of Bethune-Cookman College, ran a division of the National Youth Administration.

Outside of government the Urban League continued to lobby for economic advancement, and the NAACP pressed to make lynching a federal crime. (Though publicly against lynching and privately in favor of an antilynching bill, Roosevelt refused to make it "must" legislation to avoid losing the white southern members of Congress he needed "to save America.") In New York's Harlem, Reverend John H. Johnson organized the Citizens' League for Fair Play in 1933 to persuade white merchants to hire black clerks. After picketers blocked storefronts, hundreds of African Americans got jobs with Harlem retailers and utility companies. Racial tension over employment and housing continued to run high, and in 1935 Harlem exploded in the only race riot of the decade.

Discrimination persisted under the New Deal. Black newspapers reported hundreds of cases of NRA codes resulting in jobs lost to white workers or wages lower than white rates of pay. Disgusted editors renamed the agency "Negroes Ruined Again." Federal efforts to promote grassroots democracy often gave control of New Deal programs to local governments, where discrimination

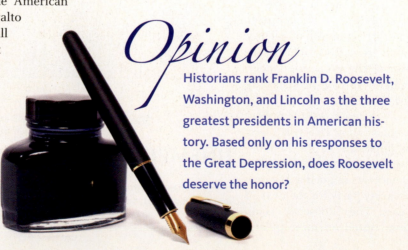

Opinion

Historians rank Franklin D. Roosevelt, Washington, and Lincoln as the three greatest presidents in American history. Based only on his responses to the Great Depression, does Roosevelt deserve the honor?

went unchallenged. New Deal showplaces like the TVA's model town of Norris, Tennessee, and the homestead village of Arthurdale, West Virginia, were closed to African Americans.

African Americans reaped some benefits from the New Deal. The WPA hired black workers for almost 20 percent of its jobs, even though African Americans made up less than 10 percent of the population. When it was discovered that the WPA was paying black workers less than whites, Roosevelt issued an executive order to halt the practice. Public Works administrator Ickes established the first quota system for hiring black Americans. By 1941 the percentage of African Americans working for the government exceeded their proportion of the population.

Civil rights never became a serious aspect of the New Deal, but for the nearly one million Mexican Americans in the United States, Latino culture sometimes frustrated meager federal efforts to help. Mexican folk traditions of self-help inhibited some from seeking aid; others remained unfamiliar with claim procedures. Still others failed to meet residency requirements. Meanwhile, low voter turnout hampered their political influence, and discrimination limited economic advancement.

In the Southwest and California, the Civilian Conservation Corps and the Works Progress Administration furnished some jobs, though fewer and for less pay than average. On Capitol Hill, Dennis Chávez of New Mexico, the only Mexican American in the Senate, channeled what funds he could into Spanish-speaking communities. But like African Americans, most Latinos remained mired in poverty. The many Mexican Americans who worked the fields as migratory laborers lay outside the reach of most New Deal programs.

Tribal Rights >>
The New Deal renewed federal interest in Indians. Among the most disadvantaged Americans, Indian families on reservations rarely earned more than $100 a year. Their infant mortality rate was the highest in the country; their life expectancy, the shortest; their education level the lowest. Their rate of unemployment was three times the national average.

In the 1930s Indians had no stronger friend in Washington than John Collier. For years he had fought as a social worker among the Pueblos to restore tribal culture. As the new commissioner of Indian affairs, he reversed the decades-old policy of assimilation and promoted tribal life. Under the Indian Reorganization Act of 1934, elders were urged to celebrate festivals, artists to work in native styles, children to learn the old languages. A special Court of Indian Affairs removed Indians from state jurisdiction. Tribal governments ruled reservations. Perhaps most important, tribes regained control over Indian land. Since the Dawes Act of 1887, the land had been allotted to individual Indians, who were often forced by poverty to sell to whites. By the end of the 1930s Indian landholding had increased.

Indians split over Collier's policies. The Pueblos, with a strong communal spirit and already functioning communal societies, favored them. The tribes of Oklahoma and

⌃ In 1937 artist Amy Jones painted life on an Iroquois reservation in the Adirondack Mountains. Indian rates for tuberculosis were high; a doctor and a nurse examine an Indian child for the disease (*left side of the painting*). On the right, Iroquois women and children weave baskets from wooden splints while Indian workers split logs to be made into splints for baskets. These themes of public health, manual labor, and Indian crafts formed powerful points of emphasis in the New Deal.

⌃ The WPA was committed to the notion of "equal pay for equal work" for men and women but also adhered to the idea of "women's work" in providing jobs for female workers. Thus most women employed by the WPA were involved with sewing, which lay at the bottom of the pay scale. Since the vast majority of women sewed by hand, the WPA made a point of training them to use machines. This 1937 WPA poster from Ohio puts Power Machine Operator at the top of its list of employable skills.

the Great Plains tended to oppose them. Individualism, the profit motive, and an unwillingness to share property with other tribe members fed resistance. So did age-old suspicion of all government programs. And some Indians such as the Navajos genuinely desired assimilation and saw tribal government as a step backward.

A New Deal for Women >> As the tides of change washed across the country, a new deal for women was unfolding in Washington. The New Deal's welfare agencies offered unprecedented opportunity for social workers, teachers, and other women who had spent their lives helping the downtrodden. They were already experts on social welfare. Several were friends with professional ties, and together they formed a network of activists in the New Deal promoting women's interests and social reform. Women served on the consumers' advisory board of the NRA, helped to administer the relief program, and won appointments to the Social Security Board.

Women also became part of the Democratic party machinery. Under the leadership of social worker Mary W. "Molly" Dewson, the Women's Division of the Democratic National Committee played a critical role in the election of 1936. Thousands of women mounted a "mouth-to-mouth" campaign, traveling from door to door to drum up support for Roosevelt and other Democrats. When the ballots

were tallied, women formed an important part of the new Roosevelt coalition.

Federal appointments and party politics broke new ground for women, but in general the New Deal abided by existing social standards. Gender equality, like racial equality, was never high on its agenda. One-quarter of all NRA codes permitted women to be paid less than men, while WPA wages averaged $2 a day more for men. The New Deal gave relatively few jobs to women, and when it did, they were often in gender-segregated trades such as sewing. Government employment patterns for women fell below even those in the private sector.

Reflecting old conceptions of reform, New Dealers placed greater emphasis on aiding and protecting women than on employing them. The Federal Emergency Relief Administration built 17 camps for homeless women in 11 states. Social security furnished subsidies to mothers with dependent children, and the WPA established emergency nursery schools (which also became the government's first foray into early childhood education). But even federal protection fell short. Social security, for example, did not cover domestic servants, most of whom were women.

The Rise of Organized Labor >> Although women and minorities discovered that the New Deal had limits to the changes it promoted, a powerful union movement arose in the 1930s by taking full advantage of the new climate. At the outset of the Depression barely 6 percent of the labor force belonged to unions. By the end of the decade, nearly a third were union members.

Though the New Deal left farmworkers officially outside its coverage, its promise of support encouraged these workers to act on their own. In California, where large agribusinesses employed migrant laborers to pick vegetables, fruit, and cotton, some 37 strikes involving over 50,000 workers swept the state after Roosevelt took office. The most famous strike broke out in the cotton fields of the San Joaquin Valley under the auspices of the Cannery and Agricultural Workers Industrial Union (CAWIU). Most of the strikers were Mexican, supported more by a complex network of families, friends, and coworkers than by the weak CAWIU. The government finally stepped in to arbitrate a wage settlement, which resulted in an end to the strike but at a fraction of the pay the workers sought.

Such government support was not enough to embolden the cautious American Federation of Labor, the nation's premier union. Historically bound to skilled labor and organized on the basis of craft, it ignored unskilled workers, who made up most of the industrial labor force, and virtually ignored women and black workers. The AFL also avoided major industries like rubber, automobiles, and steel, long hostile to unions and employing many workers with few skills.

In 1935 John L. Lewis of the United Mine Workers and the heads of seven other AFL unions announced the

⋀ During the wave of agricultural strikes in California in 1933, Mexican laborers who had been evicted from their homes settled in camps such as this one in Corcoran. The camp held well over 3,000 people, each family providing an old tent or burlap bags for habitation. Makeshift streets were named in honor of Mexican towns and heroes. By chance the field had been occupied previously by a Mexican circus, the Circo Azteca, which provided nightly entertainment.

formation of the Committee for Industrial Organization (CIO). The AFL suspended the rogue unions in 1936. The CIO, later rechristened the Congress of Industrial Organizations, turned to the unskilled. CIO representatives concentrated on the mighty steel industry, which had clung to the "open," or nonunion, shop since 1919.

In other industries the rank and file did not wait. Emboldened by the recent passage of the Wagner Act, a group of rubber workers in Akron, Ohio, simply sat down on the job in early 1936. Since the strikers occupied the plants, managers could not replace them with strikebreakers. Nor could the rubber companies call in the military or police without risk to their property. The leaders of the United Rubber Workers Union opposed the "sit-downs," but when the Goodyear Tire & Rubber Company laid off 70 workers, 1,400 rubber workers struck on their own. An 11-mile picket line sprang up outside. Eventually Goodyear settled by recognizing the union and accepting its demands on wages and hours.

The biggest strikes erupted in the automobile industry. A series of spontaneous strikes at General Motors plants in Atlanta, Kansas City, and Cleveland spread to Fisher Body No. 2 in Flint, Michigan, late in December 1936. Singing the unionists' anthem, "Solidarity Forever," workers took over the plant while wives, friends, and fellow union members handed food and

⋀ Men looking through the broken windows of an automobile plant during the wave of sit-down strikes in 1937. The windows were smashed not by the men in this photograph but by women of the newly established "Emergency Brigade" when they heard that the workers inside were being gassed. Women played a vital role in supporting the strikes, collecting and distributing food to strikers and their families, setting up a first-aid station, and furnishing day care. Women of the Emergency Brigade wore red tams and armbands with the initials "EB" as shown here.

clothing through the windows. Local police tried to break up supply lines, only to be driven off by a hail of nuts, bolts, coffee mugs, and bottles.

In the wake of this "Battle of Running Bulls" (a reference to the retreating police), Governor Frank Murphy finally called out the National Guard, not to arrest but to protect strikers. General Motors surrendered in February 1937. Less than a month later U.S. Steel capitulated without a strike. By the end of the year every automobile manufacturer except Henry Ford had negotiated with the UAW.

Bloody violence accompanied some drives. On Memorial Day 1937, 10 strikers lost their lives when Chicago police fired on them as they marched peacefully toward the Republic Steel plant. And sit-down strikes often alienated an otherwise sympathetic middle class. (In 1939 the Supreme Court outlawed the tactic.) Yet a momentous transfer of power had taken place. Union membership swelled, and the unskilled now had a powerful voice in the form of the CIO. Women's membership in unions tripled between 1930 and 1940, and African Americans also made gains. Independent unions had become a significant part of industrial America.

"Art for the Millions" ➤➤ No agency of the New Deal touched more Americans than Federal One, the bureaucratic umbrella of the WPA's arts program. For the first time, thousands of unemployed writers, musicians, painters, actors, and photographers went on the federal payroll. Public projects—from massive murals to tiny guidebooks—would make "art for the millions."

A Federal Writers Project (FWP) produced about a thousand publications. Its 81 state, territorial, and city guides were so popular that commercial publishers happily printed them. A Depression-bred interest in American history prompted the FWP to collect folklore, study ethnic groups, and record the reminiscences of 200 former slaves. Meanwhile, the Federal Music Project (FMP) employed some 15,000 out-of-work musicians. For a token charge Americans could hear the music of Bach and Beethoven. In the Federal Art Project (FAP), artists taught sculpture, painting, and carving while watercolorists and drafters painstakingly prepared the Index of American Design with elaborate illustrations of American material culture, from skillets to cigar-store Indians.

The most notable contribution of the FAP came in the form of murals. Under the influence of Mexican muralists Diego Rivera and José Clemente Orozco, American artists covered the walls of thousands of airports, post offices, and other government buildings with wall paintings glorifying local life and work. (See, for example, the mural below.) The rare treatment of class conflict later opened the FAP to charges of communist infiltration, but most of the murals stressed the enduring qualities of American life: family, work, community.

The Federal Theater Project (FTP) reached the greatest number of people—some 30 million—and aroused the most controversy. As its head, Hallie Flanagan made government-supported theater vital, daring, and relevant. *Living Newspapers* dramatized headlines of the day. Occasionally frank depictions of class conflict riled congressional conservatives, and beginning in 1938, the House Un-American Activities Committee investigated the FTP as "a branch of the Communistic organization." A year later Congress slashed its budget and brought government-sponsored theater to an end.

The documentary impulse to record life permeated the arts in the 1930s. Novels such as Erskine Caldwell's *Tobacco Road,* feature films such as John Ford's *The Grapes of Wrath,* and such federally funded documentaries as Pare Lorentz's *The River* stirred the social conscience of the country. Photographers produced an unvarnished pictorial record of the Great Depression. Their raw and

⌃ California's multiethnic workforce is captured in this detail from one of the murals that adorn Coit Tower, built in 1933 on San Francisco's Telegraph Hill. Like other American muralists, John Langley Howard drew on the work of Mexican artists such as Diego Rivera and David Alfaro Siqueiros to paint murals and frescos with political themes. Here Howard shows resolute workers rallying on May Day, an international labor holiday commemorating, among other things, the Haymarket Square Riot of 1886.

haunting photographs turned history into both propaganda and art. New Dealers had practical motives for promoting documentary realism. They wanted to blunt criticism of New Deal relief measures by documenting the distress.

REVIEW

How did the New Deal help minorities and workers?

THE END OF THE NEW DEAL (1937–1940)

"I see one-third of a nation ill-housed, ill-clad, ill-nourished," the president lamented in his second inaugural address on January 20, 1937 (the first January inauguration under a new constitutional amendment). Industrial output had doubled since 1932; farm income had almost quadrupled. But full recovery remained elusive. Over seven million Americans were still out of work, and national income was only half again as large as it had been in 1933, when Roosevelt took office. At the height of his popularity, with bulging majorities in Congress, Roosevelt planned to expand the New Deal. Within a year, however, the New Deal was largely over, drowned in a sea of economic and political troubles—many of them Roosevelt's own doing.

> **Eventually Roosevelt appointed nine Supreme Court justices. But victory came at a high price. The momentum of the 1936 election was squandered and the unity of the Democratic party destroyed.**

Packing the Courts >> As Roosevelt's second term began, only the Supreme Court clouded the political horizon. A new judicial activism, spearheaded by a conservative majority, dominated the court. It rested on a narrow view of the constitutional powers of Congress and the president. As the New Deal broadened those powers, the Supreme Court let loose a torrent of nullifications.

In 1935 the Court wiped out the NRA on the grounds that manufacturing was not involved in interstate commerce and thus lay beyond federal regulation. In 1936 it canceled the AAA, arguing that the Constitution did not permit the government to tax one group (processors) to pay another (farmers). In *Moorehead v. Tipaldo* (1936) the Court ruled that a New York minimum-wage law was invalid because it interfered with the right of workers to negotiate a contract. A frustrated Roosevelt complained that the Court had thereby created a "'no-man's land,' where no government—State or Federal" could act.

Roosevelt was the first president since James Monroe to serve four years without making a Supreme Court appointment. Among federal judges Republicans outnumbered Democrats by more than two to one in 1933. Roosevelt intended to redress the balance with legislation that added new judges to the federal bench, including the Supreme Court. The federal courts were over-burdened and too many judges "aged or infirm," he declared in February 1937. In the interests of efficiency, said Roosevelt, he proposed to "vitalize" the judiciary with new members. When a 70-year-old judge who had served at least 10 years failed to retire, the president could add another, up to 6 to the Supreme Court and 44 to the lower federal courts.

Roosevelt badly miscalculated. He regarded courts as political, not sacred, institutions and had ample precedent for altering even the Supreme Court. As recently as 1869 Congress had increased its size to nine. But in the midst of the depression-spawned crisis most Americans clung to the courts as symbols of stability. Few accepted Roosevelt's efficiency argument, and no one on Capitol Hill—with its share of 70-year-olds—believed that seven decades of life necessarily made one too infirm to work. Worse still, the proposal ignited conservative-liberal antagonisms within the Democratic party, where many conservatives abandoned him.

Suddenly the Court reversed itself. In April, *N.L.R.B. v. Jones and Laughlin Steel Corporation* upheld the Wagner Act by one vote. A month later the justices sustained the Social Security Act as a legitimate exercise of the commerce power. And when Justice Willis Van Devanter, the oldest and most conservative justice, retired later that year, Roosevelt at last made his first appointment to the Supreme Court.

With Democrats deserting him, the president accepted a substitute measure that utterly ignored his proposal to appoint new judges. Roosevelt nonetheless claimed victory. After all, the Court shifted course. And eventually he appointed nine Supreme Court justices. But victory came at a high price. The momentum of the 1936 election was squandered and the unity of the Democratic party destroyed. Opponents learned that Roosevelt could be beaten. A conservative coalition of Republicans and rural Democrats had come together around the first of several anti–New Deal causes.

The Demise of the Deal >> As early as 1936 Secretary of the Treasury Henry Morgenthau began to

plead for fiscal restraint. With productivity rising and unemployment falling, it was time to reduce spending, balance the budget, and permit business to lead the recovery. "Strip off the bandages, throw away the crutches," and let the economy "stand on its own feet," he said.

Morgenthau was preaching to the converted. Although the president had been willing to run budget deficits in the crisis, he was never comfortable with them. Still, some experts believed he was on the right track. In a startling new theory British economist John Maynard Keynes called on government not to balance the budget but to spend its way out of depression, even if it meant running in the red. When prosperity returned, Keynes argued, government could pay off its debts through taxes. This deliberate policy of "countercyclical" action (spending in bad times, taxing in good) would compensate for swings in the economy.

Keynes's theory was precisely the path chosen by several industrial nations in which recovery came more quickly than in the United States. Germany for one built its rapid recuperation on spending. When Adolf Hitler and his National Socialist (Nazi) party came to power in 1933, they went on a spending spree, constructing huge highways called *Autobahns,* enormous government buildings, and other public works. Later they ran up deficits for rearmament as they prepared for war. Between 1933 and 1939 the German national debt almost quadrupled, while in the United States it rose by barely 50 percent. For Germans, the price in lost freedoms was incalculable, but by 1936, their depression was over.

Not all nations relied on military spending. And many of them, such as Great Britain and France, had not shared in the economic expansion of the 1920s, which meant their economies had a shorter distance to rise in order to reach pre-Depression levels. Yet spending of one kind or another helped light the path to recovery in country after country. In Great Britain, for example, low interest rates plus government assistance to the needy ignited a housing boom, while government subsidies to the automobile industry and to companies willing to build factories in depressed areas slowed the slide. By 1937 British unemployment had been halved.

In the United States Roosevelt ordered cuts in federal spending early in 1937. Within six months, the economy collapsed. At the end of the year unemployment stood at 10.5 million as the "Roosevelt recession" deepened. Finally spenders convinced him to propose a $3.75 billion omnibus measure in April 1938. Facing an election, Congress happily reversed spending cuts, quadrupled farm subsidies, and embarked on a new shipbuilding program. The economy revived but never recovered. Keynesian economics was vindicated, though it would take decades before becoming widely accepted.

With Roosevelt vulnerable, conservatives in Congress struck. They trimmed public housing programs and minimum wage guarantees in the South. The president's few successes came where he could act alone, principally in a renewed attack on big business. At his urging the Justice Department opened investigations of corporate concentration. Even Congress responded by creating the Temporary National Economic Committee to examine corporate abuses and recommend revisions in the antitrust laws. These were small consolations. The president, wrote Interior Secretary Harold Ickes in August 1938, "is punch drunk from the punishment."

Vainly Roosevelt fought back in the arena of campaign politics. In the off-year elections of 1938, he tried to purge Democrats who had deserted him. The five senators he targeted for defeat all won. Republicans posted gains in the House and Senate and won 13 governorships. Democrats still held majorities in both houses, but conservatives now had the votes to block new programs. With the economy limping toward recovery, the New Deal passed into history.

The Legacy of the New Deal >> The New Deal lasted only five years, from 1933 to 1938, and it never spent enough to end the Depression. Though it pledged itself to the "forgotten" Americans, it failed the neediest among them: sharecroppers, tenant farmers, migrant workers. In many ways, it was quite conservative. It left capitalism intact and overturned few cultural conventions. Even its reforms followed the old progressive formula of softening industrialism by strengthening the state.

Yet for all its conservatism and continuities, the New Deal left a legacy of change. Under it, government assumed a broader role in the economy. To regulation was now added the complicated task of maintaining economic

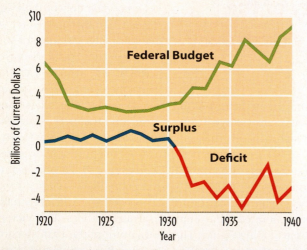

FEDERAL BUDGET AND SURPLUS/DEFICIT, 1920–1940

During the 1920s the federal government ran a modest surplus as spending dropped back sharply after World War I. Deficits grew steadily as Franklin Roosevelt's New Deal spent boldly and as revenues from taxes and tariffs continued to sink. In 1937 federal spending cuts to balance the budget reduced the deficit but brought on a recession that was quickly followed by renewed federal spending and increasing deficits.

stability—compensating for swings in the business cycle. In its securities and banking regulations, unemployment insurance, and requirements for wages and hours, the New Deal created stabilizers to avoid future breakdowns.

Franklin Roosevelt modernized the presidency. He turned the White House into the heart of government. Americans looked to the president to set the public agenda, spread new ideas, initiate legislation, and assume responsibility for the nation. The power of Congress diminished, but the scope of government grew. In 1932 there were 605,000 federal employees; by 1939 there were nearly a million (and by 1945, after World War II, some 3.5 million). The many programs of the New Deal touched the lives of ordinary Americans as never before, made them more secure, bolstered the middle class, and formed the outlines of the new welfare state.

At a time when dictators and militarists came to power in Germany, Italy, Japan, and Russia, the New Deal strengthened democracy in America. Roosevelt acted as a democratic broker, responding first to one group, then to another. And his "broker state" embraced groups previously spurned: unions, farm organizations, ethnic minorities, women. In short, during the 1930s the United States found a middle way avoiding the extremes of communism and fascism. The broker state also had limits. The unorganized, whether in city slums or in sharecroppers' shacks, too often found themselves ignored.

Under the New Deal the Democratic party became a mighty force in politics. In a quiet revolution African Americans came into the party's fold, as did workers and farmers. Political attention shifted to bread-and-butter issues. In 1932 people had argued about Prohibition and European war debts. By 1935 they were debating social security, labor relations, tax reform, public housing, and the TVA. Perhaps most important of all, Americans now assumed that in hard times government would come to their aid. With remarkable speed, the New Deal became a vital part of American life.

 REVIEW

What did the New Deal accomplish, and what did it fail to accomplish?

The Depression shook both the political and material pillars of democratic culture—even more turbulently around the world than at home. By 1939, on the eve of World War II, the Soviet Union, Germany, and Italy were firmly under the control of dictators bent on expanding

What the New Deal Did . . .

	Relief	Recovery	Reform
For the Farmer	Rural electrification Administration (1936) Farm Security Administration (1937)	Agriculture Adjustment Act (1933)	
For the Worker		National Industrial Recovery Act (1933)	National Labor Relations Act (1935) Fair Labor Standards Act (1938)
For the Middle Class	Home Owner's Loan Act (1934)		Revenue ("Wealth Tax") Act (1935) Public Utilities Holding Company Act (1935)
For the Needy	Federal Emergency Relief Act (1933) Civilian Conservation Corp (1933) Civil Works Administration (1933) National Public Housing Act (1937) Emergency Relief Appropriation Act (1935)		
For Protection Against Future Depressions			Federal Deposit Insurance Corporation (1933) Securities Exchange Act (1934) Social Security Act (1935)

New Deal chart

both their powers and their nations' territory. The number of European democracies shrank from 27 to 10. Latin America was ruled by a variety of dictators and military juntas, little different from the new despots of Europe. China suffered not only from invasion by Japan's militarists but also from the corrupt and ineffectual one-party dictatorship of Chiang Kai-shek.

The New Deal attempted to combat the Depression through the methods of parliamentary democracy, expanding government to humanize industrial society and generate prosperity. New Dealers from the president down nonetheless recognized that the federal government could not do everything. But "it bought us time to think," commented Eleanor Roosevelt in 1939. Even as she spoke those words a measure of doubt crept into her voice. "Is it going to be worthwhile?" With the threat of war on the horizon, only future generations would know for certain.

CHAPTER SUMMARY

The Great Depression of the 1930s was the longest in the history of the nation; it forced virtually all Americans to live leaner lives, and it spawned Franklin Roosevelt's New Deal.

- The Great Depression acted as a great leveler that reduced differences in income and status and left many Americans with an "invisible scar" of shame, self-doubt, and lost confidence.

- Unemployment and suffering were especially acute among agricultural migrants, African Americans, Latinos, and American Indians.
- Rates of marriage and birth declined in all social classes, and many women found themselves working additional hours inside and outside the home to supplement family incomes.
- Popular culture rallied to reinforce basic tenets of American life: middle-class morality, family, capitalism, and democracy.
- President Herbert Hoover represented a transition from the old, do-nothing policies of the past to the interventionist policies of the future. In the end his program of voluntary cooperation and limited government activism failed, and in 1932 he lost the presidency to Franklin Roosevelt.
- Roosevelt's New Deal attacked the Great Depression along three broad fronts: recovery for the economy, relief for the needy, and reforms to ward off future depressions.
- The New Deal failed to achieve full recovery but did result in lasting changes:
  - The creation of economic stabilizers such as federal insurance for bank deposits, unemployment assistance, and greater control over money and banking that were designed to compensate for swings in the economy.
  - The establishment of a limited welfare state to provide minimum standards of well-being for all Americans.

Significant Events

Herbert Hoover elected president

Repatriation of Mexicans; Scottsboro boys arrested; New York establishes first state welfare agency, Temporary Emergency Relief Administration

1928　　**1929**　　**1931**　　**1933**　　**1934**

"Great Crash" of stock market ushers in Great Depression

Franklin Roosevelt inaugurated; black blizzards begin to form Dust Bowl; Hundred Days legislation enacted

Indian Reorganization Act; Huey Long organizes Share Our Wealth Society; Father Charles Coughlin creates National Union for Social Justice

- The revitalization of the Democratic party and the formation of a powerful new political coalition of labor, urban ethnics, women, African Americans, and the South.
- The modernization of the presidency.

Additional Reading

The best overall examination of the period encompassing the Great Depression and the Second World War is David M. Kennedy's *Freedom from Fear: The American People in Depression and War, 1929–1945* (1999). For a comparative look at responses to the Great Depression, see John A. Garraty, *The Great Depression* (1987) and Wolfgang Schivelbusch, *Three New Deals: Reflections on Roosevelt's America, Mussolini's Italy, and Hitler's Germany, 1933–1939* (2006). Robert Sobel, *The Great Bull Market: Wall Street in the 1920s* (1968), is a brief, evenhanded study of the stock market and Republican fiscal policies in the 1920s. Caroline Bird, *The Invisible Scar* (1966), remains the most sensitive treatment of the human impact of the Great Depression, but it should not be read without Studs Terkel, *Hard Times: An Oral History of the Great Depression* (1970), and Robert McElvaine, *The Great Depression: America, 1929–1941* (1984), which are especially good on Depression culture and values. Joan Hoff Wilson, *Herbert Hoover: Forgotten Progressive* (1975), traces Hoover's progressive impulses before and during his presidency.

Frank Freidel, *Franklin D. Roosevelt: A Rendezvous with Destiny* (1990), is the best single-volume biography of Roosevelt, and William Leuchtenburg, *Franklin D. Roosevelt and the New Deal, 1932–1940* (1963), is the best single-volume study of the New Deal. Both fall within the liberal tradition of New Deal scholarship and are admiringly critical of Roosevelt's use of power. Jean Edward Smith's *FDR* (2007) offers a positive, if critical, reinterpretation of FDR with greater emphasis on his personal life than found in earlier biographies. For sharp criticism of New Left historians, see Paul Conkin, *The New Deal* (1967). Stephen Lawson's *A Commonwealth of Hope: The New Deal Response to Crisis* (2006) argues that the New Deal was less a makeshift reaction to the Great Depression and more a part of a longer tradition of planning and reform. Amity Schlaes, *The Forgotten Man: A New History of the Great Depression* (New York, 2007), provides a conservative critique of the New Deal that rests on stories of "forgotten" men and women and argues that its policies actually prolonged the Great Depression.

Eleanor Roosevelt is analyzed in rich detail and from a frankly feminist viewpoint in Blanche Wiesen Cook, *Eleanor Roosevelt* (1999). Susan Ware, *Beyond Suffrage: Women and the New Deal* (1981), locates a women's political network within the New Deal, and Harvard Sitkoff, *A New Deal for Blacks* (1978), studies a similar network of blacks and whites. The culture and politics of working men and women during the Great Depression are the subject of Lisabeth Cohen, *Making a New Deal: Industrial Workers in Chicago, 1919–1939* (1990). For a probing analysis of New Deal liberalism and its retreat from reform, see Alan Brinkley, *The End of Reform: New Deal Liberalism in Recession and War* (1995).

Second Hundred Days legislation; *Schecter Poultry Corporation v. United States* invalidates National Recovery Administration

Butler v. United States invalidates Agricultural Adjustment Administration (AAA); Congress of Industrial Organizations formed

Marian Anderson gives concert at Lincoln Memorial

1935 **1936** **1937** **1938** **1939**

JUSTICE ROBERTS

Roosevelt announces court-packing plan; slashes federal spending, which initiates Roosevelt recession

Fair Labor Standards Act

America's
Rise to

↗ News of battleships in flames, from the Japanese surprise attack at Pearl Harbor, sent the United States into global war.

"It was a mess," he remembered. The *USS Shaw* was in flames. The battleship *Pennsylvania*, a bomb nesting one deck above the powder and ammunition, was about to blow. When ordered to put out its fires, he told the navy officer, "There ain't no way I'm gonna go down there." Instead, he spent the rest of the day pulling bodies from the water. Surveying the wreckage the next morning, he noted that the battleship *Arizona* "was a total washout." So was the *West Virginia*. The *Oklahoma* had "turned turtle, totally upside down." It took two weeks to get all the fires out.

The war that had been spreading around the world had, until December 7, spared the United States. After the attack at Pearl Harbor panic spread up and down the West Coast. Crowds in Los Angeles turned trigger-happy. A police officer heard "sirens going off, aircraft guns firing." "Here we are in the middle of the night," he said, "there was no enemy in sight, but somebody thought they saw the enemy." In January 1942 worried officials moved the Rose Bowl from Pasadena, California, to Durham, North Carolina. Though overheated, their fears were not entirely imaginary.

Japanese submarines shelled Santa Barbara and Fort Stearns in Oregon. Balloons carrying incendiary devices caused several deaths.

Although the Japanese never mounted a serious threat to the mainland, in a world with long-range bombers and submarines, no place seemed safe. This was global war, the first of its kind. Arrayed against the Axis powers of Germany, Italy, and Japan were the Allies: Great Britain, the Soviet Union, the United States, China, and the Free French. Their armies fought from the Arctic to the southwestern Pacific, in the great cities of Europe and Asia and the small villages of North Africa

26
Globalism
1927–1945

>> **AN AMERICAN STORY**

"OH BOY"

John Garcia, a native Hawaiian, a worker at the Pearl Harbor Navy Yard in Honolulu, planned a lazy day off for Sunday, December 7, 1941. By the time his grandmother rushed in to wake him that morning at eight, he had already missed the worst of the news. "The Japanese were bombing Pearl Harbor," he recalled her yelling at him. John listened in disbelief. "I said, 'They're just practicing.'" "No," his grandmother replied. It was real. He catapulted his huge frame from the bed, ran to the front porch, hopped on his motorcycle, and sped to the harbor. >>

and Indochina, in malarial jungles and scorching deserts, on six continents and across four oceans. Perhaps as many as 100 million people took up arms; some 40 to 50 million lost their lives.

Tragedy on such a scale taught that generation of Americans that they could no longer isolate themselves from any part of the world, no matter how remote. Manchuria, Ethiopia, and Poland had once seemed far away, yet the road to war had led from those distant places to the United States. Retreat into isolation had not cured the worldwide depression or preserved the peace. As it waged a global war, the United States began to assume far wider responsibility for managing the world's geopolitical and economic systems. «

THE UNITED STATES IN A TROUBLED WORLD

The outbreak of World War II had its roots in the aftermath of World War I. Many of the victorious as well as the defeated nations resented the peace terms adopted at Versailles. Over the next two decades Germany, the Soviet Union, Italy, Poland, and Japan all sought to achieve on their own what Allied leaders had denied them during the negotiations. War debts imposed at Versailles shackled Germany's economy. As that nation struggled to recover during the Great Depression, so did all of Europe. In central and eastern Europe rivalry among fascists, communists, and other political factions led to frequent violence and instability.

Fascists took the greatest advantage of this instability. The philosophy and movement had its roots in Italy, where nationalists under Benito Mussolini gained power in the 1920s, preaching the idea of the nation as an organic community. Individuals meant little compared with the needs of the nation, fascists believed; and war kept the nation strong and served the collective interest. Adolph Hitler and his Nazis (the National Socialist German Workers' Party) went further when they assumed control of Germany in 1933. They embraced a totalitarian government, racism (especially anti-Semitism), a policy of territorial expansion to obtain *Lebensraum* (living space), and state control of an economy dedicated to making war. Japanese fascists erected a militarist state whose leaders were also bent on armed conquest. As political movements of the right, these extreme conservatives—whether fascist, national socialist, or militarist—violently opposed communism with its abolition of private property and its ideal of a classless, collectivist society. Fascists in all three nations moved against communist and labor parties at home, and abroad they sought to destroy the Soviet Union's workers' state.

Faced with this increasingly unstable world, the United States turned away from any collective action to check the fascist powers. Although their nation possessed the resources at least to ease international tensions, Americans declined to lead in world affairs, remaining outside the League of Nations.

Pacific Interests »

The effort to avoid entanglements did not mean the United States could simply ignore events abroad. In assuming colonial control over the Philippines, Americans had created a potentially dangerous rivalry with Japan over the western Pacific. So also had the American commitment to uphold China's territorial integrity, set out in the "open door" policy of 1900 (page 438). With rival Chinese warlords fighting among themselves, Japan took the opportunity to capture overseas raw materials and markets. In 1931 Japanese agents staged an explosion on a rail line in Manchuria (meant to appear as though carried out by Chinese nationalists). That act provided an excuse for Japan to occupy the whole province. A year later Japan converted Manchuria into a puppet state called Manchukuo.

Here was a direct threat to the Versailles system. But neither the major powers in Europe nor the United States was willing to risk a war with Japan over China. President Hoover would allow Secretary of State Henry Stimson only to protest that the United States would refuse to recognize Japan's takeover of Manchuria as legal. The policy of "nonrecognition" became known as the Stimson Doctrine, even though Stimson himself doubted its worth. He was right to be skeptical. Three weeks later Japan's imperial navy shelled the port city of Shanghai, seeking to expand their influence in China.

Becoming a Good Neighbor »

Growing tensions in Asia and Europe gave the United States an incentive to improve relations with nations closer to home. By the late 1920s the United States had intervened in Latin America so often that the Roosevelt Corollary (page 471) had become an embarrassment. Slowly, however, American administrations began to moderate those high-handed policies. In 1927, when Mexico confiscated American-owned properties, President Coolidge sent an ambassador to settle the dispute rather than the marines.

⌃ The Good Neighbor policy made Franklin Roosevelt unusually popular in Latin America, as this sheet music suggests. Roosevelt was the first American president to visit South America, and his diplomacy paid dividends when a largely united Western Hemisphere faced the world crisis.

In 1933, when critics compared the American position in Nicaragua to Japan's in Manchuria, Secretary Stimson ordered U.S. troops to withdraw. In such gestures lay the roots of a "Good Neighbor" policy.

Franklin Roosevelt pushed the good neighbor idea. At the seventh Pan-American Conference in 1933 his administration accepted a resolution denying any country "the right to intervene in the internal or external affairs of another." The following year he negotiated a treaty with Cuba that renounced the American right to intervene under the Platt Amendment (page 471). Henceforth the United States would replace direct military presence with indirect (but still substantial) economic influence.

As the threat of war increased during the 1930s the United States found a new Latin willingness to cooperate in matters of natural resource conservation and common defense. By the end of 1940 the administration had worked out defense agreements with every Latin American country but one. The United States faced the threat of war with the American hemisphere largely secured.

The Diplomacy of Isolationism >> During the 1920s Benito Mussolini had appealed to Italian nationalism and fears of communism to gain power in Italy.

Spinning his dreams of a new Roman empire, Mussolini embodied the rising force of fascism. His Fasci di Combattimento, or fascists, used terrorism and murder to create an "all-embracing" single-party state, outside which "no human or spiritual values can exist, let alone be desirable." Italian fascists rejected the liberal belief in political parties in favor of a glorified nation-state dominated by the middle class, small businesspeople, and small farmers.

Then on March 5, 1933, one day after the inauguration of Franklin Roosevelt, the German legislature granted Adolf Hitler dictatorial powers in Germany. Riding a wave of anticommunism and anti-Semitism, Hitler's Nazi party trumpeted similar fascist ideals, looking to unite all Germans in a Greater Third Reich. A week earlier, when the League of Nations condemned Japan for its attacks on China, the Japanese simply withdrew from the league. Its militarist leaders were intent on carving out Japan's own empire, which they called the Greater East Asia Co-Prosperity Sphere. The global rise of fascism and militarism brought the world to war.

As much as Roosevelt wanted the United States to resist aggression, he found the nation reluctant to follow. "It's a terrible thing to look over your shoulder when you are trying to lead—and to find no one there," he commented during the mid-1930s. For every step the president took toward internationalism, the Great Depression forced him home again. Programs to revive the economy gained broad support; efforts to resolve crises abroad provoked opposition. The move to noninvolvement in world affairs gained in 1935 after Senator Gerald P. Nye of North Dakota held hearings on the role of bankers and munitions makers in World War I.

merchants of death term popularized in the 1930s to describe American bankers and arms makers whose support for the Allied cause, some historians charged, drew the United States into World War I.

These "**merchants of death**," Nye's committee revealed, had made enormous profits during World War I. The committee report implied, but could not prove, that business interests had even steered the United States into war. "When Americans went into the fray," declared Senator Nye, "they little thought that they were there and fighting to save the skins of American bankers who had bet too boldly on the outcome of the war and had two billions of dollars of loans to the Allies in jeopardy."

Roused by the Nye Committee hearings, Congress debated a proposal to prohibit the sale of arms to all belligerents in time of war. Internationalists argued that an embargo should apply only to aggressor nations. Otherwise, aggressors could strike when they were better armed than their victims. The president, internationalists suggested, should use the embargo selectively. Isolationists, however, had the votes they needed. The Neutrality Act of 1935 required an impartial embargo of arms to all belligerents. The president had authority only to determine when a state of war existed.

The limitations of formal neutrality became immediately apparent. In October 1935 Mussolini ordered Italian forces into the North African country of Ethiopia. Against tanks and planes, Ethiopian troops fought back with spears and flintlock rifles. Roosevelt immediately invoked neutrality in hopes of depriving Italy of war goods. Unfortunately for Roosevelt, Italy needed not arms but oil, steel, and copper—materials not included under the Neutrality Act. When Secretary of State Cordell Hull called for a "moral embargo" on such goods, depression-starved American businesses shipped them anyway. With no effective opposition from the League of Nations or the United States, Mussolini quickly completed his conquest. In a second Neutrality Act, Congress added a ban on loans or credits to belligerents.

American non-involvement also benefited Nazi dictator Adolf Hitler. In March 1936, two weeks after Congress passed the second Neutrality Act, German troops thrust into the demilitarized area west of the Rhine River. This flagrant act violated the Treaty of Versailles. As Hitler shrewdly calculated, Britain and France did nothing, while the League of Nations sputtered out a worthless condemnation. Roosevelt remained aloof. The Soviet Union's lonely call for collective action fell on deaf ears.

Then came an attack on Spain's fledgling democracy. In July 1936 Generalissimo Francisco Franco, made bold by Hitler's success, led a rebellion against the newly elected Popular Front government. Hitler and Mussolini sent supplies, weapons, and troops to Franco's Fascists, while the Soviet Union and Mexico aided the left-leaning government. With Americans sharply divided over whom to support, Roosevelt refused to become involved. Lacking vital support, the Spanish republic fell to Franco in 1939.

Congress sought a way to allow American trade to continue (and thus to promote economic recovery at home) without drawing the nation into war itself. Under new "cash-and-carry" provisions in the Neutrality Act of 1937, belligerents could buy supplies other than munitions. But they would have to pay beforehand and carry the supplies on their own ships. If war spread, these terms favored the British, whose navy could better ensure that supplies reached England.

But the policy of cash-and-carry hurt China in 1937 when Japanese forces pushed into its southern regions. In order to give China continued access to American goods, Roosevelt refused to invoke the Neutrality Act, which would have cut off trade with

both nations. But Japan had by far the greater volume of trade with the United States. Since the president lacked the freedom to impose a selective embargo, he could only condemn Japan's invasion.

Inching toward War

>> In 1937 the three aggressor nations, Germany, Japan, and Italy, signed the Anti-Comintern Pact. On the face of it the pact pledged them only to ally against the Soviet Union. But the agreement created a Rome-Berlin-Tokyo axis that provoked growing fear of wider war. Roosevelt groped for some way to contain the Axis powers, delivering in October his first foreign policy speech in 14 months. Seeming to favor collective action, he called for an international "quarantine" of aggressor nations. Although most newspapers applauded his remarks, the American public remained skeptical, and Roosevelt remained cautious about matching words with deeds. When Japanese planes sank the American gunboat *Panay* on China's Yangtze River only two months later, he meekly accepted an apology for the unprovoked attack.

In Europe the Nazi menace continued to grow as German troops marched into Austria in 1938—yet another violation of the Versailles Treaty. Hitler then insisted that the 3.5 million ethnic Germans in the Sudetenland of Czechoslovakia be brought into the Reich. With Germany threatening to invade Czechoslovakia, the leaders of France and Britain flew to Munich in September 1938, where they struck a deal to appease Hitler. Czechoslovakia would give up the Sudetenland in return for German pledges to seek no more territory in Europe. When British

>> A company of Nazi youths parades past the Führer, Adolf Hitler (*centered in the balcony doorway*). Hitler's shrewd use of patriotic symbols, mass rallies, and marches exploited the new possibilities of mass politics.

prime minister Neville Chamberlain returned to England, he told cheering crowds that the Munich Pact would bring "peace in our time." Six months later, in open contempt for the European democracies, Hitler took over the remainder of Czechoslovakia. "Appeasement" became synonymous with betrayal, weakness, and surrender.

appeasement policy of making concessions to an aggressor nation, as long as its demands appear reasonable, in order to avoid war.

Hitler's Invasion >>

By 1939 Hitler made little secret that he intended to recapture territory Germany had lost to Poland after World War I. What then would the Soviet Union do? If Soviet leader Joseph Stalin joined the Western powers, Hitler might be blocked. But Stalin, who coveted eastern Poland, suspected that the West hoped to turn Hitler against the Soviet Union. On August 24, 1939, Russia and Germany shocked the world when they announced a nonaggression pact. Its secret protocols freed Hitler to invade Poland without fear of Soviet opposition. In turn, Stalin could extend his western borders by bringing eastern Poland, the Baltic states (Latvia, Estonia, and Lithuania), and parts of Romania and Finland into the Soviet sphere.

On the hot Saturday of September 1, 1939, German tanks and troops surged into Poland. "It's come at last," Roosevelt sighed. "God help us all." Within days France and England declared war on Germany. Stalin quickly moved into eastern Poland, where German and Russian tanks took just three weeks to crush the Polish cavalry. As Hitler consolidated his hold on eastern Europe, Stalin invaded Finland.

Once spring arrived in 1940 Hitler moved to protect his sea lanes by capturing Denmark and Norway. Soon after, German panzer divisions supported by airpower knifed through Belgium and Holland in a *Blitzkrieg*—a "lightning war." The Low Countries fell in 23 days, giving the Germans a route into France. By May a third of a million British and French troops had been driven back onto the Atlantic beaches of Dunkirk. Only a strenuous rescue effort, staged by the Royal Navy and a flotilla of yachts and fishing boats, managed to ferry them across the channel to England and safety. With the British and French routed, German forces marched to Paris.

On June 22, less than six weeks after the German invasion, France capitulated. Hitler insisted that the surrender come in the very railway car in which Germany had submitted in 1918. William Shirer, an American war correspondent standing 50 yards away, watched the dictator through binoculars: "He swiftly snaps his hands on his hips, arches his shoulders, plants his feet wide apart. It is a magnificent gesture of defiance, of burning contempt for this place and all that it has stood for in the twenty-two years since it witnessed the humbling of the German Empire."

Retreat from Isolationism >>

With France gone only Great Britain stood between Hitler and the United States. If the Nazis defeated the British fleet, what would stop the Atlantic Ocean from becoming a gateway to the Americas? Suddenly, **isolationism** seemed dangerous. Roosevelt thus abandoned impartiality in favor of outright aid to the Allies. In May 1940 he requested funds to motorize the U.S. Army (it had only 350 tanks) and build 50,000 airplanes a year (fewer than 3,000 existed, most outmoded). Over isolationist protests Congress adopted a bill for the first peacetime draft in history.

isolationism belief that the United States should avoid foreign entanglements, alliances, and involvement in foreign wars.

That summer thousands of German fighter planes and heavy bombers struck targets in England. In the Battle of Britain Hitler sought to soften up England for a German invasion. Radio reporters relayed graphic descriptions of London in flames and Royal Air Force pilots putting up a heroic defense. Such tales convinced a majority of Americans that the United States should help Britain win the war, though few favored military involvement.

In the fall of 1940 Roosevelt easily won a third term, defeating his Republican opponent, Wendell Willkie. In doing so, the president promised voters that rather than fight, the United States would become "the great arsenal of democracy." The beleaguered British, however, could no longer pay for arms under the strict provisions of cash-and-carry. So Roosevelt proposed a scheme to "lease, lend, or otherwise dispose of" arms and supplies to countries whose defense was vital to the United States. That meant sending supplies to Britain on the dubious premise that they would be returned when the war ended. Roosevelt likened "lend-lease" to lending a garden hose to a neighbor whose house was on fire. Isolationist senator Robert Taft thought a comparison to "chewing gum" more apt. After a neighbor used it, "you don't want it back." Still, in March 1941 Congress easily passed the Lend-Lease Act.

Step by step Roosevelt had led the United States to the verge of war with the Nazis. Then Hitler, as audacious as ever, broke his alliance with the Soviet Union by launching a surprise invasion of Russia in June 1941. The

"Appeasement" became synonymous with betrayal, weakness, and surrender.

<< During World War II, President Franklin Roosevelt and British Prime Minister Winston Churchill developed the closest relationship ever between an American president and the head of another government. These distant cousins shared a sense of the continuities of Anglo-American culture and of the global strategy for pursuing the war to a successful end.

Allies expected a swift collapse, but when Russian troops mounted a heroic resistance, Roosevelt extended lend-lease to the Soviet Union.

That August Roosevelt secretly met with the new British prime minister, Winston Churchill, on warships off the coast of Newfoundland. Almost every day since England and Germany had gone to war, the two leaders had exchanged phone calls, letters, or cables. Now Roosevelt and Churchill drew up the Atlantic Charter, a statement of principles that the two nations held in common. The charter condemned "Nazi tyranny" and embraced the "Four Freedoms": freedom of speech and expression, freedom of worship, freedom from want, and freedom from fear. In effect, the Atlantic Charter was an unofficial statement of war aims. Yet despite Roosevelt's increasing involvement eight of ten Americans still opposed entering the hostilities. Few in the United States suspected that an attack by Japan, not Germany, would unify America and bring it into the war.

Disaster in the Pacific >>

Preoccupied by the fear of German victory in Europe, Roosevelt sought to avoid a showdown with Japan. The navy, the president told his cabinet, had "not got enough ships to go round, and every little episode in the Pacific means fewer ships in the Atlantic." But precisely because American and European attention lay elsewhere, Japan was emboldened to expand militarily into Southeast Asia. By the summer of 1941 Japanese forces controlled the Chinese coast and all major cities. When its army marched into French Indochina (present-day Vietnam) in July, Japan stood ready to conquer all of the Southeast Asian peninsula and the oil-rich Dutch East Indies.

Roosevelt was forced to act. He embargoed trade, froze Japanese assets in American banks, and barred shipments of vital scrap iron and petroleum. Japanese leaders indicated a willingness to negotiate with the United States, but diplomats from both sides were only going through the motions. The two nations' goals were totally at odds. Japan demanded that its conquests be recognized; the United States insisted that Japan withdraw from China and renounce the Tripartite Pact with Germany and Italy. As negotiations sputtered on, the Japanese secretly prepared an attack on American positions in Guam, the Philippines, and Hawaii.

In late November American intelligence located, and then lost, a Japanese armada as it left Japan. Observing strict radio silence, the six carriers and their escorts steamed across the North Pacific. On Sunday morning, December 7, 1941, the first wave of Japanese planes roared down on the Pacific Fleet lying at anchor in Pearl Harbor. For more than an hour the Japanese pounded the ships and nearby airfields. Altogether 19 ships were sunk or battered. Practically all the 200 American aircraft were damaged or destroyed. Only the aircraft carriers, by chance on maneuvers, escaped the worst naval defeat in American history.

In Washington, Secretary of War Henry Stimson could not believe the news relayed to his office. "My God! This can't be true, this must mean the Philippines." Later that day the Japanese did attack the Philippines, along with Guam, Midway, and British forces in Hong Kong and the Malay peninsula. On December 8, Franklin Roosevelt told a stunned nation that "yesterday, December 7, 1941" was "a date which will live in infamy." America, the "reluctant belligerent," was in the war at last. Three days later Hitler declared war on the "half Judaized and the other half Negrified" people of the United States; Italy quickly followed suit.

 REVIEW

Explain why at least three major events pushed the United States to intervene in World War II.

A GLOBAL WAR

British prime minister Winston Churchill greeted the news of Pearl Harbor with shock but, even more, relief. Great Britain would no longer stand alone in the North Atlantic and the Pacific wars. "We have won the war," he thought, and that night he slept "the sleep of the saved and thankful."

As Churchill recognized, only with the Americans fully committed to war could the Allies make full use of the enormous material and human resources of the United States. Beyond that, the Allies needed to secure an alliance between the Anglo-American democracies and the Soviet Communist dictatorship that could win both the war and the peace to follow.

Strategies for War ›› Within two weeks Churchill was in Washington, meeting with Roosevelt to coordinate production schedules for ships, planes, and armaments. The numbers they announced were so large some critics openly laughed—at first. A year later combined British, Canadian, and American production boards not only met but exceeded the schedules.

Roosevelt and Churchill also planned grand strategy. Outraged by the attack on Pearl Harbor, many Americans thought Japan should be the war's primary target. But the two leaders agreed that Germany posed the greater threat. The Pacific war, they decided, would be fought as a holding action, while the Allies concentrated on Europe. In a global war, arms and resources had to be allocated carefully, for the Allies faced daunting threats on every front.

Gloomy Prospects ›› By summer's end in 1942 the Allies faced defeat. The Nazis stood outside the Soviet Union's three major cities: Leningrad, Moscow, and Stalingrad. In North Africa, General Erwin Rommel, Germany's famed "Desert Fox," swept into Egypt with his Afrika Korps to stand within striking distance of the Suez Canal—a lifeline to the resources of the British empire. German U-boats (submarines) in the North Atlantic threatened to sever the ocean link between the United States and Britain. So deadly were these "Wolfpacks" that merchant sailors developed a grim humor about sleeping. Those on freighters carrying iron ore slept above decks, since the heavily laden ships could sink in less than a minute. On oil tankers, however, sailors closed their doors, undressed, and slept soundly. If a torpedo hit, no one would survive anyway.

THE U-BOAT WAR

In the world's first truly global war, the need to coordinate and supply troops and matériel became paramount. But as German U-boats took a heavy toll on Allied shipping, it became difficult to deliver American supplies to Europe. Avoiding the North Atlantic route forced an arduous 12,000-mile journey around Africa to the Persian Gulf and then across by land. The elimination of German submarines greatly eased the shipping problem and, as much as any single battle, ensured victory.

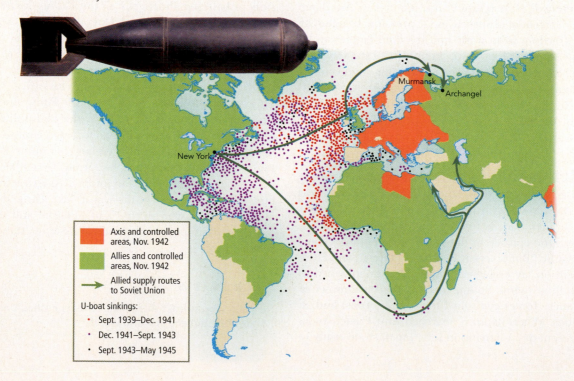

Axis and controlled areas, Nov. 1942

Allies and controlled areas, Nov. 1942

Allied supply routes to Soviet Union

U-boat sinkings:
- Sept. 1939–Dec. 1941
- Dec. 1941–Sept. 1943
- Sept. 1943–May 1945

In the Far East the Japanese navy destroyed most of the Allied fleet in the western Pacific during the Battle of Java Sea. General Douglas MacArthur, commander of American forces in the Philippines, escaped to Australia in April 1942. In what appeared to be an empty pledge, he vowed, "I shall return." The ill-equipped American and Philippine troops left on Bataan and Corregidor put up a heroic but doomed struggle. By summer no significant Allied forces stood between the Japanese and India or Australia.

Endless victories disguised fatal weaknesses within the Axis alliance. Japan and Germany never coordinated strategies. Vast armies in China and Russia drained each of both troops and supplies. Brutal occupation policies made enemies of conquered populations, which forced Axis armies to use valuable forces to maintain control and move supplies. The Nazis were especially harsh. They launched a major campaign to exterminate Europe's Jews, Slavs, and Gypsies. Resistance movements grew as the victims of Axis aggression fought back.

A Grand Alliance >>
The early defeats also obscured the Allies' strengths. Chief among these were the human resources of the Soviet Union and the productive capacity of the United States. Safe from the fighting, American farms and factories could produce enough food and munitions to supply two separate wars at once. By the end of the war American industry had turned out vast quantities of airplanes, ships, artillery pieces, tanks, and self-propelled guns, as well as 47 million tons of ammunition.

The Allies benefited, too, from exceptional leadership. The "Big Three"—Joseph Stalin, Winston Churchill, and Franklin Roosevelt—were able to maintain a unity of purpose that eluded Axis leaders. All three understood the global nature of the war. To a remarkable degree they managed to set aside their many differences in pursuit of a common goal: the defeat of Nazi Germany. At the war's height 50 countries were among the Allies, who referred to themselves as the United Nations.

To be sure, each nation had its own needs. Russian forces faced 3.5 million Axis troops along a 1,600-mile front in eastern Europe. To ease the pressure on those troops,

Stalin repeatedly called upon the Allies to open a second front in western Europe. So urgent were his demands that one Allied diplomat remarked that Stalin's foreign minister knew only four words in English: yes, no, and second front. But Churchill and Roosevelt felt compelled to turn Stalin down. After an initial surge of anger, Stalin accepted Churchill's rationale for a substitute action. That was to be a British-American invasion of North Africa at the end of 1942. Code-named Operation Torch, the North African campaign would bring British and American troops into direct combat with the Germans and stood an excellent chance of succeeding. Here was an example of how personal contact among the Big Three ensured Allied cooperation. The alliance sometimes bent but never broke.

The Naval War in the Pacific >>
Despite the decision to defeat Germany first, the Allies' earliest successes came in the Pacific. At the Battle of Coral Sea in May 1942 planes from American aircraft carriers stopped a large Japanese invading force headed for Port Moresby in New Guinea. For the first time in history two fleets fought without seeing each other. The age of naval aviation had arrived.

To extend Japan's defenses, the Japanese military ordered the capture of Midway, a small island west of Hawaii. The Americans, having decoded secret Japanese messages, were ready. On June 3, as the Japanese main fleet bore down on Midway, American planes sank four enemy carriers, a cruiser, and three destroyers. The Battle

⌃ The violence of amphibious warfare was evident on the beaches of Tarawa in 1943.

of Midway broke Japanese naval supremacy in the Pacific and stalled Japan's offensive. In August 1942 American forces went on the offensive, in the Solomon Islands east of New Guinea. With the landing of American marines on the island of Guadalcanal, the Allies started on the bloody road to Japan and victory.

Turning Points in Europe >> By the fall of 1942 Allied fortunes brightened in the European war. In Egypt at El Alamein, British forces under General Bernard Montgomery broke through Rommel's lines. Weeks later, the Allies launched Operation Torch, the

invasion of North Africa. Under the command of General Dwight D. Eisenhower, Allied forces swept eastward through Morocco and Algeria. They were halted in February 1943 at the Kasserine Pass in Tunisia, but General George S. Patton regrouped them and masterminded an impressive string of victories. By May 1943 Rommel had fled from North Africa, leaving behind 300,000 German troops.

Success in North Africa provided a stirring complement to the dogged Russian stand at Stalingrad against a vast German army. Despite huge losses, Stalin's forces went on the offensive, moving south and west through the Ukraine toward Poland and Romania.

WORLD WAR II IN EUROPE AND NORTH AFRICA

Until 1944 Soviet forces carried the brunt of the war in Europe, engaging the Axis armies across a huge front. After winning North Africa the Allies turned north to knock Italy out of the war. The final key to defeating Germany was the Anglo-American invasion of western Europe (D-Day) at Normandy (see map, page 561).

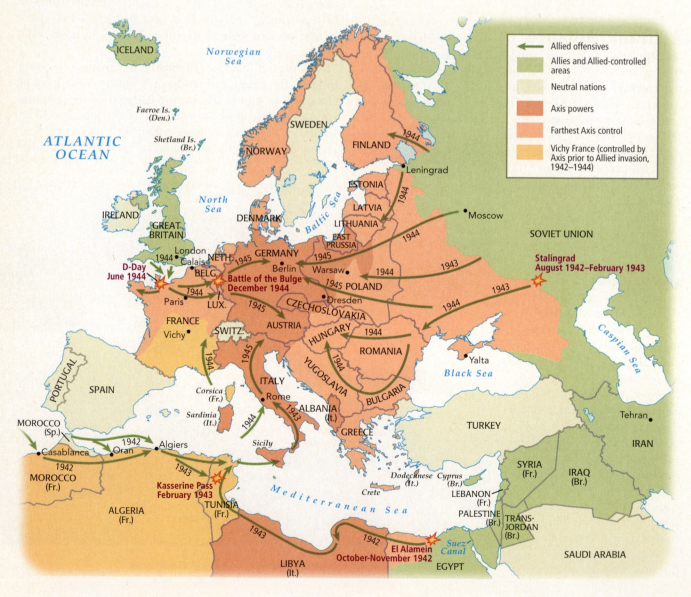

Those Who Fought

>> "The first time I ever heard a New England accent," recalled a midwesterner, "was at Fort Benning. The southerner was an exotic creature to me. The people from the farms. The New York street smarts." Mobilizing for war brought together Americans from all regions, classes, and ethnic backgrounds. More than any other social institution the army acted as a melting pot. It also offered educational opportunities and job skills. "I could be a technical sergeant only I haven't had enough school," reported one Navajo soldier in a letter home to New Mexico. "Make my little brother go to school even if you have to lasso him."

In waging the world's first global war the U.S. armed forces swept millions of Americans into new worlds and experiences. In 1941 the army had 1.6 million men in uniform. By 1945 it had more than 7 million; the navy, 3.9 million; the army air corps, 2.3 million; and the marines, 600,000. At basic training recruits were subjected to forms of regimentation—the army haircut, foul-mouthed drill sergeants, and barracks life—they had seldom experienced in other areas of America's democratic culture.

In this war, as in most, the infantry bore the brunt of the fighting and dying. They suffered 90 percent of the battlefield casualties. In all, almost 400,000 Americans died and more than 600,000 were wounded. But service in the military did not mean constant combat. Most battles were reasonably short, followed by long periods of waiting and preparation. The army used almost 2 million soldiers just to move supplies. Yet even during the lull in battle, the soldiers' biggest enemy, disease, stalked them: malaria, dysentery, typhus, and even plague. In the Pacific theater, the thermometer sometimes rose to over 110 degrees Fahrenheit.

Minorities at War

>> Minorities enlisted in unusually large numbers because the services offered training and opportunities unavailable in civilian life. Still, prejudice in the ranks remained high. The army was strictly segregated and generally assigned black soldiers to noncombatant roles. The navy accepted them only as cooks and servants. At first the air corps and the marines would not take them at all. The American Red Cross even kept "black" and "white" blood plasma separated, as if there were a difference. (Ironically, a black physician, Charles Drew, had invented the process allowing plasma to be stored.)

Despite such prejudice more than a million black men and women served. As the war progressed leaders of the black community pressured the military to ease

<< Many young soldiers, known as GIs, at first looked forward to combat. "I was going to gain my manhood," recalled one soldier. But combat hardened such troops. Donald Dickson titled his portrait of one war-weary GI *Too Many, Too Close, Too Long*.

segregation and allow black soldiers a more active role. The army did form some black combat units, usually led by white officers, as well as a black air corps unit. By mid-1942 black officers began to graduate from integrated officer candidate schools at the rate of 200 a month. More than 80 black pilots won the Distinguished Flying Cross.

For both Mexican Americans and Asian Americans the war offered an opportunity to enter the American mainstream. Putting on a uniform was an essential act of citizenship. Mexican Americans had a higher enlistment rate than the population in general. A California member of Congress observed, "as I read the casualty list from my state, I find that anywhere from one-fourth to one-third of these names are names such as Gonzales and Sanchez." Chinese Americans served at the highest rate of all groups. As Harold Liu of New York's Chinatown recalled, "for the first time Chinese were accepted as being friends. . . . All of a sudden we became part of an American dream." Korean Americans were especially valuable in the Pacific theater because many could translate Japanese.

Filipino Americans jumped at the chance to fight for the liberation of their homeland from Japanese invaders. Their loyalty had its rewards. Filipinos who volunteered became citizens. The California Attorney General reinterpreted laws that had once prevented Filipinos from owning land. Now they could buy their own farms. Jobs opened in war factories. The status of Mexican Americans and other Asian Americans improved in similar ways.

Homosexuals who wished to join the military faced a dilemma. Would their sexual orientation be discovered during the screening process? And if they were rejected and word got back to their parents or communities, would they be stigmatized? Many took that chance. Charles Rowland from Arizona recalled that he and other gay friends "were not about to be deprived the privilege of serving our country in a time of great national emergency by virtue of some stupid regulation about being gay." Those who did pass the screening test found themselves in gender-segregated bases, where life in an overwhelmingly male or female environment allowed many, for the first time in their lives, to meet like-minded gay men and women.

↑ In the face of Japanese occupation, many Filipinos actively supported the American war effort. Valentine Untalan survived capture by the Japanese and went on to serve in the American army's elite Philippine Scouts. Like a growing number of Filipinos, he moved to the United States after the war ended.

Women at War >>

World War II brought an end to the military as a male enclave that women entered only as nurses. During the prewar mobilization, Eleanor Roosevelt and other women had campaigned for a regular military organization for women. The War Department came up with a compromise that allowed women to join the Women's Army Auxiliary Corps (WAAC), but only with inferior status and lower pay. By 1943 the "Auxiliary" had dropped out of the title: WAACs became WACs, with full status, equal ranks, and equal pay. (The navy had a similar force called the WAVEs.)

Women could look with a mixture of pride and resentment on their wartime military service. Thousands served close to the battlefields, working as technicians, mechanics, radio operators, postal clerks, and secretaries. Although filling a vital need, these were largely traditional female jobs that implied a separate and inferior status. Until 1944 women were prevented by law from serving in war zones, even as noncombatants. There were women pilots, but they were restricted to shuttling planes behind the lines. At many posts WAVEs and WACs lived behind barbed wire and could move about only in groups under armed escort.

 REVIEW

What strategy did the Big Three adopt to fight the war, and when did it begin to succeed?

WAR PRODUCTION

When Pearl Harbor brought the United States into the war, Thomas Chinn sold his publishing business and devoted all his time to war work. Like many Chinese Americans, it was the first time he had worked outside Chinatown. He served as a supervisor in the Army Quartermaster Market Center, which was responsible for supplying the armed forces with fresh food as it was harvested across California. Chinn found himself coordinating cold storage warehouses across the entire state.

Food distribution was only one of many areas that demanded attention from the government. After Pearl Harbor, steel, aluminum, and electric power were all in short supply, creating bottlenecks in production lines. Roosevelt recognized the need for more direct government control of the economy.

The president used a mix of compulsory and voluntary programs to guarantee an ever-increasing supply of food, munitions, and equipment. Although slow to get underway, eventually the United States worked a miracle of production that proved every bit as important to victory as any battle fought overseas. So successful was war production that civilians suffered little deprivation.

Mobilizing for War >>

The demand for war materials created numerous production bottlenecks. To end them, the president in 1943 made Supreme Court justice James F. Byrnes the dictator

« African Americans enlisted in huge numbers. This WAC was among the first to arrive in Europe.

Selling the Sizzle When the Steak Is Missing

Why are all of these appliance images shown in picture frames?

How have oven ranges changed from the one portrayed here? Does that tell you anything about food preparation?

What is this appliance? Why do you think it isn't in homes today?

THE ART OF BETTER LIVING

Yesterday . . . Today . . . Tomorrow . . . it's Electrical Living by Westinghouse

Let's hope it's not too far away . . . that bright new day when you'll again know the lift of living electrically. And when it does come, Westinghouse will be a name to remember. It stands for the know-how and experience acquired in making 30 million pre-war electrical home appliances.

More than that . . . it stands for years of tried and tested background in making not just one or two appliances, but *twenty-two different types* of electrical servants for your home.

At the moment, we're head over heels building essential war material. And we'll stick to that job until it is done. But when the go ahead signal flashes, you can count on Westinghouse to turn out all the fine new appliances you need to banish

that "never done" feeling about housework. In war or peace, we take your homemaking problems to heart. The pre-war masterpieces shown above are just a promise of what's to come.

WESTINGHOUSE ELECTRIC & MANUFACTURING CO., MANSFIELD, O.
PLANTS IN 25 CITIES . . . OFFICES EVERYWHERE

30 MILLION PRE-WAR
Westinghouse
ELECTRIC HOME APPLIANCES
YOUR PROMISE OF STILL FINER ONES TO COME

TUNE IN JOHN CHARLES THOMAS • SUNDAY 2:30 EWT, N.B.C. • HEAR TED MALONE • MON. WED. FRI. 10:15 EWT, BLUE NETWORK

Advertisements often provide clues about what producers think people want or need. Yet during the war Westinghouse had shifted its factories to war production, no longer manufacturing home appliances. Still, the company had a message and an image to sell. Its ad copy anticipated "that bright new day when you'll again know the lift of living electrically." Not many Americans could afford that lift until the war brought back prosperity. Westinghouse was thus selling a future in which its appliances would "banish that 'never done' feeling about housework." For advertisers Roosevelt's "Four Freedoms" might well have included a fifth: the freedom to consume. Such ads hinted that the war was as much about a way of life as it was about a noble cause.

THINKING CRITICALLY

Why is the couple so formally dressed while looking at appliances? What does that suggest about the audience that the advertiser hopes to attract? How do gender stereotypes influence the differing poses of the man and the woman in the advertisement?

Credit: "The Art of Better Living" (*Life* magazine, September 25, 1944, p. 57).

---

the economy needed. His authority as director of the new Office of War Mobilization (OWM) was so great and his access to Roosevelt so direct that he became known as the "assistant president." By assuming control over vital materials such as steel, aluminum, and copper, OWM was able to allocate them more systematically. Americans learned to do without new cars and Sunday drives. Soon, the bottlenecks disappeared.

Equally crucial, industries large and small converted their factories to turning out war matériel. The "Big Three" automakers—Ford, General Motors, and

Chrysler—generated some 20 percent of all war goods, as auto factories were retooled to make tanks and planes. But small business also played a vital role. A manufacturer of model trains, for example, made bomb fuses.

War production also created new industrial centers, especially in the West. When production peaked in 1944 the aircraft industry had 2.1 million workers producing almost 100,000 planes. Most of the new plants were located around Los Angeles, San Diego, and Seattle. The demand for workers opened opportunities for many Asian workers who had been limited to jobs within their own ethnic communities. By 1943, 15 percent of all shipyard workers around San Francisco Bay were Chinese.

The government relied on large firms such as Ford and General Motors because they had experience with large-scale production. Thus, war contracts helped large corporations increase their dominance over the economy. Workers in companies with more than 10,000 employees amounted to just 13 percent of the workforce in 1939; by 1944 they constituted more than 30 percent. In agriculture a similar move toward bigness occurred. The number of people working on farms dropped by a fifth, yet productivity increased 30 percent, as small farms were consolidated into larger ones that relied on more machinery and artificial fertilizers to increase yields.

Productivity increased for a less tangible reason: pride in work done for a common cause. Civilians volunteered for civil defense, hospitals, and countless scrap drives. Children became "Uncle Sam's Scrappers" and "Tin-Can Colonels" as they scoured vacant lots for valuable trash. Backyard "victory" gardens added 8 million tons of food to the harvest in 1943; car pooling conserved millions of tires. As citizens put off buying new consumer goods, they helped limit inflation. Morale ran high because people believed that every contribution, no matter how small, helped defeat the Axis.

⌃ To fight inflation, the Office of Price Administration (OPA) imposed rationing on products in short supply. Consumers received coupons to trade for goods such as meat, shoes, and gasoline. The program was one of the most unpopular of the war.

Science Goes to War >> New technologies transformed the way the Americans fought this global war. At the battles of the Coral Sea and Midway, the navy used radar gunnery and airplanes to spot and sink enemy ships. Applied mathematics and game theory helped the Navy find and destroy the U-boats that preyed on Allied shipping. Elsewhere, improved fighter planes and

long-range bombers allowed Allied air forces to take the war to the Axis homelands. As a result, the idea of a front line lost its meaning.

In their quest to preserve democratic freedoms, scientists began to explore some of the basic forces of nature. Generals and admirals understood all too well that the fortunes of battle could turn on the weather. With the Navy's support the Massachusetts Institute of Technology created a professional program in meteorology. There, scientists applied the principles of physics to better understand climate patterns. Meteorology and other fields of geophysics provided the military with information on the winds, ocean currents, tides, and weather in far-flung theaters of the war. These efforts laid the foundation for future understanding of climate science.

No scientific quest did more to alter the relationship between humans and the natural world than the effort to

fission splitting of a nucleus of an atom into at least two other nuclei, accompanied by the release of energy. The splitting of the nucleus of the uranium isotope U-235 or its artificial cousin, plutonium, powered the atomic bomb.

build an atomic bomb. In 1938 German scientists discovered the process of nuclear **fission.** Atoms of uranium-235 when split released enormous energy. Leading physicists, many of them refugees from European fascism, understood that a fast fission reaction might be used to build a bomb. In 1939 Albert Einstein, Enrico Fermi, and Leo Szilard warned President Roosevelt that the Germans might be well on the way to creating a weapon, the use of which might determine the outcome of the war.

Concerned, Roosevelt authorized an enormous research and development effort, code-named the Manhattan Project. Over 100,000 scientists, engineers, technicians, and support staff from Canada, England, and the United States worked at 39 installations to build an atomic bomb. Yet, even as they spent over $2 billion in their quest, scientists feared the Germans might succeed before they did.

Applied science was not simply about destruction. Production mattered as well. With so many farmers off at war, increased agricultural productivity became vital. In the 1930s plant geneticists had learned to cross-pollinate corn to create new varieties. These hybrids greatly increased yields per acre. Plastics offered an alternative to natural materials such as glass, rubber, wood, steel, and copper in short supply because of the war effort; for example, commercial production of polyvinyl chloride (PVC) began modestly in 1933. Given its stability and flexibility, PVC was ideal for use in construction, plumbing, packaging, and flooring. By 1941, 120 million pounds of PVC were being manufactured annually.

Some scientific advances increased health and life expectancy. Antibiotics had their first widespread application during the war. Infectious diseases such as tuberculosis, syphilis, and pneumonia—once the scourge of armies—could now be contained. Pesticides such as DDT controlled insects that spread malaria, typhus, and other deadly and debilitating diseases. With the use of these chemicals, the health of the nation actually improved. Life expectancy increased during the 1940s an average of three years overall and by five years for African Americans. Infant mortality fell by a third.

The atomic bomb, DDT, PVC, and hybrid seeds came to represent for Americans humankind's ability to control nature. What they did not anticipate were the environmental dangers those discoveries posed. Atomic bombs spewed radiation clouds into the atmosphere. DDT controlled insect pests but killed beneficial insects and proved harmful to wildlife. Polyvinyl chloride production gave off carcinogens dangerous to humans, existed nowhere in nature, and, once discarded, took ages to degrade. The widespread use of hybrid seeds created through artificial pollination greatly reduced genetic variety. Scientists anticipated some of these dangers, but at the time they had a war to win.

War Work and Prosperity ›› Not only did
war production end the Depression; it revived prosperity. Unemployment, which stood at almost 7 million in 1940, virtually disappeared by 1944. Jeff Davies, president of Hoboes of America, reported in 1942 that 2 million of his members were "off the road." Employers, eager to overcome the labor shortage, welcomed handicapped workers. Hearing-impaired people found jobs in deafening factories; dwarfs became aircraft inspectors because they could crawl inside wings and other cramped spaces. By

Longing won't bring him back sooner...
GET A WAR JOB!
SEE YOUR U. S. EMPLOYMENT SERVICE
WAR MANPOWER COMMISSION

⌃ Propaganda poster promoting wartime employment as the way to speed a husband's return from the war.

the summer of 1943 nearly 3 million children aged 12 to 17 were working. When the war ended, average income had jumped to nearly $3,000, twice what it had been in 1939.

Organized Labor ›› Wartime prosperity brought substantial gains for unions. Still, the tensions between business and labor that marked the New Deal era continued. In 1941 alone more than 2 million workers walked off their jobs in protest. To end labor strife Roosevelt established the War Labor Board in 1942. Like the similar agency Woodrow Wilson had created during World War I, the new WLB had authority to impose arbitration in any labor dispute.

Despite the WLB, dissatisfied railroad workers in 1943 tied up rail lines in a wildcat strike. To break the impasse, the government seized the railroads and then granted wage increases. That same year the pugnacious John L. Lewis allowed his United Mine

‹‹ Douglas Aircraft's Long Beach, California, Plant. By the end of 1942 war production had ramped up sharply.

Workers to go on strike. "The coal miners of America are hungry," he charged. "They are ill-fed and undernourished." Roosevelt seized the mines and ran them for a time; he even considered arresting union leaders and drafting striking miners. But as Secretary of the Interior Harold Ickes noted, a "jailed miner produces no more coal than a striking miner." In the end the government negotiated a settlement that gave miners substantial new benefits.

Most Americans were less willing to forgive Lewis and his miners. A huge coal shortage along the East Coast had left homes dark and cold. "John L. Lewis—Damn your coal black soul," wrote the military newspaper *Stars and Stripes.* In reaction, Congress easily passed the Smith-Connolly Act of 1943. It gave the president more authority to seize vital war plants shut by strikes and required union leaders to observe a 30-day "cooling-off" period before striking.

Despite these incidents most workers remained dedicated to the war effort. Stoppages actually accounted for only about one-tenth of one percent of total work time during the war. When workers did strike, it was usually in defiance of their union leadership, and they left their jobs for just a few days.

Women Workers >>
With as many as 12 million men in uniform, women (especially married women) became the nation's largest untapped source of labor. During the high unemployment years of the Depression, both government and business had discouraged women from competing with men for jobs. Now, magazines and government bulletins began trumpeting "the vast resource of woman-power." Having accounted for a quarter of all workers in 1940, women amounted to more than a third by 1945. These women were not mostly young and single, as female workers of the past had been. A majority were either married or between 55 and 64 years old.

With husbands off at war, millions of women preferred the relative freedom of work and the additional income it provided. Black women in particular realized dramatic gains in the quality of jobs available to them. Once concentrated in low-paying domestic and farm jobs with erratic hours and tedious labor, some 300,000 rushed into factories that offered higher pay and more regular hours. Whether black or white, working women faced new stresses. The demands of a job were added to domestic responsibilities. The pressures of moving and crowded housing tore at families and communities already fearful for their men at war.

Despite the new work roles for women, the war did not create a revolution in attitudes about gender. Most Americans assumed that when the war ended, veterans would pick up their old jobs and women would return home. Surveys showed that the vast majority of Americans, male and female, continued to believe that child rearing was a woman's primary responsibility. The birthrate, which

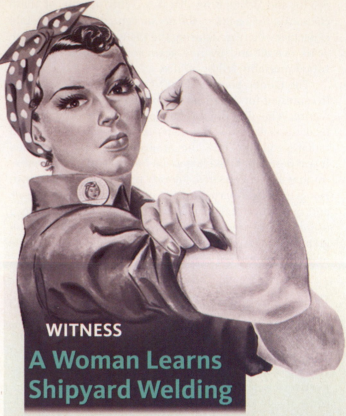

WITNESS

A Woman Learns Shipyard Welding

"I, who hate heights, climbed stair after stair till I thought I must be close to the sun. I stopped on the top deck. I, who hate confined spaces, went through narrow corridors, stumbling my way . . . into a room about four feet by ten. . . . I welded on the poop deck lying on the floor while another welder spattered sparks from the ceiling and chippers like giant woodpeckers shattered our eardrums."

—Augusta H. Clawson, *Shipyard Diary of a Women Welder* (1944)

had fallen during the Depression, began to rise by 1943 as prosperity returned.

Mobility >>
War industries attracted workers from places near and far. Vine Deloria, Jr., an American Indian, recalled that "the war dispersed the reservation people as nothing ever had. Every day, it seemed, we could be bidding farewell to families as they headed west to work in defense plants on the coast." African Americans left the South in such large numbers that cotton growers began to buy mechanical harvesters to replace their labor. The Census Bureau discovered that between Pearl Harbor in 1941 and March 1945, at least 15.3 million people (not counting those in military service) had changed their county of residence.

 **REVIEW**

How did advances in technology support the Allied war effort?

A QUESTION OF RIGHTS

President Roosevelt was determined to avoid the patriotic excesses he had witnessed during World War I: mobs menacing immigrants, appeals to spy on neighbors, harassment of pacifists. Even so, the tensions over race, ethnic background, and class differences could not be ignored. In a society in which immigration laws discriminated against Asians by race, the war with Japan made life difficult for loyal Asian Americans of all backgrounds. Black and Hispanic workers still faced discrimination in shipyards and airplane factories, much as they had in peacetime industries.

Italians and Asian Americans >> When

World War II began, about 600,000 Italian aliens and 5 million Italian Americans lived in the United States. Most still lived in Italian neighborhoods that revolved around churches, fraternal organizations, and clubs. Some had been proud of Mussolini and supported fascism. "Mussolini was a hero," recalled one Italian American, "a superhero. He made us feel special." Those attitudes changed abruptly after Pearl Harbor. During the war Italian Americans unquestioningly pledged their loyalties to the United States.

At first the government treated Italians without citizenship (along with Japanese and Germans) as "aliens of enemy nationality." They could not travel without permission, enter strategic areas, or possess shortwave radios, guns, or maps. By 1942 few Americans believed that German or Italian Americans posed any kind of danger. Eager to keep the support of Italian voters in the 1942 congressional elections, Roosevelt chose Columbus Day 1942 to lift restrictions on Italian aliens.

Americans showed no such tolerance toward the 127,000 Japanese living in the United States, whether aliens or citizens. Ironically, prejudices against them were least high in Hawaii, where the war with Japan had begun. Newspapers there expressed confidence in the loyalty of Japanese Americans, whose labor was crucial to Hawaii's economy.

On the mainland Japanese Americans remained more segregated from the mainstream of American life. State laws and local custom often threw up complex barriers. In the western states where they were concentrated around urban areas, most Japanese Americans could not vote, own land, or live in decent neighborhoods. Approximately 47,000 Japanese aliens, known as **Issei**, were ineligible for citizenship under American law. Only their children (**Nisei**) could become citizens.

Nisei American-born citizens of Japanese ancestry, contrasted with *Issei*, native-born Japanese who had moved to the United States.

⌃ Rose Carrendeno, Italian American mother of six children. The three stars indicate that her three sons are in the armed forces.

Despite such restrictions, some Japanese achieved success in small businesses such as landscaping, while many others worked on or owned farms that supplied fruits and vegetables to growing cities.

West Coast politicians pressed the Roosevelt administration to evacuate the Japanese from their communities. It did not seem to matter that about 80,000 Nisei were American citizens and that not one was ever convicted of espionage. "A Jap's a Jap . . ." commented General John De Witt, commander of West Coast defenses. "It makes no difference whether he is an American citizen or not." In response, the War Department in February 1942 drew up Executive Order 9066, which allowed the exclusion of any person from designated military areas. Under De Witt's authority, the order was applied only on the West Coast against Japanese Americans. By late February Roosevelt had agreed that both Issei and Nisei would be evacuated. But where would they go?

>> Racism against Japanese Americans was especially powerful in California.

leader A. Philip Randolph, long an advocate of greater black militancy, launched a campaign to gain entrance to jobs in defense industries and government agencies, unions, and the armed forces, all of them segregated. "The Administration leaders in Washington will never give the Negro justice," Randolph argued, "until they see masses—ten, twenty, fifty thousand Negroes on the White House lawn." In 1941 he began to organize a march on Washington.

The army began to ship the entire Japanese community to temporary "assembly centers." Most Nisei were forced to sell their property at far below market value. Furthermore, many army sites did not offer basic sanitation, comfort, or privacy. "We lived in a horse stable," remembered one young girl. Eventually, most Japanese were interned in 10 camps in remote areas of seven western states. No claim of humane intent could change the reality: these were concentration camps. Internees were held in wire-enclosed compounds by armed guards. Tar-papered barracks housed families or small groups in single rooms. Each room had a few cots, some blankets, and a single light bulb. That was home.

Some Japanese Americans protested loudly when government officials asked Nisei citizens if they would be willing to serve in the armed forces. "What do they take us for? Saps?" asked one camp prisoner. "First, they . . . run me out of town, and now they want me to volunteer for a suicide squad so I could get killed for this damn democracy." Yet thousands of Nisei did enlist, and many distinguished themselves in combat.

Concentration camps in America did not mirror the horror of Nazi death camps, but they were built on racism and fear. Worse, they violated the traditions of civil rights and liberties for which Americans believed they were fighting.

Minorities and War Work >> Minority leaders saw the irony of fighting a war for freedom in a country in which civil rights were still limited. "A jim crow army cannot fight for a free world," the NAACP declared. Labor

President Roosevelt could have issued executive orders to integrate the government, as Randolph demanded. But it took the threat of the march to make him act. He issued Executive Order 8802 in June, which forbade discrimination by race in hiring either government or defense industry workers. To carry out the policy, Order 8802 established the Fair Employment Practices Committee (FEPC). But in a society still deeply divided by racial prejudice, the new agency had only limited success in breaking down barriers against African Americans and Hispanics.

Still, the FEPC did open industrial jobs in California's shipyards and aircraft factories, which had previously refused to hire Hispanics. Thousands migrated from Texas, where job discrimination was most severe, to California, where war work created new opportunities. Labor shortages led the southwestern states to join with the Mexican government under the bracero program to recruit Mexican labor under specially arranged contracts. In Texas, in contrast, antagonism to braceros ran so deep that the Mexican government tried to prevent workers from going there. Not until late 1943 did the FEPC investigate the situation.

Black Americans faced similar frustrations. More than half of all defense jobs were closed to minorities. For example, with 100,000 skilled and high-paying jobs in the aircraft industry, blacks held about 200 janitorial positions. Unions segregated black workers or excluded them entirely. One person wrote to the president with a telling complaint: "Hitler has not done anything to the colored people—it's people right here in the United States who are keeping us out of work and keeping us down."

Eventually the combination of labor shortages, pressures from black leaders, and initiative from government agencies opened the door to more skilled jobs and higher pay. Beginning in 1943 the United States Employment Service rejected requests with racial stipulations. By 1944 blacks, who accounted for almost 10 percent of the population, held 8 percent of the jobs.

Urban Unrest >>

At the beginning of the war three-quarters of the 12 million black Americans lived in the South. Hispanic Americans, whose population exceeded a million, were concentrated in a belt along the U.S.–Mexican border. When jobs for minorities opened in war centers, African and Hispanic Americans became increasingly urban.

To ease crowding and reduce racial tensions, the government funded new housing. In Detroit federal authorities picked a site for minority housing along the edge of a Polish neighborhood. One project, named in honor of the black abolitionist Sojourner Truth, included 200 units for black families. When the first of them tried to move in, local officials had to send the National Guard to protect the newcomers from menacing Ku Klux Klan members. Riots broke out in the hot summer of 1943, as white mobs beat up African Americans riding public trolleys or patronizing movie theaters, and black protesters looted white stores. Six thousand soldiers from nearby bases finally imposed a troubled calm, but not before the riot had claimed the lives of 24 black and 9 white residents.

In southern California Anglo hostility toward Latinos focused on pachucos, or "zoot suiters." These young

⌃ A "zoot suiter" gets escorted by the police.

Hispanic men had adopted the stylish fashions of Harlem hipsters: greased hair swept back into a ducktail; broad-shouldered, long-waisted suit coats; baggy pants pegged at the ankles. The Los Angeles city council passed an ordinance making it a crime even to wear a zoot suit. In June 1943 sailors from the local navy base invaded Hispanic neighborhoods in search of zooters who had allegedly attacked servicemen. The self-appointed vigilantes grabbed innocent victims, tore their clothes, cut their hair, and beat them. When Hispanics retaliated, the police arrested them, ignoring the actions of the sailors. Irresponsible newspaper coverage made matters worse. Underlying Hispanic anger were the grim realities of poor housing, unemployment, and white racism, which added up to a level of poverty that wartime prosperity eased but in no way resolved.

Minority leaders acted on the legal as well as the economic front. The Congress of Racial Equality (**CORE**), a nonviolent civil rights group inspired by the Indian leader Mohandas K. Gandhi, used sit-ins and other peaceful tactics to desegregate some restaurants and movie theaters. In 1944 the Supreme Court outlawed the "all-white primary," an infamous device used by southerners to exclude blacks from voting in primary elections within the Democratic party. In *Smith v. Allwright* the Court ruled that since political parties were integral parts of public elections, they could not deny minorities the right to vote in primaries. Such new attitudes opened the door to future civil rights gains.

> **CORE** Congress on Racial Equality, an organization founded in 1942 that believed African Americans should use nonviolent civil disobedience to challenge segregation.

The New Deal in Retreat >>

After Pearl Harbor, Roosevelt told reporters that "Dr. New Deal" had retired in favor of "Dr. Win-the-War." Political debates, however, could not be eliminated, even during a global conflict. The growing anti–New Deal coalition of Republicans and rural Democrats saw in the war an opportunity to attack programs they had long resented. They quickly ended the Civilian Conservation Corps and the National Youth Administration, reduced the powers of the Farm Security Administration, and blocked moves to extend Social Security and unemployment benefits.

By the spring of 1944 no one knew whether Franklin Roosevelt would seek an unprecedented fourth term. Pallid skin, sagging shoulders, and shaking hands seemed open signs that he had aged too much to run. In July, a week before the Democratic convention, Roosevelt announced his decision: "All that is within me cries out to go back to my home on the Hudson River. . . . But as a good soldier . . . I will accept and serve." Conservative Democrats, however, replaced FDR's liberal vice president, Henry Wallace, with Harry S. Truman of Missouri, a loyal Democrat. The Republicans chose the moderate governor of New York, Thomas E. Dewey, to run against Roosevelt, but Dewey

IMPACT OF WORLD WAR II ON GOVERNMENT SPENDING

As the chart shows, the war spurred government spending more than the New Deal, even on nonmilitary sectors. Note that after both world wars, nonmilitary spending was higher than in the prewar years.

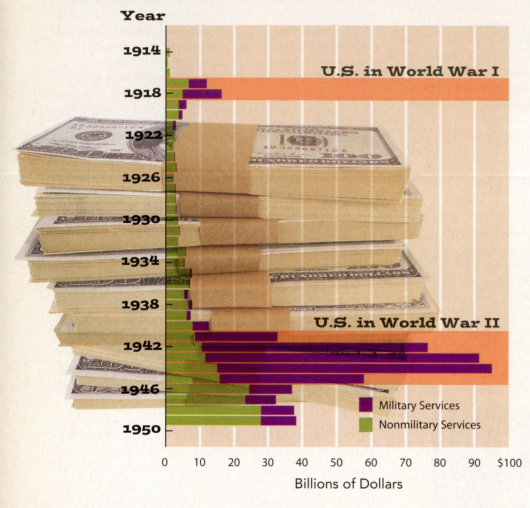

Year

U.S. in World War I

U.S. in World War II

■ Military Services
■ Nonmilitary Services

Billions of Dollars

never had much of a chance. Still, Roosevelt's margin of victory was smaller than any since 1916. Like its aging leader, the New Deal coalition was showing signs of strain.

 REVIEW

In what ways did discrimination against minorities continue after the war started?

WINNING THE WAR AND THE PEACE

In a war that stretched from one end of the globe to the other, the Allies had to coordinate their strategies on a grand scale. Which war theaters would receive equipment in short supply? Who would administer conquered territories? Inevitably, the questions of fighting a war slid into discussions of the peace that would follow. What would happen to occupied territories? How would the Axis powers be punished? If a more stable world order could not be created, the cycle of violence might never end. As Allied armies struggled mile by mile to defeat the Axis, Allied diplomacy concentrated just as much on winning the peace.

The Fall of the Third

Reich ➤➤ After pushing the Germans out of North Africa in May 1943, Allied strategists agreed to Churchill's plan to drive Italy from the war. Late in July, two weeks after a quarter of a million British and American troops had landed on Sicily, Mussolini fled to German-held northern Italy. Although Italy surrendered early in September, Germany continued to pour in reinforcements. It took the Allies almost a year of bloody fighting to reach Rome, and at the end of the campaign they had yet to break German lines. Along the eastern front, Soviet armies steadily pushed the Germans out of Russia and back toward Berlin.

General Dwight D. Eisenhower, fresh from battle in North Africa and the Mediterranean, took command of Allied preparations for Operation Overlord, the long-awaited opening of a second front in western Europe. By June 1944 all eyes focused on the coast of France, because Hitler, of course, knew the Allies would attack across the English Channel. Allied planners did their best to focus his attention on Calais, the French port city closest to the British Isles. On the morning of June 6, 1944, the invasion began—not at Calais but on the less fortified beaches of Normandy. Almost three million men, 11,000 aircraft, and more than 2,000 vessels took part in D-Day.

Luck and Eisenhower's meticulous planning favored the Allied cause. Convinced that Calais was the Allied target, Hitler delayed sending in two reserve divisions. His indecision allowed the Allied forces to secure a foothold. Still, the Allied advance from Normandy took almost two months, not several weeks as expected. Once Allied tanks

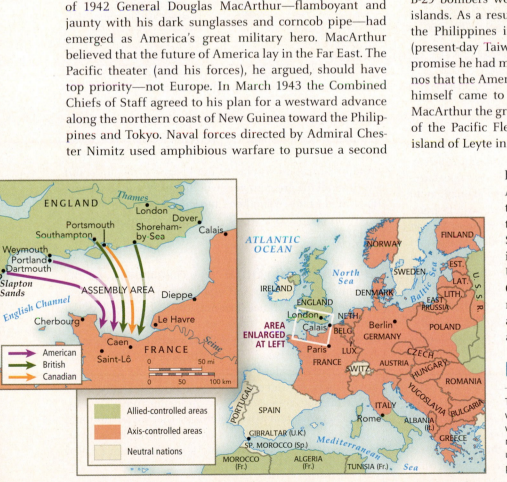

>> Landing on the coast of France under heavy Nazi machine gun fire, these American soldiers have just left the ramp of a Coast Guard landing boat.

broke through German lines, their progress was spectacular. In August Paris was liberated, and by mid-September the Allies had driven the Germans from France and Belgium. Hitler's desperate counterthrust in the Ardennes Forest in December 1944 succeeded momentarily, pushing back the Allies along a 50-mile bulge. But the "Battle of the Bulge" cost the Germans their last reserves. After George Patton's forces rescued trapped American units, little stood between the Allies and Berlin.

Two Roads to Tokyo >> In the bleak days of 1942 General Douglas MacArthur—flamboyant and jaunty with his dark sunglasses and corncob pipe—had emerged as America's great military hero. MacArthur believed that the future of America lay in the Far East. The Pacific theater (and his forces), he argued, should have top priority—not Europe. In March 1943 the Combined Chiefs of Staff agreed to his plan for a westward advance along the northern coast of New Guinea toward the Philippines and Tokyo. Naval forces directed by Admiral Chester Nimitz used amphibious warfare to pursue a second line of attack, along the island chains of the central Pacific. American submarines cut Japan's supply lines.

By July 1944 the navy's leapfrogging campaign reached the Mariana Islands, east of the Philippines. From there B-29 bombers were within range of the Japanese home islands. As a result, Admiral Nimitz proposed bypassing the Philippines in favor of a direct attack on Formosa (present-day Taiwan). MacArthur insisted on fulfilling a promise he had made "to eighteen million Christian Filipinos that the Americans would return." President Roosevelt himself came to Hawaii to resolve the impasse, giving MacArthur the green light. Backed by more than 100 ships of the Pacific Fleet, the general splashed ashore on the island of Leyte in October 1944.

The decision to invade the Philippines led to savage fighting until the war ended. As retreating Japanese armies left Manila, they tortured and slaughtered tens of thousands of Filipino civilians. The United States suffered 62,000 casualties redeeming MacArthur's pledge, but a spectacular U.S. Navy victory at the Battle of Leyte Gulf spelled the end of the Japanese Imperial Navy as a fighting force. MacArthur and Nimitz prepared to tighten the noose around Japan's home islands.

D-DAY, 1944

The final key to defeating the Nazis was the invasion of western Europe at Normandy. D-Day for the invasion was June 6, 1944, and the massive undertaking would not have been possible had the Allies been unable to use England as a base to gather their forces. Stalin supported D-Day with a spring offensive in eastern Europe.

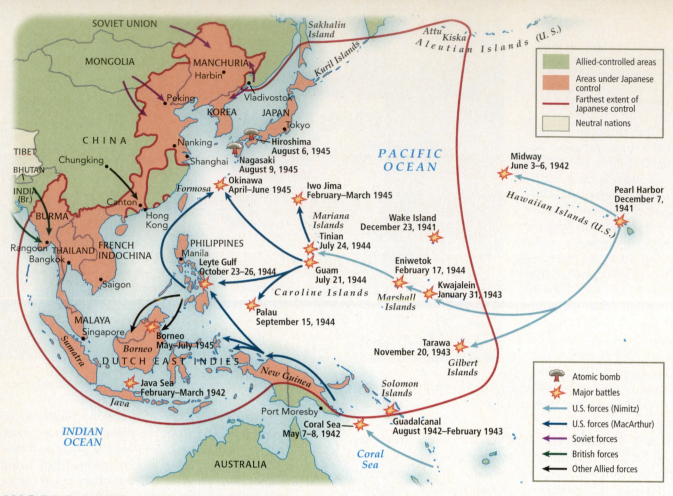

WORLD WAR II IN THE PACIFIC AND ASIA

Extraordinary distances complicated the war in the Pacific. As the map shows, American forces moved on two fronts: the naval war in the central Pacific and General MacArthur's campaign in the southwest Pacific.

Big Three Diplomacy >>

Cooperation over the postwar peace proved even knottier than planning strategies for war. Churchill believed that only a stable European balance of power, not an international agency, could preserve peace. In his view the Soviet Union was the greatest threat to upset that balance of power. Premier Joseph Stalin left no doubt that an expansive notion of Russian security defined his war aims. For future protection Stalin expected to annex the Baltic states, once Russian provinces, along with bits of Finland and Romania and about half of prewar Poland. In eastern Europe and other border areas such as Iran, Korea, and Turkey, he wanted "friendly" neighbors. It soon became apparent that "friendly" meant regimes dependent on Moscow.

Early on, Roosevelt had promoted his own version of an international balance of power, which he called the "Four Policemen." Under its framework the Soviet Union, Great Britain, the United States, and China would guarantee peace through military cooperation. But by 1944 Roosevelt was seeking an alternative to this scheme and to Churchill's wish to return to a balance of power that hemmed in the Russians. He preferred to bring the Soviet Union into a peace-keeping system based on an international organization similar to the League of Nations. But this time, all the great powers would participate, including the United States. Whether Churchill and Stalin—or the American people as a whole—would accept the idea was not yet clear.

The Road to Yalta >>

The outlines and the problems of a postwar settlement emerged during several summit conferences among the Allied leaders. In November 1943, with Italy's surrender in hand and the war against Germany going well, Churchill and Roosevelt agreed to make a hazardous trip to Teheran, Iran. There, the Big Three leaders met together for the first time. ("Seems very confident," Roosevelt said of Stalin, "very sure of himself, moves slowly—altogether quite impressive.") The president tried to charm the Soviet premier, teasing Churchill for Stalin's benefit, keeping it up "until Stalin was laughing with me, and it was then that I called him 'Uncle Joe.'"

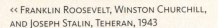
<< Franklin Roosevelt, Winston Churchill, and Joseph Stalin, Teheran, 1943

barrier to Russian expansion. The era after World War I, he believed, demonstrated that a healthy European economy required an industrialized Germany.

The Big Three made no firm decisions. For the time being, they agreed to divide Germany into separate occupation zones (France would receive a zone carved from British and American territory). These four powers would jointly occupy the German capital, Berlin, while an Allied Control Council supervised the national government.

When the Big Three turned their attention to the Far East, Stalin held a trump card. Fierce Japanese resistance on the islands of Okinawa and Iwo Jima had convinced Roosevelt that only a bloody invasion would force Japan's surrender. He thus secured a pledge from Stalin to declare war within three months of Germany's defeat. The price was high. Stalin wanted to reclaim territories that Russia had lost in the Russo-Japanese War of 1904–1906, as well as control over the Chinese Eastern and South Manchurian railroads.

The agreements reached at Yalta depended on Stalin's willingness to cooperate. In public Roosevelt put the best face on matters. He argued that the new world organization (which Stalin agreed to support) would "provide the greatest opportunity in all history" to secure a lasting peace. "We shall take responsibility for world collaboration," he told Congress, "or we shall have to bear the responsibility for another world conflict." Privately the president was less optimistic. "When the chips were down," he confessed, he doubted "Stalin would be able to carry out and deliver what he had agreed to."

Teheran proved to be the high point of cooperation among the Big Three. It was there that FDR and Churchill finally committed to the D-Day invasion Stalin had so long sought, although Churchill's promise was half-hearted at best. The British hoped to delay D-Day as long as possible in order to minimize British casualties. Stalin, for his part, promised to launch a spring offensive to pin down German troops on the eastern front. He also reaffirmed his earlier pledge to declare war against Japan once Germany was beaten.

But thorny disagreements over the postwar peace remained. That was clear in February 1945, when the Big Three met at the Russian resort city of Yalta, on the Black Sea. By then Russian, British, and American troops were closing in on Germany. Roosevelt arrived tired, ashen. At 62, limited by his paralysis, he had visibly aged. He came to Yalta mindful that although Germany was all but beaten, Japan still held out in the Pacific. Under no circumstances did he want Stalin to withdraw his promises to enter the fight against Japan and to join a postwar international organization. Churchill remained ever mistrustful of Soviet intentions. The Russians appeared only too eager to fill the power vacuum that a defeated Japan and Germany would leave.

The Allies remained most at odds about Germany's postwar future. Stalin was determined that the Germans would never invade Russia again. Many Americans shared his desire to have Germany punished and its war-making capacity eliminated. At the Teheran Conference, Roosevelt and Stalin had proposed that the Third Reich be split into five powerless parts. Churchill, however, was much less eager to bring low the nation that was the most natural

The Fallen Leader >> The Yalta Conference marked one of the last and most controversial chapters of Franklin Roosevelt's presidency. Critics charged that the concessions to Stalin were far too great: Poland had been betrayed; China sold out; the United Nations crippled at birth. Yet Roosevelt gave to Stalin little that Stalin had not liberated with Russian blood and could not have taken anyway. Four out of five Nazi soldiers killed in action died on the Eastern Front. Even Churchill, an outspoken critic of Soviet ambitions, concluded that although "our hopeful assumptions were soon to be falsified . . . they were the only ones possible at the time."

What peace Roosevelt might have achieved can never be known. He returned from Yalta visibly ill. On April 12, 1945, while sitting for his portrait at his vacation home in Warm Springs, Georgia, he complained of a "terrific headache," then suddenly fell unconscious. Two hours later Roosevelt was dead. Not since the assassination of Lincoln had the nation so grieved. Under Roosevelt's leadership government had become a protector, the president a father and friend, and the United States the leader in the struggle against Axis tyranny. Eleanor recalled how many Americans later told her that "they missed the way the President used to talk to them. . . . There was a real dialogue between Franklin and the people."

"Who the hell is Harry Truman?" the chief of staff had asked when Truman was nominated for the vice presidency in 1944. As vice president Truman had learned almost nothing about the president's postwar plans. Sensing his own inadequacies, he adopted a tough pose and made his mind up quickly. People welcomed the new president's decisiveness as a relief from Roosevelt's evasive style. Too often, though, Truman acted before the issues were clear. But he at least knew victory in Europe was at hand as Allied troops swept into Germany from the east and west.

The Holocaust >>

The horror of war in no way prepared the invading armies for their liberation of the Nazi concentration camps. **Anti-Semitism,** or

] **anti-Semitism** hatred, prejudice, oppression, or discrimination against Jews or Judaism.

prejudice against Jews and Judaism, had a long and ugly history in the Christian western world. It was particularly strong in Central Europe. As Allied troops discovered, Hitler had authorized the systematic extermination of all European Jews as well as Gypsies, homosexuals, and others considered deviant. The SS, Hitler's security force, had constructed six extermination centers in Poland. By rail from all over Europe the SS shipped Jews to die in the gas chambers.

No issue of World War II more starkly raised questions of human good and evil than what came to be known as the Holocaust. Tragically, the United States could have done more to save at least some of the 6 million Jews killed. Until the autumn of 1941 the Nazis permitted Jews to leave Europe, but few countries would accept them—including the United States. Americans haunted by unemployment feared that a tide of new immigrants would make competition for jobs even worse. After 1938 the restrictive provisions of the 1924 Immigration Act were made even tighter.

American Jews wanted to help, especially after 1942, when they learned of the death camps. But they worried that highly visible protests might only aggravate American anti-Semitism. They were also split over support for Zionists working to establish a Jewish homeland in Palestine. Roosevelt and his advisers ultimately decided that the best way to save Jews was to win the war quickly. That strategy still does not explain why the Allies did not do more: they could have bombed the rail lines to the camps, sent commando forces, or tried to destroy the death factories.

A Lasting Peace >>

Late in the summer of 1944 the Allies met at Dumbarton Oaks, a Washington estate, to lay out the structure for the proposed United Nations Organization (UNO, later known simply as the UN). An 11-member Security Council would oversee a General Assembly composed of delegates from all member nations. By the end of the first organizational meeting, held in San Francisco in April 1945, it had become clear that the United Nations would favor the Western powers in most postwar disputes.

>> In April 1945, at the concentration camp in Buchenwald, Germany, Senator Alben Barkley of Kentucky views a grisly example of the horrors of the Nazis' "final solution." As vice president under Harry Truman, Barkley urged the administration to support an independent homeland in Israel for Jews.

While the United Nations was organizing itself in San Francisco, the Axis powers were collapsing in Europe. As Mussolini attempted to escape to Germany, anti-Fascist mobs in Italy captured and slaughtered him like a pig. Adolf Hitler committed suicide in his Berlin bunker on April 30. Two weeks later General Eisenhower accepted the German surrender.

In one final summit meeting, held in July 1945 at Potsdam (just outside Berlin), President Truman met Churchill and Stalin for the first time. The three leaders agreed that Germany should be occupied and demilitarized. Stalin insisted that Russia receive a minimum of $10 billion in reparations, regardless of how much it might hurt postwar Germany or the European economy. A complicated compromise allowed Britain and the United States to restrict reparations from their zones. But in large part Stalin had his way. For the foreseeable future, Germany would remain divided into occupation zones and without a central government of its own.

Atom Diplomacy >> The issue most likely to shape postwar relations never even reached the bargaining table in Potsdam. On July 16, 1945, Manhattan Project scientists detonated their first atomic device. Upon receiving the news in Germany, Truman seemed a changed man—firmer, more confident. He "told the Russians just where they got on and off and generally bossed the whole meeting," observed Churchill. Several questions loomed. Should the United States now use the bomb? Should it warn Japan before dropping it? And perhaps equally vital, should Truman inform Stalin of the new weapon?

Over the spring and early summer of 1945 administration officials discussed the use of atomic weapons. A few scientists had recommended not using the bomb, or at least attempting to convince Japan to surrender by offering a demonstration of the new weapon's power. A high-level committee of administrators, scientists, and political and military leaders dismissed that idea. Rather than tell Stalin directly about the bomb, Truman mentioned obliquely that the United States possessed a weapon of

↟ At 0815 hours on August 6, 1945, the bomber Enola Gay dropped an atomic bomb on Hiroshima, Japan, as recorded by this photograph taken by an observation plane. Approximately 100,000 people died from the initial bomb blast, with thousands more dying from radiation poisoning. The remains of this wristwatch were found in the decimated city.

"awesome destructiveness." Stalin showed no surprise, most likely because spies had already informed him about the bomb. Privately, Truman and Churchill decided to drop the first bomb with only a veiled threat of "inevitable and complete" destruction if Japan did not surrender unconditionally. Unaware of the warning's full meaning, officials in Tokyo made no formal reply.

Some historians have charged that Secretary of State James Byrnes, a staunch anti-Communist, believed that a combat demonstration of the bomb would shock Stalin into behaving less aggressively in postwar negotiations. Most evidence, however, indicates that Truman decided to drop the bomb in order to end the war quickly. The victory in the Pacific promised to be bloody. Military leaders estimated that an invasion of Japan would produce heavy Allied casualties.

Before leaving Potsdam, Truman gave the final order for B-29s to drop two atomic bombs on Japan. On August 6 the first leveled four square miles of the city of

Opinion

Should the United States have sought an alternative to dropping the atomic bombs on Japan without a clear warning?

Hiroshima. Three days later a second exploded over the port of Nagasaki. About 140,000 people died instantly in the fiery blasts. A German priest came upon soldiers who had looked up as the bomb exploded. Their eyeballs had melted from their sockets. Tens of thousands more who lived through the horror began to sicken and die from radiation poisoning.

The two explosions left the Japanese stunned. Breaking all precedents, the emperor intervened and declared openly for peace. On September 3 a somber Japanese delegation boarded the battleship Missouri in Tokyo Bay to sign the document of surrender. World War II had ended.

 REVIEW

Over what issues did Stalin, Churchill, and Roosevelt disagree as they planned for peace?

"World War II changed everything," observed one admiral long after the war. The defeatism of the Depression gave way to the exhilaration of victory. Before the war Americans seldom exerted leadership in international affairs. After it, the world looked to the United States to rebuild the economies of Europe and Asia and to maintain peace. Not only had World War II shown the global interdependence of economic and political systems, but it had also increased that interdependence. Out of the war developed a truly international economy. At home the economy became more centralized and the role of the government larger.

Still, a number of fears loomed. Would the inevitable cutbacks in military spending bring on another depression? Would devastation in Europe and Asia produce conditions the Soviet Union could exploit for its own advantage? Did the Soviets have ambitions to undo the new global peace, much as fascism and economic instability had undone the peace of Versailles? And then there was the shadow of the atom bomb, looming over the victorious as well as the defeated. The United States might control atomic technology for the present, but what if the weapon fell into unfriendly hands? After World War II launched the atomic age, no nation, not even the United States, was safe anymore.

CHAPTER SUMMARY

World War II deepened the global interdependence of nations and left the United States as the greatest economic and military power in the world.

- As fascism spread in Europe and as militarism spread in Asia, Franklin Roosevelt struggled to help America's allies by overcoming domestic political isolation and the fervor for neutrality.
- Despite German aggression against Poland in 1939, France and the Low Countries in 1940, and the Soviet Union in 1941, the United States did not enter the war until the Japanese surprise attack on Pearl Harbor in December 1941.

Significant Events

Japan invades Manchuria; Stimson Doctrine

Munich meeting

| 1931–1932 | 1937 | 1938 | 1939 | 1940 |

HENRY STIMSON

Third Neutrality Act (cash-and-carry); Roosevelt's quarantine speech

Fall of Czechoslovakia; World War II begins in Europe

Germany launches blitzkrieg against Low Countries and France

- The alliance forged among British prime minister Winston Churchill, Soviet premier Joseph Stalin, and President Franklin Roosevelt did not swerve from its decision to subdue Germany first, even though early defeats and America's lack of preparation slowed the war effort until 1943.
- At home America's factories produced enough goods to supply the domestic economy and America's allies.
- Demands for labor created opportunities for women and minorities.
- War hysteria aggravated old prejudices and led to the internment of Japanese Americans.
- New Deal reform ended as "Dr. Win-the-War" replaced "Dr. New Deal."
- Although the successful landings in France on D-Day and the island-hopping campaign in the Pacific made it clear that the Allies would win the war, issues over Poland, Germany, and postwar boundaries raised doubts about the peace.
- The war ended with the atomic bombings of Hiroshima and Nagasaki, but not soon enough to limit the horrors of the Holocaust.

Additional Reading

A comprehensive treatment of the war years is David Kennedy, *The American People in World War II: Freedom from Fear: Part II* (2003). Robert Divine, *The Reluctant Belligerent* (2nd ed., 1979), is still excellent on the prewar diplomacy. Perhaps the most comprehensive single volume on the war is Martin Gilbert, *The Second World War: A Complete History* (2004), although Gerhard Weinberg, *The World at Arms: A Global History of World War II* (revised ed., 2005), captures the vast scale. Richard Lingeman, *Don't You Know There's a War On: The Homefront, 1941–1945* (updated ed., 2003), is a classic study. Emily Yellin, *Our Mother's War: American Women at Home and at the Front During World War II* (2005), explores the many roles women played. Tetsuden Kashmia, *Judgment Without Trial: Japanese American -Imprisonment During World War II* (2003), reveals that planning for internment of the Japanese began well before the war.

The decision to drop two atom bombs on Japan remains a topic of vigorous debate. For the racial dimension of the decision, see John Dower, *War without Mercy: Race and Power in the Pacific War* (1986). Richard Rhodes, *The Making of the Atomic Bomb* (1987), re-creates the history of the Manhattan Project. Gar Alperowitz, *The Decision to Use the Atomic Bomb* (1995), extends an interpretation he first advanced in *Atomic Diplomacy* (1965) that the Soviet Union was the planners' real target. Martin Sherwin, *A World Destroyed* (rev. ed., 1985), and J. Samuel Walker, *Prompt and Utter Destruction: Truman and the Use of the Atomic Bomb against Japan* (1997), view the decision more as a way to end the war quickly. David Holloway, *Stalin and the Bomb: The Soviet Union and Atomic Energy 1939–1956* (1994), uses Russian sources. To consult some of the original documents, see Michael B. Stoff et al., *The Manhattan Project: A Documentary Introduction to the Atomic Age* (1991).

Germany invades Soviet Union; Roosevelt and Churchill sign Atlantic Charter; Pearl Harbor attacked

D-Day invasion of France; U.S. forces return to Philippines; Battle of the Bulge; Dumbarton Oaks and Bretton Woods meetings

1941   **1942**   **1943**   **1944**   **1945**

Submarine war in the Atlantic; internment of Japanese Americans; Battle of Midway; Allied invasion of North Africa; Manhattan Project begins

Allies invade Italy; race riot in Detroit; zoot suit riots; Big Three meet at Teheran

Yalta Conference; Roosevelt dies; Truman becomes president; first United Nations Organization meeting; Germany surrenders; atom bombs dropped on Japan; World War II ends

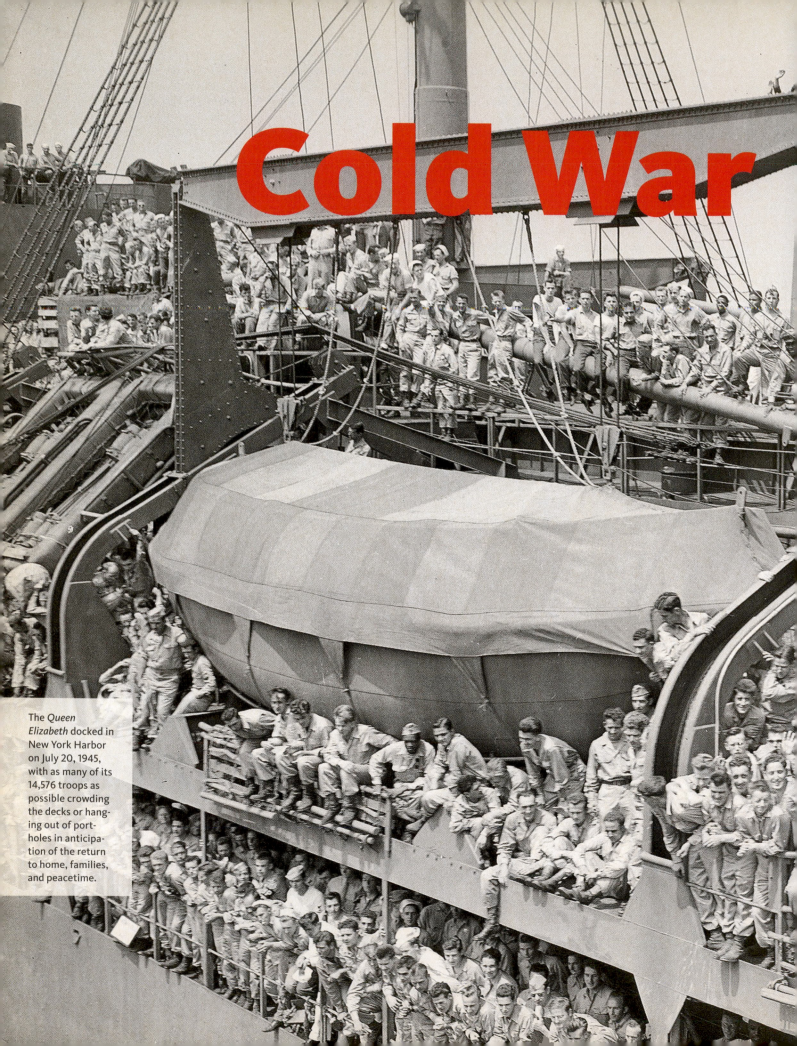

Cold War

The *Queen Elizabeth* docked in New York Harbor on July 20, 1945, with as many of its 14,576 troops as possible crowding the decks or hanging out of portholes in anticipation of the return to home, families, and peacetime.

America 27

1945–1954

>> AN AMERICAN STORY

GLAD TO BE HOME?

The war had been over for almost five months and still troopships steamed into New York. Timuel Black was packing his duffel below decks when he heard some of the white soldiers shout, "There she is! The Statue of Liberty!" >>

Black felt a little bitter about the war. He'd been drafted in Chicago in 1943, just after race riots ripped the city. His father, a strong supporter of civil rights, was angry. "What the hell are you goin' to fight in Europe for? The fight is here." He wanted his son to go with him to demonstrate in Detroit, except the roads were blocked and the buses and trains screened to prevent African Americans from coming in to "make trouble."

Instead, Black went off to fight the Nazis, serving in a segregated army. He'd gone ashore during the D-Day invasion and marched through one of the German concentration camps. "The first thing you get is the stench," he recalled. "Everybody knows that's human stench. You begin to see what's happened to these creatures. And you get—I got more passionately angry than I guess I'd ever been." He thought: if it could happen to Jews in Germany, it could happen to black folk in America. So when the white soldiers called to come up and see the Statue of Liberty, Black's reaction was, "Hell, I'm not goin' up there. Damn that." But he went up after all. "All of a sudden, I found myself with tears, cryin' and saying the same thing [the white soldiers] were saying. Glad to be home, proud of my country,

as irregular as it is. Determined that it could be better."

At the same time Betty Basye was working as a nurse in California. Her hospital treated soldiers shipped back from the Pacific: "Blind young men. Eyes gone, legs gone. Parts of the face. Burns—you'd land with a fire bomb and be up in flames." She'd joke with the men, trying to keep their spirits up, talking about times to come. She liked to take Bill, one of her favorites, for walks downtown. Half of Bill's face was gone, and civilians would stare. It happened to other patients, too. "Nicely dressed women, absolutely staring, just standing there staring." Some people wrote the local paper, wondering why disfigured vets couldn't be kept on their own grounds and off the streets. Such callousness made Basye indignant. But once the war ended, Basye had to think about her own future. "I got busy after the war," she recalled, "getting married and having my four children. That's what you were supposed to do. And getting your house in suburbia."

Yet as Betty Basye and Timuel Black soon discovered, the return to "normal" life was filled with uncertainties. The first truly global war had left a large part of Europe in ruins and the

old balance of power shattered. So great was the task of rebuilding that it soon became clear that the United States would have a central role in shaping whatever new world order emerged. Isolation seemed neither practical nor desirable in an era with the power of the Soviet Union and communism on the rise.

To blunt that threat the United States converted not so much to peace as to a "cold war" against its former Soviet ally. This undeclared war came to affect almost every aspect of American life. Abroad it justified a far wider military and economic role for the United States—not just in Europe but in the Middle East and along the Pacific Rim, from Korea to Indochina. At home it sent politicians searching the land for Communist spies and "subversives," from the State Department to the movie studios of Hollywood.

Trying to deter war in times of peace dramatically increased the role of the military-industrial-university complex formed during World War II. A people who had once resisted government intrusion into individual lives now accepted a large defense establishment. They voted, too, to maintain programs that ensured an active federal role in managing the economy. «

THE RISE OF THE COLD WAR

World War II devastated lands and people almost everywhere outside the Western Hemisphere. As the world struggled to rebuild, power that had once been centered in Europe shifted to nations on its periphery. In place of Germany, France, and England the United States and the Soviet Union emerged as the world's two reigning

superpowers—and as mortal enemies. This rivalry was not altogether an equal one. At war's end the United States had a booming economy, a massive military establishment, and the atomic bomb. In contrast, much of the Soviet Union lay in ruins.

But the defeat of Germany and Japan left no power in Europe or Asia to block the still formidable Soviet army. Many Americans feared that desperate, war-weary peoples would find the appeal of communism irresistible. If Stalin intended to extend the Soviet Union's dominion, only the United States had the economic and military might to

grasped power, they had often used violence and terror to achieve their ends. As Marxists they rejected both religion and the notion of private property, two institutions central to the American dream. Furthermore, Soviet propagandists had made no secret that they intended to export revolution throughout the world, including the United States.

The events leading to World War II caused Western leaders to fear the dangers of "appeasement." In 1938 British prime minister Neville Chamberlain's attempt at Munich to satisfy Hitler's demands on Czechoslovakia only emboldened the Nazis to expand further. After the war Secretary of the Navy James Forrestal applied the "lessons" of Munich to the new Europe. Appeasing Russian demands, he believed, would only seem like an attempt "to buy their understanding and sympathy. We tried that once with Hitler. . . . There are no returns on appeasement." To many of Truman's advisers the Soviet dictator seemed as much bent on conquest as Hitler had been.

Communist Expansion >>
During the war Stalin did make numerous demands to control territory along the Soviet borders. And with the coming of peace, he continued to push for a role in controlling the Dardanelles, the narrow straits linking Soviet ports on the Black Sea with the Mediterranean Sea. Soviet forces occupying northern Iran also lent support to rebels seeking to break away from the Iranian government. In Greece local Communists led the fighting to overturn the monarchy.

Asia, too, seemed a target for Communist ambitions. Russian occupation forces in Manchuria were turning over captured Japanese arms to Chinese Communist rebels led by Mao Zedong. Russian troops controlled the northern half of Korea. In Vietnam leftist nationalists were fighting against the return of colonial rule.

Despite Russian actions, many historians have argued, American policy makers consistently exaggerated Stalin's ambitions. At war's end much of the farmland and industry in the Soviet Union lay in ruins. When Stalin looked outward, he saw American occupation forces in Europe and Asia ringing the Soviet Union, their military might backed by a newly developed atomic arsenal. American corporations owned or controlled vast oil fields in the Middle East. Along with the French and the British, the United States was a strong presence in Southeast Asia. Given that situation, one could interpret Stalin's actions after the war as being primarily defensive, designed to counter what appeared to him a threatening American-European alliance.

More recent evidence from once-secret files of the Soviet Union suggests that despite the ravages of war, Stalin recognized that in 1945 the Soviet Union was emerging as a more powerful state. With Germany and Japan defeated, Soviet borders to the east and west were secure from invasion. Only to the south did Stalin see

^ Churchill, Truman, and Stalin met at Potsdam in July 1945. Their smiles masked serious disagreements about the shape of the postwar world.

block him. Events in the critical years of 1945 and 1946 persuaded most Americans that Stalin did have such a plan. The Truman administration concluded that "the U.S.S.R. has engaged the United States in a struggle for power, or 'cold war,' in which our national security is at stake and from which we cannot withdraw short of national suicide." What had happened that led Western leaders to such a dire view of their former Soviet allies? How did such a wide breach open between the two nations?

American Suspicions >>
Even before postwar events deepened American suspicions of the Soviets, an ideological gulf had separated the two nations. The October Revolution of 1917 shocked most Americans. They had come to view Lenin's Bolshevik revolutionaries with a mixture of fear, suspicion, and loathing. As the Communists

Opinion

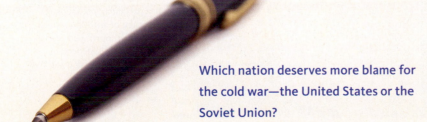

Which nation deserves more blame for the cold war—the United States or the Soviet Union?

a problem, along the border with Iran. Further, he recognized that the people of Britain and the United States had tired of fighting. Their leaders were not about to threaten the Soviet Union with war, at least in the near term. Equally significant, Soviet spies had informed Stalin in 1946 that the United States possessed only a few atom bombs, making the nuclear threat more symbolic than real. As a political realist Stalin saw an opportunity to advance the interests of the Soviet state and his own regime—as long as his actions did not risk war.

The tensions arising from the conflicting Soviet and American points of view came to a head in the first months of 1946. Stalin announced in February that the Soviet Union would act vigorously to preserve its national security. In a world dominated by capitalism, he warned, future wars were inevitable. The Russian people had to ensure against "any eventuality" by undertaking a new five-year plan for economic development.

Although some Americans thought Stalin was merely rallying Russian support for his domestic programs, others saw their worst fears confirmed. *Time* magazine, an early voice for a "get tough" policy, called Stalin's speech "the most warlike pronouncement uttered by any top-rank statesman since V-J day." "I'm tired of babying the Soviets," remarked President Truman, who in any case seldom wore kid gloves. Even his mother passed along a message: "Tell Harry to be good, be honest, and behave himself, but I think it is now time for him to get tough with someone." In March Winston Churchill warned that the Soviets had dropped an "Iron Curtain" between their satellite nations and the free world. Poland, East Germany, Romania, and Bulgaria lay behind it. Iran, Greece, Turkey, and much of Europe seemed at risk.

A Policy of Containment >> As policy makers groped for a way to deal with these developments, the State Department received a diplomatic cable extraordinary both for its length (8,000 words) and for its impact in Washington. The author was George Kennan, chargé d'affaires in Moscow and long a student of Soviet conduct.

His "long telegram" argued that Russian leaders, including Stalin, were so paranoid that it was impossible to reach any useful agreements with them. When this "instinctive Russian sense of insecurity" combined with Marxist conviction that capitalism was evil, the result was a natural tendency toward Soviet expansion, Kennan argued. Soviet power "moves inexorably . . . like a toy automobile wound up and headed in a given direction, stopping only when it meets some unanswerable force."

The response Kennan recommended was "containment." The United States must apply "unalterable counterforce at every point where [the Soviets] show signs of encroaching upon the interests of a peaceful and stable world." Kennan's analysis provided leaders in Washington with a clear strategic plan for responding to Soviet behavior. By applying firm counterpressure—diplomatic, economic, and military—the United States could block Russian aggression. Truman wholeheartedly adopted the strategy of containment.

The Truman Doctrine >> A major test of Soviet and American wills came in early 1947. As Europe reeled under severe winter storms and a depressed postwar economy, Great Britain announced that it could no longer support the governments of Greece and Turkey. Without British aid to resist them, the Communist movements within these countries seemed destined to win critical victories. Truman decided that the United States should shore up Greek and Turkish resistance. He asked Congress to provide $400 million in military and economic aid. To gain support he went before Congress in March, determined to "scare hell out of the country." The world was now divided into two hostile camps, he warned. To preserve the American way of life, the United States must step forward and help "free people" threatened by "totalitarian regimes." This rationale for aid to Greece and Turkey soon became known as the Truman Doctrine.

The Truman Doctrine marked a new level of American commitment to a cold war. Just what responsibility the Soviets had for unrest in Greece and Turkey remained

<< As American fears of Soviet intentions increased, journalists often described communism as though it were a disease, an inhuman force, or a savage predator. In April 1946 *Time* magazine, a particularly outspoken source of anti-Communist rhetoric, portrayed the spread of "infection" throughout Europe and Asia as the "Red Menace."

unclear. But Truman had linked communism with rebel movements all across the globe. That committed Americans to a relatively open-ended struggle, in which the president gained expanded powers to act when unrest threatened. Occasionally Congress would regret giving the executive branch so much power, but by 1947 anticommunism had become the dominant theme in American policy, both foreign and domestic.

The Marshall Plan >>
In promoting containment the Truman Doctrine did not aid Western Europe. There, national treasuries were empty, city streets stood dark, people starved, and factories were closed. American diplomats warned that without aid to revive the European economy, Communists would seize power in Germany, Italy, and France. If Western Europe fell, the cold war could be lost.

In June 1947 Secretary of State George C. Marshall told a Harvard commencement audience about a plan to ensure the recovery of Europe. He invited all European nations, East or West, to request assistance to rebuild their economies. Unlike Truman Marshall did not emphasize the Communist menace. Still, his massive aid plan aimed to eliminate conditions that produced the discontent that Communists often exploited. Then, too, humanitarian aid had practical benefits. As Europe recovered, so would its interest in buying American goods. Marshall did not rule out Soviet participation in the massive aid program. But he gambled—correctly—that fears of American economic domination would lead the Soviets and their allies to reject his offer. At first **neo-isolationists** in Congress argued that the United States could not afford such generosity. But when Stalin continued to solidify control of the nations behind the Iron Curtain, Congress approved the Marshall Plan, as it became known, in 1948. The blame for dividing Europe fell on the Soviet Union, not the United States. And the Marshall Plan proved crucial to Western Europe's economic recovery.

neo-isolationist an individual who after World War II believed the United States should avoid foreign entanglements.

On June 24 the Soviets suddenly blockaded land access to Berlin. Truman did not hesitate to respond: "We are going to stay, period."

Masaryk, had fallen to his death from a small bathroom window. Suicide was the official explanation, but many suspected murder.

The spring of 1948 brought another clash between the Soviets and their wartime allies, this time over Germany. There, the United States, Great Britain, and France decided to transform their occupation zones into an independent West German state. The Western-controlled sectors of Berlin, however, lay over 100 miles to the east, well within the Soviet zone. On June 24 the Soviets suddenly blockaded land access to Berlin. Truman did not hesitate to respond: "We are going to stay, period." But he did reject General Lucius Clay's proposal to shoot his way through the blockade. Instead, the United States began a massive airlift of supplies that lasted almost a year. In May 1949 Stalin lifted the blockade, conceding that he could not prevent the creation of West Germany.

Stalin's aggressive actions accelerated the American effort to use military means to contain Soviet ambitions. By 1949 the United States and Canada had joined with Britain, France, Belgium, the Netherlands, and Luxembourg to establish the North Atlantic Treaty Organization (NATO) as a mutual defense pact. For the first time since George Washington had warned against entangling alliances in his farewell address of 1793, the United States during peacetime entered into treaties of alliance with European nations.

Truman's firm handling of the Berlin crisis won him applause from both Democrats and Republicans. They were equally enthusiastic about another presidential action. Minutes after Jewish residents of Palestine announced their independence in May 1948, Truman recognized the new state of Israel. He had previously supported the immigration of Jews into Palestine, despite the opposition of oil-rich Arab states and diplomats in the State Department. The president sympathized with Jewish aspirations for a homeland. He also faced a tough campaign in 1948 in which Jewish votes would be critical. As British prime minister Clement Attlee observed: "There's no Arab vote in America, but there's a heavy Jewish vote and the Americans are always having elections."

NATO >>
American efforts to stabilize Europe placed Stalin on the defensive. In 1947 he moved against the moderate government in Hungary, which since 1945 had been chosen through relatively free elections. Soviet forces replaced the government with a Communist regime dependent on Moscow. Then in February 1948 Communists toppled the elected government of Czechoslovakia. News came that the popular Czech foreign minister, Jan

The Atomic Shield versus the Iron Curtain >>
The Berlin crisis forced Truman to consider the possibility of war. If it came, would atomic weapons again be used? That dilemma raised two other difficult questions. Should the decision to use atomic weapons rest in civilian or military hands? And was it possible to find a way to ease the atomic threat by creating an international system to control nuclear power?

COLD WAR EUROPE

By 1956 the postwar occupation of Europe had hardened into rigid cold war boundaries. The United States reacted to the presence of Soviet conventional forces in Eastern Europe by rearming West Germany and creating the NATO alliance (1949) for the defense of nations from the North Atlantic through the Mediterranean basin. The U.S.S.R. formed a counteralliance under the Warsaw Pact (1955). Although Bonn became the de facto capital of West Germany, Berlin remained the official capital and into the 1960s the focus of the most severe cold war tensions.

On the question of civilian or military control of the bomb, Truman declared he was not going to have "some dashing lieutenant colonel decide when would be the proper time to drop one." In 1946 Congress seemed to choose civilian control when it passed the McMahon Act. This bill established the Atomic Energy Commission (AEC) with control of all fissionable materials for both peacetime and military applications. The AEC was a civilian, not a military, agency, but the military maintained a central influence.

Proposals for the international control of atomic energy fell victim to cold war fears. Originally a high-level government committee proposed to Truman that the mining and use of the world's atomic raw materials be supervised by the United Nations. The committee argued that in the long run the United States would be more secure under a system of international control than by relying on its temporary nuclear monopoly. But Truman chose Bernard Baruch, a staunch cold warrior, to draw up the recommendations to the United Nations in June 1946. Baruch's proposals ensured that the United States would dominate any international atomic agency. The Soviets countered with a plan calling for destruction of all nuclear bombs and a ban on their use. Baruch had no intention of bargaining. It was either his plan or nothing, he announced. And so it was nothing. The Truman administration never seriously considered the possibility of giving up the American nuclear monopoly.

Ironically, because so much secrecy surrounded the bomb, many military planners knew little about it. Even Truman had no idea in 1946 how many bombs the United States possessed. (For the two years after Hiroshima, it was never more than a dozen.) Military planners, however, soon found themselves relying more and more on atomic weapons. The Soviet army had at its command over 260 divisions. The United States, in contrast, had reduced its forces by 1947 to little more than a single division. As the cold war heated up, American military planners were forced to adopt a nuclear strategy in the face of overwhelming superiority of Soviet forces. They would deter any Soviet attack by setting in place a devastating atomic counterattack.

By 1949, then, the cold war framed all aspects of American foreign policy. The Joint Chiefs of Staff had committed themselves to a policy of nuclear **deterrence.** Western Europe was on its way to economic recovery, thanks to the Marshall Plan. Soviet pressures on Greece and Turkey

> **deterrence** prevention of an action by fear of the consequences; during the cold war, especially among nuclear powers.

had abated. Many Americans had hopes that the United States might soon defeat communism.

Yet these successes brought little comfort. The Soviet Union was not simply a major power seeking to protect its interests and expand where opportunity permitted. In the eyes of many Americans the Soviets were determined, if they could, to overthrow the United States from either without or within. This was a war being fought not only across the globe but right in America, by unseen agents using subversive means. In this way the cold war mentality soon came to shape the lives of Americans at home much as it did American policy abroad.

 REVIEW

What were Soviet and American strategies after World War II, and what were the hot spots where these strategies clashed?

POSTWAR PROSPERITY

At war's end many business leaders feared that a sudden drop in government purchases would bring back the depressed conditions of the 1930s. Instead, despite a rocky year or two of adjusting to a peacetime economy, Americans entered into the longest period of prosperity in the nation's history, lasting until the 1970s. Even the fear of communism could not deflect Americans from the ideal of a consumer society brought about by a partnership between private enterprise and the American government.

Two forces drove the postwar economic boom. One was unbridled consumer and business spending that followed 16 years of depression and war. High war wages had piled up in savings accounts and war bonds. Eager consumers set off to find the new cars, appliances, and foods unavailable during the war. Despite the end of government wartime spending the gross national product fell less than 1 percent, and employment actually increased. Consumers had taken up the slack.

Government spending at the local, state, and federal levels provided another boost to prosperity. The three major growth industries in the decades after World War II were health care, education, and government programs. Each of these was spurred by public spending. Equally important, the federal government poured billions of dollars into the military-industrial sector. The defense budget, which fell to $9 billion in 1947, reached $50 billion by the time Truman left office. Over the longer term these factors promoting economic growth became clearer.

Hidden Costs of a Consuming Nation »

In this new consumer economy synthetic goods played a central role, promising a cheaper and more convenient life. Phosphate detergents got clothes whiter than did traditional laundry soaps. Chemical fertilizers produced greater yields in fields once treated with animal manure. The chemical giant DuPont caught the spirit of the American fascination with new wonders that promised "Better Things for Better Living . . . through Chemistry."

But the ideal of a full-employment society based on mass consumption contained flaws. The new consumer goods depended on cheap and plentiful fossil fuels, since hydrocarbons from petroleum formed the basis for many fertilizers and synthetic plastics. Much of the world's future oil resources lay in politically unstable regions such as the Middle East or in ecologically vulnerable areas such as the Gulf of Mexico. Some scientists saw nuclear energy as an alternative energy source that would fuel consumer dreams. But in 1946 an atomic test on Bikini Atoll in the South Pacific revealed that dangerous levels of radiation persisted long after an atomic blast. Atomic energy would not be the miracle source of cheap, endless power.

In 1948 the small industrial town of Donora, Pennsylvania, sent out a different warning about the cost of progress. Donora, located near Pittsburgh, was home to metal smelters and steel mills. During a five-day period an inversion layer over the town trapped a toxic brew of sulfur dioxide, carbon monoxide, and metal dust spewing from the smelters. Some twenty people died and half the town's 7,000 residents were hospitalized. Industry leaders worried that an outraged public would insist on new government controls. It preferred to view the atmosphere into which it dumped its pollution as "a useful natural resource" to be

Historian's TOOLBOX

Kix Atomic Bomb Ring of 1946

Wow, kids! For an actual, vivid, rotating 360-degree photo of one of these rings, go to www.periodictable.com/Items/084.9/index .html and click "Spin Video."

Spy story comic: espionage was a common theme in postwar popular culture. Why?

How do you react to this image? What events three years later (1949) might have made General Mills rethink the idea of promoting an atomic bomb ring (see p. 575)?

Gift and toy promotions helped to sell cereal.

It was promoted as the "Lone Ranger Atomic Bomb Ring," though the Lone Ranger, a radio and screen western hero, was in the habit of using silver bullets rather than a-bombs to fight rustlers. The ring's wearer was instructed to go into a dark room, "Slide Tail Fin off—look in Observation Lens—and you'll see frenzied flashes of light—caused by released energy of atoms splitting like crazy. . . ." Sublime breakfast cereal hooey?

Astonishingly, each ring did contain a tiny bit of polonium-210 with a half-life of only 138 days. Its stream of radioactive alpha particles caused a zinc sulfide-coated screen to light up. It was a simple version of a scientific instrument known as a spinthariscope, invented in 1903. But in 1946 the public was only slowly beginning to learn about the dangers of radiation. That would change over the

next decade, as Americans struggled to make peace with the threat of nuclear annihilation.

THINKING CRITICALLY

Does the advertisement address the issue of safety? If historians used this ad to measure public attitudes about the atomic bomb, what would it tell them? How has our perception of the bomb changed over time?

used "for the dispersion of wastes within its capacity to do so without harm to the surroundings."

A few critics argued that such ideas ignored the fundamental principles of ecology: that toxic substances entering the food chain accumulated in all living things.

Aldo Leopold, a pioneering ecologist proposed in a *Sand County Almanac* (1949) what he called a "land ethic." He observed, "we abuse the land because we see it as a commodity belonging to us" instead of "a community to which we belong," to be used with love and respect.

Americans in the postwar years were not ready to heed Leopold's warning. In any case, it took several years for the economy to make the bumpy transition from war to peace. Short-term worries trumped long-term problems.

Postwar Adjustments >> With millions of veterans looking for peacetime jobs, workers on the home front, especially women and minorities, found themselves out of jobs. War employment had given many women their first taste of economic independence. As peace came almost 75 percent of the working women in one survey indicated that they hoped to continue their jobs. But as the troops returned home, traditional cultural attitudes pushed women out of the work force. Male social scientists stressed that it was important for women to accept "more than the wife's usual responsibility for her marriage" and offer "lavish—and undemanding—affection" to returning GIs.

For minorities the end of the war brought a return of an old labor practice, "last hired, first fired." At the height of the war, over 200,000 African Americans and Hispanics had found jobs in shipbuilding. By 1946 that number had dwindled to less than 10,000. The influx of Mexican laborers under the bracero program temporarily halted. In the South, where the large majority of black Americans lived, few jobs were available.

At the same time, many Hispanic veterans who had fought for their country during the war resented returning to a deeply segregated society. Such GIs "have acquired a new courage, have become more vocal in protesting the restrictions and inequalities with which they are confronted," noted one white Texan. When a funeral director in Three Rivers, Texas, refused to open a segregated cemetery for the burial of Felix Longoria, a Mexican American soldier killed in battle, his supporters organized. Led by Dr. Hector Garcia, a former army medical officer, the American GI Forum was founded in 1948 to campaign for civil rights. Longoria was finally buried in Arlington National Cemetery after the GI Forum convinced Congressman Lyndon Baines Johnson to intervene.

Black veterans had a similar impact. Angered by violence, frustrated by the slow pace of desegregation, they breathed new energy into civil rights organizations like the NAACP and the Congress of Racial Equality. Voting rights was one of the issues they pushed. Registration drives in the South had the greatest success in urban centers like Atlanta. Other black leaders pressed for improved education. In rural Virginia, for example, a young Howard University lawyer, Spottswood Robinson, litigated cases for the NAACP to force improvement in segregated all-black schools. In one county Robinson and the NAACP even won equal pay for black and white teachers.

Out in the countryside, however, segregationists used economic intimidation, violence, and even murder to preserve the Jim Crow system. White citizens in rural Georgia lynched several black veterans who had shown the determination to vote. Such instances disturbed President Truman, who saw civil rights as a key ingredient in his reform agenda. The president was especially disturbed when he learned that police in South Carolina had gouged out the eyes of a recently discharged black veteran. Truman responded in December 1946 by appointing a Committee on Civil Rights. A year later it published its report, *To Secure These Rights.*

Discovering inequities for minorities, the committee exposed a racial caste system that denied African Americans employment opportunities, equal education, voting rights, and decent housing. But every time Truman appealed to Congress to carry out the committee's recommendations, southern senators threatened to filibuster. Their obstruction forced the president to resort to executive authority to achieve even modest results. In his most direct attack on segregation, he issued an **executive order** in July 1948 banning discrimination in the armed forces. Segregationists predicted disaster, but experience soon demonstrated that integrated units fought well and exhibited minimal racial tension.

> **executive order** declaration issued by the president or by a governor possessing the force of law.

The New Deal at Bay >> In September 1945 Harry Truman pushed boldly to extend the New Deal into the postwar era. He called for legislation to guarantee full employment, subsidized public housing, national health insurance, and a peacetime version of the Fair Employment Practices Commission to fight job discrimination. But inflation, temporary shortages of consumer goods, and a wave of strikes by autoworkers, coal miners, and railroad workers hobbled the economy. They also undermined Truman's ability to pass such liberal legislation. For two years prices rose as much as 15 percent annually. Consumers blamed the White House for not doing more to ease their burden.

With Truman's political stock falling, conservative Republicans and southern Democrats blocked the president's attempts to revive the New Deal. All the president achieved was a watered-down full-employment bill, which created the Council of Economic Advisors. The bill did establish one key principle: the government rather than the private sector was responsible for maintaining full employment. As the congressional elections of 1946 neared, Republicans pointed to production shortages and the procession of strikes by labor unions. "To err is Truman," proclaimed the campaign buttons—or, more simply, "Had enough?" Many voters had. The Republicans gained control of both houses of Congress. Not since 1928 had the Democrats fared so poorly.

Leading the rightward swing was Senator Robert A. Taft of Ohio, son of former president William Howard Taft. Bob Taft not only wanted to halt the spread of the New Deal—he wanted to dismantle it. "We have to get over the

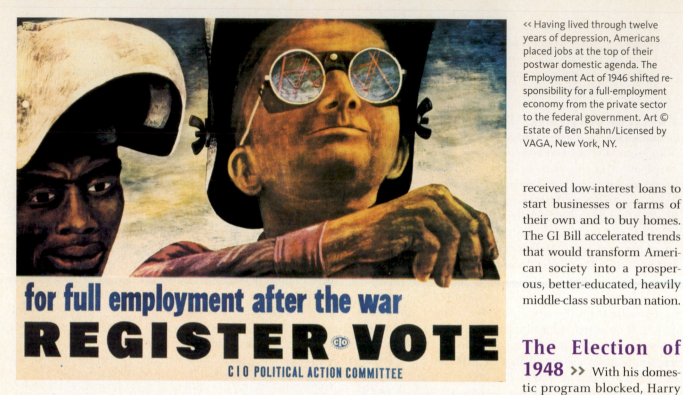

for full employment after the war
REGISTER·VOTE
CIO POLITICAL ACTION COMMITTEE

<< Having lived through twelve years of depression, Americans placed jobs at the top of their postwar domestic agenda. The Employment Act of 1946 shifted responsibility for a full-employment economy from the private sector to the federal government. Art © Estate of Ben Shahn/Licensed by VAGA, New York, NY.

received low-interest loans to start businesses or farms of their own and to buy homes. The GI Bill accelerated trends that would transform American society into a prosperous, better-educated, heavily middle-class suburban nation.

The Election of 1948 >>

With his domestic program blocked, Harry Truman faced almost certain defeat in the election of 1948. The New Deal coalition that Franklin Roosevelt had held together for so long fractured. On the left Truman was challenged by Henry Wallace, who had been a capable secretary of agriculture and vice president under Roosevelt, then secretary of commerce under Truman. Wallace wanted to pursue New Deal reforms even more vigorously than Truman did, and he continually voiced his sympathy for the Soviet Union. Disaffected liberals bolted the Democratic party to support Wallace on a third-party Progressive ticket.

Within the southern conservative wing of the party, arch-segregationists resented Truman's civil rights proposals for a voting rights bill and an antilynching law. When the liberal wing of the party passed a civil rights plank as part of the Democratic platform, delegates from several Deep South states stalked out of the convention to create the States' Rights or "Dixiecrat" party, with J. Strom Thurmond, the segregationist governor of South Carolina, as their candidate.

Republicans smelled victory. They sought to control the political center by rejecting the conservative Taft in favor of the more moderate former New York governor Thomas Dewey. Dewey proved so aloof that he inspired little enthusiasm. "You have to know Dewey well to really dislike him," quipped one critic. Still, it seemed Dewey would walk away with the race.

Truman, however, launched a stinging attack against the "reactionaries" in Congress: that "bunch of old mossbacks . . . gluttons of privilege . . . all set to do a hatchet job on the New Deal." From the rear platform of his campaign train he made almost 400 speeches in eight weeks. Over and over he hammered away at the "do-nothing" 80th

corrupting idea we can legislate prosperity, legislate equality, legislate opportunity," he said in dismissing the liberal agenda. Taft especially wished to limit the power of the unions. In 1947 he pushed the Taft-Hartley Act through Congress over Truman's veto. In the event of a strike the bill allowed the president to order workers back on the job during a 90-day "cooling-off" period while collective bargaining continued. It also permitted states to adopt "right-to-work" laws, which banned the closed shop by eliminating union membership as a prerequisite for many jobs. Union leaders hated the new law but learned to live with it, though it did hurt union efforts to organize, especially in the South.

Despite the conservative backlash most Americans continued to support the New Deal's major accomplishments: Social Security, minimum wages, and a more active role for government in reducing unemployment. The administration maintained its commitment to setting a minimum wage, raising it again in 1950 from 45 to 75 cents an hour. Social Security coverage was broadened to include an additional 10 million workers. Furthermore, a growing list of welfare programs benefited not only the poor but also veterans, middle-income families, the elderly, and students.

The most striking of these was the GI Bill of 1944, which created unparalleled opportunity for returning veterans under the "GI Bill of Rights." Those with more than two years of service received all tuition and fees plus living expenses for three years of college education. By 1948 the government was paying the college costs of almost half of all male students as over 2 million veterans went to college on the GI Bill. The increase in college graduates encouraged a shift from blue- to white-collar work and self-employment. Veterans also

Election Results Map

Candidate (Party)	Electoral Vote (%)	Popular Vote (%)
Harry S. Truman (Democratic)	303 (57)	24,105,812 (50)
Thomas E. Dewey (Republican)	189 (36)	21,970,065 (46)
Strom Thurmond (States' Rights)	3 (7)	1,169,021 (2)
Harry A. Wallace (Progressive)	—	1,157,172 (2)
Other candidates (Communist, Prohibition, Socialist Labor, Liberty)	—	272,713 —

THE COLD WAR AT HOME

Bob Raymondi, a mobster serving a prison term in the late 1940s, was no stranger to racketeering or gangland killings. In fact, he was so feared, he dominated the inmate population at Dannemora Prison. Raymondi made the acquaintance of a group of Communists who had been jailed for advocating the overthrow of the government. He enjoyed talking with people who had some education. When Raymondi's sister learned about his new friends, she was frantic. "My God, Bob," she told him, "you'll get into trouble."

Was something amiss? Many Americans seemed to believe it riskier to associate with Communists than with hardened criminals. Out of a population of 150 million the Communist party in 1950 could claim a membership of only 43,000. (More than a few of those were FBI undercover agents.) But worry about Communists Americans did. Conservatives still thought of the New Deal as "creeping socialism," only an arm's length short of communism. Leftists, they believed, controlled labor unions, Hollywood, and groups sympathetic to the New Deal. As Stalin extended Soviet control in Eastern Europe and Asia, American domestic fears grew.

ELECTION OF 1948

Congress, which, he told farmers, "had stuck a pitchfork" in their backs. On Election Day oddsmakers still favored Dewey by as much as 20 to 1. Hours before the polls closed the archconservative *Chicago Tribune* happily headlined "Dewey Defeats Truman." But the experts were wrong. Not only did the voters return Truman by over 2 million popular votes, but they gave the Democrats commanding majorities in the House and Senate.

The Fair Deal >> As he began his new term Harry Truman declared that all Americans were entitled to a "Fair Deal" from their government. He called for the enactment of such New Deal programs as national health insurance and regional TVA-style projects. Echoing an old Populist idea, Truman hoped to keep his working coalition together by forging stronger links between farmers and labor. But the conservative coalition of southern Democrats and Republicans in Congress still blocked any significant initiatives. On the domestic front Truman remained largely the conservator of Franklin Roosevelt's legacy.

REVIEW

How did the federal government promote postwar prosperity?

The Shocks of 1949 >> Nineteen forty-nine proved a pivotal year. American scientists reported in August that rains monitored in the Pacific contained traces of hot nuclear waste. Only one conclusion seemed possible: the Soviet Union possessed its own atom bomb. Senator Arthur Vandenberg, a Republican with wide experience in international affairs, summed up the reaction of many to the end of the American nuclear monopoly: "This is now a different world." Truman directed that research into a newer, more powerful hydrogen bomb continue.

Then in December came more bad news. The Nationalist government of Chiang Kai-shek fled mainland China to the offshore island of Formosa (present-day Taiwan). In January 1950 Communist troops under Mao Zedong swarmed into Beijing, China's capital city. Chiang's defeat came as no surprise to the State Department. Officials there had long regarded Chiang and his Nationalists as hopelessly corrupt and ineffective. Despite major American efforts to save his regime and stabilize China, poverty and civil unrest spread. In 1947 full-scale civil war had broken out. By February 1949 almost half of Chiang's demoralized troops had defected to the Communists. So the December defeat was hardly unexpected.

But Republicans, who had formerly supported the president's foreign policy, now broke ranks. For some time, a group of wealthy conservatives and Republican senators had resented the administration's preoccupation with Europe. Time-Life publisher Henry Luce used his magazines

△ The fall of China to the forces of Mao Zedong was one of the chilling cold war shocks of 1949.

to campaign for a greater concern for Asian affairs and especially more aid to defeat Mao Zedong. When Chiang at last collapsed, his American backers, called the China Lobby, charged the Democrats with letting the Communists win.

Worries that subversives had sold out the country were heightened when former State Department official Alger Hiss was brought to trial in 1949 for perjury. Hiss, an adviser to Roosevelt at the Yalta Conference, had been accused by former Communist Whittaker Chambers of passing secrets to the Soviet Union during the 1930s. Though the evidence in the case was inconclusive, the jury convicted Hiss for lying about his association with Chambers. And in February 1950 the nation was further shocked by news from Britain that a high-ranking physicist, Klaus Fuchs, had spied for the Russians while working on the Manhattan Project. Here was clear evidence of a conspiracy at work.

The Loyalty Crusade ➤➤ As fears of subversion and espionage mounted, President Truman sought

to protect himself from Republican accusations that he was "soft" on communism. Only days after proposing the Truman Doctrine in March 1947, the president signed an executive order establishing a Federal Employee Loyalty Program designed to guard against any disloyalty by "Reds, phonies, and 'parlor pinks.'" The order required government supervisors to certify the loyalties of those who worked below them, reporting to a system of federal loyalty review boards. The FBI was to follow up any "derogatory information" that came to light.

The system quickly got out of hand. Those accused would have no right to confront their accusers. But a few years' experience showed that it was difficult actually to prove disloyalty on the part of employees. Truman then allowed the boards to fire those who were "potentially" disloyal or "bad security risks," such as alcoholics, homosexuals, and debtors. Suspected employees, in other words, were assumed guilty until proven innocent. After some five million investigations, the program identified a few hundred employees who, though not Communists, had at one time been associated with suspect groups. Rather than calm public fears, the loyalty program gave credibility to the growing Red scare.

HUAC and Hollywood »

Hollywood, with its wealth, glamour, and highly visible Jewish and foreign celebrities, had long aroused a mixture of attraction and suspicion among traditional Americans. In 1947 the House Committee on Un-American Activities (HUAC) began to investigate Communist influences in the film industry. "Large numbers of moving pictures that come out of Hollywood carry the communist line," charged committee member John Rankin of Mississippi.

HUAC called a parade of movie stars, screenwriters, and producers to sit in the glare of its public hearings. Some witnesses, such as Gary Cooper and Ronald Reagan, were considered "friendly" because they answered committee questions or supplied names of suspected leftists. Others refused to inform on their colleagues or to answer questions about earlier ties to the Communist party. Eventually 10 uncooperative witnesses, known as the "Hollywood Ten," refused on First Amendment grounds to say whether they were or ever had been Communists. They served prison terms for contempt of Congress.

For all its probing, HUAC never offered convincing evidence that filmmakers were in any way subversive. Yet the investigation did have a chilling effect on the entertainment industry. The studios fired any actors suspected of leftist leanings, adopting a blacklist that prevented admitted or accused Communists from finding work.

⌃ The role of government informer took center-stage in this movie derived from articles in *The Saturday Evening Post.* "I had to sell out my own girl—so would you!" went the film's tagline. "I was under the toughest orders a guy could get! I stood by and watched my brother slugged . . . I started a riot that ran red with terror . . . I learned every dirty rule in their book—and had to use them—because I was a communist—but I WAS A COMMUNIST FOR THE FBI."

Since no judicial proceedings were involved, victims of false charges, rumors, or spiteful accusations found it nearly impossible to clear their names.

Suspicion of aliens and immigrants as subversives led finally to the passage, over Truman's veto, of the McCarran Act (1950). It required all Communists to register with the attorney general, forbade the entry of anyone who had belonged to a totalitarian organization, and allowed the Justice Department to detain suspect aliens indefinitely during deportation hearings. That same year a Senate committee began an inquiry designed to root out homosexuals holding government jobs. Even one "sex pervert in a Government agency tends to have a corrosive influence upon his fellow employees," warned the committee.

The Ambitions of Senator McCarthy »

By 1950 anticommunism had created a climate of fear, where irrational hysteria overwhelmed legitimate concerns. Senator Joseph R. McCarthy, a relatively unknown Republican senator from Wisconsin, saw in that fear an opportunity to improve his political fortunes. Before an audience in Wheeling, West Virginia, in February 1950 he waved a sheaf of papers in the air and announced that he had a list of 205—or perhaps 81, 57, or "a lot" of—Communists in the State Department. (No one, including the senator, could remember the number, which he continually changed.) In the following months McCarthy leveled charge after charge. He had penetrated the "iron curtain" of the State Department to discover "card-carrying Communists," the "top Russian espionage agent" in the United States, "egg-sucking phony liberals," and "Communists and queers" who wrote "perfumed notes."

In a sense, McCarthyism was the bitter fruit Truman and the Democrats reaped from their own attempts to exploit the anti-Communist mood. McCarthy, more than Truman, tapped the fears and hatreds of traditional conservatives, Catholic leaders, and neoisolationists who distrusted things foreign, liberal, or intellectual. They saw McCarthy and his fellow witch hunters as the protectors of a vaguely defined but deeply felt spirit of Americanism.

By the time Truman stepped down as president, 32 states had laws requiring teachers to take loyalty oaths. Government loyalty boards were asking employees what newspapers they subscribed to or phonograph records they collected. A library in Indiana had banned Robin Hood because the idea of stealing from the rich to give to the poor seemed too leftish. As one historian commented, "Opening the valve of anticommunist hysteria was a good deal simpler than closing it."

✔ **REVIEW**

How did Truman's actions contribute to the red scare at home and the rise of McCarthyism?

FROM COLD WAR TO HOT WAR AND BACK

As the cold war heated up during 1949 the Truman administration searched for a more assertive foreign policy. The new approach was developed by the National Security Council (NSC), an agency created by Congress in 1947 as part of a plan to help the executive branch respond more effectively to cold war crises. Rather than merely "contain" the Soviets, as George Kennan had suggested, the National Security Council wanted the United States to "strive for victory." In April 1950 the council sent Truman a document, NSC-68, which came to serve as the framework for American policy over the next 20 years.

NSC-68 called for a dramatic increase in defense spending, from $13 billion to $50 billion a year, to be paid for with a large tax increase. Most of the funds would go to rebuild conventional forces, but the NSC urged that the hydrogen bomb be developed to offset the new Soviet nuclear capacity. Efforts to carry out NSC-68 at first aroused widespread opposition. George Kennan argued that the Soviets had no immediate plans for domination outside the Communist bloc. Fiscal conservatives, both Democrat and Republican, resisted any proposal for higher taxes. All such reservations were swept away on June 25, 1950. "Korea came along and saved us," Secretary of State Dean Acheson later remarked.

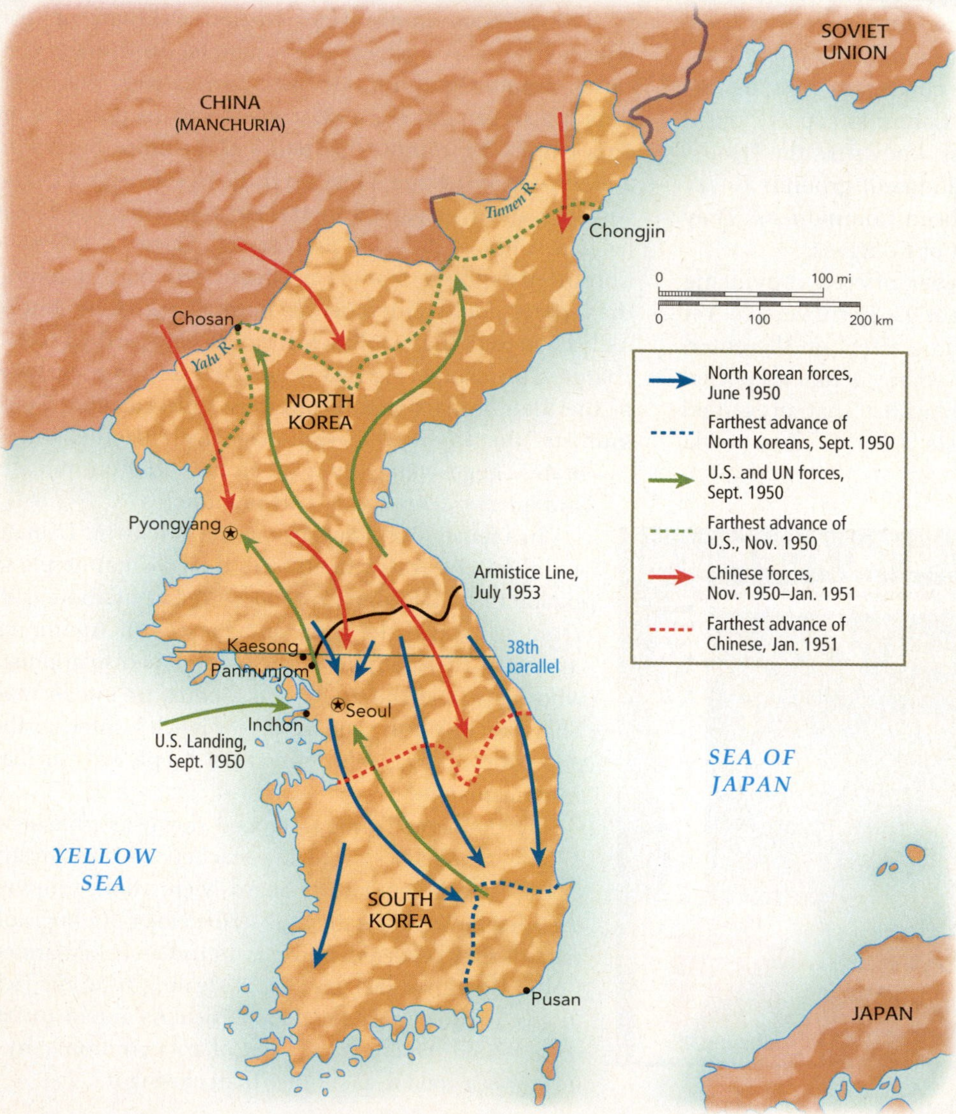

Police Action

>> In 1950 Korea was about the last place Americans imagined themselves fighting a war. Since World War II the country had been divided along the 38th parallel: the north was controlled by the Communist government of Kim Il Sung; the south, by the dictatorship of Syngman Rhee. Preoccupied with China and the rebuilding of Japan, the Truman administration's interest had dwindled steadily after the war. When Secretary of State Acheson discussed American policy in Asia for the National Press Club in January 1950, he did not even mention Korea.

On June 24 Harry Truman was enjoying a leisurely break from politics at the family home in Independence, Missouri. In Korea it was already Sunday morning when Acheson called the president. North Korean troops had crossed the 38th parallel, Acheson reported, possibly to fulfill Kim Il Sung's proclaimed intention to "liberate" South Korea. Soon Acheson confirmed that a full-scale invasion was in progress. The threat of a third world war, this one atomic, seemed agonizingly real. The United States had to respond with enough force to deter aggression, but without provoking a larger war with the Soviet Union or China.

THE KOREAN WAR

MacArthur's landing at Inchon in September 1950 helped UN forces take the offensive. The drive to the Yalu River provoked Communist China to intervene.

Map labels: SOVIET UNION · CHINA (MANCHURIA) · Tumen R. · Chongjin · Chosan · Yalu R. · NORTH KOREA · Pyongyang · Armistice Line, July 1953 · Kaesong · Panmunjom · 38th parallel · Seoul · Inchon · U.S. Landing, Sept. 1950 · YELLOW SEA · SOUTH KOREA · Pusan · SEA OF JAPAN · JAPAN

Map legend:
- North Korean forces, June 1950
- Farthest advance of North Koreans, Sept. 1950
- U.S. and UN forces, Sept. 1950
- Farthest advance of U.S., Nov. 1950
- Chinese forces, Nov. 1950–Jan. 1951
- Farthest advance of Chinese, Jan. 1951

Scale: 0 — 100 mi · 0 — 100 — 200 km

Truman did not hesitate. American troops would fight the North Koreans, though the United States would not declare war. The fighting in Korea would be a "police action" supervised by the United Nations and commanded by General Douglas MacArthur. For his part, Stalin had secretly told Kim that he did not oppose the attack, but warned that neither Russian troops nor prestige would be involved.

Truman's forceful response won immediate approval across America. Congress voted to carry out the recommendations of NSC-68. But by the time the UN authorized the police action, on June 27, North Korean forces had pinned the South Koreans within an area around Pusan (see map, page 582). In a daring counterstroke, General MacArthur launched an amphibious attack behind North Korean lines at Inchon, near the western end of the 38th parallel. Fighting eastward, MacArthur's troops threatened to trap the invaders, who fled back to the North.

⌃ Marines in North Korea wait at a roadblock on December 1, 1950. American forces retreated after the Chinese crossed the Yalu. The harsh weather added to the casualties.

The Chinese Intervene >>

MacArthur's success led Truman to a fateful decision. With the South liberated, he gave MacArthur permission to cross the 38th parallel, drive the Communists from the North, and re-unite Korea under Syngman Rhee. Such a victory was just what Truman needed with Senator Joe McCarthy on the attack at home and the 1950 congressional elections nearing. By Thanksgiving American troops had roundly defeated northern forces and were advancing toward the frozen Yalu River, the boundary between Korea and China. MacArthur, made bold by success, promised that the boys would be home by Christmas.

But on November 26, Chinese leaders made good on previous warnings as 400,000 of their troops poured across the Yalu, smashing through lightly defended UN lines. At Chosan they trapped 20,000 American and South Korean troops, inflicting one of the worst military defeats in American history. Within three weeks they had driven UN forces back behind the 38th parallel.

Truman versus MacArthur >>

Military stalemate in Korea brought into the open a simmering feud between General MacArthur and Truman. The general had

Then&Now

GEARING UP

Soldiers must carry enough equipment to face a variety of dangers and weather, yet not be slowed down or fatigued by too much gear. In Korea the American infantry soldier was armed with a semi-automatic rifle, protected by a "steel pot" helmet, and supplied with leather boots. But GIs still suffered from the cold of the Korean winter. In the Iraq War Americans soldiers used body armor, night-vision goggles, fully automatic weapons with sniper scopes, and synthetic boots—all lightweight and adapted to desert heat, arctic cold, rain, snow, and even dust storms.

The election outcome was never much in doubt. Eisenhower addressed voter unease over Korea by promising that if elected, he would go there to seek an end to the war. In the end Ike's broad smile and confident manner won him over 55 percent of the vote. "The great problem of America today," he had said during the campaign, "is to take that straight road down the middle."

Once in office Eisenhower renewed negotiations with North Korea but warned that unless the talks made speedy progress, the United States might retaliate "under circumstances of our choosing." The carrot-and-stick approach worked. On July 27, 1953, the Communists and the United Nations forces signed an armistice ending a "police action" in which nearly 34,000 Americans had died. Korea remained divided, almost as it had been in 1950. Communism had been "contained," but at a high price in human lives.

The Fall of McCarthy >> It was less clear

whether anticommunism could be contained. When Eisenhower called himself a "modern" Republican, he distinguished himself from what he called the more "hidebound" members of the GOP. Senator McCarthy's reckless antics, which at first had been directed at Democrats, began to hit Republican targets as well.

By the summer of 1953 the senator was on a rampage. He dispatched two young staff members, Roy Cohn and David Schine, to investigate the State Department's overseas information agency and the Voice of America radio stations. While there, they insisted on purging government libraries of "subversive" volumes. Some librarians, fearing for their careers, burned a number of books.

The administration's own behavior contributed to the hysteria on which McCarthy thrived. Eisenhower launched another federal loyalty campaign, which he claimed resulted in 3,000 firings and 5,000 resignations of government employees. Furthermore, a well-publicized spy trial led to the conviction of Ethel and Julius Rosenberg, a couple accused of passing atomic secrets to the Soviets. Although the evidence against Ethel was weak, the judge sentenced both Rosenbergs to the electric chair, an unusually harsh punishment even in cases of espionage. When asked to commute the death sentence to life imprisonment, Eisenhower refused, and the Rosenbergs were executed in June 1953.

In such a climate—where Democrats remained silent for fear of being called leftists and Eisenhower cautiously refused to "get in the gutter with that guy"—McCarthy lost all sense of proportion. When the army denied his staff aide David Schine a special assignment, McCarthy launched an investigation into communism in the army. Under the glare of television lights, the public had an opportunity to see McCarthy badger witnesses and make a mockery of Senate procedures. Soon after, his popularity began to slide and the anti-Communist hysteria ebbed as well. The Senate finally moved to censure him. He died three years later, destroyed by alcohol and the habit of throwing so many reckless punches.

REVIEW
On what major issues did Truman and General MacArthur disagree?

With the Democrats out of the White House for the first time since the Depression and with McCarthyites in retreat, Eisenhower did indeed seem to be leading the nation on a course "right down the middle." Still, it is worth noting how much that sense of "middle" had changed, both in terms of domestic policy and the place of the United States internationally.

Both the Great Depression and World War II made most Americans realize that the nation's economy was closely linked to the international order. The crash in 1929, with its worldwide effects, made that clear. The New Deal demonstrated that Americans were willing to give the federal government power to influence American society in major new ways. And the war led the government to intervene in the economy even more directly.

Thus when peace came in 1945, it became clear that the "middle road" did not mean a return to the laissez-faire economics of the

↗ Energetic Roy Cohn (*left*) served as the key strategist in the anticommunist campaign of Senator Joseph McCarthy (*center*). David Schine (*right*) joined the committee at Cohn's urging.

1920s. Nor would most Americans support the isolationist policies of the 1930s. "Modern" Republicans accepted social welfare programs such as Social Security and recognized that the federal government had the ability to lower unemployment, control inflation, and manage the economy in a variety of ways.

The shift from war to peace demonstrated that it was no longer possible to make global war without making a global peace. Under the new balance of power in the postwar world, the United States and the Soviet Union stood alone as "superpowers," with the potential capability to annihilate each other and the rest of the world. The United States had used its resources to rebuild the economies of Western Europe and Japan. A new global economy had begun to emerge. And the two superpowers tacitly acknowledged each other's spheres of influence: Eastern Europe and China for the Soviet Union; East Asia, Western Europe, and Latin America for the United States and its NATO allies. Much of the world, however, remained unaligned or outside the cold war boundaries. South Asia, the Middle East, Africa, and even Cuba, in America's backyard, would soon become arenas for the continuing cold war rivalry.

CHAPTER SUMMARY

The cold war between the Soviet Union and the United States affected every aspect of American domestic and foreign policy.

- Americans had long been suspicious of Soviet communism, but Stalin's aggressive posture toward Eastern Europe and the Persian Gulf region raised new fears among American policy makers.
- In response the Truman administration applied a policy of containment through the Truman Doctrine, the Marshall Plan, and NSC-68.
- The domestic transition from war to peace was slowed because of inflation, labor unrest, and shortages of goods and housing, but consumer and government spending marked the beginning of a 30-year economic expansion.
- Domestic fear of Communist subversion led the Truman administration to devise a government loyalty program and inspired the witch hunts of Senator Joseph McCarthy.

Significant Events

Civil war in Greece

1945

Truman Doctrine; Taft Hartley Act; federal loyalty oath; HUAC investigates Hollywood; Truman issues *To Secure These Rights*

1946

Kennan's "long telegram"; Republican congressional victories; Atomic Energy Commission created

1947

Marshall Plan adopted; Berlin airlift; Truman upsets Dewey

1948

Soviet atom bomb test; China falls to the Communists; NATO established

1949

- The Soviet detonation of an atomic bomb and the fall of China to the Communists, followed by the Korean War, undermined the popularity of Harry Truman and the Democrats, opening the way for Dwight Eisenhower's victory in the 1952 presidential election.

Additional Reading

A good overview of the cold war is Walter LaFeber, *America, Russia, and the Cold War* (10th ed., 2006). For the science and politics of the H-bomb see Gregg Herken, *Brotherhood of the Bomb: The Tangled Lives and Loyalties of Robert Oppenheimer, Ernest Lawrence, and Edward Teller* (2003), and Kai Bird and Martin Sherwin, *American Prometheus: The Triumph and Tragedy of J. Robert Oppenheimer* (2006). On the domestic cold war see David Halberstam, *The Fifties* (1994), and Stephen Whitfield, *The Culture of the Cold War* (1991). Robert Sklar, *Movie Made America: A Cultural History of American Movies* (rev. ed., 1994), offers insight into how the cold war affected Hollywood.

Brian Burnes, *Harry S Truman: His Life and Times* (2003), is a lively account of a president who became more popular with the passage of time. Elizabeth Edwards Spalding, *The First Cold Warrior: Harry Truman, Containment and the Remaking of Liberal Internationalism* (2006), measures Truman as an architect of the postwar world order. The best account of the man who gave his name to the red scare is David Oshinsky, *A Conspiracy So Immense: The World of Joe McCarthy* (2005). Two historians have shown how cold war politics and the civil rights movement intersected: Thomas Borstelmann, *The Cold War and the Color Line: American Race Relations in the Global Arena* (2003), and Mary Dudziak, *Cold War Civil Rights: Race and the Image of American Democracy* (2002).

Korean War begins; McCarran Act; NSC-68 adopted; Alger Hiss convicted

UN armistice ends police action in Korea; Rosenbergs executed

1950 **1951** **1952** **1953** **1954**

Truman fires MacArthur; peace talks in Korea

Eisenhower defeats Stevenson

Army-McCarthy hearings; McCarthy censured

The Suburban

28

>> **AN AMERICAN STORY**

DYNAMIC OBSOLESCENCE (THE WONDERFUL WORLD OF HARLEY EARL)

The company that epitomized the corporate culture of the 1950s was General Motors. GM executives sought to blend in rather than to stand out. They chose their suits in drab colors—dark blue, dark gray, or light gray—to increase their anonymity. Not head car designer Harley Earl. Earl brought a touch of Hollywood into the world of corporate bureaucrats. He had a closet filled with colorful suits. His staff would marvel as he headed off to a board meeting dressed in white linen with a dark blue shirt and blue suede shoes. >>

Era

1945–1963

Mr. Earl—no one who worked for him ever called him Harley—could afford to be a maverick. He created the cars that brought customers into GM showrooms across the country. Before he came to Detroit, engineering sold cars. Advertising stressed mechanical virtues—the steady ride, reliable brakes, or, perhaps, power steering. Earl made style the distinctive feature. Unlike the boxy look other designs favored, an Earl car was low and sleek, suggesting motion even when the car stood still. No feature stood out more distinctively than the fins he first put on the 1948 Cadillac. By the mid-1950s jet planes inspired Earl to design ever-more-outrageous fins, complemented by huge, shiny chrome grills and ornaments. These features served no functional purpose. Some critics dismissed Earl's designs as jukeboxes on wheels.

Earl and GM did not care. Design sold cars. "It gave [customers] an extra receipt for their money in the form of visible prestige marking for an expensive car," Earl said. The "Big Three" auto manufacturers—General Motors, Ford, and Chrysler—raced one another to redesign their annual models, the more outrageous the better. Earl once joked, "I'd put smokestacks right in the middle of the sons of bitches if I thought I could sell more cars." The goal was not a better car but what Earl called "dynamic obsolescence," or simply change for change's sake. "The 1957 Ford was great," its designer remarked, "but right away we had to bury it and start another." Even though the mechanics of cars changed little from year to year, dynamic obsolescence

^ Like a freak of evolution run riot, automotive tailfins during the 1950s were elongated until they reached the monstrous proportions of the 1959 Cadillac, which also sported bomblike taillights.

persuaded Americans in the 1950s to buy new cars in record numbers.

Fins, roadside motels, "gaseterias," drive-in burger huts, interstate highways, shopping centers, and, of course, suburbs—all these were part of a culture of mobility in the 1950s. Americans continued their exodus from rural areas to cities and from cities to the suburbs. African Americans left the South, heading for industrial centers in the Northeast, in the Midwest, and on the West Coast. Mexican Americans concentrated in southwestern cities, while Puerto Ricans came largely to New York. And for Americans in the Snow Belt, the climate of the West and South (at least when civilized by air conditioning) made the Sun Belt attractive.

The mobility was social, too. As the economy continued to expand, the size of the American middle class grew. Labor unions negotiated wage and benefits packages that moved blue-collar workers into middle-income brackets. In an era of prosperity and peace, some commentators began to speak of a **consensus**—a general

consensus point of view generally shared by a group, institution, or even a culture.

agreement in American culture, based on values of the broad middle class. In a positive light consensus reflected the agreement among most Americans about fundamental democratic values. Most citizens embraced the material benefits of prosperity as evidence of the virtue of "the American way." And they opposed the spread of communism abroad.

But consensus had its dark side. Critics worried that too strong a consensus bred a mindless conformity. Were Americans becoming too homogenized? Was there a depressing sameness in the material goods they owned, in the places they lived, and in the values they held? The baby boomers born into this era seldom agonized over such issues. In the White House President Eisenhower radiated a comforting sense that the affairs of the nation and the world were in capable hands. That left teenagers free to worry about what really mattered: a first date, a first kiss, a first job, a first choice for college, and whether or not to "go all the way" in the back seat of one of Harley Earl's fin-swept Buicks. ≪

THE RISE OF THE SUBURBS

Suburban growth accelerated sharply at the end of World War II. During the 1950s suburbs grew 40 times faster than cities, so that by 1960 half of the American people lived in them. The return of prosperity brought a baby boom and a need for new housing. Automobiles made the suburbs accessible. But the spurt in suburban growth took its toll on the cities, which suffered as the middle class fled urban areas. Many urban businesses and industries joined the exodus as well.

A Boom in Babies and in Housing >> The Great Depression caused many couples to delay beginning a family. In the 1930s birthrates had reached their low point in American history, about 18 to 19 per thousand. As prosperity returned during the war, birthrates began to rise. By 1952 they had passed 25 per thousand to reach one of the highest fertility rates in the world. New brides were also younger, which translated into increased fertility. Americans chose to have larger families, as the number with three children tripled and those with four or more quadrupled. "Just imagine how much these extra people, these new markets, will absorb—in food, in clothing, in gadgets, in housing, in services," one journalist predicted.

Historians and demographers have been hard-pressed to explain this extraordinary population bulge. It was not limited to the United States. In several other industrialized nations fertility rates also soared, Australia, New Zealand, Britain, and West Germany prime among them. Yet the long-term trend in American fertility rates was downward, as it was in other industrialized nations. Fertility rates peaked in Australia and New Zealand in 1961, and three years later, in Great Britain and West Germany. Hence the baby boom stands as an anomaly, one that remains hard to explain.

Whatever factors contributed to the baby boom, it had both immediate and long-term consequences for American society. For one, the boom in marriage and families created a need for housing. At war's end, 5 million families lived in cramped apartments or even dark basements. With the help of the GI Bill and rising incomes, the chance to own a house rather than rent became a reality for over half of American families. And it was the suburbs that offered the kind of residence most Americans idealized: a detached single-family house with a lawn.

In the 1940s inexpensive suburban housing became synonymous with the name of real estate developer William Levitt. From building houses for war workers, Levitt learned how to use mass-production techniques. In 1947 he began construction of a 17,000-house community in the New York City suburb of Hempstead. Buoyed by his success, Levitt later built developments in Bucks County, Pennsylvania, and Willingboro, New Jersey.

The typical early Levitt house was a "Cape Codder." It boasted a living room, a kitchen, a bath, and two bedrooms on the ground floor and an expansion attic, all for $7,990. None of the houses had custom details, insulation, or any features that complicated construction. "The reason we have it so good in this country," Levitt said, "is that we can produce lots of things at low prices through mass production." Uniformity in house

THE UNITED STATES BIRTHRATE, 1900–1990

Despite periods of rapid rise and fall, the nation's birthrate has shown a steady downward trend. The Depression years marked an even sharper decline as financially strapped couples deferred child rearing. Younger marriages and postwar prosperity triggered the baby boom, but in general, affluence encourages lower birthrates.

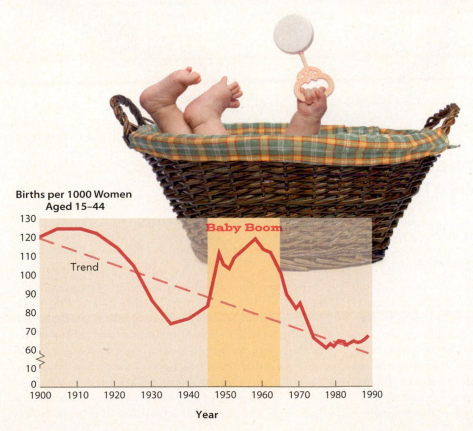

Births per 1000 Women Aged 15–44

style extended to behavior as well. Levitt discouraged owners from changing colors or adding distinctive features to the house or yard. Buyers promised to cut the grass each week of the summer and not to hang out wash on weekends.

Suburbs and Cities Transformed >>

Single-family houses with spacious lawns required plenty of open land, unlike the row houses built side by side in earlier suburban developments. That meant Levitt and other builders chose vacant areas outside major urban centers. With the new houses farther from factories, offices, and jobs, the automobile became more indispensable than ever.

As population shifted to suburbs, traffic choked old country roads. To ease congestion the Eisenhower administration proposed a 20-year plan to build a massive interstate highway system. In rallying support, Eisenhower addressed cold war fears as well, arguing that the new system would help cities evacuate in case of nuclear attack. In 1956 Congress passed the Interstate Highway Act, setting in motion the largest public works project in history. The federal government picked up 90 percent of the cost through a Highway Trust Fund, financed by special taxes on cars, gas, tires, lubricants, and auto parts.

The Interstate Highway Act had an enormous impact on American life. Average annual driving increased by 400 percent. Shopping centers, linked by the new roads, provided suburbanites with an alternative to the longer trip downtown. By 1960 more than 3,840 of them covered as much land as the nation's central business districts. Almost every community had at least one highway strip dotted with stores, bowling alleys, gas stations, and drive-in restaurants.

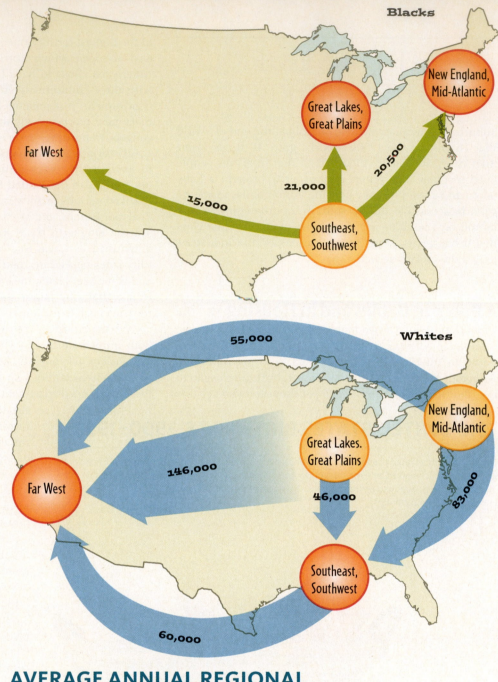

AVERAGE ANNUAL REGIONAL MIGRATION, 1947–1960

In this period African Americans were moving in significant numbers to urban centers in the Northeast, the Midwest, and the Far West. Whites were being drawn to the increasingly diversified economy of the South as well as to the new industries, stimulated by the war, in the Far West. By the 1970s, the trend had become known as the "Sun Belt" phenomenon.

The interstates affected cities in less fortunate ways. The new highway system featured beltways, ring roads around major urban areas. Instead of leading traffic downtown, the beltways allowed motorists to avoid the center city altogether. As people took to their cars, intercity rail service and mass transit declined. Seventy-five percent of all government transportation dollars went to subsidize travel by car and truck; only 1 percent was earmarked for urban mass transit. At the same time that middle-class homeowners were moving to the suburbs, many low-paying, unskilled jobs disappeared from the cities. That forced the urban poor into reverse commuting from city to suburb. All these trends made cities less attractive places to live or do business in. With fewer well-to-do taxpayers to draw on, city governments lacked the tax base to finance public services. A vicious cycle ensued that proved most damaging to the urban poor, who had few means of escape.

Much of the white population that moved to the suburbs was replaced by African Americans and Latinos. They were part of larger migrations, especially of millions of black and Latino families leaving rural areas to search for work in urban centers. Most African Americans headed for the Northeast and Upper Midwest. While central cities lost 3.6 million white residents, they gained 4.5 million African Americans. Indeed, by 1960 half of all black Americans were living in central cities.

Earlier waves of European immigrants had been absorbed by the expanding urban economy. During the 1950s, however, the flight of jobs and middle-class taxpayers to the suburbs made it difficult for African Americans and Latinos to follow the same path. In the cities fewer jobs awaited them, while declining school systems made it harder for newcomers to acculturate. In the hardest-hit urban areas, unemployment rose to over 40 percent.

In contrast, the suburbs remained beyond the reach of most minorities. Those who could afford the suburbs discovered that most real estate agents refused to show them houses; bankers would not provide mortgages. And many communities adopted either restrictive covenants or zoning regulations that kept out "undesirable" home buyers. One African American, William Myers, finally managed in 1957 to buy a house from a white family in Levittown, Pennsylvania, but the developers did not sell directly to African Americans until 1960.

Environmental Blues >> With the spread of suburbs came other growing pains. In late summer of 1956 residents of Portuguese Bend, California, learned a painful lesson about septic systems and hillside development. Houses along Palos Verde Drive South began to move—slowly at first. By October, 156 houses along with their lawns, gardens, and swimming pools had "gently slumped downhill as though they were so much custard pudding." Over time the effluent from septic systems, assisted by lawn watering, slicked the underlying layers of shale that tilted toward the nearby Pacific Ocean. With no friction to hold the soil and shale in place, gravity had done the rest. Suburbs in Washington, Cincinnati, and Pittsburgh suffered similar landslide disasters. Other misfortunes occurred where developers built in wetlands and on floodplains.

The disappearance of open space confronted many suburbanites with yet another threat to their dreams. "No more sweep of green," lamented suburban critic William Whyte, "across the hills are splattered scores of random

subdivisions, each laid out with the same dreary curves. Gone are the streams, brooks, woods, and forests that the subdivisions signs talked about." Gone, too, were habitats for birds, small mammals, fish, and amphibians.

During the suburban boom, homebuilders seldom took the environment into account. Few rural areas had zoning or building codes that restricted where and how much they could build. Less open space meant more houses. To lower land purchase costs, developers leveled hillsides, filled wetlands, and ignored flood dangers. And to lower construction costs they cleared mature trees and vegetation and scrimped on energy efficient insulation. The cost to homeowners and the environment was not at first apparent. Early suburbanites worried more about finding a home of their own at a price they could afford. Years later their desire to preserve a shred of the suburban dream would contribute to the movement to protect the environment.

 REVIEW

What factors pushed the growth of suburbs, and what were the environmental costs of pushing too hard?

THE CULTURE OF SUBURBIA

In suburban tracts across America 1950s suburbanites discovered the California Dip, the brainchild of the Lipton Company. Homemakers simply mixed Lipton's soup powder with sour cream and served it up with chips. As one commentator noted:

> Using potato chips as little shovels, you gathered up the deliciously salty but drip-prone liquid and popped it, potato chip and all, into your mouth as quickly and gracefully as possible. There was anxiety in all this—particularly the fear that a great glop of the stuff would land on your tie or the rug—but also immense satisfaction.

Lipton had discovered an ingenious way to Americanize an ethnic food. Sour cream had been a mainstay in such dishes as blintzes (thin Jewish pancakes) and borscht (an Eastern European beet soup). With an all-American name like "California Dip," sour cream's ethnic associations were left behind. The ingredient went mainstream—into the consensus.

The evolving culture of the suburbs reflected a similar process, a shucking off of ethnic associations. In many city neighborhoods, immigrant parents or grandparents lived on the same block or even in the same apartment with their children. In the suburbs, single-family dwellers often left their relatives and in-laws behind, which meant that ethnic lifestyles were less pronounced. The restrictive immigration policies of the 1920s had also reduced the number of newly arrived foreign-born Americans. Thus suburban culture reflected the tastes of the broad, mostly assimilated middle classes.

Class distinctions were more pronounced between suburban communities than within them. The upper middle class clustered in older developments, which often revolved around country clubs. Working-class suburbs sprouted on the outskirts of large manufacturing centers, where blue-collar families eagerly escaped the city. Within suburbs a more homogeneous suburban culture evolved. "We see eye to eye on most things," commented one Levittown resident, "about raising kids, doing things together with your husband . . . we have practically the same identical background."

American Civil Religion >> If suburban residents retained less of their ethnic heritages, most held on to their religious beliefs. Religion continued to be a distinctive and segregating factor during the 1950s. Catholics, Protestants, and Jews generally married within their own faiths, and in the suburbs they kept their social distance as well.

Communities that showed no obvious class distinctions were sometimes deeply divided along religious lines. Catholics attended parochial rather than public schools, formed their own clubs, and socialized less with their Protestant neighbors. Protestant and Catholic members of the same country club usually did not play golf or tennis in the same foursomes. As for Jews, one historian remarked that whereas a gulf divided many Catholics and Protestants, Jews and Gentiles "seem to have lived on the opposite sides of a religious Grand Canyon."

Although religious affiliation divided the nation along social and residential lines, most Americans agreed that religious commitment was an essential part of their lives. "Our government makes no sense unless it is founded on a deeply religious faith," President Eisenhower declared, "and I don't care what it is." In short, any religion was better than none. Historians have referred to this generalized adherence to faith as American civil religion. Each Friday afternoon the host of TV's "Howdy Doody Show," Buffalo Bob Smith, urged his young viewers to worship "at the church or synagogue of your choice."

Americans took that advice to heart as church membership rose to over 50 percent for the first time in the twentieth century. As of 1957 the Census Bureau reported that 96 percent of the people asked cited a specific affiliation when asked, "What is your religion?" Many leaders saw religion as a weapon in the Cold War. After all, Communists were avowed atheists. Prominent clergy pointed out that the Pledge of Allegiance was so secular that any young Soviet child could recite it. So in 1954 Congress added to the Pledge's "one nation indivisible" the phrase "under God."

Patriotic and anti-Communist themes were strong in the preaching of clergy who pioneered the use of television. Billy Graham, a Baptist revival preacher, first attracted

↑ In *Easter Morning*, Norman Rockwell satirized the contrasting conformities of suburban life. The sheepish father, no doubt forced to wear suits all week, prefers a shocking red bathrobe, a cigarette, and the Sunday paper to the gray flannel lockstep of his church-bound family.

national attention at a tent meeting in Los Angeles in 1949. Following in the tradition of nineteenth-century revivalists like Dwight Moody, Graham soon achieved even wider impact by televising his meetings. Though no revivalist, the Roman Catholic bishop Fulton J. Sheen made the transition from a radio to a television ministry. In his weekly program he extolled traditional values and attacked communism.

"Homemaking" Women in the Workaday World >> The growth of a suburban culture revealed a contradiction in the lives of middle-class women. Never before were their traditional roles as housewives and mothers so central to American society. Yet never before did more women join the workforce outside the home.

For housewives the single-family suburban home required more labor to keep clean. At the same time the baby boom left suburban mothers with more children to tend and less help from relatives and grandparents, who less often lived nearby. Increased dependence on automobiles made many a suburban housewife the chauffeur for her family By the 1950s housewives doing "errands" replaced milkmen and grocers making deliveries.

Yet between 1940 and 1960 the percentage of wives working outside the home doubled, from 15 to 30 percent. While some women took jobs simply to help make ends meet, more than financial necessity was involved.

>> To housewife and mother many suburban women of the 1950s added the role of chauffeur. Husbands who once walked to work and children who walked to school now needed to be delivered and picked up. The average suburban woman spent one full working day each week driving and doing errands.

Middle-class married women went to work as often as lower-class wives, and women with college degrees were the most likely to get a job. Two-income families were able to spend far more on extras: gifts, education, recreation, and household appliances. In addition, women found status and self-fulfillment in their jobs, as well as a chance for increased social contacts.

More women were going to college, too, but that increased education did not translate into economic equality. The median wage for women was less than half that for men—a greater gap than in any other industrial nation. The percentage of women holding professional jobs actually dropped between 1950 and 1960.

The Flickering Gray Screen >> The new medium of television fit perfectly into suburban lifestyles. It provided an ideal way to entertain families at home as well as sell them consumer goods.

The entrance of television into the American mainstream came only after World War II. In 1949 Americans owned only a million televisions; by 1960 more Americans, some 46 million, had televisions than had bathrooms. Attendance began dropping at movie theaters and sports arenas. As downtown theaters closed, popular suburban drive-ins allowed whole families to enjoy movies in the comfort of their cars. But even that novelty failed to draw viewers away from their televisions.

In 1948 politics moved into the television age, as the networks covered both the Democratic and Republican conventions. Two years later, they televised hearings on organized crime chaired by Senator Estes Kefauver. Some thirty million viewers watched senators grill mobster Frank Costello about his criminal organization and its ties to city governments. Millions more watched Senator Joseph McCarthy's ill-fated attack on the army in 1954. With such a large audience, television clearly had the potential to shape the nation's politics. But the networks did not want controversy to drive away advertisers. By the mid-1950s hostile reaction to coverage of McCarthy led them to downgrade public affairs programs. They relied instead on telefilm dramas, quiz shows, sports, and situation comedies.

 REVIEW

How did religion, the role of women, and television each help to define suburban culture?

THE POLITICS OF CALM

In presiding over these changes in American society, President Dwight David Eisenhower projected an aura of paternal calm. Pursuing "modern Republicanism," the new president sought consensus, not confrontation. No longer would conservatives like Robert Taft call for a repeal of the New Deal and a return to laissez-faire capitalism. Eisenhower declared that he was "conservative when it comes to money and liberal when it comes to human beings."

The Eisenhower Presidency >> Eisenhower had been raised in a large Kansas farm family. His parents, though poor, offered him a warm, caring home steeped in religious faith. In an era of organizational men, Eisenhower succeeded by mastering the military's bureaucratic politics. In the placid years between the two world wars, the skills "Ike" demonstrated at golf, poker, and bridge often proved as valuable as his military expertise. Yet these genial ways could not hide his ambition or his ability to judge character shrewdly. It took a gifted organizer to coordinate the D-Day invasion and to hold together the egocentric Allied generals who pushed east to Berlin.

As president, Eisenhower supported key New Deal programs. He even agreed to increases in Social Security, unemployment insurance, and the minimum wage. He accepted a small public housing program and a modest federally supported medical insurance plan for the needy. But as a conservative, Eisenhower remained uncomfortable with big government. Thus he rejected more far-reaching liberal proposals on housing and universal health care through the Social Security system.

Eisenhower was more reluctant to imitate New Deal efforts to stimulate the economy. FDR and Truman had established a tradition of activism: when the economy faltered, they used deficit spending and tax cuts to stimulate it. Eisenhower preferred to reduce federal spending and

Point of View

Television and Abundance

"Things. Things to look at. New things. The latest things. High style. The glass door lets [Lucille Ball of *I Love Lucy*] peep into her oven: she loves it because it lets her see inside. And seeing is absolutely central to the meaning of the 1950s. The only thing wrong with movies was that they weren't TV, offering a free look at the contents of other peoples' lives, and houses, on demand."

KARAL ANN MARLING *As Seen on TV: The Visual Culture of Everyday Life in the 1950s*

the government's role in the economy. When a recession struck in 1953–1954, the administration was concerned more with balancing the budget and holding inflation in line than with reducing unemployment through government spending.

Eisenhower was pragmatic in other areas. When major projects called for federal leadership, as with the Highway Act, he supported them. In 1954 he signed the St. Lawrence Seaway Act, which joined the United States and Canada in an ambitious engineering project to open the Great Lakes to ocean shipping. Like the highway program, the seaway

was fiscally acceptable because the funding came from user tolls and taxes rather than from general revenues.

A pragmatic approach to farm policy proved more difficult. Farmers made up a major Republican voting bloc. The popularity of crop subsidies and modern technology among farmers made it difficult to regulate agricultural production. Even when farmers cut back acreage, they discovered that automated harvesters, fertilizers, and new varieties of plants actually increased farm output. In an age of continuing centralization, more and more small farms were being replaced by agribusinesses. As economic power concentrated in these large commercial farming operations, so did their political muscle to protect farm subsidies.

Despite occasional setbacks Eisenhower remained popular. Although he suffered a major heart attack in 1955, voters gladly reelected him in 1956. But poor economic performance took its toll. In the wake of the 1954 recession Congressional Democrats gained a 29-member majority in the House and a 1-vote edge in the Senate. Never again would Eisenhower work with a Republican majority. In 1958, when recession again dragged down the economy, the mid-term elections gave Democrats an even more commanding advantage. Modern Republicanism did not put down deep roots beyond Eisenhower's White House.

The Conglomerate World >> Corporate America welcomed the administration's probusiness attitudes as well as the era's general prosperity. Wages for the average worker rose over 35 percent between 1950 and 1960. Business and labor leaders negotiated generous wage and benefits packages that minimized the strikes of earlier eras. At the same time, the economic distress of the 1930s had led corporate executives to devise new ways to minimize the danger of economic downturns. In various ways, each of the approaches sought to minimize shocks in specific markets by expanding the size of corporations.

One expansion strategy took the form of diversification. In the 1930s industrial giant General Electric had concentrated largely in one area: equipment for generating electric power and light. When the Depression struck, GE found its markets evaporating. The company responded by entering markets for appliances, X-ray machines, and elevators—all products developed or enhanced by the company's research labs. In the postwar era General Electric

<< Eisenhower was a popular president, but his health created widespread public concern. He suffered a mild heart attack in September 1955, and timely surgery on a bowel obstruction the following June saved his life. Despite his age and ill health, the president was easily reelected in 1956. Here he recuperates after the 1955 heart attack, at an army hospital in Denver.

diversified even further, into nuclear power, jet engines, financial services, and television. Diversification was most practical for large industrial firms, whose size allowed them to support extensive research and development.

Conglomeration often turned small companies into giants. Unlike earlier horizontal and vertical combinations, **conglomerate** mergers could join companies with seemingly unrelated products. Over a 20-year period International Telephone and Telegraph branched out from its basic communications business into banking, hotels and motels, car rental, home building, and insurance. Corporations also became multinational by expanding their overseas operations or buying out potential foreign competitors. Large integrated oil companies such as Mobil and Standard Oil of New Jersey developed huge oil fields in the Middle East and markets around the free world.

> **conglomerate** corporation whose various branches or subsidiaries are either directly or indirectly spread among a variety of industries, usually unrelated to one another.

One aid to managing these modern corporate giants was the advent of electronic data processing. In the early 1950s computers were virtually unknown in private industry. But banks and insurance companies saw the new mainframe computers of International Business Machines (IBM) as an answer to their need to manipulate huge quantities of records and statistical data. Manufacturers, especially in the petroleum, chemical, automotive, and electronics industries, began to use computers to monitor their production lines, quality control, and inventory.

 REVIEW

In what ways did President Eisenhower show his pragmatic approach to governing?

CRACKS IN THE CONSENSUS

In the 1950s many corporations advertised a cultural consensus just as much as the products they sold. They praised prosperity as a reflection of an American way of life. "What was good for the country, was good for General Motors," GM's president assured the nation. Not all Americans were persuaded of the virtues of consensus and business leadership. Intellectuals and artists found in corporate culture a stifling conformity that crushed individual creativity. On the fringes of society, the Beats scorned traditional behavior and values. Closer to the mainstream, a new generation of musicians created rock and roll, which became the sound of youthful rebellion.

Critics of Mass Culture >> In Levittown, New Jersey, a woman who had invited her neighbors to a

cocktail party eagerly awaited them dressed in newly fashionable Capri pants—a tight-fitting calf-length style. Alas, one early-arriving couple glimpsed the woman through a window. What on earth was the hostess wearing? Pajamas? Who in their right mind would entertain in pajamas? The couple sneaked home, afraid they had made a mistake about the day of the party. They telephoned another neighbor, who anxiously called yet others on the guest list. The neighbors finally mustered enough courage to attend the party. But when the hostess later learned of their misunderstanding, she put her Capri pants in the closet for good. Levittown was not ready for such a change in fashion.

Was America turning into a vast suburban wasteland, where the neighbors' worries over Capri pants would stifle all individuality? Many highbrow intellectuals derided the homogenized lifestyle created by mass consumption, conformity, and **mass media.** Critics such as Dwight Macdonald sarcastically attacked the culture of the suburban middle classes: Reader's Digest Condensed Books and uplifting film spectacles such as *The Ten Commandments.* "Midcult," Macdonald called it, which was his shorthand for uninspired middlebrow culture.

> **mass media** forms of communication designed to reach a vast audience, generally a nation state or larger, without personal contact between the senders and receivers.

Other critics charged that the skyscrapers and factories of giant conglomerates housed an impersonal world. In large, increasingly automated work-places, skilled laborers seemed little more than caretakers of machines. Large corporations required middle-level executives to submerge their personal goals in the processes and work routines of a large bureaucracy. David Riesman, a sociologist, condemned stifling conformity in *The Lonely Crowd* (1950). In nineteenth-century America, Riesman argued, Americans had been "inner directed." It was their own consciences that formed their values and drove them to seek success. In contrast, modern workers had developed a personality shaped not so much by inner convictions as by the opinions of their peers. The new "other-directed" society of suburbia preferred security to success. "Go along to get along" was its motto.

William Whyte carried Riesman's critique from the workplace to the suburb in *The Organization Man* (1956). Here he found rootless families, shifted from town to town by the demands of corporations. (IBM, went one standard joke, stood for "I've Been Moved.") The typical "organization man" was sociable but not terribly ambitious. He sought primarily to "keep up with the Joneses" and the number of consumer goods they owned. He lived in a suburban "split-level trap," as one critic put it, one among millions of "haggard" men, "tense and anxious" women, and "the gimme kids."

No doubt such portraits were overdrawn and overly alarmist. Many suburbanites put up with the constraints of conformity because they preferred the convenience of mass production goods. But the critics were on to something. Behind the impersonal façade of bureaucratic organizations and suburban tract houses, millions of Americans experienced a growing sense of discontent.

Juvenile Delinquency, Rock and Roll, and Rebellion >>

Young Americans were among suburbia's sharpest critics. Dance crazes, outlandish clothing, slang, rebelliousness, and sexual precociousness—all these behaviors challenged middle-class respectability. More than a few educators warned that America had spawned a generation of rebellious "juvenile delinquents." Psychologist Frederic Wertham told a group of doctors, "You cannot understand present-day juvenile delinquency if you do not take into account the pathogenic and pathoplastic [infectious] influence of comic books." Others laid the blame on films and the lyrics of popular music.

The center of the new teen culture was the high school. Whether in consolidated rural school districts, new suburban schools, or city systems, the large, comprehensive high schools of the 1950s were often miniature melting pots where middle-class students were exposed to, and often adopted, the style of the lower classes. They wore jeans and T-shirts, challenged authority, and defiantly smoked cigarettes, much like the motorcycle gang leader portrayed by Marlon Brando in the film *The Wild One* (1954).

In many ways the debate over juvenile delinquency was an argument about social class and, to a lesser degree, race. When adults complained that "delinquent" teenagers dressed poorly, lacked ambition, were irresponsible and sexually promiscuous, these were the same arguments traditionally used to denigrate other outsiders—immigrants, the poor, and African Americans. Nowhere were these racial and class undertones more evident than in the hue and cry that greeted the arrival of rock and roll.

Before 1954 popular music had been divided into three major categories: pop, country and western, and rhythm and blues. A handful of major record companies with almost exclusively white singers dominated the pop charts. On one fringe of the popular field was country and western, often split into cowboy musicians such as Roy Rogers and Gene Autry and the hillbilly style associated with Nashville. The music industry generally treated rhythm and blues as "race music," whose performers and audience were largely black. Each of these musical traditions, it is worth noting, grew out of regional cultures. As the West and the South merged into the national culture, so these musical subcultures were gradually integrated into the national mainstream.

By the mid-1950s the distinctiveness of the three styles began to blur. Singers on the white pop charts recorded a few songs from country and from rhythm and blues. The popularity of crossovers such as "Sh boom," "Tutti Frutti," and "Earth Angel" indicated that a major shift in taste and market was under way. Lyrics still reflected the pop field's preoccupation with young love, marriage, and happiness, but the music now vibrated with the rawer, earthier style of rhythm and blues. Country and western singer Bill Haley brought the new blend to the fore in 1954 with "Shake, Rattle, and Roll," the first rock song to reach the top ten on the pop charts.

And then—calamity! Millions of middle-class roofs nearly blew off with the appearance in 1955 of the rhythmic and raucous Elvis Presley. By background Elvis was a country boy whose musical style combined elements of gospel, country, and blues. But it was his hip-swinging, pelvis-plunging performances that electrified teenage audiences. To more conservative adults Presley's long hair, sideburns, and tight jeans seemed menacingly delinquent, an expression of hostile rebellion. What they often resented but rarely admitted was

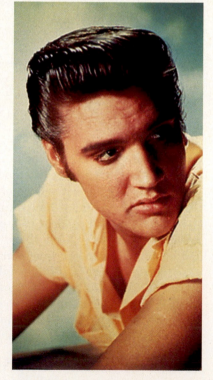

⌃ The King, Elvis Presley

⌃ James Dean in *Rebel without a Cause*. Dean was just 24 when he died in a car crash in 1955, but he remained a symbol of youthful discontent.

that Elvis looked lower class, sounded black, and really could sing.

Beyond the frenetic rhythms of rock and roll, and even farther beyond the pale of suburban culture, a subculture flourished known as the beat generation. In run-down urban neighborhoods and college towns this motley collection of artists, intellectuals, musicians, and middle-class students dropped out of mainstream society. In dress and behavior the "beats" self-consciously rejected what they viewed as the excessive spiritual bankruptcy of America's middle-class culture. They were nonconformists in a conformist world. Cool urban "hipsters"—especially black jazz musicians such as John Coltrane and Sonny Rollins—were their models. They read poetry, listened to jazz, explored Oriental philosophy, and experimented openly with drugs, mystical religions, and sex.

✔ **REVIEW**

Why did social critics worry about conformity in the 1950s?

NATIONALISM IN AN AGE OF SUPERPOWERS

One source of the Beats' dismay with modern society was the dark shadow of the atom bomb. Along the Iron Curtain of Eastern Europe and across the battle lines of northern Asia, the Soviet-American cold war settled into an uneasy stalemate. But World War II had also disrupted Europe's colonial relationships. As nationalists in the Middle East, Africa, and Southeast Asia fought to gain independence, the two superpowers competed for their allegiance. Across the globe the Eisenhower administration sought ways to prevent the Soviet Union from capturing national independence movements. To do so, it sometimes used the threat of nuclear war to block Communist expansion in Europe or Asia.

To the Brink? >> Eisenhower, no stranger to world politics, shared the conduct of foreign policy with

Opinion

Why did rock and roll arouse so much controversy?

his secretary of state, John Foster Dulles. Coming from a family of missionaries and diplomats, Dulles had within him a touch of both. He viewed the Soviet-American struggle in almost religious terms, as a fight between good and evil. Eisenhower was less hostile toward the Soviets. In the end, the two men's differing temperaments led to a policy that seesawed from confrontation to conciliation.

The Republican Party was divided over issues of national security. As a centrist Eisenhower sought to compromise between those who favored a more aggressive policy to defeat Communism and those who worried that big defense meant big government. Dulles wanted the United States to aid in liberating the "captive peoples" of Eastern Europe and other Communist nations. However, Eisenhower was equally determined to cut back military spending and troop levels in order to keep the budget balanced. The president was sometimes irked at the "fantastic programs" the Pentagon kept proposing. "If we demand too much in taxes in order to build planes and ships," he argued, "we will tend to dry up the accumulations of capital that are necessary to provide jobs for the million or more new workers that we must absorb each year."

Rather than rely on costly conventional forces, Eisenhower and Dulles used the threat of massive nuclear retaliation to intimidate the Soviets into behaving less aggressively. Dulles insisted that Americans not shrink from the threat of nuclear war: "If you are scared to go to the brink, you are lost." And as Secretary of Treasury George Humphrey put it, a nuclear strategy was much cheaper—"a bigger bang for the buck." Henceforth American foreign policy would have a "new look," though behind the more militant rhetoric lay an ongoing commitment to containment.

Brinkmanship in Asia >> Moving beyond talk of **brinkmanship** to concrete action did not prove easy. When Dulles announced American intentions to "unleash" Chiang Kai-shek to attack mainland China from his outpost on Taiwan (formerly Formosa), China threatened to invade Taiwan. At that, Eisenhower ordered the Seventh Fleet into the area to protect rather than unleash Chiang. If the Communists attacked, Dulles warned bluntly, "we'll have to use atomic weapons."

brinkmanship policy of using the threat of nuclear war in order to persuade an opponent to back down.

Nuclear weapons also figured in the American response to a crisis in Indochina. There, Vietnamese forces led by Ho Chi Minh were fighting the French, who had reestablished their colonial rule at the end of World War II. Between 1950 and 1954, the United States provided France with over $1 billion in military aid in Vietnam. Eisenhower worried that if Vietnam fell to a Communist revolutionary such as Ho, other nations

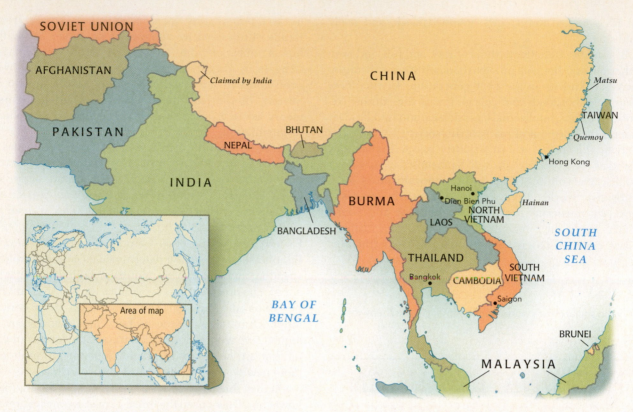

ASIAN TROUBLE SPOTS

After the Geneva Accords divided Indochina into North and South Vietnam, Secretary of State Dulles organized the Southeast Asia Treaty Organization (SEATO) to resist Communist aggression in Southeast Asia. In addition to the conflict in Vietnam, tensions were fueled by the mutual hostility between mainland Communist China and Chiang Kai-shek's Taiwan, as well as the offshore islands Quemoy and Matsu.

of Southeast Asia would follow. "You have a row of dominoes set up," the president warned; "you knock over the first one [y]ou could have the beginning of a disintegration that would have the most profound influences."

Worn down by a war they seemed unable to win, the French in 1954 tried to force a final showdown with Ho Chi Minh's army at Dien Bien Phu. (For a map of Vietnam, see page 634.) Finding themselves besieged and near defeat, the French pleaded for more American aid. Admiral Arthur Radford, head of the Joint Chiefs of Staff, proposed a massive American air raid, perhaps even using tactical nuclear weapons. But again Eisenhower pulled back. The idea of American involvement in another Asian war aroused opposition from both allies and domestic political leaders.

In May 1954 the garrison at Dien Bien Phu collapsed under the seige. At an international peace conference in Geneva, Switzerland, the French negotiated the terms of their withdrawal. Ho Chi Minh agreed to pull his forces north of the 17th parallel, temporarily dividing the nation into North and South Vietnam. Because of Ho's broad popularity, he seemed assured an easy victory in elections scheduled for within the next two years. Dulles, however, viewed any Communist victory as unacceptable, even if the election was democratic. He convinced Eisenhower

to support a South Vietnamese government under Ngo Dinh Diem. Dulles insisted that Diem was not bound by the Geneva Accords to hold any election—a position the autocratic Diem eagerly supported. To help keep him in power, the United States sent a military mission to train South Vietnam's army. The commitment was small, but a decade later it would return to haunt Americans.

The Superpowers >> Korea, Taiwan, Indochina—to Dulles and Eisenhower, the crises in Asia and elsewhere could all be traced back to the Soviet dictatorship. But in March 1953 Soviet dictator Joseph Stalin died. Power soon fell to Nikita Khrushchev, a party stalwart with a formidable intellect and peasant origins in the farm country of Ukraine. In some ways Khrushchev resembled another farm-belt politician, Harry Truman. Both were unsophisticated yet shrewd, earthy in their sense of humor, energetic, short-tempered, and largely inexperienced in international affairs. Khrushchev kept American diplomats off balance. At times genial and conciliatory, he would suddenly become demanding and boastful.

Khrushchev moderated some of the excesses of the Stalin years. At home, he gradually shifted the Soviet economy toward production of consumer goods. Internationally, he called for an easing of tensions and reduced forces in Europe, hoping to make Western Europeans less dependent on the United States. In Washington the administration was unsure of how to receive the new overtures. Conservatives kept the spirit of McCarthyism alive, so that compromise with the Soviets risked provoking their wrath. It was actually Winston Churchill who suggested that the Russians might be serious about negotiating. In 1955 the Americans, British, French, and Soviets met in a conference at Geneva, Switzerland. Although little came of the summit other than a cordial "spirit of Geneva," the meeting hinted that a cooling in the arms race was possible.

Nationalism Unleashed >> The spirit of Geneva did not long survive new nationalist upheavals. Khrushchev's moderation encouraged nationalists in Soviet-controlled Eastern Europe to push for greater independence. Riots erupted in Poland, while in Hungary students took to the streets demanding that a coalition government replace the puppet regime established by Stalin. At first Moscow accepted the new Hungarian government and began to remove Soviet tanks. But when Hungary announced it was withdrawing from the Warsaw Pact, the tanks rolled back into Budapest to crush the uprising in October 1956. The United States protested but did nothing to help liberate the "captive nations." For all its tough talk, the "new look" foreign policy recognized that the Soviets possessed a sphere of influence where the United States would not intervene.

Nationalist movements also flourished in the Middle East. When a nationalist government in Iran seemed to lean toward the Soviets, Eisenhower approved a covert CIA operation in 1953 to oust the government and restore a firm ally, Shah Mohammad Reza Pahlavi. Eisenhower and Dulles also worried about the actions of Egyptian leader Gamal Abdel Nasser. Dulles had promised American aid to help Nasser build the Aswan Dam, a massive power project on the Nile River. But when Nasser formed an Arab alliance against the young state of Israel and pursued economic ties with the Warsaw bloc, Dulles withdrew the American offer of aid. In 1956 Nasser angrily countered by seizing the British-owned Universal Suez Canal Company. The company ran the waterway through which tankers carried most of Europe's oil.

Events then moved quickly. Israel, alarmed at Nasser's Arab alliance, invaded the Sinai peninsula of Egypt on October 29—the same day Hungary announced it was leaving the Warsaw Pact. Three days later French and British forces seized the canal in an attempt to restore their own interests and prestige. Angered that his allies had not consulted him, Eisenhower joined the Soviet Union in supporting a United Nations resolution condemning Britain, France, and Israel and demanding an immediate cease-fire. By December American pressures forced Britain and France to remove their forces. Few events placed as much strain on the Western alliance as the Suez crisis. At the same time, Nasser had demonstrated the potential force of Third World nationalism.

Given the unstable situation in the Middle East, Eisenhower convinced Congress to give him the authority to use force against any Communist attack in that region. What became known as the Eisenhower Doctrine allowed the president in times of crisis to preempt Congress's power to declare war. Anti-Communism had led many conservatives to overcome their fear of a powerful presidency. In 1958 Eisenhower used his authority to send U.S. marines into Lebanon, a small nation that claimed to have been infiltrated by Nasser's supporters. Since no fighting had yet occurred, sunbathers on the beaches of Beirut, Lebanon's capital, were startled as 5,000 combat-clad marines stormed ashore. In the end, the crisis blew over, and the American forces withdrew. Dulles claimed that the United States had once again turned back the Communist drive into the emerging nations. In reality, nationalism more than communism had been at the root of Middle Eastern turmoil.

Nationalist forces were also in ferment in Latin America, where only 2 percent of the people controlled 75 percent of the land. Repressive dictatorships exercised power, and foreign interests—especially American ones—dominated Latin American economies. In 1954 Eisenhower authorized the CIA to send a band of Latin American mercenaries into Guatemala to overthrow a nationalist government there. Similar economic tensions beset Cuba, where the United States owned 80 percent of the country's utilities and operated a major naval base at Guantánamo Bay. A disgruntled middle-class lawyer, Fidel Castro, gained the support of impoverished peasants in Cuba's mountains and, in January 1959, drove the deeply corrupt and pro-American dictator from power.

⌃ Fidel Castro was initially welcomed when he arrived in Washington, D.C., shortly after taking power in Cuba in 1959.

At first many Americans applauded the revolution, welcoming Castro when he visited the United States. But Eisenhower was distinctly cool to the cigar-smoking Cuban, who had filled key government positions with Communists, launched a sweeping agricultural reform, and confiscated American properties. Retaliating, Eisenhower embargoed Cuban sugar and mobilized opposition to Castro in other Latin American countries. Cut off from American markets and aid, Castro turned to the Soviet Union.

The Response to Sputnik ≫ Castro's turn
to the Soviets seemed all the more dangerous because of Soviet achievements in their missile program. In 1957 they stunned America by orbiting the first space satellite, dubbed *Sputnik*. By 1959 the Soviets had crash-landed a much larger payload on the moon. If the Russians could target the moon, surely they could launch nuclear missiles against America. In contrast, the American space program suffered so many delays and mishaps that rockets exploding on launch were nicknamed "flopniks" and "kaputniks."

How had the Soviets managed to catch up with American technology so quickly? Some Americans blamed the schools, especially weak programs in science and math. In 1958 Eisenhower joined with Congress to enact a National Defense Education Act, designed to strengthen graduate education and the teaching of science, math, and foreign languages. At the same time, crash programs to build basement fallout shelters sought to protect Americans in case of a nuclear attack. Democrats charged that the administration had allowed the United States to face an unacceptable "missile gap."

Thaws and Freezes ≫ Throughout this series of crises, each superpower found it difficult to interpret the other's motives. The Russians exploited nationalist revolutions where they could—less successfully in Egypt, more so in Cuba. "We will bury you," Khrushchev admonished Americans, though it was unclear whether he meant through peaceful competition or military confrontation. More menacingly, in November 1958 he demanded that the Western powers withdraw all troops from West Berlin within six months. Berlin would then become a "free city," and the Western powers could negotiate further access to it only with East Germany, a government the West had refused to recognize. When Eisenhower flatly rejected the ultimatum, Khrushchev backed away from his hard-line stance.

Rather than adopt a more belligerent course, Eisenhower determined to use the last 18 months of his presidency to improve Soviet-American relations. The shift in policy was made easier because Eisenhower knew from American intelligence (but could not admit publicly) that the "missile gap" was not real. While willing to spend more on missile development, he refused to heed the calls for a crash defense program at any cost. Instead, he took a more conciliatory approach by inviting Khrushchev to visit the United States in September 1959. Though the meetings produced no significant results, they eased tensions.

In May Eisenhower's plans for a return visit to the Soviet Union were abruptly canceled. Only weeks earlier the Russians had shot down a high-altitude U-2 American spy plane over Soviet territory. At first Eisenhower claimed the plane had strayed off course during weather research, but Khrushchev sprang his trap: the CIA pilot, Gary Powers, had been captured alive. The president then admitted that he had personally authorized the U-2 overflights for reasons of national security.

⌄ Even before the launch of *Sputnik* in 1957, Americans had begun devising fallout shelters for protection from the effects of a nuclear attack. This one was exhibited in 1955.

Growing Up in the Shadow of the Bomb

"And so whenever the civil defense sirens interrupted my school days with their apocalyptic howls, I folded my papers neatly and filed into the hallway and squatted in front of the lockers with my head between my knees and my hands on the back of my neck, like everyone else . . . Properly prepared, we were told, [we] could expect a 97 percent chance of survival—a figure universally recognized as a lie."

— Lawrence Wright,
In the New World (1987)

That episode ended Eisenhower's hopes that his personal diplomacy might create a true thaw in the cold war. Yet a less mature president might have led the United States into more severe conflict or even war. Eisenhower was not readily impressed by the promises of new weapons systems. He left office with a warning that too much military spending would lead to "an unwarranted influence, whether sought or unsought" by the **military-industrial complex** at the expense of democratic institutions.

> **military-industrial complex** combination of the U.S. armed forces, arms manufacturers, and associated political and commercial interests, which grew rapidly during the cold war era.

 REVIEW

How did President Eisenhower's "New Look" foreign policy affect American actions in Asia, the Middle East, and Latin America?

THE COLD WAR ON A NEW FRONTIER

The 1960 election promised to bring the winds of change to Washington. The opponents—Vice President Richard Nixon and Senator John F. Kennedy of Massachusetts—were the first major presidential candidates born in the twentieth century. At age 43 John Fitzgerald Kennedy would be the youngest person ever elected to the office. Nixon was just four years older. The nation needed to find "new frontiers," Kennedy proclaimed. His rhetoric was noble, but the direction in which he would take the nation was far from clear.

The Election of 1960 >>

The biggest issue of the campaign was social as much as political. Jack Kennedy was a Roman Catholic out of Irish Boston, and no Catholic had ever been elected president. Conservative Protestants, many concentrated in the heavily Democratic South, were convinced that a Catholic president would never be "free to exercise his own judgment" if the pope ordered otherwise. Kennedy confronted the issue head-on, addressing an association of hostile ministers in Houston. "I believe in an America where the separation of church and state is absolute," he said, "—where no Catholic prelate would tell the President (should he be Catholic) how to act, and no Protestant minister would tell his parishioners how to vote." House Speaker Sam Rayburn, an old Texas pol, was astonished by Kennedy's bravura performance. "My God! . . . He's eating them blood raw."

Vice President Nixon ran on his political experience and reputation as a staunch anti-Communist. His

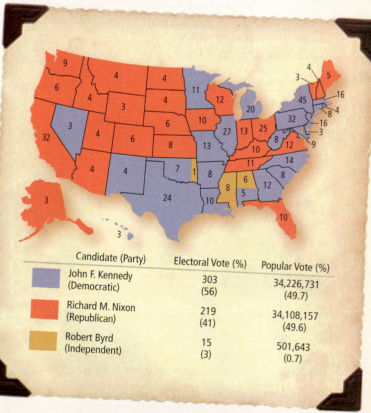

Candidate (Party)	Electoral Vote (%)	Popular Vote (%)
John F. Kennedy (Democratic)	303 (56)	34,226,731 (49.7)
Richard M. Nixon (Republican)	219 (41)	34,108,157 (49.6)
Robert Byrd (Independent)	15 (3)	501,643 (0.7)

ELECTION OF 1960

campaign faltered in October as unemployment rose. Nixon was also hurt by a series of televised debates with Kennedy—the first broadcast nationally. Despite his debating skill, Nixon was overtired, and his Lazy Shave makeup failed to hide his five-o'clock shadow. Election Day saw the largest turnout in 50 years: 64 percent of all voters. Out of 68.3 million ballots cast, Kennedy won by a margin of just 118,000. The whisker-thin victory was made possible by strong Catholic support in key states. "Hyphenated" Americans—Hispanic, Jewish, Irish, Italian, Polish, and German—voted Democratic in record numbers, while much of the black vote that had gone to Eisenhower in 1956 returned to the Democratic fold.

The Hard-Nosed Idealists of Camelot »

Many observers compared the Kennedy White House to Camelot, King Arthur's magical court. A popular musical of 1960 pictured Camelot as a land where skies were fair, men brave, women pretty, and the days full of challenge. With similar vigor, Kennedy surrounded himself with bright, energetic advisers. Touch football games on the White House lawn displayed a rough-and-tumble playfulness, akin to Arthur's jousting tournaments of old.

In truth, Kennedy was not a liberal by temperament. Handsome and intelligent, he possessed an ironic, self-deprecating humor. Yet in Congress, he had led an undistinguished career, supported Senator Joe McCarthy, and earned a reputation as a playboy. He joined a faction of Democrats who wanted to overcome the Republican advantage on national security issues. To woo the liberals Kennedy surrounded himself with a distinguished group of intellectuals and academics.

Robert Strange McNamara typified the pragmatic, liberal, but anti-Communist bent of the new Kennedy team. Steely and brilliant, McNamara was one of the postwar breed of young executives known as the "whiz kids." As a Harvard Business School professor and later as president of Ford Motors, he specialized in using new quantitative tools to streamline business. As the new secretary of defense, McNamara intended to find more flexible and efficient ways of conducting the cold war.

Kennedy liked men like this—witty, bright, intellectual—because they seemed comfortable with power and were not afraid to use it. If Khrushchev spoke of waging guerrilla "wars of liberation," Americans could play that game, too. The president's leisure reading reflected a similar adventurous taste: the popular James Bond spy novels. Agent 007, with his license to kill, was sophisticated, a cool womanizer (as even Kennedy continued to be), and ready to use the latest technology to deal with Communist villains. Ironically, Bond demonstrated that there could be plenty of glamour in being "hard-nosed" and pragmatic. That illicit pleasure was the underside, perhaps, of Camelot's high ideals.

The (Somewhat) New Frontier at Home »

It proved more difficult to take bold initiatives at home than abroad. Kennedy and his advisers had no broad vision for reform. They preferred to tackle problems one by one. In making domestic policy Kennedy found himself hemmed in by a Democratic Congress dominated by conservatives. As a result the president's legislative achievements were modest. He passed a bill providing some financial aid to depressed industrial and rural areas. But on key issues, including civil rights, aid to education, and medical health insurance, Kennedy made no headway.

He wavered, too, on how to manage the economy. The president's liberal advisers favored increased government spending to reduce unemployment, even if that meant a budget deficit. Even so, Kennedy believed that prosperity for big business spelled growth for the whole nation. Thus the president asked Congress to ease antitrust restrictions and grant investment credits and tax breaks—actions that pleased corporate interests. But he was convinced that the

⌃ The urbane John F. Kennedy was associated with both King Arthur (*left*, played by Richard Burton in the 1960 musical) and the spy James Bond (played by Sean Connery, *right*). Kennedy and his advisers prided themselves on their pragmatic, hard-nosed idealism. But while Bond used advanced technology and covert operations to save the world, in real life such approaches had their downside, as the growing civil war in Vietnam would demonstrate.

government needed to limit the power of both large corporations and unions to set prices and wages. The alternative was an inflationary spiral in which wage increases would spark price increases followed by even higher wage demands.

To prevent such a spiral the Council of Economic Advisors proposed that steel manufacturers agree to hold down prices if labor unions agreed to limit an increase in their wages. When the large steel corporations broke their part of the informal bargain by sharply raising steel prices, Kennedy angrily called for investigations into price fixing and shifted Pentagon purchases to smaller steel companies that had not raised prices. The intense pressure caused the big companies to drop the price increases but soured relations between the president and the business community.

Kennedy's Cold War >>
During the 1952 election Republicans exploited the stalemate in Korea, the fall of China, and the fear of domestic communism to suggest that the Democrats could not protect the nation's security. Once elected Kennedy was determined not to be seen as soft on communism. The cold war contest, he argued, had shifted from the traditional struggle over Europe to the developing nations in Asia, Africa, and Latin America. The

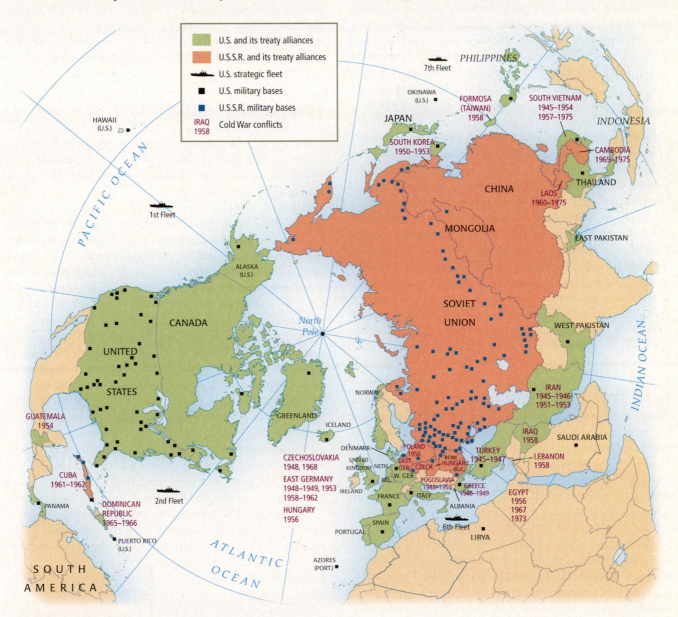

THE WORLD OF THE SUPERPOWERS

This map shows the extent of the cold war Soviet and American military buildup. The United States established a worldwide network of bases and alliances surrounding Soviet bloc nations that extended from Japan and South Korea, South Vietnam, Pakistan, and Turkey in Asia to the nations of the NATO alliance in Europe. Soviet efforts to expand its influence in the Third World led to the creation of an outpost in Cuba. Around these strategic perimeters, hot spots and centers of crisis continued to simmer.

United States should be armed with a more flexible range of military and economic options.

The Alliance for Progress, announced in the spring of 1961, reflected the Kennedy approach. He promised to provide $20 billion in foreign aid to Latin America over 10 years—about four times the aid given under Eisenhower. In return Latin American nations would agree to reform unfair tax policies and begin agricultural land reforms. If successful the alliance would discourage future Castro-style revolutions. With similar fanfare the administration set up the Peace Corps. This program sent idealistic young men and women to Third World nations to provide technical, educational, and public health services. Under the alliance, most Peace Corps volunteers were assigned to Latin America.

To back the new economic policies with military muscle, the Pentagon directed jungle warfare schools, both in North Carolina and in the Canal Zone. The programs were designed to train Latin American police and paramilitary groups as well as American special forces like the Green Berets. If the Soviets or their allies entered wars of liberation, United States commandos would be ready to fight back.

Kennedy believed, too, that the Soviets had made space the final frontier of the cold war. Only a few months after the president's inauguration, a Russian cosmonaut orbited the world for the first time. In response Kennedy challenged Congress to authorize a manned space mission to the moon that would land by the end of the decade. In February 1962 John Glenn circled the earth three times in a "fireball of a ride." Gradually, the American space program gained on the Russians'.

Cold War Frustrations >>
Kennedy had little success in countering "wars of liberation." The Eisenhower administration had authorized the CIA to overthrow Fidel Castro's Communist regime in Cuba, 90 miles south of Florida. Eager to establish his own cold war credentials, Kennedy approved an attack by a 1,400-member army of Cuban exiles in April 1961. The invasion turned into a mismanaged disaster. The poorly equipped rebel forces landed at the swampy Bay of Pigs, and no discontented rebels flocked to their support. Within two days Castro's army had rounded them up. Taking responsibility for the fiasco, Kennedy suffered a bitter humiliation.

Kennedy's advisers took a similar covert approach in South Vietnam. There, the American-backed prime minister, Ngo Dinh Diem (see page 600), grew more unpopular by the month. South Vietnamese Communists, known as the National Liberation Front (NLF), waged a guerrilla war against Diem with support from North Vietnam. Buddhists and other groups backed the rebellion, since Diem, a Catholic, ruthlessly persecuted them. In May 1961, a

If the Soviets or their allies entered wars of liberation, United States commandos would be ready to fight back.

month after the Bay of Pigs invasion, Kennedy secretly ordered 500 Green Berets and military advisers to Vietnam to prop up Diem. By 1963 the number of "military advisers" had risen to more than 16,000.

As the situation degenerated, Diem's corruption and police-state tactics made it unlikely he could defeat the Vietcong. Thus the Kennedy administration tacitly encouraged the military to stage a coup. The plotters captured Diem and, to Washington's surprise, shot him in November 1963. Despite Kennedy's policy of pragmatic idealism, the United States found itself mired in a Vietnamese civil war, in which it had no clear strategy for winning.

Confronting Khrushchev >>
Vietnam and Cuba were just two areas in the Third World where the Kennedy administration sought to battle Communist forces. But the conflict between the United States and the Soviet Union soon overshadowed developments in Asia, Africa, and Latin America.

In June 1961 a summit held in Vienna gave the president his first chance to take the measure of Nikita Khrushchev. For two long days, Khrushchev was brash and belligerent. East and West Germany must be reunited, he demanded. The problem of Berlin, where dissatisfied East Germans were fleeing to the city's free western zone, must be settled within six months. Kennedy left Vienna worried that the Soviet leader perceived him as weak and inexperienced. By August events in Berlin confirmed his fears. The Soviets threw up a heavily guarded wall sealing off the enclave of West Berlin from the rest of the eastern zone. Despite American protests, the wall stayed up.

Tensions with the Soviet Union also led the administration to rethink the American approach to nuclear warfare. Under the Dulles doctrine of massive retaliation, almost any incident threatened to trigger a full launch of nuclear missiles. Kennedy and McNamara sought to establish a "flexible response doctrine" that would limit the level of a first nuclear strike and thus leave room for negotiation.

But what if the Soviets launched a first-strike attack to knock out American missiles? A flexible response policy required that enough American missiles survive in order to retaliate. So McNamara began a program to bury missile sites underground and develop submarine-launched missiles. **Mutually assured destruction (MAD)** would deter a Soviet threat. The new approach resulted in a 15 percent increase in the 1961 military budget, compared with only 2 percent increases during the last two years of Eisenhower's term.

mutually assured destruction (MAD) national defense strategy in which a nuclear attack by one side would inevitably trigger an equal response leading to the destruction of both the attacker and the defender.

The Missiles of October >>

The peril of nuclear confrontation became dramatically clear in the Cuban missile crisis of October 1962. President Kennedy had warned repeatedly that the United States would treat any attempt to place offensive weapons in Cuba as an unacceptable threat. Khrushchev pledged that the Soviet Union had no such intention but bristled privately at this concession. In May 1962 he ordered the building of a secret nuclear base in Cuba. Throughout the summer the buildup went largely undetected by Americans. But by October 14 overflights of Cuba by U-2 spy planes had uncovered the offensive missile sites. Kennedy was outraged.

For a week American security advisers secretly debated a course of action. The Joint Chiefs of Staff urged air strikes against the missile sites, and at first Kennedy agreed. "We're certainly going to . . . take out these . . . missiles," he said. But other advisers pointed out that the U-2 flights had not photographed all of Cuba. What if there were more concealed bases with missiles ready to fire? The Soviets could then launch an atomic attack on the United States despite the air strikes. Kennedy finally chose the more restrained option of a naval blockade to intercept "all offensive military equipment under shipment to Cuba."

On October 22 word of the confrontation began to leak out. "CAPITAL CRISIS AIR HINTS AT DEVELOPMENTS ON CUBA, KENNEDY TV TALK IS LIKELY," headlined the *New York Times.* In Moscow, Soviet leaders were convinced that an American invasion of Cuba was likely. "The thing is we were not going to unleash war," a nervous Khrushchev complained, "we just wanted to intimidate them, to deter the anti-Cuban forces." Americans were stunned that evening by the president's television address.

Over the next few days tensions mounted as a Soviet submarine approached the line of American ships. On October 25 the navy stopped an oil tanker. Several Soviet ships reversed course. In Cuba, Soviet general Issa Pliyev assumed the worst—that in addition to the blockade, an American invasion of Cuba was being secretly prepared. The attack was expected "in the night between October 26 and October 27 or at dawn on October 27," he said, in a coded message to Moscow. Equally ominously, he added, "We have taken measures to disperse 'techniki' [the nuclear warheads] in the zone of operations." In other words, Pliyev was making his nuclear missiles operational.

The morning of October 27 alarmed Soviet technicians detected a U-2 spy plane over Cuba. Was this the beginning of the expected attack? General Pliyev had issued strict instructions not to use force without his go-ahead, but when the air defense command looked to consult him, he could not be found, and the U-2 would leave Cuban

⌃ The discovery of Soviet offensive missile sites in Cuba, revealed by low-level American reconnaissance fights, led to the first nuclear showdown of the cold war. For several tense days in October 1962 President Kennedy met with his National Security Council to debate the proper course of action.

airspace at any moment. Soviet officers went ahead and shot it down, killing its pilot.

Meanwhile, Kennedy was seeking urgently to resolve the crisis through diplomatic channels. Worried that events might spiral out of control, the president put off a decision on the U-2 incident until the following morning.

⌃ The *Women Strike for Peace* organization spoke out during the Cuban missile crisis.

He decided to accept a secret offer from Khrushchev to remove Soviet missiles, in return for an American pledge not to invade Cuba. Kennedy also gave private assurances that U.S. missiles pointed at the Soviet Union, stationed in Turkey, would be removed within half a year. In Moscow, Khrushchev agreed reluctantly to the deal, telling his advisers somberly that there were times to advance and times to retreat, and this time "we found ourselves face to face with the danger of war and of nuclear catastrophe, with the possible result of destroying the human race." The face-off ended on terms that saved both sides from overt humiliation.

The nuclear showdown prompted Kennedy to seek ways to control the nuclear arms race. "We all inhabit this small planet," he warned in June 1963. "We all breathe the same air. We all cherish our children's future. And we are all mortal." The administration negotiated a nuclear test ban with the Soviets, prohibiting all aboveground nuclear tests. At the same time, Kennedy's prestige soared for "standing up" to the Soviets.

 REVIEW

How did crises in Berlin and Cuba push President Kennedy to change cold war policies?

The Cuban missile crisis was the closest the world had come to "destroying the human race," in Khrushchev's words. Such a close call sobered the superpowers. It did not, however, end the cold war. Ahead lay long, bloody regional wars—for the United States, in Vietnam; for the Soviet Union, in Afghanistan; and elsewhere, between Israel and its Arab neighbors. Conservatives would continue to press for victory in the cold war, but never again would the two superpowers stand so close to the brink of an atomic war. The nuclear anxieties of the 1950s—so much a part of the suburban era—gave way to different, equally urgent concerns in the 1960s.

CHAPTER SUMMARY

At midcentury, during an era of peace and prosperity, the United States began to build a new social and political agenda.

- Automobiles and the culture of the highways helped bind Americans to one another in a "consensus" about what it meant to be an American.
- Highways made possible rapid suburban growth.
- Suburbs proved popular with the growing white-collar middle class.
- Consensus in suburbs blurred class distinctions and promoted the notion of "civil religion."
- Suburban life nurtured the ideal of the woman who found fulfillment as a homemaker and a mother, even though more women began to work outside the home.
- President Eisenhower resisted the demands of conservatives to dismantle the New Deal and of liberals to extend it, in favor of moderate, or "middle-of-the-road," Republicanism.

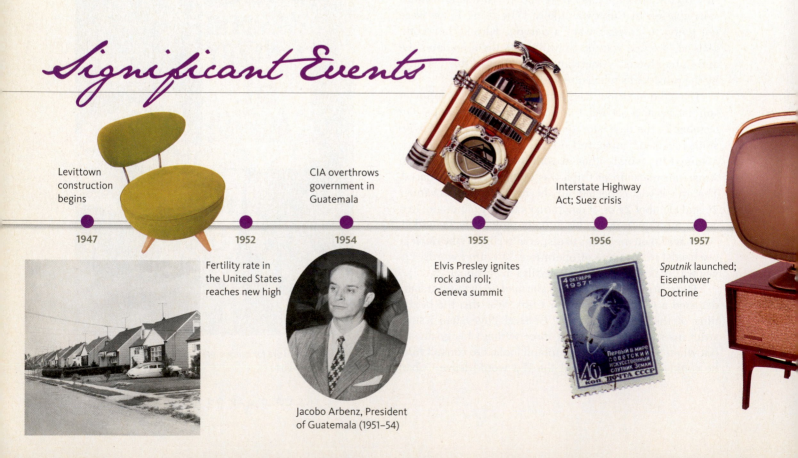

Significant Events

Levittown construction begins — 1947

Fertility rate in the United States reaches new high

CIA overthrows government in Guatemala — 1952 — 1954

Jacobo Arbenz, President of Guatemala (1951–54)

Elvis Presley ignites rock and roll; Geneva summit — 1955

Interstate Highway Act; Suez crisis — 1956

Sputnik launched; Eisenhower Doctrine — 1957

- Cracks in the consensus appeared among discontented intellectuals and among teenagers who, through Elvis Presley and new teen idols, discovered the power of rock and roll.
- Efforts to more vigorously contain the U.S.S.R. and communist China through a policy of "brinkmanship" proved difficult to apply because of growing Third World nationalism.
- Eisenhower held back from using tactical nuclear weapons during crises in Vietnam and Taiwan.
- Successful CIA operations in Iran and Guatemala encouraged American policy makers to use covert operations more frequently.
- Postcolonial nationalism contributed to crises in Hungary, Egypt, and Cuba, where President Kennedy was embarrassed by the failure of an invasion attempt to overthrow Fidel Castro.
- Relations between the two superpowers thawed gradually but not without recurring confrontations between the United States and the Soviet Union.
- Under Eisenhower, the Soviet success with *Sputnik* increased fears that the United States was vulnerable to missile attacks, while the U-2 spy plane incident worsened relations.
- John F. Kennedy proved willing to use covert operations as well as diplomatic and economic initiatives like the Peace Corps and the Alliance for Progress.
- The construction of Soviet missile bases 90 miles from American shores triggered the Cuban missile crisis of 1962, the closest the United States and the Soviet Union ever came to nuclear war.

Additional Reading

David Halberstam profiles suburban America engagingly in *The Fifties* (1994); using suburban Orange County, California, as her focus, Lisa McGirr, looks at conservative grassroots organization in *Suburban Warriors: The Origins of the New American Right* (2001). For a fresh environmental perspective, see Adam Rome, *The Bulldozer in the Countryside; Suburban Sprawl and the Rise of American Environmentalism* (2001). Karal Ann Marling, *As Seen on TV: The Visual Culture of Everyday Life in the 1950s* (1998), dissects the popular aesthetics of the era. For popular culture, see Glenn Altschuler, *All Shook Up: How Rock and Roll Changed America* (2003). As a corrective to the view of women in the 1950s popularized by Betty Friedan, *The Feminine Mystique* (1963), see the provocative essays in Joanne Meyerowitz, ed., *Not June Cleaver: Women and Gender in Postwar America* (1994).

Fred Greenstein, *The Hidden Hand Presidency: Eisenhower as Leader* (rev. ed., 1994), contradicts the view of Ike as a bumbling president. Historians have also refurbished Kennedy's reputation. See, for example, Graham Allison, *The Essence of Decision: Explaining the Cuban Missile Crisis* (2nd ed., 1999), and Warren Bass, *Support Any Friend: Kennedy, the Middle East, and the Making of the U.S. Israel Alliance* (2003). Two fine books on Kennedy and Vietnam are Fredrik Logevall, *Choosing War: The Lost Chance for Peace and the Escalation of War in Vietnam* (2003), and David Kaiser, *American Tragedy: Kennedy, Johnson, and the Origins of the Vietnam War* (2002).

Marines sent into Lebanon; Berlin crisis

1958

Castro seizes power in Cuba; Khrushchev visits United States

1959

Soviet Union captures CIA pilot; Kennedy elected president

1960

Eisenhower warns of military-industrial complex; Bay of Pigs invasion; Berlin Wall built

1961

Cuban missile crisis

1962

On August 28, 1963, more than 250,000 demonstrators joined the great civil rights march on Washington. Although the day belonged to Martin Luther King, Jr., the movement's most prominent leader, ordinary Americans both black and white played key roles in initiating the civil rights crusade.

Civil Rights

29

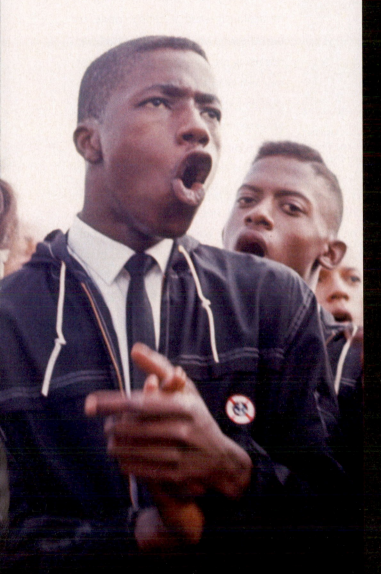

>> **AN AMERICAN STORY**

TWO ROADS TO INTEGRATION

Six-year-old Ruby knew the lessons. She was to look straight ahead—not to one side or the other—and especially not at them. She was to keep walking. Above all, she was not to look back once she'd passed, because that would encourage them. Ruby knew these things, but it was hard to keep her eyes straight. The first day of school, her parents came, along with federal marshals to keep order. And all around hundreds of angry white people were yelling things like, "You little nigger, we'll get you and kill you." Then she was within the building's quiet halls and alone with her teacher. She was the only person in class: none of the white students had come. As the days went by during that autumn of 1960, the marshals stopped walking with her but the hecklers still waited. And once in a while Ruby couldn't help looking back, trying to see if she recognized the face of one woman in particular.

Ruby's parents were not social activists. They signed their daughter up for the white school in this New Orleans neighborhood because "we thought it was for all the colored to do, and we never thought Ruby would be alone." Her father's white employer fired him; letters and phone calls threatened the family. Through it all Ruby seemed >>

and Uncivil Liberties

1947–1969

^ Overton Park Zoo in Memphis, Tennessee, was segregated, like thousands of other public facilities throughout the South in the late 1950s. In the case of the zoo, Tuesdays were "colored" days, the only time when blacks could attend—except if the Fourth of July fell on a Tuesday. Then "colored" day was moved to Thursday.

to take things in stride, though her parents worried that she was not eating well. Often she left her school lunch untouched or refused anything other than packaged food such as potato chips. It was only after a time that the problem was traced to the hecklers. "They tells me I'm going to die, and that it'll be soon. And that one lady tells me every morning I'm getting poisoned soon, when she can fix it." Ruby was convinced that the woman owned the variety store nearby and would carry out her threat by poisoning the family's food.

Over the course of a year white students gradually returned to class and life settled into a new routine. By the time Ruby was 10 she had developed a remarkably clear perception of herself. "Maybe because of all the trouble going to school in the beginning I learned more about my people," she told Robert Coles, a psychologist studying children and the effects of segregation. "Maybe I would have anyway; because when you get older you see yourself and the white kids; and you find out the difference. You try to forget it, and say there is none; and if there is you won't say what it be. Then you say it's my own people, and so I can be proud of them instead of ashamed."

The new ways were not easy for white southerners either—even those who saw the need for change. One woman, a teacher from Atlanta, recalled for Robert Coles the summer 10 years earlier, when she went to New York City to take courses in education. There were black students in her dormitory, an integrated situation she was not used to. One day as she stepped from her shower, so did a black student from the nearby stall. "When I saw her I didn't know what to do," the woman recalled. "I felt sick all over, and frightened. What I remember—I'll never forget it—is that horrible feeling of being caught in a terrible trap, and not knowing what to do about it. . . . My sense of propriety was with me, though—miraculously—and I didn't want to hurt the woman. It wasn't her that was upsetting me. I knew that, even in that moment of sickness and panic." So she ducked back into the shower until the other woman left.

It took most of the summer before she felt comfortable eating with black students. Back in Atlanta she told no one about her experiences. "At that time people would have thought one of two things: I was crazy (for being so upset and ashamed) or a fool who in a summer had become a dangerous 'race mixer.'" She continued to love the South and to defend its traditions of dignity, neighborliness, and honor, but she saw the need for change. And so in 1961 she volunteered to teach one of the first integrated high school classes in Atlanta. "I've never felt so useful," she concluded after two years; ". . . not just to the children but to our whole society. American as well as Southern. Those children, all of them, have given me more than I've given them."

For Americans in all walks of life, the changes that swept the United States in the 1960s were wrenching.

From the schoolrooms and lunch counters of the South to the college campuses of the North, from eastern slums to western migrant labor camps, American society was in ferment.

On the face of it, such agitation seemed a dramatic reversal of the placid 1950s. Turbulence and controversy had overturned stability and consensus. Yet the events of the 1960s grew naturally out of the social conditions that preceded them. The civil rights movement was brought about not by a group of farsighted leaders in government but by ordinary folk who sought change, often despite the reluctance or even fierce opposition of people in power. After World War II grassroots organizations such as the NAACP for blacks and the American GI Forum for Latinos acted with a new determination. Both peoples sought to achieve the equality of opportunity promised by the American creed. «

THE CIVIL RIGHTS MOVEMENT

The struggle of African Americans for equality during the postwar era is filled with ironies. By the time barriers to legal segregation in the South began to fall, millions of black families were leaving for regions where discrimination was less easily challenged in court. The South they left behind was in the early stages of an economic boom. The cities to which many migrated had entered a period of decline. Yet, as if to close a circle, the rise of large black voting blocs in major cities created political pressures that forced the nation to dismantle the worst legal and institutional barriers to racial equality.

The Changing South and African Americans >>

Before World War II, 80 percent of African Americans lived in the South. Most raised cotton as sharecroppers and tenant farmers. But the war created a labor shortage at home, as millions went off to fight and others to armament factories. This shortage gave cotton growers an incentive to mechanize cotton picking. In 1950 only 5 percent of the crop was picked mechanically; by 1960 at least half was. Tenant farmers, sharecroppers, and hired labor of both races left the countryside for the city.

The national level of wages also profoundly affected southern labor. When federal minimum wage laws forced lumber or textile mills to raise their pay scales, the mills no longer expanded. In addition, steel and other industries with strong national unions and manufacturers with plants around the country set wages by national standards. That brought southern wages close to the national average by the 1960s. As the southern economy grew, what had for many years been a distinct regional economy integrated into the national economy.

As wages rose and unskilled work disappeared, job opportunities for black southerners declined. New high-wage jobs were reserved for white southerners, since outside industries arriving in the South made no effort to change local patterns of discrimination. So the ultimate irony appeared. As per capita income rose and industrialization brought in new jobs, black laborers poured out of the region in search of work. They arrived in cities that showed scant tolerance for racial differences and little willingness or ability to hire unskilled black labor.

The NAACP and Civil Rights >>

In the postwar era the National Association for the Advancement of Colored People (NAACP) led the legal fight against racial segregation. Their hard-hitting campaign reflected the increased national political influence of African Americans as they migrated out of the South. No longer could northern politicians readily ignore the demands that black leaders made for greater equality. At first, however, the NAACP focused its campaign on the courts.

Thurgood Marshall was the association's leading attorney. Marshall had attended law school in the 1930s at Howard University in Washington. There, the law school's dean, Charles Houston, was in the midst of revamping the school and turning out sharp, dedicated lawyers. Not only was Marshall sharp; he had the common touch as well. "Before he came along," one observer noted, "the principal black leaders—such men as Du Bois and James Weldon Johnson and Charles Houston—didn't talk the language of the people. They were upper-class and upper-middle-class Negroes. Thurgood Marshall was of the people. . . . Out in Texas or Oklahoma or down the street here in Washington at the Baptist church, he would make these

> **The civil rights movement was brought about not by a group of farsighted leaders in government but by ordinary folk who sought change.**

rousing speeches that would have 'em all jumping out of their seats."

During the late 1930s and early 1940s Marshall toured the South (in "a little old beat-up '29 Ford"), typing out legal briefs in the backseat, trying to get teachers to sue for equal pay, and defending blacks accused of murder in a Klan-infested county in Florida. He was friendly with whites and not shy. Black citizens who had never even considered the possibility that a member of their race might win a legal battle "would come for miles, some of them on mule-back or horseback, to see 'the nigger lawyer' who stood up in white men's courtrooms."

For years NAACP lawyers supported members of the community willing to risk their jobs, property, and lives to challenge segregation. But the NAACP chose not to attack head-on the Supreme Court decision (*Plessy v. Ferguson,* 1896) that permitted "separate but equal" segregated facilities. They simply demonstrated that a black college or school might be separate, but it was hardly equal if it lacked a law school or even indoor plumbing.

⌃ Thurgood Marshall

The *Brown* Decision >>

In 1950 the NAACP changed tactics: it would now try to convince the Supreme Court to overturn the separate but equal doctrine itself. Oliver Brown of Topeka, Kansas, was one of the people who provided a way. Brown was bothered that his daughter Linda had to walk past an all-white school on her way to catch the bus to her segregated black school. A three-judge federal panel rejected Brown's suit because the schools in Topeka, while segregated, did meet the legal standards for equality. The NAACP appealed the case to the Supreme Court and, in 1954, won a striking decision. *Brown v. Board of Education of Topeka* overturned the lower court ruling and overthrew the doctrine of "separate but equal."

Marshall and his colleagues succeeded in part because of a change in the Court itself. The year before, President Eisenhower had appointed Earl Warren, a liberal Republican from California, as chief justice. Warren, a forceful advocate, managed to persuade even his reluctant judicial colleagues that segregation as defined in *Plessy* rested on an insupportable theory of racial supremacy. The Court ruled unanimously that separate facilities were inherently unequal. To keep black children segregated solely on the basis of race, it ruled, "generates a feeling of inferiority as to their status in the community that may affect their hearts and minds in a way unlikely ever to be undone."

At the time of the *Brown* decision, 21 states and the District of Columbia operated segregated school systems. All had to decide, in some way, how to comply with the new ruling. The Court allowed some leeway, handing down a second ruling in 1955 that required states to carry out desegregation "with all deliberate speed." Some border states reluctantly decided to comply, but in the Deep South, many pledged die-hard defiance. In 1956, a "Southern Manifesto" was issued by 19 U.S. senators and 81 representatives: they intended to use "all lawful means" to reestablish legalized segregation.

Latino Civil Rights >>

Mexican Americans also considered school desegregation a key to their civil rights campaign. After World War II, only 1 percent of children of Mexican descent graduated from Texas high schools. Two Latino organizations, the American GI Forum and the League of United Latin American Citizens (LULAC, see page 518), supported legal challenges to the Texas system of school segregation.

In 1947 the superintendent in the town of Bastrop, Texas, had refused a request to enroll first-grader Minerva Delgado in a nearby all-white school. Civil rights activist Gus Garcia, a legal adviser to both LULAC and the GI Forum, helped bring a case on Minerva's behalf against the school district. But before *Delgado et al. v. Bastrop et al.* could even be tried, a Texas judge ordered an end to segregated schools beyond the first grade (the exception was based on the assumption that the youngest Mexican American children needed special classes to learn English). Delgado served notice that Mexicans would no longer accept second-class citizenship. It also served as a precedent in *Brown v. Board of Education* in 1954.

Two weeks before the Supreme Court made that landmark civil rights ruling, it also decided a case of great importance to Latinos. Unlike African Americans, Latinos did not face a Jim Crow system of laws imposing segregation. Throughout the Southwest the states recognized just

Opinion

How did the cold war influence the response to the civil rights movement?

two races: black and white. That left Mexican Americans in legal limbo. Though legally grouped with whites, by longstanding social custom they were barred from many public places, could not serve on juries, and faced widespread job discrimination. To remedy the situation, Mexican Americans had to establish themselves in the courts as a distinct class of people. Only then could they seek legal remedies.

An opportunity to make that point arose in the case of Pete Hernández, who had been convicted of murder by an all-white jury in Jackson County, Texas. As Gus Garcia and other Mexican American attorneys realized, no Mexican American had served on a Jackson jury in the previous 25 years. Taking a leaf from the tactics of Thurgood Marshall, they appealed the Hernández case before the Supreme Court, hoping to extend to Mexicans the benefits of the Fourteenth Amendment's equal protection clause.

The key to the Hernández case was ingenious but direct. Lawyers for Texas argued that because Mexicans were white, a jury without Mexicans was still a jury of peers. Yet the courthouse in which Hernández was convicted had two men's rooms. One said simply "MEN." The other had a crude, hand-lettered sign that read "COLORED MEN" and below that, in Spanish, "HOMBRES AQUÍ" ["MEN HERE"]. As one of Garcia's colleagues recalled: "In the jury pool, Mexicans may have been white, but when it came to nature's functions they were not." Such examples of discrimination persuaded the Supreme Court, in *Hernández v. Texas,* to throw out the state's argument. "The Fourteenth Amendment is not directed solely against discrimination due to a 'two-class theory,' that is, based on differences between 'white' and Negro," ruled Chief Justice Earl Warren. Warren's reasoning made it possible for Latinos to seek redress as a group rather than as individuals.

⚑ Attorney Gus Garcia (left) was one of the key leaders of the American GI Forum, founded by Mexican American veterans to pursue their civil rights. He and his colleagues successfully appealed the conviction of Pete Hernández (center) before the Supreme Court in 1954.

A New Civil Rights Strategy ⟩⟩ Neither the *Brown* nor the *Hernández* decision ended segregation, but they combined with political and economic forces to usher in a new era of southern race relations. In December 1955 Rosa Parks, a 43-year-old black civil rights activist, was riding the bus home in Montgomery, Alabama. When the driver ordered her to give up her seat for a white man, as Alabama Jim Crow laws required, she refused. Police took her to jail and eventually fined her $14.

Determined to overturn the law, a number of women from the NAACP, led by Jo Ann Robinson, met secretly at midnight to draft a letter of protest:

> Another Negro woman has been arrested and thrown into jail because she refused to get up out of her seat on the bus and give it to a white person. . . . Until we do something to stop these arrests, they will continue. The next time it may be you, or you or you. This woman's case will come up Monday. We are, therefore, asking every Negro to stay off the buses on Monday in protest of the arrest and trial.

Thousands of copies of the letter were distributed, and the Monday **boycott** was such a success it was extended indefinitely. Many in the white community, in an effort to halt the unprecedented black challenge, resorted to various forms of legal and physical intimidation. No local insurance agent would insure cars used to carpool black workers. A bomb exploded in the house of the Reverend Martin Luther King, Jr., the key boycott leader. Still the boycotters held out until November 13, 1956, when the Supreme Court ruled that bus segregation was illegal.

boycott tactic used by protestors, workers, and consumers to pressure business organizations through a mass refusal to purchase their products or otherwise do business with them.

The triumph was especially sweet for Martin Luther King, Jr., whose leadership in Montgomery brought him national fame. Before becoming a minister at the Dexter Street Baptist Church, King had had little personal contact with the worst forms of white racism. He had grown up in the relatively affluent middle-class black community of Atlanta, Georgia, the son of one of the city's most prominent black ministers. He attended Morehouse College, an academically respected black school in Atlanta, and Crozer Theological Seminary in Philadelphia before entering the doctoral program in theology at Boston University. As a graduate student King embraced the pacifism and nonviolence of the Indian leader Mohandas Gandhi and the activism of Christian reformers of the progressive era.

As boycott leader, King had the responsibility to rally support without triggering violence. Since local officials were all too eager for any excuse to use force, King's nonviolent approach proved an effective strategy. "In our protest there will be no cross burnings. No white person will be taken from his home by a hooded Negro mob and brutally murdered." And he evoked the Christian and republican ideals that would become the themes of his civil rights crusade. "If we protest courageously, and yet with dignity and Christian love," he said, "when the future history books are written, somebody will have to say, 'There lived a race of people, of black people, of people who had the moral courage to stand up for their rights. And thereby they injected a new meaning into the history of civilization.'"

Indeed, the African Americans of Montgomery did set an example of moral courage that attracted national attention and rewrote the pages of American race relations. King and his colleagues were developing the tactics needed to launch a more aggressive phase of the civil rights movement.

Little Rock and the White Backlash >>

The civil rights spotlight moved the following year to Little Rock, Arkansas. There, reluctant white officials had adopted a plan to integrate the schools with a most deliberate lack of speed. Nine black students were scheduled to enroll in September 1957 at the all-white Central High School. Instead, the school board urged them to stay home. Governor Orval Faubus, generally a moderate on race relations, called out the Arkansas National Guard on the excuse of maintaining order. President Eisenhower, who had refused to endorse the *Brown* decision, tacitly supported Faubus in his defiance of court-ordered integration by remarking that "you cannot change people's hearts merely by laws."

Still, the Justice Department could not let Faubus defy the federal courts, and it won an injunction against the governor. But when the nine blacks returned to school on September 23, a mob of a thousand abusive protesters greeted them. So great was national attention to the crisis that Eisenhower felt compelled to send in a thousand federal troops and take control of the National Guard. For one year the Guard preserved order until Faubus, in a last-ditch maneuver, closed all the schools. Only in 1959, under the pressure of another federal court ruling, did the Little Rock schools reopen and resume the plan for gradual integration.

In the face of such attitudes King and other civil rights leaders recognized that the skirmishes of Montgomery and Little Rock were a beginning, not the end. Cultural attitudes and customs were not about to give way overnight. Black leaders were unable to achieve momentum on a national scale until 1960. Then, a series of spontaneous demonstrations by young people changed everything.

✔ REVIEW

In what way did the *Brown* and *Hernández* cases promote the cause of civil rights?

A MOVEMENT BECOMES A CRUSADE

On January 31, 1960, Joseph McNeill got off the bus in Greensboro, North Carolina, a freshman on the way back to college. When he looked for something to eat at the lunch counter, the waitress gave the familiar reply. "We don't serve Negroes here."

It was a refrain repeated countless times and in countless places. Yet for some reason this rebuke particularly offended McNeill. He and his roommates had read a pamphlet describing the 1955 bus boycott in Montgomery, Alabama. They decided it was time to make their own protest against segregation. Proceeding the next day to the "whites only" lunch counter at a local store, they sat politely waiting for service. Rather than comply, the

⌃ Angry white students, opposed to integration, menace black students during a recess at Little Rock's Central High. This civil rights crisis was the first covered by television. For weeks NBC correspondent John Chancellor took a chartered plane daily from Little Rock to Oklahoma City to deliver film footage for the nightly news program. Such national attention made people outside the South more sensitive to civil rights issues.

manager closed the counter. Word of the action spread. A day later—Tuesday—the four students were joined by 27 more. Wednesday, the number jumped to 63, Thursday, to over 300. Came the weekend, 1,600 students rallied to plan further action. Within two weeks, the courage of the Greensboro students had inspired 15 **sit-ins** across the South. By year's end, 70,000 people had demonstrated; thousands had gone to jail.

> **sit-in** form of direct action in which protesters nonviolently occupy and refuse to leave an area.

The campaign for black civil rights gained momentum not so much by the power of national movements as through a host of individual decisions by local groups and citizens. When New Orleans schools were desegregated in 1960, young Ruby's parents had not intended to make a social statement. But once involved, they refused to back down. The students at Greensboro had not been approached by the NAACP but acted on their own initiative.

Riding to Freedom >>

Of course, organizations channeled these discontents and aspirations, especially those directed by a new generation of younger activists. Martin Luther King's Southern Christian Leadership Conference (SCLC) hinted at these more direct challenges to the social order. King continued to advocate nonviolent protest: "To resist without bitterness; to be cursed and not reply; to be beaten and not hit back." A second organization, the Congress of Racial Equality (CORE), was even more prepared to force nonviolent confrontations with the segregationist system. A new group, the Student Non-Violent Coordinating Committee (SNCC, pronounced "Snick"), grew out of the Greensboro sit-in. SNCC represented the militant, younger generation of black activists, impatient with the slow pace of reform.

In May 1961 CORE director James Farmer led a group of black and white "freedom riders" on a bus trip from Washington to New Orleans. They intended to focus national attention on the inequality of segregated facilities. Violent southern mobs gave the freedom riders the kind of attention they feared. In South Carolina, thugs beat divinity student John Lewis as he tried to enter an all-white waiting room. Mobs in Anniston and Birmingham, Alabama, assaulted the freedom riders as police ignored the violence. One of the buses was burned.

Sensitive to the power of conservative southern Democrats, President Kennedy tried to avoid sending federal forces to protect the demonstrators. But his hopes were dashed. From a phone booth outside the bus terminal, John Doar, a Justice Department official in Montgomery, relayed the horror to Attorney General Robert Kennedy:

> Now the passengers are coming off. They're standing on a corner of the platform. Oh, there are fists; punching! A bunch of men led by a guy with a bleeding face are beating them. There are no cops. It's terrible! It's terrible! There's not a cop in sight. People are yelling. "There those niggers are! Get 'em; get 'em!" It's awful.

Appalled, Robert Kennedy ordered in 400 federal marshals, who barely managed to hold off the crowd. King, addressing a meeting in town, phoned the attorney general to say that their church had been surrounded by a mob that was throwing rocks and carrying firebombs. "I said that we were doing the best that we could," Kennedy later recalled, "and that he'd be as dead as Kelsey's nuts if it hadn't been for the marshals and the efforts that we made."

Both Kennedys understood that civil rights was the most divisive issue the administration faced. The president needed the votes of African Americans and liberals to win reelection. Yet an active federal role threatened to drive white southerners from the Democratic party. Thus Kennedy hedged on his promise to introduce civil rights legislation. He assured black leaders that executive orders

⌃ In May 1961 a mob in Montgomery, Alabama, surrounded the Negro First Baptist Church where Martin Luther King, Jr., was leading an all-night vigil. King put in a call to Attorney General Robert Kennedy, who sent 400 federal marshals to keep order.

would eliminate discrimination in the government and in businesses filling government contracts. He appointed several blacks to high positions and five, including Thurgood Marshall, to the federal courts. But the freedom riders, by their bold actions, forced the Kennedys to do more.

Civil Rights at High Tide >> By the fall of 1961 Robert Kennedy had persuaded SNCC to shift its energies to voter registration, which he assumed would stir up less violence. Voting booths, Kennedy noted, were not like schools, where people would protest, "We don't want our little blond daughter going to school with a Negro."

↑ In Birmingham, Alabama, firefighters used high-pressure hoses to disperse civil rights demonstrators. The force of the hoses was powerful enough to tear bark off trees. Photographs like this one aroused widespread sympathy for the civil rights movement.

Despite the Kennedys' desire to defuse tensions, confrontation increased anyway. A federal court ordered the segregated University of Mississippi to admit James Meredith, a black applicant. When Governor Ross Barnett personally blocked Meredith's registration in September 1962, Kennedy ordered several hundred federal marshals to escort Meredith into a university dormitory. The marshals were met by a mob, which shot out street lights and threw rocks and bottles. The president finally sent in federal troops, but not before 2 people were killed and 375 wounded.

In Mississippi President Kennedy had begun to lose control of the civil rights issue. The House of Representatives, influenced by television coverage of the violence, introduced a number of civil rights measures. And in 1963 Martin Luther King led a group to Birmingham, Alabama, to force a showdown against segregation. From a prison cell there he produced one of the most eloquent documents of the civil rights movement, his "Letter from Birmingham Jail." Addressed to local ministers who had called for an end to confrontation, the letter defended the use of civil disobedience. The choice, King warned, was not between obeying the law and nonviolently breaking it to bring about change. It was between his way and streets "flowing with blood," as frustrated black citizens turned toward more militant ideologies.

Once freed, King led new demonstrations. Television cameras were on hand that May as Birmingham police chief "Bull" Connor, a man with a short fuse, unleashed attack dogs, club-wielding

police, and fire hoses powerful enough to peel the bark off trees. When segregationist bombs went off in African American neighborhoods, black mobs retaliated with their own riot, burning a number of shops and businesses owned by white citizens. In the following 10 weeks more than 750 protests and marches erupted in 186 cities and towns, both North and South. King's warning of streets "flowing with blood" no longer seemed far-fetched.

WITNESS

Living Scared in Mississippi

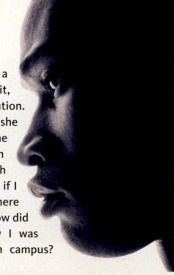

"[While I was attending college] I got a letter from Mama with dried-up tears on it, forbidding me to go the [NAACP] convention. . . . She said if I didn't stop that shit she would come to Tougaloo and kill me herself. . . . She said the sheriff had been by, telling her I was messing around with that NAACP group. She said he told her if I didn't stop it, I could not come back there any more. . . . Then it occurred to me—how did the sheriff or anyone at home know I was working with the NAACP chapter on campus? Somehow they had found out. . . ."

—Anne Moody, *Coming of Age in Mississippi* (1968)

Kennedy sensed that he could no longer compromise on civil rights. "If [an American with dark skin] cannot enjoy the full and free life all of us want," he asked Americans, "then who among us would be content to have the color of his skin changed and stand in his place? Who among us would then be content with counsels of patience and delay?" The president followed his words with support for a strong civil rights bill to end segregation and protect black voters. When King announced a massive march on Washington for August 1963, Kennedy objected that it would undermine support for his bill. "I have never engaged in any direct action movement which did not seem ill-timed," King replied. Faced with the inevitable, Kennedy convinced the organizers to use the event to promote the administration's bill, much to the disgust of militant CORE and SNCC factions.

On August 28, 250,000 people gathered at the Lincoln Memorial to march in support of civil rights and racial harmony. Appropriately, the day belonged to King. In the powerful tones of a southern preacher, he reminded the crowd that the Declaration of Independence was a promise that applied to all people, black and white. "I have a dream," he cried, that one day "all of God's children, black men and white men, Jews and Gentiles, Protestants and Catholics, will be able to join hands and sing in the words of the old Negro spiritual, 'Free at last! Free at last! Thank God Almighty, we are free at last!'"

⌃ June 14, 1963—Attorney General Robert F. Kennedy speaks to a crowd of African Americans and whites through a megaphone outside the Justice Department; a sign supporting the Congress of Racial Equality is prominently displayed.

civil rights received the greatest national coverage when white, not black, demonstrators were killed. They wondered, too, how Lyndon Johnson, a consummate southern politician, would approach the civil rights programs.

The new president, however, saw the need for action. Just as the Catholic issue had tested Kennedy's ability to lead, Johnson was convinced that if he failed on civil rights, "I'd be dead before I could ever begin." On his first day in office, he promised one civil rights leader after another that he would pass Kennedy's bill. Despite a southern filibuster in the Senate, the Civil Rights Act of 1964 became law. Embodying the provisions of the Kennedy bill, it barred discrimination in public accommodations like lunch counters, bus stations, and hotels. It also prohibited employers from discriminating by race, color, religion, sex, or national origin.

The Civil Rights Act, however, did not strike down literacy tests and other laws used to prevent black citizens from voting. With King and other black leaders keeping up the pressure, President Johnson persuaded Congress to pass a strong Voting Rights Act in August 1965. The act outlawed literacy tests and permitted federal officials to monitor elections in many southern districts. With some justice Johnson called the act "one of the most monumental laws in the entire history of American freedom." Within a five-year period black voter registration in the South jumped from 35 to 65 percent.

The Fire Next Time >> Civil rights politics
fractured the Democratic party. The president scheduled a trip to Texas to recoup some southern support. On November 22, 1963, the people of Dallas lined the streets for his motorcade. Suddenly a sniper's rifle fired several times. Kennedy slumped into his wife's arms, fatally wounded. His assassin, Lee Harvey Oswald, was caught several hours later. Oswald seemed a mysterious figure. Emotionally unstable, he had spent several years in the Soviet Union. But his actions were never fully explained, because only two days after his arrest—in full view of television cameras—he was gunned down by a disgruntled nightclub operator named Jack Ruby.

In the face of such violence, many Americans came to doubt that gradual reform or nonviolence could hold the nation together. Younger black leaders observed that

Black Power >> But
even the new civil rights laws did not strike at the **de facto segregation** found outside the South. This was segregation not spelled out in laws but practiced through unwritten custom. In large areas of America, African Americans were locked out of suburbs, kept out of decent schools, barred from clubs, and denied all but the most menial jobs. Nor did the Voting Rights Act deal with the sources of urban black poverty. The median income for urban black residents was about half of what white residents earned.

In such an atmosphere, militants sharply questioned the liberal goal of integration. Since the 1930s

de facto segregation
spatial and social separation of populations brought about by social behavior rather than by laws or legal mechanisms.

Point of View

King's Final Months

"Still . . . [in the Poor People's Campaign of 1968, Martin Luther] King's messianic vision seemed only to wheel out farther, reaching beyond the nation to embrace now almost deliriously the world itself. The social crisis in America, he declared, was 'inseparable from an international emergency which involves the poor, the dispossessed, the exploited of the whole world. . . .' It was as if . . . he had come to feel laden with all the planet's grief—famines, massacres, maraudings of war, the slums not only of Chicago, but of Cairo and Culcutta and Lima—all the earth's cruelty and anguish. Even as the Poor People's Campaign seemed foundering, he had begun appealing for a yet vaster and climactic movement to accomplish a wholly new global community beyond class, tribe, race, nation—'a world unity in which all barriers of caste and color are abolished.'"

MARSHALL FRADY *Martin Luther King, Jr.: A Life*

the Nation of Islam religious sect, dedicated to complete separation from white society, had attracted as many as 100,000 members, mostly young men. During the early 1960s the sect drew wider attention through the efforts of Malcolm X. Provocative, shrewd, and charismatic, Malcolm had learned the language of the downtrodden from his own experience as a former hustler, gambler, and prison inmate. His militancy alarmed whites, though by 1965 he was in fact becoming more moderate. He accepted integration but emphasized black community action. After breaking with the Black Muslims, Malcolm was gunned down by rivals.

By 1965 even CORE and SNCC had begun to give up working with white liberals for nonviolent change. If black Americans were to liberate themselves fully, militants argued, they could not merely accept rights "given" to them by whites: they had to claim them. Some members began carrying guns to defend themselves. In 1966 Stokely Carmichael of SNCC gave the militants a slogan—"Black Power"—and the defiant symbol of a gloved fist raised in the air.

⋀ MALCOLM X

In its moderate form, the black power movement encouraged African Americans to recover their cultural roots, their African heritage, and a new sense of identity. African clothes and natural hairstyles became popular. On college campuses black students pressed universities to hire black faculty, create black studies programs, and provide segregated social and residential space.

For black militants, on the other hand, violence became a revolutionary tool. The Black Panther party of Oakland, California, called on the black community to arm. Panther leader Huey Newton and his followers openly brandished shotguns and rifles as they patrolled the streets protecting blacks from police harassment. After a gun battle with police left a wounded Newton in jail, Eldridge Cleaver assumed leadership of the party. But even at the height of their power, the Panthers never counted more than 2,000 members nationwide.

Violence in the Streets ⟩⟩ No

ideology organized the frustration and despair that existed in the ghettos. Often, a seemingly minor incident such as an arrest or an argument on the streets would trigger an eruption of violence. A mob would gather, and police cars and white owned stores would be firebombed or looted. Riots broke out in Harlem and Rochester, New York, in 1964; the Watts area of Los Angeles in 1965; Chicago in 1966; and Newark and Detroit in 1967. It took nearly 5,000 troops to end the bloodiest rioting in Detroit, where 40 died, 2,000 were injured, and 5,000 were left homeless.

To most white Americans the violence was unfathomable and inexcusable. Martin Luther King, still pursuing the tactics of nonviolence, was saddened by the destruction but came to understand the anger behind it. Touring Watts only days after the riots, he was approached by a band of young blacks. "We won," they told him proudly. "How can you say you won," King countered, "when thirty-four Negroes are dead, your community is destroyed, and whites are using the riot as an excuse for inaction?" The youngsters were unmoved. "We won because we made them pay attention to us."

For Lyndon Johnson, ghetto violence and black militance mocked his efforts to achieve racial progress. The Civil Rights and Voting Rights acts were essential parts of the "Great Society" he hoped to build. In that regard he had achieved a legislative record virtually unequaled by any other president in the nation's history. What Kennedy had promised, Johnson delivered. But the anger exploding in the nation's cities exposed serious flaws in the theory and practice of liberal reform.

 REVIEW

How did SCLC and SNCC differ in their tactics for promoting civil rights?

CIVIL RIGHTS: PATTERNS OF PROTEST AND UNREST

The first phase of the civil rights movement was confined largely to the South, where the freedom riders of 1961 dramatized the issue of segregation. Beginning in the summer of 1964, urban riots brought the issue of race and politics home to the entire nation. Severe rioting followed the murder of Martin Luther King, Jr., in 1968, after which the worst violence subsided.

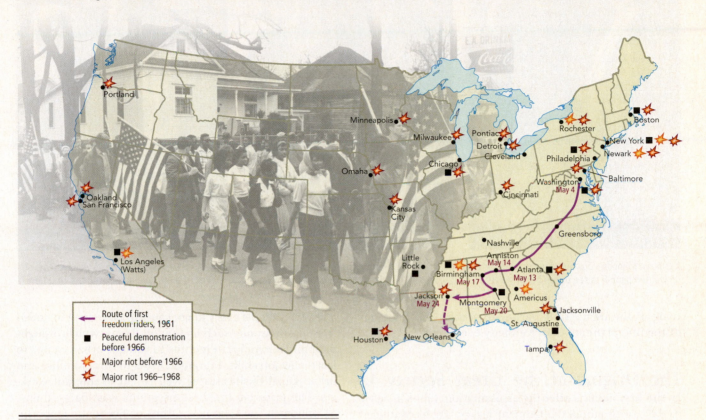

Portland
Minneapolis
Milwaukee
Pontiac
Detroit
Cleveland
Rochester
Boston
New York
Newark
Philadelphia
Baltimore
Chicago
Omaha
Oakland
San Francisco
Kansas City
Cincinnati
Washington May 4
Greensboro
Los Angeles (Watts)
Nashville
Little Rock
Anniston May 14
Atlanta May 13
Birmingham May 17
Americus
Jacksonville
Jackson May 24
Montgomery May 20
St. Augustine
Houston
New Orleans
Tampa

→ Route of first freedom riders, 1961
■ Peaceful demonstration before 1966
✦ Major riot before 1966
✦ Major riot 1966–1968

LYNDON JOHNSON AND THE GREAT SOCIETY

Like the state he hailed from, Lyndon Baines Johnson was in all things bigger than life. His gifts were greater, his flaws more glaring. Insecurity was his Achilles' heel and the engine that drove him. If Kennedy had been good as president, Johnson would be "the greatest of them all, the whole bunch of them." The president was sometimes driven to ask why so few people genuinely liked him; once a courageous diplomat actually answered; "Because, Mr. President, you are not a very likable man."

Johnson was born in the hill country outside Austin, Texas, where the dry, rough terrain only grudgingly yielded up a living. He arrived in Washington in 1932 as an ardent New Dealer who loved the political game. As majority leader of the Senate after 1954, Johnson was regarded as a moderate conservative who knew what strings to pull to get the job done. On an important bill, he latched on to the undecided votes until they succumbed to the famous "Johnson treatment," a combination of arguments, threats,

rewards, and patriotic appeals. (Once, before meeting with Johnson, President Eisenhower pleaded with his attorney general, William Rogers, to run interference: "Bill, if Lyndon tries to get around my desk, block him off. I can't stand it when he grabs me by the lapel.")

Despite his compulsion to control every person and situation, Johnson was best at hammering out compromises among competing interest groups. To those who served him well he could be loyal and generous. And as president, he cared sincerely about society's underdogs. His support for civil rights, aid to the poor, education, and the welfare of the elderly arose out of genuine conviction. In that sense he stood squarely in the liberal political tradition that flowered during the 1960s. Like the New Dealers of the 1930s and the progressives before them, liberals were pragmatic reformers who wished to refine rather than overturn capitalism. Like Franklin Roosevelt and John F. Kennedy, Johnson believed that the government could and should actively manage the economy in order to soften the boom-and-bust swings of capitalism. Like progressives from the turn of the century, Johnson looked to improve society by applying the intelligence of "experts." With the nation still in shock over the Kennedy assassination, Johnson possessed the horse-trading skills—and the leverage with the southern

⌃ Lyndon Johnson's powers of persuasion were legendary. He applied the "Johnson treatment" (as here, in 1957, to Senator Theodore Green) whenever he wanted people to see things his way. Few could say no, as he freely violated their personal space and reminded them who dominated the situation.

wing of the Democratic party—to accomplish far more of the liberal dream than Kennedy ever could.

The Origins of the Great Society »

In the first months after the assassination, Johnson acted as the conservator of the Kennedy legacy. "Let us continue," he told a grief-stricken nation. Liberals who had dismissed Johnson as an unprincipled power broker came to respect the energy he showed in quickly steering Kennedy's Civil Rights Act and tax cut legislation through Congress.

Kennedy had come to believe that prosperity alone would not ease the plight of America's poor. In 1962 Michael Harrington's book *The Other America* brought attention to the persistence of poverty despite the nation's affluence. Harrington focused attention on the hills of Appalachia, which stretched from western Pennsylvania south to Alabama. In some counties a quarter of the population survived on a diet of flour and dried-milk paste supplied by federal surplus food programs. Under Kennedy, Congress had passed a new food stamp program as well as laws designed to revive the economies of poor areas.

Robert Kennedy also headed a presidential committee to fight juvenile delinquency in urban slums by involving the poor in **community action** programs.

community action programs designed to identify and organize local leaders to take steps to alleviate poverty and crime in their neighborhoods.

It fell to Lyndon Johnson to fight Kennedy's "war on poverty." By August 1964 this master politician had driven through Congress the most sweeping social welfare bill since the New Deal. The Economic Opportunity Act addressed almost every major cause of poverty. It included training programs such as the Job Corps, which brought poor and unemployed recruits to rural or urban camps to learn new job skills. It granted loans to rural families and urban small businesses as well as aid to migrant workers. The price tag for these programs was high—almost $1 billion to fund the new Office of Economic Opportunity (OEO). Unfortunately the speed Johnson demanded in implementing the programs led in more than one instance to confusion, conflict, and waste.

The Election of 1964 »

In 1964, however, these flaws were not yet evident. Johnson's political stock remained high as he announced his ambition to forge a "Great Society," in which poverty and racial injustice no longer existed. The chance to fulfill his dreams seemed within reach, for the Republicans nominated Senator Barry Goldwater of Arizona as their presidential candidate. Though ruggedly handsome and refreshingly candid, Goldwater believed that government should not dispense welfare, subsidize farmers, or aid public education. He was so determined to combat the spread of communism that he favored a nuclear showdown, if necessary, to achieve victory. Few Americans subscribed to such conservative views.

Thus the election produced the landslide Johnson craved. Carrying every state except Arizona and four in the Deep South, he received 61 percent of the vote. Democrats gained better than two-to-one majorities in the Senate and House. The president moved rapidly to exploit the momentum.

The Great Society >>

In January 1965 Johnson announced a legislative vision that would extend welfare programs on a scale beyond even Franklin Roosevelt's New Deal. By the end of 1965 some 50 bills had been passed, many of them major pieces of legislation.

As a former teacher Johnson believed better schools would compensate the poor for their disadvantages at home. Under the Elementary and Secondary School Act, students in low-income school districts were to receive educational equipment, money for books, and enrichment programs like Project Head Start for nursery-school-age children. As schools scrambled to spend federal money, they paid more for middle-class educational professionals' salaries than on resources for disadvantaged students.

Johnson also pushed through the Medicare Act to provide the elderly with health insurance to cover their hospital costs. Studies had shown that older people used hospitals three times more than other Americans did and generally had incomes only half as large. Since Medicare made no provision for the poor who were not elderly, Congress also passed a program called Medicaid. Participating states would receive matching grants from the federal government to pay the medical expenses of those on welfare or those too poor to afford medical care.

The Great Society also reformed immigration policy in ways that showed how much global economics and culture had changed since 1924, when the National Origins Act was passed. That act had embodied the deeply Euro-centric orientation of American society, providing that almost all the annual admissions quota of 154,000 went to northern Europeans. Asians were barred almost entirely.

By 1965 the United States was a more diverse society. The Immigration Act of 1965 abolished the national origins system. Besides increasing annual admissions to 170,000, it gave marked preference to reuniting families of those immigrants already in the United States—so much so that some observers nicknamed it the "brothers and sisters act." Asians and Eastern Europeans were among its prime beneficiaries. Such liberal provisions were offset, however, by prejudice toward Latin Americans. Many in Congress feared a massive influx of poverty-stricken workers from south of the border. Hence the new act capped arrivals from the Western Hemisphere at 120,000 annually. Johnson's immigration reform thus reflected the shifting balance of the global economy.

Nor did Johnson, in his efforts to outdo the New Deal, slight the environment. By the mid-1960s many Americans had become increasingly concerned about smog from factories and automobiles; lakes and rivers polluted by detergents, pesticides, and industrial wastes; and the disappearance of wildlife. The insecticide DDT provided a prime example of such concerns. For years public health and agriculture officials had viewed DDT as a kind of magic bullet that could wipe out disease-spreading insects and pests such as the boll weevil that attacked crops. Deemed harmless, the chemical was sprayed regularly on farmland, forests, golf courses, beaches, and even around people.

Scientist and nature writer Rachel Carson argued against such casual and wholesale use. "The contamination of man's total environment with such substances of incredible harm," most significantly the pesticide DDT, she wrote in her 1962 book *Silent Spring,* could "alter the very material of heredity upon which the shape of the future depends." More fundamentally, Carson challenged the popular belief that humans could improve on nature through science and technology. "The 'control of nature'," she wrote, "is a phrase conceived in arrogance, born of the Neanderthal age of biology and philosophy when it was supposed that nature exists for the convenience of man. . . ." She advocated a biocentric approach in which humans sought harmony with the natural world. Her critics dismissed her as romantic or even hysterical. One linked her to "the organic gardeners, the anti-fluoride leaguers, the worshippers of 'natural foods' . . . and other pseudo-scientists and faddists."

But the outcry sparked by *Silent Spring* could not be suppressed. The Kennedy administration formed a committee to study the problem and it largely vindicated Carson. "The elimination of the use of persistent toxic pesticides should be the goal," the investigators concluded. More important, Carson taught Americans to think ecologically. She showed the interconnection of living things and how toxic chemicals moved through the food chain,

△ Convinced that pesticides such as DDT posed no threat to humans, public health and agriculture officials sprayed people and land with a reckless abandon that compelled Rachel Carson to advocate curbs on pesticide use.

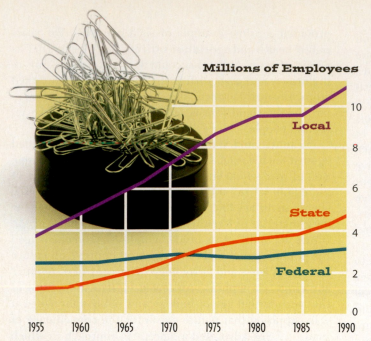

Millions of Employees

Local

10

8

State

6

4

Federal

2

0

1955   1960   1965   1970   1975   1980   1985   1990

GROWTH OF GOVERNMENT, 1955–1990

Government has been a major growth industry since World War II. Most people think of "big government" as federal government. But even during the Great Society, far more people worked in state and local government.

affecting beneficial and harmful insects alike, as well as birds, animals, and humans.

Carson's alarm helped inspire a broad movement to protect the environment, and Congress, prodded by Lyndon Johnson, took note. In 1964 and 1965 it established pollution standards for interstate waterways and provided funds for sewage treatment and water purification. New laws tightened standards on air pollution. In addition Congress passed the National Wilderness Preservation System Act to set aside 9.1 million acres of wilderness as "forever wild."

The Great Society produced more legislation and more reforms than the New Deal. It also carried a higher price tag than anyone predicted. Economic statistics suggested that general prosperity, boosted by the tax cut bill, did more to fight poverty than all the OEO programs. Conservatives and radicals alike objected that the liberal welfare state was intruding into too many areas of people's lives.

For all that, the Great Society was the high-water mark of a trend toward activist government that had grown steadily since the progressive era and the Great Depression. While Americans continued to pay lip service to the notion that government should remain small and interfere little in citizens' lives, no strong movement emerged to eliminate Medicare or Medicaid. Few Americans disputed the right of the government to regulate industrial pollution or to control the excesses of large corporations or powerful labor unions. In this sense, the tradition of liberalism prevailed, whatever Johnson's failings.

The Reforms of the Warren Court »

Although Lyndon Johnson and Congress led the liberal crusade in the 1960s, the Supreme Court played an equally significant role. Until Chief Justice Earl Warren retired in 1969, the Court continued to hand down landmark decisions in broad areas of civil liberties and civil rights.

In 1960 the rights of citizens accused of a crime but not yet convicted were often unclear. Those too poor to afford lawyers could be forced to go to trial without representation. Often they were not informed of their constitutional rights when arrested. In a series of decisions, the Court ruled that the Fourteenth Amendment provided broad guarantees of **due process** under the law. *Gideon v. Wainwright* (1963), an appeal launched by a Florida prisoner, made it clear that all citizens were entitled to legal counsel in any case involving a possible jail sentence. In *Escobedo v. Illinois* (1964) and *Miranda v. Arizona* (1966), the Court declared that individuals detained for a crime must be informed of the charges against them, of their right to remain silent, and of their right to have an attorney present during questioning. Though these decisions applied to all citizens, they were primarily intended to benefit the poor, who were most likely to be in trouble with the law and least likely to understand their rights.

due process constitutional concept, embodied in the Fifth and Fourteenth Amendments, that no person shall be deprived of life, liberty, or property without legal safeguards such as being present at a hearing, having an opportunity to be heard in court, having the opportunity to confront hostile witnesses, and being able to present evidence.

Other decisions promoted a more liberal social climate. In *Griswold v. Connecticut* (1964) the Warren Court overturned a nineteenth-century law banning the sale of contraceptives or medical advice about their use. The Court also demonstrated its distaste for censorship by greatly narrowing the legal definition of obscenity. A book had to be "utterly without redeeming social value" to permit censorship. And the Court strengthened the constitutional separation of church and state by ruling in *Engel v. Vitale* (1962) that prayers could not be read in public schools.

Banning official school prayer may have been one of the Court's most controversial decisions; *Baker v. Carr* (1962) was one of its most far-reaching. Most states had not redrawn their legislative districts to reflect the growth of urban and suburban population since the nineteenth century. The less populated (and most often conservative) rural areas elected the most legislators. In *Baker v. Carr* the Court ruled that the states must redraw legislative lines to follow as closely as possible the principle of "one person, one vote."

 REVIEW

What were three major legislative achievements of Johnson's Great Society?

YOUTH MOVEMENTS

In 1964 some 800 students from Berkeley, Oberlin, and other colleges met in western Ohio to be trained for the voter registration campaign in the South. Middle-class students who had grown up in peaceful white suburbs found themselves being instructed by protest-hardened SNCC coordinators. The lessons were sobering. When beaten by police, the SNCC staff advised, assume the fetal position—hands protecting the neck, elbows covering the temples. That minimized injuries from night-sticks. A few days later, grimmer news arrived. Three volunteers who had left for Mississippi two days earlier had already been arrested by local police. Now they were reported "missing." Six weeks later, their mangled bodies were found, bulldozed into the earthworks of a freshly finished dam.

By the mid-1960s conservatives, civil rights organizations, and the poor were not the only groups rejecting liberal solutions. Dissatisfied members of the middle class—and especially the young—had joined them. The students who returned to campus from the voter registration campaign that summer of 1964 were the shock troops of a much larger movement.

Activists on the New Left >> More than
a few students had become disillusioned with the slow pace of reform. Tom Hayden, from a working-class family in a suburb of Detroit, went to college at the University of Michigan, then traveled to Berkeley, and soon joined civil rights workers in Mississippi. Along with other radical students, Hayden helped form Students for a Democratic Society (SDS). Members of SDS gave up on change through the electoral system. Direct action was needed if the faceless, bureaucratic society of the "organization man" were to be made truly democratic. SDS advocated a "participatory democracy" that made full use of sit-ins, protest marches, and confrontation.

These discontents surfaced most dramatically in the Free Speech Movement at the University of California's Berkeley campus. To people like Tom Hayden and those in the SDS, Berkeley was a bureaucratic monster, enrolling more than 30,000 students who filed into large impersonal halls to endure lectures from remote professors. In the fall of 1964, when university police tried to remove a recruiter for CORE, thousands of angry students surrounded a police car for 32 hours.

To Mario Savio, a graduate student in philosophy and veteran of the Mississippi Freedom summer, the issue was clear: "In our free-speech fight, we have come up against what may emerge as the greatest problem of our nation—depersonalized, unresponsive bureaucracy." When the university's president, Clark Kerr, threatened to expel Savio, 6,000 students took control of the administration building, stopped classes with a strike, and convinced many faculty members to join them. Kerr backed down, placing no limits on free speech on campus except those that applied to society at large. But the lines between students and administrators had been drawn. The rebellious spirit spread to other major universities like Michigan, Yale, and Columbia, and then to campuses across the nation.

Political activism on college campuses was not limited to students on the left. The clean-cut members of Young Americans for Freedom (YAF) criticized students in the Free Speech Movement as beatniks, liberals, and Communists. To YAF Eisenhower's "middle-of-the-road Republicanism" and Kennedy's liberalism were both forms of "statism." Growth of government, these young conservatives believed, threatened individual liberty and freedom. Their hero, Barry Goldwater, embodied the **libertarian** values and anti-Communism they

> **libertarian** advocate of a minimalist approach to governing, in which the freedom of private individuals to do as they please ranks paramount.

⌃ Edie Black from Smith College was one of hundreds of middle-class students who volunteered during Freedom Summer of 1964. Here she teaches in a school at Mileston, Mississippi. Many students returned to their campuses in the fall radicalized, ready to convince others to join them in finding alternatives to "the system."

cherished. Undaunted by Goldwater's defeat in 1964, YAF was the seedbed of a new generation of conservatives who gained control of the Republican party in the 1970s.

Vatican II and American Catholics >>

Catholics played a prominent role in the creation of YAF. Many Catholics and conservatives condemned the secular trends of modern life as a threat to their traditional faith. But other American Catholics sought a greater engagement with the currents of change. They were pleased when, in October 1962, Pope John XXIII summoned church leaders to a reformist ecumenical council, popularly known as Vatican II.

Pope John instructed the council to weigh issues facing the world in the 1960s, including poverty, nuclear war, atheism, and birth control. He wished, as well, to bring the church hierarchy into closer touch with lay members and the modern world in which they lived. Although Pope John died before the council finished, his successor, Pope Paul VI, supported changes that would transform the church. Gone were "fish Fridays" and Saturday confessions. Priests would now face the congregation, not the altar, and deliver their services in English, not Latin. In

ecumenism movement encouraging unity among religions, especially among Christian denominations and between Christians and Jews.

addition, Vatican II encouraged Catholics to reach out to other Christians in a spirit of **ecumenism.**

The reforms initiated by John XXIII inspired many Catholics to activism both inside and outside the church. Fathers Daniel and Philip Berrigan were among a number of priests and nuns who joined antipoverty and antiwar movements. Some female Catholics sought a greater role for women in religious life. As one historian concluded, "Catholics live in a different world since the Council."

The Rise of the Counterculture >> Spiritual matters also aroused less-religious rebels who found their culture too materialistic and shallow. These alienated students began to grope toward spiritual, nonmaterial goals. "Turn on to the scene, tune in to what is happening, and drop out of high school, college, grad school, junior executive," advised Timothy Leary, a Harvard psychology professor who also dropped out. Those who heeded Leary's call to spiritual renewal rejected politics for a lifestyle of experimentation with music, sex, and drugs. Observers labeled their movement a "counterculture."

The counterculture of the 1960s had much in common with earlier religious revival and utopian movements. It admired the quirky individualism of Henry David Thoreau. Like Thoreau, it turned to Asian philosophies such as Zen Buddhism. Like Brook Farm and other nineteenth-century utopian communities, the new "hippie" communes sought perfection along the fringes of society.

Communards "learned how to scrounge materials, tear down abandoned buildings, use the unusable," as one member of the "Drop City" commune put it. Sexual freedom became a means to liberate members of the counterculture from the repressive inhibitions that distorted the lives of their "uptight" parents. Drugs appeared to offer access to a higher state of consciousness or pleasure. Timothy Leary began experimenting with hallucinogenic mushrooms in Mexico and soon moved on to LSD. The drug "blew his mind," he announced, and he became so enthusiastic in making converts that Harvard blew him straight out of its hallowed doors. By 1966 Leary was lecturing across the land on the joys of drug use.

Where Leary's approach to LSD was cool and contemplative, novelist Ken Kesey (*One Flew over the Cuckoo's Nest*) embraced it with antic frenzy. His ragtag company of druggies and freaks formed the "Merry Pranksters" at Kesey's home outside San Francisco. Writer Tom Wolfe chronicled their travels in

psychedelic characterized by or generating shifts in perception and altered states of awareness, often hallucinatory, and usually brought on by drugs such as LSD, mescaline, or psilocybin.

The Electric Kool-Aid Acid Test as the Pranksters headed east on a **psychedelic** school bus in search of Leary. Their example inspired others to drop out.

The Rock Revolution >> In the 1950s rock and roll defined a teen culture preoccupied with young love, cars, and adult pressures. One exception was the Kingston Trio, which in 1958 popularized folk music and historical ballads, especially among college audiences. As the interest in folk music grew, the lyrics increasingly focused on social or political issues. Bob Dylan joined other folk singers in the civil rights march on Washington in 1963, singing "We Shall Overcome" and "Blowin' in the Wind." Their music reflected the activist side of the counterculture as they sought to provoke their audiences to political commitment. Dylan, who had played his songs of social protest on an unamplified guitar, shocked fans in 1965 by donning a black leather jacket and shifting to a "folk rock" style featuring an electric guitar. His new songs seemed to suggest that the old America was almost beyond redemption.

In 1964 a new sound, imported from England, exploded on the American scene. The Beatles, four musicians from Liverpool, attracted frenzied teen audiences everywhere they played. Along with other English groups, like the Rolling Stones, the Beatles reconnected American audiences with the rhythm-and-blues roots of rock and roll. And, like Dylan's, their style influenced pop culture almost as much as their music. After a spiritual pilgrimage to India, they returned to produce *Sergeant Pepper's Lonely Hearts Club Band,* possibly the most influential album of the decade. It blended sound effects with music, alluded to trips taken with "Lucy in the Sky with Diamonds" (LSD), and welcomed listeners into a turned-on

^ The Beatles had a major impact on men's style as well as on popular music. This 1963 photo shows their "mod" look popular first in England. Later they adopted a hippie look.

world. Out in San Francisco, bands such as the Grateful Dead pioneered "acid rock" with long pieces aimed at echoing drug-induced states of mind.

The debt of white rock musicians to rhythm and blues led to increased integration in the music world. Before the 1960s black rhythm and blues bands played primarily to black audiences in segregated clubs or over black radio stations. Black artists such as Little Richard, Chuck Berry, and Ray Charles wrote many hit songs made popular by white performers. The rising black social and political consciousness gave rise to "soul" music. Blacks became "soul brothers" and "soul sisters," and for the first time their music was played on major radio stations. One black disk jockey

^ Rock groups such as the Grateful Dead were closely associated with the drug culture. LSD inspired the genre of psychedelic art that adorned album covers and posters with freaked-out lettering that seemed to dazzle and dance even if the viewer had not inhaled or ingested. The album here is titled *American Beauty*.

described soul as "the last to be hired, first to be fired, brown all year round, sit-in-the-back-of-the-bus-feeling." Soul was the quality that expressed black pride and separatism. Out of Detroit came the Motown sound, which combined elements of gospel, blues, and big-band jazz.

The West Coast Scene >> The vibrant counterculture also signaled an increasing importance of the West Coast in American popular culture. In the 1950s the shift of television production from the stages of New York to the film lots of Hollywood helped establish Los Angeles as a communications center. San Francisco became notorious as a center of the beat movement. By 1963 the "surfing sound" of West Coast rock groups such as the Beach Boys and Jan and Dean had made southern California's preoccupation with surfing and cars into a national fad.

Before 1967 Americans were only vaguely aware of another West Coast phenomenon, the "hippies." But in January a loose coalition of drug freaks, Zen cultists, and political activists banded together to hold the first well-publicized "Be-In." The beat poet Allen Ginsberg was on hand to offer spiritual guidance. The Grateful Dead and Jefferson Airplane, acid rock groups based in San Francisco, provided entertainment. An unknown organization called the Diggers somehow managed to supply free food and drink, while the notorious Hell's Angels motorcycle gang policed the occasion. In that way the Bay Area emerged as a spiritual center of the counterculture.

In the summer of 1969 all the positive forces of the counterculture converged on Bethel, New York, in the Catskill Mountains resort area, to celebrate the promise of peace, love, and freedom. The Woodstock Music Festival attracted 400,000 people to the largest rock concert ever organized. For one long weekend the audience and performers joined to form an ephemeral community based on sex, drugs, and rock and roll. Even then, the counterculture was dying. Violence intruded on the laid-back urban communities that hippies had formed. Organized crime and drug pushers muscled in on the lucrative trade in LSD, amphetamines, and marijuana. Bad drugs and addiction took their toll. Free sex often became an excuse for exploitation, loveless gratification, and even rape.

Furthermore, what failure could not doom was finished off by success. Much that once seemed outrageous in the hippie world was soon absorbed into the mainstream marketplace. Rock groups became big business enterprises commanding huge fees. Yogurt, granola, and herbal teas appeared on supermarket shelves. Ironically, much of the world that hippies forged was embraced and tamed by the society hippies had rejected.

 REVIEW

How did the following elements influence the counterculture: drugs, music, religion?

Despite such disillusionments at the end of the decade, the civil rights movement changed the United States in fundamental ways. Although de facto segregation and racism remained entwined in American life, segregation as a legal system had been overturned. No longer was it enshrined by the decisions of the highest court in the land, as it had been in *Plessy v. Ferguson*. And the rise of black power—in both its moderate and radical forms—reflected a political and cultural current that was international as well as national. In Africa the drive for civil rights revolved around the effort to overthrow the imperial powers of Europe. In colony after colony African nationalists fought for their independence, with Ghana leading the way in 1957. Too often the new governments devolved into dictatorships; while in South Africa the white regime maintained a system of *apartheid* that strictly segregated the races and smothered black political and economic progress. But colonial empires continued to fall across the globe.

The United States granted independence to its principal Asian colony, the Philippines, in 1946. Yet Americans, too, found themselves ensnared by the conflicts of colonialism. More than any other single factor, a growing war in France's former colony, Vietnam, destroyed the promise of Lyndon Johnson's Great Society and distracted from the campaign for civil rights. After 1965 the nation divided sharply as the American military role in Southeast Asia grew. Radicals on the left looked to rid America of a capitalist system that promoted race and class conflict at home and imperialism and military adventurism abroad. Conservatives who supported the war called for a return to more traditional values, such as law and order. Both the left and the right attacked the liberal center. Their combined opposition helped undermine the consensus Lyndon Johnson had worked so hard to build.

CHAPTER SUMMARY

Largely excluded from the prosperity of the 1950s, African Americans and Latinos undertook a series of grassroots efforts to gain the legal and social freedoms denied them by racism and, in the South, an entrenched system of segregation.

- Early postwar campaigns focused on legal challenges to the system, winning victories in the Supreme Court decisions of *Brown v. Board of Education* and *Hernández v. Texas.*
- Later in the 1950s Martin Luther King and other civil rights activists used new techniques of protest, such as the boycott to desegregate the bus system in Montgomery, Alabama.
- Continued resistance by white southerners sparked a school integration dispute in Little Rock, Arkansas.
- Beginning in 1960 widespread grassroots efforts from black churches, students, and political groups accelerated the drive for an end to segregation.

Significant Events

Hernández v. Texas; Brown v. Board of Education
1954

Montgomery bus boycott begun
1955

Little Rock crisis
1957

Greensboro sit-ins
1960

CORE freedom rides begin
1961

JAMES MEREDITH

James Meredith desegregates University of Mississippi; *Engel v. Vitale; Baker v. Carr*
1962

- Violence against sit-ins, Freedom Rides, voter registration drives, and other forms of nonviolent protest made the nation sympathetic to the civil rights cause.
- In the wake of the assassination of President Kennedy, Lyndon Johnson persuaded Congress to adopt the Civil Rights Act of 1964 and the Voting Rights Act of 1965.
- The Supreme Court under Chief Justice Earl Warren expanded civil liberties through its Gideon, Escobedo, and Miranda decisions, and also eased censorship, banned school prayer, and increased voting rights.
- Lyndon Johnson delivered on the liberal promise of his Great Society through his 1964 tax cut, aid to education, Medicare and Medicaid, wilderness preservation, and urban redevelopment and through the many programs of his war on poverty.
- Johnson's liberal reforms did not satisfy student radicals, minority dissidents, feminists, gays, and the counterculture whose members sought to transform America into a more just and less materialistic society.

Additional Reading

Steven Lawson, Charles Payne, and James Patterson provide an excellent overview in *Debating the Civil Rights Movement, 1945–1968* (2006). Also useful is Robert Weisbrot, *Freedom Bound: A History of America's Civil Rights Movement* (1990). Though exhaustive in detail (nearly 3,000 pages in all), Taylor Branch's three-volume biography of Martin Luther King, Jr., is superb: *Parting the Waters, America in the King Years, 1954–1963* (1988); *Pillar of Fire: America in the King Years, 1963–65* (1998); and *At the Edge of Canaan: America in the King Years, 1965–1968* (2006). The prominent role of women, sometimes slighted, receives its due in Bettye Collier-Thomas and V. P. Franklin, eds., *Sisters in the Struggle: African-American Women in the Civil Rights–Black Power Movements* (2001). Latino civil rights movements are covered in Henry A. J. Ramos, *American G.I. Forum* (1998), and F. Arturo Rosales, *Chicano! The History of the Mexican-American Civil Rights Movement* (1997).

Todd Gitlin, *The Sixties* (1987), set the early tone for books that are part history and part memoir. Terry Anderson, *The Movement and the Sixties* (1995), offers a view that is both politically engaged and scholarly. Mark H. Lytle, *The Gentle Subversive: Rachel Carson, Silent Spring and the Rise of the Environmental Movement* (2007) provides a brief biographical approach. For a narrative overview also consult Lytle, *America's Uncivil Wars: The Sixties Era from Elvis to the Fall of Richard Nixon* (2006). Robert Dallek, *An Unfinished Life: John F. Kennedy, 1917–1963* (2003), draws a portrait that balances Kennedy's virtues and vices. The best recent biography of Lyndon Johnson is Randall Woods, *LBJ: Architect of Ambition* (2006).

Escobedo v. Illinois; Griswold v. Connecticut; Civil Rights Act passed; Economic Opportunity Act; Wilderness Preservation System Act; Johnson defeats Goldwater; Berkeley Free Speech Movement; Beatles introduce British rock

Black Panthers battle Oakland, California, police; first Be-In

1963   1964   1965   1967   1969

March on Washington; *Gideon v. Wainwright*; Kennedy assassinated

Johnson launches the Great Society; Voting Rights Act; Watts riots; Malcolm X assassinated; Medicare and Medicaid acts

Woodstock Music Festival

ELDRIDGE CLEAVER

The Vietnam Era

1963–1975

In Vietnam helicopters gave infantry unusual mobility—a critical element in a war with no real front line, because troops could be quickly carried from one battle to another. These soldiers await a pickup amid rice paddies south of Saigon.

30

>> **AN AMERICAN STORY**

WHO IS THE ENEMY?

Vietnam from afar: it looked like an emerald paradise. Thomas Bird, an army rifleman sent there in 1965, recalled his first impression: "A beautiful white beach with thick jungle background. The only thing missing was naked women running down the beach, waving and shouting 'Hello, hello, hello.'" Upon landing, Bird and his buddies were each issued a "Nine-Rule" card outlining proper behavior toward the Vietnamese. "Treat the women with respect, we are guests in this country and here to help these people." >>

But who were they helping and who were they fighting? When American troops searched out Vietcong forces, the VC generally disappeared into the jungle beyond the villages and rice fields. John Muir, a marine rifleman, walked into a typical hamlet with a Korean lieutenant. To Muir the place looked ordinary, but the Korean had been in Vietnam awhile. "We have a little old lady and a little old man and two very small children," he pointed out. "According to them, the rest of the family has been spirited away . . . either been drafted into one army or the other. So there's only four of them, and they have a pot of rice that's big enough to feed fifty people. And rice, once it's cooked, will not keep. They gotta be feeding the VC." Muir watched in disbelief as the lieutenant set the house on fire. The roof "started cooking off ammunition, because all through the thatch they had ammunition stored."

GIs soon learned to walk down jungle trails with a cautious shuffle, looking for a wire or a piece of vine that seemed too straight. "We took more casualties from booby traps than we did from actual combat," recalled David Ross, a medic. "It was very frustrating because how do you fight back against a booby trap? You're just walking along and all of a sudden your buddy doesn't have a leg. Or you don't have a leg." Yet somehow the villagers would walk the same paths and never get hurt. Who was the enemy and who the friend?

The same question was being asked half a globe away, on the campus of Kent State University on May 4, 1970. By then the Vietnam War had dragged on for more than five years, driving President Lyndon Johnson from office and embroiling his successor, Richard Nixon, in controversy. When Nixon expanded the war beyond Vietnam into Cambodia, protest erupted even at Kent State, just east of Akron, Ohio. Opposition to the war had become so intense in this normally apolitical community that 300 students had torn the Constitution from a history text and, in a formal ceremony, buried it. "President Nixon has murdered it," they charged. That evening demonstrators spilled into the nearby town, smashed shop windows, and returned to campus to burn down an old army ROTC building. Governor James Rhodes ordered in 750 of the National Guard. Student dissidents were the "worst type of people we harbor in America," he announced. "We are going to eradicate the problem."

When demonstrators assembled for a rally on the college commons, the Guard ordered them to disperse. Whether they had the authority to do so was debatable. The protesters stood their ground. Then the guardsmen advanced, wearing full battle gear and armed with M-1 rifles, whose high-velocity bullets had a horizontal range of almost two miles. Some students scattered; a few picked up rocks and threw them. The guardsmen suddenly fired into the crowd, many of whom were students passing back and forth from classes. Incredulous, a young woman knelt over Jeffrey Miller; he was dead. By the time calm was restored, three other students had been killed and nine more wounded, some caught innocently in the Guard's indiscriminate fire.

News of the killings swept the nation. At Jackson State, a black college in Mississippi, antiwar protesters seized a women's dormitory. On

⌃ Nguyen Ai Quoc, who became Ho Chi Minh, once worked at London's posh Carlton Hotel in the pastry kitchen of the renowned chef Escoffier. But he was soon swept up in socialist and nationalist politics, appearing at the Versailles Peace Conference (*left*) to plead for an independent Vietnam. Ho spent a lifetime in anticolonialist and revolutionary activity and became a revered leader of his people (*right*). He died in 1969, six years before his dream of a united Vietnam became a reality.

May 14 state police surrounding the building opened fire without provocation, killing two more students and wounding a dozen. In both incidents the demonstrators had been unarmed. The events at Kent State and Jackson State turned sporadic protests against the American invasion of Cambodia into a nationwide student strike. Many students believed the ideals of the United States had been betrayed by those forces of law and order sworn to protect them.

Who was the friend and who the enemy? Time and again the war in Vietnam led Americans to ask that question. Not since the Civil War had the nation been so deeply divided. As the war dragged on, debate moved off college campuses and into the homes of middle Americans, where sons went off to fight and the war came home each night on the evening news. As no other war had, Vietnam seemed to stand the nation on its head. When American soldiers shot at Vietnamese "hostiles," who could not always be separated from "friendlies," or when National Guardsmen fired on their neighbors across a college green, who were the enemies and who were the friends? «

THE ROAD TO VIETNAM

For several thousand years Vietnam had struggled periodically to fight off foreign invasions. Buddhist culture had penetrated eastward from India. More often Indochina faced invasion and rule by the Chinese from the north. After 1856 the French entered as a colonial power, bringing with them a strong Catholic tradition.

Ho Chi Minh was one Vietnamese who hoped to throw off French influence as well as the Chinese. Since the end of World War I, he had worked to create an independent Vietnam. After World War II he organized a guerrilla war against the French, which finally led to their defeat at Dien Bien Phu in 1954 (page 600). He agreed at the Geneva peace conference to withdraw his forces north of the 17th parallel in return for a promise to hold free elections in both the North and the South. The Americans, having supported the French struggle against Ho, helped install Ngo Dinh Diem in South Vietnam. They then supported Diem's decision not to hold elections, which Ho's followers seemed sure to win. Frustrated South Vietnamese Communists—the Vietcong—renewed their guerrilla war. "I think the Americans greatly underestimate the determination of the Vietnamese people," Ho remarked in 1962, as President Kennedy was committing more American advisers to South Vietnam.

Lyndon Johnson's War » For Kennedy, Vietnam had been just one of many anti-Communist skirmishes his activist advisers wanted to fight. As attention focused increasingly on Vietnam, he came to discount President Eisenhower's "domino theory" that if Diem's pro-Western government fell to the Communists, the other nations of Southeast Asia would collapse one after the other. Still, he saw a Communist victory as unacceptable. But what to do? Even 16,000 American "advisers"

had been unable to help the unpopular Diem, who was executed by a military coup in November 1963, which had the tacit support of the United States. When Kennedy was assassinated a few weeks later, the problem of Vietnam was left to Lyndon Johnson.

Johnson's political instincts told him to keep the Vietnam War at arm's length. He felt like a catfish, he remarked, who had "just grabbed a big juicy worm with a right sharp hook in the middle of it." Johnson's heart was in his Great Society programs. Yet fear of the political costs of defeat in Vietnam led him steadily toward deeper American involvement.

Until August 1964 American advisers had focused on training and supporting the South Vietnamese army, which fought the Vietcong reluctantly. North Vietnam, for its part, had been infiltrating men and supplies along the Ho Chi Minh Trail, a network of jungle routes threading through Laos and Cambodia into the highlands of South Vietnam. With the Vietcong controlling some 40 percent of South Vietnam, Johnson strategists decided to relieve the South by increasing pressure on North Vietnam itself.

American ships patrolling the Gulf of Tonkin began to provide cover for secret South Vietnamese raids against the North. On August 2, three North Vietnamese patrol boats exchanged fire with the American destroyer *Maddox*. Two nights later, in inky blackness and a heavy thunderstorm, a second incident occurred. But a follow-up investigation could not be sure whether enemy ships had even been near the scene. President Johnson was not pleased. "For all I know our navy might have been shooting at whales out there," he remarked privately.

Whatever his doubts, the president publicized both incidents as "open aggression on the high sea" and ordered retaliatory air raids on North Vietnam. He did not disclose that the navy and South Vietnamese forces had been conducting secret military operations at the time. When Johnson then asked for the authority to take "all necessary measures" to "repel any armed attack" on American

Ho Chi Minh Trail

Major battles of Tet offensive

CHINA

NORTH VIETNAM

BURMA

Lao Cai

Dien Bien Phu

Thai Nguyen

Hanoi

Haiphong

GULF OF TONKIN

Mekong R.

Luang Prabang

PLAIN OF JARS

Thanh Hoa

Gulf of Tonkin incident Aug. 1964

Hainan

LAOS

Vinh

Vientiane

SOUTH CHINA SEA

Ping R.

Yom R.

Po Sak R.

THAILAND

Mekong R.

Mun R.

Con Thien
Sepone   Quang Tri
Khe Sanh   Hue

Da Nang

My Lai Massacre March 16, 1968

Quang Ngai

Dak To
Kon Tum

Bangkok

CAMBODIA

Tonle Sap

Pursat

Mekong R.

CENTRAL HIGHLANDS

Pleiku

Qui Nhon

SOUTH VIETNAM

Nha Trang

Da Lat

GULF OF THAILAND

Phnom Penh

Chau Doc

PLAIN OF REEDS

Song Be

Saigon

Ben Tre

Can Tho

Mekong River Delta

0   200 mi
0   200   400 km

THE WAR IN VIETNAM

For the United States one strategic problem was to locate and destroy the supply routes known as the Ho Chi Minh Trail. Rugged mountains and triple canopy jungles hid much of the trail from aerial observation and attack.

withdraw. In theory **escalation** would increase military pressure to the point at which further resistance would cost more than the enemy was willing to pay. By taking

> **escalation** process of steady intensification, rather than a sudden or marked increase, applied to the increasing American military presence in Vietnam.

gradual steps the United States would demonstrate its resolve to win while leaving the door open to negotiations.

The theory that made so much sense in the White House did not work well in practice. Each stage of American escalation only hardened the resolve of the Vietcong and North Vietnamese. When a Vietcong mortar attack in February killed seven marines stationed at Pleiku airbase, Johnson ordered U.S. planes to begin bombing North Vietnam.

Restricted air strikes did not satisfy more hawkish leaders. Retired Air Force chief of staff Curtis LeMay complained, "We are swatting flies when we should be going after the whole manure pile." In March Johnson ordered Operation Rolling Thunder, a systematic bombing campaign aimed at bolstering confidence in South Vietnam and cutting the flow of supplies from the North. Rolling Thunder achieved none of its goals. American pilots could seldom spot the Ho Chi Minh Trail under its dense jungle canopy. Equally discouraging, South Vietnamese leaders quarreled among themselves and jockeyed for power instead of uniting against the Vietcong.

Once the Americans established bases from which to launch the new air strikes, these too became targets for guerrilla attacks. General William Westmoreland, the chief of American military operations in Vietnam, requested combat troops to defend the bases. Johnson's decision to send 3,500 marines proved to be a crucial first

forces and to "prevent future aggression," Congress overwhelmingly passed what became known as the Tonkin Gulf Resolution.

Senator Ernest Gruening of Alaska, one of only two lawmakers to vote no, objected that the resolution gave the president "a blank check" to declare war, a power the Constitution reserved to Congress. Johnson insisted that he had limited aims. But with his victory in the 1964 election the president felt free to exploit the powers the resolution gave him.

Rolling Thunder >> In January 1965 Johnson received a disturbing memorandum from Bundy and McNamara. "Both of us are now pretty well convinced that our present policy can lead only to disastrous defeat," they said. The United States should either increase its attack—*escalate* was the term coined in 1965—or simply

step toward Americanizing the war. Another 40,000 soldiers arrived in May and 50,000 more by July.

McNamara ordered that the escalation be carried out in a "low-keyed manner to avoid undue concern and excitement in the Congress and in domestic public opinion." He worried also about how China and Russia might react. By 1966 almost 185,000 American troops had landed—and the call for more continued. In 1968, at the height of the war, 536,000 American troops were being supported with helicopters, jet aircraft, and other advanced military technologies. This was "escalation" with a vengeance.

REVIEW

Why did Lyndon Johnson choose to escalate the war in Vietnam, and how did he do it?

SOCIAL CONSEQUENCES OF THE WAR

The impact of the war fell hardest on the baby-boom generation of the 1950s. As these young people came of age, draft calls for the armed services were rising. At the same time, the civil rights movement and the growing counterculture were encouraging students to question the goals of establishment America. Whether they fought in Vietnam or protested at home, supported the government or demonstrated against it, eventually these baby boomers—as well as Americans of all ages—were forced to take a stand on Vietnam.

The Soldiers' War >> Most Americans sent to Vietnam were chosen by the draft. Under the Selective Service System, as it was called, many young people in the middle and upper classes could avoid service: college students or those working in "critical" occupations, such as teachers and engineers. As the war escalated, the draft was changed so that some students were called up through a lottery system. Still, those who knew the medical requirements might be able to produce a doctor's affidavit

certifying a weak knee, flat feet, or bad eyes—all grounds for flunking the physical. Of the 1,200 men in Harvard's class of 1970, only 56 served in the military, and only 2 of them in Vietnam.

The poorest and least educated were also likely to escape service, because the Armed Forces Qualification Test and the physical often screened them out. Thus the sons of blue-collar America were most likely to accept Uncle Sam's letter of induction. Once in uniform, Hispanic and black Americans who had fewer skills were more often assigned to combat duty. The draft also made it a relatively young man's war. The average age of soldiers serving in Vietnam was 19, compared with an average of 26 for World War II.

Most American infantry came to Vietnam ready and willing to fight. But physical and psychological hardships took their toll. An American search-and-destroy mission would fight its way into a Communist-controlled hamlet, clear and burn it, and move on—only to be ordered back days or weeks later because the enemy had moved in again. Since success could not be measured in territory gained, the measure became the "body count": the number of Vietcong killed. Unable to tell who was friendly and who was hostile, GIs sometimes took out their frustrations on innocent civilians. Officers counted those victims as Vietcong in order to inflate the numbers that suggested the Americans were winning.

Most Americans assumed that superior military technology could guarantee success. But technology alone could not tell friend from foe. Since the Vietcong routinely mixed with the civilian population, the chances for deadly error increased. Bombs of napalm (jellied gasoline) and white phosphorus rained liquid fire from the skies,

>> The Vietcong often fought in small groups, using the dense vegetation to cover their movements. These suspects faced an arduous interrogation as U.S. soldiers tried to learn more about the location of Vietcong units.

coating everything from village huts to the flesh of flee-ing humans. Since the enemy could hide in the jungle, the Americans made war on its vegetation. American planes spread more than 100 million pounds of defoliants that destroyed more than one-third of South Vietnam's timberlands—an area approximately the size of the state of Rhode Island. The long-term health and ecological effects were severe. The military benefits were minimal.

⌃ Before and after. The devastating impact of American bombing and use of defoliants such as Agent Orange on the Vietnamese countryside.

By 1967 the war was costing more than $2 billion a month. The United States dropped more bombs on Viet-nam than it had during all of World War II. After one air attack on a Communist-held provincial capital, Ameri-can troops walked into the smoldering ruins. "We had to destroy the town in order to save it," an officer explained. As the human and material costs of the war increased, that statement stuck in the minds of many observers. What sense was there in a war that saved people by burn-ing their homes?

The War at Home ›› As the war dragged on

such questions provoked anguished debate among Ameri-cans, especially on college campuses. Faculty members held "teach-ins" to explain the issues to concerned stu-dents. Scholars familiar with Southeast Asia questioned every major assumption the president used to justify esca-lation. The United States and South Vietnam had brought on the war, they charged, by violating the Geneva Accords of 1954. Moreover, the Vietcong were an indigenous rebel force with legitimate grievances against Saigon's corrupt government. The war was a civil war among the Viet-namese, not an effort by Soviet or Chinese Communists to conquer Southeast Asia, as Eisenhower, Kennedy, and Johnson had claimed.

hawks and doves nicknames for the two opposing posi-tions in American policy dur-ing the war in Vietnam. Hawks supported the escalation of the war and a "peace with honor." Doves argued that the United States had wrongly intervened in a civil war and should withdraw its troops.

By 1966 national lead-ers had divided into oppos-ing camps of "**hawks**" and "**doves.**" The hawks argued that America must win in Vietnam to save Southeast Asia from communism, to preserve the nation's pres-tige, and to protect the lives of American soldiers fight-ing the war. Most Americans supported those views. The doves were nonetheless a prominent minority. Afri-can Americans as a group were far less likely than white Americans to support the war. Some resented the diver-sion of resources from the cities to the war effort. Many black Americans' heightened sense of racial consciousness led them to identify with the Vietnamese people. Martin Luther King, SNCC, and CORE all opposed the war. Heavy-weight boxing champion Muhammad Ali, a black Muslim, refused on religious grounds to serve in the army, even though the decision cost him his title.

By 1967 college students and faculty turned out in crowds to express their outrage: "Hey, hey, LBJ, how many kids have you killed today?" Over 300,000 people demonstrated in April 1967 in New York City. Some col-lege protesters even burned their draft cards in defiance of federal law. In the fall more violent protests erupted as antiwar radicals stormed a draft induction center in Oakland, California. The next day 55,000 protesters ringed the Pentagon in Washington. Again, mass arrests followed.

As protests flared, key moderates became increas-ingly convinced the United States could not win the war. Senator William Fulbright of Arkansas was among them. Having helped President Johnson push the Tonkin Gulf Resolution through the Senate, Fulbright now held hear-ings sharply critical of American policy.

Defense Secretary Robert McNamara became the most dramatic defector. For years the statistically minded sec-retary struggled to quantify the success of the war effort. By 1967 McNamara had become skeptical. If Americans were killing 300,000 Vietnamese, enemy forces should be shrinking. Instead, intelligence estimates indicated that North Vietnamese infiltration had risen from 35,000 a year in 1965 to 150,000 in 1967. McNamara came to have deep moral qualms about continuing the war indefinitely. "The picture of the world's greatest superpower killing or seriously injuring 1,000 noncombatants a week, while trying to pound a tiny, backward nation into submission on an issue whose merits are hotly disputed, is not a pretty one," he advised. When Johnson, who did not want to be remembered as the first American leader who lost a war, continued to side with the hawks, McNamara resigned.

> **"You can kill ten of my men for every one I kill of yours . . . even at those odds, you lose and we win." (Ho Chi Minh)**

As the war's cost soared to more than $50 billion a year, it fueled a rising inflation. Medicare, education, housing, and other Great Society programs raised the domestic budget sharply too. Through it all Johnson refused to raise taxes, even though wages and prices rose rapidly. From 1965 to 1970 inflation jumped from about 2 percent to around 4 percent. The economy was headed for trouble.

 REVIEW

What factors complicated conducting the war in Vietnam and managing the war at home?

THE UNRAVELING

Almost all the forces dividing America seemed to converge in 1968. Until January of that year, most Americans had reason to believe General Westmoreland's estimate of the war. There was, he suggested, "light at the end of the tunnel." Johnson and his advisers, whatever their private doubts, in public painted an optimistic picture. With such hope radiating from Washington, few Americans were prepared for the events of the night of January 30, 1968.

Tet Offensive ▶▶ As the South Vietnamese began their celebration of Tet, the Vietnamese lunar New Year, Vietcong guerrillas launched a series of concerted attacks. Assault targets included Saigon's major airport, the South Vietnamese presidential palace, and Hue, the ancient Vietnamese imperial capital. Most unnerving to Americans, 19 Vietcong commandos blasted a hole in the American embassy compound in Saigon and stormed in. They fought in the courtyard until all 19 lay dead. One reporter, stunned by the carnage, compared the courtyard to a butcher shop.

Tet must rank as one of the great American intelligence failures, on a par with the failure to anticipate Japan's attack on Pearl Harbor or China's intervention in the Korean War. For nearly half a year the North Vietnamese had lured American troops away from Vietnam's cities into pitched battles at remote outposts. As American forces dispersed, the Vietcong infiltrated major population centers. A few audacious VC, disguised as South Vietnamese soldiers, even hitched rides on American jeeps and trucks. Though surprised by the Tet offensive, American and South Vietnamese troops repulsed most of the assaults. General Westmoreland announced that the Vietcong's "well-laid plans went afoul."

In a narrow military sense Westmoreland was right. The enemy had been driven back, sustaining perhaps 40,000 deaths. Only 1,100 American and 2,300 South Vietnamese soldiers had been killed. But Americans at home received quite another message. Tet created a "credibility gap" between the administration's optimistic reports and the war's harsh reality. The president had repeatedly claimed that the Vietcong were on their last legs. Yet as Ho Chi Minh had coolly informed the French after World War II: "You can kill ten of my men for every one I kill of yours . . . even at those odds, you will lose and I will win." Respected CBS news anchor Walter Cronkite drew a gloomy lesson of Tet for his national audience: "To say that we are mired in stalemate seems the only realistic, yet unsatisfactory, conclusion."

The Tet offensive sobered Lyndon Johnson as well as his new secretary of defense, Clark Clifford. Clifford was a Johnson loyalist and a believer in the war. But as he reviewed the American position in Vietnam, he could get no satisfactory answers from the Joint Chiefs of Staff, who had requested an additional 206,000 troops. "How long would it take to succeed in Vietnam?" Clifford recalled asking them:

> They didn't know. How many more troops would it take? They couldn't say. Were two hundred thousand the answer? They weren't sure. Might they need more? Yes, they might need more. Could the enemy build up [their own troop strength] in exchange? Probably. So what was the plan to win the war? Well, the only plan was that attrition would wear out the Communists, and they would have had enough. Was there any indication that we've reached that point? No, there wasn't.

LEVELS OF U.S. TROOPS IN VIETNAM (AT YEAR END)

This graph suggests one reason why protest against the war increased after 1964, peaked by 1968, and largely ended after 1972.

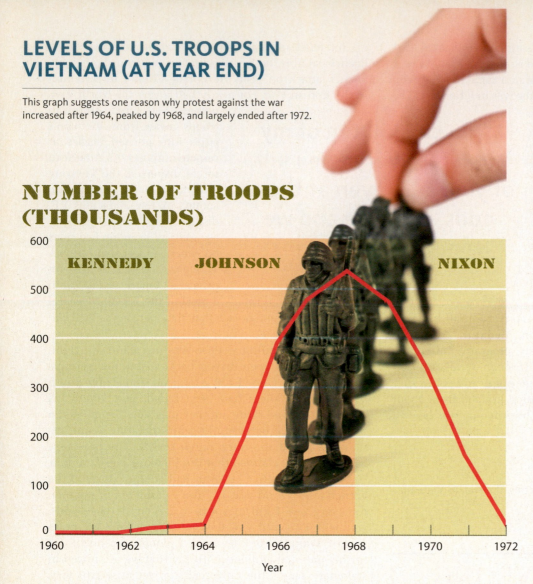

NUMBER OF TROOPS (THOUSANDS)

KENNEDY   JOHNSON   NIXON

600
500
400
300
200
100
0

1960   1962   1964   1966   1968   1970   1972

Year

an announcement that bombing raids against North Vietnam would be halted, at least partially, in hopes that peace talks could begin. They were still trying to write an ending when Johnson told them, "Don't worry; I may have a little ending of my own." On March 31 he supplied it, announcing: "I have concluded that I should not permit the presidency to become involved in the partisan divisions that are developing in this political year. . . . Accordingly I shall not seek, and I will not accept, the nomination of my party for another term as your president."

The announcement shocked nearly everyone. The Vietnam War had pulled down one of the savviest, most effective politicians of the era. North Vietnam responded to the speech by sending delegates to a peace conference in Paris, where negotiations quickly bogged down. And American attention soon focused on the chaotic situation at home, where all the turbulence, discontent, and violence of the 1960s seemed to be coming together.

Clifford decided to build a case for de-escalation. To review policy, he formed a panel of "wise men," respected pillars of the cold war establishment. The war could not be won, they concluded, and Johnson should seek a negotiated settlement.

Meanwhile, the antiwar forces had found a political champion in Senator Eugene McCarthy from Wisconsin. McCarthy was something of a maverick, who wrote poetry in his spare time. He announced that no matter how long the odds, he intended to challenge Lyndon Johnson in the 1968 Democratic primaries. Idealistic college students got haircuts and shaves in order to look "clean for Gene" as they campaigned for McCarthy in New Hampshire. Johnson won the primary, but his margin was so slim (300 votes) that it amounted to a stunning defeat. To the anger of McCarthy supporters, Robert Kennedy, John Kennedy's younger brother, quickly announced his own antiwar candidacy.

"I've got to get me a peace proposal," the president told Clifford. White House speechwriters put together

The Shocks of 1968 >> On April 4 Martin Luther King, Jr., traveled to Memphis to support striking sanitation workers. He was relaxing on the balcony of his motel when James Earl Ray, an escaped convict, fatally shot him with a sniper's rifle. King's campaign of nonviolence was overshadowed by the violent reaction to his murder. Riots broke out in ghetto areas of the nation's capital; by the end of the week, disturbances rocked 125 more neighborhoods across the country. Then on the evening of June 5 a disgruntled Arab nationalist, Sirhan Sirhan, assassinated Robert Kennedy. Running in opposition to the war, Kennedy had just won a crucial primary victory in California.

The deaths of King and Kennedy pained Americans deeply. In their own ways, both men exemplified the liberal tradition, which reached its high-water mark in the 1960s. King had retained his faith in a Christian theology of nonviolence. He sought reform for the poor of all races without resorting to the language of the fist and the gun. Robert Kennedy had come to reject the war his brother

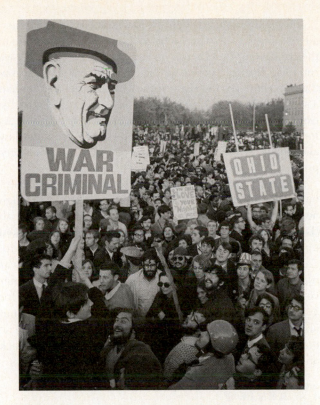

Despite the liberal achievements of the Great Society, antiwar protestors vilified Lyndon Johnson.

mayor's blessing, turned on the crowd in what a federal commission later labeled a police riot. In one pitched battle, many officers took off their badges and waded into the crowd, nightsticks swinging, chanting "Kill, kill, kill." Reporters, medics, and other innocent bystanders were injured; at 3 A.M. police invaded candidate Eugene McCarthy's hotel headquarters and pulled some of his assistants from their beds.

With feelings running so high, President Johnson did not dare appear at his own party's convention. Theodore White, a veteran journalist covering the assemblage, scribbled his verdict in a notebook as police chased hippies down Michigan Avenue. "The Democrats are finished," he wrote.

Revolutionary Clashes Worldwide »

The clashes in Chicago seemed homegrown, but they took place against the backdrop of a global surge in radical, often violent, student upheavals. In 1966 Chinese students were in the vanguard of Mao Zedong's Red Guards, formed to enforce a Cultural Revolution that sought to purge China of all bourgeois cultural influences. Although that revolution persecuted millions among the educated classes and left the country in economic shambles, Mao became a hero to radicals outside China. Radicals also lionized other revolutionaries who took up arms: Fidel Castro and Che Guevara in Cuba and Ho Chi Minh in Vietnam.

Radical targets varied. In Italy students denounced the official Marxism of the Soviet Union and the Italian Communist party. French students at the Sorbonne in Paris rebelled against the university's efforts to discipline political activists. Students in Czechoslovakia launched a full-scale rebellion, known as Prague Spring, against the Soviet domination of their nation—until Soviet tanks crushed the uprising. Though the agenda varied from country to country, virtually all student revolutionaries condemned the American war in Vietnam.

had supported, and he seemed genuinely to sympathize with the poor and minorities. At the same time, he was popular among traditional white ethnics and blue-collar workers. Would the liberal political tradition have flourished longer if these two charismatic figures had survived the turbulence of the 1960s?

Once violence silenced the most distinct liberal voices, it became clear that Democrats would choose Hubert Humphrey to replace Lyndon Johnson. Humphrey had begun his career as a progressive and a strong supporter of civil rights. But as Johnson's loyal vice president, he was intimately associated with the war and the old-style liberal reforms that could never satisfy radicals. The Republicans had chosen Richard Nixon, a traditional anti-Communist now reborn as the "new," more moderate Nixon. As much as radicals disliked Johnson, they truly abhorred Nixon, "new" or old.

Chicago, where the Democrats met for their convention, was the fiefdom of Mayor Richard Daley, long a symbol of machine politics. Daley was determined that the dissatisfied radicals who poured into Chicago would not disrupt "his" Democratic convention. The radicals were equally determined that they would. For a week the police skirmished with demonstrators: police clubs, riot gear, and tear gas versus the demonstrators' eggs, rocks, and balloons filled with paint and urine. When Daley refused to allow a peaceful march past the convention site, the radicals marched anyway, and then the police, with the

Whose Silent Majority? »

Radicals were not the only Americans alienated from the political system in 1968. Governor George Wallace of Alabama sensed the frustration among the "average man on the street, this man in the textile mill, this man in the steel mill, this barber, this beautician, the policeman on the beat." In running for president, Wallace sought the support of blue-collar workers and the lower middle classes.

Wallace had first come to national attention in 1963, when he barred integration of the University of Alabama. Briefly, he pursued the Democratic presidential nomination in 1964. For the race in 1968 he formed his own American Independent party. Wallace's enemies were the "liberals, intellectuals, and long hairs [who] have run this country for too long." Wallace did not simply appeal to law and order, militarism, and white backlash; he was too sharp for that. With roots in southern Populism, he called for federal job-training programs, stronger unemployment benefits, national health insurance, a higher minimum wage, and a further extension of union rights. Many Robert Kennedy voters shifted to Wallace. A quarter of all union members backed him.

Richard Nixon, too, sought the votes of disgruntled Democratic voters, especially in the once solidly Democratic South. Republicans, of course, had been condemned by the Populists of old as representatives of the money power, but Nixon himself had modest roots. He came from a middle-class family and at Duke Law School was so pinched for funds that he lived in an abandoned toolshed. His dogged hard work earned him the somewhat dubious nickname of "iron pants." And Nixon well understood the disdain ordinary laborers felt for "kids with beards from the suburbs" who seemed always to be insisting, protesting, *demanding.* Nixon believed himself a representative of the **"silent majority,"** as he later described it, not a vocal minority.

silent majority phrase coined by President Richard Nixon in a 1969 speech, referring to the large number of Americans who supported his policies but did not express their views publicly.

He thus set two goals for his campaign: to distance himself from President Johnson on Vietnam and to turn Wallace's "average Americans" into a Republican majority.

The Vietnam issue was delicate, because Nixon had generally supported the war. As he told one aide, "I've come to the conclusion that there's no way to win the war. But we can't say that, of course. In fact, we have to seem to say the opposite." During the campaign he hinted that he had a secret plan to end the war but steadfastly refused to disclose it. He pledged only to find an honorable solution. As for Wallace's followers, Nixon promised to promote "law and order" while cracking down on "pot," pornography, protest, and permissiveness.

Hubert Humphrey had the more daunting task of surmounting the ruins of the Chicago convention. All through September antiwar protesters dogged his campaign with "Dump the Hump" posters. Although Humphrey picked up steam late in the campaign (partly by cautiously criticizing Johnson's war policies), the last-minute surge was not enough. Nixon captured 43.4 percent of the popular vote to 42.7 percent for Humphrey and 13.5 percent for Wallace. Some voters had punished the Democrats not just for the war but also for supporting civil rights. The majority of the American electorate had turned its back on liberal, activist government.

✔ REVIEW

What events in 1968 made that year a turning point in the war in Vietnam and in politics at home?

ELECTION OF 1968

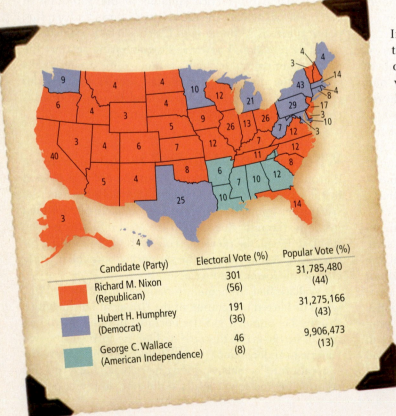

Candidate (Party)	Electoral Vote (%)	Popular Vote (%)
Richard M. Nixon (Republican)	301 (56)	31,785,480 (44)
Hubert H. Humphrey (Democrat)	191 (36)	31,275,166 (43)
George C. Wallace (American Independence)	46 (8)	9,906,473 (13)

THE NIXON ERA

In Richard Nixon Americans had elected two men to the presidency. The public Nixon appeared to be a traditional small-town conservative who cherished individual initiative, chamber-of-commerce capitalism, Fourth-of-July patriotism, and middle-class propriety. The private Nixon was a troubled man. His language among intimates was caustic and profane. He waxed bitter toward those he saw as enemies. Never a natural public speaker, he was physically rather awkward—a White House aide once found toothmarks on a "child-proof" aspirin cap the president had been unable to pry open. The public Nixon seemed to search out challenges—"crises" to face and conquer.

Vietnamization—and Cambodia

>> A settlement of the Vietnam "crisis" thus became one of Nixon's first priorities. He found a congenial ally in National Security Advisor Henry Kissinger. Kissinger, an intensely ambitious Harvard academic, shared with the new president a global vision of foreign affairs. Like Nixon, Kissinger had a tendency to pursue his

ends secretly, circumventing the traditional channels of government such as the State Department.

Both men wanted to end the war but insisted on "peace with honor." That meant leaving a pro-American South Vietnamese government behind. The strategy Nixon adopted was "Vietnamization," a gradual withdrawal of American troops as a way to advance peace talks in Paris. The burden of fighting would shift to the South Vietnamese army. Critics likened this strategy to little more than "changing the color of the corpses." All the same, as the media shifted their focus to the peace talks, the public had the impression the war was winding down.

At the same time, Nixon hoped to drive the North Vietnamese into negotiating peace on American terms. Quite consciously, he traded on his reputation as a cold warrior who would stop at nothing. As he explained to his chief of staff, Robert Haldeman:

> I call it the Madman Theory, Bob. I want the North Vietnamese to believe that I've reached the point where I might do anything to stop the war. We'll just slip the word to them that, "for God's sake, you know Nixon is obsessed about Communists. We can't restrain him when he's angry—and he has his hand on the nuclear button"—and Ho Chi Minh himself will be in Paris in two days begging for peace.

In the spring of 1969 the president launched a series of bombing attacks against North Vietnamese supply depots inside neighboring Cambodia. Johnson had refused to widen the war in this manner, fearing domestic reaction. Nixon simply kept the raids secret.

The North Vietnamese refused to cave in. Ho Chi Minh's death in 1969 changed nothing. His successors continued to reject any offer that did not end with complete American withdrawal and an abandonment of the South Vietnamese military government. Once again Nixon turned up the heat. Over the opposition of his secretaries of defense and state, he ordered American troops into Cambodia to wipe out North Vietnamese bases there. On April 30, 1970, he announced the "incursion" of American troops, proclaiming that he would not allow "the world's most powerful nation" to act "like a pitiful helpless giant."

The wave of protests that followed included the fatal clashes between authorities and students at Kent State and Jackson State as well as another march on Washington by 100,000 protesters. Congress was upset enough to repeal the Tonkin Gulf Resolution, a symbolic rejection of Nixon's invasion. After two months American troops left Cambodia, having achieved little.

Fighting a No-Win War >> For a time Vietnamization seemed to be working. As more American

troops went home, the South Vietnamese forces improved modestly. But for American GIs still in the country, morale became a serious problem. Why were the "grunts" in the field still being asked to put their lives on the line, when it was becoming clear there would be no victory? The anger surfaced increasingly in incidents known as "fragging," in which GIs threw fragmentation grenades at officers who pursued the war too aggressively.

Nor could the army isolate itself from the trends dividing American society. Just as young Americans "turned on" to marijuana and hallucinogens, so soldiers in Vietnam used drugs. Black GIs brought with them from home the issues of black power. One white medic noticed that when Muhammad Ali refused to be drafted African Americans in his unit began "to question why they were fighting the Honky's war against other Third World people."

The Move toward Détente >> Despite Nixon's insistence on "peace with honor," Vietnam was not a war he had chosen to fight. And both Kissinger and Nixon recognized that by 1968 the United States no longer had the resources to dominate international relations around the globe. The Soviet Union remained their prime concern. Ever since Khrushchev had backed down at the Cuban missile crisis in 1962, the Soviets had steadily expanded their nuclear arsenal. The Vietnam war also diverted valuable military and economic resources from easing instability in the Middle East, and other Third World regions.

In what the White House labeled the "Nixon Doctrine," the United States would shift some of the military burden for containment to other allies: Japan in the Pacific, the shah of Iran in the Middle East, Zaire in central Africa, and the apartheid government in South Africa. At the same time, Nixon and Kissinger looked for new ways to contain Soviet power not simply through nuclear deterrence but through negotiations to ease tensions. This policy was named, from the French, **détente**.

Kissinger and Nixon looked to ease tension by linking separate cold war issues. The arms race burdened the Soviet economy; why not offer American concessions on nuclear missiles? In return, the Soviets would be asked to put pressure on North Vietnam to negotiate an end to the war. Nixon also decided to reach out to Mao Zedong, the ruler of Communist China. When the Soviets saw the United States drawing closer to their old rival China, they would likely cooperate in order to discourage the Americans from enlarging Chinese power. Playing this "China card" was a significant break from Nixon's conservative past. Republicans had long viewed the Soviet Union and China as part of a monolithic Communist conspiracy.

> **détente** relaxation of strained relations between nations, especially among the United States, the Soviet Union, and China in the 1970s and late 1980s.

<< Richard Nixon's trip to China included this visit to the Great Wall. Precisely because he had been so staunch an anti-Communist, Nixon appreciated the enormous departure his trip marked in Sino-American relations.

To further this new strategy, Kissinger slipped off to China on a secret mission and then reappeared having arranged a trip to China for the president. During that visit in early 1972, Nixon pledged to normalize relations, a move the public enthusiastically welcomed.

Later that year Nixon achieved more of his push for détente. In May he traveled to the Soviet Union to join Premier Leonid Brezhnev in signing the first Strategic Arms Limitation Treaty (SALT I). In the agreement, both sides pledged to limit the number of intercontinental ballistic missiles (ICBMs) each side would deploy, as well as agreeing not to develop a new system of antiballistic missiles (ABMs).

Americans were pleased at the prospect of lower cold war tensions. But it was not clear that the linkages achieved in Moscow and Beijing would help free the United States from its war in Vietnam.

 **REVIEW**

How did Richard Nixon both escalate the war in Vietnam and wind it down?

THE NEW IDENTITY POLITICS

The liberal tradition had long embraced a belief in the common humanity of all Americans. Lyndon Johnson expressed the notion pungently, updating Shakespeare's Shylock with a Texas twang: "They cry the same tears, they feel hungry the same, they bleed the same." Differences among individuals, liberals argued, came not from race or gender but from cultural circumstances and historical experiences. Out of such beliefs, civil rights advocates committed themselves to an integrated America.

But just as Vietnam weakened the liberal consensus on the need to contain communism, minority activism challenged liberal assumptions on integration. The emerging politics of the late 1960s substituted a model of **pluralism** for the unified one sought by integrationists. Traditionally, Latino civil rights groups such as LULAC and World War II veterans in the American GI Forum had looked to assimilate into American society. Now minorities began to forge identities in opposition to the prevailing culture. By 1970 black nationalists had abandoned integration for the politics of black pride. To these activists the qualities that distinguished black Americans were what made them distinct—their music, clothing, hairstyles, and religion. In similar ways radical feminists, Latinos, Native Americans, and gays demanded that the nation respect and protect their essential differences.

pluralism idea that identity cannot be reduced to a single shared essence. The philosophy contrasts with the belief, in American politics, that citizens should assimilate into a more uniform cultural identity of shared values.

To some degree the Supreme Court had already granted that point in both the *Brown* and *Hernández* decisions of 1954 (see pages 614–615). In each case the Court declared that Latinos and African Americans had suffered not simply as individuals but as groups. To correct past injustices, identity politics called for positive steps—what the Johnson Administration called **affirmative action**—to repair the damage done by past injustices.

affirmative action practice of actively seeking to increase the number of racial and ethnic minorities, women, persons in a protected age category, persons with disabilities, and disabled veterans in a work place or school.

Latino Activism >> The distinct identities of minorities became more visible owing to a new wave of immigration in the 1950s and 1960s from Puerto Rico, Mexico, and Cuba. Historical and cultural ethnic differences among the three major Latino groups made it difficult to develop a common political agenda. Still, some activists did seek a greater unity.

After World War II a weak island economy and the lure of prosperity on the mainland brought more than a million Puerto Ricans into New York City. As citizens of the United States, they could move freely to the mainland and back home again. That dual consciousness discouraged

Historian's TOOLBOX

Farm Workers' Altar

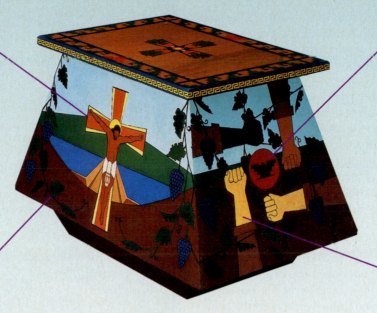

The crucifix suggests that the migrant worker is Catholic. Protestant Christians traditionally used the symbol of the cross without Jesus.

This is the flag of the United Farm Workers, designed at the request of César Chávez. Use the Internet to find out more about the altar's symbolism. What key words would you choose in your search?

The grape leaves decorating the altar remind people of the UFW's grape boycott.

What do the different skin tones of the arms suggest?

Historians use art works as a lens through which they can view the beliefs and values of an era. This altar was created by artist Emanuel Martínez at a time when the United Farm Workers were engaged in a campaign for the right to negotiate labor contracts with grape growers. In 1968 César Chávez held a 24-day hunger strike that ended successfully with the celebration of mass. This altar was used at the ceremony, which was attended by farm workers as well as civil rights supporters, including Senator Robert F. Kennedy. The altar thus had symbolic overtones for the occasion. Most Mexican American farm workers were devout Catholics, just as many early African American civil rights activists shared a Protestant faith. But other symbols suggest the complexity of the movement's belief system, with allegiance to union activity and political struggle, as well as the movement's connection to Aztec and mestizo traditions of Mexico.

THINKING CRITICALLY

Why would it be appropriate to end a hunger strike with a mass? What other cultural echoes in this decade resonate from the image of a raised, closed fist? In what ways do those symbols link to the "new identity politics"?

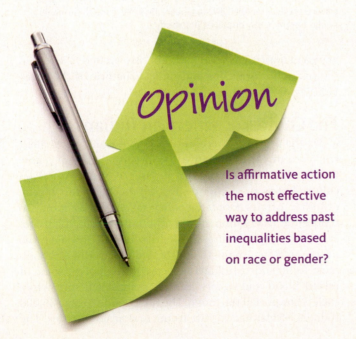

Opinion

Is affirmative action the most effective way to address past inequalities based on race or gender?

many from establishing deep roots stateside. Equally important, the newcomers were startled to discover that, whatever their status at home, on the mainland they were subject to racial discrimination and often segregated into urban slums. Light-skinned migrants escaped those conditions by blending into the middle class as "Latin Americans." The Puerto Rican community thereby lost some of the leadership it needed to assert its political rights.

Still, during the 1960s the urban barrios gained greater political consciousness as groups such as *Aspira* adopted the strategies of civil rights activists and organizations such as the Black and Puerto Rican Caucus created links with other minority groups. The Cubans who arrived in the United States after Fidel Castro came to power in 1959—some 350,000 over the course of the decade—forged fewer ties with other Latinos. Most settled around Miami. An unusually large number came from Cuba's professional, business, and government class and were racially white and politically conservative.

Mexican Americans, however, constituted the largest segment of the Latino population. Until the 1940s most were farmers and farm laborers in Texas, New Mexico, and California. But during the 1950s the process of mechanization pushed them toward the cities—some 85 percent of the population by 1969. With urbanization came a slow improvement in the quality of jobs held. A body of skilled workers, middle-class professionals, and entrepreneurs emerged.

Yet Mexican agricultural workers continued to face harsh working conditions and meager wages. Attempts to unionize faltered partly because workers migrated from job to job and strikebreakers were easily imported. In 1963 a soft-spoken but determined farmworker, César Chávez, recruited fellow organizers Gil Padilla and Dolores Huerta to make another attempt. Their efforts over the next several years led to the formation of the United Farm Workers labor union.

Chávez, like Martin Luther King, proclaimed an ethic of nonviolence. Also like King, he was guided by a deep religious faith (Roman Catholicism in the case of Chávez and most Mexican American farmworkers). During a strike of Mexican and Filipino grape workers in the summer of 1966, Chávez led a 250-mile march on Sacramento. ("Dr. King had been very successful" with such marches, he noted.) Seeking additional leverage, the union used consumers as an economic weapon by organizing a boycott of grapes in supermarkets across the nation. Combined with a 24-day hunger strike by Chávez—a technique borrowed from Gandhi—the boycott forced growers to negotiate contracts with the UFW beginning in 1970.

Just as King found his nonviolent approach challenged by more radical activists, Chávez saw a new generation of Mexican Americans take up a more aggressive brand of identity politics. Many began calling themselves Chicanos. Like blacks, Chicanos saw themselves as a people whose heritage had been rejected, their labor exploited, and their opportunity for advancement denied. In Denver Rodolfo "Corky" Gonzales laid out a blueprint for a separatist Chicano society, with public housing set aside for Chicanos and the development of economically independent barrios. "We are Bronze People with a Bronze Culture," declared Gonzales. "We are a Nation. We are a union of free pueblos. We are Aztlán."

The new activism came from both college and high school students. Like others of the baby-boom generation, Mexican Americans attended college in increasing numbers. In addition, Lyndon Johnson's Educational Opportunity Programs, part of the War on Poverty, brought higher education to thousands more Latinos. By 1968 some 50 Mexican American student organizations had sprung up on college campuses. In Los Angeles that year thousands of Chicano high school students walked out to protest substandard educational conditions. Two years later La Raza Unida (The Race United) launched a third-party movement to gain power in communities in which Chicanos

⌃ Living conditions were harshest for Mexican Americans among agricultural workers. César Chávez mobilized migrant workers into the United Farm Workers union. Here he meets with Dolores Huerta, his vice-president in the UFW in January 1968. Note the three iconic symbols prominently displayed in the office.

were a majority. The more militant "Brown Berets" adopted the paramilitary tactics and radical rhetoric of the Black Panthers.

The Choices of American Indians ≫ Ironically, the growing strength of the civil rights movement created a threat to Indian tribal identities. Liberals came to see Indian reservations not as oases of Native American culture but as rural ghettos. During the 1950s the Bureau of Indian Affairs adopted a policy called "termination." To reduce the reservation system, the Bureau would cut federal services, gradually sell off tribal lands, and push the people into the "mainstream" of American life. Although most full-blooded Indians objected to the policy, some of mixed blood and others already assimilated into white society supported the move. The relocation of some 35,000 Indians accelerated a shift from rural areas to cities. The

urban Indian population, which had been barely 30,000 in 1940, reached more than 300,000 by the 1970s.

Still, the activism of the 1960s inspired Indian leaders to shape their own political agenda. In 1968 urban activists in Minneapolis created AIM, the American Indian Movement. A year later like-minded Indians living around San Francisco Bay formed Indians of All Tribes. Because the Bureau of Indian Affairs refused to address the problems of urban Indians, more militant members of the organization seized the abandoned federal prison on Alcatraz Island in San Francisco Bay. The Alcatraz action inspired calls for a national Pan-Indian rights movement.

Then in 1973 AIM organizers Russell Means and Dennis Banks led a dramatic takeover of a trading post at Wounded Knee, on a Sioux reservation in South Dakota. Ever since white cavalry gunned down over a hundred Sioux in 1890 (page 367), Wounded Knee had symbolized for Indians the betrayal of white promises and the bankruptcy of reservation policy. Even more, Wounded Knee now demonstrated how difficult it was to achieve unity when so many tribes were determined to go their own ways. Other Indians did not support the militant takeover of Wounded Knee, and federal officers soon forced its occupiers to leave. The movement splintered further as more than 100 different organizations were formed during the 1970s to pursue reform at the local, state, and federal levels.

Asian Americans >>

In striking down the old quota system the 1965 Immigration Reform Act led to a sharp increase in the numbers of immigrants from Asia. Asians who in 1960 made up less than 1 percent of the American population (about a million people) were by 1985 2 percent (about five million). This new wave included many middle-class professionals, a lower percentage of Japanese, and far more newcomers from Southeast and South Asia. Earlier civil rights reforms had swept away the legal barriers to full citizenship that had once stigmatized Asians.

Many Americans saw these new immigrants as "model minorities." They possessed skills in high demand, worked hard, were often Christian, and seldom protested. The 1970 census showed Japanese and Chinese Americans with incomes well above the median for white Americans. Such statistics, however, hid fault lines within communities. Although many professionals assimilated into the American mainstream, agricultural laborers and sweatshop workers remained trapped in poverty. And no matter how much Anglos praised their industry, Asian Americans still wore what one sociologist defined as a "racial uniform." They were nonwhites in a white society.

Few Americans were aware of Asian involvement in identity politics. That was in part because the large majority of Asian Americans lived in just three states—Hawaii, California, and New York. Further, Asian Americans were less likely to join the era's vocal protests. Nonetheless Asian students did join with African Americans, Chicanos, and Native Americans to advocate a "third world revolution" against the white establishment. Asian students, too, wanted a curriculum that recognized their histories and cultures.

Gay Rights >>

In 1972 Black Panther Huey Newton observed that homosexuals "might be the most oppressed people" in American society. Certainly Newton was qualified to recognize oppression when he saw it. But by then a growing number of homosexuals had embraced liberation movements that placed them among minorities demanding equal rights.

Even during the "conformist" 1950s gay men founded the Mattachine Society (1951) to fight anti-homosexual attacks and to press for wider public acceptance. Lesbians formed a similar organization, the Daughters of Bilitis, in 1955. Beginning in the mid-1960s, more radical gay and lesbian groups began organizing to raise individual consciousness and to establish a gay culture in which they felt free. One group called for "acceptance as full equals . . . basic rights and equality as citizens; our human dignity; . . . [our] right to love whom we wish."

The movement's defining moment came on Friday, June 27, 1969, when New York police raided the Stonewall Inn, a Greenwich Village bar. Such

<< In 1890 the U.S. cavalry killed 146 Indians at Wounded Knee, South Dakota. In 1973 members of the American Indian Movement seized the hamlet of Wounded Knee, making it once again a symbol of conflict.

raids were common enough: the police regularly harassed gays and lesbians by raiding the places where they gathered. This time the patrons fought back, first with taunts and jeers, then with paving stones and parking meters. Increasingly, gay activists called on homosexuals to "come out of the closet" and publicly affirm their sexuality. In 1974 gays achieved a major symbolic victory when the American Psychiatric Association removed homosexuality from its list of mental disorders.

Feminism >>

Organized struggle for women's rights and equality in the United States began before the Civil War. Sustained political efforts had won women the vote in 1920. But the women's movement of the 1960s and 1970s began to push for equality in broader, deeper ways.

Writer Betty Friedan was one of the earliest to voice dissatisfaction with the cultural attitudes that flourished after World War II. Even though more women were entering the job market, the media routinely glorified housewives and homemakers while discouraging those who aspired to independent careers. In *The Feminine Mystique* (1963) Friedan identified the "problem that has no name," a dispiriting emptiness in the midst of affluent lives. "Our culture does not permit women to accept or gratify their basic need to grow and fulfill their potentialities as human beings."

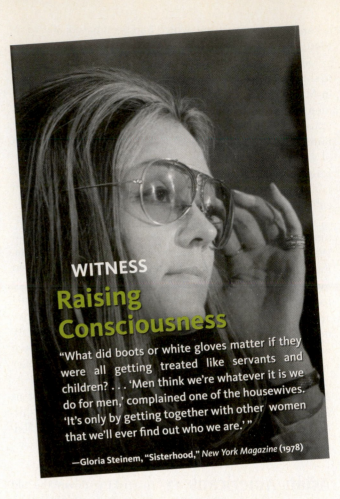

WITNESS

Raising Consciousness

"What did boots or white gloves matter if they were all getting treated like servants and children? . . . 'Men think we're whatever it is we do for men,' complained one of the housewives. 'It's only by getting together with other women that we'll ever find out who we are.'"

—Gloria Steinem, "Sisterhood," *New York Magazine* (1978)

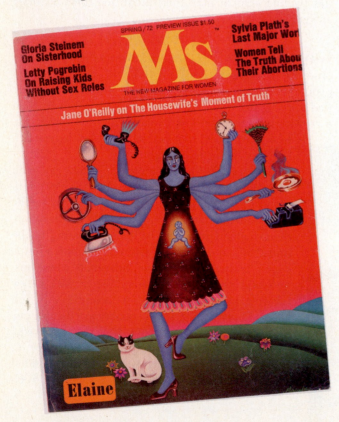

The creation of *Ms.* magazine in 1972 gave feminists a means to reach a broader audience. The cover of its first issue used the image of a many-armed Hindu goddess to satirize the many roles of the modern housewife.

The Feminine Mystique gave new life to the women's rights movement. The Commission on the Status of Women appointed by President Kennedy proposed the 1963 Equal Pay Act and helped add gender to the forms of discrimination outlawed by the 1964 Civil Rights Act. Women also assumed an important role in both the civil rights and antiwar movements. They accounted for half the students who went south for the "Freedom Summers" in 1964 and 1965. But even women who joined the protests of the 1960s often found themselves belittled and limited to providing menial services such as cooking and laundry. Casey Hayden, a veteran of SDS and SNCC, told her male comrades that the "assumptions of male superiority are as widespread . . . and every much as crippling to the woman as the assumptions of white superiority are to the Negro."

By 1966 activist women were less willing to remain silent. Friedan joined a group of 24 women and 2 men who formed the National Organization for Women (NOW). In arguing that "sexism" was much like racism, they persuaded President Johnson in 1967 to include women along with African Americans, Hispanics, and other minorities as a group covered by federal affirmative action programs.

Broader social trends established a receptive climate for the feminist appeal. After 1957 the birthrate began a rapid decline; improved methods of contraception, such as the birth control pill, permitted smaller families. By

1970 an unprecedented 40 percent of all women were employed outside the home. Education also spurred the shift from home to the job market, since higher educational levels allowed women to enter an economy oriented increasingly toward white-collar service industries rather than blue-collar manufacturing.

Equal Rights and Abortion >>

As its influence grew, the feminist movement translated women's grievances into a political agenda. In 1967 NOW proclaimed a "Bill of Rights" that called for maternity leave for working mothers, federally supported day-care facilities, child care tax deductions, and equal education and job training. But feminists divided on two other issues: the passage of an Equal Rights Amendment to the Constitution and a repeal of state antiabortion laws.

At first support seemed strong for an Equal Rights Amendment that forbade all discrimination on the basis of gender. In 1972 both the House and the Senate passed the Equal Rights Amendment (ERA) virtually without opposition. Within a year 28 of the necessary 38 states had approved the ERA. It seemed only a matter of time before 10 more state legislatures would complete its ratification. Many in the women's movement also applauded the Supreme Court's decision, in *Roe v. Wade* (1973), to strike down 46 state laws restricting a woman's access to abortion. In his opinion for the majority, Justice Harry Blackmun observed that a woman in the nineteenth century had "enjoyed a substantially broader right to terminate a pregnancy than she does in most states today." As legal abortion in the first three months of pregnancy became more readily available, the rate of maternal deaths from illegal operations, especially among minorities, declined.

But the early success of the Equal Rights Amendment and the feminist triumph in *Roe v. Wade* masked underlying divisions among women's groups. *Roe v. Wade* triggered a sharp backlash from many Catholics, Protestant evangelicals, and socially conservative women. Their opposition inspired a crusade for a "right to life" amendment to the Constitution. A similar conservative reaction breathed new life into the "STOP ERA" crusade of Phyllis Schlafly, an Illinois political organizer. Although a professional working-woman herself, Schlafly believed that women should embrace their traditional role as homemakers subordinate to their husbands. "Every change [that the ERA] requires will deprive women of a right, benefit, or exemption that they now enjoy," she argued. By 1979 supporters of ERA were forced to admit that they would not succeed in convincing the necessary three-fourths of the state legislatures to ratify the amendment.

 **REVIEW**

In what ways were the movements for the rights of Latinos, Indians, Asian Americans, gays, and women similar and in what ways different?

VALUE POLITICS: THE CONSUMER AND ENVIRONMENTAL MOVEMENTS

Among those seeking to change America were reformers who defined themselves by their ideas and values rather than by personal identity. Where many participants in identity politics viewed themselves as outsiders, consumer advocates and environmentalists generally came from the social mainstream. Still, they shared with the counterculture a worry that excessive materialism wasted resources and generated pollution, while too many corporations exploited the public through misleading advertising and shoddy, even dangerous, products.

Technology and Unbridled Growth >>

As early as 1962 marine biologist Rachel Carson had warned in *Silent Spring* against the widespread use of chemical pesticides, especially DDT. Though chemical companies sought to discredit her work as shrill and unreliable, a presidential commission vindicated her conclusions. Pesticides were only one aspect of what environmentalists considered misguided technology. A report issued in 1965 indicated that every river near an urban area in the United States was polluted, save one (the St. Croix near St. Paul, Minnesota). Certainly, anyone with a sense of irony could not help marveling that the industrially fouled Cuyahoga River running through Cleveland, Ohio, burst into flames in 1969. Smog, radioactive fallout, lethal pesticides, and polluted rivers were the by-products of a society wedded to technology and unbridled economic growth.

To consumer advocates, rising fatality rates on American highways signaled another kind of corporate failure. Besides contributing to smog and other forms of pollution, many automobiles were inherently dangerous to their occupants. That was a conclusion announced by an intense young reformer, Ralph Nader, in his 1965 exposé *Unsafe at Any Speed*. Nader's particular target was the rear-engine Chevrolet Corvair. General Motors' internal studies confirmed crash data that the Corvair tended to flip over during turns or skidded uncontrollably. Though the company fixed the problem, it also hired private investigators to try to discredit Nader.

The company picked the wrong target. Nader was the son of immigrant Lebanese parents who supported their son's success at Princeton and Harvard Law School. He lived simply and had no vices. And when he discovered GM's campaign against him, he successfully sued. GM's embarrassed president publicly apologized, but by then Nader had become a counterculture hero. In 1966 Congress passed the

National Traffic and Motor Vehicle Safety Act and the Highway Safety Act. For the first time the government required seatbelts and set safety standards for cars, tires, and roads.

With the money from his lawsuit Nader founded a consumer advocacy organization in 1969, the Center for the Study of Responsive Law. His staff of low-paid but eager lawyers, student interns, and volunteers investigated a wide range of consumer and environmental issues. "Nader's Raiders," as his staff was called, shared their leader's view that it was time for corporations "to stop stealing, stop deceiving, stop corrupting politicians with money, stop monopolizing, stop poisoning the earth, air and water, stop selling dangerous products, stop exposing workers to cruel hazards." In the tradition of progressive reform Nader looked to an interventionist government and informed citizen-consumers to regulate corporate behavior.

Many environmentalists, too, had links to the progressive era and the idea that government action could police corporate irresponsibility and preserve scenic and natural wonders for the benefit of future generations. What made modern environmentalism distinct was a growing focus on the field of ecology. Since the early twentieth century, this biological science had demonstrated how closely life processes throughout nature depended on one another. New groups such as the Environmental Defense Fund (EDF) and Friends of the Earth used legal challenges and civil disobedience to advocate for nature. Inspired by Rachel Carson's *Silent Spring,* the EDF filed lawsuits in Michigan and Wisconsin to have DDT declared a toxin subject to state regulation.

Barry Commoner, a politically active biologist, argued in his book *The Closing Circle* (1971) that modern society courted disaster by trying to "improve on nature." American farmers, for example, greatly increased their crop yields by switching from animal manures to artificial fertilizers. But the change consumed large quantities of energy, raised costs, often left soils sterile, and polluted nearby water. By the 1970s chemical discharges had virtually killed Lake Erie. Technology might prove profitable in the short run, Commoner argued, but in the long run modern methods were bankrupting the environment.

Political Action >>
While he was no friend of liberal reform, President Nixon sensed that these value movements had broad popular appeal. His administration supported the passage of the National Environmental Policy Act of 1969, which required environmental impact statements for all major public projects. And in 1970 Nixon established the Environmental Protection Agency (EPA), whose first major act recognized Rachel Carson's campaign by banning most domestic uses of DDT. The president also signed a bill establishing an Occupational Safety and Health Agency (OSHA) to enforce health and safety standards in the workplace, and Clean Water and Clean Air Acts.

On April 22, 1970, millions of Americans demonstrated their commitment to a healthy environment as

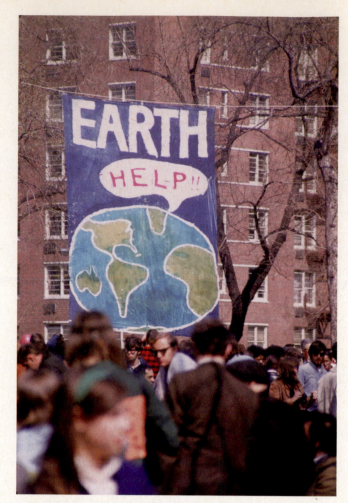

⌃ The first Earth Day, 1970

they celebrated the first Earth Day. For a few hours, pedestrians strolled city streets closed to motor vehicles, school children planted trees and picked up litter, and college students demonstrated. The enthusiasm reflected the movement's dual appeal: it was both practical in seeking to improve the quality of air, water, and earth and spiritual in celebrating the unity of living things. But Senator Gaylord Nelson of Wisconsin, who helped bring Earth Day about, appreciated the occasion's more radical implications. "The Establishment sees this as a great big antilitter campaign. Wait until they find out what it really means . . . to clean up our earth."

The Legacy of Identity and Value Politics >>
Earth Day did not signal a consensus on an environmental ethic. President Nixon, for one, was unwilling to impose regulations that stifled growth, especially when facing a troubled economy. Radical activists "aren't really one damn bit interested in safety or clean air," he commented to one industry group. "What they are interested in is destroying the system." If he faced "a flat choice between jobs and smoke," nature would be the loser.

<< After *Apollo 11* reached the moon in 1969, President Richard Nixon told the astronauts "this is the greatest week in the history of the world since the creation." Reverend Billy Graham took exception to this rhetorical flourish. What about Christ's birth, his death, and his resurrection, he asked the President. "Tell, Billy," Nixon instructed his chief of staff, "RN referred to a week, not a day."

approach to equality tended to fragment rather than unify the nation. It divided liberals from activists farther to the left and signaled that reform had reached its high-water mark, even as white men continued to earn more than women or minorities. The road to equality—whether in the workplace, schools, or even the bedroom—remained a fault line along which the nation would divide.

The End of the War >> Like identity politics, the continuing debate over Vietnam revealed the divisions in American society. A peace settlement there eluded President Nixon because the North Vietnamese continued to reject any peace agreement that left the South Vietnamese government in power. Unwilling to send back American troops, in May 1972 Nixon instead ordered North Vietnam's major port, Haiphong, mined and blockaded, along with a sustained bombing campaign. In December

Nixon's political instincts were shrewd. Rather than fight the tides of reform, he rode those that were popular, basking for example, in the triumphant *Apollo 11* moon landing in 1969. At the same time he resisted those such as affirmative action that offended Republicans and traditional Democrats. Both the 1968 and 1972 presidential elections revealed a shift in political power toward the southern and western rims of the United States where traditional values flourished and where whites, in the wake of the civil rights revolution, were deserting the Democrats in droves. These were the voters Nixon courted, in what he sometimes referred to as his "southern strategy" to replace the old New Deal coalition with a new Republican majority. By the early 1970s his silent majority worried more about job security than clean air and water. As one bumper sticker declared: "Out of work? Hungry? Eat an environmentalist."

The president sought to channel a similar backlash against identity politics. Conservatives opposed many of the era's reforms, including the Equal Rights Amendment, the integration of private clubs, and the use of racial and gender quotas for jobs and college admissions. Merit, not race or gender, should determine an individual's opportunities, they argued. Ethnic identity organizations such as the Italian American Civil Rights League spoke out against affirmative action for minorities.

Yet even critics could not deny that political and social activists had brought a sense of empowerment to people who had long seen themselves as "other" Americans who had been excluded. The reforms of the 1960s opened doors to jobs, careers, and avenues of success previously closed to all but white males. Inevitably, however, a pluralistic

⌃ Members of Nixon's "Silent Majority" resented antiwar and minority group protestors. This man, who lost his son in Vietnam, attacks "America's noisy scum."

he launched an even greater wave of attacks, as American planes dropped more bombs in 12 days than they had during the entire campaign from 1969 to 1971.

Ironically South Vietnamese leaders threw up the greatest obstacle to a settlement, for they were rightly convinced that General Thieu's regime would not last once the United States departed. But by January 1973, with Kissinger back in Paris, a treaty was finally arranged. Three months later the last American units were home.

 REVIEW

What were the philosophies behind the consumer and environmental movements, and how well did they succeed in the political arena?

PRAGMATIC CONSERVATISM

In August 1969 4,000 angry white union workers marched on city hall in Pittsburgh, Pennsylvania. There, a confrontation with police turned violent, leaving 50 protestors injured and 200 under arrest. A month later the scene repeated itself in Chicago, where hundreds of construction workers "slugged it out with 400 policemen." In both cases the issue was the "Philadelphia Plan" for affirmative action. Under it, the Nixon administration adopted the rule set forth under Lyndon Johnson in 1967 that government funding would be provided only if contractors' bids had "the result of producing minority group representations in all trades and in all phases of the construction project." The building trades unions wanted to know why they had been singled out when so many other industries did not meet those goals. Race played a role as well. "Why should these guys be given special consideration, just because they happen to be black?" one angry worker asked.

By 1969 affirmative action had become a political hot potato and Richard Nixon knew it. Over the course of his first term the president charted a pragmatic course, preserving and even expanding popular entitlements such as social security, seeking a middle ground on civil rights and affirmative action, while following the liberal tides in areas such as environmental protection.

Nixon's New Federalism >> Nixon envisioned his New Federalism as a conservative counter to liberal programs run by the federal government. Passed in 1972, a revenue sharing act distributed $30 billion over five years in federal block grants to state and local governments. Instead of the funds being earmarked for specific purposes, localities could decide which problems needed attention and how best to attack them. A similar approach influenced aid to individuals. In the past, liberal programs from the New Deal to the Great Society often provided specific services to individuals: job retraining programs, Head Start programs for preschoolers, food supplement programs for nursing mothers. Republicans argued that such a "service strategy" too often assumed that federal bureaucrats best understood what the poor needed. Nixon favored an "income strategy," which gave recipients money to spend it as they saw fit. Such grants were meant to encourage initiative, increase personal freedom, and reduce government bureaucracy. Even if Nixon was determined to reverse the liberalism of the 1960s, critics were wrong to dismiss him as a knee-jerk conservative.

Stagflation >> Ironically, a worsening economy forced Nixon to adopt liberal remedies. By 1970 the nation had entered its first recession in a decade. Traditionally a recession brought a decrease in demand for goods and a rise in unemployment as workers were laid off. Manufacturers then cut prices in order to encourage demand for their goods and cut wages in order to preserve profit margins. But in the recession of 1970, while unemployment rose as economists would have expected, wages and prices were also rising in an inflationary spiral—a condition described as "stagflation."

Unfriendly Democrats labeled the phenomenon "Nixonomics," although in truth Lyndon Johnson had brought on inflation by refusing to raise taxes to pay for the war and for Great Society social programs. In addition, wages continued to rise partly because powerful unions had negotiated automatic cost-of-living increases into their contracts. Similarly, where a few large corporations dominated an industry, like steel and oil, prices and wages ignored market forces and continued to rise as demand and employment fell.

Mindful that his own "silent majority" were the people most pinched by the slower economy, Nixon decided that unemployment posed a greater threat than inflation. Announcing "I am now a Keynesian," he adopted a deficit budget designed to stimulate the growth of jobs. More surprising, in August 1971 he announced that to provide short-term relief, wages and prices would be frozen for 90 days. For a Republican to advocate wage and price controls was near heresy, almost as heretical as Nixon's overtures to China. For a year federal wage and price boards enforced the ground rules for any increases until the economy grew again. Controls were lifted in January 1973. As in foreign policy, Nixon had reversed long-cherished policies to achieve practical results.

Social Policies and the Court >> Affirmative action, school prayer, contraception, criminal rights, obscenity, and school busing were all issues on which Supreme Court decisions offended the silent majority. By and large the liberal Court placed rights and liberties

ahead of traditional values and law enforcement. The justices recognized, for example, that 15 years after its *Brown v. Board of Education* decision, most school districts remained segregated. In white neighborhoods, parents opposed having their children bused to more distant, formerly all-black schools as part of a plan to achieve racial balance. Although black parents for their part worried about how their children might be treated in hostile white neighborhoods, by and large they supported busing as a means to better education.

Under Nixon, federal policy on desegregation took a 180-degree turn. In 1969 the Justice Department supported lawyers for Mississippi who asked the Supreme Court to delay an integration plan. The Court not only rejected that proposal but two years later ruled, in *Swann v. Charlotte-Mecklenburg Board of Education* (1971), that busing, balancing ratios, and redrawing school district lines were all acceptable ways to achieve integration. Given the continuing liberal activism of the Court, the president looked to change its direction by filling vacancies with more conservative justices. He replaced Chief Justice Earl Warren in 1969 with Warren Burger, a jurist who had no wish to break new ground. When another vacancy occurred in 1969, Nixon tried twice to appoint conservative southern judges with reputations for opposing civil rights and labor unions. Congress rejected both. In the end, the president nominated Minnesotan Harry Blackmun, a moderate judge of unimpeachable integrity. Two more conservative appointments guaranteed that the Court would no longer lead the fight for minority rights. But neither would it reverse the achievements of the Warren Court.

Triumph and Revenge >>

As the election of 1972 approached, Nixon's majority seemed to be falling into place, especially after the Democrats nominated Senator George McGovern of South Dakota under new party rules for selecting delegates to the convention. No longer did party bosses handpick the delegates. Minorities, women, and young people all received proportional representation. McGovern's nomination gave Nixon the split between "us" and "them" he sought. The Democratic platform embraced all the activist causes that the silent majority resented. It called for immediate withdrawal from Vietnam, abolition of the draft, amnesty for war resisters, and a minimum guaranteed income for the poor.

By November the only question that remained to be settled was the size of Nixon's majority. An unsolved burglary at the Watergate complex in Washington, D.C., while vaguely linked to the White House, had not touched the president. Nixon received almost 61 percent of the popular vote.

Yet the overwhelming victory did not relieve the urge to settle scores. In his political battles, Nixon exhibited a tendency to see issues in terms of a very personal "us against them." With his consent (and with Lyndon Johnson's before him), the FBI and intelligence agencies conducted a covert, often illegal war against antiwar groups and political opponents. "We have not used the power in the first four years, as you know," he remarked to his chief of staff, H. R. Haldeman, during the campaign. "We haven't used the Bureau [FBI] and we haven't used the Justice Department, but things are going to change now. And they are going to change and they're going to get it, right?" The administration began compiling an "enemies list"—everyone from television news correspondents to student activists—to be targeted for audits by the Internal Revenue Service or other forms of harassment.

In truth, Nixon had already begun to abuse his presidential powers. In June 1971 *The New York Times* published a secret, often highly critical military study of the Vietnam War, soon dubbed the *Pentagon Papers*. Angry that such information had become public, the president authorized a secret group known as "the plumbers" to burglarize a psychiatrist's office. The doctor had been treating Daniel Ellsberg, the disillusioned official who had leaked the *Pentagon Papers,* and the burglars hoped to find records that were personally damaging.

> ### In his political battles, Nixon exhibited a tendency to see issues in terms of a very personal "us against them."

Nixon also took his battle to Congress. When Democrats passed a number of programs the president opposed, he simply refused to spend the appropriated money. By 1973 Nixon had used this policy of "impoundment" to cut some $15 billion out of more than 100 federal programs. The courts eventually ruled that impoundment was illegal.

Break-In >>

Nixon's fall from power began with what seemed a minor event. In June 1972 burglars entered the Democratic National Committee headquarters, located in Washington's plush Watergate apartment complex. The five burglars did seem an unusual lot. They wore business suits and carried bugging devices, tear-gas guns, and more than $2,000 in crisp new 100-dollar bills. One had worked for the CIA. Another was carrying an address book whose phone numbers included that of a Howard Hunt at the "W. House." Nixon's press secretary dismissed the break-in as "a third-rate burglary attempt," and Nixon himself announced that a thorough investigation had concluded "no one on the White House staff . . . was involved in this

very bizarre incident. What really hurts in matters of this sort is not the fact that they occur," the president continued. "What really hurts is if you try to cover up."

In January 1973 the burglars went on trial along with former White House aides E. Howard Hunt, Jr., and G. Gordon Liddy. Judge John Sirica was not satisfied with the defendants' guilty plea. He wanted to know who had directed the burglars and why "these 100-dollar bills were floating around like coupons."

Facing a stiff jail sentence, one of the Watergate burglars admitted that the defendants had been bribed to plead guilty and that they had perjured themselves to protect higher government officials. The White House then announced on April 17 that all previous administration statements on the Watergate scandal had become "inoperative." Soon after, the president accepted the resignations of his two closest aides, H. R. Haldeman and John Ehrlichman. He also fired John Dean, his White House counsel, after Dean agreed to cooperate with prosecutors.

To the Oval Office >> Over the summer of
1973 a string of officials testified at televised Senate hearings. Each witness took the trail of the burglary and its cover-up higher into White House circles. Then John Dean gave his testimony. Young, with a Boy Scout's face, Dean declared in a quiet monotone that the president had personally been involved in the cover-up. Still, the testimony remained Dean's word against the president's until Senate committee staff discovered, almost by chance, that since 1970 Nixon had been secretly recording all conversations and phone calls in the Oval Office. The reliability of Dean's testimony was no longer central, for the tapes could tell all.

Obtaining that evidence proved no easy task. In an effort to restore confidence in the White House, Nixon agreed to the appointment of a special prosecutor, Harvard law professor Archibald Cox, to investigate the new

Watergate disclosures. When Cox subpoenaed the tapes, the president refused to turn them over, citing executive privilege and matters of national security. The courts, however, overruled this position.

As that battle raged and the astonished public wondered if matters could possibly get worse, they did. Evidence unrelated to Watergate revealed that Vice President Spiro Agnew had systematically solicited bribes, both as governor of Maryland and while serving in Washington. He resigned the vice presidency in October. Under provisions of the Twenty-fifth Amendment, Nixon appointed Representative Gerald R. Ford of Michigan to replace Agnew.

Meanwhile, when Special Prosecutor Cox demanded the tapes, the president offered to submit written summaries instead. Cox rejected the offer and on Saturday night, October 20, Nixon fired Cox. Reaction to this "Saturday Night Massacre" was overwhelming: 150,000 telegrams poured into Washington, and by the following Tuesday, 84 House members had sponsored 16 different bills of impeachment. The beleaguered president agreed to hand over the tapes. And he appointed Texas lawyer Leon Jaworski as a new special prosecutor. By April 1974 Jaworski's investigations led him to request additional tapes. Again the president refused, although he grudgingly supplied some 1,200 pages of typed transcripts of the tapes.

Even the transcripts damaged the president's case. Littered with cynicism and profanity, they revealed Nixon talking with his counsel John Dean about how to "take care of the jackasses who are in jail." When Dean estimated it might take a million dollars to buy their silence, Nixon replied, "We could get that. . . . You could get a million dollars. And you could get it in cash. I know where it could be gotten."

Even those devastating revelations did not produce the "smoking gun" demanded by the president's defenders. When Special Prosecutor Jaworski petitioned the Supreme Court to order release of additional tapes, the Court in *United States v. Nixon* ruled unanimously in Jaworski's favor.

Resignation >> The end came quickly. The House
Judiciary Committee adopted three articles of impeachment, charging that Nixon had obstructed justice, had abused his constitutional authority in improperly using

federal agencies to harass citizens, and had hindered the committee's investigation.

The tapes produced the smoking gun. Conversations with Haldeman on June 23, 1972, only a few days after the break-in, showed that Nixon knew the burglars were tied to the White House staff and knew that his attorney general had acted to limit an FBI investigation. Not willing to be the first president convicted in a Senate impeachment trial, Nixon resigned on August 8, 1974. The following day Gerald Ford became president. "The Constitution works," Ford told a relieved nation. "Our long national nightmare is over."

Had the system worked? In one sense, yes. For the first time a president had been forced to leave office and numerous members of his administration served prison terms for crimes related to the break-in and cover-up. Yet the corrupt campaign practices that financed Watergate continue to plague the political system. The system works, as the Founding Fathers understood, only when citizens and public servants respect the limits of government power.

▲ Nixon's farewell; his daughter Tricia looks on.

 REVIEW

In what ways was Richard Nixon a conservative, and why did he adopt some liberal policies?

THE ROAD'S END FOR VIETNAM AND LIBERALISM

Healing did not come easily to a land scarred by the upheavals of the 1960s. The unpretentious Ford made himself readily available to the media. But as an unelected president, he had no popular mandate. Only a month into office and without any warning, he granted Richard Nixon a full pardon for any crimes he might have committed. Ford hoped to put Watergate behind the nation rather than look backward in recrimination. But the pardon succeeded only in deepening the nation's cynicism, because Nixon would never face prosecution nor assume responsibility for his crimes.

A Post-Imperial President >> For their part, the Democrats controlling Congress were determined to rein in the imperial presidency. The War Powers Act,

already passed in 1973, required that the president consult Congress whenever possible before committing troops to the battlefield, report to Congress within two days of taking action, and withdraw troops after 60 days unless Congress voted to retain them.

Reports of widespread abuses by the nation's intelligence services strengthened congressional resolve to rein in the executive branch. Hearings revealed that the CIA had routinely violated its charter forbidding it to spy on Americans at home. Abroad, the agency had attempted to assassinate foreign leaders in Cuba, the Congo, South Vietnam, and the Dominican Republic. The FBI had also used illegal means to infiltrate and disrupt domestic dissidents. J. Edgar Hoover had authorized an (unsuccessful) operation to drive Martin Luther King to suicide. Determined to eliminate future abuses, the Senate established committees to oversee intelligence operations.

Hemmed in by a newly assertive Congress, Ford relied on Henry Kissinger's guidance in foreign policy. The secretary of state perceived himself as a realist who could not avoid offending idealists on the political left and right. Quoting the German writer Goethe, Kissinger explained, "If I had to choose between justice and disorder, on the one hand, and injustice and order, on the other, I would always choose the latter."

During the final years of Nixon's administration Kissinger followed that maxim, certainly (with the president's blessing), by ordering the CIA to finance a military coup in Chile in 1973. The coup overthrew the democratically elected socialist leader, Salvador Allende Gossens. Allende died in the coup, and a brutally oppressive military regime assumed power. Kissinger argued that the United States had the right to limit democratic disorder in Latin America, in order to guard against the evils of Communism.

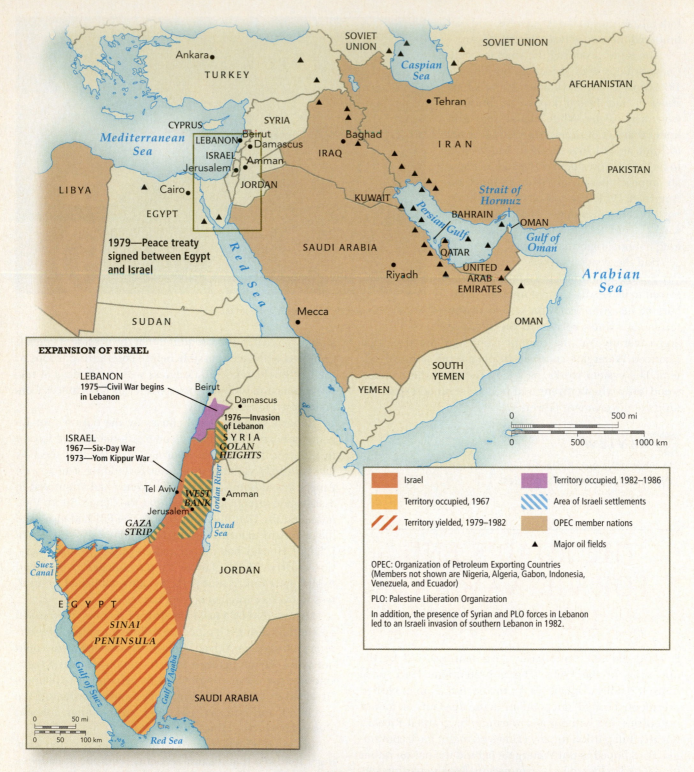

EXPANSION OF ISRAEL

LEBANON
1975—Civil War begins
in Lebanon

1976—Invasion
of Lebanon

ISRAEL
1967—Six-Day War
1973—Yom Kippur War

SYRIA
GOLAN
HEIGHTS

Beirut

Damascus

Tel Aviv

Amman

WEST
BANK

Jordan River

Jerusalem

GAZA
STRIP

Dead
Sea

JORDAN

Suez
Canal

EGYPT

SINAI
PENINSULA

Gulf of Suez

Gulf of Aqaba

SAUDI ARABIA

Red Sea

0   50 mi
0   50 100 km

Ankara

TURKEY

SOVIET
UNION

Caspian
Sea

SOVIET UNION

AFGHANISTAN

CYPRUS

Mediterranean
Sea

SYRIA

Beirut
LEBANON
Damascus
ISRAEL
Amman
Jerusalem
JORDAN

Tehran

Baghad

IRAQ

I R A N

PAKISTAN

LIBYA

Cairo

EGYPT

1979—Peace treaty
signed between Egypt
and Israel

Red Sea

KUWAIT

SAUDI ARABIA

Riyadh

Mecca

Persian Gulf

BAHRAIN

QATAR

UNITED
ARAB
EMIRATES

Strait of
Hormuz

OMAN

Gulf of
Oman

Arabian
Sea

OMAN

SUDAN

YEMEN

SOUTH
YEMEN

0   500 mi
0   500   1000 km

■ Israel		▨ Territory occupied, 1982–1986
■ Territory occupied, 1967		▨ Area of Israeli settlements
▨ Territory yielded, 1979–1982		■ OPEC member nations
		▲ Major oil fields

OPEC: Organization of Petroleum Exporting Countries
(Members not shown are Nigeria, Algeria, Gabon, Indonesia,
Venezuela, and Ecuador)

PLO: Palestine Liberation Organization

In addition, the presence of Syrian and PLO forces in Lebanon
led to an Israeli invasion of southern Lebanon in 1982.

OIL AND CONFLICT IN THE MIDDLE EAST, 1948–1988

After World War II the Middle East became a vital geopolitical region beset by big-power rivalry and complicated by local, tribal, ethnic, and religious divisions and political instability. Much of the world's known oil reserves lie along the Persian Gulf. Proximity to the former Soviet Union and vital trade routes such as the Suez Canal have defined the region's geographic importance. Revolutions in Iran and Afghanistan, intermittent warfare between Arabs and Jews, the unresolved questions of Israel's borders and a Palestinian homeland, the disintegration of Lebanon, and a long, bloody war between Iran and Iraq were among the conflicts that unsettled the region. In addition, the presence of Syrian and PLO forces in Lebanon led to an Israeli invasion of southern Lebanon in 1982.

Energy and the Middle East >>
Kissinger also looked to manage the effects of an energy crisis brought to a head by events in the Middle East. The United States and its allies had long depended on Middle Eastern oil and, as Americans' appetite for energy grew, so did its dependence on foreign sources. Low oil prices discouraged conservation or the use of alternative energy sources. Prime among the nation's foreign suppliers were the 13 nations making up the Organization of Petroleum Exporting Countries (OPEC)—and chief among those were seven Arab states and Iran.

The importance of that supply became clear in the autumn of 1973, when on Yom Kippur, the holiest day of the Jewish year, troops from Egypt and Syria launched a surprise attack on Israel. The seven Arab members of OPEC supported Egypt and Syria by imposing a boycott on oil exports to countries seen as friendly to the Israelis. Lasting from October 1973 to March 1974, the boycott staggered the western nations and Japan. The price of crude oil had been rising in any case, from under $2 a barrel in 1972 to over $12 by 1976. As the price of petroleum soared, so did the cost of carbon-based plastics used in a huge range of products from phonograph records to raincoats to tires. Inflation rose to an annual rate of 14 percent. Meanwhile, with gasoline scarce, motorists found themselves waiting in line for hours at the pump, in hopes of purchasing a few gallons.

The oil crisis pushed many cities toward financial disaster. In October 1975 New York announced it was near bankruptcy and petitioned the Ford administration for relief. When the president refused, the *New York Daily News* headline blared, "Ford to City: Drop Dead." The administration did eventually extend a loan, but not before the political damage had been done.

To ease the crisis Kissinger mediated the conflict between Israel and the Arab states. In negotiating he flew back and forth so often between Jerusalem in Israel and Cairo in Egypt that observers nicknamed his plane the "Yo-Yo express" and Kissinger's efforts "shuttle diplomacy." Eventually, the Israelis agreed to withdraw from the west bank of the Suez Canal and to disengage from Syrian troops along the Golan Heights, which overlooked Israel. An uncertain peace returned, and OPEC lifted its boycott. The following year Congress addressed the energy crisis by ordering electric utilities to switch from expensive oil to more abundant and cheaper (though more polluting) coal. The new legislation also ordered the auto industry to improve the efficiency of its cars and created a strategic petroleum reserve as one means of managing future disruptions on a short-term basis.

Limits across the Globe >>
The energy crisis was only one factor limiting American ambitions at home and abroad. The United States also faced mounting competition from industries in Europe and in the emerging economies of the Pacific rim (Japan, South Korea, Taiwan, Hong Kong, Singapore, and the Philippines). Lower wages there convinced many American manufacturers to move high-wage jobs overseas. The AFL-CIO complained that as skilled and high-pay union jobs disappeared, what remained would be "a nation of hamburger stands, a country stripped of its industrial capacity . . . a nation of citizens busily buying and selling hamburgers and root beer floats."

Both Ford and Henry Kissinger looked to ease America's economic burdens by further détente with the Soviet Union. The Soviet economy, like the American, was mired in stagnation. In two summit meetings, the second held at Helsinki, Finland, in 1975, the two superpowers established the framework for a second strategic arms limitation treaty (SALT II).

Still, the agreement provided no way out of the morass halfway across the globe, where in January 1975 North Vietnamese forces had renewed their offense against the South. President Ford implored Congress to grant $1 billion in emergency aid, warning as earlier presidents had that if Vietnam fell, nations all over the world would doubt American commitments. This time, few people accepted the domino theory. "My God, we're all tired of it, we're sick to death of it," exclaimed one citizen in Oregon. "55,000 dead and $100 billion spent and for what?" In April 1975 Saigon fell, amid scenes of desperate Americans and South Vietnamese fighting to squeeze onto evacuation helicopters.

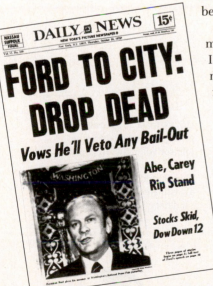

✕ As the energy crisis contributed to New York City's near-bankruptcy, Gerald Ford at first opposed federal assistance. New Yorkers were not amused.

> ✔ **REVIEW**
> What impact did the OPEC boycott have on the United States at home and abroad?

"The enemy must fight his battles far from his home base for a long time," a Vietnamese strategist once wrote. "We must further weaken him by drawing him into protracted campaigns. Once his initial dash is broken, it will be easier to destroy him." The enemy in question was not the Americans, nor the French, but the Mongol invaders of 1284 C.E. The strategy of resistance and attrition that kept the Chinese at bay for centuries also defeated the United States. Between 1961 and 1973 the war cost billions in national treasure, and left some 57,000 soldiers dead and over 300,000 wounded. The cost to Southeast Asia was even more incalculable. Much of the land lay devastated, and some 6.5 million South Vietnamese had become refugees along with 3 million Laotians and Cambodians. In excess of 3 million Vietnamese soldiers and civilians died during the war.

Defeat in Vietnam marked the end of liberalism triumphant and offered a stark reminder of the limits of American power. No longer did most Americans believe that the world could be remade in their image. While the United States waged its futile war in Vietnam, power had shifted to the growing economies of Europe and the Pacific rim and to the members of OPEC. If Richard Nixon had not overreached, he might have replaced the liberal creed with a new conservative approach to government. But Nixon had exceeded the limits of presidential power in his desire for mastery, just as liberalism exceeded its limits in the quagmire of Lyndon Johnson's war. The rise of a new conservative tide would have to wait for a new quest to restore America's power and prestige.

CHAPTER SUMMARY

Though presidents from Truman to Nixon sent American forces to Indochina, Vietnam was Lyndon Johnson's war, and the political divisions it caused ended both his presidency and the consensus on liberal reform.

- To force the North Vietnamese to negotiate, Johnson escalated the American war effort, pouring in troops and bombing North Vietnam heavily.
- As the nation divided into prowar hawks and antiwar doves, the Vietcong's Tet offensive shocked Americans. In the face of opposition Johnson abandoned his reelection campaign.
- In the wake of the assassinations of Martin Luther King and Robert Kennedy, Hubert Humphrey became the Democrats' presidential nominee. But riots at the Chicago convention so damaged Humphrey's candidacy that Richard Nixon won the election, promising a "peace with honor" in Vietnam.
- A wide range of minorities—Latinos, Indians, Asian Americans, gays, and feminists—adopted identity politics as a way to claim their full civil rights.
- Mexican American migrant workers led by César Chávez established a farmworkers' union, the UFW, while a rising generation of Latino students adopted more militant techniques for establishing a Chicano identity.
- Though often divided by tribal diversity, militant Native Americans called attention to the discrimination faced by Indians in urban settings as well as on reservations.
- Feminists campaigned for civil and political equality as well as to change deep-seated cultural attitudes of a "patriarchal" society.

Significant Events

French defeated at Dien Bien Phu; Geneva accords

1954

Tonkin Gulf incident

Rolling Thunder begins bombing of North Vietnam; Ralph Nader's *Unsafe at Any Speed*

1964

1965

BETTY FRIEDAN

César Chávez campaign; National Organization of Women established

1966

U.S. Vietnam troop levels peak at 536,000; Tet offensive; Johnson withdraws from presidential race; Martin Luther King, Jr., and Robert Kennedy assassinated; George Wallace candidacy; Nixon wins election

1968

- In addition to reform movements based on identity, the value politics of environmentalists and consumer advocates extended the spirit of reform.
- White House involvement in the Watergate break-in and the president's subsequent cover-up led to the first resignation of an American president.
- President Gerald Ford inherited an office weakened by scandal, an economy in recession, and a Congress determined to rein in an "imperial presidency."
- An energy crisis brought on by Arab-Israeli conflict and an oil boycott by the OPEC nations worsened an already ailing American economy.
- Secretary of State Henry Kissinger used shuttle diplomacy to bring an uneasy peace to the Middle East. He and President Ford sought to ease diplomatic tensions by pursuing détente with the Soviet Union.
- The fall of Vietnam after three decades of debilitating war left liberal ideals in disarray, though Nixon's overreaching in the White House temporarily forestalled a resurgence of conservatism in the United States.

Additional Reading

Two books—David Kaiser, *American Tragedy: Kennedy, Johnson, and the Origins of the Vietnam War* (2000), and Fred Logevall, *Choosing War: The Last Chance for Peace and the Escalation of War in Vietnam* (1999)—trace the road to full U.S. involvement in Vietnam. Among those who lay the blame with Lyndon Johnson see Michael Hunt, *Lyndon Johnson's Cold War Crusade in Vietnam, 1945–1968* (1997), and Lloyd Gardner, *Pay Any Price: Lyndon Johnson and the Wars for Vietnam* (1997). H. W. Brands, *The Foreign Policies of Lyndon Johnson: Beyond Vietnam* (1999), reminds us that the president faced other issues. For the soldiers' experience, look at the classic by Michael Herr, *Dispatches* (1977), and David Maraniss, *They Marched Into Sunlight: War and Peace, Vietnam and America, October 1967* (2004).

Keith Olsen, *Watergate: The Presidential Scandal That Shook America* (2003), is a lively brief account of Nixon's fall, while Stanley Kutler, *The Wars of Watergate: The Last Crisis of Richard Nixon* (1992), provides more detail. For an argument that the 1970s were more significant than the 1960s see Bruce Shulman, *The Seventies: The Great Shift in American Culture, Society, and Politics* (2002). Gender politics are widely explored in Ruth Rosen, *The World Split Open: How the Modern Women's Movement Changed America* (2001). Excellent on the environmental movement is Robert Gottlieb, *Forcing the Spring: The Transformation of the American Environmental Movement* (1996).

For a fresh, nonpartisan look at Richard Nixon see Melvin Small, *The Presidency of Richard Nixon* (2003), or Richard Reeves, *President Nixon: Alone in the White House* (2002). A dissenter from the camp of Kissinger admirers is Jussi Hanhimaki, *The Flawed Architect: Henry Kissinger and American Foreign Policy* (2004).

GERALD FORD

Nixon adopts wage and price controls; Pentagon Papers published

Thieu government falls in South Vietnam

1970

1971

1972

1973

1974

1975

First Earth Day; U.S. troops invade Cambodia; NOW organizes Strike for Equality; Clean Air and Water acts; repeal of Tonkin Gulf resolution

Nixon policy of détente; Watergate burglary

Vietnam peace treaty; *Roe v. Wade*; AIM supporters occupy Wounded Knee

House adopts articles of impeachment; Nixon resigns; Ford becomes president; Kissinger Arab-Israeli diplomacy; Ford pardons Nixon

The Conservative Challenge

1976–1992

Completed in 1980, the year former California governor Ronald Reagan was elected president, the Crystal Cathedral in Orange County, California, symbolized the rising influence of conservatives and evangelical Christians in American life and politics. Though the church's theology was traditional, it used the most modern techniques of the mass media to spread its message.

31

>> AN AMERICAN STORY

THE NEW AMERICAN COMMONS

In the early 1970s San Diego city officials looked out at a downtown that was growing seedier each year as stores and shoppers fled to the suburban malls that ringed the city. Nor was San Diego an exception. Across the nation many once-thriving downtown retail centers became virtual ghost towns at the close of the business day. But San Diego found a way to bounce back. At the core of the redevelopment plan was Horton Plaza, a mall with the look of an Italian hill town. Stores with stucco facades fronted twisting pedestrian thoroughfares where Renaissance arches lured customers to upscale stores like Banana Republic, to jewelers, and to sporting goods shops. Jugglers and clowns wandered the streets, while guitarists serenaded passersby. Horton Plaza soon ranked just behind the zoo and Sea World as San Diego's prime tourist attraction. By 1986 it was drawing more than 12 million shoppers and tourists.

With their soaring atriums, lavish food courts, and splashing fountains, malls became the cathedrals of American material culture. Shopping on Sunday rivaled churchgoing as the weekly family ritual. Whereas >>

⌃ Minnesota's Mall of America, opened in 1992, became the largest mall in the United States and the ultimate cathedral of consumption.

American youth culture centered on the high school in the 1950s and on college campuses in the 1960s, in the 1970s and 1980s it gravitated toward mall fast-food stores and video amusement arcades. By 1985, when Horton Plaza opened, the United States boasted more shopping centers (25,000) than it did either school districts or hospitals.

Malls as cathedrals of consumption reflected a society turning away from social protest to more private means of fulfillment. Some individuals adopted a consumerist or material path, being the first in the neighborhood to own a microwave, gas grill, or VCR. Evangelical religion offered others redemption in the prospect of being "born again." Still others extolled the virtues of traditional family values. Through private charity and volunteerism they proposed to replace the support provided by the modern welfare state. Along less orthodox paths, the "human potential movement" taught techniques such as yoga and Transcendental Meditation as means to inner fulfillment.

Given the twin calamities of Watergate and Vietnam, it was perhaps not surprising that so many Americans expressed discontent and a spiritual hunger. One opinion poll reported that some 70 percent of those surveyed agreed that "over the last 10 years, this country's leaders have consistently lied to the people." President Jimmy Carter, the devout former governor from Georgia who succeeded Gerald Ford in the White House, saw the problem as a "crisis of confidence . . . at the very heart and soul and spirit of our national will." Similarly Carter's successor, Ronald Reagan, sought in 1981 to reverse that widespread pessimism and restore national confidence. He evoked a vision of the United States as a "city upon a hill" that would inspire the rest of the world through its strong actions and abiding virtues. In doing so Reagan deliberately echoed language Puritan leader John Winthrop used to describe the seventeenth-century Massachusetts Bay Colony.

Could the move to a more conservative, more private, less government-oriented approach restore the commonwealth that Reagan's rhetoric hailed? At times John Winthrop's austere vision seemed to have morphed into a city on a hill with climate control, where the piped-in music and cheery fast-food courts served to banish all social problems to a land far beyond the parking lots. Yet issues that remained unresolved in the 1970s could not be ignored in the 1980s. The nation's environment faced new crises—the pollution from toxic waste dumps, damage from acid rain, and accidents at nuclear power plants—while feminists, gay and lesbian activists, and minority groups all pushed to reduce discrimination and extend their rights. Civil rights activist Jesse Jackson spoke for many who resisted the conservative faith in small government. Instead he championed diversity and tolerance and urged that government, not the private sector, was the most effective agent for cleaning up the environment, creating jobs, reducing urban violence and solving public health crises such as the newly arisen AIDS epidemic.

In the end neither liberals nor conservatives succeeded in imposing their visions on the American nation. Even so, the move rightward, both politically and culturally, dominated the post-Watergate years. More than any other political figure, Ronald Reagan tapped the public's feelings of both resentment and hope. He confounded his critics with a capacity to sustain broad support for his image of a born-again America. ≪

THE CONSERVATIVE REBELLION

In California Howard Jarvis, a retired businessman, had for years promoted tax-cutting referenda on the state ballot. While those measures failed to attract widespread support, Jarvis's efforts to reduce property taxes did. In the case of property taxes, the issue was equity, not simply lower taxes. Small homeowners often paid taxes at much higher rates than large property owners and businesses. Hence, the extremely conservative Jarvis began to frame his antigovernment agenda in populist terms: his supporters, he claimed, were the small interests and individuals: teachers, blue-collar workers, and "a great number of Negroes." His group, the United Organizations of Taxpayers (UOT) received no money from oil companies, bankers, land speculators, or insurance companies.

Tax Revolt >>

By the late 1970s California was ripe for the Jarvis rebellion. Inflation imposed a crushing burden on middle and lower class homeowners. At the same time their taxes rose steadily. An old radical and union organizer described state politicians and bureaucrats as "those leeches who must have more and more taxes." Such mounting anger helped UOT collect 1.25 million signatures to place Proposition 13 on the ballot in 1978. The measure cut property taxes 57 percent and made it difficult for the state and local legislatures to raise taxes in the future. Opponents warned that the loss of revenue would force school closings, job losses, and reduced police and fire protection, but the measure passed with widespread support.

The tax rebellion spread across the nation. Over the next four years 12 states passed similar resolutions, while many legislatures cut public spending and taxes, hoping to avoid the voters' wrath. Even liberal Massachusetts capped local property taxes and prevented future increases of more than 2½ percent. Increasing numbers of Americans no longer embraced the liberal consensus that activist government could solve the nation's problems and promote progress.

The Diverse Evangelical World

>> But the conservative rebellion was not merely the child of a faltering economy, stagnating wages, and a resistance to paying taxes. The social ferment of the 1960s had taken its toll on spiritual life. During that decade mainline Protestant churches struggled over how religious beliefs should engage with civil rights, the war in Vietnam, issues of sex and gender, and more liberated lifestyles. As more congregations embraced liberal definitions of faith, many Protestants found themselves yearning for a more traditional religious experience. These disaffected moved in large numbers from long established denominations such as Presbyterians and Congregationalists to evangelical churches. By the mid-1980s some 36 percent of Americans described themselves as "born again." Many Catholics and Jews also resisted the liberalization of their faith.

Among evangelicals, sects such as the Southern Baptists and Assemblies of God attracted large national memberships, but their real focus was local, centered in church communities. Such congregations insisted that salvation came through a spiritual rebirth (being "born again") after a person had acknowledged sinfulness and embraced Christ's atonement. Evangelical tradition encouraged proselytizing by the faithful, often in the form of revivals and spiritual awakenings. Finally, most evangelicals anticipated the rapture, when Christ would return to transport true believers into his Father's kingdom. These shared beliefs, when combined with a commitment to piety, put evangelicals squarely at odds with modern society. They imposed a strict personal morality, often insisted on the central role of fathers in the family, and in some churches forbade such worldly evils as dancing, cosmetics, movies, gambling, and premarital sex.

Though evangelicals condemned much of modern culture, many preachers advocated a "prosperity theology" that encouraged economic success. They also used the media to spread the word, none more effectively than Pat Robertson, the son of a Virginia politician. Robertson, a magnetic Southern Baptist, used cable and satellite broadcasts to expand the Christian Broadcast Network into a media empire. His *700 Club* reached an audience of millions and inspired his colleague Jim Bakker to launch the even more popular *Praise the Lord Club*—PTL for short. Although the content featured gospel singing, fervent

Point of View

The Transforming Seventies

"Most Americans regard the seventies as an eminently forgettable decade—an era of bad clothes, bad hair, and bad music impossible to take seriously. . . . Contemporaries dismissed it as a 'Pinto' decade," referring to Ford's mysteriously exploding compact car. . . . The impression could hardly be more wrong. The Seventies transformed American economic and cultural life as much as, if not more than the revolution in manners and morals of the 1920s and the 1960s."

BRUCE J. SCHULMAN *The Seventies: The Great Shift in American Culture, Society, and Politics*

preaching, faith healing, and speaking in tongues, the format mirrored that of major network talk shows, opening with a Christian monologue, conversations with celebrity guests, and musical entertainment.

The Catholic Conscience >>

American Catholics faced their own decisions about the lines between religion and politics. In the 1960s a social activist movement had arisen out of the church council known as Vatican II (see page 626). Its reforms also sought to modernize the church, reducing the amount of Latin in the mass and encouraging greater participation by lay people.

Disturbed by these currents Catholic conservatives found support when the charismatic John Paul II assumed the papacy in 1979. Vigorous, outgoing and warm, Pope John Paul nonetheless reined in the modern trends of Vatican II. He ruled against a wider role for women in the church hierarchy and stiffened church policy against birth control. These rulings put him at odds with many American Catholics. The American church also faced a crisis as fewer young men and women chose celibate lives as priests and nuns.

Though conservative Catholics and Protestant evangelicals could be wary of one another, they shared certain views. Both groups lobbied for the government to provide federal aid to parochial schools and Fundamentalist academies. Even more strongly they were united by their opposition to abortion. John Paul reaffirmed the church's teaching that all life began at conception and that abortion amounted to murder of the unborn. Evangelicals, long suspicious of the power of secular technology and science, attacked abortion as another instance in which science had upset life's natural moral order.

Moving Religion into Politics >>

Since many evangelicals believed that the apocalypse—the end times of the world—were fast approaching, before the 1970s they saw little reason to reform society. Many refused even to vote. Gradually that apolitical stance weakened. A number of Supreme Court decisions, beginning with the ban on school prayer in *Engel v. Vitale* (1962) struck conservatives as an attack on their faith, but none more so than *Roe v. Wade*. If an unborn fetus was fully human, was it not necessarily endowed with both a soul and with human rights? Here was a case where government policy seemed to threaten faith and family. So also did the teaching of Darwinian evolution and sex education in the schools.

Once abortion and education issues brought them into politics, evangelicals began to organize. In 1977 the Reverend Jerry Falwell from Lynchburg, Virginia, joined his fellow Baptist preacher, Tim LaHaye of San Diego, to fight for the repeal of a gay rights ordinance in Miami, Florida. LaHaye and his wife Beverly, a writer, had formed the Concerned Women of America (CWA), a "pro-family" organization that by the 1980s claimed more members than the National Organization of Women. The LaHayes were outspoken opponents of homosexuality and pornography. Under their leadership, CWA crusaded against abortion, no-fault divorce laws, and the Equal Rights Amendment.

Their ally, the Reverend Falwell, epitomized the entrepreneurial gifts of many preachers of prosperity theology. His daily radio broadcasts and Sunday television show, the *Old Time Gospel Hour,* reached over a million listeners. His home church ran multiple Sunday services to accommodate a congregation of 17,000. And when he and LaHaye defeated the gay rights ordinance in Miami, they went on to form the Moral Majority, a political action organization, which Falwell described as "pro-life, pro-family, pro-morality, and pro-American." The Moral Majority also shared the conservative opposition to labor unions, environmental reform, and most government-based social welfare programs.

The Media as Battleground >>

Both evangelicals and political conservatives believed the mass media corrupted family values. Its permissive, even positive portrayal of unmarried women, premarital sex and drug use, profanity, homosexuality, nudity, and violence offended their moral sensibilities. The conservative determination to censor media content clashed with a liberal commitment to free speech and toleration for diversity.

Hollywood movies had long pushed the boundaries of acceptable content, but by the 1970s television began to introduce more controversial and politicized programming.

<< During the late 1970s and the 1980s conservatives increasingly spoke out against abortion and in favor of the right to life for an unborn fetus. Adopting the tactics of protest and civil disobedience once common to radicals in the 1960s, they clash here with pro-choice demonstrators outside Faneuil Hall in Boston.

In 1971 producer Norman Lear introduced *All in the Family,* whose main character, Archie Bunker, embodied the blue-collar backlash against liberal and permissive values. The ultimate male chauvinist, Archie treated his wife Edith like a servant, clashed with his modestly rebellious daughter Gloria, and heaped verbal abuse on his leftist Polish-American son-in-law. All things liberal or cosmopolitan—"Hebes," "Spics," and "Commie Crapola"— became targets for Archie's coarse insults. Despite its popularity the show was attacked from both the left and the right. Many conservatives who shared Archie's values found the language offensive, while some minority leaders charged that the show legitimized the prejudices it attacked.

The most popular sitcom of the 1970s, *M*A*S*H* (for Mobile Army Surgical Hospital), was also the most liberal. Set in a hospital unit during the Korean War, the show criticized the politicians who mired the United States in Vietnam. As the show evolved over ten years, it reflected changing liberal sensibilities. "Hawkeye" Pierce and his fellow surgeons began the series as hard-drinking, womanizing foes of war and the military. Ten years later they still hated the army and war, but they had become more vulnerable and in touch with their emotions. And head nurse Margaret "Hot Lips" Houlihan was transformed from a flag-waving martinet into a woman seeking a career and respect in a man's world. The irreverence central to the show's appeal angered conservatives, who argued that *M*A*S*H* demonstrated how secular liberal values dominated the media. A similar bias, they believed, warped movies, newspapers, and popular music.

 REVIEW

Why did evangelical Christians become more politically active in the 1970s, and what tactics did they use?

JIMMY CARTER: RESTORING THE FAITH

In the escalating war between liberal and conservative forces, James Earl "Jimmy" Carter succeeded in his quest for the presidency because he did not fit neatly into either camp. Carter represented a new breed of Southern governors—they came from the Sun Belt, not the Cotton Belt; they were economic progressives, not segregationists. At the same time, Carter had credentials conservatives could appreciate. He was a former Navy man and nuclear engineer, a peanut farmer from the thoroughly southern town of Plains, Georgia, and had served as Georgia's governor. More unusual still, Carter openly declared his faith as a "born again" Christian, a term largely unused outside evangelical circles.

When he began campaigning only 2 percent of Americans outside his home state had heard of him. Carter turned his outsider's status to advantage by promising to bring honesty and openness to a nation still smarting from Watergate. "I will not lie to you," he assured voters. President Ford, for his part, had to fight off a challenge from his party's right wing, led by Ronald Reagan, a former California governor, movie actor, and television host. Reagan grew up as a New Deal Democrat, but deeply held concerns with high income taxes and Communism had turned him toward conservative causes. In the election Carter beat Ford by a slim margin.

The Search for Direction >> On Inauguration Day Jimmy Carter redeemed his pledge to bring simplicity and directness to Washington politics. Rather than the usual limousine ride down Pennsylvania Avenue, Carter and his family walked. The imperial presidency, he made

⌃ Over its 11 years the cast of M*A*S*H introduced many new characters. Among the few in the original cast who appeared in all 11 years were Loretta Swit ("Hot Lips" Houlihan), Alan Alda (Hawkeye Pierce, *seated*), Jamie Farr (the cross-dressing Maxwell Q. Klinger, *upper right*), and William Christopher (Father Mulcahy, *upper left*).

clear, was a thing of the past. But Congress was equally determined to rein in the executive branch. To succeed in governing, Carter and his brash Georgia outsiders would have to prove they could swim among the political sharks.

Carter brought to the office disciplined work habits, a mastery of detail, and a wealth of plans to address the energy crisis, economic stagnation, the financial woes of major cities, and a host of foreign policy issues. What he and his advisors had not decided was how to set priorities. Veteran politicians warned not to try too much too soon, but Carter admitted, "it's almost impossible for me to delay something that I see needs to be done." Almost immediately the president called for the elimination of 19 expensive pork barrel water projects as financially wasteful and environmentally destructive. The move stunned even Democrats, who liked bringing home funds to their communities. They promptly threatened to bury his other legislative proposals unless he backed down, which he was forced to do.

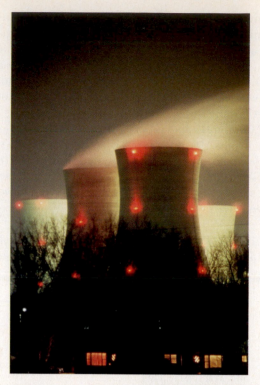
⌃ Cooling towers at Three Mile Island nuclear reactor

Energy and the Environment ›› Regardless of Carter's political skills, the times demanded that he address two related issues: the environment and skyrocketing energy prices. Those issues were in constant tension, since satisfying energy needs required the use of natural resources, just at the time when the need to protect them had become more evident.

Carter did strengthen the Environmental Protection Agency as well as the clean air and water regulations enforced by the EPA. And he championed legislation to create a Superfund that could spend $1 billion a year to clean up toxic waste sites.

Problems arose, however, when environmental and energy policies clashed. The harsh winter of 1977–1978 that greeted the new administration drove the price of heating oil even higher. Carter responded with a comprehensive National Energy Program. It outlined measures environmentalists favored to promote conservation, such as "gas guzzler" taxes, new efficiency standards for building materials and appliances, and solar tax credits. And to please the oil and gas industries, the president recommended a complex plan to deregulate gas and oil prices so they would find their "true value." Carter urged Congress to move quickly, calling his energy bill "the moral equivalent of war." He had not counted on the determination of special interests to block

virtually every provision he proposed. Eighteen months later Congress approved only deregulation, some conservation tax credits, and a new cabinet-level Department of Energy. No comprehensive national policy on energy ever emerged.

But what sort of energy policy made sense? Environmentalists and energy producers clashed over the most beneficial course of action. A 1977 report of the National Academy of Sciences warned that the consumption of fossil fuels—oil, gasoline, natural gas, and coal—might well be causing long-term changes in the earth's climate, leading to a potentially catastrophic global warming. A *New York Times* headline announced, "Scientists Fear Heavy Use of Coal May Bring Adverse Climate Shift." Neither scientists nor energy companies were yet prepared to recommend specific policies to regulate and limit the greenhouse gases—carbon dioxide prime among them—produced when fossil fuels were burned.

Some utility companies argued for nuclear power plants, since fission energy emitted no carbon dioxide. That was an option few environmentalists could accept. No solution yet existed to dispose of the radioactive wastes nuclear plants generated when they produced electricity. Then in March 1979 a plume of radioactive steam spewed from an overheated nuclear reactor at Three Mile Island in Pennsylvania. Local authorities evacuated some 100,000 panicked residents from nearby communities. After the Three Mile Island incident the prospects for nuclear power dimmed. While existing nuclear plants continued to operate, the accident insured that no new ones would be built for decades to come.

The Sagging Economy ›› Throughout the 1970s wages stagnated, unemployment rose, and so did inflation, spurred by rising energy costs, falling industrial productivity, and foreign competition. Carter at first proposed stimulating the economy with a series of popular tax rebates. And he pleased progressive politicians by finding new funding for federal programs such as food stamps, Social Security, Medicare, and Medicaid.

But these attempts to cushion the blow of hard times were countered by the president's fiscal conservatism. Confronted by the large deficit from the Nixon and Ford years, Carter canceled his proposed tax rebates. "Government cannot solve our problems," he insisted, nor "eliminate poverty, or provide a bountiful economy, or reduce inflation, or save our cities, or cure illiteracy or provide energy." That sentiment, spoken by a Democrat, indicated how successful conservatives had been in promoting their ideas.

Foreign Policy: Principled or Pragmatic? »

In foreign policy, Jimmy Carter again gravitated between conservative and liberal impulses, between being practical and being idealistic. Like Nixon and Kissinger, Carter recognized that the United States had neither the strength nor the resources to impose its will in a postcolonial world. But unlike his conservative critics, Carter viewed the threat of Soviet strength with greater skepticism. Too often, he believed, a knee-jerk fear of Soviet power led Americans to support right-wing dictators, no matter how brutal or corrupt, simply because they professed to be anticommunist.

Carter insisted that the United States should assume a moral posture by giving human rights a higher priority. He spoke out publicly on behalf of political prisoners and reduced foreign aid to some dictatorships (though strategic allies such as the Philippines under the autocratic Ferdinand Marcos were largely spared). Argentinean Nobel Peace Prize winner Adolfo Pérez Esquivel claimed he owed his life to Carter's policies. Hundreds of other journalists and dissidents, who routinely faced imprisonment, torture, and even murder, benefited as well.

Carter also eased decades of distrust toward Yankee imperialism by negotiating a treaty to turn over to Panama control of the Canal Zone, the 10-mile-wide strip that the United States administered under a perpetual lease. For many conservatives, Carter's initiative offered further evidence of declining American power. Presidential hopeful Ronald Reagan condemned the proposed treaty as "appeasement," while Senator S. I. Hayakawa of California quipped: "It's ours; we stole it fair and square." Despite such criticisms the Senate ratified the final agreement in 1978.

For conservatives, however, Carter's real test lay in his relations with the Soviet Union. The president's first impulse was to continue the policy of détente scorned by the right wing. The Soviet Union's economy had long been saddled by inefficient industries and obligations to poor client states such as Cuba, Vietnam, and East Germany. Premier Leonid Brezhnev became even more willing to negotiate after the Carter administration announced he would extend diplomatic recognition to communist China—playing "the China card" as Kissinger and Nixon once had. In 1979 Carter and Soviet Premier Brezhnev agreed on SALT II, finalizing talks on strategic arms limitation set in motion by President Ford. Although neither side agreed to scrap its major weapon systems, conservatives still attacked the treaty as a sell-out, and stalled its approval in the Senate.

The Middle East: Hope and Hostages »

Throughout the cold war, instability in the oil-rich Middle East continually threatened to set off a larger conflict. Secular dictators in Iran, Egypt, Syria, and Iraq vied with autocratic monarchies in Saudi Arabia, Kuwait, Jordan, and the Arab emirates. Tensions simmered between rival Islamic religious sects, the Sunnis and Shi'ites, while at the same time all the Arab nations were united in their hostility toward Israel.

American policy for the region pulled in two directions. On the one hand, the United States wanted to insure the free flow of Middle Eastern oil to the industrial world; on the other, it was committed to the survival of Israel. The energy crises of the 1970s heightened the tensions within these goals, as did Israel's decision to refuse Palestinian demands for a homeland in the West Bank. The diplomatic impasse eased somewhat when Egyptian president Anwar Sadat traveled to Israel to meet Israeli president Menachem Begin. Sensing an opportunity to promote peace, Carter invited the two leaders to Camp David in September of 1978.

⌃ It was at Camp David, in private talks sponsored by President Jimmy Carter (*center*), that Egyptian president Anwar el-Sadat (*left*) and Israeli prime minister Menachem Begin (*right*) hammered out a "Framework for Peace in the Middle East" as a first step toward ending decades of war and mistrust.

For 13 days the two antagonists argued, while Carter kept them at the table. Each feared the consequence of giving the other side too much. Finally, they struck a limited compromise: Sadat would recognize Israel; Israel would return the Sinai Peninsula to Egypt. On the question of a Palestinian state in the West Bank and Gaza, Begin would not yield. Even so, the discussions had been historic. Begin and Sadat shared the Nobel Peace Prize for their courageous diplomacy, but it could just as well have gone to Carter, who brokered the peace.

Amid the turmoil of the Middle East, the Shah of Iran had long seemed a stabilizing force. But in the autumn of 1978 Shi'ite fundamentalists rebelled against his rule. Long dismayed by the increasing westernization of their society, they found the presence of tens of thousands of non-Muslim American military advisers particularly offensive. When the shah's regime collapsed in February 1979, the religious leader Ayatollah Ruhollah Khomeini established an Islamic republic. Later that year, after the United States admitted the ailing Shah to an American hospital for medical treatment, several hundred Iranian students stormed the U.S. embassy in Tehran and took 53 Americans hostage. Though this act violated every convention of western diplomacy, the United States was helpless to respond.

A President Held Hostage >>
While American policymakers debated how to respond to the Khomeini regime, the Soviet Union faced Islamic fundamentalists in their own southern republics. In Afghanistan Islamic rebels had toppled a pro-Soviet regime, leading Leonid Brezhnev to order a Soviet invasion of its neighbor to the south. President Carter condemned the invasion, but there was little the United States could do. As a symbolic gesture he announced that the United States would boycott the 1980 Olympics in Moscow.

Once again, the problem of energy dependence interacted with the region's political instability to create a political crisis. Nightly newscasts aired the spectacle of "America Held Hostage" in Iran. And the turbulence in the Middle East set off another round of OPEC oil price increases. Soaring energy costs soon drove up inflation to near 14 percent and some interest rates above 20 percent. Chrysler Corporation, the nation's third leading car manufacturer, teetered on the edge of bankruptcy and was saved only by a federally guaranteed loan.

With polls giving Carter a negative rating of 77 percent, the president once again moved right. He revived the cold war rhetoric of the 1950s and accelerated the development of new classes of nuclear weapons. But whereas the CIA in 1953 had successfully overthrown an Iranian government, an airborne mission launched in April 1980 to rescue the hostages ended in disaster. Eight marines died when two helicopters and a plane collided in Iran's central desert in the midst of a blinding sandstorm. The United States, as even the president admitted, was mired in "a crisis of confidence."

The administration's mistakes had no doubt contributed to it. Yet the obstacles to projecting American power internationally were not simply a result of Carter's mismanagement. Vietnam had demonstrated the clear limits of what U.S. forces could accomplish in distant lands, while the long lines for expensive gas rose from an energy crisis decades in the making. The problems in the Middle East had proved intractable over many centuries. Finally, Carter could not be blamed for the reluctance of Americans to sacrifice personal comforts for the general good. American culture had long defined wealth as having more, not wanting less. In 1980 the discouraged electorate discovered in Ronald Reagan a political leader who shared that faith.

 REVIEW

How did Jimmy Carter's presidency demonstrate that he could be both liberal and conservative in his approach to governing?

PRIME TIME WITH RONALD REAGAN

The recession of the 1970s and the accompanying runaway inflation brought about a major political realignment, only the third since the Civil War. Republicans undermined the Democrats' New Deal coalition and established a conservative majority that would dominate American politics for at least three decades. In the 1980 presidential campaign, Ronald Reagan asked Americans, "Are you better off now than you were four years ago?" Many thought not, as Reagan swept the election with an unexpectedly large majority. The fight against inflation and high taxes would be the cornerstone of his administration, a strategy that replaced the liberals' central concern with using federal policy to ease unemployment.

The Great Communicator >>
Reagan's message was clear. "It is time to reawaken the industrial giant, to get government back within its means, and to lighten the punitive tax burden." To both liberals and conservatives this signaled the onset of what came to be called "the Reagan Revolution." Liberals feared—and conservatives hoped—that the revolution meant a harder line on cold war issues and an assault on a wide range of social programs and regulations at home. What both groups ignored at first were the moderating forces at work. As governor of California, Reagan had showed a willingness to accommodate, at times increasing both spending and taxes. The liberal *Washington Post* commented that the new president was not someone who allowed rigid ideas to block flexible policies. Equally important, noted the *Post,* almost anyone who met him thought he was "a nice guy, a happy secure person who likes himself and most other people."

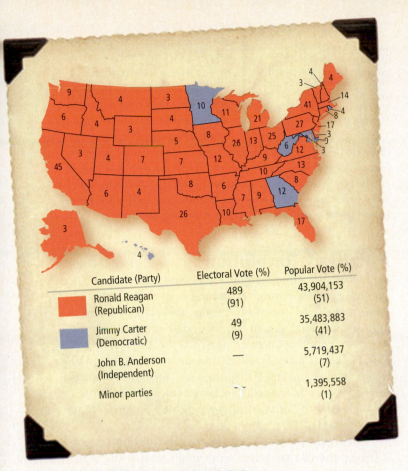

Candidate (Party)	Electoral Vote (%)	Popular Vote (%)
Ronald Reagan (Republican)	489 (91)	43,904,153 (51)
Jimmy Carter (Democratic)	49 (9)	35,483,883 (41)
John B. Anderson (Independent)	—	5,719,437 (7)
Minor parties		1,395,558 (1)

ELECTION OF 1980

In other ways Reagan contradicted expectations. With his jaunty wave and jutting jaw, he projected an aura of physical vitality and movie-star good looks. Yet at 69 he was the oldest person to become president, and no one since Calvin Coolidge slept as soundly or as often. Such serenity marked his refusal to become bogged down in the details of his job. Outsiders applauded his "hands-off" style after four years under Jimmy Carter, whose obsession with policy details led critics to say he missed the forest for the trees. Reagan set the direction of his administration, leaving the rest to his advisors. Sometimes that left him in the dark about major programs. Donald Regan, his first Treasury Secretary, once noted: "The Presidential mind was not cluttered with facts."

The effectiveness of Reagan's message was no accident. The president had honed his public speaking skills as an actor, as a spokesperson for General Electric, and as a politician. His communications staff planned everything from the president's words to a speech's location and camera angles down to the lighting. But the elaborate preparation also depended on Reagan's discipline as a performer. The president understood as well as his staff how to use a battlefield, a classroom, or the flag to communicate a hopeful message.

Luck played a role as well. Problems that handcuffed Carter seemed to ease on Reagan's watch. The day he took office Iran announced it would release the American hostages after 444 days of captivity. Three aging Russian leaders, beginning with Leonid Brezhnev in 1982, died suddenly, thereby greatly reducing the influence of the Soviet Union. And when a disturbed gunman shot Reagan in the chest two months after his inauguration, the wounds were not life threatening. Even Reagan's critics admired his courage in the face of death.

The Reagan Agenda >>

In addition to luck, however, Reagan viewed the economic downturn as an excellent reason to push for his revolution in government. That agenda called for massive tax cuts, deregulation of the economy, and a reduction in spending for social programs. Only the military would be spared the budget cutters' axe, because the president planned a forceful foreign policy to contain Soviet power.

A commitment to **supply-side economic** theory became the cornerstone of the Reagan revolution. Supply-side advocates argued that high taxes and government regulation stifled business. The key to revival lay in a large tax cut—a politically popular proposal, though economically controversial. Lower tax revenues would not increase the massive and growing federal budget deficits, insisted supply-side economist Arthur Laffer. His calculations suggested that lower tax rates would stimulate the economy so greatly, that tax revenues would actually grow, thanks to higher profits and a renewed prosperity. Broad cuts in social programs would further reduce deficits.

> **supply-side economics** theory that emphasizes tax cuts and business incentives to encourage economic growth rather than deficit spending to promote demand.

After little more than half a year in office, Congress handed the president most of the cuts he requested. The Economic Recovery Tax Act (ERTA) lowered income tax rates over the next three years by 25 percent, capital gains from the sale of stock by 40 percent, and investment income rates by 28 percent. Taxpayers in the highest brackets were far and away the biggest winners. At the same time Reagan signed the Omnibus Budget Reconciliation Act, which slashed some $35 billion spent on government programs. *The Wall Street Journal* hailed the two measures as a "spectacular tax victory," and news commentators suggested that Reagan had ended 50 years of liberal government.

Liberal government relied on the support of big labor. Here, too, Reagan struck a decisive blow. In 1981, members of PATCO, the air controllers union, struck against what they claimed were dangerous and debilitating working conditions. PATCO workers were, however, both highly paid and public service employees. Reagan declared their strike illegal and, without addressing the issues they raised, summarily fired them. Large corporations seized on the antiunion climate to wrest significant concessions on wages and work rules.

Many conservatives dismissed warnings of global warming, viewing environmental policies as essentially a strategy to regulate business. Under Reagan the National Climate Program Office, created during the Carter years, became "an outpost in enemy territory." Anne Gorsuch, the new head of the Environmental Protection Agency, cut her agency's budget so drastically, it almost ceased to function. The EPA filed no new enforcement cases against hazardous waste sites, even though the agency knew of some 18,000 that qualified for clean-up under the Superfund law passed during Carter's final year in office.

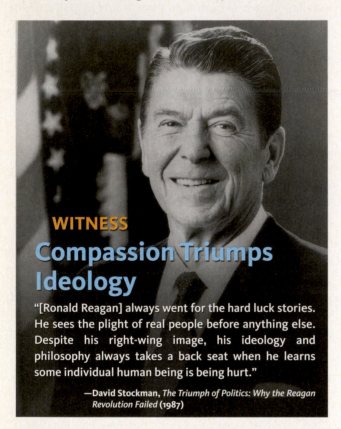

Compassion Triumps Ideology

"[Ronald Reagan] always went for the hard luck stories. He sees the plight of real people before anything else. Despite his right-wing image, his ideology and philosophy always takes a back seat when he learns some individual human being is being hurt."

—David Stockman, *The Triumph of Politics: Why the Reagan Revolution Failed* (1987)

The Occupational Safety and Health Administration was also severely cut back, ending its efforts to set health and safety standards and regulate toxic work environments. Workers were at particular risk in plants that produced polyvinyl chloride (PCV) and related plastics used in a wide array of consumer products. Members of OCAW, (the Oil, Chemical, and Atomic Workers union) had documented chemical wastes that the German firm BASF dumped into the Mississippi River at its Louisiana plant. There, they constantly smelled "this chlorine all day, twenty-four hours a day, depending on what job you're working at." When OCAW called a strike to gain improved wages and safer working conditions, the company locked the workers out for five years. OSHA was no longer interested in pursuing such cases.

Before being appointed Reagan's Secretary of the Interior, James G. Watt had fought environmentalists and federal regulations. An evangelical Christian and a

sagebrush rebels group of western cattlemen, loggers, miners, developers, and others who argued that federal ownership of huge tracts of land and natural resources violated the principle of states' rights.

self-proclaimed "**sagebrush rebel**," Watt had long wanted to force the Department of the Interior to open the public grazing lands, forests, and wilderness to private development. His abrasive style (he once denied the Beach Boys a permit to perform, because he considered their music immoral) offended so many people he resigned in 1983. Scandal forced EPA director Gorsuch to resign the same year, but the campaign continued to reduce or eliminate environmental regulation.

A Halfway Revolution >> Soon after the tax cuts went into effect evidence emerged that supply-side predictions of booming tax revenues were not materializing. Continued recession, rising interest rates, and a mounting federal deficit compounded the problem. So Reagan reversed course and accepted the Tax Equity and Fiscal Responsibility Act of 1982, a measure including $98 billion in tax increases disguised as "revenue enhancements." A year later Social Security reform led to further tax increases. In both cases Regan allowed pragmatism to trump ideology.

After reversing course on tax cuts, the economy began a strong upturn that extended through both of the president's terms in office. Labor productivity improved, inflation subsided to 4.3 percent, unemployment fell, and the stock markets rose sharply. Falling energy costs played a major role as OPEC members exceeded their production quotas. Having sold for as much as $30 per barrel, prices for crude oil fell as low as $10.

The benefits of an improved economy were distributed unevenly across economic classes and regions. For the wealthiest Americans the 1980s were the best of times. The top 1 percent commanded a greater share of wealth (37 percent) than at any time since 1929. Their earnings per year were 25 times greater than the 40 percent of Americans at the bottom of the economic ladder. Still, good times meant new jobs—over 14.5 million. Three million of these were concentrated in unskilled, minimum wage areas such as hotels, fast-food restaurants, and retail stores. High-paying jobs in financial services, real estate, insurance, and law went largely (70 percent) to white males. Only 2 percent went to African Americans.

outsourcing the contracting of goods or services from outside a company or organization in order to maintain flexibility in the size of the organization's work force.

The 1980s also saw an acceleration of the trend toward **outsourcing**, or relocating, high-wage industrial jobs to low-wage areas such as Mexico and Asia. Given its commitment to free markets and free trade, the Reagan administration resisted pressure to develop a plan to keep jobs at home. Thus even as the economy grew and

POVERTY IN AMERICA, 1970–1993

Social Security and other income supplements to older Americans reduced their rate of poverty. For all other traditionally impoverished groups the prosperity of the Reagan-Bush years left them slightly worse off than in 1980. The charts also indicate that poverty was most severe for unwed or divorced mothers and their children, and people of color.

Percent of Group Living in Poverty

- Single Mothers with Children
- Children under 18
- Persons Aged 65 and Over

(y-axis: 0, 10, 20, 30, 40, 50; x-axis: 1970, 1975, 1980, 1985, 1990, 1993)

Percent of Group Living in Poverty

- Black
- Hispanic
- White

(y-axis: 0, 10, 20, 30, 40, 50; x-axis: 1970, 1975, 1980, 1985, 1990, 1993)

Year

sectors. In general new technology workers were much younger and better educated. The media began referring to young, upwardly mobile, urban professionals as Yuppies—part of the younger generation that rejected the antimaterialistic values of their Hippie forebears. To Gen-Xers, those born after 1963 (the end of the baby boom), computers and other electronic devices seemed second nature. Computerization and information technologies streamlined the workplace so that the time it took to develop and bring new products to market fell sharply, along with the cost. Increased productivity also reduced the demand for low-skill workers. By contrast, demand for workers with education and technical skills rose (as did wages) and thereby increased the income gap between those at the top and bottom of the labor market.

In an economy in which brains displaced brawn, educated women were among the big winners. Not only did they find more jobs in high tech areas and computerized offices, but they also greatly increased their presence in law, medicine, business, and other professional schools. Still, many women continued to flow into lower-paying jobs in health care, education, social services, and government. The net result was that well-educated women gained far more economic independence and a more substantial political voice, while women with fewer skills and less education saw their earnings eroded. Single mothers with children, many who worked in low-wage jobs, were the nation's most impoverished group.

Job displacement in the 1980s had a devastating impact on two other groups, African American men and organized labor. Beginning in the 1970s black males lost much of the gains they had made over the previous three decades. The decline in the unionized manufacturing industries such as steel and autos struck hardest at the older industrial cities where blacks had gained a foothold in the economy. Often lacking the education required in the technology sector, black men had difficulty finding new jobs and many simply dropped out of the labor market. Sociologists began to describe an underclass, trapped in poverty, while middle class blacks escaped devastated urban neighborhoods.

As manufacturing declined so, too, did membership in unions. Labor organized 27 percent of all workers in 1953, 20 percent in 1980, 16 percent in 1990. Only the increase in the number of unionized government workers helped offset the shrinkage in the industrial sector. Deregulation made matters worse. With increased competition in the airlines, trucking, and telecommunications industries (all areas where membership had been strong), unions were forced to make concessions on wages and benefits. A two-tier system emerged in which younger workers received lower pay and hence had less incentive to join unions. A shrinking membership reduced labor's political clout, weakened the Democratic Party, and spurred the conservative revolution.

inflation dropped below 2 percent, unemployment persisted at over 6 percent, and poverty levels ranged from 11 to 15 percent. Cuts in programs such as food stamps, Medicaid, and school lunches increased the burden on the poor.

Winners and Losers in the Labor Market »

Several characteristics distinguished workers in the new technology industries from those in older industrial

Many high technology companies build headquarter complexes much like college campuses. Oracle, a business software systems company, built this gleaming complex in Redwood City, California, part of what has come to be known as Silicon Valley.

 **REVIEW**

What were the major goals of the Reagan Revolution?

STANDING TALL IN A CHAOTIC WORLD

Ronald Reagan's view of world affairs was primal. "The Soviet Union underlies all the unrest in the world," he stated in his 1980 campaign. Thus he made the defeat of the Communist menace a central mission of his administration. To that end he believed Americans must put Vietnam behind them and once again stand tall in the world. Although he was pleased to see the Soviet threat dissolving by the end of his years in office, the president also discovered that firmness and military force alone were not sufficient to calm regional crises across the world.

The Military Buildup >>
Reagan described the Soviet Union as the "evil empire." His plan to defeat that enemy centered on a massive buildup of the American military. Whereas Richard Nixon had thought the United States needed enough force to fight one and one-half wars at any time, Reagan pushed for enough to fight three and one-half around the globe. That required expenditures of over $1.6 trillion in his first five years (Carter had planned for $1.2 trillion). The combination of massive defense spending and tax cuts created huge deficits.

The massive military buildup not only created debt, it also expanded the federal government that conservatives were so eager to reduce. Cost overruns and wasteful spending were yet another problem. Exposés of $600 toilet seats and $7,000 coffee pots symbolized spending run amok. Worse yet were the multibillion-dollar weapons systems that were unneeded. Air Force planners, for example, persuaded Congress to fund the B-2 bomber, a plane costing $2 billion each and designed to penetrate Soviet air defenses. Only later did investigators determine that those Soviet air defenses did not exist. In general, advocates of the defense buildup exaggerated Soviet capabilities in order to pressure Congress to appropriate money.

Controversy arose, too, when Reagan's tough-talking defense planners spoke out about winning any nuclear exchange with the Soviet Union. In *Nuclear Winter* author Jonathan Schell warned that no one would win a nuclear war, in which debris in the atmosphere would create conditions fatal to all life on earth. Such warnings revived the antinuclear movement across East Asia, Europe, and America. Bishops of the American Catholic Church felt moved to announce their opposition to nuclear war.

Disaster in the Middle East >>
The Middle East continued to be a flashpoint of U.S.-Soviet tensions when in 1982 Israel invaded neighboring Lebanon to destroy missiles supplied by Syria, a Soviet client state. Israeli General Ariel Sharon also used the invasion to strike a decisive blow against forces of the Palestine Liberation Organization (PLO) that were camped in Lebanon. As the Israeli offensive bogged down, however, international outrage over the killing of Palestinians in Israeli-controlled camps forced Sharon to withdraw his troops.

Reagan then decided to send American troops to Beirut, Lebanon's capital, to protect the Palestinians and keep the peace between warring Christian and Muslim factions. Unfamiliar with the terrain or the politics, the Americans were drawn into supporting Christian militias. Muslim radicals responded by bombing the American Embassy and then, in October 1983, a U.S. marine barracks. Some 239 troops died. Confronting a chorus of criticism, including some from his own Defense Department, Reagan withdrew American troops from Lebanon.

The president also groped for a response to terrorist attacks and hostage-taking by Islamic fundamentalists. In response to repeated hijackings and other provocations, the president was forceful and uncompromising: "Let terrorists beware: . . . our policy will be one of swift and effective retribution." But against who should the United States seek retribution? Intelligence agencies had only sketchy profiles of the many terrorist factions and their political allies. In 1986 the president launched an attack against Libya, which sponsored terrorism. But so, too, did Syria and Iran, against whom the administration did nothing.

Frustrations in Central America >>   At first, Reagan found he could stand tall closer to home. On the pretext of protecting American medical students studying on the Caribbean island of Grenada, American troops crushed a band of pro-Cuban rebels and evacuated the students, who were hardly at risk. But the action in Grenada was largely symbolic.

More challenging was a campaign to overthrow the left-wing Sandinista government in Nicaragua. The president justified arming the anti-Sandinista "Contras," as aid

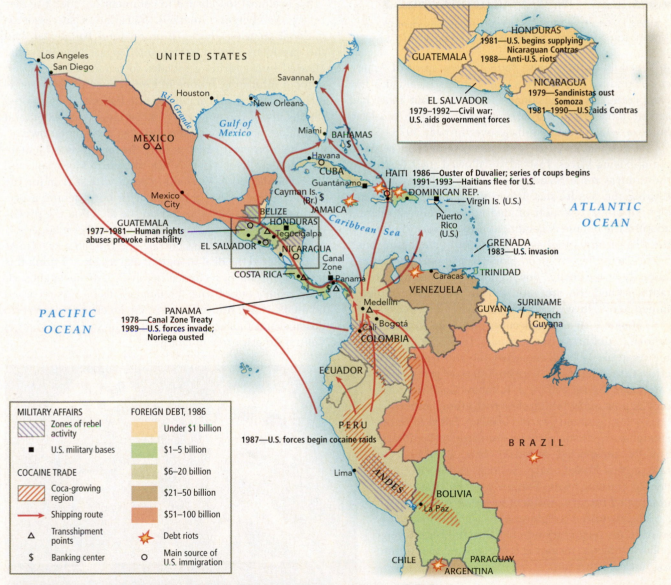

CENTRAL AMERICAN CONFLICTS, 1974–1990

President Reagan's attempts to overthrow the Sandinista government in Nicaragua focused American attention on Latin America. So, too, did the staggering debts Latin countries owed to American banks. A sharp rise in the drug trade also destabilized the region, as the Medellin drug cartel in Colombia shipped drugs through havens in Panama and the Bahamas into the United States. In December 1989 President Bush invaded Panama and brought the nation's leader, Manuel Noriega, to the United States to trial for drug trafficking charges.

In 1984, civil rights activist Jesse Jackson became the second African-American to run a national campaign for the presidency.

to "freedom fighters" who battled in the spirit of America's Founding Fathers. True, the Contras included a few democrats and disillusioned Sandinistas, but most had served in the brutal and corrupt dictatorship of Anastasio Somoza, which the Sandinistas overthrew in 1979.

Reagan had no desire to broker a settlement between the opposing forces. Instead, he allowed the CIA to help the Contras mine Nicaragua's harbor, in hopes of destabilizing the Sandinistas. When the mines damaged foreign ships—a violation of international law—Congress adopted the Boland Amendment, which explicitly forbade the CIA or "any other agency or entity involved in intelligence activities" to spend money to support the Contras "directly or indirectly." Bowing to criticism, Reagan reluctantly signed the measure, though he remained determined to overthrow the Sandinistas.

Though Reagan's reelection had been expected, the campaign did bring two surprises. In the Democratic primaries Jesse Jackson mounted the most successful effort to that date by an African American presidential candidate. But his call for a "Rainbow Coalition" uniting the poor and working class with ethnic minorities, family farmers, and gay and lesbians failed to attract enough mainstream support, even among Democrats. Equally unexpected, Mondale chose Geraldine Ferraro, a New York Congresswoman, as his vice presidential running mate. Ferraro was the first woman nominated for vice president by either major party.

The victorious Reagan and his advisers looked forward in his second term to tackling stubborn foreign policy problems, including terrorism and the continuing nuclear arms race.

The Iran-Contra Connection >> By mid-1985 Reagan policymakers felt two major frustrations. First, Congress had forbidden any support of the Contras in Central America, and second, Iranian-backed terrorists continued to hold hostages in Lebanon.

In the summer of 1985 a course of events was set in motion that eventually linked these two issues.

The president made it increasingly clear that he wanted to find a way to free the remaining hostages. National Security Adviser Robert McFarlane suggested opening a channel to "moderate factions" in the Iranian government. If the United States sold Iran a few weapons, the grateful moderates might use their influence in Lebanon to free the hostages. But an agreement to exchange arms for hostages would violate the president's vow never to pay ransom to terrorists. Still, over the following year, four secret arms shipments were made to Iran. One hostage was set free.

Reagan's secretaries of state and defense both had strongly opposed the notion of trading arms for hostages. "This is almost too absurd to comment on," Defense Secretary Weinberger remarked. McFarlane's successor as national security adviser, Admiral John Poindexter, had the president sign a secret intelligence "finding" that allowed him and his associates to pursue their mission without informing anyone in Congress or even the secretaries of defense and state. Because the president ignored the details of foreign policy, McFarlane, Poindexter, and their aides had assumed the power to act on their own.

The man most often pulling the strings was Lieutenant Colonel Oliver "Ollie" North, an aide to McFarlane and later Poindexter. A Vietnam veteran with a flair for the dramatic, North was impatient with bureaucratic procedures. In January 1986 he hit on the idea that the profits made selling arms to Iran could be secretly siphoned off to buy weapons for the Contras. The Iranian arms dealer who brokered the deal thought it a great idea. "I think this is now, Ollie, the best chance, because . . . we never get such good money out of this," he laughed, as he was recorded on a tape North himself made. "We do everything. We do hostages free of charge; we do all terrorists free of charge; Central America free of charge."

Oliver North successfully took the offensive in his testimony before the congressional committee investigating the Iran-Contra scandals. Here North delivers a pro-Contra lecture to the committee.

Cover Blown >>

Through the fall of 1986 both operations remained hidden from view until a Lebanese newspaper exposed the Iranian arms deal. Astonished reporters besieged the administration, demanding to know how secret arms sales to a terrorist regime benefited the president's antiterrorist campaign. As the inquiry continued, the link between the arms sales and the Contras was discovered.

The press nicknamed the scandal "Irangate," comparing it to Richard Nixon's Watergate affair. But Irangate raised more troubling issues. During Watergate Nixon had led the cover-up to save his own political skin. But during the Iran-Contra congressional hearings, Admiral Poindexter testified that he had kept Reagan in ignorance "so that I could insulate him from the decision and provide some future deniability for the president if it ever leaked out." In that way, Iran-Contra revealed a presidency out of control. An unelected segment within the government had taken upon itself the power to pursue its own policies beyond legal channels.

From Cold War to Glasnost >>

Because few members of Congress wanted to impeach a genial president, the hearings came to a sputtering end. Reagan's popularity returned, in part because of substantial improvement in Soviet-American relations. By the 1980s the Soviet Union was far weaker than American experts, including the CIA, had ever recognized. The Soviet economy stagnated; the Communist party was mired in corruption. The war in Afghanistan had become a Soviet Vietnam. By accelerating the arms race Reagan placed additional pressure on the U.S.S.R.

In 1985 a fresh spirit entered the Kremlin. Unlike the aged leaders who preceded him, Mikhail Gorbachev was young and saw the need for reform within the Soviet Union. Gorbachev's fundamental restructuring, or *perestroika,* set about improving relations with the United States. He reduced military commitments and adopted a policy of openness (*glasnost*) about problems in the Soviet Union. In October the two leaders held their second summit in Reykjavík, Iceland. Gorbachev dangled the possibility of abolishing all nuclear weapons. Reagan was receptive to the idea, but in the end did not accept so radical

opinion

Which was the greater threat to constitutional principles, Watergate or Irangate?

⌃ In October 1986 President Reagan and General Secretary Mikhail Gorbachev met for arms talks at Reykjavik, Iceland. At their second summit meeting Gorbachev proposed that the two superpowers agree to "the liquidation of nuclear weapons." Reagan liked that ambitious goal (considerably more than his skeptical advisers), but he was unable to agree because he wanted to continue development of an antiballistic missile system.

a proposal. Even so, a summit in Moscow two years later eliminated an entire class of nuclear missiles with ranges of 600 to 3,400 miles. Both sides agreed to allow on-site inspections of missile bases and the facilities where missiles would be destroyed.

Thus, as the election of 1988 approached, the president could claim credit for improved relations with the Soviet Union. Loyalty to Ronald Reagan made Vice President George H. W. Bush the Republican heir apparent. The Democratic challenger, Governor Michael Dukakis of Massachusetts, pointed out how much the poor and even many middle-class Americans had lost during the 1980s. But Bush put the lackluster Dukakis on the defensive. With the economy reasonably robust, Bush won by a comfortable margin. The Reagan agenda remained on track.

✓ REVIEW

How did Reagan's foreign policy try to overcome the legacy of Vietnam?

AN END TO THE COLD WAR

President George Herbert Walker Bush was born to both privilege and politics. The son of a Connecticut senator, he attended an exclusive boarding school and Yale University. His background made him part of the East Coast establishment often scorned by more populist Republicans. Yet once the oil business lured Bush to Texas, he became a Goldwater Republican and ran unsuccessfully for the Senate in 1964. Foreign policy interested him far more than domestic politics, though in the end, inattention to domestic issues proved his undoing as the economy slid into recession.

A Post–Cold War Foreign Policy >> To

the astonishment of most Western observers, Mikhail Gorbachev's reform policies led not only to the collapse of the Soviet empire but also to the breakup of the Soviet Union itself. In December 1988 Gorbachev spoke in the United Nations of a "new world order." To that end he began liquidating the Soviet cold war legacy, as the last Russian troops began leaving Afghanistan and then Eastern Europe.

Throughout 1989 Eastern Europeans began to test their newfound freedom. In Poland, Hungary, Bulgaria, Czechoslovakia, and, most violently, Romania, Communist dictators fell from power. Nothing more inspired the world than the stream of celebrating East Germans pouring through the Berlin Wall in November 1989. Within a year the wall, a symbol of Communist oppression, had been torn down and Germany reunified. Although Gorbachev struggled to keep together the 15 republics that made up the Union of Soviet Socialist Republics, the forces of nationalism and reform pulled it apart. The Baltic republics—Lithuania, Latvia, and Estonia—declared their independence in 1991. Then, in December, the Slavic republics of Ukraine, Belarus, and Russia formed a new Commonwealth of Independent States. By the end of December eight more of the former Soviet republics had joined the loose federation. Boris Yeltsin, the charismatic president of Russia, became the Commonwealth's dominant figure. With no Soviet Union left to preside over, Gorbachev resigned as president.

Although President Bush increasingly supported Gorbachev's reforms, he did so with caution. Even if he had wished to aid Eastern Europe and the new Commonwealth states, soaring deficits at home limited his options. The administration seemed to accept the status quo in Communist China, too. When in June 1989 China's aging leadership crushed students rallying for democratic reform in Beijing's Tiananmen Square, Bush muted American protests.

The fall of the Soviet Union signaled the end of a cold war that, over the span of half a century, had threatened a

⋀ The Berlin Wall had stood since August 1961 as a symbol of cold war tensions. Thus Americans joined these Germans in celebrating the Wall's destruction. At long last the cold war seemed to be at an end.

nuclear end to human history. At a series of summits with Russian leaders, the United States and its former rival agreed to sharp reductions in their stockpiles of nuclear weapons. The Strategic Arms Reduction Treaty (or START, concluded in July 1991) far surpassed the limits negotiated in earlier SALT talks. By June 1992 Bush and Yeltsin had agreed to even sharper cuts.

The Gulf War >> With two superpowers no longer facing off against each other, what would the "new world order" look like? If anything, regional crises loomed larger. Instability in the Middle East produced the greatest foreign policy challenge. From 1980 to 1988 Iran and Iraq had battered each other in a debilitating war. During those years the Reagan administration assisted Iraq with weapons and intelligence, until at last it won a narrow victory over Iran's fundamentalists. But Iraq's ruthless dictator, Saddam Hussein, had run up enormous debts. To ease his financial crisis, Hussein cast a covetous eye on his neighbor, the small oil-rich sheikdom of Kuwait. In August 1990, 120,000 Iraqi troops invaded and occupied Kuwait, catching the Bush administration off guard. Would Hussein stop there?

"We committed a boner with regard to Iraq and our close friendship with Iraq," admitted Ronald Reagan. Embarrassed by having supported the pro-Iraqi policy, Bush was determined to thwart Hussein's invasion of Kuwait. He likened the Iraqi leader to Hitler and coordinated a United Nations–backed economic boycott. Increasing the pressure further, he deployed half a million American troops in Saudi Arabia and the Persian Gulf. By November Bush had won a resolution from the UN Security Council permitting the use of military force if Hussein did not withdraw.

On January 17, 1991, planes from France, Italy, Britain, Saudi Arabia, and the United States began bombing Baghdad and Iraqi bases. Operation Desert Storm had begun. After weeks of merciless pounding from the air, ground operations shattered Hussein's vaunted Republican Guards in less than 100 hours. In an act of spite, Hussein resorted to ecoterrorism. His forces set Kuwait's oil fields ablaze and dumped huge quantities of crude oil into the rich Persian Gulf ecosystem. It did him no good: by the end of February Kuwait was liberated, and nothing stood between Allied forces and Iraq's capital, Baghdad. Bush was unwilling to advance that far—and most other nations in the coalition agreed. If Hussein were toppled, it was not clear who in Iraq would fill the vacuum of power.

Domestic Doldrums >> Victory in the Gulf War boosted the president's popularity so high that aides brushed aside the need for any bold domestic program. "Frankly, this president doesn't need another single piece of legislation, unless it's absolutely right," asserted John Sununu, his cocky chief of staff. "In fact, if Congress wants to come together, adjourn, and leave, it's all right with us." That attitude suggested a lack of direction that proved fatal to Bush's reelection hopes.

At first Bush envisioned a domestic program that would soften the harsher edges of the Reagan revolution. He promised to create a "kinder, gentler" nation. Yet pressures from conservative Republicans kept the new president from straying too far in the direction of reform. When delegates from 178 nations met at an "Earth Summit" in Rio de Janeiro in 1992, the president opposed efforts to draft stricter rules to lessen the threat of global warming. Bush did sign into law the sweeping Clean Air Act passed by Congress in 1990. But soon after,

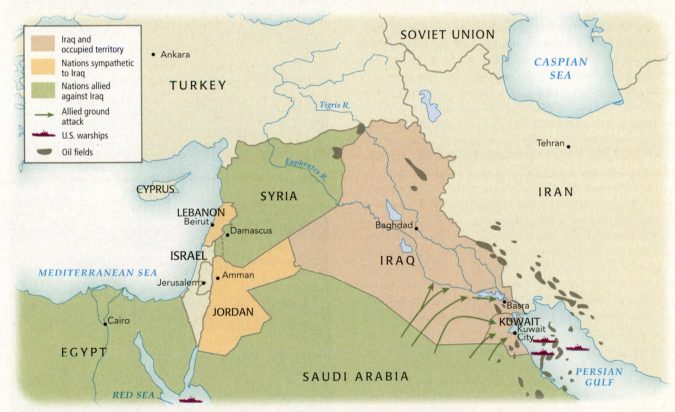

WAR WITH IRAQ: OPERATION DESERT STORM

When Saddam Hussein invaded oil-rich Kuwait on August 2, 1990, the United States formed a coalition to force out the Iraqis. (Although Turkey was not a formal member, it allowed its airfields to be used. Israel remained uninvolved to avoid antagonizing Arab coalition members.) The coalition launched Operation Desert Storm in January 1991; land forces invaded on February 24, routing Iraqi troops, who left Kuwait in ruin and its oil fields aflame.

Vice President Dan Quayle established a "Council on Competitiveness" to rewrite regulations that corporations found burdensome.

Similarly, the president called for reform of an educational system whose quality had declined through the 1980s. But, while he convened a well-publicized "Education Summit" in 1989, the delegates issued a modest set of goals only after the president was urged to do so by his cochair at the summit, Governor Bill Clinton of Arkansas.

The Conservative Court >> Although Presidents Reagan and Bush both spoke out against abortion, affirmative action, the banning of prayer in public schools, as well as other conservative social issues, neither made action a legislative priority. Even so, both presidents shaped social policy through their appointments to the Supreme Court. Reagan placed three members on the bench, including in 1981 Sandra Day O'Connor, the first woman to sit on the high court. Bush nominated two justices. As more liberal members of the Court retired (including William Brennan and Thurgood Marshall), the decisions handed down became distinctly more conservative. The appointment of Antonin Scalia gave the Court its most outspoken conservative.

In 1991 the Senate hotly debated President Bush's nomination of Clarence Thomas, an outspoken black conservative and former member of the Reagan administration. The confirmation hearings became even more contentious when Anita Hill, a woman who had worked for Thomas, testified that he had sexually harassed her. Women's groups blasted the all-male Judiciary Committee for keeping Hill's allegations private until reporters uncovered the story. Thomas and his defenders accused his opponents of using a disgruntled woman to help conduct a latter-day lynching. In the end the Senate narrowly voted to confirm, and Thomas joined Scalia as one of the Court's most conservative members.

Evidence of the Court's changing stance came most clearly in its attitude toward affirmative action—those laws that gave preferred treatment to minority groups in order to remedy past discrimination. State and federal courts and legislatures had used techniques such as busing and the setting of quotas—minimum proportional shares of minorities or women as part of an institution's makeup—to overturn past injustices. As early as 1978, however, the Court began to set limits on affirmative action. In *Bakke v. Regents of the University of California* (1978), the majority ruled that college admissions staffs could not set fixed quotas, although they could still use race as a guiding factor in trying to create a more diverse student body. Increasingly, the Court made it easier for white citizens to challenge affirmative action programs. At the same time it set higher standards for those who wished to put forward a claim of discrimination.

"An amorphous claim that there has been past discrimination in a particular industry cannot justify the use of an unyielding racial quota," wrote Justice O'Connor in 1989.

Disillusionment and Anger >> Ronald Reagan had given a sunny face to conservatism. He had assured voters that if taxes were cut, the economy would revive and deficits would fall. He promised that if "big government" could be scaled back, there would be a new "morning in America." Yet a decade of hands-off conservative leadership left the deficit ballooning and state and local governments larger than ever with fewer resources to address the nation's needs. A growing number of Americans felt that the institutions of government had come seriously off track. Indeed, such cynicism was fueled by the attacks on big government by Reagan and Bush.

⌃ As the AIDS epidemic spread in the 1980s, quilts such as these expressed sorrow for lost friends and loved ones. The quilts also served to raise public awareness of the need for a more effective policy to aid the afflicted and fight the disease.

A series of longer-term crises contributed to this sense of disillusionment. One of the most threatening centered on the nation's savings and loan institutions. By the end of the decade these thrifts were failing at the highest rate since the Great Depression. Reagan's advisers as well as members of Congress ignored the warnings that fraud and mismanagement were increasing sharply. Only during the Bush administration did it become clear that the cost of rebuilding the savings banks and paying off huge debts might run into hundreds of billions of dollars.

The late 1980s also brought a public health crisis. Americans were spending a higher percentage of their resources on medical care than were citizens in other nations, yet they were no healthier. As medical costs soared, more than 30 million Americans had no health insurance. The crisis was worsened by a fatal disorder that physicians began diagnosing in the early 1980s: acquired immunodeficiency syndrome, or AIDS. With no cure available, the disease threatened to take on epidemic proportions not only in the United States but also around the globe. Yet because the illness at first struck hardest at the male homosexual community and intravenous drug users, many groups in American society were reluctant to address the problem.

Bank failures, skyrocketing health costs, anger over poverty and discrimination—none of these problems by itself had the power to derail the conservative revolution. Still, the various crises demonstrated how pivotal government had become in providing social services and limiting the abuses of powerful private interests in a highly industrialized society.

The Election of 1992 >>

In the end, George Bush's inability to rein in soaring government deficits proved most damaging to his reelection prospects. "Read my lips! No new taxes," he pledged to campaign audiences in 1988. But the president and Congress remained at loggerheads over how to reach the holy grail of so many conservatives: a balanced budget. In 1985 Congress had passed the Gramm-Rudman Act, establishing a set of steadily increasing limits on federal spending. By 1990 the law's automatic spending limits were threatening popular programs such as Medicare. To preserve them, Bush agreed to a package of new taxes along with budget cuts. Conservatives felt betrayed, and in the end, the deficit grew larger all the same.

As the election of 1992 approached, unemployment stood at more than 8 percent, penetrating to areas of the economy not affected by most recessions. Statistics showed that wages for middle-class families had not increased since the early 1970s and had actually declined during Bush's presidency. Many Reagan Democrats seemed ready

to return to the party of Franklin Roosevelt, who had mobilized an activist government in a time of economic crisis.

The Democrats nominated Governor Bill Clinton of Arkansas to challenge Bush in the presidential election. Clinton arose out of the ranks of the baby-boomers born after World War II. Like many of his generation he had opposed the war in Vietnam and experimented with marijuana (but "did not inhale," he assured skeptical reporter). In the campaign he accused Bush of failing to combat the recession. "It's the economy, stupid!" read the sign tacked up at his election headquarters. Clinton painted himself as a new kind of Democrat: centrist, independent of liberal interest groups and willing to work with business.

At the voting booth middle-of-the-road voters turned to Clinton and, in smaller numbers, to third-party challenger H. Ross Perot. Clinton captured 43 percent of the popular vote (to Bush's 38 and Perot's 19) in the largest turnout—55 percent—in 20 years. The election of four women to the Senate, including the first African American woman, Carol Moseley Braun, indicated that gender had become an electoral factor.

 REVIEW

What steps did Reagan, Gorbachev, and Bush take to stop the arms race and end the cold war?

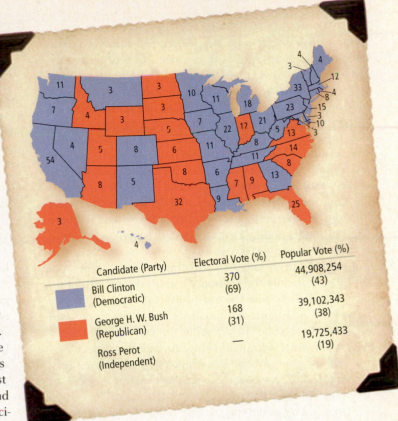

Candidate (Party)	Electoral Vote (%)	Popular Vote (%)
Bill Clinton (Democratic)	370 (69)	44,908,254 (43)
George H. W. Bush (Republican)	168 (31)	39,102,343 (38)
Ross Perot (Independent)	—	19,725,433 (19)

The 1992 election left the fate of the conservative revolution unresolved. Under Reagan and Bush the economy had grown and inflation had subsided. Yet prosperity benefited mostly those at the upper end of the income tax scale. Most Americans saw their financial situation stagnate or grow worse. Reagan and Bush had both supported a conservative social agenda that sought to restrict abortion rights, return prayer to the schools, and end affirmative action, but neither had done much to advance those goals. Both presidents weakened the capacity of the federal government to implement social programs.

In foreign affairs Reagan and Bush presided over the end of the cold war. Despite a growing isolationist sentiment among Democrats and Republicans, both presidents had shown a willingness to assert American power—in Libya, Lebanon, Nicaragua, and the Persian Gulf. Domestically the economy had grown and inflation had subsided, despite the most recent recession. Yet this prosperity had benefited mostly those at the upper end of the income scale. In pursuing the conservative creed both presidents significantly weakened the capacity of the federal government to implement social programs. No longer did Americans expect Washington to solve all the issues of the day.

How, then, would the nation meet the needs of an increasing number of poor, minority, elderly, and immigrant Americans? And what role would the United States play in the post–cold war era, when it stood as the lone superpower in the world arena? Those were questions for president-elect Bill Clinton as he sought to lead the United States into the post-cold war world.

CHAPTER SUMMARY

During the years of the Carter, Reagan, and Bush administrations, the nation's political and social agenda was increasingly determined by a conservative movement, including newly politicized evangelical Christians, that sought to restore traditional religious and family values, patriotism, and a more limited role for government.

- Jimmy Carter, unable to end the recession at home, pursued success abroad with a human rights policy and the negotiation of the Camp David Accords between Israel and Egypt—only to have the Soviet invasion of Afghanistan and the Iranian hostage crisis undermine his foreign policy.
- Ronald Reagan led the conservative tide with a program to limit the power of labor unions, reduce government regulation, lower taxes, and sharply increase spending on the military.
- Despite a revived economy, Reaganomics had two undesirable outcomes: huge government budget deficits and a growing gap in income between the rich and poor.
- Conservative appointments to the federal judiciary and the Supreme Court led to decisions increasing limits on government intervention in the areas of civil rights, affirmative action, abortion rights, and the separation of church and state.
- Reagan's efforts to "stand tall" in foreign policy led to the Iran-Contra scandal, which revealed a broad pattern of illegal arms shipments to right-wing rebels

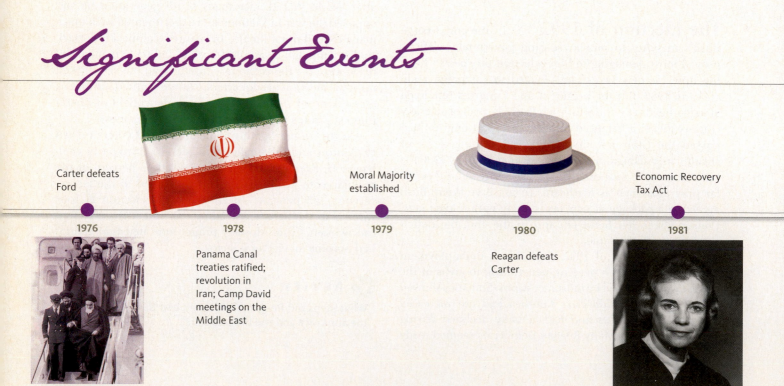

Significant Events

Carter defeats Ford

1976

Panama Canal treaties ratified; revolution in Iran; Camp David meetings on the Middle East

1978

Moral Majority established

1979

Reagan defeats Carter

1980

Economic Recovery Tax Act

1981

SANDRA DAY O'CONNOR

in Nicaragua and the trading of arms to Iran in an unsuccessful attempt to win the release of hostages in Lebanon—actions for which the president was sharply criticized but not impeached.

- Both Reagan and George Bush welcomed reforms set in motion by Mikhail Gorbachev that led by 1991 to the breakup of the Soviet Union, reductions in nuclear arms, and an end to the cold war.
- In the post–cold war era regional conflicts proved more troublesome as Iraq's invasion of Kuwait led Bush to form a UN coalition that routed the forces of Saddam Hussein in Operation Desert Storm.
- For George Bush a continuing recession, high budget deficits, and high unemployment undermined his bid for reelection.

Additional Reading

Bruce Shulman, *The Seventies* (2002), follows the transition from the 1960s to the Reagan era. An intriguing new look at the same subject is Philip Jenkins, *Decade of Nightmares: The End of the Sixties and the Making of Eighties America* (2006). An even-handed treatment of Jimmy Carter is Robert A. Strong, *Working in the World:*

Jimmy Carter and the Making of American Foreign Policy (2000). Two books that do justice to Ronald Reagan and the politics of the right are John Ehrman, *The Eighties: America in the Age of Reagan* (2006), and Gil Troy, *Morning in America: How Ronald Reagan Invented the 1980s* (2005). Considering the transformation into the digital world is Fred Turner, *From Counterculture to Cyberculture: Stewart Brand,* The Whole Earth Catalogue *and the Rise of Digital Utopianism* (2006).

Randall Balmer, *Mine Eyes Have Seen the Glory: A Journey Into the Evangelical Subculture in America* (2006), offers the perspectives of someone raised in the evangelical tradition. The issue of income inequality is well explained in Frank Levy, *The New Dollars and Dreams: American Incomes and Economic Change* (1999). Racial currents of the era are powerfully conveyed in Nicholas Lemann, *The Promised Land* (1995). The reasonably friendly treatment of George H. W. Bush by Ryan Barilleaux and Mark Rozell, *Power and Prudence: The Presidency of George H. W. Bush* (2004), can moderate the often insightful Kevin Phillips, *American Dynasty: Aristocracy, Fortune, and the Politics of Deceit* (2004). On the first Gulf War see Alberto Bin, Richard Hill, and Archer Jones, *Desert Storm: A Forgotten War* (1998).

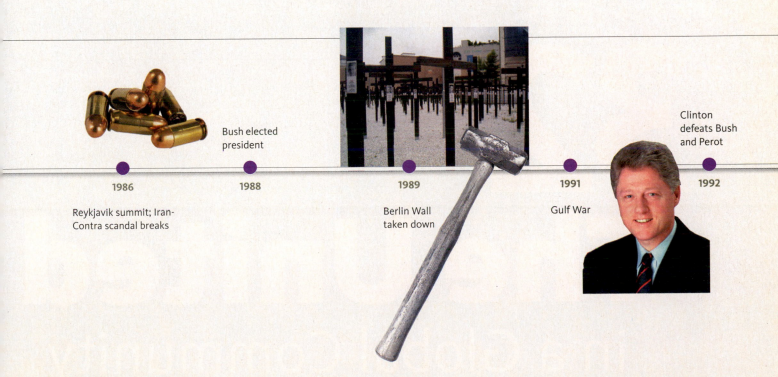

1986 — Reykjavik summit; Iran-Contra scandal breaks

1988 — Bush elected president

1989 — Berlin Wall taken down

1991 — Gulf War

1992 — Clinton defeats Bush and Perot

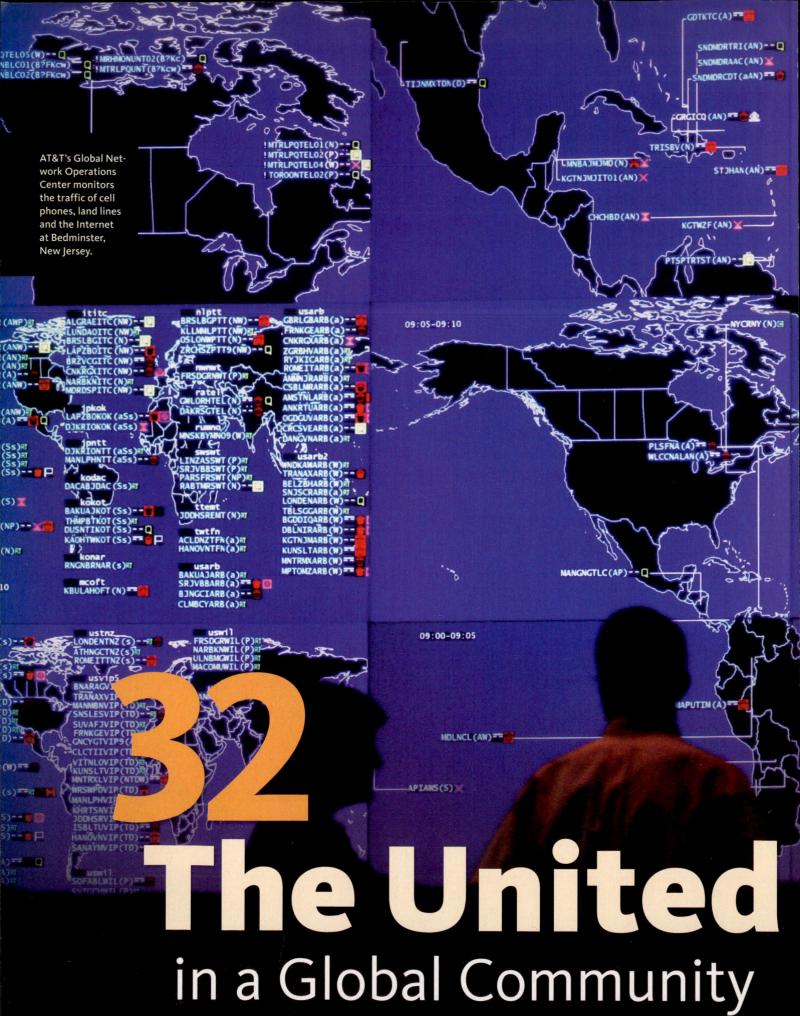

AT&T's Global Network Operations Center monitors the traffic of cell phones, land lines and the Internet at Bedminster, New Jersey.

32

The United
in a Global Community

States

1989–Present

>> **AN AMERICAN STORY**

OF GROCERY CHAINS AND MIGRATION CHAINS

Juan Chanax had never been far from San Cristobal, a small village in the Guatemalan highlands. In that region, some two thousand years earlier, his Mayan ancestors had created one of the world's great civilizations. During the twentieth century, San Cristobal had escaped the political upheavals that disrupted much of Guatemala. Still, by the 1970s Chanax, a weaver, struggled to support his young family. Work at a nearby American textile factory brought steady wages, but scarcely enough to survive on. The coming of the factory alerted him to a larger world outside his mountain village. In 1978 he decided that the only way he could help his sick son and improve himself—to *"superarme,"* as he put it—was to go north. Chanax made his way to Houston, Texas, with little more than a letter introducing him to several Guatemalans. Through them he learned of a maintenance job at a Randall's supermarket. >>

In the late 1970s high oil prices had brought a boom to Houston. And as the city grew, Randall's expanded with it. That expansion meant plenty of low-wage jobs for people like Chanax, even though he had almost no education and had entered the United States illegally. Randall's did not want just any low-wage workers. The chain specialized in high-priced goods in fancy suburban stores. Its upscale customers received valet parking, hassle-free shopping, and service from uniformed employees. Shortly before Chanax began work, one of Randall's managers had a falling out with several African American employees. When the manager criticized their work, they argued heatedly, until one employee finally threw a mop at the manager and quit.

The incident proved to be Chanax's opportunity. Unlike the worker who stormed out, Chanax was willing to do any job without complaint. The minimum wage was more than twice what he earned in Guatemala. Within several weeks he began to wire money home to his family. And when the manager said Randall's would soon need more workers, Chanax arranged for his brother-in-law and an uncle to come north. Over time Randall's began to hire Guatemalans exclusively.

Within five years more than a thousand Mayans from San Cristobal were working at Randall's. A single person had created what scholars call a migration chain. Through Chanax, the supermarket chain had found access to a minimum-wage workforce who would perform willingly—in the company's words—as "cheerful servants." The Mayans, in turn, found opportunities unavailable in Guatemala. In the process Chanax and other early immigrants had become department managers and supervising assistants. Many of their wives worked as maids and servants in the homes of Houston's upper-income communities.

⚹ By the mid-1990s over a quarter of a million laborers worked in Southern California's garment industry, many of them recently arrived immigrants from Mexico or Central America. "Very often we work until eight or nine at night the six days and then work a half day Sunday," commented one. Chicano artist Yolanda López celebrates the virtues of a hard-working seamstress by portraying her as the Virgin of Guadalupe, the traditional patron saint of Mexico.

In many ways Juan Chanax and his fellow Guatemalans mirrored the classic tale of immigrants realizing the American dream. In suburban Houston they formed their own community in an area that came to be known as Las Americas. There, various Central American immigrant groups established churches and social clubs amid some 90 apartment complexes that a decade or two earlier had housed mostly young, single office workers. The growth of Las Americas in the late twentieth century echoed the pattern of immigrants who had come to the United States at the century's opening.

Yet those patterns had changed in important ways, too. Although cities remained the mecca of most immigrants, many newcomers of the 1980s and 1990s settled in suburban areas, particularly in the West and Southwest. Industrial factories had provided the lion's share of work in the 1890s, but a century later the service industries—grocery stores, fast-food chains, janitorial positions—absorbed many more of the new arrivals. Even the faces had changed, as European immigrants found themselves outnumbered by Latinos from Mexico and Central America as well as by Asians from the Philippines, China, Korea, Southeast Asia, and the Indian subcontinent, not to mention increasing numbers of Arabs, Africans, and Eastern Europeans. The broad geographic range reflected perhaps the most important shift in immigration: its truly global character. Transportation and communications networks tied immigrants to their home countries more strongly than in the past, allowing immigrants like Juan to keep in touch with former neighbors and relatives by phone as well as mail. Immigrants continued to participate in home-country politics more easily; they could wire money instantly to relatives and even build homes thousands of miles away where one day they planned to retire.

The global nature of immigration was only one aspect of an American society more tightly linked to the world community. With the end of the cold war, diplomacy shifted toward the need to manage regional conflicts. The international economy forged equally close links: the effects of a financial collapse in Thailand or a bank default in France could spread to other countries in a matter of weeks or even days. Finally, the dawn of the twenty-first century witnessed a communications revolution as the Internet tied together correspondents, consumers, manufacturers, and information systems. The movement of people, financial capital, and data around the globe forced a nation of nations to adapt itself to an increasingly global community—one in which terror also played a defining role. ≪

THE NEW IMMIGRATION

The Immigration Act of 1965 (page 623) altered the face of American life—perhaps more than any other legislation from Lyndon Johnson's Great Society. Those who passed the act did not expect such far-reaching changes, for they assumed that Europeans would continue to predominate among newcomers. Yet reform of the old quota system opened the way for a wave of immigrants unequaled since the beginning of the century.

More than 20 million immigrants arrived legally in the United States between 1990 and 2010, and millions more illegally. The greatest numbers came from Asia (People's Republic of China, the Philippines, and India) and Latin America (Mexico, Cuba, and Colombia). Immigrants settled largely in seven states: California, New York, Florida, Texas, Pennsylvania, New Jersey and Illinois. The influx raised the nation's foreign-born population to about 12 percent—a significant percentage, though lower than the high-water mark of 20 percent in 1900. The numbers were especially concentrated among the young. As of 2010 a quarter of the residents of the United States under 18 were immigrants or immigrants' children. When the nation prospered in the 1990s, Americans welcomed these newcomers as a vital source of new workers. But when the economy went into recession in 2008, immigration once again became a divisive political issue.

PROJECTED POPULATION SHIFTS, 1980–2050

The 6.5 million immigrants who arrived between 1990 and 1998 accounted for 32 percent of the increase in the total U.S. population. Census figures project an increasing racial and ethnic diversity. White population is projected to drop from 80 percent in 1980 to about 53 percent in 2050, with the nation's Latino population rising most sharply.

⌃ Sikhs—seen marching here in the New York City annual Sikh Day Parade in 2003—trace their origins to India's Punjab region.

The New Look of America—Asian Americans ≫

In 1970, 96 percent of Asian Americans were Japanese, Chinese, or Filipino. By the year 2000, those same three groups made up only about half of that group, as Asian Indians, Koreans, and Vietnamese joined the incoming stream. The newcomers also varied dramatically in economic background, crowding both ends of the economic spectrum.

The higher end included many Chinese students who, beginning in the 1960s, sought out the United States for a college education, then found a job and stayed, eventually bringing in their families. "My brother-in-law left his wife in Taiwan and came here as a student to get his Ph.D. in engineering," explained Subi Lin Felipe. "After he received his degree, he got a job in San Jose. Then he brought in a sister and his wife, who brought over one of her brothers and me. And my brother's wife then came." Asian Indians were even more acculturated upon arrival because about two-thirds entered the United States with college degrees already in hand. Indian engineers played a vital role in the computer and software industries. Similarly, Korean and Filipino professionals took skilled jobs, particularly in medical fields.

Yet Asian immigrants also included those on the lower rungs of the economic ladder. Among the new wave of Chinese immigrants, or San Yi Man, many blue-collar workers settled in the nation's Chinatowns, where they worked in restaurants or sewed in sweatshops. Without education and language skills, often in debt to labor contractors, most remained trapped in Chinatown's ethnic economy. Refugees from war and revolution in Southeast Asia often made harrowing journeys.

Even highly educated Asian immigrants often found it difficult to land jobs in their professions. To American observers, Korean shopkeepers seemed examples of success, when in fact such owners often enough had been professionals forced into the risky small-business world. One Filipino surgeon, unable to open up his own medical practice, found himself working as a restaurant meat cutter, for employers who had no idea of his real occupation. "They thought I was very good at separating meat from the bone," he commented ironically. In addition, the children of many immigrants found it difficult to adapt to American life. Schools reported significant numbers of Asian American students who were failing. Members of this "lost generation" were most often

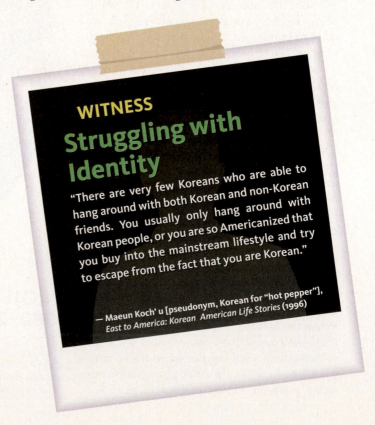

WITNESS

Struggling with Identity

"There are very few Koreans who are able to hang around with both Korean and non-Korean friends. You usually only hang around with Korean people, or you are so Americanized that you buy into the mainstream lifestyle and try to escape from the fact that you are Korean."

— Maeun Koch' u [pseudonym, Korean for "hot pepper"], *East to America: Korean American Life Stories* (1996)

the children of families who entered the United States with little education and few job skills.

The New Look of America—Latinos ››

Like Asian Americans, Latinos in the United States constituted a diverse mosaic, reflecting dozens of immigrant streams. Although the groups shared a language, they usually settled in distinct urban and suburban barrios across the United States. Such enclaves provided support to newcomers and an economic foothold for newly established businesses. Money circulated within a community; the workers and owners of an ethnic grocery, for example, spent their wages at neighboring stores, whose profits fueled other immigrant businesses in a chain reaction.

Washington Heights, at the northern tip of New York City, followed that path after nearly a quarter of a million Dominicans settled there during the 1970s and 1980s. Shopkeepers' stereos boomed music of trumpets and congas, while peddlers pushed heavily loaded shopping carts through busy streets, crying "¡A peso! ¡A peso!" ("For a dollar!"). In addition, Dominican social clubs planned dances or hosted political discussions. Similarly, in Miami and elsewhere in South Florida, Cuban Americans created their own self-sustaining enclaves. A large professional class and strong community leadership brought prosperity and political influence.

Along the West Coast, Los Angeles was the urban magnet for many Latino (and Asian) immigrants. Mexicans had long flocked to East Los Angeles, and in the 1990s it remained convenient to the jobs in factories, warehouses, and railroad yards across the river. Many Mexican Americans now owned their own businesses and homes. But beginning in the mid-1980s and 1990s the neighborhood of MacArthur Park became the focal point for the newest immigrants from Mexico and Central America.

Illegal Immigration ››

Because Mexico and the United States shared a long common border—and an equally long history of intermingling of peoples and cultures—many Mexicans entered the United States illegally. But illegal immigration increased during the 1980s as Central Americans joined the northward flow. By 1985, the number of illegal immigrants in the United States was estimated at anywhere from 2 to 12 million.

Congress attempted to stem that tide by passing the Immigration and Control Act of 1986. Tightened border security was coupled with a requirement that American employers certify their workers as legal residents. At the same time, illegal immigrants who had arrived before 1986 were granted amnesty and allowed to become legal residents. In the end, however, the law failed to create the clean slate Congress had hoped for. Worried about a labor shortage, California's fruit and vegetable growers lobbied for exceptions to the rules. Furthermore, the many immigrants who became legal under the new law sought to reunite their families, bringing in wives and children illegally. By 2006 the illegal population of Latinos in the United States exceeded 8 million.

Links with the Home Country ››

In an increasingly interdependent world, the new immigrants found it easier to maintain links with their points of origin. Pacoima, the small suburban barrio outside Burbank, California, boasted 13 different currency exchanges to handle the funds that immigrants wired home to relatives. By 1992 the amount of funds sent worldwide was so great that it was surpassed in volume only by the currency flows of the global oil trade.

Religious Diversity ››

The new immigration also reshaped America's religious faiths. During the 1950s, most Americans' sense of religious diversity encompassed the mainline Protestant churches, Roman Catholicism, and Judaism. But immigrants brought with them not only their own brands of Christianity and Judaism but also Buddhist, Hindu, and Islamic beliefs. By 2009 there were perhaps 2 to 3 million Muslims in the United States. Many had emigrated from Arab states, but adherents from South Asia made up an even greater number. Buddhists and Hindus numbered about a million adherents each.

Mainline Protestants and Catholics changed as well. The Presbyterian Church (U.S.A.) increased its Korean-speaking congregations from about 20 in 1970 to over 350 by the turn of the century. In New York City, Episcopalian services were held in 14 different languages. And Catholic churches increasingly found themselves celebrating mass in both English and Spanish. Such arrangements took place not only in urban congregations such as the Church of the Nativity in South Central Los Angeles (where Latinos alternated services with African Americans) but increasingly even in rural areas, like Columbus Junction, Iowa, whose Catholic church was energized by Mexican Americans working in a nearby meat-processing plant.

✔ **REVIEW**

What are the major sources of immigration over the past two decades, and how has the composition of those immigrants changed?

THE CLINTON PRESIDENCY

With the presidential inauguration of 1993, William Jefferson Clinton became the first baby boomer to occupy the White House. His wife, Hillary Rodham Clinton, would be the most politically involved presidential wife since Eleanor Roosevelt. Like so many couples of their generation, the Clintons were a two-career family. Both trained as lawyers at Yale University during the tumultuous early

<< President Clinton's most ambitious reform aimed to overhaul the nation's health care system to provide all Americans with basic health care (along with a card to guarantee it). Despite the card's intended resemblance to the ID for the popular Social Security program, medical interest groups lobbied successfully to defeat the proposal.

1970s. Bill chose politics as his career, becoming governor in his home state of Arkansas, while Hillary mixed private practice with public service. Their marriage had not been easy. Revelations of Clinton's sexual affairs almost ruined his presidential campaign.

Clinton envisioned himself as an activist president. He pledged to revive the economy and rein in the federal deficit, which had grown enormously during the Bush-Reagan years. Beyond that, he called for systematic reform of the welfare and health care systems as well as measures to reduce the increasing violence that too often had turned urban neighborhoods into war zones. An activist executive could achieve much, he believed, especially if he brought "a disciplined, aggressive agenda" to the job.

But the new president's desire for major legislative initiatives ran up against the election results of 1992. Clinton had received just 43 percent of the popular vote, while the Republicans had narrowed the Democratic majorities in Congress. Furthermore, the president's high energy levels did not always seem to be directed solely at his political agenda. One observer shrewdly noted that there were two Bill Clintons—the idealistic young man from Hope, Arkansas (his hometown), and the boy from Hot Springs (his mother's home). The latter was a resort town associated with the seamier side of Arkansas high life. With increasing frequency, the leadership mustered by the idealistic politician from Hope seemed to be undermined by the character flaws of the boy from Hot Springs.

The New World Disorder >> Clinton hoped
to concentrate on domestic rather than foreign affairs. He discovered that the "new world order," hailed by both Mikhail Gorbachev and George Bush, seemed more like a world of regional disorders. In Russia, President Boris Yeltsin struggled to bring stability from out of chaos, yet market reforms failed to revive a stagnant economy. Elsewhere in the world, ethnic and nationalist movements

provoked a number of regional crises. By using American power in a limited way, Clinton gained considerable public support.

In sub-Saharan Africa, brutal civil wars broke out in both Somalia and Rwanda. As president-elect, Clinton had supported President Bush's decision in December 1992 to send troops to aid famine-relief efforts in Somalia. But attempts to install a stable government proved difficult. Tragically, the United States as well as European nations failed to intervene in Rwanda before more than a million people were massacred in 1994.

Instability in Haiti pushed the president to take a bolder approach closer to home. In 1991 Haitian military leaders had forced their country's elected president, Jean-Bertrand Aristide, into exile. The harsh rule that followed sent over 35,000 refugees fleeing toward the United States, often in homemade boats and rafts. When a UN-sponsored economic embargo failed to oust the military regime, the Security Council in 1994 approved an invasion of Haiti by a multinational force. American troops proved crucial in convincing the military to leave. A smaller UN force stayed on to maintain order as new elections returned Aristide to the presidency.

Yugoslavian Turmoil >> Europe's most intractable trouble spot proved to be Yugoslavia, a nation divided by ethnic rivalries within a number of provinces, including Serbia, Croatia, Kosovo, and Bosnia. After Bosnia became independent in 1992 both Serbs and Croats, but especially the Serbs, resorted to what was euphemistically referred to as "ethnic cleansing"—the massacre of rival populations—to secure control. The United States at first viewed the civil war in Yugoslavia as Europe's problem. But as the civilian death toll mounted to a quarter of a million, the conflict became difficult to ignore. Nobel Peace Prize winner and Holocaust survivor Elie Wiesel beseeched President Clinton to "stop the bloodshed. . . . Something, anything, must be done."

Still, the ghosts of Vietnam loomed. Many members of Congress feared the prospect of American troops bogged down in a distant civil war. By 1995 Clinton had committed the United States to support NATO bombing of Serb forces, and when Bosnian and Croatian forces began to win back territory, the Serbs agreed to peace talks to be held in Dayton, Ohio. The Dayton Accords created separate Croatian, Bosnian, and Serbian nations. Some 60,000 NATO troops, including 20,000 Americans, moved into Bosnia to enforce the peace. Clinton had intervened successfully without the loss of American lives. In the spring of 1999 Serbian atrocities led him to participate in another successful intervention by NATO forces, this time in Kosovo.

Middle East Peace >>

Clinton also worked to mediate conflict in the Middle East. Sporadic protests and rioting by Palestinians in the Israeli-occupied territories of Gaza and the West Bank gave way in the 1990s to negotiations. At a ceremony hosted by the president in 1993, Palestinian leader Yasir Arafat and Israeli prime minister Itzak Rabin signed a peace agreement permitting self-rule for Palestinians in the Gaza Strip and in Jericho on the West Bank. In 1995 Arafat became head of the West Bank Palestinian National Authority.

Still, a full settlement remained elusive. The assassination of Prime Minister Rabin in 1995 by an angry Orthodox Jew began a period of increased suspicion on both sides, as extremists sought to derail the peace process. Clinton's efforts to broker a settlement continued until he left office in January 2001, but he was unable to bring the Israelis and Palestinians together. Whether in the Middle East, Eastern Europe, Africa, or the Caribbean, such regional crises demonstrated how difficult a new global "world order" would be to maintain.

Recovery without Reform at Home >>

Throughout Clinton's presidency the nation experienced a powerful economic expansion, which sustained his popularity despite a sexual scandal and attacks by conservatives. But the increasing prosperity did not provide Clinton enough headway to enact his major reform goal, overhauling the nation's health care system.

Reversing the deficits of the Reagan and Bush years was the new president's first domestic goal. He also proposed investments to stimulate the economy and repair the nation's decaying public infrastructure. In contrast, Presidents Reagan and Bush had cut funds to rebuild schools, roads, dams, bridges, and other public structures. In August 1993 a compromise budget bill passed by only a single vote in the Senate, with Republicans blocking the stimulus portion of Clinton's program. Still, deficit reduction was a significant achievement.

Victory in the budget battle provided Clinton the necessary leverage to pass NAFTA, the North American Free Trade Agreement. With the promise of greater trade and more jobs, the pact linked the United States economy more closely with those of Canada and Mexico. The president also helped supporters of gun control overcome the opposition of the National Rifle Association to pass the Brady Bill, which required a five-day waiting period on gun purchases.

Health care reform topped Clinton's legislative agenda. A task force led by Hillary Rodham Clinton developed a plan to provide health coverage for all Americans, including the 37 million who in 1994 remained uninsured. But a host of interest groups rallied to defeat the proposal, especially small businesses that worried that they would bear the brunt of the system's financing.

If the Clintons' plan had passed, the president and the Democratic majority in Congress might have boasted that government was responding to some of the long-term problems facing American society. But the failure of health care reform heightened the perception of an ill-organized administration and a Congress content with the status quo. The 1994 mid-term elections confirmed the public's anger over political gridlock, as Republicans captured majorities in both the House and the Senate.

The Conservative Revolution Reborn >>

When the new Congress assembled, the combative Speaker of the House, Newt Gingrich of Georgia, proclaimed himself a "genuine revolutionary." Gingrich used the first hundred days of the new session to vote on ten proposals from his campaign document "The Contract with America." The contract proposed a balanced-budget amendment, tax cuts, and term limits for all members of Congress. To promote family values, an anticrime package included a broader death penalty and welfare restrictions aimed at reducing teen pregnancy. Although the term limits proposal did not survive, the other nine proposals were passed by the House.

"When you look back five years from now," enthused Republican governor Tommy Thompson of Wisconsin, "you're going to say 'they came, they saw, they conquered.'" But the Senate was in a less revolutionary mood and the public worried about what Gingrich and his rebels proposed. To balance the federal budget while still cutting taxes, they planned to reduce Medicare expenditures while allowing premiums to double. They also sought to roll back environmental protections for endangered species, pollution controls set up by the Clean Water Act, and restrictions on mining, ranching and logging on public lands.

When Clinton threatened to veto the Republican budget, Republicans forced a confrontation by shutting down the federal government. The elderly on Social Security, travelers at National Parks, and soldiers on active duty all felt the consequences and Congress retreated.

In the end, the president outmaneuvered the Republicans by preempting their agenda. In 1995, he proposed his own route toward a balanced budget and the following year signed into law a sweeping reform of welfare. The bill ended guaranteed federal aid to poor children, and turned over such programs to the states. Food stamp spending was cut, and the law placed a five-year limit on payments

⌃ "I am a genuine revolutionary," House Speaker Newt Gingrich proclaimed, and the newly elected Republican freshmen in Congress led the charge to complete the Reagan revolution. By clothing Newt's followers as stiff-armed, flag-waving militarists, illustrator Anita Kunz recalls Mussolini's overzealous Black Shirts.

to any family. Under the idea of welfare-to-work, most adults receiving payments had to find work within two years. With a robust economy in full swing, voters readily supported Bill Clinton's reelection bid in 1996. Clinton became the first Democrat since Franklin Roosevelt to win a second term in the White House.

Women's Issues >>

As first lady, Hillary Rodham Clinton used her influence to promote opportunity for women and to draw attention to feminist issues. Bill Clinton shared many of his wife's concerns, and appointed Ruth Bader Ginsburg to the Supreme Court as well as three women to his cabinet, including Janet Reno as attorney general. In 1997 he named Madeleine Albright as the first female secretary of state.

Both Clintons supported a woman's right to control her decisions on reproduction, an issue that remained hotly contested. Because antiabortion conservatives had been unable to secure the repeal of *Roe v. Wade,* they sought to limit its application as much as possible.

More problematic for feminists was the Supreme Court decision in the 1991 case of *UAW v. Johnson Controls.* Since *Muller v. Oregon* in 1908 (page 450), the Court had accepted as constitutional those laws that gave women special protection based on their biological differences from men. Using this standard, Johnson Controls had a policy barring women workers from manufacturing batteries, because lead fumes in the workplace might damage an unborn fetus. The workers' union challenged the policy, noting that fertile men who faced reproductive risks in the workplace were not restricted. The Court agreed with the union, ruling that the emphasis on biological differences denied women an "equal employment opportunity." Justice Harry Blackmun wrote that a woman's decision as to whether her "reproductive role is more important to herself and her family than her economic role" was one for her to make on her own.

Many feminists hailed the decision as a step toward workplace equality. Feminist scholar Cynthia Daniels saw it as more ambiguous. Should laws recognize biological difference, or should they uphold equality? As Daniels argued: "To ignore difference is to risk placing women in a workplace designed by and for men, with all of its

hazards and lack of concern for the preservation of life and health." Yet rules that recognized difference had in the past reinforced "those assumptions and economic structures which form the foundation of women's inequality."

Scandal >>

Almost every two-term president has faced some crisis in his second term. Watergate brought down Richard Nixon, and the Iran-Contra controversy tarnished Reagan. Bill Clinton's scandal was in some ways more puzzling. At once smaller and more personal, it nonetheless threatened him with the ultimate constitutional sanction: **impeachment,** conviction, and removal from office.

impeachment the Constitutional process whereby members of the House of Representatives bring charges against a government official for "Treason, Bribery, or other high Crimes and Misdemeanors." If impeached, the individual is tried before the Senate, where a vote of two-thirds is needed to convict. Conviction results in removal from office.

Conservative Republicans who disliked Clinton's politics were generally even more offended by his moral lapses. Many referred to him derisively as "Slick Willie." During his first term they pressured Attorney General Reno to appoint Kevin Starr as a special prosecutor to investigate the president's involvement in an old Arkansas real estate venture known as Whitewater. Years of digging and millions of dollars later neither Starr nor two Senate committees had produced any evidence of wrongdoing. Then in January 1998 Starr hit what looked like an investigative jackpot. Linda Tripp, a former Bush administration appointee, had secretly taped her conversations with White House intern Monica Lewinsky. Lewinsky said that she and the president had an affair in the White House.

Keeping the existence of the tapes a secret, Starr deposed the president and Lewinsky about their relationship. Both swore under oath that they had not had "sexual relations." Then news leaked about the tapes. News pundits generally agreed that the president would have to resign or face impeachment—if not for his indiscretion with Lewinsky, then for lying under oath. After cross-examining Clinton before a grand jury, Starr recommended the president be impeached for perjury, obstruction of justice, and witness tampering.

To the astonishment of the news media, polling indicated that impeachment had little public support. Although Clinton had clearly engaged in behavior most Americans found inappropriate or even repugnant, they seemed to draw a line between public and private actions. The Republicans pressed their attack anyway. Along party lines, a majority in the House voted three articles of impeachment for lying to the grand jury, suborning perjury, and orchestrating a cover-up. In January 1999 the matter went to the Senate for trial, with Chief Justice of the United States William Rehnquist presiding.

Unlike with the Watergate scandals, in which Richard Nixon resigned because a bipartisan consensus had determined that impeachment was necessary, the accusers and defenders of Bill Clinton divided along partisan lines. The Senate voted to acquit, with five Republicans joining all 45 Senate Democrats in the decision.

The Politics of Surplus >> The impeachment controversy left the president weakened, but hardly powerless. Throughout the political tempest the nation's economy grew strongly. By 1999 the rate of unemployment had dropped to 4.1 percent, the lowest in nearly 30 years. Furthermore, as the economy expanded, federal tax receipts grew with it. By 1998 Bill Clinton faced a situation that would have seemed improbable a few years previous—a budget surplus. By balancing the budget the president had appropriated a key Republican issue.

Hanging by a Chad: The Election of 2000 >> Al Gore, who had loyally served as Bill Clinton's vice president, received the Democratic presidential nomination in 2000. Both Gore and his Republican opponent, George W. Bush (the son of former president George H. W. Bush) ran centrist, cautious campaigns. By election night many pollsters predicted a race "too close to call," but they were not prepared for the razor-thin margin. The outcome came down to Florida, where, two days after the election, Bush led by just 300 votes. Nationwide, Gore held a lead of 500,000 in the popular vote, but without Florida's 25 electoral votes neither candidate could claim a majority in the Electoral College. The 9,000 votes that went to Green party candidate Ralph Nader most likely cost Gore a clear victory in the state.

Evidence immediately surfaced of voting irregularities: complicated and hard-to-read ballots and punch-card machines so antiquated that they failed to fully perforate many ballots, leaving behind what would become known as "hanging chads." More serious charges alleged that the state had actively suppressed voting in heavily black counties.

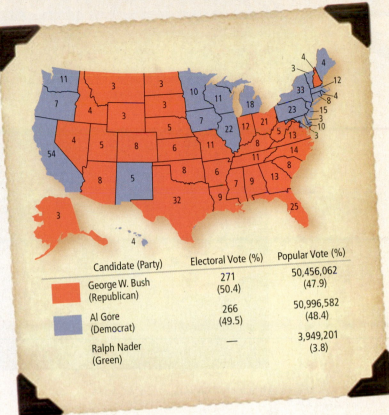

Candidate (Party)	Electoral Vote (%)	Popular Vote (%)
George W. Bush (Republican)	271 (50.4)	50,456,062 (47.9)
Al Gore (Democrat)	266 (49.5)	50,996,582 (48.4)
Ralph Nader (Green)	—	3,949,201 (3.8)

ELECTION OF 2000

After weeks of legal challenges, the U.S. Supreme Court decided the question of how to recount Florida's ballots. In *Bush v. Gore,* the Court's conservative majority, all Republican appointees, ruled 5–4 to end the recount. The Supreme Court, rather than the American electorate, cast the deciding votes to make George W. Bush the president of the United States.

 REVIEW

What were President Clinton's greatest successes and failures in foreign and domestic policy?

THE UNITED STATES IN A NETWORKED WORLD

In 1988 economist Lawrence Summers was working on the presidential campaign of Michael Dukakis. At a meeting in Chicago, the staff assigned him a car with a telephone. Summers was so impressed, he called his wife "to tell her I was in a car with a phone." A decade later as a member of the Clinton administration, he visited a village in Africa's Ivory Coast which could be reached only by dugout canoe. As Summers stepped into the canoe for his

Mapping the Internet

Color of lines and height of arcs indicate the intensity of web traffic as of the mid 1990s; the hotter the colors (orange, yellow) the greater the traffic.

Note which areas of the world are shown in black.

Why is the southern tip the only colored area of Africa?

How does this map suggest a potential source of tension between the Islamic and Western nations?

The Internet is not so much a single vast network, but a network of networks. It grew out of the efforts of the United States government to link major research and defense centers with a communications system that could survive a nuclear attack. The networks it joins now range from small home and office users, to universities, large corporations, and national governments. Probably no phenomenon in the recent past has done more to create a truly global economy. Stephen G. Eick

of Bell Laboratories created this map, based on 1993 data, to visually portray the flows of Internet traffic. Experts estimate that about a quarter of the world's people (almost 2 billion) have access to the worldwide web (www). Though many people think of the web and the Internet as the same thing, they are not. Hardware and software create the Internet (much like a railroad), while documents, sites, and other electronically accessible information make up the Web.

THINKING CRITICALLY

What would be another way to graph the information on this map? In what ways do you anticipate that the map would change if it were brought up to date? In what ways is the Internet similar to earlier systems of communication (that is, telephone, telegraph) and transportation (that is, railroads, airlines, interstate highways)? In what ways different?

return trip, an aide handed him a cell phone: "Washington has a question for you." The man who once marveled at a phone in his car in Chicago 10 years later expected one in his dugout in the African interior.

The Internet Revolution ›› Like Summers,

Americans at the end of the twentieth century were linked to a global communications network almost anywhere they went. This interconnectivity had been driven by a revolution in microchip technologies.

By the mid-1980s small businesses, homes, and schools were using personal computers for word processing, graphic design, and spreadsheets that tracked personal and financial data. Ten years later desktop computers could boast more power than the mainframes of the 1950s.

Most Internet pioneers shared a democratic vision of the web as open and free to all. Users could communicate without restriction and find access to any form of

information. Such openness was the bane of authoritarian governments, which found it difficult to control public opinion in a world in which information flowed freely. But the web's unregulated format raised legal, moral, and political questions as well. By 1999 five million sites were in operation—among them the dispensers of pornography, hate speech, and even instructions on how to build atomic bombs. A number of politicians and civic groups called for the censorship of the more extreme web content. Others argued that the greater danger lay in allowing the Internet to become dominated by large telecommunications companies. These advocates called for legislation protecting "Net neutrality."

Equally intriguing was the emergence of a new virtual culture. Computer engineers competed to devise the most effective algorithms to power search engines, a business that Google soon dominated. And through Internet browsers and other software, individuals could chat, find a job, download music, buy and sell merchandise or locate potential mates. Within 10 years, political blogs offered instant responses to the issues of the day. Grassroots organizations formed mass social and political movements using email and networking sites such as Facebook and Twitter. Virtual communities came into being in cyberspace. No longer did people have to turn to major media outlets to stay in touch with the news.

The revolution in microchip technologies contributed substantially to the economic expansion of the 1990s. In 1998 e-commerce alone generated some 482,000 jobs. Whereas in 1965 businesses committed just 3 percent of their spending to high technology, they committed 45 percent in 1996. That increase contributed to a significant rise in labor productivity. Improved productivity in turn proved to be a critical factor behind economic growth. Business-to-business sales went from $40 billion in 1998 to some $1.1 trillion by 2007, while retail sales approached $400 billion.

American Workers in a Two-Tiered Economy >> The benefits of prosperity were not evenly distributed, however. Economists described the United States after the 1980s as a two-tiered labor market in which most increases in earning went to people with the highest wages. Despite prosperity, the median income of American families was barely higher in 1996 than in 1973. Indeed, the earnings of the average white male worker actually fell. Only because so many women entered the job market did the family standard of living remain the same. In the early 1970s some 37 percent of women worked outside the home; in 1999 about 57 percent did.

Education was a critical factor in determining winners in the high-tech, global economy. Families with college-educated parents were three times more likely to have home access to the Web than were those families in which parents' education ended with high school. Because average education levels were relatively lower among African Americans and Latinos (and relatively higher among Asian Americans), the computer divide took on a racial cast as well. But the implications went beyond mere access to the web and its wealth of information and commerce. More important, the high-wage sector of the computer economy required educated workers, and the demand for them drove up those workers' salaries.

Most semiskilled and unskilled workers saw little growth in earnings despite full employment. Unlike computer programmers or corporate executives who were in high demand, low-skill workers were not able to increase their earnings simply by switching jobs. Some economists concluded that "the most important economic division is not between races, or genders,

or economic sectors, but between the college-educated and the non-college-educated."

African Americans and the Persistence of the Racial Divide >> In the 1990s the highest-paid celebrity in the world was an African American—Michael Jordan. Oprah Winfrey, also an African American, was the highest-paid woman in America. Although the situation of African Americans had improved vastly since the 1950s, race still mattered—as the case of black motorist Rodney King showed.

In 1991 Los Angeles police, all white, arrested King, for speeding and drunken driving. As King lay on the ground, four officers proceeded to beat him with nightsticks more than 50 times. When blacks complained about such police brutality, public officials often ignored them. But this time a man in a nearby apartment videotaped the beating, which the news media broadcast to the entire nation. Yet, the following year, an all-white suburban jury acquitted the officers, concluding that King had been threatening and that the officers had acted within their authority.

The verdict enraged the African American community in Los Angeles, where widespread riots erupted for three days. It was the worst civil disturbance in Los Angeles history. By the time order was restored nearly 2,000 people had been injured, 40 people had died, over 4,500 fires burned, and $500 million of property had been looted, damaged, or destroyed.

At first glance the riot appeared to be much like the one that had decimated Watts, a rundown area of Los Angeles, in 1965. Poor African Americans had lashed out in frustration at white racism. In fact, the 1992 riots were multiracial in character, exposing divisions in Los Angeles's multicultural communities. Rioters, both black and Latino, damaged over 2,000 small groceries, liquor stores, and other businesses run by Korean American immigrants. African

⩔ The Los Angeles riots of 1992 revealed divisions in the city's multicultural communities of African Americans, Latinos, and Asian Americans.

Americans also attacked Latinos; and after the first day, Latinos joined in the disturbances. But there was a revealing pattern. In the more established Latino communities of East Los Angeles, where families had more to lose, residents remained quiet or worked actively to maintain the peace. In contrast, fires and looting destroyed many businesses in the MacArthur Park area, where the newest Latino immigrants lived. Thus the 1992 riots exposed tension and competition among ethnic groups.

African Americans in a Full-Employment Economy >>

By the late 1990s African Americans in increasing numbers were benefitting from a decade of economic expansion. Home ownership reached 46 percent, and employment increased from around 87 percent in 1980 to nearly 92 percent in 1998. African Americans in greater numbers rose up the ladder in corporate America. Many started their own businesses. Within the nation's inner cities, crime and poverty decreased, especially rates of murder and violence. Births to unwed mothers reached a postwar low. Fewer blacks lived below the poverty level and fewer were on welfare.

Civil rights leaders remained concerned, however, about the continued opposition to affirmative action. In 1996 California voters passed a ballot initiative, Proposition 209, that eliminated racial and gender preferences in hiring and college admissions. The leading advocate for Proposition 209 was a conservative black businessman, Ward Connerly. Connerly argued that racial preferences demeaned black and other minority students by setting up a double standard that patronizingly assumed minorities could not compete on an equal basis. In any case, Proposition 209 had a striking effect. Enrollments of Latinos and blacks at the elite California university campuses and professional schools dropped sharply. Similar laws banning racial preference in admissions produced similar declines at leading state universities in Texas, Washington, and Michigan.

The Supreme Court did not fully address the issue of affirmative action until 2003, when it ruled on the University of Michigan's admissions program, in *Gratz v. Bollinger.* The Court argued that Michigan's point system was unconstitutional, because it gave minorities preference in undergraduate admissions. At the same time, the Court approved a separate program used by the university's law school, which allowed race as a consideration in the admissions process. In so doing the justices allowed the nation's public universities as well as other institutions to take race into account in less overt ways. Affirmative action had been reduced in scope, but not abolished.

Global Pressures in a Multicultural America >>

Clearly the changes wrought by the new global economy affected not just the immigrant enclaves but American culture as a whole. Salsa rhythms became part of the pop culture mainstream, and Latino foods competed with Indian curries, Japanese sushi, and Thai takeout.

But the mix of cultures was not always benign. Nativists of the early twentieth century succeeded in sharply restricting immigration. During the 1990s restriction again became a goal of those citizens worried that if the United States became too diverse, it would lose its national identity. In 1990 Lawrence Auster published *The Path to National Suicide,* in which he complained of the "browning of America." In California, opponents of immigration supported Proposition 187, a ballot initiative that denied health, education, and welfare benefits to illegal aliens. Despite the opposition of most major religious, ethnic, and educational organizations, the measure passed with a lopsided 59 percent of the vote. In the end, the proposition did not go into effect because a federal judge ruled unconstitutional the provision denying education to children of illegal aliens.

Traditionally, nativist conflicts pit the dominant majority culture against the minority cultures of more recent arrivals. But in a multicultural society, such polar opposites often break down. In 1998 yet another ballot initiative passed in California (Proposition 227), mandating that schools phase out all their bilingual education programs. Students would be granted only one year of English-language immersion courses before receiving all instruction in English. Both white and Latino voters approved the proposition by nearly 62 percent. And the measure itself had been proposed after a group of Spanish-speaking parents boycotted their elementary school until it agreed to teach their children to read and write in English.

In 2006 immigration and especially the status of millions of illegal aliens became a hotly debated issue. On the one hand, immigrant groups proclaimed their loyalty to the United States and asked Congress to make it possible for them to become citizens. On the other hand, advocates of a more restrictive policy insisted that illegal immigration imposed a heavy burden on wages and government services. Since aliens earned less than natives, these workers were also more likely to need means-tested government benefits such as Medicaid and food stamps.

The question of how the United States will manage its borders remains unresolved. Even the idea of a "nation" takes on new meaning in a global economy in which jobs, people, and goods move wherever markets for them exist. As international migrations bring new people to America's shores, the American political system will continue to evolve ways of encompassing a diversity that now reflects the entire world.

 **REVIEW**

How did the Internet and multiculturalism reflect a new global order?

TERRORISM IN A GLOBAL AGE

Along the northeast coast of the United States September 11, 2001, dawned bright and clear. In the World Trade Center, Francis Ledesma was sitting in his office on the sixty-fourth floor of the South Tower when a friend suggested they go for coffee. In the cafeteria he heard and felt a muffled explosion: a boiler exploding, he thought. But then he saw bricks and glass falling by the window. When he started to head back to his office for a nine o'clock meeting, his friend insisted they leave immediately. Out on the street Francis saw the smoke and gaping hole where American Airlines Flight 11 had hit the North Tower. At that moment a huge fireball erupted as United Airlines Flight 175 hit their own South Tower. "We kept looking back," Francis recalled as they escaped the area, "and then all of a sudden our building, Tower 2, collapsed. I really thought that it was a mirage."

That was only the beginning of the horror. Shortly after takeoff from Dulles Airport American Airlines Flight 77 veered from its path and crashed into the Pentagon. Several passengers on United Airlines Flight 93 from Newark to San Francisco heard the news over their cell phones before hijackers seized that plane. Rather than allow another attack, passengers stormed the cockpit. Moments later the plane crashed into a wooded area of western Pennsylvania.

From a secure area at Barksdale Air Force Base in Louisiana, President George W. Bush addressed a shaken nation. He called the crashes a "national tragedy" and condemned those responsible. "Freedom itself was attacked this morning by a faceless coward, and freedom will be defended," he assured the American people.

Not since Pearl Harbor had the United States experienced such a devastating strike on its homeland. Most directly the tragedy claimed approximately 3,000 lives. More than 20,000 residents living in lower Manhattan had to evacuate their homes. The attack had broader economic consequences as well. Before September 11 the booming economy of the 1990s was already showing signs of strain, as overextended Internet companies retrenched

⌃ The cold war of the 1950s had imagined a Manhattan like this: debris everywhere, buildings in ruin, the city shrouded in smoke and fumes. On September 11, 2001, however, disaster on such a large scale came not from confrontation with another superpower but through the actions of international terrorists. The attack made clear that in a post–cold war world, global threats could come from small groups as well as powerful nations.

or went out of business. The World Trade Center attack pushed the nation into a recession. Added to those economic worries were new fears for security. The attacks were not the work of enemy nations but of an Arab terrorist group known as al Qaeda, led by a shadowy figure, Saudi national Osama bin Laden. After the World Trade Center attack, the United States focused less on the danger from other nations and more on terrorism, initiated by smaller groups, both subnational and international.

A Conservative Agenda at Home ≫ The crisis of September 11, 2001, energized George W. Bush. Before the attacks, his administration seemed to lack direction. Bush's claim to leadership was shaky partly because of the contested presidential election. Among his critics the president had a reputation as a person who took little interest in complex domestic issues and almost none in foreign policy. Yet his easy self-assurance contrasted sharply with Bill Clinton's more frenetic style.

Although the new president's inaugural address promised a moderate course, his administration moved sharply to the right. Traditionally, presidents, no matter whether liberal or conservative, govern from the center. Pollster Karl Rove persuaded Bush to rule as a conservative.

opinion

Is torture justified against potential enemies, when the United States is under threat from terrorists?

Vice President Richard Cheney pushed an agenda designed to accumulate power in the presidency. Secretary of State Donald Rumsfeld wanted to build a military prepared for local and regional conflicts in the post–cold war world. All of Bush's advisors favored massive tax cuts, fewer social programs, and less government regulation, especially of the environment. When Vice President Cheney brought energy industry leaders together in the summer of 2001 to discuss policy, he included no one from the environmental community.

The Bush administration pressed a conservative plan for school accountability through the use of standardized tests. Some liberals joined the president in January 2002 when he signed into law the "No Child Left Behind" initiative. Yet while the bill allowed for $18 billion in funding, the administration asked for only $12 billion, leaving much of the burden for new program on financially strapped state and local governments. Evangelical Christians were pleased with the president's proposal for "faith-based initiatives" that would provide public funds to churches involved in education and social work. Critics complained that such aid blurred the line separating church and state.

Tax cuts formed the cornerstone of the Bush agenda. Many conservatives wanted lower taxes in order to limit the government's ability to initiate new policies—a strategy referred to as "starving the beast." With a recession looming, Bush defended his proposals as a means to boost the economy and create jobs. Congress supported the proposed cuts, passing the first in 2001 and another the following year. Massive size did not alone make these tax bills controversial. In fact the cuts did little to create jobs and those in high income brackets received most of the benefits. Further, tax cuts turned the federal budget surpluses of the late 1990s into massive deficits.

Unilateralism in Foreign Affairs >> Even

before the events of September 11, the president rejected multilateralism—the policy of working together with international allies—that had guided American presidents, including his father, since World War II. Bush was determined that the United States would play a global role largely on its own terms. In particular conservatives bitterly distrusted the United Nations as rife with corruption and an impediment to forceful action.

The administration's unilateral approach became clear when it rejected the 1997 Kyoto Protocol on global warming to which 178 nations had subscribed. "We have no interest in implementing that treaty," announced Christie Whitman, head of the Environmental Protection Agency. She argued that compliance would add an unfair burden on American energy producers. Environmentalists around the globe protested the decision. With only 4 percent of the world's population, the United States produced about 25 percent of the Earth's greenhouse gas emissions.

The tragedy of September 11 reoriented American foreign policy priorities. At home the president was careful to distinguish between the majority of "peace-loving" Muslims and "evil-doers" such as Osama bin Laden. But he made it clear that the enemy was "a radical network of terrorists" and that governments around the world had a simple choice: "Either you are with us or you are with the terrorists."

In a war with so many shadowy opponents, it was not easy to agree on which radical groups most threatened American security. The network worked underground, spread across dozens of nations and in most cases was not a network at all. Even the states hospitable to al Qaeda proved hard to single out. Afghanistan was an obvious target. It was the seat of the Taliban, extreme Islamic fundamentalists, and the haven of bin Laden. Yet 15 of the 19 hijackers in the World Trade Center attacks hailed from Saudi Arabia, long an ally of the United States.

The Roots of Terror >> Before September 11

Americans had paid little attention to terrorist movements. Indeed, a only a few American radicals had resorted to terrorism. In 1995 Timothy McVeigh, a right-wing terrorist, detonated a bomb that killed 161 people in the federal building in Oklahoma City. Yet that event was shocking precisely because, in the United States, it was relatively rare.

Most terrorists resort to violence not because they are strong, but because they are weak. By attacking civilians and creating widespread fear they hope to undermine the legitimacy of governments and force their enemies to recognize their grievances. In both Northern Ireland and Israel, two centers of recent terrorist activities, the ruling governments possessed far more power than the insurgents.

While booming populations and high unemployment in the Middle East fostered terrorist movements, ironically it was the cold war—and, indirectly, the United States— that provided terrorists with training and weapons. During the early 1980s the Soviet Union was bogged down in its war in Afghanistan. The CIA, with help from Pakistan, Saudi Arabia, and the United Kingdom, encouraged Muslims from all over the world to join the Afghan rebels. One of the militants who journeyed to Afghanistan was Osama bin Laden, a devout Muslim and son of a Saudi business leader. During the 1980s bin Laden founded al Qaeda to forge a broad-based alliance of Arab rebels. When Iraq invaded Kuwait in 1990, bin Laden was dismayed that the Saudis allowed the United States to use its lands to invade Iraq. It was not the kind of holy war he had imagined. From his hidden camps in Afghanistan he began directing a terror network to strike back.

Bin Laden's organization differed from previous terrorist movements in that it had no national home—unlike the Irish Republican Army, which struggled to unify Ireland, or Palestinians, who wanted an independent state of their own. Al Qaeda's primary motivation was religious rather than nationalist.

The group's anti-American campaign began with a bombing at the World Trade Center in 1993. Further attacks occurred in places far from the United States. Twice the Clinton administration retaliated against al Qaeda with missile attacks; once it narrowly missed killing bin Laden himself in one of his Afghan camps.

The War on Terror: First Phase >> The military offensive against terrorism began in early October 2001. Despite American demands to deliver bin Laden "dead or alive," the Taliban rulers of Afghanistan refused. The United States then launched air attacks followed by an invasion, which quickly brought down the Taliban. The United States established a coalition government in Kabul to help in the slow and uncertain process of rebuilding Afghanistan. Although bin Laden managed to escape, this first stage of the war on terrorism went well. The president's approval ratings remained high and Afghans celebrated the end of Taliban rule, particularly women, whose rights had been severely restricted by the regime.

Domestically the war on terrorism faced a daunting task. The United States was an open society, where citizens expected to travel freely and valued their privacy. A month after the World Trade Center attacks the vulnerability of American society was further exposed by the deaths of five people from letters tainted with anthrax virus sent through the postal system. Evidence eventually pointed to a domestic rather than foreign source of the virus, but widespread fears led the administration to propose the USA Patriot Act. Congress passed it so quickly, some members did not even read the bill before voting for it. The act broadly expanded government powers to use electronic surveillance, monitor bank transactions (to fight money laundering), and investigate suspected terrorists.

Beyond locating and arresting terrorists, an effort was set in motion to secure vital systems of transportation, communication, and energy production. To coordinate new measures, Bush created the cabinet-level Department of Homeland Security,

The War in Iraq >> With the war in Afghanistan ended, the president's focus shifted from Osama bin Laden to Iraq's brutal dictator, Saddam Hussein. Indeed, neoconservatives in the Bush administration had long wished to overthrow Hussein, even before the September 11 attacks. Regime change in Iraq they argued would promote democracy in the Middle East and protect Israel. The only question, Deputy Defense Secretary Paul Wolfowitz acknowledged, "was whether [invading Iraq] should be in the immediate response or whether [the president] should concentrate simply on Afghanistan first."

Bush and his administration built the case for war against Iraq. "If we know Saddam Hussein has dangerous weapons today—and we do—," he proclaimed, "does it make any sense for the world to wait . . . for the final proof, the smoking gun that could come in the form of a mushroom cloud?" The president had already laid the groundwork for a policy of not waiting, by asserting that the United States would be "ready for preemptive action when necessary to defend our liberty and to defend our lives." In fact, much of the evidence for WMDs was based on what administration officials, including the president, knew was faulty intelligence.

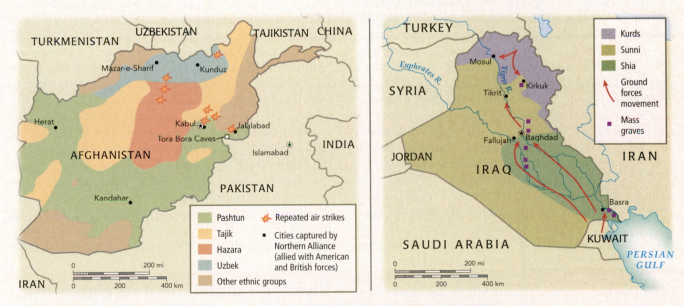

THE WAR ON TERROR: AFGHANISTAN AND IRAQ

In Afghanistan al Qaeda forces were concentrated in the mountainous region along the border with Pakistan. Ethnic and religious divisions influenced allegiances in both wars. In Iraq the most severe resistance to American occupation occurred from around Baghdad to Fallujah in the west and Tikrit to the north. In this "Sunni triangle," Sunni Muslims had prospered more under Saddam Hussein than had Shi'a Muslims to the south.

This **doctrine of preemption**—announcing that the United States might attack before it was itself attacked—

doctrine of preemption war undertaken in anticipation of imminent attack or invasion by another nation or in hopes of gaining a strategic advantage when war seems unavoidable.

was a major departure from the cold war policy of containment. "A preventive war, to my mind, is an impossibility," President Eisenhower declared in 1954. But Bush argued that, in an era in which terrorist enemies struck without warning, containment would no longer work. With midterm elections looming in October 2002 the president persuaded Congress to pass a joint resolution giving him full authority to take military action against Iraq if he deemed it necessary.

UN weapons inspectors, however, reported that they could find no evidence of WMDs or programs to build them. The Security Council refused to support an American resolution giving the United States the authority to lead a UN-sponsored invasion. Only the United Kingdom, Spain, and Italy, among the major powers, were willing to join the United States.

On March 19, 2003, without a UN mandate, a "coalition of the willing" (30 nations, though the actual troops were virtually all American and British) attacked Iraq. The invasion was accomplished with amazing speed and precision. Within days U.S. forces were halfway to Baghdad. On May 1 Bush announced an end to major combat operations. Coalition casualties (135 dead and 1,511 wounded) were remarkably low.

A Messy Aftermath >>
Although a large majority of Americans supported the invasion of Iraq, a vocal minority had opposed the war. Some believed that a doctrine of preemption was not only morally wrong, but also dangerous. If the United States felt free to invade a country, what was to stop other nations from launching their own wars, justified by similar doctrines of preemption? Opponents also pointed out that no solid evidence linked the secular Saddam Hussein with the religious al Qaeda.

The administration found it impossible to ignore the practical problems arising out of swift victory. Ethnic and

Shi'ite and Sunni two major branches of Islam. After the death of the Prophet Muhammad most believers accepted the tradition of having their leader chosen by community consensus (the Sunni branch), but a minority supported the claim of Ali, the Prophet's cousin. Over the years theological differences have separated Shi'ite and Sunni Muslims as well.

religious factions divided Iraq—**Shi'ite** Muslims in the southeast, **Sunni** Muslims around Baghdad, and Kurds in the north. Without Saddam's tyranny to hold the country together, the burden of peacekeeping fell to the American military. By the fall of 2004 more than 1,000 Americans and coalition allies had died preserving the peace—more than five times the 172 killed in winning the war. In addition, the United States had spent over half a billion dollars in a futile search for the weapons of mass destruction. Hussein had never possessed the technology to build them.

Even the creation of a provisional Iraqi government in June 2004 did not stop the violence from spreading. Meanwhile, the American cost of the war had risen to over $120 billion, at a time when the federal deficit at home was exceeding $550 billion.

The intangible costs of the war were also high. In the spring of 2004 Americans were stunned to learn that Iraqi prisoners of war being held in the Abu Ghraib prison near Baghdad had been abused and tortured by American soldiers guarding them. The Bush administration blamed a handful of "bad apples" in the military. In reality the administration had encouraged such abuses. The Justice Department's Office of Legal Counsel prepared a memo that argued that cruel, inhuman, or degrading acts might not be classified as torture.

The Second Term >>
For President Bush the war on terror became the center of his reelection campaign. Bush's Democratic opponent, Senator John Kerry of Massachusetts, criticized the administration for mishandling the war, but was tarred with "flip-flopping" on the issue. (He voted for one funding request, he noted, before he voted against it.) Although the outcome of the election came down once again to a single state—this time Ohio—Bush won both the popular and the electoral vote.

With Republican control of all three branches of government, the moment seemed opportune to promote long sought conservative goals. Bush began with a politically

privatize transferral of an economic enterprise or public utility from the control of the government into private ownership.

risky campaign to **privatize** Social Security. He argued that the federal retirement system faced insolvency if steps were not taken to fix it, before baby boomers began to retire. But he met stiff opposition, even from some in his own party, to his proposal to create individual retirement accounts. Critics worried that individuals risked losing their nest eggs if they chose unwisely, whereas the existing system guaranteed a return, even if it was less spectacular.

The president exerted the most significant impact on conservative values by appointing two justices to the Supreme Court, John Roberts and Samuel Alito. In 2007 the Court issued a number of decisions demonstrating that the Court indeed had moved to the right. By a 5–4 majority, it weakened campaign finance laws that set limits on how much individuals or parties could contribute, limited free speech on the part of students in schools, and protected religious groups offering social programs financed by public funds.

Disasters Domestic and Foreign >>
Bush's early second-term failures on Social Security and tax cuts proved to be no more than a headwind to his popularity—compared to the gale from Hurricane Katrina. That storm slammed into the Gulf Coast in September 2005, smashing New Orleans's levees and inundating the city. Most well-to-do citizens escaped before the storm, but no one

had made adequate provision to evacuate the elderly, disabled, and poor, most of whom were African American. For days desperate survivors hung to rooftops. Well over a thousand died, while tens of thousands huddled in the damaged Superdome sports arena.

The president at first seemed disengaged from the crisis. Nor was Administration prepared to act decisively. Headed by an incompetent political appointee, the Federal Emergency Management Agency (FEMA) suffered from staff and budget cuts. Much of the nation looked on in disbelief and anger as Gulf Coast residents waited helplessly for federal relief. Over three years later, much of the city lay in ruins and many residents had never returned. Katrina reminded Americans that there are some problems that only an effective government can address.

Halfway across the globe in Iraq sectarian violence between Shi'a and Sunni Muslims threatened to erupt into a full civil war. As critics charged that the administration lacked a coherent exit strategy, in 2007 Bush changed course, by ordering more troops to Iraq—a surge—rather than a withdrawal. The surge temporarily reduced violence, but political stability remained elusive, while the Taliban in Afghanistan posed a growing threat.

Suddenly the impregnable Republican stranglehold on Washington seemed to slip. Voters voiced their displeasure in the 2006 congressional elections, not only with the handling of the war and the administration's stumbles dealing with Katrina but also with a series of financial and sexual scandals that tarred Republicans. Democrats took control of both the House and Senate.

Collapse >> As President Bush's popularity plummeted, the Democrats sensed even greater possibilities in 2008. And then the economy went into freefall. Over the previous decade, banks, investment firms, and hedge funds had poured trillions of dollars into unregulated mortgage-backed securities. Lenders routinely granted mortgages to prospective homeowners who possessed virtually no assets and little capacity to make monthly payments. One fruit picker in California received a $750,000 mortgage, though he earned just $14,000 a year. Financial markets bundled such subprime mortgages with other forms of debt, creating financial instruments that were so complicated, few bankers recognized their underlying risks.

As the housing market contracted, many of these securities proved worse than worthless. On September 15, 2008, the huge Lehman Brothers investment bank suddenly filed for bankruptcy. The following day the Federal Reserve authorized $85 billion in loans to keep insurance giant American International Group (AIG) afloat. Nine days later the Office of Thrift Supervision closed Washington Mutual Bank, the nation's largest savings and loan association. Frightened banks refused to make loans even to financially sound corporations, leaving the nation facing its worst economic disaster since the Great Depression.

The Bush administration, which normally championed the free market, hastily extended massive government

 A plea from New Orleans residents threatened by Hurricane Katrina.

loans to save the banking system. The Troubled Asset Relief Program (TARP) allowed the Treasury Department to purchase or insure up to $700 billion of mortgages and securities ("toxic assets" with no evident value) in order to stabilize financial markets. Later the administration modified the program to invest money directly into troubled banks. Critics complained that while desperate homeowners faced foreclosure, the government bailed out those who had created the problem in the first place.

The 2008 election played out against this global financial crisis. For the Democrats, Hillary Clinton had entered the presidential race as the odds-on favorite, with high name recognition and long experience in government. However Barack Obama, a junior Senator from Illinois, had electrified the party with an arousing speech to the 2004 convention. He possessed the advantages of relative youth—he was 47 when he ran—as well as the hard-nosed skills of a former community organizer. Even more striking, Obama was an African American, born in Hawai'i to a white mother and Kenyan father. Obama overcame Clinton in a strongly contested primary season and then, with his running mate, Senator Joe Biden of Delaware, went on to defeat the Republican nominee, Senator John McCain of Arizona, and his vice presidential nominee Governor Sarah Palin of Alaska.

Forty-five years after Martin Luther King, Jr., shared his dreams of freedom on the Washington Mall, the United States had elected the first African American as its president.

✔ **REVIEW**

What issues made the Republicans vulnerable in the 2008 election?

OBAMA: HOPE VERSUS PRAGMATISM

A young president, an energetic wife with her own credentials as a lawyer, and the hopes of millions that he could restore the nation's fortunes—what could have been more promising? But Barack Obama had to set aside much of his campaign agenda to deal with the crises he faced in the short term. The financial system remained in free fall, millions faced job loss and eviction their homes, and major corporate icons such as General Motors and Chrysler stood on the brink of bankruptcy. Abroad, no timetable existed to bring American troops back from Iraq. Worse yet, pressure mounted to redeploy troops to nearby Afghanistan where Taliban insurgents threatened the governments in Kabul and neighboring Pakistan.

Obama moved quickly in February 2009 to propose measures designed to stimulate the collapsing economy: tax cuts, expanded unemployment benefits and social welfare provisions, as well as spending on education, health care, and infrastructure. The stimulus package carried a $787 billion price tag. Republicans dismissed it as ineffective federal spending that burdened the national debt; none would vote for it in the House and only three in the Senate. Liberals warned that more than a trillion in spending might be needed to fully prime the economy.

Similar partisanship complicated Obama's pledge to reform the nation's bloated health care system. Americans paid far more for medical care than any other nation, but were no healthier. Over 40 million people had no health insurance, and rising unemployment threatened millions more with loss of coverage. Many Republicans had supported the idea of reform—Republican presidential candidate Mitt Romney had actually established a comprehensive plan similar to Obama's when he was governor of Massachusetts—but Congressional Republicans staunchly opposed any deal. After a year of bitter negotiation, the Democrats passed a major bill in March 2010. "He had won ugly—without a single Republican—but won all the same," wrote columnist Jonathan Alter. Among the program's many initiatives, provisions extended Medicaid to some 16 million relatively poor people, guaranteed coverage for children, and prevented insurers from denying coverage because of "preexisting conditions."

With the president's support, Congress also passed what many observers considered "the toughest financial reform" since the aftermath of the Great Depression. Among other provisions, the law established a consumer protection agency to rein in abuses by credit card companies.

The milestones in health care and financial reform did not translate into popularity for either the president or the Democrats. On many other issues Obama followed a pragmatic middle course that left many unhappy. He did so partly because of personal style—one of low-key

⌃ Barack Obama on election night 2008 with his family

accommodation—and partly because of Republican obstruction. (Senate Republicans threatened to filibuster the Democratic majority 256 times from 2007–2010, compared with 130 times the Democrats threatened during the Republican-controlled Congress from 2003–2007.) On the one hand, the president ended the American combat role in Iraq by his previously announced deadline of August 2010. On the other, he poured an additional 30,000 troops into Afghanistan and Pakistan to fight Taliban insurgents, with little to show for the effort. He angered some conservatives by banning waterboarding, a practice authorized by the Bush administration. Civil libertarians, however, were angered because he kept "extraordinary rendition," the practice of sending terror suspects to other nations that practice torture, in place. Obama pushed the Pentagon and Congress to abandon "don't ask, don't tell" policy for gays in the military; yet he declined to take executive action on the matter. In a surprise, Congress voted in December 2010 to end the practice.

As the midterm elections of 2010 approached, poll numbers for Obama and the Democrats were down. Fed up with business as usual in Washington, and convinced that Obama was a dangerous socialist, disgruntled conservatives and independents formed a loosely coordinated alliance dubbed the Tea Party movement. Members, like the original demonstrators in Boston in 1773, protested high taxes. They wanted less government, not more, in their lives, although many also demanded a more active federal crackdown on illegal immigration and opposed any reduction in Social Security benefits.

Short, Medium, Long >>

Events force every individual—the president no less than anyone—to calibrate their actions in relation to short-term, medium, and long-term goals. Short-term crises such as the financial collapse of 2008 demanded immediate attention. With health care and financial reform, Obama could claim medium-term victories—to have put in place reforms that had been unsuccessfully attempted over the course of several decades.

Global warming, however, seemed to pose the greatest threat over the long term, for both the nation and the world. Conservatives and industry leaders were frequently skeptical of the scientific evidence suggesting that the earth's warming was man-made or even a threat, although George Bush acknowledged the dangers in his 2007 State of the Union address. Scientists predicted that the increase in global temperatures could raise sea levels as much as a meter by the end of the century. Such a rise would threaten many of the world's major cities, from Miami to Alexandria, Egypt, to Ho Chi Minh City in Vietnam. The future of close to a billion people living in low-lying coastal flood plains might depend

ENVIRONMENTAL STRESSES ON THE GULF OF MEXICO

The oil spill of 2010, caused by an explosion at the British Petroleum deepwater drilling rig, spread oil through the gulf, in both surface and underwater plumes. There are currently over 3,800 active oil rig platforms in the Gulf of Mexico. But the gulf had already been plagued by a hypoxic zone, where it is impossible for marine life to life. The zone, which has existed for decades, is created when fertilizers from farm fields are washed into the Mississippi River system and flushed into the gulf along with storm runoff and treated sewage. This problem has persisted for decades. Which problem receives the most attention, the short- or the long-term?

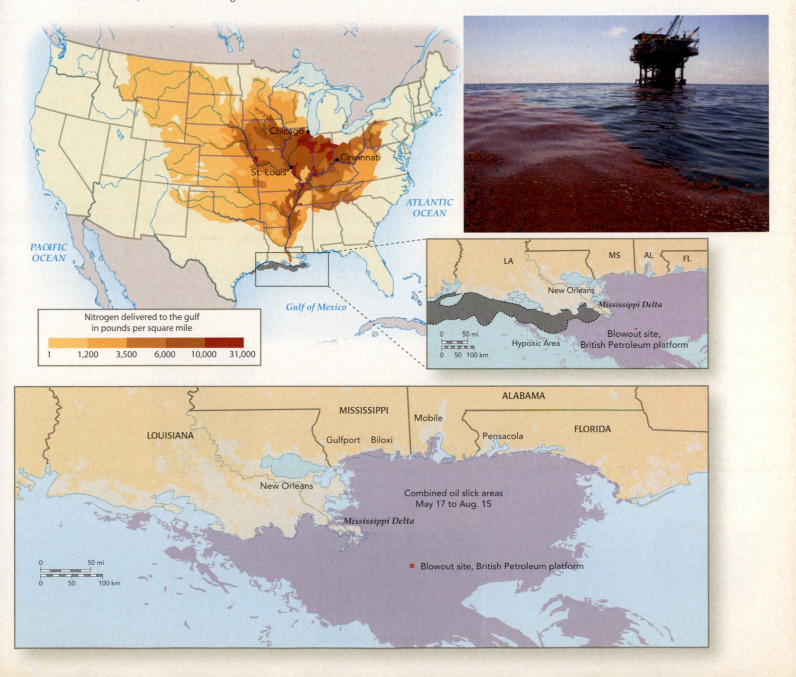

on decisions about greenhouse gases made in capitals as far-flung as Washington, Beijing, New Delhi, Mexico City, and Brussels. Barack Obama supported a proposal for **cap-and-trade legislation** to encourage factories to reduce the production of greenhouse gases. But a surprise visit in 2009 to a climate change conference in Copenhagen sparked little progress in forging any new international agreements with teeth. And at home, opposition from Republicans and Democrats hailing from energy-producing states placed cap-and-trade legislation on an indefinite hold.

cap-and-trade legislation would cap the amount of greenhouse gases factories could release into the atmosphere. Firms cutting emissions below those levels would receive credits, which they could trade for payments from lagging companies, rewarding firms that helped the environment.

Short-term environmental crises did receive attention, as when a deepwater oil-rig operated by British Petroleum (BP) exploded in April 2010 and began spewing oil into the Gulf of Mexico, in what became the biggest accidental marine oil spill in history. Many scientists saw the spill as an ecological disaster comparable to the Dust Bowl in the 1930s. It took almost four months before the company, working in conjunction with other oil companies, government agencies and scientists, finally capped the well. Even so, the plumes of spilled oil added the gulf's woes, since it was already plagued by a 'hypoxic zone' of lifeless water created by fertilizers and other human effluents washed down the Mississippi River.

REVIEW

List the major problems dealt with by the Bush and Obama administrations, and rank them as short-, medium- or long-term crises. How successfully can they be addressed?

Can the republic's political system manage longer-term crises that develop over decades? Half a century ago, as marine biologist Rachel Carson researched her book *Silent Spring,* she saw how a single species, humans, had "acquired significant power to alter the nature of [their] world." The instruments of that power included chemicals and radiation polluting air, earth, rivers, and seas. Since then the supply of clean, fresh water for human consumption and irrigation has shrunk. Overfishing and pollution have reduced much of the world's once-rich fisheries. Desertification and soil erosion threaten human populations with starvation. AIDS, malaria, and other epidemic diseases have raised worldwide public health concerns. As Nobel Prize-winning humanitarian and naturalist Albert Schweitzer once ruefully observed: "Man can hardly even recognize the devils of his own creation."

With the world's largest economy, the United States must play a central role in addressing these problems. Still, as John Kennedy warned almost 50 years ago, Americans alone cannot "right every wrong or reverse every adversity." The threats America faces are truly global in scope, and so must be the solutions. Echoing Kennedy, whom she much admired, Carson argued: "I think we're challenged as mankind has never been challenged before, to prove our maturity and our mastery, not of nature, but of ourselves."

CHAPTER SUMMARY

Over the past two decades the United States has become increasingly involved in economic, financial, and demographic relationships that increased both the nation's diversity and global interdependence.

- The Immigration Act of 1965 opened the United States to new waves of immigration hailing from South and Southeast Asia as well as more traditional flows from China, Japan, and the Philippines.
- Both legal and illegal immigrants from Mexico, Cuba, and Central America contributed to the growing Latino population, settling in urban and suburban barrios.

Significant Events

Immigration and Control Act

1986

Rodney King verdict; Los Angeles riots; Bill Clinton elected

Health care reform fails; Republicans win control of Congress

1992

Welfare reform adopted

1994

1996

Senate acquits Clinton of impeachment charges

1998

Supreme Court ends Florida recount; George W. Bush elected

2000

Terrorists destroy the World Trade Center; United States attacks Afghanistan's Taliban regime

2001

- During the Clinton and Bush presidencies Islamic radicalism and terrorism as well as regional conflicts in the Middle East, Eastern Europe, Africa, and the Caribbean replaced cold war rivalry as the central challenge of foreign policy.
- A divided and (after the elections of 1994) hostile Congress limited President Clinton's legislative program aimed at health care, education, and welfare reform. The campaign of Republicans to impeach President Clinton ended when the Senate failed to convict the president.
- The growth of the Internet, the World Wide Web, social networks, and e-commerce was part of a revolution in communications and information management made possible by advances in microchip and computer technology.
- President George W. Bush advanced a conservative agenda in domestic affairs, revolving around lower taxes, education reform, and faith-based initiatives in social policy. In foreign policy he pursued a unilateralist approach that led him to reject the Kyoto Protocol on global warming.
- The attacks of September 11 gave new stature to the president, as he declared war on Al Qaeda and global terrorism.
- The Bush administration launched a successful attack on Afghanistan's Taliban regime in 2001, before invading Iraq, in a preemptive war.
- Hurricane Katrina, the protracted wars in Afghanistan and Iraq, and the collapse of the housing and financial markets undermined public confidence in the Bush administration.
- Voter dissatisfaction allowed Democrats to gain control of the House and Senate in 2006 and send Barack Obama to the White House in 2008.
- A weak economy, ongoing wars in Iraq and Afghanistan, and political factionalism in Congress limited President Obama's ability to deliver on his promise to bring "change" to Washington.
- Over a unified Republican opposition, Obama legislated a stimulus package and reform of the nation's health care system and financial markets but failed to make headway on climate change.

Additional Reading

Accounts of the most recent past often reflect the partisan spirit of those engaged in ongoing controversies. Sidney Blumenthal, *The Clinton Wars* (2003), is an insider's unabashed defense of the Clintons. Richard Posner, a federal judge, takes on two judicial controversies—impeachment in *An Affair of State: The Investigation and Trial of President Clinton* (1999) and the Gore-Bush controversy in *Breaking the Deadlock* (2003). Joseph Stiglitz, *The Roaring Nineties: A New History of the World's Most Prosperous Decade* (2004), offers a liberal perspective on economic inequalities. On multiculturalism and the prospects for democracy, see Alan Wolf, *Does American Democracy Still Work?* (2006). Richard Alba and Victor Nee, *Remaking America: Assimilation and Contemporary Immigration* (2003), argues that today's immigrants are following the same path as those in the early twentieth century.

Jacob Hacker and Paul Pierson, *Off Center: The Republican Right and the Erosion of American Democracy* (rev. ed. 2006), capture Karl Rove's strategy to create a conservative majority. Lawrence Wright, *The Looming Tower: Al-Qaeda and the Road to 9/11* (2006), makes the case that Osama bin Laden purposely drew George Bush into a trap. Ron Suskind, *The One Percent Doctrine* (2006), uses CIA sources to follow the road to war in Iraq. Tom Englehart, *The American Way of War: How Bush's War Became Obama's* (2010), explains the difficulty of getting out of Afghanistan and Iraq. Michael Lewis, *The Big Short* (2010), retraces the financial meltdown. Spencer Weart, *The Discovery of Global Warming* (2008), is a fascinating look at the science of global warming.

NANCY PELOSI

Financial crisis; Bush adopts TARP measures; Barack Obama elected

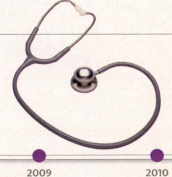

2003

2005

2006

2008

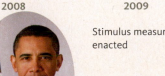

2009

2010

Department of Homeland Security created; United States and the "Coalition of the Willing" invade Iraq

Hurricane Katrina devastates the Gulf Coast

Democrats win control of Congress

Stimulus measures enacted

Health care and financial reform passed

Appendix

- **The Declaration of Independence**
- **The Constitution of the United States of America**

The Declaration of Independence

The Unanimous Declaration of the Thirteen United States of America

When, in the course of human events, it becomes necessary for one people to dissolve the political bands which have connected them with another, and to assume, among the powers of the earth, the separate and equal station to which the laws of nature and of nature's God entitle them, a decent respect to the opinions of mankind requires that they should declare the causes which impel them to the separation.

We hold these truths to be self-evident, that all men are created equal; that they are endowed by their Creator with certain unalienable rights; that among these, are life, liberty, and the pursuit of happiness. That, to secure these rights, governments are instituted among men, deriving their just powers from the consent of the governed; that, whenever any form of government becomes destructive of these ends, it is the right of the people to alter or to abolish it, and to institute a new government, laying its foundation on such principles, and organizing its powers in such form, as to them shall seem most likely to effect their safety and happiness. Prudence, indeed, will dictate that governments long established, should not be changed for light and transient causes; and, accordingly, all experience hath shown, that mankind are more disposed to suffer, while evils are sufferable, than to right themselves by abolishing the forms to which they are accustomed. But, when a long train of abuses and usurpations, pursuing invariably the same object, evinces a design to reduce them under absolute despotism, it is their right, it is their duty, to throw off such government and to provide new guards for their future security. Such has been the patient sufferance of these colonies, and such is now the necessity which constrains them to alter their former systems of government. The history of the present King of Great Britain is a history of repeated injuries and usurpations, all having, in direct object, the establishment of an absolute tyranny over these States. To prove this, let facts be submitted to a candid world:

He has refused his assent to laws the most wholesome and necessary for the public good.

He has forbidden his governors to pass laws of immediate and pressing importance, unless suspended in their operation till his assent should be obtained; and, when so suspended, he has utterly neglected to attend to them.

He has refused to pass other laws for the accommodation of large districts of people, unless those people would relinquish the right of representation in the legislature; a right inestimable to them, and formidable to tyrants only.

He has called together legislative bodies at places unusual, uncomfortable, and distant from the depository of their public records, for the sole purpose of fatiguing them into compliance with his measures.

He has dissolved representative houses repeatedly for opposing, with manly firmness, his invasions on the rights of the people.

He has refused, for a long time after such dissolutions, to cause others to be elected; whereby the legislative powers, incapable of annihilation, have returned to the people at large for their exercise; the state remaining, in the meantime, exposed to all the danger of invasion from without, and convulsions within.

He has endeavored to prevent the population of these States; for that purpose, obstructing the laws for naturalization of foreigners, refusing to pass others to encourage their migration hither, and raising the conditions of new appropriations of lands.

He had obstructed the administration of justice, by refusing his assent to laws for establishing judiciary powers. He has made judges dependent on his will alone, for the tenure of their offices, and the amount and payment of their salaries.

He has erected a multitude of new offices, and sent hither swarms of officers to harass our people, and eat out their substance.

He has kept among us, in time of peace, standing armies, without the consent of our legislatures.

He has affected to render the military independent of, and superior to, the civil power.

He has combined, with others, to subject us to a jurisdiction foreign to our Constitution, and unacknowledged by our laws; giving his assent to their acts of pretended legislation:

For quartering large bodies of armed troops among us:

For protecting them by a mock trial, from punishment, for any murders which they should commit on the inhabitants of these States:

For cutting off our trade with all parts of the world:

For imposing taxes on us without our consent:

For depriving us, in many cases, of the benefit of trial by jury:

For transporting us beyond seas to be tried for pretended offences:

For abolishing the free system of English laws in a neighboring province, establishing therein an arbitrary government, and enlarging its boundaries, so as to render it at once an example and fit instrument for introducing the same absolute rule into these colonies:

For taking away our charters, abolishing our most valuable laws, and altering, fundamentally, the powers of our governments:

For suspending our own legislatures, and declaring themselves invested with power to legislate for us in all cases whatsoever.

He has abdicated government here, by declaring us out of his protection, and waging war against us.

He has plundered our seas, ravaged our coasts, burnt our towns, and destroyed the lives of our people.

He is, at this time, transporting large armies of foreign mercenaries to complete the works of death, desolation, and tyranny, already begun, with circumstances of cruelty and perfidy scarcely paralleled in the most barbarous ages, and totally unworthy the head of a civilized nation.

He has constrained our fellow citizens, taken captive on the high seas, to bear arms against their country, to become the executioners of their friends, and brethren, or to fall themselves by their hands.

He has excited domestic insurrections amongst us, and has endeavored to bring on the inhabitants of our frontiers, the merciless Indian savages, whose known rule of warfare is an undistinguished destruction of all ages, sexes, and conditions.

In every stage of these oppressions, we have petitioned for redress, in the most humble terms; our repeated petitions have been answered only by repeated injury. A prince, whose character is thus marked by every act which may define a tyrant, is unfit to be the ruler of a free people.

Nor have we been wanting in attention to our British brethren. We have warned them, from time to time, of attempts made by their legislature to extend an unwarrantable jurisdiction over us. We have reminded them of the circumstances of our emigration and settlement here. We have appealed to their native justice and magnanimity, and we have conjured them, by the ties of our common kindred, to disavow these usurpations, which would inevitably interrupt our connections and correspondence. They, too, have been deaf to the voice of justice and consanguinity. We must, therefore, acquiesce in the necessity which denounces our separation, and hold them as we hold the rest of mankind, enemies in war, in peace, friends.

We, therefore, the representatives of the United States of America, in general Congress assembled, appealing to the Supreme Judge of the world for the rectitude of our intentions, do, in the name, and by the authority of the good people of these colonies, solemnly publish and declare, that these united colonies are, and of right ought to be, free and independent states: that they are absolved from all allegiance to the British Crown, and that all political connection between them and the state of Great Britain is, and ought to be, totally dissolved; and that, as free and independent states, they have full power to levy war, conclude peace, contract alliances, establish commerce, and to do all other acts and things which independent states may of right do. And, for the support of this declaration, with a firm reliance on the protection of Divine Providence, we mutually pledge to each other our lives, our fortunes, and our sacred honor.

The foregoing Declaration was, by order of Congress, engrossed, and signed by the following members:

New Hampshire
New York
Delaware
North Carolina
Josiah Bartlett
William Floyd
Caesar Rodney
William Hooper
William Whipple
Philip Livingston
George Read
Joseph Hewes
Matthew Thornton
Francis Lewis
Thomas M'Kean
John Penn
Lewis Morris

Massachusetts Bay
New Jersey
Maryland
South Carolina
Samuel Adams
Richard Stockton
Samuel Chase
Edward Rutledge
John Adams
John Witherspoon
William Paca
Thomas Heyward, Jr.
Robert Treat Paine
Francis Hopkinson
Thomas Stone
Thomas Lynch, Jr.
Elbridge Gerry
John Hart
Charles Carroll,
of Carrollton
Arthur Middleton
Abraham Clark

Rhode Island
Pennsylvania
Virginia
Georgia
Stephen Hopkins
Robert Morris
George Wythe
Button Gwinnett
William Ellery
Benjamin Rush
Richard Henry Lee
Lyman Hall
Benjamin Franklin
Thomas Jefferson
George Walton

Connecticut
John Morton
Benjamin Harrison
Roger Sherman
George Clymer
Thomas Nelson, Jr.
Samuel Huntington
James Smith
Francis Lightfoot Lee
William Williams
George Taylor
Carter Braxton
Oliver Wolcott
James Wilson
George Ross

Resolved, That copies of the Declaration be sent to the several assemblies, conventions, and committees, or counsils of safety, and to the several commanding officers of the continental troops; that it be proclaimed in each of the United States, at the head of the army.

The Constitution of the United States of America[1]

We the People of the United States, in Order to form a more perfect Union, establish Justice, insure domestic Tranquility, provide for the common defence, promote the general Welfare, and secure the Blessings of Liberty to ourselves and our Posterity, do ordain and establish this CONSTITUTION for the United States of America.

ARTICLE I

SECTION 1. All legislative Powers herein granted shall be vested in a Congress of the United States, which shall consist of a Senate and House of Representatives.

SECTION 2. The House of Representatives shall be composed of Members chosen every second Year by the People of the several States, and the Electors in each State shall have the Qualifications requisite for Electors of the most numerous Branch of the State Legislature. No Person shall be a Representative who shall not have attained to the Age of twenty-five Years, and been seven Years a Citizen of the United States, and who shall not, when elected, be an Inhabitant of that State in which he shall be chosen.

[Representatives and direct Taxes[2] shall be apportioned among the several States which may be included within this Union, according to their respective Numbers, which shall be determined by adding to the whole Number of free Persons, including those bound to Service for a Term of Years, and excluding Indians not taxed, three fifths of all other Persons.][3] The actual Enumeration shall be made within three Years after the first Meeting of the Congress of the United States, and within every subsequent Term of ten Years, in such Manner as they shall by Law direct. The Number of Representatives shall not exceed one for every thirty Thousand, but each State shall have at Least one Representative; and until such enumeration shall be made, the State of New Hampshire shall be entitled to chuse three, Massachusetts eight, Rhode- Island and Providence Plantations one, Connecticut five, New York six, New Jersey four, Pennsylvania eight, Delaware one, Maryland six, Virginia ten, North Carolina five, South Carolina five, and Georgia three. When vacancies happen in the Representation from any State, the Executive Authority thereof shall issue Writs of Election to fill such Vacancies. The House of Representatives shall chuse their Speaker and other Officers; and shall have the sole Power of Impeachment.

SECTION 3. The Senate of the United States shall be composed of two Senators from each State, chosen by the Legislature thereof, for six Years; and each Senator shall have one Vote.

Immediately after they shall be assembled in Consequence of the first Election, they shall be divided as equally as may be into three Classes. The Seats of the Senators of the first Class shall be vacated at the Expiration of the second Year, of the second Class at the Expiration of the fourth Year, and of the third Class at the Expiration of the sixth Year, so that one-third may be chosen every second Year; and if Vacancies happen by Resignation, or otherwise, during the Recess of the Legislature of any State, the Executive thereof may make temporary Appointments until the next Meeting of the Legislature, which shall then fill such Vacancies. No Person shall be a Senator who shall not have attained to the Age of thirty Years, and been nine Years a Citizen of the United States, and who shall not, when elected, be an Inhabitant of that State for which he shall be chosen.

The Vice President of the United States shall be President of the Senate, but shall have no vote, unless they be equally divided.

The Senate shall chuse their other Officers, and also a President pro tempore, in the absence of the Vice President, or when he shall exercise the Office of President of the United States.

The Senate shall have the sole Power to try all Impeachments. When sitting for that purpose they shall be on Oath or Affirmation. When the President of the United States is tried, the Chief Justice shall preside: And no person shall be convicted without the Concurrence of two thirds of the Members present.

Judgment in Cases of Impeachment shall not extend further than to removal from Office, and disqualification to hold and enjoy any Office of honor, Trust, or Profit under the United States: but the Party convicted shall nevertheless be liable and subject to Indictment, Trial, Judgment, and Punishment, according to Law.

1 This version follows the original Constitution in capitalization and spelling. It is adapted from the text published by the United States Department of the Interior, Office of Education.

2 Altered by the Sixteenth Amendment.

3 Negated by the Fourteenth Amendment.

SECTION 4. The Times, Places and Manner of holding Elections for Senators and Representatives, shall be prescribed in each State by the Legislature thereof; but the Congress may at any time by Law make or alter such Regulations, except as to the Places of Chusing Senators. The Congress shall assemble at least once in every Year, and such Meeting shall be on the first Monday in December, unless they shall by Law appoint a different Day.

SECTION 5. Each House shall be the Judge of the Elections, Returns and Qualifications of its own Members, and a Majority of each shall constitute a Quorum to do Business; but a smaller number may adjourn from day to day, and may be authorized to compel the Attendance of absent Members, in such Manner, and under such Penalties, as each House may provide.

Each House may determine the Rules of its Proceedings, punish its Members for disorderly Behaviour, and, with the Concurrence of two thirds, expel a Member. Each House shall keep a Journal of its Proceedings, and from time to time publish the same, excepting such Parts as may in their Judgment require Secrecy; and the Yeas and Nays of the Members of either House on any question shall, at the Desire of one fifth of those Present, be entered on the Journal.

Neither House, during the Session of Congress, shall, without the Consent of the other, adjourn for more than three days, nor to any other Place than that in which the two Houses shall be sitting.

SECTION 6. The Senators and Representatives shall receive a Compensation for their Services, to be ascertained by Law, and paid out of the Treasury of the United States. They shall in all Cases, except Treason, Felony, and Breach of the Peace, be privileged from Arrest during their Attendance at the Session of their respective Houses, and in going to and returning from the same; and for any Speech or Debate in either House, they shall not be questioned in any other Place.

No Senator or Representative shall, during the Time for which he was elected, be appointed to any civil Office under the Authority of the United States, which shall have been created, or the Emoluments whereof shall have been increased, during such time; and no Person holding any Office under the United States shall be a Member of either House during his continuance in Office.

SECTION 7. All Bills for raising Revenue shall originate in the House of Representatives; but the Senate may propose or concur with Amendments as on other bills. Every Bill which shall have passed the House of Representatives and the Senate, shall, before it become a Law, be presented to the President of the United States; If he approve he shall sign it, but if not he shall return it, with his Objections, to that House in which it shall have originated, who shall enter the Objections at large on their Journal, and proceed to reconsider it. If after such Reconsideration two thirds of that House shall agree to pass the bill, it shall be sent, together with the objections, to the other House, by which it shall likewise be reconsidered, and if approved by two thirds of that House, it shall become a Law. But in all such Cases the Votes of both Houses shall be determined by Yeas and Nays, and the Names of the Persons voting for and against the Bill shall be entered on the Journal of each House respectively. If any Bill shall not be returned by the President within ten Days (Sundays excepted) after it shall have been presented to him, the Same shall be a Law, in like Manner as if he had signed it, unless the Congress by their Adjournment prevent its Return, in which Case it shall not be a Law. Every Order, Resolution, or Vote to which the Concurrence of the Senate and House of Representatives may be necessary (except on a question of Adjournment) shall be presented to the President of the United States; and before the Same shall take Effect, shall be approved by him, or being disapproved by him, shall be repassed by two thirds of the Senate and House of Representatives, according to the Rules and Limitations prescribed in the Case of a Bill.

SECTION 8. The Congress shall have Power To lay and collect Taxes, Duties, Imposts and Excises, to pay the Debts and provide for the common Defence and general Welfare of the United States; but all Duties, Imposts and Excises shall be uniform throughout the United States;

To borrow money on the credit of the United States;

To regulate Commerce with foreign Nations, and among the several States, and with the Indian Tribes;

To establish an uniform rule of Naturalization, and uniform Laws on the subject of Bankruptcies throughout the United States; To coin Money, regulate the Value thereof, and of foreign Coin, and fix the Standard of Weights and Measures;

To provide for the Punishment of counterfeiting the Securities and current Coin of the United States;

To establish Post Offices and post Roads; To promote the Progress of Science and useful Arts, by securing for limited Times to Authors and Inventors the exclusive Right to their respective Writings and Discoveries;

To constitute Tribunals inferior to the Supreme Court;

To define and punish Piracies and Felonies committed on the high Seas, and Offenses against the Law of Nations;

To declare War, grant Letters of Marque and Reprisal, and make Rules concerning Captures on Land and Water;

To raise and support Armies, but no Appropriation of Money to that Use shall be for a longer Term than two Years;

To provide and maintain a Navy;

To make Rules for the Government and Regulation of the land and naval forces;

To provide for calling forth the Militia to execute the Laws of the Union, suppress Insurrections and repel Invasions;

To provide for organizing, arming, and disciplining the Militia, and for government such Part of them as may be employed in the Service of the United States, reserving to the States respectively, the Appointment of the Officers, and the Authority of training the Militia according to the discipline prescribed by Congress;

To exercise exclusive Legislation in all Cases whatsoever, over such District (not exceeding ten Miles square) as may, by Cession of particular States, and the acceptance of Congress, become the Seat of the Government of the United States, and to exercise like Authority over all Places purchased by the Consent of the Legislature of the State in which the Same shall be, for the Erection of Forts, Magazines, Arsenals, Dock-yards, and other needful Buildings;—And

To make all Laws which shall be necessary and proper for carrying into Execution the foregoing Powers, and all other Powers vested by this Constitution in the Government of the United States, or in any Department or Officer thereof.

SECTION 9. The Migration or Importation of such Persons as any of the States now existing shall think proper to admit, shall not be prohibited by the Congress prior to the Year one thousand eight hundred and eight, but a tax or duty may be imposed on such Importation, not exceeding ten dollars for each Person.

The privilege of the Writ of Habeas Corpus shall not be suspended, unless when in Cases of Rebellion or Invasion the public Safety may require it.

No bill of Attainder or ex post facto Law shall be passed.

No capitation, or other direct, Tax shall be laid unless in Proportion to the Census or Enumeration herein before directed to be taken.

No Tax or Duty shall be laid on Articles exported from any State.

No Preference shall be given by any Regulation of Commerce or Revenue to the Ports of one State over those of another: nor shall Vessels bound to, or from, one State, be obliged to enter, clear, or pay Duties in another.

No Money shall be drawn from the Treasury, but in Consequence of Appropriations made by Law; and a regular Statement and Account of the Receipts and Expenditures of all public Money shall be published from time to time.

No Title of Nobility shall be granted by the United States: And no Person holding any Office of Profit or Trust under them, shall, without the Consent of the Congress, accept of any present, Emolument, Office, or Title, of any kind whatever, from any King, Prince, or foreign State.

SECTION 10. No State shall enter into any Treaty, Alliance, or Confederation; grant Letters of Marque and Reprisal; coin Money; emit Bills of Credit; make any Thing but gold and silver Coin a Tender in Payment of Debts; pass any Bill of Attainder, ex post facto Law, or Law impairing the Obligation of Contracts, or grant any Title of Nobility.

No State shall, without the Consent of the Congress, lay any Imposts or Duties on Imports or Exports, except what may be absolutely necessary for executing its inspection Laws; and the net Produce of all Duties and Imposts, laid by any State on Imports or Exports, shall be for the use of the Treasury of the United States; and all such Laws shall be subject to the Revision and Control of the Congress.

No state shall, without the Consent of Congress, lay any duty of Tonnage, keep Troops, or Ships of War in time of Peace, enter into any Agreement or Compact with another State, or with a foreign Power, or engage in War, unless actually invaded, or in such imminent Danger as will not admit of delay.

ARTICLE II

SECTION 1. The executive Power shall be vested in a President of the United States of America. He shall hold his Office during the Term of four years, and, together with the Vice President, chosen for the same Term, be elected, as follows:

Each State shall appoint, in such Manner as the Legislature thereof may direct, a Number of Electors, equal to the whole Number of Senators and Representatives to which the State may be entitled in the Congress: but no Senator or Representative, or Person holding an Office of Trust or Profit under the United States, shall be appointed an Elector.

[The Electors shall meet in their respective States, and vote by Ballot for two persons, of whom one at least shall not be an Inhabitant of the same State with themselves. And they shall make a List of all the Persons voted for, and of the Number of Votes for each; which List they shall sign and certify, and transmit sealed to the Seat of the Government of the United States, directed to the President of the Senate. The President of the Senate shall, in the Presence of the Senate and House of Representatives, open all the Certificates, and the Votes shall then be counted. The Person having the greatest Number of Votes shall be the President, if such Number be a Majority of the whole Number of Electors appointed; and if there be more than one who have such Majority, and have an equal Number of Votes, then the House of Representatives shall immediately chuse by Ballot one of them for President; and if no Person have a Majority, then from the five highest on the List the said House shall in like Manner chuse the President. But in chusing the President, the Votes shall be taken by States, the Representation from each State having one Vote; a quorum for this Purpose shall consist of a Member or Members from two-thirds of the States, and a Majority of all the States shall be necessary to a Choice. In every Case, after the Choice of the President, the Person having the greatest Number of Votes of the Electors shall be the Vice President. But if there should remain two or more who have equal votes, the Senate shall chuse from them by Ballot the Vice President.]⁴

The Congress may determine the Time of chusing the Electors, and the Day on which they shall give their Votes; which Day shall be the same throughout the United States.

No person except a natural-born Citizen, or a Citizen of the United States, at the time of the Adoption of this Constitution, shall be eligible to the Office of President; neither shall any Person be eligible to that Office who shall not have attained to the Age of thirty-five years, and been fourteen Years a Resident within the United States.

In Case of the Removal of the President from Office, or of his Death, Resignation, or Inability to discharge the Powers and Duties of the said Office, the same shall devolve on the Vice President, and the Congress may by Law provide for the Case of Removal, Death, Resignation, or Inability, both of the President and Vice President, declaring what Officer shall then act as President, and such Officer shall act accordingly, until the disability be removed, or a President shall be elected.

The President shall, at stated Times, receive for his Services a Compensation, which shall neither be increased nor diminished during the Period for which he shall have been elected, and he shall not receive within that Period any other Emolument from the United States, or any of them.

Before he enter on the execution of his Office, he shall take the following Oath or Affirmation:—"I do solemnly swear (or affirm) that I will faithfully execute the Office of President of the United States, and will, to the best of my Ability, preserve, protect, and defend the Constitution of the United States."

SECTION 2. The President shall be Commander in Chief of the Army and Navy of the United States, and of the Militia of the several States, when called into the actual Service of the United States; he may require the Opinion, in writing, of the principal Officer in each of the executive Departments, upon any subject relating to the Duties of their respective Offices, and he shall have Power to Grant Reprieves and Pardons for Offenses against the United States, except in Cases of Impeachment.

He shall have Power, by and with the Advice and Consent of the Senate, to make Treaties, provided two-thirds of the Senators present concur; and he shall nominate, and by and with the Advice and Consent of the Senate, shall appoint Ambassadors, other public Ministers and Consuls, Judges of the supreme Court, and all other Officers of the United States, whose Appointments are not herein otherwise provided for, and which shall be established by Law: but the Congress may by Law vest the Appointment of

such inferior Officers, as they think proper, in the President alone, in the Courts of Law, or in the Heads of Departments.

The President shall have Power to fill up all Vacancies that may happen during the Recess of the Senate, by granting Commissions which shall expire at the End of their next Session.

SECTION 3. He shall from time to time give to the Congress Information of the State of the Union, and recommend to their Consideration such Measures as he shall judge necessary and expedient; he may, on extraordinary occasions, convene both Houses, or either of them, and in Case of Disagreement between them, with respect to the Time of Adjournment, he may adjourn them to such Time as he shall think proper; he shall receive Ambassadors and other public Ministers; he shall take care that the Laws be faithfully executed, and shall Commission all the Officers of the United States.

SECTION 4. The President, Vice President and all civil Officers of the United States, shall be removed from Office on Impeachment for, and Conviction of, Treason, Bribery, or other high Crimes and Misdemeanors.

ARTICLE III

SECTION 1. The judicial Power of the United States, shall be vested in one supreme Court, and in such inferior Courts as the Congress may from time to time ordain and establish. The Judges, both of the supreme and inferior Courts, shall hold their Offices during good Behaviour, and shall, at stated Times, receive for their Services, a Compensation, which shall not be diminished during their Continuance in Office.

SECTION 2. The judicial Power shall extend to all Cases, in Law and Equity, arising under this Constitution, the Laws of the United States, and Treaties made, or which shall be made, under their Authority;—to all Cases affecting ambassadors, other public ministers and consuls;—to all cases of admiralty and maritime Jurisdiction;— to Controversies to which the United States shall be a Party;—to Controversies between two or more States;—between a State and Citizens of another State;⁵ —between Citizens of different States—between Citizens of the same State claiming Lands under Grants of different States, and between a State, or the Citizens thereof, and foreign States, Citizens, or Subjects. In all Cases affecting Ambassadors, other public Ministers and Consuls, and those in which a State shall be Party, the supreme Court shall have original Jurisdiction. In all the other Cases before mentioned, the

---

4 Revised by the Twelfth Amendment.

5 Qualified by the Eleventh Amendment.

supreme Court shall have appellate Jurisdiction, both as to Law and Fact, with such Exceptions, and under such Regulations as the Congress shall make.

The trial of all Crimes, except in Cases of Impeachment, shall be by Jury; and such Trial shall be held in the State where the said Crimes shall have been committed; but when not committed within any State, the Trial shall be at such Place or Places as the Congress may by Law have directed.

SECTION 3. Treason against the United States, shall consist only in levying War against them, or in adhering to their Enemies, giving them Aid and Comfort. No Person shall be convicted of Treason unless on the Testimony of two Witnesses to the same overt Act, or on Confession in open Court.

The Congress shall have power to declare the Punishment of Treason, but no Attainder of Treason shall work Corruption of Blood, or Forfeiture except during the Life of the Person attainted.

ARTICLE IV

SECTION 1. Full Faith and Credit shall be given in each State to the public Acts, Records, and judicial Proceedings of every other State. And the Congress may by general Laws prescribe the Manner in which such Acts, Records and Proceedings shall be proved, and the Effect thereof.

SECTION 2. The Citizens of each State shall be entitled to all Privileges and Immunities of Citizens in the several States.

A Person charged in any State with Treason, Felony, or other Crime, who shall flee from Justice, and be found in another State, shall on demand of the executive Authority of the State from which he fled, be delivered up, to be removed to the State having Jurisdiction of the crime. No Person held to Service or Labour in one State, under the Laws thereof, escaping into another, shall, in Consequence of any Law or Regulation therein, be discharged from such Service or Labour, but shall be delivered up on Claim of the Party to whom such Service or Labour may be due.

SECTION 3. New States may be admitted by the Congress into this Union; but no new State shall be formed or erected within the Jurisdiction of any other State; nor any State be formed by the Junction of two or more States, or parts of States, without the Consent of the Legislatures of the States concerned as well as of the Congress. The Congress shall have Power to dispose of and make all needful Rules and Regulations respecting the Territory or other Property belonging to the United States; and nothing in this Constitution shall be so construed as to Prejudice any Claims of the United States, or of any particular State.

SECTION 4. The United States shall guarantee to every State in this Union a Republican Form of Government, and shall protect each of them against Invasion; and on Application of the Legislature, or of the Executive (when the Legislature cannot be convened) against domestic Violence.

ARTICLE V

The Congress, whenever two-thirds of both Houses shall deem it necessary, shall propose Amendments to this Constitution, or, on the Application of the Legislatures of two-thirds of the several States, shall call a Convention for proposing Amendments, which, in either Case, shall be valid to all Intents and Purposes, as part of this Constitution, when ratified by the Legislatures of three-fourths of the several States, or by Conventions in three-fourths thereof, as the one or the other Mode of Ratification may be proposed by the Congress; Provided that no Amendment which may be made prior to the Year One thousand eight hundred and eight shall in any Manner affect the first and fourth Clauses in the Ninth Section of the first Article; and that no State, without its Consent, shall be deprived of its equal Suffrage in the Senate.

ARTICLE VI

All Debts contracted and Engagements entered into, before the Adoption of this Constitution, shall be as valid against the United States under this Constitution, as under the Confederation.

This Constitution, and the Laws of the United States which shall be made in Pursuance thereof; and all Treaties made, or which shall be made, under the Authority of the United States, shall be the supreme Law of the Land; and the Judges in every State shall be bound thereby, any Thing in the Constitution or Laws of any State to the Contrary notwithstanding.

The Senators and Representatives before mentioned, and the Members of the several State Legislatures, and all executive and judicial Officers, both of the United States and of the several States, shall be bound by Oath or Affirmation to support this Constitution; but no religious Tests shall ever be required as a qualification to any Office or public Trust under the United States.

ARTICLE VII

The Ratification of the Conventions of nine States shall be sufficient for the Establishment of this Constitution between the States so ratifying the same.

Done in Convention by the Unanimous Consent of the States present the Seventeenth Day of September in the Year of our Lord one thousand seven hundred and Eighty seven, and of the Independence of the United States of America the Twelfth. In Witness whereof We have hereunto subscribed our Names.[6]

GEORGE WASHINGTON
PRESIDENT AND DEPUTY FROM VIRGINIA

New Hampshire	**Massachusetts**	**Connecticut**	**Georgia**
New Jersey	**Pennsylvania**	George Clymer	James Wilson
Delaware	**Maryland**	Pierce Butler	James Madison, Jr.
North Carolina	**South Carolina**	William Samuel Johnson	William Few
John Langdon	Nathaniel Gorham	Thomas FitzSimons	
William Livingston	Benjamin Franklin		**New York**
George Read	James McHenry	**Virginia**	Gouverneur Morris
William Blount	John Rutledge	Roger Sherman	Abraham Baldwin
Nicholas Gilman	Rufus King	Jared Ingersoll	Alexander Hamilton
David Brearley	Thomas Mifflin	John Blair	
Gunning Bedford, Jr.	Daniel of St. Thomas Jenifer		
Richard Dobbs Spaight	Charles Cotesworth Pinckney		
William Paterson	Robert Morris		
John Dickinson	Daniel Carroll		
Hugh Williamson	Charles Pinckney		
Jonathan Dayton			
Richard Bassett			
Jacob Broom			

Articles in Addition to, and Amendment of, the Constitution of the United States of America, Proposed by Congress, and Ratified by the Legislatures of the Several States, Pursuant to the Fifth Article of the Original Constitution[7]

[AMENDMENT I]

Congress shall make no law respecting an establishment of religion, or prohibiting the free exercise thereof; or abridging the freedom of speech, or of the press; or the right of the people peaceably to assemble, and to petition the Government for a redress of grievances.

[AMENDMENT II]

A well regulated Militia, being necessary to the security of a free State, the right of the people to keep and bear Arms shall not be infringed.

[AMENDMENT III]

No Soldier shall, in time of peace, be quartered in any house, without the consent of the Owner, nor in time of war, but in a manner to be prescribed by law.

6 These are the full names of the signers, which in some cases are not the signatures on the document.

7 This heading appears only in the joint resolution submitting the first ten amendments, known as the Bill of Rights.

[AMENDMENT IV]

The right of the people to be secure in their persons, houses, papers, and effects, against unreasonable searches and seizures, shall not be violated, and no Warrants shall issue, but upon probable cause, supported by Oath or affirmation, and particularly describing the place to be searched, and the persons or things to be seized.

[AMENDMENT V]

No person shall be held to answer for a capital or otherwise infamous crime, unless on a presentment or indictment of a Grand Jury, except in cases arising in the land or naval forces, or in the Militia, when in actual service in time of War or public danger; nor shall any person be subject for the same offence to be twice put in jeopardy of life or limb; nor shall be compelled in any criminal case to be a witness against himself, nor be deprived of life, liberty, or property, without due process of law; nor shall private property be taken for public use, without just compensation.

[AMENDMENT VI]

In all criminal prosecutions, the accused shall enjoy the right to a speedy and public trial, by an impartial jury of the State and district wherein the crime shall have been committed, which district shall have been previously ascertained by law, and to be informed of the nature and cause of the accusation; to be confronted with the witnesses against him; to have compulsory process for obtaining witnesses in his favour, and to have the Assistance of Counsel for his defence.

[AMENDMENT VII]

In suits at common law, where the value in controversy shall exceed twenty dollars, the right of trial by jury shall be preserved, and no fact tried by a jury, shall be otherwise reexamined in any Court of the United States, than according to the rules of the common law.

[AMENDMENT VIII]

Excessive bail shall not be required, nor excessive fines imposed, nor cruel and unusual punishments inflicted.

[AMENDMENT IX]

The enumeration of the Constitution, of certain rights, shall not be construed to deny or disparage others retained by the people.

[AMENDMENT X]

The powers not delegated to the United States by the Constitution, nor prohibited by it to the States, are reserved to the States respectively, or to the people. [Amendments I–X, in force 1791.]

[AMENDMENT XI] [8]

The Judicial power of the United States shall not be construed to extend to any suit in law or equity, commenced or prosecuted against one of the United States by Citizens of another State, or by Citizens or Subjects of any Foreign State.

[AMENDMENT XII] [9]

The Electors shall meet in their respective States and vote by ballot for President and Vice-President, one of whom, at least, shall not be an inhabitant of the same State with themselves; they shall name in their ballots the person voted for as President, and in distinct ballots the person voted for as Vice-President, and they shall make distinct lists of all persons voted for as President, and of all persons voted for as Vice-President, and of the number of votes for each, which lists they shall sign and certify, and transmit sealed to the seat of the government of the United States, directed to the President of the Senate;—The President of the Senate shall, in the presence of the Senate and House of Representatives, open all the certificates and the votes shall then be counted;—The person having the greatest number of votes for President, shall be the President, if such number be a majority of the whole number of Electors appointed; and if no person have such majority, then from the persons having the highest numbers not exceeding three on the list of those voted for as President, the House of Representatives shall choose immediately, by ballot, the President. But in choosing the President, the votes shall be taken by states, the representation from each state having one vote; a quorum for

8 Adopted in 1798.
9 Adopted in 1804.

this purpose shall consist of a member or members from two-thirds of the states, and a majority of all the states shall be necessary to a choice. And if the House of Representatives shall not choose a President whenever the right of choice shall devolve upon them, before the fourth day of March next following, then the Vice-President shall act as President, as in the case of the death or other constitutional disability of the President.—The person having the greatest number of votes as Vice-President, shall be the Vice-President, if such number be a majority of the whole number of Electors appointed, and if no person have a majority, then from the two highest numbers on the list, the Senate shall choose the Vice-President; a quorum for the purpose shall consist of two-thirds of the whole number of Senators, and a majority of the whole number shall be necessary to a choice. But no person constitutionally ineligible to the office of President shall be eligible to that of Vice-President of the United States.

[AMENDMENT XIII][10]

SECTION 1. Neither slavery nor involuntary servitude, except as a punishment for crime whereof the party shall have been duly convicted, shall exist within the United States, or any place subject to their jurisdiction.

SECTION 2. Congress shall have power to enforce this article by appropriate legislation.

[AMENDMENT XIV][11]

SECTION 1. All persons born or naturalized in the United States, and subject to the jurisdiction thereof, are citizens of the United States and of the State wherein they reside. No State shall abridge the privileges or immunities of citizens of the United States; nor shall any State deprive any person of life, liberty, or property, without due process of law; nor deny to any person within its jurisdiction the equal protection of the laws.

SECTION 2. Representatives shall be apportioned among the several States according to their respective numbers, counting the whole number of persons in each State, excluding Indians not taxed. But when the right to vote at any election for the choice of electors for President and Vice-President of the United States, Representatives in Congress, the Executive and Judicial officers of a State, or the members of the Legislature thereof, is denied to any of the male inhabitants of such State, being twentyone years of age, and citizens of the United States, or in any way abridged, except for participation in rebellion, or other crime, the basis of representation therein shall be reduced in the proportion which the number of such male citizens shall bear to the whole number of male citizens twenty-one years of age in such State.

SECTION 3. No person shall be a Senator or Representative in Congress, or elector of President and Vice- President, or hold any office, civil or military, under the United States, or under any State, who, having previously taken an oath, as a member of Congress, or as an officer of the United States, or as a member of any State legislature, or as an executive or judicial officer of any State, to support the Constitution of the United States, shall have engaged in insurrection or rebellion against the same, or given aid or comfort to the enemies thereof. But Congress may by a vote of two-thirds of each House, remove such disability.

SECTION 4. The validity of the public debt of the United States, authorized by law, including debts incurred for payment of pensions and bounties for services in suppressing insurrection or rebellion, shall not be questioned. But neither the United States nor any State shall assume or pay any debts or obligation incurred in aid of insurrection or rebellion against the United States, or any claim for the loss or emancipation of any slave; but all such debts, obligations, and claims shall be held illegal and void.

SECTION 5. The Congress shall have the power to enforce, by appropriate legislation, the provisions of this article.

[AMENDMENT XV][12]

SECTION 1. The right of citizens of the United States to vote shall not be denied or abridged by the United States or by any State on account of race, color, or previous condition of servitude—

SECTION 2. The Congress shall have power to enforce this article by appropriate legislation.

[AMENDMENT XVI][13]

The Congress shall have power to lay and collect taxes on incomes, from whatever source derived, without apportionment among the several States, and without regard to any census or enumeration.

10 Adopted in 1865.
11 Adopted in 1868.
12 Adopted in 1870.
13 Adopted in 1913.

[AMENDMENT XVII] [14]

The Senate of the United States shall be composed of two Senators from each State, elected by the people thereof, for six years; and each Senator shall have one vote. The electors in each State shall have the qualifications requisite for electors of the most numerous branch of the State legislatures.

When vacancies happen in the representation of any State in the Senate, the executive authority of such State shall issue writs of election to fill such vacancies: Provided, That the legislature of any State may empower the executive thereof to make temporary appointments until the people fill the vacancies by election as the legislature may direct. This amendment shall not be so construed as to affect the election or term of any Senator chosen before it becomes valid as part of the Constitution.

[AMENDMENT XVIII] [15]

SECTION 1. After one year from the ratification of this article the manufacture, sale, or transportation of intoxicating liquors within, the importation thereof into, or the exportation thereof from the United States and all territory subject to the jurisdiction thereof for beverage purposes is hereby prohibited.

SECTION 2. The Congress and the several States shall have concurrent power to enforce this article by appropriate legislation.

SECTION 3. This article shall be inoperative unless it shall have been ratified as an amendment to the Constitution by the legislatures of the several States, as provided in the Constitution, within seven years from the date of the submission hereof to the States by the Congress.

[AMENDMENT XIX] [16]

The right of citizens of the United States to vote shall not be denied or abridged by the United States or by any State on account of sex.

Congress shall have power to enforce this article by appropriate legislation.

14 Adopted in 1913.

15 Adopted in 1918.

16 Adopted in 1920.

[AMENDMENT XX] [17]

SECTION 1. The terms of the President and Vice-President shall end at noon on the 20th day of January, and the terms of Senators and Representatives at noon on the 3d day of January, of the years in which such terms would have ended if this article had not been ratified; and the terms of their successors shall then begin.

SECTION 2. The Congress shall assemble at least once in every year, and such meeting shall begin at noon on the 3d day of January, unless they shall by law appoint a different day.

SECTION 3. If, at the time fixed for the beginning of the term of the President, the President elect shall have died, the Vice-President elect shall become President. If a President shall not have been chosen before the time fixed for the beginning of his term or if the President elect shall have failed to qualify, then the Vice-President elect shall act as President until a President shall have qualified; and the Congress may by law provide for the case wherein neither a President elect nor a Vice-President elect shall have qualified, declaring who shall then act as President, or the manner in which one who is to act shall be selected, and such person shall act accordingly until a President or Vice-President shall have qualified.

SECTION 4. The Congress may by law provide for the case of the death of any of the persons from whom the House of Representatives may choose a President whenever the right of choice shall have devolved upon them, and for the case of the death of any of the persons from whom the Senate may choose a Vice-President whenever the right of choice shall have devolved upon them.

SECTION 5. Sections 1 and 2 shall take effect on the 15th day of October following the ratification of this article.

SECTION 6. This article shall be inoperative unless it shall have been ratified as an amendment to the Constitution by the legislatures of three-fourths of the several States within seven years from the date of its submission.

17 Adopted in 1933.

[AMENDMENT XXI][18]

SECTION 1. The eighteenth article of amendment to the Constitution of the United States is hereby repealed.

SECTION 2. The transportation or importation into any State, Territory, or possession of the United States for delivery or use therein of intoxicating liquors, in violation of the laws thereof, is hereby prohibited.

SECTION 3. This article shall be inoperative unless it shall have been ratified as an amendment to the Constitution by conventions in the several States, as provided in the Constitution, within seven years from the date of the submission hereof to the States by the Congress.

[AMENDMENT XXII][19]

No person shall be elected to the office of the President more than twice, and no person who has held the office of President, or acted as President, for more than two years of a term to which some other person was elected President shall be elected to the office of the President more than once.

But this Article shall not apply to any person holding the office of President when this Article was proposed by the Congress, and shall not prevent any person who may be holding the office of President, or acting as President, during the term within which this Article becomes operative from holding the office of President or acting as President during the remainder of such term.

This article shall be inoperative unless it shall have been ratified as an amendment to the Constitution by the legislatures of three-fourths of the several states within seven years from the date of its submission to the states by the Congress.

[AMENDMENT XXIII][20]

SECTION 1. The District constituting the seat of Government of the United States shall appoint in such manner as the Congress may direct:

A number of electors of President and Vice-President equal to the whole number of Senators and Representatives in Congress to which the District would be entitled if it were a State, but in no event more than the least populous State; they shall be in addition to those appointed by the States, but they shall be considered, for the purpose of the election of President and Vice-President, to be electors appointed by a State; and they shall meet in the District and perform such duties as provided by the twelfth article of amendment.

SECTION 2. The Congress shall have power to enforce this article by appropriate legislation.

[AMENDMENT XXIV][21]

SECTION 1. The right of citizens of the United States to vote in any primary or other election for President or Vice- President, for electors for President or Vice-President, or for Senator or Representative in Congress, shall not be denied or abridged by the United States or any state by reason of failure to pay any poll tax or other tax.

SECTION 2. The Congress shall have the power to enforce this article by appropriate legislation.

[AMENDMENT XXV][22]

SECTION 1. In case of the removal of the President from office or of his death or resignation, the Vice-President shall become President.

SECTION 2. Whenever there is a vacancy in the office of the Vice President, the President shall nominate a Vice President who shall take office upon confirmation by a majority vote of both Houses of Congress.

SECTION 3. Whenever the President transmits to the President Pro Tempore of the Senate and the Speaker of the House of Representatives his written declaration that he is unable to discharge the powers and duties of his office, and until he transmits to them a written declaration to the contrary, such powers and duties shall be discharged by the Vice-President as Acting President.

SECTION 4. Whenever the Vice-President and a majority of either the principal officers of the executive departments or of such other body as Congress may by law provide, transmit to the President Pro Tempore of the Senate and the Speaker of the House of Representatives their written declaration that the President is unable to discharge the powers and duties of his office, the Vice

18 Adopted in 1933.
19 Adopted in 1951.
20 Adopted in 1961.

21 Adopted in 1964.
22 Adopted in 1967.

President shall immediately assume the powers and duties of the office as Acting President.

Thereafter, when the President transmits to the President Pro Tempore of the Senate and the Speaker of the House of Representatives his written declaration that no inability exists, he shall resume the powers and duties of his office unless the Vice President and a majority of either the principal officers of the executive departments or of such other body as Congress may by law provide, transmit within four days to the President Pro Tempore of the Senate and the Speaker of the House of Representatives their written declaration that the President is unable to discharge the powers and duties of his office. Thereupon Congress shall decide the issue, assembling within forty-eight hours for that purpose if not in session. If the Congress, within twenty-one days after receipt of the latter written declaration, or, if Congress is not in session, within twenty-one days after Congress is required to assemble, determines by two-thirds vote of both Houses that the President is unable to discharge the powers and duties of his office, the Vice President shall continue to discharge the same as Acting President; otherwise, the President shall resume the powers and duties of his office.

[AMENDMENT XXVI][23]

SECTION 1. The right of citizens of the United States, who are eighteen years of age or older, to vote shall not be denied or abridged by the United States or by any State on account of age.

SECTION 1. The Congress shall have power to enforce this article by appropriate legislation.

[AMENDMENT XXVII][24]

No law, varying the compensation for the services of the Senators and Representatives, shall take effect, until an election of Representatives shall have intervened.

23 Adopted in 1971.
24 Adopted in 1992.

Credits

Text Credits

CHAPTER 24: Figure: Declining World Trade, 1929–1933 from *World in Depression, 1929–1939* by Charles P. Kindleberger. Copyright 1986 by University of California Press Books. Reproduced with permission of the University of California Press via Copyright Clearance Center.

CHAPTER 28: Figure: Average Annual Regional Migration, 1947–1960 from Frank Levy, "Major U.S. Migration Flows in the late 1940s and 1950s (persons per year)." In *Dollars and Dreams: The Changing American Income Distribution*, Figure 6.1. © 1987 Russell Sage Foundation, 112 East 64th Street, New York, NY 10021. Reprinted with permission.

CHAPTER 31: Figure: Poverty in America, 1970–1993 from Frank Levy, "Official Poverty Rates for Children, the Elderly, and the General Population." In *The New Dollars and Dreams: American Incomes and Economic Change*, Figure 7.11. © 1998 Russell Sage Foundation, 112 East 64th Street, New York, NY 10021. Reprinted with permission.

Photo Credits

334–335: Library of Congress; 336: *A Visit from the Old Mistress,* by Winslow Homer, 1876. Oil on canvas, 18x24 1/8". Smithsonian American Art Museum, Washington, DC/Art Resource, NY; 337: Harper's Weekly; 338 L: Library of Congress; 338 R: Library of Congress (LC-USZ62-130976); 339: Library of Congress; 340 T: Puck, 1890; 345: © Bettmann/Corbis; 347: Library of Congress; 348: The Granger Collection, New York; 349 B: Library of Congress (ppmsca22453); 352 L: Library of Congress (3b50366u); 352 C: The New-York Historical Society (50475); 352 R: Library of Congress; 353 L: The New-York Historical Society (50475); 353 C: © Brand X Pictures/Jupiter Images; 353 R: Library of Congress; 354–355: Omni-Photo Communications, Inc.; 357: National Archives; 358: Library of Congress (LC-USZ62-79320); 360 T: Courtesy of the Billy Graham Center Museum; 360 B: LSU in Shreveport, Noel Memorial Library, Archives and Special Collections 361, 362: Library of Congress; 366 T: Library of Congress (3b03310); 366 B: The Montana Historical Society; 367: The Institute of Texan Cultures, San Antonio, Texas; 368: Library of Congress (LC-W7-938); 371: Photograph of Mr. and Mrs. David Hilton and children. North of Weissert, rural Custer County, Nebraska, c. 1880. Solomon D. Butcher Collection, Nebraska State Historical Society, Lincoln.; 373 T: Image courtesy of Circus World Museum, Baraboo, Wisconsin; 373 B: Library of Congress (LC-USZC4-4706); 374 BL: © Comstock/Jupiter Images; 374 TL: © Photodisc/Getty Images; 374 BR: Library of Congress; 374 TR: Kansas State Historical Society (E185.1878.1); 375 BL: Library of Congress (LC-DIG-ppmsca-07783); 375 T: Library of Congress (LC-USZ62-51120); 375 BR: USDA Photograph Archives; 376–377: © Bettmann/Corbis; 379 T: Ramplett/iStockphoto; 379 B: New York Public Library; 380: Texas Energy Museum, Beaumont, Texas; 381 T: The Granger Collection, New York; 381 B: CMCD/Getty Images; 386: Library of Congress; 388: Collier's, 1905; 390: Brown Brothers; 391, 393: Library of Congress; 394: Deutsches Historisches Museum; 395: Library of Congress; 396 L: Library of Congress (LC-DIG-pga-01926); 396 C: Library of Congress; 396 R: WildStock/Alamy; 397 L: Library of Congress; 397 CL: Library of Congress (LC-USZ62-75191); 397 CR: Library of Congress (LC-USZ62-75202); 397 R: © Stockbyte; 398–399: Yale University Art Gallery/Art Resource, NY; 400: National Archives; 401, 402, 404, 405, 406: Library of Congress; 407 TL: Library of Congress (3a47363); 407 TR: Division of Political History, National Museum of American History, Smithsonian Institution (2004–26275); 407 B: Library of Congress (3a03368); 408: George Wesley Bellows (American 1882–1925), *The Sawdust Trail*, 1916. Oil on Canvas 63 x 45 1/8 in. Milwaukee Art Museum, Purchase, Layton Art Gallery L1964.7 Photography by P. Richard Eells.; 409, 410, 411: Library of Congress; 412: Courtesy of The Winterthur Library (RBR NK2740 R32 PF tc); 413 L: University of Chicago; 413 R: © Nick Anderson; 414: Library of Congress (LC-USZ62-95730); 415: *Blackboard* 1877 by Winslow Homer. © 2000 Board of Trustees, National Gallery of Art, Washington, Gift (Partial and Promised) of Jo Ann and Julian Gans, Jr., in honor of the 50th Anniversary of the National Gallery of Art; 416: Library of Congress; 417: Harpers New Monthly Magazine, May 1893; 418: *Sixth Avenue Shoppers* by Everett Shinn. Pastel and watercolor on board, 21 x 26 1/2". Santa Barbara Museum of Art, Gift of Mrs. Sterling Morton for the Preston Morton Collection; 419: Image courtesy of Circus World Museum, Baraboo, Wisconsin with permission from Ringling Bros. and Barnum & Bailey ® THE GREATEST SHOW ON EARTH®; 420 BL: Library of Congress; 420 C: Library of Congress (LC-DIG-steres-1s01730); 420 BR: Library of Congress (LC-DIG-steres-1s01730); 421 TL: Underwood & Underwood/Corbis; 421 C: Library of Congress (LC-USZ62-550050); 421 TR: Library of Congress (LC-USZ62-20621); 422–423: Stock Montage/Getty Images; 425: Library of Congress (9ppmsca19299); 427: Courtesy of the California History Room, California State Library, Sacramento, California; 428: Courtesy of Cornell University Library, Ithaca, NY; 429, 430, 431, 432, 434: Library of Congress; 436: James Steidl/iStockphoto; 438: Philip P. Choy, Professor of Asian American Studies at San Francisco State University ; 440: Chicago Historical Society (ICHi-08428); 444 BL: Library of Congress (LC-USZC4-769); 444 TL: Library of Congress (LC-DIG-dwpbh-04440); 444 TR: Illustration of the pistol of Charles Guiteau by James Dabney McCabe; 444 BR: © Photodisc/Gety Images; 445 BL: Library of Congress (3a10261u); 445 C: Library of Congress (LC-DIG-npcc-27728); 445 BR: Library of Congress (3g03917u); 446–447: The Granger Collection, New York; 448: Brown Brothers; 451: Library of Congress; 452 T: Library of Congress 452 B: Royalty Free/Corbis; 453, 454, 455: Library of Congress; 456 : *Without Sanctuary: Lynching Photography in America*, plates 25 and 26; 459 T: Brown Brothers; 459 B, 460, 461: Library of Congress; 462: Courtesy of The Bancroft Library, University of California, Berkeley; 465: Culver Pictures, Inc.; 466 L: Library of Congress (LC-USZ62-13025); 466 C: Hemera Technologies/Jupiter Images; 466 R: Library of Congress; 467 L: Library of Congress; 467 R: Library of Congress; 468–469: Snark/Art Resource, NY; 471: Artist Unknown, *Japanese. News Runners Rushing in with the Latest*, Japanese, Late Meiji era. Color lithograph; ink on card stock. Museum of Fine Arts, Boston, Leonard A. Lauder Collection of Japanese Postcards, 2002.1581; 473: Brown Brothers; 476: National Archives; 479 : Rare Book, Manuscript, and Special Collections Library, Duke University (n967); 480 L: © Hulton-Deutsch Collection/Corbis; 480 R:USAF/AP Images; 481 T: National Archives; 481 B: Sascha Burkard/iStockphoto; 483: Cartoon by D.C. Boonzaier in "Die Burger," October 16, 1918.; 486: International News Photos, Inc.; 487 T: Library of Congress; 487 B: Culver Pictures, Inc.; 488 L: Library of Congress; 488 C: Library of Congress (LC-USZ62-118281); 488 R: Library of Congress (LC-USZC4-1502); 489 L: Library of Congress (LC-USZ62-13554); 489 C: Library of Congress (LC-USZC4-9869); 489 R: © Photodisc/Gety Images; 490–491, 492: © Bettmann/Corbis; 493: Nebraska State Historical Society (RG2183-1933-0411-1); 494: "A Man is Known by the Car He Keeps", Saturday Evening Post, Jan. 24, 1925; 496: Library of Congress (LC-USF34-030662-D); 497: Library of Congress; 498: © Bettmann/Corbis; 499: Library of Congress; 500: *Blues,* (detail) 1929 by Archibald John Motley, Jr. Photograph ©1993 The Art Institute of Chicago. All Rights Reserved. Lent by Archie Motley and Valerie Gerrard Browne, 41.1988. Reproduced with the permission of the estate of the artist; 502: Library of Congress; 503: Research Division of the Oklahoma Historical Society; 504: Courtesy of Christine Lesiak/NET Television 24.14; 508: Mark Evans/iStockphoto; 510 L: Library of Congress (3c11278u); 510 C: © Photodisc; 510 R: Library of Congress (LC-B201-5202-13); 511 L: Library of Congress (LC-USZ62-111391); 511 C: Library of Congress (LC-DIG-ggbain-38216); 511 R: Library of Congress (LC-USZ62-74748); 512–513: Library of Congress (LC-DIG-fsac-1a34169); 514: Brown Brothers; 515: Library of Congress; 516: Radio designed by Harold van Doren and J.G. Rideout. Made by Air-King Products CO., Brooklyn, 1930–33. The Brooklyn Museum of Art, purchased with funds donated by The Walter Foundation, [85.9] Photograph, Scott Hyde.; 517 L: Library of Congress, FSA/OWI Collection, (LC-DIG-fsa-8b27276); 517 R: Library of Congress, 519: *Home Relief Station* 1935–36 by Louis Ribak. Collection of Whitney Museum of American Art, NY. Purchase. 36.148. Photograph © 2000: Whitney Museum of American Art. Courtesy of the Mandelman-Ribak Foundation.; 520: *Riot at Union Square* ,1947 [date depicted: March 6, 1930] by Peter Hopkins. Oil on canvas. Museum of the City of New York, Gift of the Artist, 66.82; 522 T: Library of Congress (LC-USZ62-25812); 522 B: Martin McEvilly/The New York Daily News; 525: Library of Congress; 527: © Condé Nast Archive/Corbis; 528 T: Library of Congress; 529: USDA Photo Archives; 531: Amy Jones; 532: Library of Congress (LC-USZC2-5665); 533 T: Courtesy of The Bancroft Library, University of California, Berkeley; 533 C: Walter P. Reuther Library, Wayne State University; 533 B: State Archives of Michigan, #05060; 534: *California Industrial Scenes,* (detail) 1934, by John Langley Howard. Coit Tower, San Francisco. Photograph, Don Beatty; 537 TL: P Wei/iStockphoto; 537 TC: David Hardman/iStockphoto; 537 CL: Oleg Kulakov/iStockphoto; 537 BL: Benjamin Brandt/iStockphoto; 537 BC: Anton Zhukov/iStockphoto; 537 BR: Keith Webber, Jr./iStockphoto; 538 BL: Library of Congress (3a25105u); 538 TL: © IT Stock/PunchStock; 538 BR: © Ingram Publishing/Fotosearch; 538 TR: Library of Congress; 539 L: Library of Congress (LC-DIG-npcc-10611); 539 R: Library of Congress (LC-USZ62-130313); 540–541: Photo by Time Life Pictures/Department Of

Defense (DOD)/Time Life Pictures/Getty Images; **542**: National Archives; **544**: © 1942 Edward B. Marks Music Company. Copyright renewed. All rights reserved. Photograph courtesy Franklin Delano Roosevelt Library, Hyde Park, New York.; **545, 547**: © Corbis; **548**: ©Christine Balderas/iStockphoto; **549**: Royalty Free/Corbis; **551**: *Too Many, Too Close, Too Soon,* by Donald Dickson. US Army Center of Military History/Army Art Collection; **552 T**: Courtesy James W. Davidson; **552 B**: National Archives; **553**: Westinghouse; **554, 555**: National Archives; **556**: Royalty Free/Corbis; **557, 558**: Library of Congress; **559**: © Bettmann/Corbis; **560**: Comstock Images/Alamy; **561**: National Archives; **563**: Library of Congress; **564**: National Archives; **565 TL**: © Brian Brake/Photo Researchers, Inc.; **565 TR**: National Archives; **566 L**: Library of Congress (LC-USZ62-54011); **566 C**: Comstock Images/Alamy; **566 R**: Library of Congress (LC-USZC2-819); **567 BL**: Library of Congress (LC-USE6-E-005418); **567 TL**: Library of Congress; **567 BR**: © Ingram Publishing/Fotosearch; **567 TR**: © Digital Archive Japan/Alamy; **568–569**: Tony Camerano/AP Images; **571 T**: The Truman Presidential Museum & Library; **572**:AP Images; **578**: *For Full Employment After the War Register to Vote,* 1944 by Ben Shahn. The Museum of Modern Art, New York. Gift of the CIO Political Action Committee. Digital Image © The Museum of Modern Art/Licensed by SCALA/Art Resource, NY, Art © Estate of Ben Shahn/Licensed by VAGA, New York, NY; **580**: © Baldwin H. Ward & Kathryn C. Ward/Corbis; **581**: © Warner Bros./Photofest; **583 T**: National Archives; **583 BL**: © Bettmann/Corbis; **583 BR**: The Department of Defense; **584**: Janis Christie/Getty Images; **585**: Eve Arnold/Magnum Photos, Inc.; **586 TL**: Department of Energy Office of History and Heritage; **586 BR**: Economic Cooperation Administration; **586 TR**: Mila Zinkova; **587 L**: Library of Congress; **587 C**: Private Collection; **587 R**: Library of Congress; **588–589**: Courtesy of the Advertising Archive; **590**: Michael Melford; **591**: ©James Steidl/iStockphoto; **594**: Printed by permission of the Norman Rockwell Family Agency. Copyright © 1959 the Norman Rockwell Family Entities. Courtesy Curtis Publishing.; **595**: *Catching the 8:05,* by Thornton Utz. ©1953 SEPS: Licensed by Curtis Publishing, Indianapolis, IN. All Rights Reserved. www.curtispublishing.com.; **596**: © Bettmann/Corbis; **598 L**: © Warner Bros./Photofest; **598 R**: © Bettmann/Corbis; **601**: © Bettmann/Corbis; **602 T**: Library of Congress; **602 B**: AP Images; **603**: Royalty Free/Corbis; **604 L, R**: Photofest; **604 C**: © Corbis; **607 T**: © Corbis; **607 B**: Library of Congress; **608 BL**: Library of Congress; **608 TL**: © Comstock Images/Alamy; **608 CL**: © Bettmann/Corbis; **608 TR**: Brand X Pictures/PunchStock; **608 CR**: Library of Congress; **608 R**: © Classio PIO/Fotosearch; **609 BL**: Library of Congress (LC-U9-1472E-36); **609 T**: © Ingram Publishing/Superstock; **609 BC, BR**: Image Club; **610–611**: © Steve Schapiro/Corbis; **612**: © Ernest C. Withers, Courtesy Panopticon Gallery, Boston, MA; **614 T**: Library of Congress (ppmsca 01271); **615**: Texas A & M University, Bell Library, Special Collections & Archives, Dr. Hector Garcia Papers, Corpus Christi, TX; **616**: Burt Glinn/Magnum Photos, Inc.; **617**: © Bettmann/Corbis; **618 T**: Charles Moore/Black Star/Stock Photos; **618 B**: Getty Images; **619**: Library of Congress; **620 B**: AP Images; **621**: Library of Congress (LC-DIG-ppsca-08102); **622** : George Tames/New York Times, 1957; **623**: © Bettmann/Corbis; **624**: Daniel Bobrowsky/iStockphoto; **625**: © 1976 Matt Herron/Take Stock; **627 T**: © Bettmann/Corbis; **627 B**: © 1970 Warner Bros. Records WS1893. Artwork by

Kelly-Mouse Studios; **628 L**: Library of Congress (LC-USZ62-109643); **628 C**: © Ingram Publishing/Alamy; **628 R**: Library of Congress (LC-DIG-ppmsca-04292); **629 L**: C Squared Studios/Getty Images; **629 BL**: Library of Congress; **629 R**: Library of Congress (LC-USZ62-95480); **629 BR**: © Photodisc/Getty Images; **630–631**: © Tim Page/Corbis; **632 L**: AFP/Getty Images; **632 R**: © Bettman/Corbis; **635**: © Tim Page/Corbis; **636**: AP Images; **638**: Andrius Grigalinas/iStockphoto; **639**: UPI/Bettmann/Corbis; **642**: Bettmann/Corbis; **643 T**: *Farm Workers' Altar,* 1967, by Emanuel Martinez. Acrylic on wood. 37 1/2 x 53 x 35 1/2 in. Gift of the International Bank of Commerce in honor of Antonio R. Sanchez, Sr. Smithsonian American Art Museum (1992.95)/Art Resource, NY; **644**: Arthur Schatz/Time Life Pictures/Getty Images; **645**: © Corbis; **646 L**: Courtesy of MS. Magazine; **646 R**: Library of Congress; **648**: Hulton Archive/Getty Images; **649 T**: Digital Vision/Getty images; **649 B**: Bill Ray/Time Life Pictures/Getty Images; **652**: AP Images; **653**: National Archives; **655**: New York Daily News; **656 BL**: US Navy Historical Center/Washington Navy Yard; **656 TL**: © Digital Archive Japan/Alamy; **656 BC**: Ryan McVay/Getty Images; **656 TR**: Library of Congress (LC-USZ62-115884); **656 BR**: © PhotoDisc/Getty Images; **657 C**: © PhotoDisc; **657 R**: Library of Congress; **658–659**: © JP Laffont/Sygma/Corbis; **660**: AP Images; **662**: © Bettmann/Corbis; **663**: Photofest; **664**: © Wally McNamee/Corbis; **665**: Wally McNamee/Woodfin Camp & Associates; **668**: Library of Congress (LC-USZ62-13040); **669 T**: Buffington/Getty Images; **669 L**: Stockphoto4u/iStockphoto; **669 C**: eyecrave/iStockphoto; **669 B**: Ivar Teunissen/iStockphoto; **670**: © Gerald French/Corbis; **672 T**: David Hume Kennerly/Getty Images; **672 B**: AP Images; **673 T**: David Hume Kennerly/Getty Images; **674**: Lutz Schmidt/AP Images; **676**: © Reuters/Corbis; **678 TL**: © Digital Archive Japan/Alamy; **678 TR**: Steve Cole/Getty images; **678 BR**: Library of Congress (LC-USZ62-86846); **679 TL**: © Comstock Images/Alamy; **679 BL**: © PhotoDisc; **680–681**: © Ed Murray/Star Ledger/Corbis; **682**: Yolanda M. Lopez; **683**: Ryan McVay/Getty Images; **684 T**: Jennifer Szymaszek/AP Images; **684 B**: Bülent Gültek/iStockphoto; **686**: © Jeffrey Markowitz/Sygma/Corbis; **688**: Illustration by Anita Kunz for the New Yorker Magazine. Anita Kunz Limited. Reproduced by permission of the artist.; **690**: Stephen G. Eick/Advizor Solutions; **691**: © Peter Turnley/Corbis; **693 T**: © Mark M. Lawrence/Corbis; **693 B**: Courtesy of Apple Inc.; **697**: David J. Phillip/AP Images; **698**: Doug Mills/The New York Times, November 5, 2008; **699**: © Julie Dermansky/Corbis; **700 L**: © Comstock/Punchstock; **700 C**: Dirck Halstead/Time Life Pictures/Getty Images; **700 R**: Digital Vision Ltd./SuperStock; **701 TL**: © Ingram Publishing/Alamy; **701TC**: © Stefan Zaklin/Corbis; **701 B**: Library of Congress (LC-DIG-ppbd-00358); **701 TR**: Photodisc/Getty Images.

Photo Credits (Design Elements)

Pages **367 T, 439, 488, 528, 620, 661**: Chris Schrameck/Getty Images; **341 B**: Torsten Stahlberg/iStockphoto; **364, 389, 401 B, 426**: © Lars Christensen/Cutcaster; **449, 477, 501, 530**: © Nataliya Hora/iStockphoto; **565 B, 571 B, 599, 614 B**: © Olivier Blondeau/iStockphoto; **643 B, 673 B**: © Floortje/iStockphoto.

Index

National Organization of Women (NOW),
    646–647
National Origins Acts, 503, 623
National Recovery Administration (NRA),
    524–525
National War Labor Board (NWLB), 480
National Woman Suffrage Association, 498
National Woman's party, 453
nativism, 408–409, 409, 502, 502–503, 692
NATO. *See* North Atlantic Treaty Organization
navalism, 436–437, 441m, 471–472
navy, 476, 540–541, 540–542, 547, 549, 549–550
Nazis, 520, 543, 544, 549
Nelson, Gaylord, 648
neo-isolationist, 573
Neutrality Act of 1935, 544–545
New England Kitchen, 450
New Federalism, 650
New Orleans, growth of, 402, 402m
New York City, 398, 398–399, 408, 411
New York Stock Exchange, 381, 384, 508
the New Deal
    agriculture planning and, 525, 525–526
    art for millions and, 534, 534–535
    Cold War and, 577–578, 578
    democratic Roosevelts and, 522, 522
    dissent from, 526–527, 527
    election of 1936, 529
    Great Depression, American people and,
        529, 529–535, 531–534
    Great Depression and early stages of,
        521–526, 522, 523m–524m, 525
    Great Depression and end of, 535–538,
        536–537
    Great Depression and second, 526–529,
        527–528
    industrial recovery planning and, 524–525
    legacy of, 536–537, 536–537
    limited reach of, 530–531
    organized labor's rise and, 532–534, 533
    saving banks and, 522–523
    second hundred days of, 527–529, 528
    tribal rights and, 531, 531–532
    unemployment relief and, 523–524, 524m
    Western water and, 530
    women and, 532
    World War II and, 559–560, 560
Nez Percé, 366
Nicaragua, 472, 671m, 671–672
Nicholas II (czar), 477
Nimitz, Chester, 561
Nineteenth Amendment, 446, 454, 481
NIRA. *See* National Industrial Recovery Act
Nisei, 557–558, 558
Nixon, Richard, 603m, 603–604, 639,
    648–649
    fighting no-win war and, 641
    move toward détente, 641–642, 642
    pragmatic conservatism and, 650–653,
        652–653
    Vietnam era and, 640–642, 642
    Vietnamization, Cambodia and, 640–641
    Watergate and, 651–653, 652–653
NLRB. *See* National Labor Relations Board
N.L.R.B. v. Jones and Laughlin Steel Corpora-
    tion, 535
NLU. *See* National Labor Union

Nobel Prize, 471, 500–501, 665, 665–666, 686,
    700
normal schools, 416
North, Oliver, 672, 672
North Atlantic Treaty Organization (NATO),
    573
the North, 348–349
NOW. *See* National Organization of Women
NRA. *See* National Recovery Administration
Nuclear Winter (Schell), 670
NWLB. *See* National War Labor Board
Nye, Gerald P., 544

O

Oakley, Annie, 373
Obama, Barack, 698, 698–700, 699, 699m
O'Connor, Sandra Day, 676
oil, 380, 380, 699m, 699–700
    Middle East and, 654m, 655, 655
    trust, 385–386
Oliver, Joe ("King"), 500
Operation Desert Storm, 674, 675m
outsourcing, 668
Over Here: The First World War and American
    Society (Kennedy, D. M.), 488

P

Pacific, 443m, 543, 547, 549, 549–550, 562m
Padilla, Gil, 644
padrones, 381–382
Palestine, 564, 573. *See also* Israel
Palin, Sarah, 697
Palmer, A. Mitchell, 487–488
Panama Canal, 438, 470m, 470–471, 473m, 488
pandemics, 483, 483–484, 484m
panics, 424
    of 1873, 349
Pankhurst family, 453
Parks, Rosa, 615
Parsons, Charles, 398, 398–399
Patent Office, U.S., 379
patents, 379
Patrons of Husbandry, 429
Patton, George S., 561
Paul, Alice, 453, 480
peace
    globalism, winning war and, 560–566, 561,
        561m–562m, 563–565
    imperialism, debate over empire and,
        441–442, 441n2
    Middle East and, 687
    Roosevelt, F. D., for, 562–564, 563
    U.S. and lost, 484–488, 485m, 486–487
    winning World War II and, 560–566, 561,
        561m–562m, 562–564
    World War I, preparedness, and election of
        1916, 476–477, 477m
    World War II and lasting, 564–565
Pearl Harbor, 540–542, 540–542, 547
Pendleton Act, 426
Pentagon Papers, 651
perestroika, 673
Perkins Gilman, Charlotte, 451–452
Perot, H. Ross, 677, 677m
Pershing, John "Black Jack," 473–474, 482

petroleum, 379. *See also* oil
Philippine-American War, 442
Philippines, 440–442, 441n2, 561–562, 562m.
    See also Filipino Americans
Pinchot, Forester, 461–462, 463
Pingree, Hazen, 457
plantations, 335
    post war Georgia, 342, 342, 342m
    Southern mistresses on, 336, 336
Platt Amendment, 471, 544
Plessy v. Ferguson, 361, 614, 628
Pliyev, Issa, 607
Plunkitt, George Washington, 398–400
pluralism, 642
plurality, 428
Poindexter, John, 672–673
police action, 582m, 582–583
political machines, 406
political parties, 425–426. *See also specific*
    parties
political system, 424. *See also* value politics
    African American response and, 434,
        434–435
    battle of standards and, 432, 432–433
    campaign, election and, 433m, 433–434,
        433n1
    depression of 1893, 431–432
    dreams of commercial empire and, 438–439
    farmers' revolt and, 428–431, 429–430
    ferment in states and cities and, 428, 428
    imperialism, European-style and
        American, 436
    imperialism and, 436–443, 437m, 438, 440,
        441m, 443m
    imperialism shapers and, 436–438, 437m,
        438
    issues, 426–427
    Jim Crow politics and, 434
    McKinley's White House and, 435
    new realignment and, 431–432, 431–435,
        433m, 434
    parties in, 425–426
    political stalemate and, 425, 425
    politics of paralysis in, 425, 425–428, 427
    rumblings of unrest and, 432
    significant events, 444–445
    visions of empire and, 435–439, 436,
        437m, 438
    White House from Hayes to Harrison and,
        427, 427–428
Poole, Elijah (Elijah Muhammad), 518
Pope, John (general), 364
population increase, 419, 501m, 502–503, 503
Populism, 428, 431
Populists, 426, 430–432, 430–434, 444
poverty, 358, 359m, 451, 451, 537, 537, 622,
    669, 669
Powderly, Terence V., 392
Powell, John Wesley, 363–364, 366
pragmatic conservatism
    break-in and, 651–652
    Nixon's New Federalism of, 650
    oval office and, 652, 652
    resignation and, 652–653, 653
    social policies, the Court and, 650–651
    stagflation and, 650
    triumph and revenge for, 651